MOON

D0039635

PROVENCE

JAMIE IVEY

Contents

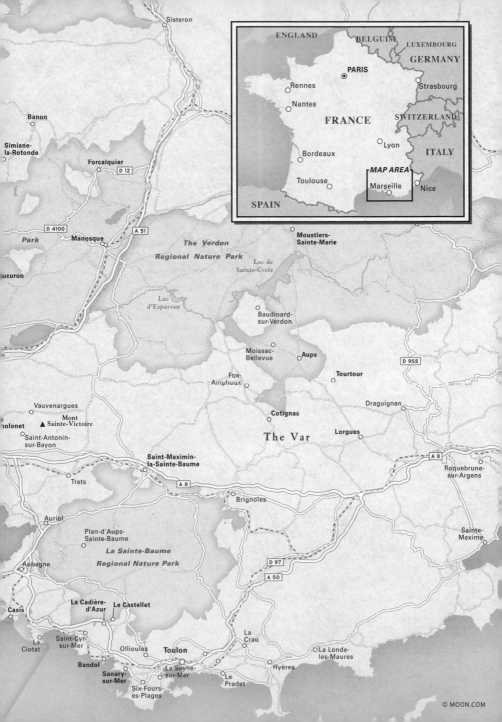

Sisteron

Banon

Simiane-
la-Rotonde

Forcalquier   D 12

Park   D 4100

Manosque   A 51

ucuron

The Verdon
Regional Nature Park

Moustiers-
Sainte-Marie

Lac de
Sainte-Croix

Lac
d'Esparron

Baudinard-
sur-Verdon

Moissac-
Bellevue   Aups

Fox-
Amphoux   D 955

Tourtour

Vauvenargues

Mont
▲ Sainte-Victoire

Draguignan

holonet

Saint-Antonin-
sur-Bayon

Cotignac

The Var

Lorgues

Saint-Maximin-
la-Sainte-Baume   A 8

Trets   A 8   Roquebrune-
sur-Argens

Brignoles

Auriol

Plan-d'Aups-
Sainte-Baume   Sainte-
Maxime

Aubagne   La Sainte-Baume
Regional Nature Park   D 97

A 50

Casis

La Cadière-
d'Azur   Le Castellet

La
Ciotat

La
Crau   La Londe-
les-Maures

Saint-Cyr-
sur-Mer   Ollioules   Toulon

Bandol   La Seyne-
sur-Mer   Le
Pradet   Hyères

Sanary-
sur-Mer

Six-Fours-
es-Plages

Inset map (France):

ENGLAND   BELGIUM   LUXEMBOURG
GERMANY

PARIS ✴   Strasbourg

Rennes

Nantes   SWITZERLAND

FRANCE

Lyon   ITALY

Bordeaux

Toulouse   *MAP AREA*

SPAIN   Marseille   Nice

DISCOVER

Provence

People have found it impossible to agree on the geographic boundaries of Provence. Some insist on a "golden triangle" of land around the major cities of Aix-en-Provence, Arles, and Avignon. It's here that you will find the most celebrated sites: the arched glory of the Arles Roman arena and the vaulted splendor of the Palais des Papes. And it's here that you'll tread in the footsteps of Van Gogh and Cézanne, the painters who define Provence in the popular imagination.

By contrast, some are adamant that Provence stretches almost as far north as Lyon. This is where you first encounter the scent of the south, wild thyme and rosemary, mixed with the sweet sticky smell of pine trees.

For others the geography of Provence is shaped by its food and wine. Imagine yourself on a market morning. The smells are evocative: bread fresh from the oven; bundles of dried lavender harvested under the watchful eye of Mont Ventoux; a grilled leg of Sisteron lamb slowly turning on the rotisserie. People move from stand to stand thinking of the perfect accompaniment for a glass of rosé: perhaps some wild boar *saucisson* (dry, cured sausage) from the pine forests of the Var or an oozing morsel of Banon goat's cheese. Then again, why not some

Clockwise from top left: lavender bouquets in a market in Gordes; a water wheel in L'Isle-sur-la-Sorgue; village houses in Roussillon; the Cours Mirabeau in Aix-en-Provence; the remains of a ship jut from the side of a Toulon apartment building; Moustiers-Sainte-Marie village.

anchovies that have been plucked from the sea just off Marseille, or some olives ripened below the medieval fortress at Les Baux-de-Provence. If all the right food is on sale, many are prepared to allow they're in Provence.

Photographers, artists, and nature enthusiasts, however, insist the most important factor is not food, but the presence of Provence's mystical light. No one can doubt that hiking through the Calanques next to the glittering Mediterranean is a high-definition experience. Yet just a few hundred kilometers up the coast near Montpellier, the piercing clarity vanishes.

The unifying theme that runs through all these different views of Provence is that, whatever the precise boundaries, life in Provence hovers on the verge of sensory overload. This guide covers the major cities of Aix-en-Provence, Arles, Avignon, and Marseille, and the regional nature parks of the Luberon, Les Alpilles, the Camargue, and the Verdon Gorge. In addition, it will take you from the sweet-smelling lavender fields of Haute Provence to the pungent, earthy truffle markets of the northern Vaucluse, and from the beach in Bandol, where light-hearted rosé wines almost seem to wink back at you, to the robust and legendary reds of Châteauneuf-du-Pape. Good-natured quibbling from the locals aside, this area forms the most truly unforgettable region of France: La Provence.

Clockwise from top left: the Petit Colorado ocher mine; a home in Arles; Pont du Gard; a narrow street in Simiane-La-Rotonde.

10 TOP
EXPERIENCES

1 Strolling down the **Cours Mirabeau** in Aix, a street that epitomizes Provence in its beauty, history, café society, and centuries-old plane trees (page 194).

2 Experiencing the wonder and reverence induced by **Palais des Papes.** New technology has revived the splendor of touring this vast Gothic palace (page 37).

3 Imagining gladiators, clashing metal, and the smell of sweat and blood at Arles' **Roman arena** (page 85).

4 Getting up close and personal with local wildlife, including rare wading birds, flamingos, bulls, and white horses, on a **Camargue Safari** (page 110).

^ ^
^ ^ ^

5 **Wine tasting in the Northern Vaucluse,** hopping between Châteauneuf-du-Pape (page 55) and Vacqueyras, Gigondas, and Rasteau (page 63) to discover the region's stellar reds.

6 Village hopping through the **Petit and Grand Luberon.** This is Provence at its most alluring; the hills of the Luberon hold numerous charming villages in their soft embrace (page 152).

7 Smelling the intoxicating pine forests, olive groves, vines, and wild herbs among the jagged bare rocks of **Les Alpilles Regional Nature Park** (page 113).

8 Visiting the daring, futuristic **MuCEM,** a glass box containing a museum of Mediterranean culture, one of the many architectural projects transforming the reputation of Marseille (page 241).

9 Exploring the **Verdon Gorge,** especially via kayak. At 700 meters (2,296 feet) deep and 25 kilometers (15.5 miles) long, it's an awe-inspiring demonstration of the power of nature over time (page 289).

10 Walking through the waving seas of the **lavender fields of Haute Provence,** with picturesque villages rising like islands, and shoals of bees darting this way and that (page 179).

Planning Your Trip

Where to Go

Avignon and the Vaucluse

The busy metropolitan outskirts of Avignon give way to a walled medieval interior. The main draw is the world-famous **Palais des Papes,** closely followed by the **Pont Saint-Bénézet,** whose arches famously stretch only halfway across the Rhône. Day trips to the **Pont du Gard** Aqueduct and **Châteauneuf-du-Pape** vineyards are a must. Nearby **L'Isle-sur-la-Sorgue** is an antique lover's mecca and a great base to explore north toward **Mont Ventoux.**

Arles, the Camargue, and Les Alpilles

For the locals here, life is all about bull running and bull fighting. There are plenty of other reasons to recommend the region, including major Roman sites and the Van Gogh art trail. **Saint-Rémy-de-Provence** and **Arles** are filled with shady restaurants, art galleries, and boutique shops. Don't miss the surrounding countryside, which is dominated by rocky peaks and a pungent combination of pine forests, olive groves, and vineyards. In the nearby **Camargue Regional Nature Park,** a wildlife safari takes you to hidden salty marshlands filled with flamingos and herds of the iconic white horses.

The Luberon and the Lavender Fields of Haute Provence

The **Luberon Regional Nature Park** is a rural idyll, dotted with renowned villages such as **Lourmarin, Ménerbes, Gordes,** and **Bonnieux.** Depending on the time of year, the

a high plateau in Haute Provence

Chapter Divisions

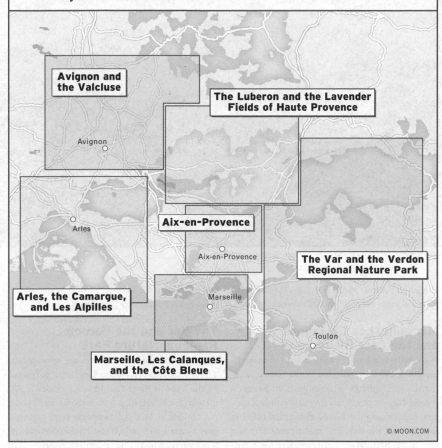

© MOON.COM

fields will be full of melons, pumpkins, drifting blossoms, or vines sagging with fruit. Thanks to the closeness between man and nature, simple pleasures are elevated to the unforgettable; a goat's cheese salad and a glass of wine can taste every bit as good as a Michelin-star meal. The hills are crisscrossed with cycle and hiking routes and dotted with vineyards to visit. In late July and early August, the lure of lavender in full bloom calls visitors to the high plateaus of **Haute Provence.**

Aix-en-Provence

The city, rather than any given sight or museum, is the star. Time in Aix passes almost unnoticed. Most visits begin underneath the shady canopy of the plane trees on the wide café-lined **Cours Mirabeau** and end in the old town amid a maze of cobbled streets and small squares adorned with trickling fountains. Don't miss a visit to **Cézanne's workshop** or the chance to see his work at the **Musée Granet.** The countryside surrounding Aix is dominated by Cézanne's most

late summer lavender at the base of Mont Sainte-Victoire

cherished subject, **Mont Sainte-Victoire,** plus plentiful vineyards and small Provençal villages.

Marseille, Les Calanques, and the Côte Bleue

Marseille is a loud, brash, in-your-face melting pot of cultures, founded by the Greeks, and, thanks to centuries of immigration, France's second-biggest city. Sparkling new cultural centers, hidden neighborhoods, fishermen offering the catch of the day, and restaurants offering *vrai* (true) bouillabaisse all compete for attention. To the east is the **Calanques National Park,** perhaps the most scenic, unspoiled stretch of Mediterranean coast remaining in France. Accessible largely either on foot or by boat, the Calanques are a series of rocky inlets cut into the coastline. To the west is the beautiful and more accessible **Côte Bleue,** a section of coast that also

boasts its own Calanques, as well as one of the most beautiful railway lines in Provence.

The Var and the Verdon Regional Nature Park

Sometimes clichéd descriptions are appropriate: The **Verdon Gorge**—the limestone gorge cut by the Verdon River that in some places is 700 meters (2,296 feet) high—does momentarily take your breath away. Cooler summer temperatures, great water sports, and traditional Provençal villages such as **Moustiers-Sainte-Marie** make the Verdon Regional Nature Park a popular destination in high summer. Farther south, Var villages such as **Cotignac** and **Tourtour** offer an authentic Provençal feel and easy access to the Côte d'Azur. The **Var resorts** between **Bandol** and **Toulon** are just as scenic as their more celebrated Riviera counterparts and a lot less busy.

Cooking holidays are increasingly popular in Provence. You could build a whole week around cooking classes or just schedule half a day. Cookery classes are often combined with market tours, with the ingredients being purchased in the market. Here are some of the best classes available:

LUBERON

- **La Petit Maison** (Cucuron, www.lapetite-maisondecucuron.com) fills up well in advance, so book well ahead to ensure a place on one of Eric Sapet's popular cookery courses. A list of upcoming courses is published three months in advance. They take place every Saturday morning, starting at 10am. Each course is followed by a sit-down lunch with wine, when you can enjoy the fruits of your labor. As many noncooking friends can join you as you like. The price is €80 per person, including the meal and wine.

AIX, SAINT-REMY-DE-PROVENCE, AND MARSEILLE

- **Provence Gourmet** (www.provence-gourmet.fr) offers a friendly home cooking experience with local chef Gilles. Gilles was born and raised in Marseille and lived in the United States for four years. His courses often include vineyard visits and market visits, in addition to the cooking class. Prices from €160.

THE VAR

- **Hostellerie Berard** (www.hotel-berard.com/en/page/cookery-classes-provence.4.html) in La Cadière d'Azur on the Var coast offers gastronomic stays, where rooms can be booked along with cookery classes. Nonresidents can also join the Saturday morning cooking class. Ingredients are selected from the kitchen garden, and then with the aid of the hotel's chefs, students prepare classic Provençal dishes. The price is €155 per person, including a meal at the end of all the work.

When to Go

Summer

The period between **July 14** and **August 14** is by far the busiest and hottest in Provence. Sightseeing can be oppressive under the beating heat of the summer sun. Most tourists in these months get out and about early, doing as much as they can before lunch, and then spend the afternoon by the pool. Restaurants are busier, the weekend traffic on the autoroutes is terrible, and at the seaside there's hardly a spare inch of beach. The first two weeks in July and the last two in August are slightly quieter, and a good option for determined sunseekers who want to avoid the worst of the crowds. July is also the best time to see the **lavender fields** in full bloom.

Spring and Fall

Spring and autumn are a delight. **April-June** and **September-October** are perhaps the best months to visit. The sun is usually shining, and the Provençal countryside looks its most beautiful. In early spring the fields fill with the wild blossoms of almond and cherry trees. In autumn the vines turn a magnificent range of russet and golden colors. It's the perfect time of year for activities like cycling, hiking, and kayaking. The roads are quiet, so it's easy to get from sight to sight.

Winter

In **December,** when the weather can still be mild, the towns, cities, and villages begin gearing up for Christmas. Lights go up at the beginning of the

fishing harbor Vallon des Auffes, Marseilles

month, and special **Christmas markets** take place on an almost daily basis. Gourmands start salivating at the thought of **truffles,** the so-called black diamonds of Provence, which grow in the ground under oak trees between mid-December and the end of February. Christmas itself is a gastronomic festival of seafood, *foie gras,* and those truffles.

In **January** and **February,** it's best to base yourself in a city. The towns and villages of Provence can be exceedingly quiet, and it gets quite cold, with nighttime temperatures often falling below 32°F (0°C). If you love hiking and cycling, then it's still a good time to visit. The sky is often almost impossibly blue. By the seaside, it's not unusual for people to sunbathe in sheltered spots, and the brave even swim.

By **March** the countryside is slowly stirring into life, vines sprout with an urgent vigor, and the fruit trees begin to blossom. The markets fill up with traders, and village shops and restaurants reopen. Everyone seems happy as the tourist season begins.

Before You Go

Passports and Visas

The latest visa requirements can be checked at the France Diplomatie website (www.diplomatie. gouv.fr/en/coming-to-france). The site offers a "visa wizard" that will quickly tell you your requirements. Here is a summary of the situation at time of writing:

Nationals from the **United States, Canada,** **Australia,** and **New Zealand** can enter France and stay for up to 90 days without a visa. Stays of more than 90 days require a visa and proof of income and medical insurance. Citizens of **EU-member countries** who have a valid passport and national identity card can travel freely to France. **British** nationals should check visa requirements once the United Kingdom has exited

If You Have...

ONE WEEK

Pick a central base for three or four nights such as L'Isle-sur-la-Sorgue in the Vaucluse. From here you can explore the cities of Arles and Avignon and the Luberon Nature Park. For the remaining nights, stay in Aix-en-Provence, enjoy the city, and add either a day trip to the coast or one to the Gorges du Verdon. If you are traveling in July or early August, make sure you see the lavender fields on the Valensole plateau on the way to the Gorge.

TWO WEEKS

Divide your time between the coast and inland. Once again, pick a central base. Saint-Rémy-de-Provence is another good alternative. With your second week, spend a couple of nights on the Côte Bleue, catching the train into Marseille to explore the city. Then stay in Cassis, visit the Calanques and one of the seaside resorts of Bandol, Saint-Cyr, or Sanary-sur-Mer.

THREE WEEKS

Plan to stay a couple of nights in each of the big cities: Aix, Arles, Avignon, and Marseille. Explore the cities and the neighboring sights, such as Mont Sainte-Victoire near Aix, the Camargue near Arles, Châteauneuf-du-Pape and the Pont du Gard from Avignon, and the Calanques near Marseille. Spend the second week in the heart of the Provençal countryside. Choose among the villages of the Luberon, Les Alpilles Nature Park, northern Vaucluse, or inland Var, which all share a similar relaxed Provençal atmosphere. For the third week, divide your time between the Gorge du Verdon and the Var Coast.

the European Union. South African nationals require a short-stay visa for visits up to 90 days, and a long-stay visa if the traveler plans to stay more than 90 days.

What to Pack

What should go into your suitcase very much depends on when you visit. In addition to weather-appropriate clothing and other necessities, don't forget a plug adapter for your electronic devices. European outlets take round, two-prong plugs.

Transportation

By Air

Most travelers will arrive at either Marseille or Nice airport. Both have low-cost terminals as well as regular scheduled flights to all major destinations in Europe.

For transatlantic passengers, Marseille Airport has direct flights with Air Canada and Air Transat to Montreal. For other North American destinations, travelers must fly to common hubs such as Paris, London, or Amsterdam and then take a connecting flight to Marseille.

Alternatively, North Americans can fly from New York direct to Nice, which is approximately a 1-hour drive from the area covered in this book. Flights are offered by Delta and newcomer La Compagnie.

For Australians the quickest way to get to the South of France is a flight to Dubai. From Dubai, Emirates flies direct to Nice. Alternatively, there are direct flights to Nice from Hong Kong.

There are no direct flights to the South of France from South Africa. South Africans should fly to London, Amsterdam, or Paris and pick up a connecting flight.

Avignon Airport is a low-cost hub that has flights to and from Birmingham and Southampton in the UK. **Nîmes Airport,** a 45-minute drive from Avignon, is a low-cost hub with flights to and from Stansted and Luton airports near London. Farther into the Languedoc, **Montpellier Airport,** which is a 60-minute drive from Avignon, also offers flights to multiple UK destinations, as well as Paris, Berlin, Copenhagen, and Dublin.

By Train

Provence is directly connected by a **TGV line** to Paris. Hourly TGV trains stop at the major cities of Avignon (under three hours from Paris), Aix-en-Provence, and Marseille.

Eurostar operates a weekend service from May to mid-October from London to Avignon.

The outward journey is nonstop, but the return journey requires getting off the train at Lille for passport control.

By Car

The main route to Provence from the north is the **A7 autoroute,** which runs between Lyon, Avignon, and Aix-en-Provence. It is nicknamed the Autoroute du Soleil. During weekends in the summer months of July and August, it is advisable to find alternative routes because the stretch between Avignon and Lyon becomes one long traffic jam.

The **A8 autoroute** runs from the Italian border near Nice to Aix-en-Provence, and the **A9** runs from just outside Avignon to the Spanish border near Barcelona.

Roman tile work in Vaison-la-Romaine

The Best of Provence

The itinerary recommended below is relatively ambitious. You will need a car, and it's intended as a happy combination of history and culture, blending inland Provence with a dash of the coast, and mixing in plenty of stops that will satisfy gourmands. For some there may be too much travel from place to place, so adapt as necessary and, above all, don't forget to leave time to sit in a café, preferably with a pastis, and watch the world go by.

Day 1

Start in **Avignon.** An early TGV (bullet train) from Paris will get you there in time for lunch at the **Carrés du Palais** restaurant. In the afternoon, tour the **Palais des Papes** and cross the river to **Villeneuve-lès-Avignon** for a view back over the city and of the famous **Pont d'Avignon** (Pont Saint-Bénézet). Stay overnight in the **Clos Saluces** bed-and-breakfast and make it your base for the first three days.

Day 2

Rise bright and early for breakfast in the verdant garden of Clos Saluces and then head out into the countryside around Avignon. History buffs will love a morning trip to the **Pont du Gard Roman Aqueduct.** On the way back to Avignon in the afternoon, stop off at **Châteauneuf-du-Pape** to sample the luxurious velvety reds.

Day 3

Tour the hill villages of the **Luberon Nature Park.** Be sure to include Gordes, Goult, and Roussillon as stop-off points. If you have time, go and see the **Abbey de Senanque,** just outside Gordes. It is particularly worth the detour in early summer when the lavender is in bloom. Eat lunch on the terrace of the **L'Esprit des Romarins** restaurant overlooking Gordes. In the afternoon head back to Avignon via **L'Isle-sur-la-Sorgue.** Walk along the banks of the **River**

view across the Rhône of Pont Saint-Bénézet toward Avignon

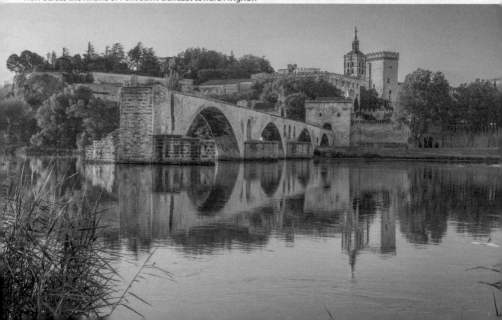

Sorgue, enjoying the tumbling water wheels and browsing the renowned **antiques shops.**

Day 4

Head to **Arles** and prepare for some serious culture. Visit the Roman theater and Roman arena as well as the Fondation Van Gogh. Then head out into the Camargue for a late lunch at **La Chassagnette,** followed by flamingo spotting at the **La Capelière** nature reserve. Drive to Aix-en-Provence and stay overnight in the **Hotel des Augustins.**

Day 5

In the morning explore **Aix-en-Provence** by following the **Cézanne walking trail.** Have lunch at **Les Deux Garcons** on the Cours Mirabeau before enjoying a cultural afternoon visiting the **Musée Granet** or the **Hotel Caumont,** or both.

Day 6

Head north to the **Gorges du Verdon,** stopping at the **Valensole Plateau** en route to see

the lavender (July/early August). Wander the picturesque streets of **Moustiers-Sainte-Marie,** before driving the head-spinning **Corniche Sublime** in the afternoon. If there is time, rent a paddleboat from one of the beaches on **Lac de Sainte-Croix.** Return to Aix.

Day 7

Head to Cassis, and either hike out into **Les Calanques,** or catch a boat from the port. Enjoy a bouillabaisse portside either for lunch or as the sun dips below the horizon. If you have time, visit **Domaine Paternel** to pick up some of the finest white wine and rosé in Provence.

Finally, if you happen to leave Provence via Marseille Airport, the **Calanque de Méjean** is a 20-minute drive away. Depending on the time of day, enjoy either a drink, lunch, or supper at the **Mange Tout** restaurant while gazing out to sea. It's a magical place to start or end your trip.

If you manage most of the above in seven days, consider yourself an honorary Provençal.

a boat leaves from bay to open sea in Les Calanques

Lavender in Haute Provence and Beyond

Haute Provence is rightly considered the best place to see lavender. Rows of the lavender roll like waves over the horizon, creating a shimmering purple haze. Besides Haute Provence's best spots (page 179), here are a few other ways to experience lavender throughout the region:

- Taste lavender ice cream in almost any ice cream shop. In particular, look out for the sumptuous lavender ice cream produced by artisan glacier Scaramouche in Cereste in the Luberon. It's available in restaurants across Provence, including **Les Sudistes** in Apt (page 156).

- **Bastide,** a shop in Aix-en-Provence, specializes in simple, clean beauty products made from Provençal ingredients, such as lavender honey bodywash (page 207).

- The drive to the **Domaine des Masques** winery in Pays d'Aix-en-Provence may be bumpy, but rewards with rows of lavender lining the road to the old farmhouse and wine-making facilities (page 223).

- Paraglide over the Verdon's purple lavender fields with the experts at **Verdon Passion** (page 297).

Haute Provence is famous for its lavender.

- Even in urban Marseille, you can get a whiff of lavender at the **Cruise Passenger Market,** where it's stacked by the bundle along the quayside (page 253).

Best of the Outdoors and Nature

Provence is perfect for both serious outdoor enthusiasts and people who prefer a leisurely stroll. Enthusiasts who love nothing better than filling their holiday with activities will be thrilled at the breadth of hiking, kayaking, biking, and birdwatching available here.

Hiking

- Head off for a bracing walk along the **Digue de la Mer sea wall**, departing from Saintes-Maries beach in the Camargue (page 101).

- Enjoy sweeping views and look for the Luberon's Egyptian vulture after hiking the 30-minute trail up to **Fort de Buoux** (page 157).

- Walk the exhilarating two-kilometer **Sentier de Petit Prince** along the steep drops and sweeping views of the Port-Miou calanque (page 268).

- Hike the iconic **Sentier de l'Imbut**, which plunges you into the heart of the Gorges du Verdon (page 296).

Artist Trail

Two of the greatest artists ever to have lived—Paul Cézanne and Vincent Van Gogh—spent great chunks of their career painting Provence. These two artists can legitimately be called the forefathers of modern art. Their unique appreciation and interpretation of Provence's famed light paved the way for the Fauvist and Cubist movements.

Cézanne was based in Aix, and Van Gogh moved between Arles and Saint-Rémy-de-Provence. Split a week's stay between Aix and Arles to see their work and the places that inspired them.

CÉZANNE

- Cézanne originals are on display in the **Musée Granet** in Aix-en-Provence (page 200).

- The **Cézanne Atelier**, on the outskirts of Aix, has been restored to mirror its condition during the years before the artist died; those familiar with his work may recognize objects that appeared in many of his paintings (page 200).

- The **Footsteps of Cézanne Walk** allows visitors a window into the artist's life in Aix. You can either join the weekly guided group or pick up a map and follow the route yourself (page 204).

- **Le Jas de Bouffan,** also just outside Aix, was Cézanne's family home, where he completed almost 30 works (page 202).

VAN GOGH

- At least one Van Gogh is always on show at the **Fondation Vincent Van Gogh** in Arles (page 89).

Abbaye Montmajour

- The **Van Gogh Walking Tour,** also in Arles, gives visitors a chance to walk in the footsteps of the year the artist spent in the city (page 93).

- The artist voluntarily checked into the mental institute at **Monastere St Paul de Mausole** in Saint-Rémy-de-Provence, where he completed many paintings (page 113).

- Van Gogh obsessively painted the **Abbaye Montmajour** in Fontvieille more than 50 times, drawn by the way the huge building imposes itself on the landscape (page 124).

Kayaking

- Rent a kayak and go with the flow down the **River Sorgue,** stopping for a refreshing swim in the summer (page 74).

- Hugging the coast in a kayak is a wonderful way to see **the Calanques,** just east of Marseille (page 270).

Biking

- Take the 2-hour **Cavalon Velo Route** from Coustellet to Castellet, taking in some of the Luberon's most picturesque villages (page 155).

- Rent a bike and ascend **Mont Ventoux.** There's no shame in taking an e-bike, as the White Giant of Provence gets the knees of even professional cyclists quaking with fear (page 68).

Bird-Watching

- Spot flamingos and other avian wildlife on a 90-minute bird-watching walk at the **Ornithological Park of Pont de Gau** (page 109).

- Head out into the wilds in the back of a Land Rover to see Camargue white horses, bulls, and plentiful birdlife on a **Camargue safari** (page 110).

Camping

- Sleep outside near the renowned Luberon village of **Lourmarin** at **Les Hautes Prairies** campground, which has tent sites and cabins (page 171).

- Pitch a tent in the heart of the **Luberon Nature Park** at beautiful **Camping des Sources,** located just outside of Gordes (page 147).

- View **Les Alpilles** from **Monplaisir campsite,** which is a short walk from the charming town of Saint-Rémy-de-Provence (page 120).

Wine Tasting

Visiting a vineyard should be an intimate experience. Ideally you'll meet the owner or a member of the family, or a staff member involved in the wine making. You should be able to wander in the vines and crouch down and crumble the soil between your fingers. Poking your head into the cellar where the wine is made is always fun. Usually, there's a pungent smell of fermentation. If you are lucky, your host will plunge a long pipette (known as the thief) into a barrel of maturing wine and let you taste. The best way to ensure a good visit is to **call in advance** and express an interest in the wines of the vineyard. If you do so, you'll be greeted with open arms and plentiful bottles to taste. The following is a suggested three-day itinerary to sample some of the best wines in Provence.

Day 1

Arrive in Avignon. Rent a car and immediately head 30 minutes north to **Châteauneuf-du-Pape.** The suburbs of Avignon give way to a sea of vines on either side of the Rhône. Upon arrival at Châteauneuf, head to the tasting rooms of

Provence grape harvest

Beaurenard. As well as a Châteauneuf-du-Pape, there's an excellent Rasteau full of spices and ripe fruit available at €15 a bottle. Have lunch at **Le Pistou**, a popular choice in the center of town. There's a small terrace and a cozy dining room.

In the afternoon, head into the nearby **Dentelles de Montmirail.** Stop at **Domaine Goubert** just outside Gigondas, where the wine is full of undertones of tobacco. Stay at **Hotel les Florets** outside Gigondas. Jump in the pool before an indulgent supper.

Day 2

Explore the village of **Gigondas** in the morning before driving an hour to Fontvieille. Have lunch at the **Cave les Alpilles.** The Cave is principally a wine shop rather than a restaurant, and so no markup is charged on the extensive wine list. A good plat du jour is served, plus cheeses and cold meats. After lunch, drive 1 hour through the olive groves east toward the Luberon. Stop outside Bonnieux at vineyard **Château Canorgue,** where there are more than 10 different wines to taste.

Drop out of the Petit Luberon to the village of Lourmarin in the southern Luberon. Stay at the village center **Moulin de Lourmarin.** Explore the village and then pop 2 kilometers (1.25

miles) up the road for a tasting at **Domaine La Cavale,** which offers cellar tours and tastings of local wines, as well as great wines from around the world.

Day 3

Drive 1 hour south to **Domaine des Masques,** just outside Aix-en-Provence. To reach the vineyard, you will drive up a dirt track for 5 kilometers (3 miles). This road takes you on to a stretch of rock known as the Cengle, or belt, which encircles the base of **Mont Sainte-Victoire.** This high plateau has only one vineyard, which makes outstanding and well-priced reds, whites, and rosés. Afterward, enjoy lunch at the nearby restaurant **Le Saint-Estéve,** which overlooks Mont Sainte-Victoire.

Then head south for another hour to **Domaine Tempier** outside Bandol. There's no fanfare or grand buildings, but this modest vineyard happens to make one of the best reds in Provence. The center of the domaine is a simple house surrounded by vines set at the end of a row of trees. The tasting room has a family feel and the aged red is some of the best you are ever likely to taste. Afterward, stay at the **Hotel Delos** on the Plage Renécros in Bandol.

one of many wine cellars in Provence

The Best Seaside Restaurants in Provence

The first secret to finding a good beach restaurant is choosing one in an out-of-the-way location, far from the crowds. Usually the spots are idyllic. Second, a beach restaurant should be a no-nonsense affair, serving fresh, simply prepared dishes. What could be better than a glass of rosé, the Mediterranean glinting in the sun, and a plate of fried calamari with lemon and aioli? It's paradise on a plate. This book is full of little beach bars where you can enjoy this experience. Here are my favorites:

MARSEILLE, LES CALANQUES, AND CÔTE BLEUE

- In Marseille, escape from the crowds to the hidden Vallon des Auffes inlet and eat sensational bouillabaisse at **Chez Fonfon** (page 257).

- The **Pergola** restaurant in the Calanque de Niolon just outside Marseille feels like you've escaped from the rest of the world (page 277).

- **Mange Toute** also just outside Marseille in the Calanque Méjean offers an idyllic setting and basic, no-frills service (page 278).

- At **Le Château** in Calanque de Sourmiou, diners with a reservation have the luxury of driving their cars down to the seaside. Everyone else must walk (page 273).

fresh fish from tides to table

COASTAL VAR

- **La Table de Nans,** just outside Saint-Cyr-sur-Mer in Var, serves sublime food in a sublime setting (page 317).

- **O Petit Monde** and **Kima Plage** on Plage Portissol in Sanary-sur-Mer both offer great food accompanied by the sound of breaking waves on the nearby rocks (pages 326 and 325).

Avignon and the Vaucluse

Readers of this guide who are planning a trip to Europe might find themselves with the same tricky choice that Pope Clement V faced back at the beginning of the 14th century when he was trying to pick a location for the papal court: which city to choose, Rome or Avignon?

Perhaps it was a glass of the local red (now known as Châteauneuf-du-Pape) that nudged Clement toward Avignon. The blessings of the region must have been evident in every sip of the intoxicating, velvety wine whose high levels of alcohol have been known to induce a state of almost transcendental rapture in today's top tasters. The rest, as they say, is history. The immense, fortress-like Palais des Papes was thrown up in just 20 years and it is now the main reason people visit Avignon.

Highlights

Look for ⭐ to find recommended sights, activities, dining, and lodging.

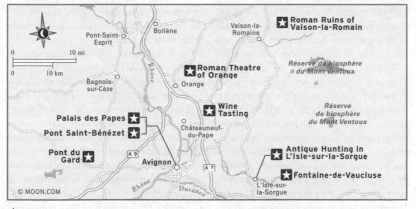

⭐ **Palais des Papes:** In the early 14th century, Pope Clement V opted for Avignon as a base for the papal court rather than Rome. The finery of this medieval Gothic palace has been revived with the magic of technology, and a tour of the building induces wonder, reverence, and a hint of trepidation (page 37).

⭐ **Pont Saint-Bénézet:** A reported miracle worked by a shepherd boy spurred construction of this iconic bridge completed in 1185 (page 43).

⭐ **Pont du Gard:** Pick your own superlative. Whatever word you alight on will barely do justice to this 275 meter (902 feet) long, 49 meter (160 feet) high Roman aqueduct. For a close-up view of this ancient engineering masterpiece, rent a kayak (page 52).

⭐ **Wine Tasting:** Châteauneuf-du-Pape is the blockbuster name, but also allow time to visit the vineyards of Gigondas, Vacqueyras, Rasteau, and Beaumes-de-Venise. The countryside, as well as the wine, is a delight (page 55 and 63).

⭐ **Roman Theatre of Orange:** Seating 10,000 people, this amphitheater is unique thanks to its surviving stage wall. It comes alive every summer with a major opera festival (page 58).

⭐ **Roman Ruins of Vaison-la-Romain:** Vaison has one of the most impressive and extensive collections of Roman ruins in Provence, including the remains of a residential quarter and a theater (page 61).

⭐ **Antique Hunting in L'Isle-sur-la-Sorgue:** Indulge in some of the best antique shopping in the whole of France against a backdrop of churning waterwheels (page 72).

⭐ **Fontaine-de-Vaucluse:** The source of the River Sorgue is the largest karst spring in France. It's a deep cavern from which, at certain times of year, clear cold water explodes in a bubbling torrent (page 73).

Avignon has long been one of the principal gateways to Provence. Until the late 15th century the power of the French crown ended on the western bank of the Rhône. To the east, the counts of Provence held power. These days with its airport and fast TGV links to Paris, Avignon is a popular starting point for visitors to Provence, not least because the surrounding countryside of the Vaucluse offers plenty of nearby attractions.

L'Isle-sur-la-Sorgue boasts some of the best antique shopping in France; the area around Orange and Vaison-la-Romaine offers impressive Roman ruins; and nearby Richerenches, the truffle capital of Provence, sets the pulses of gourmands racing. Then there's Mont Ventoux: Known as the white giant, this 1,909-meter (6,263-foot) high mountain is a cycling mecca, with aficionados coming from all over to attempt the most legendary climb in the road bike world. For the less energetic there's no shortage of Provençal feel in the perched hill villages, trickling fountains, and pretty, plane-tree-lined squares dotting the region. In such an environment, eating out is as much a visual as it is a gastronomic pleasure. Of course, you'll probably need something to sip while admiring the views, but beware: The gargantuan wine lists of restaurants can seem daunting. Châteauneuf-du-Pape might be the most internationally well-known of the local wines, but the villages of Gigondas, Vacqueyras, Rasteau, and Beaumes-de-Venise, clustered together in a region known as the Dentelles de Montmirail, also produce wines of stunning quality.

All things considered, just like Clement V, you may conclude that Rome can wait.

PLANNING YOUR TIME

A two-night stay in Avignon allows plenty of time to explore the city, and could include a half-day excursion to **Châteauneuf-du-Pape** or the **Pont du Gard.** One could also easily spend a day each in **L'Isle-sur-la-Sorgue, Orange, Vaison-la-Romaine, Mont Ventoux,** and the **Dentelles de Montmirail.** Avignon can easily be used as a base to explore the entire region, as can L'Isle-sur-la-Sorgue, which also benefits from being adjacent to the Luberon.

Visitors who like the conveniences of a city should opt for Avignon as their base. There are plenty of options for restaurants, shops, and entertainment. Those who like a more relaxed atmosphere should choose L'Isle-sur-la-Sorgue. It's a small town that is easy to navigate and is blessed by the soothing sound of the **River Sorgue,** which runs alongside the main streets. Visitors looking for a rustic Provençal feel should head to the villages of the Dentelles de Montmirail, where the pace of life is much slower and the countryside dominated by sweeping expanses of vines.

Traveling from north or south in the region is quick thanks to the **A7** autoroute. When traveling east or west, allow more time because the roads are smaller.

Itinerary Ideas

THE BEST OF AVIGNON AND THE VAUCLUSE

Day 1

1 Make the sumptuous **Maison sur La Sorgue** in L'Isle-sur-la-Sorgue your base to explore the region.

Previous: Pont d'Avignon and the Palais des Papes on the Rhône River at sunrise; Coté Parc antique shop in L'Isle-sur-la-Sorgue; ancient tower at Châteauneuf-du-Pape.

The Best of Avignon and the Vaucluse

DAY ONE
1. Maison sur La Sorgue
2. Palais des Papes
3. Les Halles Food Market
4. Rocher des Doms
5. Châteauneuf-du-Pape
6. Le Vivier

DAY TWO
1. Fontaine-de-Vaucluse
2. Kayak Vert
3. Au Fil du Temps
4. Antique shops
5. Café Fleurs

DAY THREE
1. Vaison-la-Romain
2. Nez
3. Mont Ventoux
4. Carré d'Herbes

© MOON.COM

2 Head into nearby Avignon on the D901 (40-minute drive), and explore the city, visiting the magnificent **Palais des Papes** and the Pont d'Avignon.

3 Shop for lunch provisions among the colorful stalls at **Les Halles Food Market.**

4 Enjoy a picnic at the **Rocher des Doms** garden, overlooking the Place du Palais.

5 Leave Avignon, and head north for 20 minutes on the D907 to **Châteauneuf-du-Pape** for an afternoon of wine tasting.

6 Return on the D192 to L'Isle-sur-la-Sorgue for supper at **Le Vivier** restaurant on the banks of the River Sorgue.

Day 2

1 Rise early and visit the source of the River Sorgue 10 minutes' drive away, taking the D25 to **Fontaine-de-Vaucluse.**

2 Canoe down the river with **Kayak Vert.** The descent starts just outside Fontaine-de-Vaucluse and takes two hours.

3 Have lunch 20 minutes away in nearby Pernes-les-Fontaines (take the D25 and the D938) at **Au Fil du Temps.** Later, work off the calories by visiting as many of the town's 40 fountains as possible.

4 Return to L'Isle-sur-la-Sorgue on the D938 and explore the town's **antique shops.**

5 Have supper in the excellent **Café Fleurs** in the center of town.

Day 3

1 Drive north and satisfy your inner historian by visiting the Roman ruins at **Vaison-la-Romaine** (D938). Drive time is just under an hour.

2 Enjoy lunch in Gigondas, 20 minutes away just off the D977, and sample the excellent local wine on offer at **Nez.**

3 Drive to the summit of **Mont Ventoux** for the best view in Provence. Allow 30 minutes' drive time to reach Bédoin from Gigondas, and then another 30 minutes to get from there to the summit. Adrenalin junkies can hire a descent bike and meet their more timid friends back at base camp in Bédoin.

4 Return to L'Isle-sur-la-Sorgue (40 minutes on the D938), and round off the three days with supper in the atmospheric **Carré d'Herbes.**

Avignon

Avignon is many things to many different people. To tourists it will always be the City of the Popes, visited for the Palais des Papes and the romance of a kiss on the Pont d'Avignon (also known as the Pont Saint-Bénézet). To oenophiles it is the capital of the Côtes du Rhône wine region, an area that produces some of the world's most renowned reds. For thespians Avignon is the home of one of Europe's top performing arts festivals. Visit in summer and the streets will be alive with theater troupes promoting their shows. Finally, it's a university city with a large student population sustaining plentiful bars and clubs. The result is that Avignon is a city with many faces. It boasts wonderful museums, many of which are free to visit. The Musée du Petit Palais and the Musée Calvet are highlights, but with no admission price, all museums merit a quick visit.

Avignon is also home to some of the finest historic hotels in Provence, with new chic retreats opening every year. Yet the pressure of having so many different people to please means that away from the main streets and squares the city can feel a little run-down. Even so, there is a sense of innovation and creativity. Pop-up shops selling artisan designs of furniture, clothes, and more are common, and the plentiful theaters host year-round events such as dance and yoga classes. Adding to the allure is a vibrant restaurant scene on and around the various church squares that are a legacy of Papal rule.

ORIENTATION

The **historic center** of Avignon, where you will spend nearly all of your time, is surrounded by 4 kilometers (2.5 miles) of walled ramparts. Inside the walls you will discover a pleasant mixture of church squares, cafés, shops, restaurants, museums, and historic sites. The bus station and central train station (for local trains, not TGV/bullet trains, which arrive farther out) are located opposite **Porte de La République,** just outside the walls. From there a broad avenue (Cours Jean Jaurès and then rue de La République) runs south to north through the historic center, arriving at **Place de l'Horloge.** This Place is home to the town hall and the 19th-century Opera House, and is considered the heart of the city. Just to the north is the **Place du Palais,** the **Palais des Papes,** and the entrance to the **Pont d'Avignon.** The main road running from west to east, branching off the bottom of Place de l'Horloge, is rue Carnot.

SIGHTS

★ Palais des Papes

Place du Palais; tel. 04 32 74 32 74;
www.palais-des-papes.com; daily Sept. 1-Nov. 1
9am-7pm, Nov. 2-Feb. 29 9:30am-5:45pm, March
9am-6:30pm, Apr. 1-June 30 9am-7pm, July 9am-8pm,
Aug. 9am-8:30pm; €12, €10 reduced, under 8 free

The Palais des Papes has long been one of Provence's must-see sights, illustrating the story of the papal cities of Avignon and Rome. The sheer size and scale of the Palais are impressive, and that's before you learn it was built inside 20 years. Between 1335 and 1352, successive popes Benedict XII and Clement VI oversaw the construction.

The Palais des Papes is a stark monolith of forbidding stone that also served as a fortress and inquisitional court. Little remains of the original furnishings, but holding up the Histopad tablet (provided with the entrance fee) allows visitors to travel back 700 years: Ghosts of cardinals sit in chairs, banquetting tables are laden with roast chickens, and the faded frescoes on the walls are suddenly brought to life. Children can play a special treasure hunt game on the Histopad, searching for coins hidden in objects from the Palais's past.

Musée du Petit Palais

Palais des Archevêques, Place du Palais;
tel. 04 90 86 44 58; www.petit-palais.org;
Wed.-Mon. 10am-1pm and 2pm-6pm; free

Built between 1318 and 1320, the Petit Palais predates its big brother on the other side of the square by a decade or so. It was purchased by Pope Benedict XII in 1335 for use as the Episcopal Palace during construction of the Palais des Papes. It now houses a remarkable collection of 13th- to 15th-century paintings and sculptures. Viewed after a tour of the Palais des Papes, the museum is an enriching experience, sketching in the cultural background at the time of the Avignon Popes, and following the art world in its then illusive quest to introduce perspective.

Musée Calvet

65 rue Joseph Vernet; tel. 04 90 86 33 84;
www.musée-calvet.org;
Wed.-Mon. 10am-1pm and 2pm-6pm; free

The Musée Calvet contains a large eclectic mix of paintings, sculptures, and archaeological

Avignon and the Vaucluse Area

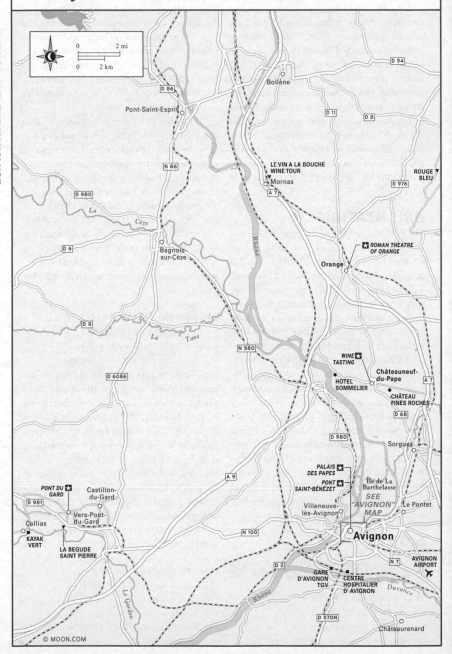

0   2 mi

0   2 km

D 94

Bollène

D 86

Pont-Saint-Esprit

N 86

D 11

D 8

LE VIN A LA BOUCHE
WINE TOUR

ROUGE
BLEU

D 980

Mornas

A 7

D 976

La Cèze

D 6

Bagnols-
sur-Cèze

★ ROMAN THEATRE
OF ORANGE

Orange

D 9

La Tave

N 580

D 6086

WINE ★
TASTING

Châteauneuf-
du-Pape

A 7

HOTEL
SOMMELIER

CHÂTEAU
FINES ROCHES

D 68

D 980

Sorgues

A 9

PALAIS ★
DES PAPES

PONT ★
SAINT-BÉNÉZET

Île de La
Barthelasse

SEE
"AVIGNON"
MAP

Le Pontet

PONT DU ★
GARD

Castillon-
du-Gard

Villeneuve-
lès-Avignon

D 981

Vers-Pont-
du-Gard

Avignon

Collias

N 100

KAYAK
VERT

LA BEGUDE
SAINT PIERRE

N 7

AVIGNON
AIRPORT ✈

D 2

GARE
D'AVIGNON
TGV

CENTRE
HOSPITALIER
D'AVIGNON

Durance

Le Gardon

Rhône

D 570N

Châteaurenard

© MOON.COM

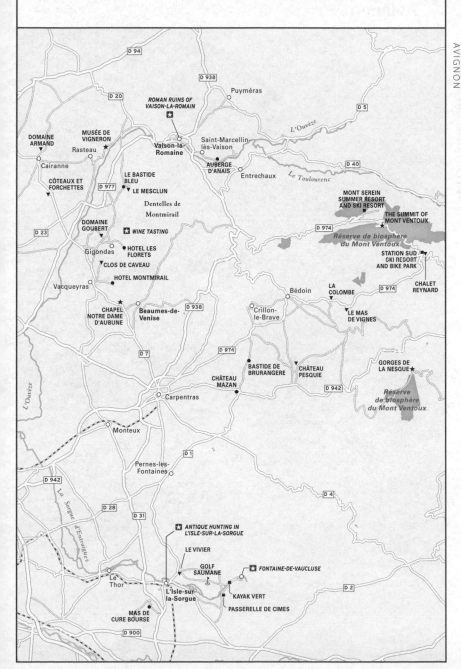

D 94

D 938

D 20

ROMAN RUINS OF
VAISON-LA-ROMAIN ★

Puyméras

D 5

DOMAINE
ARMAND

MUSÉE DE
VIGNERON ★

Rasteau

Vaison-la-
Romaine

Saint-Marcellin-
lès-Vaison

L'Ouvèze

D 40

Cairanne

CÔTEAUX ET
FORCHETTES ▼

LE BASTIDE
BLEU

D 977

● LE MESCLUN

AUBERGE
D'ANAIS

Entrechaux

Le Toulourenc

Dentelles de
Montmirail

D 23

DOMAINE
GOUBERT ▼

★ WINE TASTING

● HOTEL LES
FLORETS

MONT SEREIN
SUMMER RESORT
AND SKI RESORT

THE SUMMIT OF
MONT VENTOUX
★

D 974

Réserve de biosphère
du Mont Ventoux

Gigondas

● CLOS DE CAVEAU

● HOTEL MONTMIRAIL

STATION SUD
SKI RESORT
AND BIKE PARK

D 974

CHALET
REYNARD

Vacqueyras

Bédoin

LA
COLOMBE ▼

CHAPEL ★
NOTRE DAME
D'AUBUNE

Beaumes-de-
Venise

D 938

Crillon-
le-Brave

● LE MAS
DE VIGNES

GORGES DE
LA NESQUE ★

D 7

D 974

BASTIDE DE
BRURANGERE ●

CHÂTEAU
PESQUIE ▼

Réserve
de biosphère
du Mont Ventoux

L'Ouvèze

CHÂTEAU
MAZAN ●

D 942

Carpentras

Monteux

D 1

Pernes-les-
Fontaines

D 942

D 28

D 31

D 4

ANTIQUE HUNTING IN
★ L'ISLE-SUR-LA-SORGUE

La Sorgue d'Entraigues

LE VIVIER

GOLF
SAUMANE

★ FONTAINE-DE-VAUCLUSE

Le
Thor

L'Isle-sur-
la-Sorgue

■ KAYAK VERT

PASSERELLE DE CIMES

D 2

MAS DE
CURE BOURSE ●

D 900

Avignon

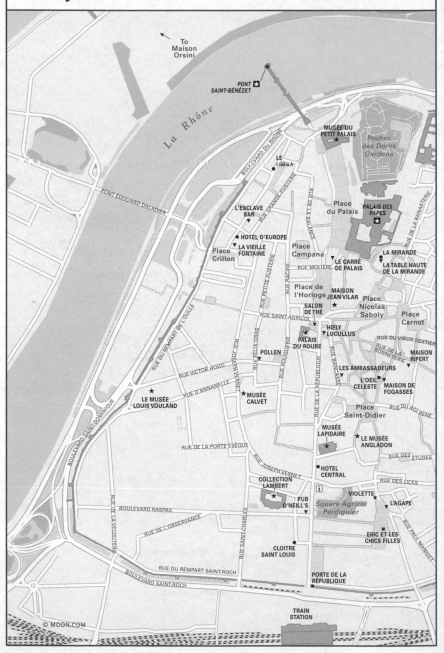

To
Maison
Orsini

La Rhône

PONT
SAINT-BÉNÉZET

PONT ÉDOUARD DALADIER

BOULEVARD DU RHÔNE

MUSÉE DU
PETIT PALAIS

*Rocher
des Doms
Gardens*

LE LIMAS

L'ESCLAVE
BAR

RUE GRANDE FUSTERIE

RUE DE LA BALANCE

Place
du Palais

PALAIS DES
PAPES

RUE DE LA BANASTERIE

HÔTEL D'EUROPE

LA VIEILLE
FONTAINE

Place
Crillon

Place
Campana

Place de
l'Horloge

RUE MOLIÈRE

LE CARRÉ
DE PALAIS

LA MIRANDE

LA TABLE HAUTE
DE LA MIRANDE

RUE PETITE FUSTERIE

RUE RACINE

MAISON
JEAN VILAR

Place
Nicolas
Saboly

Place
Carnot

SALON
DE THÉ

RUE SAINT-AGRICOL

HIELY
LUCULLUS

RUE DU VIEUX SEXTIER

RUE DE LA
BONNETERIE

MAISON
RIPERT

RUE FÉLIX GRAS

PALAIS
DU ROURE

POLLEN

RUE JOSEPH VERNET

LES AMBASSADEURS

RUE BANCASSE

L'OEIL
CELESTE

MAISON DE
FOGASSES

RUE VICTOR HUGO

RUE D'ANNANELLE

RUE BOUQUERIE

RUE DE LA RÉPUBLIQUE

Place
Saint-Didier

RUE DU ROI RENE

LE MUSÉE
LOUIS VOULAND

MUSÉE
CALVET

MUSÉE
LAPIDAIRE

LE MUSÉE
ANGLADON

BOULEVARD SAINT-DOMINIQUE

RUE DE LA PORTE ÉVÊQUE

HÔTEL
CENTRAL

RUE DES ÉTUDES

COLLECTION
LAMBERT

RUE JOSEPH VERNET

RUE DES LICES

PUB
O'NEILL'S

VIOLETTE

*Square Agricol
Perdiguier*

L'AGAPE

RUE SAINT-CHARLES

BOULEVARD RASPAIL

RUE DE L'OBSERVANCE

RUE DE LA VELOUTIÈRE

ERIC ET LES
CHICS FILLES

RUE PAUL MANIVET

CLOITRE
SAINT LOUIS

RUE DU REMPART SAINT-ROCH

BOULEVARD SAINT-ROCH

PORTE DE LA
RÉPUBLIQUE

© MOON.COM

TRAIN
STATION

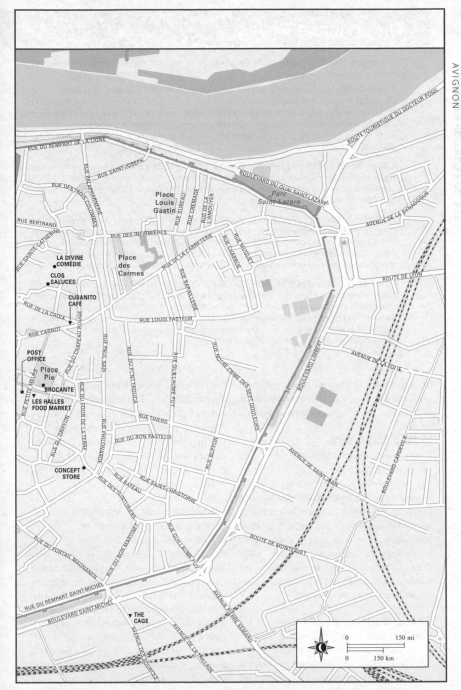

ROUTE TOURISTIQUE DU DOCTEUR PONS

RUE DU REMPART DE LA LIGNE

RUE SAINT-JOSEPH

BOULEVARD DU QUAI SAINTE LAZARE

RUE DES TROIS COLOMBES

RUE PALAPHARNERIE

Parc
Saint-Lazare

AVENUE DE LA SYNAGOGUE

RUE BERTRAND

Place
Louis
Gastin

RUE SUREAU

RUE CRÉMADE

RUE DE LA
L'AMOUVER

RUE DES INFIRMIÈRES

RUE SAINTE CATHERINE

**LA DIVINE
COMÉDIE**

Place
des
Carmes

RUE DE LA CARRETERIE

RUE HUGUET

ROUTE DE LYON

**CLOS
SALUCES**

RUE CHARRUE

**CUBANITO
CAFÉ**

RUE BAFAILLERIE

RUE DE LA CROIX

RUE LOUIS PASTEUR

RUE CARNOT

AVENUE DE LA FOI

**POST
OFFICE**

RUE DU CHAPEAU ROUGE

RUE PAUL SAIN

RUE DU P'NT TROUCA

RUE GUILLAUME PUY

RUE NOTRE-DAME DES SEPT DOULEURS

BOULEVARD LIMBERT

**Place
Pie**

BROCANTE

RUE PETITE MEILLE

**LES HALLES
FOOD MARKET**

RUE DU TOUR DE LA TERRE

RUE PHILONARDE

RUE THIERS

RUE BUFFON

RUE DU GRIFFON

RUE DU BON PASTEUR

AVENUE DE SAINT-JEAN

**CONCEPT
STORE**

RUE BATEAU

RUE SAINT-CHRISTOPHE

RUE DES TEINTURIERS

BOULEVARD CARDEVILA

RUE DU PORTAIL MAGNANEN

RUE DU BON MARTINET

RUE GUILLAUME DU

ROUTE DE MONTFAVET

RUE DU REMPART SAINT-MICHEL

BOULEVARD SAINT-MICHEL

AVENUE PIERRE SEMARD

**THE
CAGE**

AVENUE DE LA TRILLADE

AVENUE PIERRE SEMARD

AVENUE DES SOURCES

0   150 mi

0   150 km

The Avignon Popes

The history surrounding the Palais des Papes can seem convoluted. Here's a quick timeline to get you up to speed.

- **The Babylonian Captivity of the Church (1309-1377):** During this period, popes resided in Avignon, supposedly under the undue influence of the French crown, indulging in corruption and debauchery reminiscent of Babylon around 600 BC. It all began with Pope Clement V, who happened to be in France at the time of his election. A roving papal court was quite normal back in the day, so Clement headed to Avignon, then under the control of the Duchy of Naples.

- **Construction of the Palais des Papes (1334-1352):** Construction of the Palais des Papes started under Clement V's successors Benedict XII (1334-42) and Clement VI (1342-52). The wealthy Clement VI also purchased the entire city of Avignon from the Duchy of Naples for 80,000 florins.

- **Return to Rome (1377):** Finally, the silver-tongued St. Catherine of Siena persuaded Gregory XI to abandon the delights of southern France and return to Rome, ending the Babylonian captivity of the church. This 68-year slice of history is not to be confused with the actual Babylonian captivity (note the absence of the church qualifier), which, as we all know, was the period of time that Hebrew leaders spent locked up in licentious Babylon around 600 BC.

- **The Papal or Western Schism (1378-1417):** Are you with me so far? Next came the Papal or Western Schism (which has nothing to with the Great Schism of 1054 between the churches of the East and West). Within a year a new pope, Urban VI (Gregory died soon after his return to Rome), provoked some of his cardinals into electing an alternative pope back in Avignon. For another 40 years or so, the Catholic church had two popes, meaning that for more than a century there was a sitting Pope in Avignon.

finds, including an Egyptian collection. It's located in a spacious, airy 18th-century palace, and you don't have to pay a cent to enjoy it.

Musée Lapidaire

27 rue de la République; tel. 04 90 85 75 38;
www.musée-lapidaire.org;
Tues.-Sun. 10am-1pm and 2pm-6pm; free

Housed in an old Jesuit chapel on the main shopping street, the museum is a pleasant place to stumble upon. Luring you in from the doorway is an open view of the overflow archaeological collection of the Musée Calvet. Once again the museum is free, allowing some visitors to dip in for a cursory 10 minute tour, while others linger much longer.

Palais du Roure

3 rue Collège du Roure; tel. 04 13 60 50 01;
www.avignon.fr/ma-ville/culture-et-tourisme/
avignon-musées; Tues.-Sun. 10am-1pm and 2pm-6pm; free

Between 1469 and 1908, this hôtel particulier (lavish town house) was the home of the Baroncelli family. The impressive gothic palace was christened the Palais du Roure by Provençal poet Frédéric Mistral in the 19th century. Today it is a center for Provençal culture, history, traditions, language, and literature. There is a large collection of bells collected by Jeanne de Flandreysy.

Le Musée Louis Vouland

17 rue Victor Hugo; tel. 04 90 86 03 79;
www.vouland.com; Tues.-Sun. 2pm-6pm, closed Jan.;
€6, reduced €4, children under 14 free

Named after its founder, Avignon industrialist Louis Vouland, who died in 1973, the museum houses a varied collection of art and furnishings that belonged to the French aristocracy during the pre- and post-revolutionary eras, with a particular focus on Provençal works. The atypical layout makes the visit feel like a tour of a decadently furnished private house rather than a museum.

Collection Lambert

5 rue Violette; tel. 04 90 16 56 20;
www.collectionlambert.fr; Sept.-May Tues.-Sun.
11am-6pm, July and Aug. 11am-7pm; €10, reduced €8,
6-11 €2, under 6 free

Housed in two hôtel particuliers, the Collection Lambert is something of a haven from the busy bustling streets of the city. The collection is composed of 20th- and 21st-century contemporary art donated to the state by Yvon Lambert, including works by Claire Fontaine, Robert Ryman, and Bertrand Lavier. Excellent temporary exhibitions are also staged.

Le Musée Angladon

5 rue Laboureur; tel. 04 90 82 29 03;
https://angladon.com; Apr. 1-Oct. 31, Tues.-Sun. 1-6
pm, Nov. 1-March 31 Tues.-Sat. 1pm-6 pm, closed Jan.;
€8, reduced €6, children 4-14 €1.50

Picasso, Sisley, Van Gogh, Cézanne, Degas: The list reads like a who's who of the art world. The paintings form part of the collection of courturier Jacques Doucet (1853-1929). Doucet's great-nephew Jean Angladon and Angladon's wife Paulette Martin established the museum as a place for the public to enjoy intimate experiences with some of the great works of modern art.

★ Pont Saint-Bénézet (Pont d'Avignon)

Pont d'Avignon, Boulevard de la Ligne;
tel. 04 32 74 32 74; www.avignon-pont.com; Sept.
1-Nov. 1 9am-7pm, Nov. 2-Feb. 29 9:30am-5:45pm,
March 9am-6:30pm, April 1-June 30 9am-7pm,
July 9am-8pm, Aug. 9am-8:30pm; €5, reduced €4,
joint ticket with Palais des Papes €14

Every monument needs a great backstory, and few have better ones than the Pont d'Avignon. In 1177 Saint-Bénézet, a young shepherd boy, was out tending his sheep when there was an eclipse. The sky blackened, but in the enveloping darkness, a light shone. It was a vision, a message from God calling Bénézet to build a bridge over the Rhône. Angels, he was told, would watch his flock because he had a mightier task. People laughed at the shepherd boy claiming to be a divinely appointed bridge builder. They laughed no more when he placed the first stone, a boulder so massive that no man could lift it.

Wealthy backers flocked to support the miracle worker and a 22-arch, 900-meter (2,952-foot) bridge was completed. Unfortunately, God's blessing did not last forever. Parts of the bridge were swept away in successive floods and rebuilding work continued over the centuries, until in 1688 the city finally accepted the inevitable and let the bridge fall to ruin. Its fame today is as much a product of the children's song "Sur La Pont d'Avignon" as it is of the legend of Saint-Bénézet. The song dates back to the 17th century, and the original version is more likely to have mentioned people dancing under the bridge—where the arches crossed the Île de la Barthelasse—than on it.

The Pont d'Avignon is accessed via rue Ferruce, which leads to the Place du Palais. Stairs take you up the tower to the level of the bridge. A ramp and lift facilitate disabled access. An audio guide accompanies the visit, which lasts about an hour. There's also a small exhibition where you can see a short computer-generated film with a 3D reconstruction of the bridge through the ages. Afterward an accompanying film describes the technical background and research that went into reconstruction. In addition to learning about the legend and history of the bridge, you'll enjoy a beautiful view of Avignon. And if you are with your partner, the end of the bridge is a nice place to share a romantic kiss!

Maison Jean Vilar

8 rue de Mons; tel. 04 90 86 59 64;
https://maisonjeanvilar.org;
Tues.-Sat. 11am-6pm; €6, under 18 free

Jean Vilar started the Avignon Theatre Festival in 1947 (see events). He died in 1973, and in 1979 the Hotel Crochans was acquired by the city of Avignon to house the documents related to creating the festival and to serve as a center for events and exhibitions leading up to the festival. If you love theater and are unable

1

2

3

to make a visit during the festival, then exploring the Jean Vilar archive is a welcome consolation.

Villeneuve-lés-Avignon

Villeneuve-lés-Avignon; www.villeneuvelezavignon.fr

A short taxi or bus ride (Line 11 from Cours President Kennedy) takes you across the river to Villeneuve-lés-Avignon. Until 1790 Avignon itself belonged to either the papacy or the Duchy of Naples, and the French crown exercised its authority from the town of Villeneuve on the opposing bank. These days Villeneuve is a prosperous suburb of Avignon, offering excellent views back across the river, particularly from the Fort Saint André. Place Jean Jaurès is a nice shady square for lunch.

GUIDED TOURS

AVIGNON GOURMET TOUR

Avignon City Center,
meeting point confirmed on reservation;
tel. 06 35 32 08 96; www.avignongourmetours.com;
March 20-Oct. 31 daily; from €49

A guilt-free way to sample the best local produce is to take a walking tour. You'll enjoy tasting olive oil, cheeses, and plentiful Côtes du Rhône wine. A vigorous walk between the stops eases the conscience.

NOCTAMBULES D'AVIGNON

Avignon City Center, meeting point confirmed on
reservation; tel. 06 14 23 41 31;
www.lesnoctambulesdavignon.com/en;
info@lesnoctambulesdavignon;
Apr.-late Sept. daily 9:30pm; €50

Four different themed night tours are offered: Papal History, Past and Present, Christians and Bourgeoise, and City Squares. For those wishing to avoid the hot summer sun, these tours are a great option. Different tours are offered on different nights, so check the online calendar for availability.

1: The Sorgue river runs through the town of L'Isle-sur-la-Sorgue. 2: Roman aqueduct at Pont du Gard, a UNESCO World Heritage Site 3: The imposing Palais des Papes was constructed between 1335 and 1352.

SPORTS AND RECREATION

Parks

ÎLE DE LA BARTHELASSE

The residents of Avignon head to this park to escape the crowds. It's located on a large island in the middle of the Rhône and is popular with cyclists and walkers. The views back toward Avignon are beautiful. In the summer a **shuttle boat** runs every half hour from Boulevard du Quai de La Ligne, a short distance upriver from Pont Saint Bénézet, across to the Île. Alternatively the Park can be accessed from Pont Edouard Daladier.

THE ROCHER DES DOMS GARDEN

Overlooking the Place du Palais is this delightful garden. Once again it's a good spot for views, this time across the Rhône to Villeneuve-lés-Avignon. The garden is also ideal for a picnic in the shade and there's a small snack bar. Children will love the playground.

Cycling

RAMPART CIRCULAR

A 4-kilometer (2.5-mile) cycle route has been created around the old city wall. The route also extends over the Pont Edouard Daladier and onto Île de la Barthelasse. The circular route hugs the Rhône before turning inland and heading through the administrative center of the city. The route can be picked up at any point along the city walls. Try starting at Place Crillon, just off the Place du Palais.

VELOPOP

Avignon stations include Place Pie, Hotel de Ville, Carmes, Port Saint Lazare, Porte Thiers, Porte Lambert, Jaurès; tel. 08 10 45 64 56;
€1 access fee and €0.50 for every half hour

Avignon operates a bike rental scheme as part of its transport service. Locate a station, enter your credit card details and mobile phone number, and you will be sent a code to unlock a bike. After use, return the bike to any Velopop station.

ENTERTAINMENT AND EVENTS

AVIGNON FESTIVAL AND AVIGNONLEOFF

Various venues across town; www.festival-avignon. com; runs for three weeks from end of the first week in July; free to €50, depending on performance

Created in 1947 the Avignon Festival is one of the most important contemporary performing arts festivals in the world. Sixty shows are produced across 40 venues, attracting an audience of 155,000 people. Shows range from dance, to theater, to comedy, to mime, readings, and films. The festival is so successful, it has spawned a more riotous and irreverent baby brother, Avignonleoff (www.avignonleoff.com), which puts on 1,000 shows across town. The majority of the shows are in French, and hunting for English-language performances can seem like looking for a needle in a haystack. However, it is worth persevering. Plus many events, such as dance, don't require any language skills and are often performed in unforgettable venues such as the courtyard of the Palais des Papes. The websites for both the Avignon Festival and Avignonleoff are available in English and contain full program information.

VIBRATIONS

Palais des Papes; https://avignon-vibrations.com/language/en; Aug. 14-Oct. 14 nightly 9:15pm and 10:15pm

This summer light show on walls of Palais des Papes is aimed at all ages. Images of the Pont du Gard interchange with dancing whales, ice cream cones raining down on lavender fields, and flamenco dancing. It's all a touch bizarre but somehow it works, no doubt thanks to the high courtyard of the Palais des Papes, which provides the perfect environment for this enchanting extravaganza.

SHOPPING

BROCANTE

Place Pie; Tuesday and Thursday 8am-5pm

Twice a week year round, 30 *brocante* (secondhand) traders set up in the picturesque Place Pie. From antique mirrors to limited-edition books, there are always surprises, and it's always fun browsing.

ERIC ET LES CHICS FILLES

7 Place des Corps Saints; tel. 04 90 82 54 67; Tues.-Sat. 10am-7pm

Nine different designers present their collections of clothing, knitwear, jewelery, bags, and textiles in a funky creative space.

L'OEIL CELESTE

48 rue des Fourbisseurs; tel. 04 90 85 29 12; Tues.-Sat. 10.15am-12.30pm and 2.30pm-7pm

Designer Patricia Gauthier has put together a collection of silver jewellery using stones, gemstones, and minerals from around the world.

CONCEPT STORE

16 Place de La Principale; tel. 04 90 85 29 86; Mon. 1:30pm-7pm, Tues.-Sat. 10am-7pm

Offering a curated range of limited-edition or one-of-a-kind fashion and design items, this is a great place to pick up something unusual for the home.

FOOD

Regional Cuisine

LA VIEILLE FONTAINE

12 Place Crillon, Hotel Europe; tel. 04 90 14 76 76; www.heurope.com; Tues.-Sat. 12:30pm-1:30pm and 7:30pm-9:30pm; €38-€58

La Vieille Fontaine is a destination gastronomic restaurant located on the grounds of the luxurious Hotel Europe. Provençal cooking tends to be hearty but not always refined; here the emphasis is on elevating regional dishes with the use of modern cooking techniques. The menu changes regularly; representative dishes include *foie gras* (goose or duck liver) and beet mousse, and asparagus with mussels. Book in the summer to ensure a table on the terrace next to the old fountain.

1: Posters cover everything during the Avignon Festival. **2:** shopping in Les Halles

★ L'AGAPE

21 Place Corps Saints; tel. 04 90 85 04 06;
www.restaurant-agape-avignon.com;
Tues.-Sat. noon-2pm and 7:30pm-9:30pm; €27-30

A great location on a pretty square, seasonal good value menus, a convivial atmosphere, and inventive cooking make this one of the most popular restaurants in the city. Try the roasted duckling with white beans, swiss chard, and a cocoa sauce and you'll be back the next day for seconds. Reserve in advance, particularly in season.

LA TABLE HAUTE DE LA MIRANDE

4 Place de L'Amirande; tel. 04 90 14 20 20;
www.lamirande.com; Tues., Wed., Fri. and Sat.
evening 8pm to 10:30pm; €95 menu including wine

Avignon's most famous luxury hotel offers an unforgettable dining experience. Gather around chef Severine Sagnet's table, which seats 14, and experience her farm-to-table cooking style while making friends with locals and travelers. Booking is essential for this intimate and one-of-a-kind experience.

HIELY LUCULLUS

5 rue de La République; tel. 04 90 86 17 07;
www.hiely-lucullus.com; Thurs.-Mon. noon-1:30pm
and 7:30pm-9:30pm; €27-32

Food is a very serious business at Hiely Lucullus. In the upstairs dining room just off the main shopping street, every detail has been refined. The crisp table linen and polished cutlery impress before you even sit down. Presentation of dishes, such as saddle of rabbit stuffed with olives served with a chicken jus sauce, is immaculate. Reservations are advisable.

POLLEN

3 bis rue de la Petite Calade; tel. 04 86 34 93 74;
http://pollen-restaurant.fr;
Mon.-Fri. noon-1:30 and 7:30pm-9:30pm; €28-58

Chef Mathieu Desmaret left the Hotel Europe to set up his own gastronomic restaurant. Pollen opened in 2018 to great reviews. Signature dishes include mackerel with grilled vegetables and a citron and ginger dressing. The vibe is cool, modern, and minimalist, with a clientele of serious foodies who love nothing better than chatting about what's on the plate in front of them.

MAISON DE FOGASSES

37 rue des Fourbisseurs;
tel. 04 90 87 25 02;
www.maison-de-fogasses; Thurs.- Sat.
7:30pm-9:30pm, Sunday noon-3pm; €20-30

Corinne Guyon has opened up an old town house, parts of which date to the 13th century,

fresh pastries at the market

to the general public. There are apartments to rent and a popular restaurant in the leafy garden. Try the lavish Sunday brunch, when the table almost sags with the weight of salads, hams, cheeses, and sweet and savory dishes. Reservations, particularly for brunch, are recommended.

Bistros
LE CARRÉS DU PALAIS

1 Place du Palais; tel. 04 65 00 00 01;
www.carredupalais.fr;
daily noon-2:30pm and 7:30pm-9:30pm; €26- 30
Situated in the old Bank of France building, the Carré offers a wine school, a wine bar, and a large bistro with a terrace facing the Place du Palais with a view of the Palais des Papes. Matching whatever you order from the seasonal menu with the perfect glass of Côtes du Rhône is the house speciality.

MAISON RIPERT

28 rue de La Bonneterie;
tel. 04 90 27 37 97 12:30pm-1:30pm and
7:30pm-9:30pm, closed Sun. and Wed.; €26-30
Set in an old patisserie shop dating back to 1820, the interior is a delight, with wooden chairs, checked tablecloths, and gilded mirors. Occasional photo exhibitions and jazz music add to the atmosphere. The menu is fairly standard bistro fare with dishes such as lamb shank and duck breast. Reservations are advisable during the tourist season.

Cafés and Light Bites
SALON DE THÉ

2 rue de La République;
daily 7:30am-7:30pm;
€3.50 for a pastry
Right in the tourist center of Avignon, this old-fashioned café is a great place to stop for a bite. Pick a pastry from the delectable selection on display inside, then take your ticket and a seat on the terrace. You can enjoy your sugar fix while watching the shoppers parade by on the main drag.

VIOLETTE

30 Place Saint Corps; tel. 04 90 47 45 50;
Tues.-Sat. 7:30am-7:30pm; pastries from €3
This café with a funky vibe is a good place for a snack, from sandwiches to *pain au chocolat* (chocolate-filled croissant) to delicious cakes and pastries. It's located on one of Avignon's pretty church squares, and you can either eat in or take your delicacy to a nearby shady bench and watch the world pass by.

Markets
LES HALLES FOOD MARKET

18 Place Pie; tel. 04 90 27 15 15;
www.avignon-leshalles.com; Tues.-Sat. 6am-2pm
Even if you have just eaten, or started a diet, a visit to Les Halles is a must. This covered market is like a window into the French soul. The pride that each of the market traders takes in the produce and the care with which it is arranged speak to the French people's enduring relationship with the land and their cuisine. There's color everywhere, not just in the fruit and vegetables but also in the interchanges between clients and stall holders; recipes are swapped, and cooking tips are shared. In one corner there's an oyster bar, and every Saturday at 11am a chef gives a cooking demonstration. There's also a cooking school-cum-restaurant run by American chef Jonathan Chiri (www. jonathanchiri.com).

BARS AND NIGHTLIFE
THE CAGE

1 avenue des Sources; tel. 04 90 27 00 84;
www.thecage.fr; Thurs.-Sun. 10:30pm till late; €10
admission, €8 drinks
This popular nightclub has regular theme evenings, such as kitsch and '80s music. Visiting DJs really get the local crowd going with techno nights.

L'ESCLAVE BAR

12 rue des Limas; tel. 04 90 85 14 91; www.facebook.
com/esclavebar; Open Mon.-Sat. and Sunday in
summer 11:45pm till late; alcoholic drinks €8
L'Esclave is Avignon's only city center gay bar.

Tuesday is karaoke night, and it is particularly popular.

LES AMBASSADEURS

27 rue Bancasse; tel. 04 90 86 31 55;
www.clublesambassadeurs.fr; Thurs.-Sun. 10:30pm till
late; free admission, drinks from €8

Cozy booths surround the usually packed dance floor of Les Ambassadeurs. Dress well to make it past the doorman.

CUBANITO CAFÉ

51 rue Carnot; tel. 04 90 86 98 04;
www.cubanitocafeavignon.com, Tues.-Sun.
5pm-1:30am; drinks from €4, tapas from €5

A restaurant, tapas bar, dance club, and dance school all rolled into one. Themed nights are raucous with scantily clad Brazilian dancers up on the bar swaying and grinding.

PUB O'NEILL'S

38 cours Jean Jaurès; tel. 04 32 76 33 40;
daily 10am-1:30am; drinks from €3.50

This roudy Irish bar has weekly live bands on Monday night and shows all the major sporting events.

ACCOMMODATIONS
€50-100
HOTEL CENTRAL

31 rue de La République; tel. 04 90 86 07 81;
www.hotel-central-avignon.com; €89 d

Hotel Central offers 35 simply furnished rooms with Wi-Fi, air-conditioning, and ensuite bathrooms. The main shopping street is just out the front door. There's a small garden and outside terrace. For cyclists there's secure storage for their bikes. The nearest parking is Jean Jaurès.

€100-200
CLOITRE SAINT LOUIS

20 rue du Portail Boquier; tel. 04 90 27 55 55;
www.cloitre-saint-louis.com; €100 d

Choose between the historic cloister building or the modern annex at this city center hotel with a pool. All rooms are ensuite with contemporary furnishings, Wi-Fi, and air-conditioning. The hotel has private parking for €15 per night. The courtyard is particularly charming with centuries-old plane trees shading a moss-covered fountain. Dining outside next to the old city walls is an atmospheric pleasure.

LE LIMAS

51 rue de Limas; tel. 06 69 00 60 37;
www.le-limas-avignon.com; €140 d

This four-bedroom bed-and-breakfast right in the historic heart of Avignon has a pretty roof terrace overlooking the Palais des Papes. In the summer months it's perfect for a croissant and coffee. All rooms have air-conditioning, ensuite bathrooms, and Wi-Fi. The nearest parking is the underground Palais des Papes.

MAISON ORSINI

21 rue Montée de la Tour, Villenueve Les Avignon;
tel. 06 82 27 65 94; www.maisonorsini.com; €170 d

So often in Provence, it is better to be on the outside looking in. The view from the terrace of the Maison Orsini over the Rhône to the Palais des Papes makes the stay. There's a large selection of rooms and apartments, all comfortably furnished with ensuite bathrooms, Wi-Fi, and air-conditioning. There's a charming courtyard restaurant where you can enjoy the sunset and there's parking on site.

Over €200
★ CLOS SALUCES

11 rue Saluces; tel. 06 72 75 49 37;
www.leclossaluces.fr; €240 d

It took three years to renovate this beautiful 19th-century town house close to the Palais des Papes. The interior decor is a rich mixture of vintage furnishings and objects from the 1950s to the 1970s. All rooms have ensuite bathrooms and Wi-Fi, and there's a verdant garden. The nearest parking is the underground Palais des Papes.

HOTEL D'EUROPE

12 Place Crillon; tel. 04 90 14 76 76;
www.heurope.com; €260 d

Former guests at this luxury city center hotel

include Charles Dickens and Jackie Kennedy. All rooms have ensuite bathrooms and Wi-Fi, but at the lower end of the price range they can be a little cramped. Chandeliers, period paintings, furniture, and tapestries all help to create an ambiance that reminds guests of, but does not overplay, the history of the city. Parking is €20 per day.

★ LA MIRANDE

4 Place de L'Amirande; tel. 04 90 14 20 20; www.la-mirande.fr; €355 d

There's a French Downton Abbey feel to staying at La Mirande. Pieces of exquisite French decorative arts are everywhere; some even hide secrets like the mirror televisions. La Mirande is the byword for luxury in Avignon, and as you would expect all rooms have Wi-Fi, ensuite bathrooms, and air-conditioning.

LA DIVINE COMÉDIE

16 Impasse Jean Pierre Gras; tel. 06 77 06 85 40; www.la-divine-comedie.com; €400 d

Boasting the largest private garden in Avignon, with a 15-meter (49-foot) swimming pool and wellness center, this five-suite guest house, is the latest addition to Avignon's canon of luxury retreats. The inside drips with antique furniture, but has also been rewired to provide high-speed Wi-Fi everywhere. All suites have air-conditioning and ensuite bathrooms. Parking is available on site.

INFORMATION AND SERVICES

TOURIST OFFICE

41 Cours Jean Jaurès; tel. 04 32 74 32 74; www.avignon-tourisme.com; Mon.-Sat. 9am-6pm, Sun. 10am-1pm

Avignon's central tourist office has English-speaking staff who can help with anything from finding accommodations to getting tickets for events. The office is stocked with helpful maps and brochures that cover not just Avignon but also the surrounding countryside.

CENTRE HOSPITALIER D' AVIGNON

305 rue Raoul Follereau; tel. 04 32 75 33 33; www.ch-avignon.fr

Located to the south of the city near the TGV station, the hospital has a 24-hour emergency service.

POST OFFICE

2 rue Petite Meuse; tel. 04 32 75 33 339; Mon.-Fri. 9am-noon and 2pm-5pm

On the corner of the attractive Place Pie in the center of Avignon, the post office offers the standard services for sending letters and packages, both within France and internationally.

GETTING THERE
By Train

The **TGV station** is on Avenue de la Gare in the Courtine district southwest of the city center. It takes about 2 hours and 40 minutes to travel to Avignon from **Paris.** It takes 1 hour to get there from **Lyon** and 30 minutes from **Marseille.** The price of a TGV train varies hugely depending on how far ahead you book and when you travel. Complicating matters further, there is a new low-cost TGV service called Ouigo, which offers a no-frills service between the cities. If you travel in the week in the middle of the day, it is possible to pick up a train from Avignon to Paris for as little as €25. Travel in peak times and the same journey could cost you more than €200. There are new direct TGV connections between Avignon and Barcelona, Madrid, Frankfurt, Geneva, and Amsterdam. A train connection from the TGV station to the city center runs 35 times a day; the journey time is 5 minutes on a TER regional train. The city center train station on Boulevard Saint Roch just outside the town walls offers connections to local towns such as Carpentras.

By Plane

Avignon airport (335 Avenue Clément Ader, Avignon-Montfavet; www.avignon.aeroport.fr) has direct flights to Southampton, Birmingham, and London May-September.

Bus Line 30 connects the airport and the city center. The larger **Marseille Provence airport** is 45 minutes' drive away.

By Car

The city sits at the heart of the motorway network. It is located on the A7 and A9 autoroutes, and the national N7 and N100 routes. Traveling from **Paris** to Avignon by car takes just under 7 hours on the A6 and A7 autoroutes. From **Arles,** take the D2; the journey is 45 kilometers (28 miles) and takes about 50 minutes. From **Aix-en-Provence,** take the A7 for 88 kilometers (54 miles); the trip takes an hour and 10 minutes. From **Marseille,** take the A7 covering 105 kilometers (65 miles) in an hour and 10 minutes

The suburbs of Avignon can be off-putting when arriving by car. Plentiful traffic lights and roundabouts cause congestion. Tower blocks and shopping centers crowd the roadside, and the city center—with its narrow lanes and pedestrian areas—can be difficult to negotiate with a car. So, you will be better off parking your car while you enjoy central Avignon. The best parking for access to the historic center is the Palais des Papes, located on the north side of the city on the banks for the Rhône. There are also parking lots outside the city center, at Île Piot and Parking Les Italiens,which are free of charge. A park-and-ride bus takes you to the city center.

GETTING AROUND

Most people will find that the easiest way to get around Avignon is to **walk.** Many of the roads are pedestrian-friendly and the distances between sights are relatively short.

Electric shuttle buses connect the out-of-town parking lots on Île Piot and Parking Les Italiens to the city center. Within the city **La Baladine,** seven-seat electic vehicles travel through the city center. A ride costs €0.50 and you simply need to wave your hand for the vehicle to stop, and get on. **Velopop cycles** are available for rent from 17 cycle stations across Avignon.

Around Avignon

SIGHTS

★ **Pont du Gard**

400 Route du Pont du Gard, Vers-Pont-du-Gard

A short hop over the Rhône from Avignon is the Pont du Gard Roman Aqueduct. At nearly 50 meters (164 feet) tall and 490 meters (1,607) long, this was the highest aqueduct of the Roman world, boasting 47 arches at the time of its construction. Its job was to carry water to the city of Nîmes 25 kilometers (15.5 miles) away. The sheer scale of the endeavor provokes most people to pause in their stride, stop, and stare. The three-tier aqueduct was built with 50,000 tons of stone. A visit includes entry to the on-site museum, which delves into the science of how the Romans managed to construct such a behemoth. For children there's a dedicated learning-through-play area, where they can assume various roles from Roman engineer to archaeologist. Surrounding parkland is a pleasant spot for a picnic lunch. Alternatively there's a snack bar, bistro, and restaurant. To drive to Pont du Gard from Avignon, take the N100, covering 26 kilometers (16 miles) in 28 minutes.

RECREATION

KAYAK VERT

8 Chemin de Saint-Vincent, Collias;
tel. 04 66 22 80 76; www.kayakvert.com; descends
every 30 minutes June-Sept., 9am-5pm, reserve in
advance.; €23, reduced €19, children 6-12 €12

An alternative fun way to see the Pont is to kayak from Collias. The trip downstream takes a couple of hours, and all the effort is rewarded by an unparalleled view of the Pont from beneath its arches. The company then provides coaches to take you back upriver.

FOOD
LA BEGUDE SAINT PIERRE
D981, Vers Pont du Gard; tel. 04 66 02 63 60; www. hotel-begude-saint-pierre.com; Tues.-Sat. noon-1:30pm and 7:30pm-9:30pm; €26 two-course menu

Just 2 kilometers (1.25 miles) from the Pont, this semi-gastronomic restaurant is located in the garden of a hotel. Relax away from the crowds on a terrace overlooking the pool and enjoy classic bistro dishes such as lamb filet with a red wine sauce and roasted vegetables. The old stone walls of the farmhouse add a rustic touch. Service is warm and friendly, with a clientele of hotel residents and passing tourists.

CLOS DE VIGNES
9 place du 8 mai 1945, Castillon de Gard; tel. 04 66 37 02 26; www.leclosdesvignes30.fr; Fri.-Tues. noon-2:30pm and 7:30pm-9pm; €26 two-course menu

Situated in the sleepy village of Castillon de Garde, the Clos de Vigne boasts an attractive vine-covered terrace. The cooking is excellent, although some local dishes such as Veal's Head can be challenging. For less adventurous diners, there's always a safer option such as steak with pepper sauce.

The Vaucluse

Cheaper, quieter, and more authentic than the tourist hotspots, the northern Vaucluse is an area of Provence that is often overlooked by visitors. Yet at Orange and Vaison-la-Romaine are Roman ruins that can compete with those in Arles, and dotted throughout the Dentelles de Montmirail are picturesque villages that rival those in the Luberon or Les Alpilles. Added to this are three unique reasons to visit. First, L'Isle-sur-la-Sorgue is a town unlike any other in Provence. It is built at the branching of the Sorgue river, and a network of canals and bridges link its pretty streets, earning this town the nickname the Venice of Provence. The sight of the waterwheels (there are still 20 turning throughout the town) is alone worth a visit, but most people come for the antiques, from chandeliers to leather club armchairs to smaller items such as kitchen tools; browsing the stores is an utter pleasure.

Second, there's Mont Ventoux, which dominates the skyline of Provence. It's visible from the Luberon, Arles, Les Alpilles, and throughout the northern Vaucluse, peaking between trees and jutting majestically above other lesser peaks. There is no better way to understand the geography of Provence than standing on its summit. How you get to the top is up to you, but note the ascent once famously killed a professional cyclist in the Tour de France, so if in doubt, drive. In the winter the two small ski resorts near the summit tend to have snow from late December until the end of February.

Finally, although the vignerons of Bandol on the Var coast might quibble, the southern Rhône is the finest wine-producing region in Provence. Be careful though, and check the alcohol content listed on the label, because these days some wines contain as much as 15.5 percent alcohol, which is practically the level of a fortified wine. The effect can be not so much to loosen your tongue as to unravel it and lasso it around a nearby tree.

ORIENTATION
The Vaucluse stretches from its capital, Avignon, in the west, north along the banks of the Rhône, passing the nearby wine-producing village of **Châteauneuf-du-Pape** toward the town of **Orange** 30 kilometers (19 miles) away. Orange is famed for its Roman Theatre. To the northwest of Orange is another celebrated Roman site, **Vaison-la-Romaine,** and south of Vaison is the small mountain chain,

the **Dentelles de Montmirail**. Here you will find well-known **wine-producing villages** such as Gigondas, Vacqueyras, Rasteau, and Beaumes-de-Venise. Immediately to the east of the Dentelles is the unmissable highest mountain in Provence: **Mont Ventoux.** Head south from Mont Ventoux and you'll encounter the ever-churning waterwheels of the renowned antiques center of **L'Isle-sur-la-Sorgue**. The Vaucluse, in fact, extends farther east from here, into the Luberon, an area covered later in this guide.

CHÂTEAUNEUF-DU-PAPE

The construction of Châteauneuf's eponymous château was started under Pope John XII in 1317. Today the ruins of its walls still sit proudly on the hill above the village. However, the wine industry that the Avignon Popes nurtured survives. Look carefully at the fields of vines and you will see round stones surrounding the bases of the vines. These were left behind after the retreat of an ancient sea. Today they soak up the heat of the sun during the day and act like radiators at night, keeping the soil around the vines warm, speeding the maturation of the grapes and maintaining moisture in the soil. All of this helps to produce sumptuous red wines. Upon arrival in Châteauneuf-du-Pape, you'll see that the outskirts of the village are dominated by the tasting rooms of the major vineyards. Once you have had a few nips of wine, the village is worth exploring. Head up the hill toward the château, and then duck off the main drag to find picturesque and sleepy side streets.

TOP EXPERIENCE

★ Wine Tasting
MAISON BROTTE
Avenue Saint-Pierre de Luxembourg; tel. 04 90 83 59 44; www.brotte.com; April 15-Oct. 15, 9am -1pm and 2pm-7pm, June-mid-Sept. 9am-7pm, Oct. 15-Apr. 14,

9am-noon and 2pm-6pm; free tasting
On the outskirts of Châteauneuf-du-Pape, this domaine offers the most informative overall visit. A small museum has been created presenting an explanation of the unique terroir of Châteauneuf-du-Pape. Reds and whites from Châteauneuf and throughout the Rhône valley can be tasted.

LA CAVE FAMILLE PERRIN
1 rue du Portail; tel. 04 90 02 15 54; www.beaucastel.com/en; Mon.-Sat. 10am-6:30pm; free tasting
Like many Châteauneuf producers, the Perrin family have moved their tasting room into the village. While it is a shame not to see the grounds of Château Beaucastel, the range of wines to taste makes up for the disappointment, including the blockbuster rosé Miraval, famously created by Brad Pitt and Angelina Joli. You can taste some white wines, as well as the more expensive Châteauneuf-du-Pape reds; bottles of aged Châteauneuf exceed €50 each.

BEAURENARD
10 Avenue Saint Pierre de Luxembourg; tel. 04 90 83 71 79; www.beaurenard.fr; Mon.-Fri. 9am-noon and 1:30pm-5:30pm; free tasting
This renowned producer has a tasting room and wine cellar near the entrance to town. If you want to take a tour of the cellar it helps to phone in advance, but you can taste the estate's wines without a reservation. In addition to Châteauneuf-du-Pape, there's an excellent Rasteau full of spices and ripe fruit available for €15 a bottle.

ANDRE MATTIEU
3bis, route de Courthézon; tel. 04 90 83 72 09; www.domaine-andre-mathieu.com; Mon.-Sat. 9am-5pm; free tasting
Visiting Domaine Mattieu is an intimate experience, unlike some of the other large producers who can afford to create tasting rooms separate from their châteaus. You'll meet the wine grower and see the land where the vines are growing. Prices for a bottle of Châteauneuf start around €20.

1: Fontaine-de-Vaucluse 2: the vineyards and landscape surrounding Châteauneuf-du-Pape

★ VINADEA

8 rue Maréchal Foch;

tel. 04 90 83 79 60; www.vinadea.com;

daily 10am-12:30pm and 2pm-6pm; free tasting

This shop is recommended by locals as the best place to buy and taste wine. More than 200 different wines are on sale from Châteauneuf and surrounding appellations, and different bottles are opened every day for free tastings. In 2019, the shop will see the opening of a wine bar, wine museum, and artistic exhibition space in the old caves adjacent to the shop. Prices per bottle are the same as, or very close to, the the retail price in the vineyard.

Tours
WINE PRESTIGE TOUR

Pickup and drop-off available for addresses within 10 kilometers (6.2 miles) of Châteauneuf-du-Pape; tel. 06 83 53 39 79; https://wineprestigetour.com; daily; €90 half day, €140 full day

Pierre Fernandez was born in Châteauneuf-du-Pape. His grandmother was one of the first female winemakers in the appellation, and he's a qualified sommelier. In other words, what he doesn't know about the wines of the region isn't worth knowing. Tours are friendly and informative, and Pierre's connections open doors (and bottles) that would otherwise be closed to the public.

AVIGNON WINE TOUR

Pickup and drop-off available for addresses within Avignon; tel. 06 28 05 33 84; www.avignon-wine-tour.com; weekly tours include Châteauneuf-du-Pape on Wednesday; €130 per day

Francois Marcou leads wine tours throughout Provence. As you would expect from a former hotelier and restaurateur, he's charming and very knowledgeable about wine. The tour includes tastings at four vineyards and a lunch stop.

Festivals
VERRAISON FESTIVAL

Throughout the village; www.chateauneuf-du-pape-tourisme.fr; first weekend in August

To celebrate the ripening of the grapes, Châteauneuf holds a huge party. There's usually a medieval banquet and a "Papal" procession. In a village where it's never hard to find a drink, it becomes impossible to move without having a glass thrust in to your hands.

Food
LE VERGER DES PAPES

Rue Montée du Château; tel. 04 90 83 50 40; Mon.-Sun. noon-1:30pm and 7:30pm-9pm; €15-25

Nestled in the heights of Châteauneuf-du-Pape, in the lea of the ruined walls of the old château, Le Verger des Papes is a village stalwart. The menu (lunch only) is well thought out, with something for everyone, including—somewhat unusually for France—a good vegetarian option of zucchini cake, served with a Nyon olive biscuit and a creamed garlic sauce. Reservations are necessary in the summer season.

CHÂTEAU FINES ROCHES

1901 Route de Sorgues; tel. 04 90 83 70 23; www.Châteaufinesroches.com; daily noon-2pm and 7pm-9pm; €32 lunch menu; €44 evening menu

The restaurant boasts a lovely terrace overlooking the vines and lures an audience of well-heeled oenophiles. The cooking is good but not overly creative. Dishes might include a poached filet of guinea fowl or grilled fish in a butter sauce. Be careful because the excellent wine list quickly bumps up the bill.

LE PISTOU

15 rue Joseph Ducos; tel. 04 90 83 71 75; http://lepistou-restaurant.e-monsite.com; Tues.-Sun. noon-2pm and 7pm-9pm; €15-26

This restaurant is a popular choice in the center of town. There's a small terrace and a cozy dining room. The menu offers comfort food like pork in mustard sauce as well as more exotic dishes like wok-cooked prawns with pineapple. In season it's worth reserving.

LA MERE GERMAINE

3 rue Commandant Lemaître; tel. 04 90 22 78 34;
http://lameregermaine.fr/fr; €19 plat du Jour, €30
menu

Located in the dining room of a village center hotel, this restaurant is full of old-world atmosphere. Tiled floors, leather banquettes, and a wooden bar all add to the traditional feel. The food is competitively priced and well-prepared, relying on French classics such as *foie gras* and veal chops. It's not normally necessary to reserve.

Accommodations
HOTEL SOMMELIER

2268 Route de Roquemaure D17 Grange Neuve;
tel. 09 70 35 60 29; www.la-sommellerie.fr; €155 d

Three kilometers (1.85 miles) outside Châteauneuf, with its own pool and restaurant, this hotel is a good place from which to explore the surrounding vineyards. The 16 rooms all have Wi-Fi, air-conditioning, and ensuite bathrooms. There are two large family suites. Most rooms overlook the swimming pool, which nestles snuggly beneath the picturesque ivy covered walls of the L-shaped hotel building.

HOTEL GARBURE

3 rue Joseph Ducos; tel. 04 90 83 75 08;
www.logishotels.com/fr/hotel/hotel-la-garbure-6270?partid=661; €100 d

This friendly, centrally located hotel also has a popular restaurant. With only eight bedrooms (all with ensuite bathrooms and Wi-Fi) it's worth reserving well in advance. The rooms are colorfully decorated in typical Provençal style, and the stone walls of the hotel building add a touch of historical ambiance. Private parking is available, and numerous wine tastings await just up the street.

★ CHÂTEAU FINES ROCHES

1901 Route de Sorgues; tel. 04 90 83 70 23;
www.Châteaufinesroches.com; €199 d

This hotel is set in a picturesque 19th-century château, completely surrounded by vines. Views from the turret room out across the countryside are magnificent. All 11 rooms have ensuite bathrooms, Wi-Fi, and air-conditioning. There's an on-site restaurant with a terrace looking out to Chateauneuf and Mont Ventoux. The pool area offers similar sweeping views. Services offered by the hotel include soothing massages to take away the strains of a long day of sightseeing.

Getting There and Around
BY BUS

From **Avignon, Transvaucluse Line 2** runs to Sorgues (see www.sudmobilite.fr); this part of the journey can also be made by train from the Avignon central station. From Sorgue, a connecting bus **(Line 23)** takes you to Châteauneuf-du-Pape. The journey, including the connection, takes just over 1 hour and costs €4. Using the train as a substitute where necessary, there are five services a day. Line 23 also runs five times a day between Châteauneuf-du-Pape and Orange; the trip takes 25 minutes and costs €2. Consult www.sudmobilite.fr for full bus timetables.

BY CAR

From **Avignon** to Châteauneuf-du-Pape, take the D907; the trip is 17 kilometers (10.5 miles) and takes 23 minutes. From **Orange,** take the D68 for 10 kilometers (6.2 miles); the drive takes 16 minutes. If you're coming from **Vaison-la-Romaine,** take the D977; the journey is 35 kilometers (21.75 miles) and takes 40 minutes; and from **L'Isle-sur-la-Sorgue,** take the D16 31 kilometers (19.25 miles) and you will arrive in 43 minutes.

The village of Châteauneuf-du-Pape is best explored on foot, but you will also want to see the surrounding area. If you do not have a car, consider renting a bike to get out and about in the vineyards. Bicycles are available for rent from **Sun-e-bike** (Rue des Consuls, Châteauneuf-du-Pape, tel. 07 58 14 33 97, www.location-velo-provence.com).

ORANGE

Few tourists who whizz past Orange on the Autoroute du Soleil on the way to the coast ever think of stopping. The enlightened ones get to experience a historic town with a medieval center, and a couple of major Roman monuments. Stop for longer than a night, though, and you'll need to get out and explore the surrounding countryside. Finding your way around is relatively easy. The historic center is ringed by the busy N7 and D976 roads. The Roman Arc de Triomphe is located on the N7 just as it approaches the town from the north. The Roman Theatre (Théâtre Antique) is at the southern end of the historic center.

Sights

★ ROMAN THEATRE OF ORANGE (THÉÂTRE ANTIQUE)

Rue Madeleine Roch; www.theatre-antique.com; daily Jan.-Feb. and Nov.-Dec. 9:30am-4:30pm; €9.50, reduced €7.50, price includes admission to the art and history museum, virtual reality headset €5

Academic study of Roman theater continues to explore why performances took place, who performed, and who watched, and central to the understanding of the art form is the theater in Orange. Built around 1 BC, it is the only Roman theater in the world whose stage wall is still standing. The wall measures 103 meters (338 feet) long and 36 meters (118 feet) high.

Spaced along both the interior and exterior façade are entrance and exit points for the actors. Above the principal door is a statue of the Emperor Augustus. A new contemporary-style roof has been added to protect the wall and ensure good acoustic quality for the performances that continue to take place. In Roman times, a canvas covering would have been stretched above the stage, protecting actors and the 10,000-strong audience from the heat. A visit today includes an excellent audio guide that adds historical color, plus the Ghosts of the Theatre performance: a multi-media presentation depicting the different ways the theater has been used through the ages.

MUSÉE D'ART ET D'HISTOIRE

Rue Madeleine Roch; www.theatre-antique.com/en/ discovering-site/orange-museum; daily Jan.-Feb. and Nov.-Dec. 9:45am-12:30pm and 1:30pm-4:30pm, March and Oct. 9:45am-12:30pm and 1:30pm-5:30pm, April-May and Sept. 9:15am-6pm, June-Aug. 9:15am-7pm; €5.50, reduced €4.50

Orange might seem like a small sleepy town, but its history is fascinating. Here's a snippet of what you can discover at the town museum: Orange began life as the Roman town of Aurisio in 35 BC. During the reign of the

the Roman theatre in Orange

French King Charlemagne (742-814) it became the home of the Counts of Orange, a dynasty that ruled The Netherlands during the 16th century. In 1689 William of Orange acceded to the English throne. The Oranges certainly gained ground, also giving their names to West, East, and South Orange in New Jersey, and the Orange Free State in South Africa.

ARC DE TRIOMPHE

Av L'Arc de Triomphe; always open

In the Middle Ages, the Triumphal Roman Arch of Orange was incorporated into the town walls. Crossbow men, taking the medieval equivalent of a cigarette break, apparently peppered the façade with bolts, accounting for the pockmarking all across the face of the monument. Those with more respect for history can study the engravings depicting naval battles, spoils of war, and Roman battles against Gauls and Germanic tribes. The arch, built during the reign of Augustus (27 BC to AD 14) is now found in a small park where the N7 road splits as it enters Orange.

Entertainment and Events
CHORÉGIES D'ORANGE

Théâtre Antique, rue Madeleine Roche; www.choregies.fr; beginning of July to beginning of August

Dating back to 1860 the *chorégies* are thought to make up the oldest surviving music festival in France. The format has changed over the years, and now concentrates exlusively on opera, with around six performances taking place over a one-month period. Booking early is essential to secure a seat to watch international opera stars performing in the capitvating venue of the Roman Theatre.

Food
LE PARVIS

55 cours Pourtoules; tel. 04 90 34 82 00; https://leparvisorange.com; Tues.-Sat. noon-1:30pm and 7:30pm-9pm; menus €21-48

Under the new ownership of Nicolas and Delphine Jay since the beginning of 2018, this restaurant is building a reputation for beautiful, tasty plates of food. Rumor has it

that a Michelin star is on its way. Tourists and locals enjoy dishes like filet mignon of pork with sweet potato mash, curried zucchinim and cider vinegar. Reservations in advance during the main tourist season are advisable.

AU PETIT PATIO

58 Cours Aristide-Briand; tel. 04 90 29 69 27; Mon.-Sat. noon-1:30pm and 7pm-9:30pm; €19 lunchtime menu

Au Petit Patio offers fun bistro cooking and an attractive outside terrace. The menu is based around Provençal favorites, with a slight bias toward fish. Popular with locals, the atmosphere is convivial, and it's sensible to reserve, particularly in the evenings in season.

A LA MAISON

4 Place des Cordeliers; tel. 04 90 60 98 83; Tues.-Sat. noon-2pm and 7pm-10:30pm, Mon. 7pm-10:30pm; €12-25

A la Maison is located in a quiet spot a few streets from the Roman Theatre, next to a bubbling fountain. The menu is fairly typical of most Provençal cafés, offering salads, and grilled meat and fish. You'll receive a warm welcome, and the food is freshly prepared.

Accommodations
L'HERBIER

8 Place aux Herbes; tel. 04 90 34 09 23; €80 d

This is an excellent value two-star hotel in the historic center of Orange. It's located on a pretty square, and has a pleasant terrace, surrounded by a stone wall, where breakfast is served. All rooms have ensuite bathrooms and Wi-Fi. The nearest parking is near the Roman Theatre.

AU VIN CHAMBRE

15 Avenue Frederic Mistral; tel. 04 88 84 12 19; www.auvinchambre.com; €150 d

Here's one for the oenophiles: This boutique hotel has its own wineshop selling a curated selection from across France. The hotel has five suites, all with ensuite bathrooms and Wi-Fi, plus there's a large garden with a pool, table tennis, and a petanque court. There's also a

Truffles: The Black Diamond of Provence

Provence is home to one of the most expensive gastronomic delicacies in the world: the *tuber melanosporum*, or black truffle. Depending on harvesting conditions, the price for 1 kilo (2.2 pounds) of truffle can near 1,000 euros, hence the affectionate nickname, black diamond.

Part of the fun of eating truffles, and the justification for the price, is the associated mystique. The fact that truffles are so hard to find means they are all the more prized. As a fungus, they can only grow from trees (usually oak) infected with a specific virus. In the soil underneath such trees, a thin thread attaches the truffle to its host tree. Truffles are also very choosy about exactly when they grow. In general, truffle season is December to February. For a bumper harvest, rain in spring needs to be followed by a dry summer and a cold winter. Then there's the lunar cycle: Some hunters insist on a full moon before they will go out foraging.

To find truffles an expert dog is a must, ideally suckled from birth on a mother who has had truffle oil rubbed on her nipples. All this effort is worthwhile because truffles taste majestic. Grated over some scrambled eggs, stirred into a pasta or risotto, or even mixed with a little butter in a baked potato, the truffle transforms everyday food into a banquet.

WHERE TO FIND TRUFFLES

- **Richerenches:** Thanks to a combination of soil and climate, the small village of Richerenches in the northern Vaucluse is the center of Provençal truffle production. Every Saturday from mid-November to the end of March, Richerenches hosts **a truffle market,** luring restaurant buyers from across France (page 354).

- **Hotel Montmirail** (Route de Montmirail, Vacqueras; www.hotelmontmirail.com): This hotel in the Dentelles hosts truffle-themed weekends in January and February, with truffle-hunting demonstrations and truffle-themed menus (page 66).

- **Maison du Truffe** (Place de l'Horloge, Menerbes; www.vin-truffe-luberon.com): Groups can organize truffle hunting demonstrations and truffle-themed cooking classes at this restaurant and activity center in Menerbes in the Luberon. Or stop by the shop for truffle-themed gifts (page 165).

- **Maison de la Truffe d'Aups et du Verdon** (1 Place Martin Bidoure, Aups; http://maisondelatruffe-verdon.fr): The informative, multisensory exhibits at Maison de La Truffe explain where and how truffles grow and examine the lives of truffle hunters in the Var. There's even a dedicated children's truffle discovery game (page 305).

restaurant on site, though it's a short walk to the center of Orange. Private parking is €12 a night.

Getting There

BY TRAIN
The Orange **train station** (www.oui.sncf) is located on Rue Pierre Semard. There are 23 trains a day running between Orange and Avignon. The journey time is around 20 minutes and costs €6.60.

BY BUS
Transvaucluse line 4 from **Vaison-la-Romaine** runs hourly, and the bus departs from the train station; the trip takes an hour and costs €2. **Line 23** from **Châteauneuf-du-Pape** runs six times a day and departs from La Republique; it takes 25 minutes and costs €2. **Line 2** to **Avignon** runs twice an hour and departs from Rue Pourtoules, taking 1 hour and costing €2. Consult www.sudamobilite.fr for full timetables of trans-vaucluse buses.

BY CAR
To reach Orange from **Avignon** take the A7. The journey is 34 kilometers (21 miles) and takes 35 minutes. From **Vaison-la-Romaine,** take the D977; the journey is 29 kilometers (18

miles) and takes 35 minutes. From **L'Isle-sur-la-Sorgue,** take the A7 for 50 kilometers (31 miles); the trip will take about 45 minutes.

VAISON-LA-ROMAINE

Vaison is a thriving small town. It's split in two by the Ouvèze River. On the hill to the south is the medieval town. Here the streets are narrow and cobbled, and the houses are made of stone. Every now and then there's also a shady square with a plane tree and a fountain. The medieval town tends to be quieter than the new town, which is on the opposite side of the river where the land is flat, and the town has grown out from the main tourist sight, the Roman remains that give Vaison its name. In summer Vaison is a fun, lively, artistic place to visit, with the Roman theater hosting a major dance festival.

Sights
★ ROMAN RUINS

Rue Burrus; www.vaison-la-romaine.com/spip. php?rubrique30; Nov.-Dec. and Feb. 10am-noon and 2pm-5pm; Mar. and Oct. 10am-12:30pm and 2pm 5:30pm, April May 9:30am 6pm; June Sept. 9:30am-6:30pm; €9 including all historic sites, children 10-17 €4

As is the case throughout Roman Provence, the Ligurian civilization arrived first, establishing a settlement on the hilly side of the Ouvèze river. Under the Romans, Vaison moved to the plain on the opposite side of the river, with the bridge (just off the D977) being completed around 1 BC. The main Roman remains are a few minutes' walk from the bridge on either side of rue Burrus. The two different Roman neighborhoods, named Puymin and Vilasse, are visible from the road. Paying the entrance fee allows you to wander amid the ruins of Roman streets and examine up close the floor plans of houses, including bathing rooms and the remains of mosaic tiles. On the Puymin site there is also a museum that holds decorative articles and tools discovered during the dig, as well as a Roman theater, which is testament to the wealth of Vaison at the time.

CATHEDRAL NOTRE-DAME DE NAZARETH AND CLOISTERS

Rue Alphonse Daudet; www.vaison-la-romaine.com/ spip.php?rubrique218; June-Sept. 9:30am-6pm; cathedral free, cloisters €9 with Roman ruins

This cathedral was built on the site of a former Roman temple, and you can still see the Roman columns supporting the exterior wall. It almost looks like the ancient temple wants to erupt from the earth and displace the Christian church. Inside, the cathedral is simply decorated and the most aesthetically pleasing part of a visit is seeing the cloisters, which surround a small garden at the northern end of the cathedral.

Entertainment and Events
DANCE FESTIVAL

Théâtre Antique; tel. 0649 42 02 88; www.vaison-danses.com; late June-late July; €10-48

Throughout this month-long festival, there are performances to suit all tastes, from ballet to modern dance, and even hip-hop performances from students at the local dance school. Performances start at 10pm, and the old Roman theater provides a memorable backdrop to the shows.

Food
★ BISTRO DU'O

Rue Gaston Gevaudan; tel. 04 90 41 72 90; www.bistroduo.fr; Tues.-Sat. noon-2pm and 7pm-10pm; menus €38-68

This is an address for serious foodies. Under a high vaulted ceiling, dishes that are almost too beautiful to eat make you paradoxically long to devour them the moment they arrive. A salmon gravalax topped with citrus fruits is the weakness of many. Expect the locals dining next to you to spend the entire meal earnestly debating the elusive flavors of the dishes.

LE MOULIN A HUILE

1 quai Maréchal Foch; tel. 04 90 36 04 56; www.lemoulinahuile84.fr; Thurs.-Sun. 12:15pm-1:45pm and 7:15pm-8:45pm; €29 two-course menu

In a lovely setting on the Ouvèze river, this

gastronomic institution is a good place to stop and enjoy a meal. Descriptions on the menu are simplistic ("vegetables from my garden," "Ventoux pork,") but the finished plates are intricately prepared. Reserve ahead in season to be sure of a table.

THE GIROCEDRE
4 rue de Portalet, Puymeras;
tel. 04 90 46 50 67;
www.legirocedre.fr;
Wed.-Sun. noon-2pm and 7pm-9:30pm; €18-20

Five kilometers (3 miles) north of Vaison, this restaurant is particularly popular on summer evenings when cooking is done over an open wood fire. Simple dishes such as lamb chops and rib of beef get the char-grill treatment. The outside dining area garlanded with outdoor lights is an enchanting place to eat.

Accommodations
AUBERGE D'ANAIS
132 Chemin de Anais, Le Peyréras, Route de
Saint-Marcellin, Entrechaux;
tel. 04 90 36 20 06;
www.aubergeanais.com; €100 d

Ten kilometers (6 miles) south of Vaison-a-Romaine, this small seven-bedroom hotel is surrounded by vines and olive trees. There's a large pool and a good restaurant. All rooms have Wi-Fi and are ensuite. The overall ambience is one of pared-down simplicity, with the beauty of the location being the prime reason to stay.

LE BEFFROI
2 rue de l'Évêché; tel. 04 90 36 04 71;
www.le-beffroi.com; €120 d

Located in medieval Haute Vaison, Le Beffroi offers plenty of period charm with oak-beamed ceilings and traditional *terre cuite* (baked earth) tiled floors. The hotel is split between two different buildings, so families should make a point to request rooms close together. All rooms have Wi-Fi and ensuite bathrooms. There's a pool in the garden.

Getting There
BY CAR
To reach Vaison from **Avignon,** take the A7 and D977. The trip is 52 kilometers (32 miles) and takes 54 minutes. From **Orange,** take the D23 and D977, covering 30 kilometers (18.6 miles) in 33 minutes; and from **L'Isle-sur-la-Sorgue,** take the D977, covering 55 kilometers (34 miles) in 50 minutes.

BY BUS
This region is not very well-served by public transport, but **Transvaucluse line 4** runs between Orange and Vaison-la-Romaine 10 times a day, passing through the Dentelles villages of Seguret and Sablet, and costing €2. The bus stop is on Avenue de La Choralies in Vaison La Romaine. The stop in Orange is the train station on Rue Pierre Semard. Consult www.sudmobilite.fr for full bus timetables.

DENTELLES DE MONTMIRAIL
Paradise for wine lovers, hikers and mountain climbers, the Dentelles are a range of limestone rocks folded upward during the Jurassic age. Their name stems from a resemblance to the seemingly haphazard collection of pins on a lace-making board. On the south western slopes of the Dentelles are the renowned red wine producing villages of Gigondas, Vacqueyras, and Beaumes-de-Venise. The last is known for its sweet muscat as well as its red wine. Across the Ouvèze river are the winemaking villages of Rasteau and Cairanne.

Sights
CHÂTEAU AND HOSPICE GIGONDAS
Montée du Château and Places des Vignerons,
Gigondas; accessible all day

Gigondas is such a lovely small village that its name in Roman times was Jocanditus, meaning "joy." Following the Montée du Château, a marked path takes you past dry stone terraces planted with historic grape varieties and Mediterranean plants to the ruins of the château at the top of the hill. Also of interest is the old hospice, now used to house art exhibitions. There is also an adjoining sculpture walk.

CHAPEL NOTRE DAME D'AUBUNE
Chemin de Notre Dame D'Aubune, Beaumes-de-Venise; tel. 04 90 62 94 39; Tues. 10am-noon

Even if you don't happen to be in Beaumes on a Tuesday morning when the chapel opens its doors, it's worth taking the road adjoining the Canal de Carpentras to take a quick look from the outside. The chapel was built in the 12th century and is one of the finest examples of Provençal Romanesque art. Legend has it that just after the building was completed, the devil threw a rock down from the hillside to crush the building. Thankfully, the Virgin Mary appeared and caught the missile. There is a small medieval garden to explore on the grounds of the chapel.

MUSÉE DE VIGNERON
Route de Vaison-la-Romaine, Rasteau; tel. 04 90 46 11 75; 10am-6pm, closed Sun. and Tues.

This is worth a visit for true wine buffs. The walls of the seven different rooms are filled with every sort of historical wine-making tool imaginable. There's an explanation of the geology and main grape varieties of the region,

and a tasting room to sample the wines of Beaurenard.

★ Wine Tasting
DOMAINE GOUBERT
235 Chemin de Jardinieres, Gigondas; tel. 04 90 65 86 38; www.lesgoubert.fr/; Mon.-Fri. 9am-noon and 2pm- 6pm

The oldest parts of this vineyard date back to the 17th century, making the building one of the first to be constructed outside the village walls. The domaine has been in the same family for generations and produces fantastic Gigondas, full of ripe fruit flavors, spices, and an undertone of tobacco.

CLOS DE CAVEAU
1560 Chemin de Caveau, Vacqueyras; tel. 04 90 65 85 33; www.closdecaveau.com; daily in summer 10am-noon and 2pm-7pm, Sept.-April weekdays only same hours

In 2004 pyschologist Henri Bugener quit his job in London and moved to Clos de Caveau outside Vacqueyras. It's a domaine with a history, having once been owned by renowned wine writer Steven Spurrier. These days it's a friendly place to visit, with a 1.4-kilometer

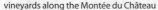

vineyards along the Montée du Château

(0.9-mile) wine trail that winds through the different varietals of grapes. The signature Vacqueyras red tastes of ripe fruit and plums with a touch of mint.

DOMAINE ARMAND

Route de Saint Roman de Malegarde, Cairanne;
tel. 04 90 30 81 50; www.domaine-armand.com;
Mon.-Sat. 9am-noon and 2pm-6pm

This small 38-hectare (94-acre) family domaine offers competively priced Cairanne and Rasteau, both at around €10 a bottle. It's not the most visually attractive vineyard to visit, but the passion of the Armand family for the wine they produce is more than evident. The wines are heady and structured with plenty of ripe fruit notes.

ROUGE BLEU

Le Petit Alcyon, La Bouillon, Saint Cecile Les Vignes;
tel. 07 61 00 47 92; www.rouge-bleu.com; Mon.-Sat.
9am-noon and 2pm-6pm

Co-owner Caroline Jones spent her early career in the wine industry in her native Australia. In 2012 she bought Rouge Bleu with her French partner Thomas Bertrand. Together they are dedicated to making natural wines, almost completely cutting out chemical use in the fields and during the vinification process. The resulting wines are wonderfully expressive of the land. Caroline and Thomas welcome help in the field at all times of year, so call ahead if you want to consider volunteering.

LE VIN A LA BOUCHE WINE TOUR

33 Grand Rue, Mornas; tel. 04 90 46 90 80; www.
levinalabouche.com; €125 a day (minimum 2 people)

Celine Viany attended France's most prestigious wine university before becoming a sommelier and working in some of Provence's most exclusive restaurants. She now runs informative wine tours, specializing in the Côtes du Rhône region. Her professional contacts are excellent, which means that clients get to enjoy bottles that casual tasters never experience.

Sports and Recreation
LE ROCHER DU MIDI HIKE

Maps and information from Tourist Office,
5 rue du Portail, Gigondas; tel. 04 90 65 85 46;
www.ventouxprovence.fr/fileadmin/mediatheque/
ventoux-provence/document/gigondas-rando-
dentelles-430.pdf

Try this 5-kilometer (3-mile) walk out into the vines from the center of Gigondas. It follows along the Routes des Dentelles toward the Rocher du Midi. The Rocher (rock) is a natural viewpoint and picnic spot that offers a lovely panorama of the Dentelles, the Cévennes, and Mont Ventoux. The path is marked and relatively flat, with a total climb of only 200 meters (656 feet). Most hikers complete the walk in just under two hours. Be sure to take a hat because there is not much shade.

DENTELLES CYCLE ROUTE

Beaumes de Venise Tourist Office 140 Place du
Marche, Beaumes de Venise; tel. 04 90 62 94 39;
www.ventouxprovence.fr/fileadmin/mediatheque/
ventoux-provence/document/velo-au-pied-des-
dentelles.pdf

Departing from Beaumes-de-Venise, follow the cycle route in the direction of Lafare. The circular route covers 21 kilometers (13 miles) and takes approximately 2 hours. There are extensive views of the Dentelles, the terraced vineyards, and the hill villages of Lafare and La Roque Alric. As you leave Beaumes you also pass the eerie shape of Rocalinaud, a rock formed from the sand on the bottom of a prehistoric sea, subsequently eroded by the wind over the years. The ruins of Château Barroux are also passed on the route.

BENOIT IGOULEN BIKE HIRE

Beaumes-de-Venise; tel. 04 90 62 93 35;
www.igoulen-location-velo.fr; daily 8am-8pm;
from €18 for a half day

This well-established shop in the center of Beaumes rents road, mountain, and electric bikes. The shop also provides advice on routes.

Wine Festivals

GIGONDAS SUR TABLE

Gigondas; tel. 04 90 37 79 60;
www.gigondas-vin.com;
promotion@gigondas-vin.com; mid-July (usually
16th); €50 per person.

At first glance the price may seem high. However the evening, which needs to be reserved in advance, includes tastings of wines from all the Gigondas domaines, complemented by food prepared by the top local chefs. Fine wine and great food; it couldn't be more French!

VACQUEYRAS FETE DU VIN

Vacqueyras, www.fetedesvins-vacqueyras.fr;
two days in mid-July (usually July 13-14);
free wine tasting, $50 meal

The festival involves two days of free wine tasting in the streets of Vacqueyras with a procession of vignerons, bands, and a holy Mass, all rounded off by a grand gourmet meal on the second day. As always in this wine-producing area, remember the wines are not only delicious, but also high in alcohol. Consume in moderation.

LA NUIT DU VIN

Rasteau; www.rasteau.fr/aoc-rasteau/evenements/
la-nuit-du-vin; Aug. 14 5pm; €5

The vignerons of Rasteau join together every year to provide an unforgettable evening. The €5 price buys you a tasting glass, and you can then wander from table to table sampling wines from more than 20 different vineyards. There's music, food trucks, and children's amusements to keep the party going.

CAIRANNE WINE FESTIVAL

Cairanne; www.rhone-wines.com;
mid-July (usually July 22) 4pm

Pay €5 for your tasting glass and wander from stall to stall enjoying wine from all the different vineyards. To keep you going, there's plenty of music and food, and depending on how much you drink, dancing.

Food

L'OUSTALET

Place Gabrielle Andeol, Gigondas;
tel. 04 90 65 85 30; www.loustalet-gigondas.com/en;
Tues.-Sat. noon-2pm and 7pm-9pm; €32-42

Wine and food are viewed as inseparable in this gastronomic temple in the heart of Gigondas. The wine list includes more than 100 different producers, so don't be afraid to ask for help. The cooking is excellent, and tastes even better on the terrace. Try something light in the summer, like John Dory with almond milk and girolles.

★ NEZ

Place du Rouvis, Gigondas; tel. 04 90 28 59 99;
Mon.-Sat. 11am-1:30pm and 6pm-9pm; €12-18

The formula is simple: Compile a wine list full of the best producers in the region, upend a few wine barrels and turn them into high tables, mix in some simple dishes like beef carpaccio and pesto linguine, and you end up with a convivial place for a meal. Nez is a small wine bar. so reserve ahead to avoid disappointment.

LE MESCLUN

Rue des Poternes, Seguret; tel. 04 90 46 93 43;
Thurs.-Tues. 12:15pm-1:30pm and 7:15pm-9pm, closed
Tues. and Sun. evening, and all day Wed.; €22-25

Benefiting from a lovely shady terrace, high in the village with views out over the vines, Le Mesclun is brimming with Provençal atmosphere. The presentation of the food is immaculate, and the menu a showpiece for the flavors of the south. Try the pigeon roasted in wild Provençal herbs. Booking is advisable in season.

AUBERGE SAINT ROCH

9 route de Caromb, Rasteau; tel. 04 90 65 08 21;
www.auberge-saintroch-84.fr; Fri.-Wed.
12:15pm-1:30pm and 7:15pm- 8:45pm;
€21 two-course lunch menu.

The interior decor definitely needs an update, but this small restaurant remains ever popular with the villagers. Expect traditional cooking in dishes such as saddle of lamb with crusty lamb sweet breads. There's a small terrace. Reservations are only necessary in the summer season.

CÔTEAUX ET FORCHETTES

3340 route de Carpentras, Croisement de la Couranconne, Cairanne; tel. 04 90 66 35 99; www.côteauxetforchettes.com; Wed.-Sat. and Tues. noon-2pm and 7pm-9pm, Sun. and Mon. noon-2pm, closed Thurs; €26 three-course lunch, €33 and €49 evening menus

The terrace of the Côteaux et Forchette is so close to the vines that in the summer you can smell the sugar rising in the grapes as you eat. Inventive internationally influenced cooking pulls in a crowd of locals and in-the-know tourists. The filet of trout with a zucchini quinoa and a coulis of rocket (arugula) wasabi packs a punch. Reservations advisable in season.

Accommodations
HOTEL MONTMIRAIL

Route de Montmirail, Vacqueras; tel. 04 90 65 84 01; www.hotelmontmirail.com; €100 d

After a hard day of wine tasting, grab a few hours of sunshine next to the pool before enjoying a meal in the garden restaurant. Rooms are simply furnished, and all have Wi-Fi and ensuite bathrooms. In January and February the hotel offers special truffle-themed weekends, with truffle-hunting demonstrations and truffle-themed menus.

HOTEL LES FLORETS

1243 Route des Florets, Gigondas; tel. 04 90 65 85 01; www.hotel-lesflorets.com/en; €120 d

Located in the countryside just outside Gigondas, this small hotel has a picturesque pool and restaurant with an excellent reputation. Rooms all have ensuite bathrooms and Wi-Fi. Although not overly luxurious, Les Florets feels like a hidden haven, a place where an afternoon can easily slip by as you lounge by the pool with a good book, before enjoying an indulgent evening meal.

★ LES REMPARTS

74 Cours Louis Pasteur, Beaumes-de-Venise; tel. 04 90 62 75 49; www.lamaisondesremparts.com; €230 d

This is a great base from which to explore the surrounding countryside and vineyards. There are five immaculately decorated, spacious rooms all with ensuite bathrooms and Wi-Fi, and a garden with a lovely pool. Views from the Secret de Brume room over the Dentelles and Mont Ventoux are magnificent.

LE BASTIDE BLEU

Route de Sablet, Seguret; tel. 04 90 46 83 43; www.bastidebleue.com; €80 d

From its shady courtyard restaurant serving local food and wine, to the stone walls and blue shutters of the building, the bastide exudes Provençal charm. It's relatively inexpensive, and all seven rooms have ensuite bathrooms and Wi-Fi. There's also a pool to enjoy, and two of the rooms are larger and can accommodate families. The nearby village of Seguret is one of the most attractive in the area.

Getting There and Around
BY CAR

The **D977** and the **D938** are the main roads that encircle the Dentelles, taking you to Vaison-la-Romaine as you head north, and the town of Carpentras as you travel south. Vaison-la-Romaine is 55 kilometers (34 miles) from Avignon and 30 kilometers (19 miles) from Orange. Carpentras is 28 kilometers (17 miles) from Avignon and 26 kilometers (16 miles) from Orange.

BY BUS

The region is not very well-served by public transport. **Transvaucluse line 4** runs between **Orange** (departing from the train station on Rue Pierre Semard) and **Vaison-la-Romaine** (departing from Avenue des Choralies) 10 times a day, passing through the Dentelles villages of **Seguret** and **Sablet.** Consult www.sudmobilite.fr for up-to-date timetables of transvaucluse buses.

MONT VENTOUX AND AROUND

Some people, when they see a mountain, have an immediate urge to climb to the top. Others are happy to enjoy the scenic view from afar. Whichever camp you fall into, Mont Ventoux provides a majestic backdrop to a holiday in this area. Bédoin, the main village at the base of the mountain, is an attractive place that bustles with activity thanks to the daily influx of cyclists preparing to take on the climb to the summit. The Monday market is one of the largest in the Vaucluse. High up near the peak of Mont Ventoux, the Mont Serein resort offers hiking, pony riding, and plenty of children's activities. In the winter Mont Serein becomes one of the mountain's two ski resorts. Back down at the foot of the mountain, the little-known Gorge de la Nesque is a scenic excursion for a day.

Sights
THE SUMMIT OF MONT VENTOUX
Col des Tempetes, Mont Ventoux

It's wise to check the weather forecast before setting off for the summit of Mont Ventoux. Motorists (and brave, extremely fit cyclists) depart from either Malaucene or Bédoin, taking the D974 in both cases. From December to the end of March the road is often closed due to snow. Mont Ventoux is some 1,909 meters (6,263 feet) high and geologically, if not geographically, is part of the same mountain chain as the Alps. Besides snow, the other meteorological threat is the wind. Even at ground level, the mistral (strong seasonal wind) is a fearsome foe for cyclists. At the summit a gust can knock people off their bikes or feet. The last part of the road, as it turns through the bare limestone rock near the summit, is called the Col de Tempetes, which translates as Canyon of the Storms. When the wind blows, this final approach is often closed. The good news is that, once you reach the summit, you can justifiably claim to have seen the best panorama in Provence.

GORGES DE LA NESQUE
D942, Villes sur Auzon

The baby sibling of the Gorges du Verdon is accessed by taking the D942 between Villes-sur-Auzon and Castelleras. The road is narrow and the gorge cut by the River Nesque is precipitous enough to set your heart pumping. In places the drop is 400 meters (1,312 feet), and it feels impossible to reconcile the geological feature with the tiny trickle of the River Nesque. Indeed, halfway along the gorge, the

Gorges de la Nesque canyon pass

Nesque, almost as if it were ashamed of itself, disappears underground to reappear farther south at Fontaine-de-Vaucluse. Note that the road is also a favorite with cyclists, so progress can be slow.

Sports and Recreation
BÉDOIN LOCATION CYCLE HIRE
20 Route de Malaucen, Bédoin;
tel. 04 90 65 94 53; www.Bédoin-location.fr;
daily 8:30am-6:30pm; from €35 for a half day
Bikes and advice for all riding skill levels are available here, including electric bikes to ease your way to the summit, and descent bikes for those who want the buzz of coming down without the hassle of going up. If Mont Ventoux, the "beast of Provence" is too ambitious for you, the shop proposes plenty of other routes.

STATION SUD BIKE PARK
Chalet Reynard, Route de Mont Ventoux, Bédoin; tel. 04 90 65 63 95;
www.stationventouxsud.com/bike-park.php;
opening time depend on weather, call for information; €14 per day
At 1,500 meters (4,921 feet) Station Sud, one of Mont Ventoux's winter ski resorts, is transformed during the summer into a bike park. Cyclists use the ski lifts to climb the mountain, then descend cross-country trails of varying difficulty.

MONT SEREIN SUMMER RESORT
Station du Mont Serein, Beaumont du Ventoux;
tel. 04 90 63 42 02; www.stationdumontserein.com/
saison/activite-ete; daily in summer except in the case of high winds; price depends on activity
Mont Serein is a great place for a family day out in the summer. Escape the extreme heat of lowland Provence and enjoy walking and horseriding trails. There are also trampolines and a downhill go-kart descent to keep the kids occupied. The GR4 walking trail passes the station on its way to the summit. The walk from the station to the top takes 1 hour and 30 minutes.

SUNSET MONT VENTOUX
Office de Tourisme, 1 Route de Malaucène, Bédoin;
tel. 04 90 65 63 95; www.ventouxprovence.fr/
reportages/mont-ventoux/rando-coucher-du-soleil-sur-le-mont-ventoux.html; weekly in tourist season, enquire at Bédoin tourist office for details
Meet with a guide outside the Bédoin Tourist Office before traveling together to Chalet Reynard at 1,500 meters (4,921 feet). From there the walk departs at 7pm. Over the next two hours the color gently fades from the sun, and the shadows lengthen on the slopes of the mountain. Deer can usually be seen foraging on the bare scree near the summit. Finally around 9pm, watch from the summit as the light is turned off across Provence.

STATION SUD SKI RESORT
Chalet Reynard, Route de Mont Ventoux, Bédoin;
tel. 04 90 65 63 95; www.stationventouxsud.com/
ski-ventoux.php; opening time depends on weather, call for information; €12 per day
In Avignon there is a saying: *"Qui ski Ventoux, ski partout,"* meaning the person who skis Mont Ventoux can ski anywhere. The weather is often bitter, the snow conditions icy, and the wind often too high for the lifts to work. Still, if you are brave enough, there are 7 kilometers (5.3 miles) of pistes, with five beginner runs and two intermediate runs.

MONT SEREIN SKI RESORT
Station du Mont Serein, Beaumont du Ventoux;
tel. 04 90 63 42 02; www.stationdumontserein.com/;
opening time depends on weather, call or visit website for information; €17 per day
This is the bigger of the two stations with 12 kilometers (7.45 miles) of pistes, eight lifts, and more challenging skiing, with expert and intermediate runs, as well as easier slopes. Access in the winter is from Malaucene only.

Entertainment and Events
BÉDOIN MONDAY MARKET
Avenue Barral des Baux, Bédoin
The largest market around Mont Ventoux takes place in Bédoin every Monday. There's a nice mix of food, and arts and crafts items,

The Tour de France and Mont Ventoux

cycling to the top of Mont Ventoux

The Tour de France is the annual cycle race that the French nation obsesses over every July. For three weeks, every detail of every stage is scrutinized. Experts agree that the tour is won or lost on the climbs and there's none more fearsome than Mont Ventoux. The white giant of Provence was first added to the rota of Tour stages in 1951, and now appears on the list every four years or so. The battle to reach its summit first has pushed countless riders to exhaustion and revealed the depths of their determination and courage. Nobody suffered more than Englishman Tom Simpson, who fell from his bike in the desert of scree near the summit and died of exhaustion. A gravestone now marks the spot.

Watching the Tour pass is an incredible experience. Spectators arrive as much as a few days before the passage of the cyclists. Super-fans camp by the roadside to secure the best view. On the actual day, excitement mounts as police outriders secure the route, followed by a caravan of trucks decorated by tour sponsors that distribute free gifts to the crowd. After that, the cyclists pass in an instant of sporting perfection, apparently untroubled by the preternatural effort required to propel a bike at speed over immense distances. In just one or two seconds it's over, but it's worth it, because the Tour is as important psychologically to France as any of its national monuments. Check the Tour website (www.letour.fr) for details of the stages. At least one stage always passes through Provence every summer.

There are plenty of places to satisfy your inner professional cyclist around Mont Ventoux. Here are a few:

- **The Summit of Mont Ventoux:** Whether you get there by the power of your own legs or with the assistance of an e-bike, the view from the top is amazing.

- **Gorges de la Nesque:** The D942 between Villes-sur-Auzon and Castelleras is a favorite with cyclists, with thrilling views of the gorge.

- **Station Sud Bike Park:** A ski resort turned into a cross-country bike park for adrenaline junkies.

including olive wood chopping boards and locally made jewelry.

Wineries
CHÂTEAU PESQUIE
1365Bis route de Flassan, Mormoiron;
tel. 04 90 61 94 08; www.châteaupesquie.com;
Mon.-Sat. 10am-noon and 2pm-6pm
A regal line of centuries-old plane trees lines the road leading up to the impressive château. Running right up to the foot of the balustraded terrace are formal gardens overlooked by Mont Ventoux. Inside the tasting room, every detail has been thought out, including toys to keep the kids amused. The chardonnay is lovely and buttery, and the reds really pack an alcoholic punch.

Food
CHALET REYNARD
Route du Mont Ventoux, Bédoin;
tel. 04 90 61 84 55; www.chalet-reynard.fr;
Wed.-Mon. noon-3pm; €15-30
This well-known café has recently opened a semi-gastronomic restaurant on its first floor. There, hikers, bikers, and skiers in winter can sample specialities such as truffle omelette and melted Mont d'Or cheese impregnated with truffles. It's mountain food for mountain people. The climb to this height is long, so it's wise to reserve.

LE MAS DE VIGNES
15 Chemin Des Jas, Route de Mont Ventoux, Bédoin;
tel. 04 90 65 63 91; www.restaurant-lemasdesvignes.
fr; Wed.-Sun. noon-2pm and 7pm-9pm, Mon.- Tues.
7pm-9pm.; €38 or €50 menus
Five kilometers (3 miles) outside Bédoin, 500 meters up the slopes of Mont Ventoux, is Le Mas De Vignes restaurant. In-the-know diners enjoy dishes such as fish of the day with sauteed vegetables and a coconut curry sauce. The view from the terrace is worth the visit alone. Book ahead in season.

LA COLOMBE
3890 Route du Mont Ventoux, Bédoin; tel. 04 90 65 61 20; www.la-colombe.fr; Fri.- Sat. noon-1:30pm
and 7pm-9:30pm, Sun. noon-1:30pm, Tues.-Thurs. 7pm-9:30pm; €19 lunch menu, €38 dinner
This charming small restaurant just outside Bédoin offers a lunchtime menu that changes daily, and evening menus that change with the availability of local seasonal products. Expect pork from Mont Ventoux and plenty of truffles in season. Depending on whether you arrive before or after an ascent of the white giant, there is a spacious terrace for you to relax or collapse. Reserve in season, particularly in the evening.

Accommodations
CHÂTEAU MAZAN
Rue Napoléon, Mazan; tel. 04 90 69 62.61;
www.Châteaudemazan.com; €160 d
Birthplace of the Marquis de Sade's father and uncle, this château was built around 1720. It has been converted into an atmospheric 30-bedroom hotel, chock-full of antiques. In the summer there's a romantic restaurant on the château's terrace. All rooms have Wi-Fi, air-conditioning, and ensuite bathrooms.

BASTIDE DE BRURANGERE
137 Chemin des Rols, Mazan; tel. 06 75 24 59 29;
http://labastidedebrurangere.com; €220 d
Located just outside the town of Mazan, this old farmhouse is now a boutique hotel. There are five bedrooms, each with ensuite bathrooms and Wi-Fi. Nice touches include two pools, one overflowing into the other, and spa treatments to restore the legs and spirits of weary cyclists.

★ HOTEL CRILLON-LE-BRAVE
Place de l'Eglise, Crillon-le-Brave; tel. 04 90 65 61 61;
www.crillonlebrave.com; €450 d
Crillon-le-Brave is a perched village just outside Bédoin. It's now dominated by a luxury hotel that occupies eight different houses in the small village. Each room is individually decorated with antique furniture, and many boast large picture windows. There are two restaurants, a pool with a view, and countless hidden corners to escape to. All rooms have

Getting There and Around
BY CAR
To reach Bédoin from **Avignon,** take the D942 and the D974, covering 40 kilometers (25 miles) in 45 minutes. From **L'Isle-sur-la-Sorgue,** take the D163; the journey is 31 kilometers (19 miles) and takes 40 minutes. From **Orange,** take the D974 for 37 kilometers (23 miles); it will take 45 minutes. From **Vaison-la-Romaine,** take the D938; the trip is 22 kilometers (13.5 miles) and takes 30 minutes.

BY BUS
Transcove Line L (www.transcove.com) runs eight times a day between Carpentras, Mazan, Crillon-le-Brave and Bédoin. The bus takes 45 minutes to reach Bédoin and costs around €4.

L'ISLE-SUR-LA-SORGUE AND FONTAINE-DE-VAUCLUSE
Built on an island created by the branching of the Sorgue River, L'Isle sur la Sorgue is a vibrant market town that draws visitors from miles around thanks to its fame as an antique center. Markets on Thursday (Provençal) and Sunday (antiques and Provençal goods) are extremely popular. A visit midweek when the antique shops tend to close is a good time to enjoy the beauty of the town. Bridges and waterwheels are hidden away in unexpected places, and over a coffee on a riverside terrace, there's always the spectacle of ducks paddling furiously to avoid being swept downstream. For more aquatic experiences, the nearby village of Fontaine-de-Vaucluse is located at the bubbling source of the Sorgue, and the village of Pernes-les-Fontaine is best-known for its 41 public fountains.

Sights
EGLISE NOTRE DAME DES ANGES
Place de la Liberté, L'Isle-sur-la-Sorgue;
Mon.-Fri. 10am-noon and 3pm-6pm
The boutique-filled streets of L'Isle-sur-la-Sorgue, wind away from the river toward a large, open central square that is dominated by the Eglise Notre Dame des Anges. Built in the 12th century, the church was extended and renovated in the Italian style during the 18th century. The exterior, which gives onto Place de La Liberté, is relatively plain, but inside the scale is impressive. The stalls and chapels are particularly fine examples of the baroque style

with plentiful use of vibrant colors, such as rich blues and decadent gold.

★ Antique Hunting

The main antique shops in L'Isle-sur-la-Sorgue line the southern bank of the river, and a pleasant hour can easily be spent hopping from one to another. Note that most antique shops are closed Tuesday-Thursday.

LE VILLAGE DES ANTIQUAIRES DE LA GARE

2 Avenue de l'Égalité, L'Isle-sur-la-Sorgue;
tel. 04 90 38 04 57;
www.levillagedesantiquairesdelagare.com;
Fri.-Mon. 10am-7pm

Probably the best of several antique villages (collections of small antique shops in the same building) to be found around the town, this complex has a nice relaxed atmosphere with the traders sipping on wine and gossiping while waiting for the next sale. Leather club sofas, chandeliers, and mirrors, are among the eclectic items on sale.

RAMIS ANTIQUITES

Le Quai de La Gare, 4 avenue Julien Guigue,
L'Isle-sur-la-Sorgue;
tel. 06 09 33 43 68;
www.ramisantiquites.com;
Fri. 2pm-7pm and Sat.-Mon. 10am-7pm

Tables, paintings, sculptures and other exceptional works of art are for sale over the two floors of this showroom set in a historic town house. The collection is at the higher end of the price range available in the town.

HOTEL DONGIER

15 Espl. Robert Vasse, L'Isle-sur-la-Sorgue;
tel. 04 90 21 50 24;
http://hoteldongierantiquites.fr/1.aspx;
Fri.-Mon. 10am-7pm

Grouped together in this 18th-century town house is a wonderful collection of antiques. At times it feels more like a museum than a shop, because entire walls are filled with oil paintings and some of the furniture dates back to the 16th century.

LA COURS DE CRÉATEURS

11 rue Carnot, L'Isle-sur-la-Sorgue;
tel. 06 35 41 15 31; Fri.-Mon. 10am-7pm

There's a nice mix of brocante, pop art, vintage items, and contemporary artisan goods in this co-operative shop set in an old convent. Prices are more reasonable than in some of the more upscale shops.

CANDY AND CLOUD

9 rue Carnot, L'Isle-sur-la-Sorgue;
www.candyandcloud.com; Tues.-Sun. 10am-7pm

A collection of funky objects from home clearances and brocante markets fill this colorful shop. There are also some contemporary home decor wares mixed in.

L'ISLE AUX BROCANTES

7 avenue des 4 otages, L'Isle-sur-la-Sorgue;
tel. 06 20 10 58 15; www.lileauxbrocantes.com;
Fri. 2pm-7pm and Sat.-Mon. 10am-7pm

There can be few more pleasant places to shop for antiques. Cross over a little bridge and enter a shady square ringed with the stands of 40 or so dealers. If it all gets too much, there's an on-site restaurant to relax and consider the pros and cons of a purchase. The website is an excellent resource to identify potential purchases in advance of a visit.

WEEKLY MARKET

Quai Jean Jaurès, Place de la Liberté and throughout town, L'Isle-sur-la-Sorgue; Thurs. and Sun.

L'Isle-sur-la-Sorgue has two weekly markets. On Thursday morning the market is smaller and concentrates mainly on food. On Sunday, the town comes to a stop with a combined food and antique market. It's great fun because you never know quite what you might find from glorious antique furniture to 3.5-meter (12-foot) tall mock space rockets.

BI-ANNUAL ANTIQUE FAIR

L'Isle-sur-la-Sorgue; Easter weekend and Aug. 15

Twice a year the number of antique dealers in L'Isle-sur-la-Sorgue swells from 300 to 700 when 400 traveling dealers join the resident sellers, creating one of the largest antique fairs in the world. Almost every inch of pavement is filled with traders selling anything from small old-fashioned coffee grinding machines to tables, beds, and chests of drawers. There is quite literally something for everyone. Part of the fun is haggling, which is best done with a smile on your face and a readiness to walk away if the price is not right. An estimated 120,000 people flock to each of these two fairs, so parking is far from easy, and reservations are imperative at hotels and restaurants.

Hiking
★ FONTAINE-DE-VAUCLUSE

Fontaine-de-Vaucluse; www.oti-delasorgue.co.uk/
en-ot-delasorgue/en-principal/discover/land-heritage/
our-villages/fontaine-de-vaucluse; parking €3-5

Natural springs are usually pretty unimpressive sights. However, Fontaine-de-Vaucluse, outside L'Isle-sur-la-Sorgue, is much more than a spring. Visit at the right time of year (late autumn and late spring) and there is quite literally a fountain of water gushing from the ground. You can hear the roar from the village of Fontaine-de-Vaucluse 1 kilometer (0.6 miles) away from the source. An easy 20-minute walk up a level rocky path

with a slight incline at the end takes you to the spring. The experience varies dramatically, depending on flow levels that can be checked on the tourist office website. Either water cascades from a rocky hole in the ground, plunging down the valley, or you can peer down through a gap in the rocks into a still, mirror-like pool of water. The spring can discharge up to 700,000,000 cubic meters of water a year, making it the fifth-largest karst spring in the world.

THE FOUNTAIN WALK OF PERNES LES FONTAINES

Start at Tourist Office, Place Gabriel Moutte 84210,
Pernes-les-Fontaines; tel. 04 90.61 31 04;
www.tourisme-pernes.fr/uploads/Document/
circuit-des-fontaines.pdf

In the 18th century, Pernes was transformed by the discovery of the Saint Roch source. Suddenly it was possible to bring water to every corner of the town. Four commemorative fountains were built to celebrate: Cormoran; Souchet; Reboul, and Hopital. As the saying goes, there's no such thing as too much of a good thing, and so the industrious people of Pernes kept on investing in fountains. Today there are 41 public fountains and an estimated 60 private ones.

Fontaine-de-Vaucluse near the river source

Don't expect to be wowed by great torrents of cascading water; the fountains of Pernes are largely simple affairs, but it's fun to pick up a map for the circular walk, which starts and finishes at the tourist office, and tick off the fountains as you go. Good places to pause include, the Museum of the Resistance and Hotel de Cheylus, which contains the only remaining example of a Jewish ritual bathing area in the Vaucluse. There are two different routes, one taking 1 hour, and the other 1 hour and 30 minutes. Pernes is built on a slight hill. Provided you pick the right side of the street, it's usually possible to stay in the shade. For lunch before or after the walk, try **Restaurant Au Fil du Temps** (51 place Louis Giraud; tel. 04 90 30 09 48).

SORGUE WATERWHEEL WALK
Place de la Liberté, L'Isle-sur-la-Sorgue;
www.oti-delasorgue.co.uk/detail/e3e810570970c26d
692f459156ea08b6/322566
Up until the 16th century, the traditional trades of L'Isle-sur-la-Sorgue (wool and silk weaving) were done by hand. New waterwheel technology then gradually transformed the work, providing power to factories. Around 60 waterwheels were in use by the 19th century. Today nearly 20 remain, dotted around the town, slowly churning the water. Invariably, they are coated by heavy moss, which softens their appearance and brings greenery right into the center of town. Pick up a map from the tourist office to follow the Parcours des Roues, a 2-kilometer (1.25-mile) walk that takes about 25 minutes.

Other Sports and Recreation
KAYAK VERT
Avenue Robert Garcin, Fontaine-de-Vaucluse;
tel. 04 90 20 35 44; www.canoevaucluse.com;
June- Aug., descents every 30 minutes, 10am-5pm.
Out of season groups by appointment; from €20
adults, €15 children 12-18, €10 6-12
Kayaking down the emerald-green, icy cold waters of the Sorgue is a great escape from

the summer heat. The 2-hour route is picturesque as you float through wooded countryside, past bathers and picnickers. You can nose into the back gardens of houses on the river and even jump out for a swim in various places. It is advisable to have an adult in the boat with children because the water can flow quickly and there are frequent overhanging branches.

PASSERELLE DE CIMES
Route de Cavaillon, Lagnes; tel. 04 90 38 56 87;
https://accrobranche-vaucluse.com; check online
reservation system for available times; €20 all
courses, €12 medium-level courses
This activity is like an obstacle course in the trees. Catering for all levels, and starting with children as young as 4, Passerelle de Cimes is one of the best accrobranching centers in the region. The black advanced courses really are only for the brave.

GOLF SAUMANE
1141 route de Fontaine-de-Vaucluse,
Saumane-de-Vaucluse; tel. 04 90 20 20 65;
www.golfdesaumane.fr; €60 green fee
Just along the road from L'Isle-sur-la-Sorgue is this picturesque parkland golf course. As you might expect on a course close to the Sorgue, there are plenty of water hazards.

Food
LE VIVIER
800 Cours Fernande Peyre, L'Isle-sur-la-Sorgue;
tel. 04 90 38 52 80; www.levivier-restaurant.com;
Wed.-Sun. 12:30pm-1:30pm and 7:30pm-9:30pm,
closed Sat. lunchtime and Mon.-Tues.; €30 all mains
Le Vivier offers inventive high-quality food on the banks of the River Sorgue 1 km (.6 miles) or so from the center of town. There's a large terrace overlooking the river, and three-course menus range from €30 to €60. Fish is a specialty; for example, try the perch with wild rice, seaweed and clam broth. For a Michelin-star restaurant, the atmosphere is noticeably relaxed and not too fussy. In the summer season reservations are advisable.

OLIVE ET RAISINS

2 Rue Theodore Aubanel, L'Isle-sur-la-Sorgue;
tel. 04 90 21 17 36; www.olive-et-raisin.com;
Tues.-Sun. 9:30am-7:30pm; €18-34 for two people

This little deli on the banks of the Sorgue has a small restaurant and offers takeaway picnic hampers. Food is served on sharing plates, and there's an almost infinite choice of nibbles: *saucisson* (dry, cured sausage), cured hams, *foie gras,* pickled artichokes, cheeses, etc. Tables are limited, so book in advance to secure a seat.

CAFÉ FLEURS

9 rue Théodore Aubanel, L'Isle sur-la-Sorgue;
tel. 04 90 20 66 94; www.cafefleurs.com;
Thurs.-Mon. noon-2pm and 7:30pm-9:30pm; €23-33

L'Isle-sur-la-Sorgue is rarely quiet. The restaurant tables along the river quickly fill with crowds. To escape the throng and enjoy refined dining in a quiet courtyard, try the Café des Fleurs. The beef fillet with grated summer truffle is perfectly accompanied by the house wine, a red Côtes du Rhône from the owner's vineyard. In the summer season, reservations are advisable.

★ LE CARRÉ D'HERBES

13 avenue des Quatre Otages, L'Isle-sur-la-Sorgue;
tel. 04 90 38 23 97; www.lecarredherbes.eu;
Fri.-Tues. noon-2:30pm and 7pm-9:30pm; €20-24

Unfortunately, every time I have been in L'Isle-sur-la-Sorgue, this restaurant has been closed. However, friends rave about the lunchtime three-course menu and they book well in advance to secure a table for Sunday lunch (the day of the main market). They recommend the lamb with sun-dried tomatoes and eggplant cannelloni.

SUMMER FLOATING MARKET

First Sunday in August; from 7:30am

Once upon a time the fishermen who lived along the Sorgue river used to pole their narrow low-bottomed boats into L'Isle-sur-la-Sorgue to sell their fish. In the Provençal language, the boats were called *nego chin,* the less than optimistic translation of which is "dog drowner." This tradition has been revived, although in this one-off event it is more likely to be melons, olives, and wine rather than fish on sale. Making a purchase is not easy: First there are the crowds to negotiate and then the large drop down to the boats. Overeager shoppers have been known to tumble into the river! Due to these hazards the floating market is more of a spectacle than a serious opportunity to shop. Arrive early to avoid the crowds and see the boats pulled up by the banks, filled with their goods.

Accommodations

HOTEL LES NÉVONS

205 Chemin des Névons, L'Isle-sur-la-Sorgue;
tel. 04 90 20 72 00; www.hotel-les-nevons.com; €90 d

This large hotel offers exceptional value just a few minutes' walk from the center of the town. The decor is basic but there's secure parking (which is something of a luxury in busy L'Isle-sur-la-Sorgue) and a roof-top pool. All rooms have ensuite bathrooms, air-conditioning, and Wi-Fi. It's not the place for those who love Provençal character, but the Nevons remains a practical, no-nonsense choice.

MAS DE CURE BOURSE

120 Chemin de la Serre, L'Isle-sur-la-Sorgue;
tel. 04 90 38 16 58; www.masdecurebourse.com; €110 d

This 17th-century post house has plenty of charm. Located a five-minute drive from the town, the hotel is nestled in verdant parkland planted with lavender and roses. There's a pool, private parking, and on-site restaurant, All rooms are decorated in the Provençal style and have ensuite bathrooms, Wi-Fi and air-conditioning.

★ MAISON SUR LA SORGUE

6 Rue Rose Goudard, L'Isle-sur-la-Sorgue;
tel. 06 87 32 58 68;
www.lamaisonsurlasorgue.com; €300 d

As you would expect in L'Isle-sur-la-Sorgue, this guesthouse is overflowing with antiques and collectables from around the world. The four rooms, all with ensuite bathrooms and Wi-Fi, are exceptionally spacious and beautifully designed. The location in the center of town is perfect. It's the perfect base for a refined and cosseted stay.

Getting There
BY TRAIN
L'Isle-sur-la-Sorgue train station (https://en.oui.sncf/en) is located just off Avenue de l'Egalité. Trains run 10 times a day from Avignon's central station on Boulevard Saint Roch; singles cost €5.20, and the journey takes just over half an hour

BY BUS
Transvaucluse **Line 6** from **Avignon** runs 10 times a day from the train station on Boulevard Saint Roch; it takes 44 minutes and costs €2.60, arriving on Cours Emile Zola in L'Isle-sur-la-Sorgue. For more information, www.sudmobilite.fr has full timetables of transvaucluse buses.

BY CAR
To reach L'Isle-sur-la-Sorgue from **Avignon** take the D942, traveling 30 kilometers (18.65 miles) in 38 minutes. From **Orange,** take the A7, covering 46 kilometers (28.5 miles) in 33 minutes. From **Vaison-la-Romaine,** take the D938; the journey is 48 kilometers (30 miles) and takes 57 minutes.

Arles, the Camargue, and Les Alpilles

Arles is a town blessed by culture. It's overflow-ing with Roman monuments, immortalized in paintings such as *The Night Café* by Vincent Van Gogh, and boasts world-class museums and art galleries. It's full of fountains and squares, chic boutiques, and famous chefs, all of which combine to make it a quintessentially Provençal destination. Yet Arles is also the gateway to the Camargue, and the home of bull fighting in the region. A wild Camarguaise spirit underlies everything, and frequently escapes during the city's many unmissable festivals and fairs.

Driving out of Arles, you cross into the Camargue wetland delta. In low-lying fields, black bulls lower their horns and paw the ground. Rare migratory birds arrow overhead. Mosquitos swarm and the mistral

Highlights

Look for ★ to find recommended sights, activities, dining, and lodging.

★ **Les Arènes:** The cries of the gladiators echo through the ages thanks to the superbly preserved architecture of this 2nd-century Roman arena (page 85).

★ **Fondation Van Gogh:** Changing collections celebrate Van Gogh's artistic legacy, and there is always an original or two on display (page 89).

★ **Luma Arles:** A multimillion-euro redevelopment of an old railway repair yard into a space for artistic exchange will change the face of Arles forever; the Frank Gehry skyscraper is impossible to miss (page 93).

★ **Parc Ornithologique du Pont de Gau:** Get up close with the flamingos at this bird park with hides and marked trails (page 109).

★ **Camargue Safari:** Whether you ride in the back of a jeep or on a horse, an official safari is the best way to see the Camargue wildlife (page 110).

★ **Glanum:** Visualize the everyday life of a Roman citizen in the ruins of this fortified town outside Saint-Rémy-de-Provence. Particularly impressive are the mausoleum and the triumphal arch (page 117).

★ **Carrières des Lumières:** This old bauxite mine is now used for high-quality large-scale art projections set to music (page 126).

© MOON.COM

Arles, the Camargue, and Les Alpilles

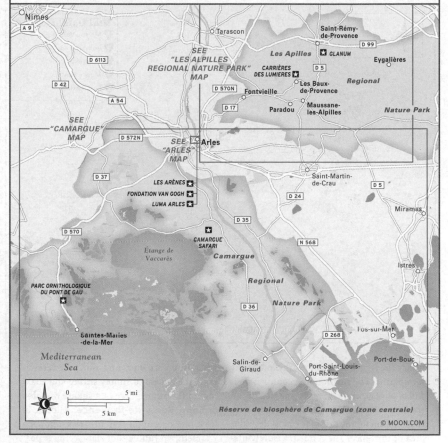

© MOON.COM

wind howls. Stop at one of the many roadside restaurants and you'll often discover a guitarist playing flamenco music. Wine flows, couples dance, and there are feats of eating and drinking that make a party anywhere else in Provence look like a dull workplace affair. The flamboyant culture of the wild, windswept, waterlogged nature reserve makes a statement: This is the Camargue. Don't be fooled by the pink flamingos and the picturesque white horses: Life is hard here, and we dance today because tomorrow is unknown.

The Rhône crossing near Port-Saint-Louis-du-Rhône in the Camargue toward Les Alpilles is made via a small ferry pulled by a chain. The journey takes five minutes, during which passengers are transported from one Provençal universe to another. Les Alpilles is epitomized by its main town, Saint-Rémy-de-Provence. It is a gorgeous place, all cobbled streets, plane trees, and chic cafés sheltering

Previous: Arles is located on a bend in the Rhône; the Roman arena in Arles; Beaucaire medieval Old Town and view of Chateau Royal de Beaucaire.

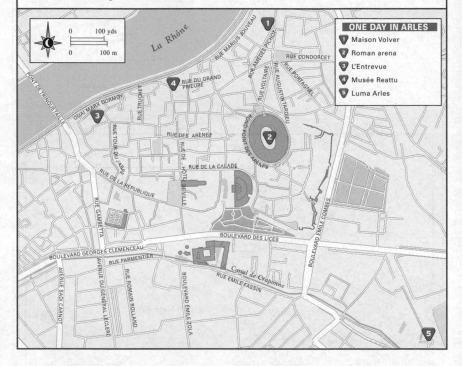

One Day in Arles

ONE DAY IN ARLES
1 Maison Volver
2 Roman arena
3 L'Entrevue
4 Musée Reattu
5 Luma Arles

under the jagged peaks of nearby low, rocky mountains. The surrounding countryside is full of olive groves, vineyards, and wealthy attractive villages. As a result the area vies with the Luberon for the title of the most desirable area of Provence. The refined, leisurely lifestyle on offer is in sharp contrast to that of the Camargue.

PLANNING YOUR TIME

The rich cultural heritage of the region means planning ahead is crucial. All the main sights are within 1 hour's drive of each other or less. However, the list of things to do is long. Visiting all the Roman sights alone could easily take a week. Identify in advance what interests you, and don't underestimate the appeal of simply sitting and soaking up the atmosphere in a square in **Arles** or **Saint-Rémy-de-Provence.** Allocate at least one overnight stay in Arles, allowing yourself two full days of sightseeing if possible. An overnight stay is also recommended to experience the beauty and variety of the **Camargue:** Sunset and sunrise are the best times to watch wildlife and appreciate the majestic light. In **Les Alpilles,** a visit to **Saint-Rémy-de-Provence** and its related sights is worth at least another day, and village hopping, olive oil, and wine tasting could easily take up another.

Itinerary Ideas

ONE DAY IN ARLES

1 Enjoy an indulgent breakfast on the terrace of **Maison Volver,** just a few hundred meters from the Roman arena.

2 Tour the **Roman arena** before the crowds, while rehearsing a few Russell Crowe quotes from the film *Gladiator.*

3 Stroll through Arles toward the river, passing the Roman baths before having lunch on the terrace of the **L'Entrevue** overlooking the Rhône.

4 Pop next door to the **Musée Reattu,** being sure to study the poignant text of Van Gogh's letter to Gauguin, written following the argument that led Van Gogh to cut off his ear.

5 Finish the day with a sunset picnic in the newly sprouting park that surrounds **Luma Arles.** Admire the play of light on the metal cladding of the Frank Gehry building.

TWO DAYS IN LES ALPILLES AND THE CAMARGUE

Day 1

1 After an overnight stay in the Mas de Carassins boutique hotel, take a 5-minute walk into **Saint-Rémy-de-Provence** for breakfast and explore the town.

2 Have lunch at **Bistrot Decouverte** on the bustling ring road.

3 Spend the afternoon visiting the Roman ruins of **Glanum** adjacent to the hotel.

4 Return to **Mas de Carassins** for supper by the pool, gazing at Les Alpilles as the light fades from the rocks.

Day 2

1 Leave Saint-Rémy-de-Provence and head toward Arles and into the Camargue on the D570, arriving at **Saintes-Maries-de-la-Mer** in about an hour.

2 Park the car at Plage l'Est just outside the town, and walk out onto the **Digue seawall** for an invigorating seaside stroll.

3 Explore the town and have a light lunch of fried seafood at **Pica Pica.**

4 Take a **wildlife safari** either on horseback or in a four-wheel-drive vehicle to see the bulls, white horses, and flamingos up close.

5 Stay overnight at **Mas de La Fouque** just outside town, spotting birdlife out on the *etang* (lake).

Two Days in Les Alpilles and the Camargue

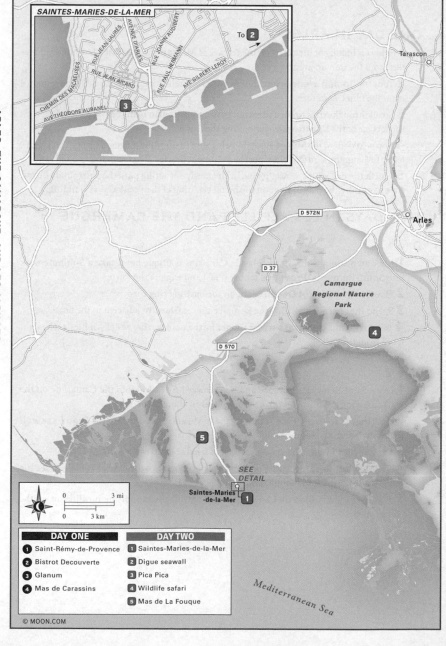

SAINTES-MARIES-DE-LA-MER

RUE JEAN AICARD
RUE JEAN JAURÈS
AVENUE D'ARLES
RUE JOANN AUDIBERT
RUE PAUL HERMANN
AVE GILBERT LEROY
CHEMIN DES MAGRUSES
AVE THÉODORE AUBANEL

To **2**

Tarascon

D 572N

Arles

D 37

Camargue
Regional Nature
Park

4

D 570

5

SEE
DETAIL

Saintes-Maries
-de-la-Mer **1**

0   3 mi
0   3 km

Mediterranean Sea

DAY ONE	DAY TWO
1 Saint-Rémy-de-Provence	**1** Saintes-Maries-de-la-Mer
2 Bistrot Decouverte	**2** Digue seawall
3 Glanum	**3** Pica Pica
4 Mas de Carassins	**4** Wildlife safari
	5 Mas de La Fouque

© MOON.COM

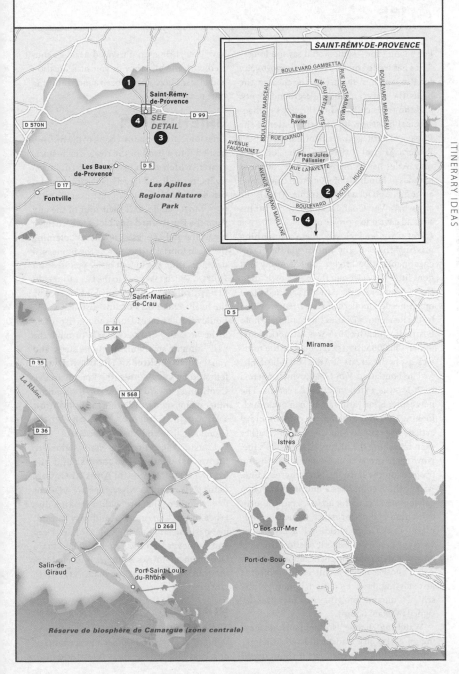

SAINT-RÉMY-DE-PROVENCE

BOULEVARD GAMBETTA
BOULEVARD MARCEAU
RUE DU PETIT PUITS
RUE NOSTRADAMUS
BOULEVARD MIRABEAU
RUE CARNOT
Place Favier
AVENUE FAUCONNET
Place Jules Pélissier
RUE LAFAYETTE
AVENUE DURAND MAILLANE
BOULEVARD
VICTOR HUGO
2
To **4**

1
Saint-Rémy-
de-Provence
4 SEE
DETAIL
3
D 570N
D 99
Les Baux-
de-Provence
D 5
D 17
Fontville
Les Apilles
Regional Nature
Park
Saint-Martin-
de-Crau
D 5
D 24
Miramas
D 35
La Rhône
N 568
Istres
D 36
D 268
Fos-sur-Mer
Salin-de-
Giraud
Port-Saint-Louis-
du-Rhône
Port-de-Bouc
Réserve de biosphère de Camargue (zone centrale)

Arles

For a long time—some would say too long—Arles has traded on its past. It's the go-to city for Roman sites: the arena, the theater, the baths, the graveyard, the underground crypts, and the finds collected in the city's archaeological museum. It's also the center of the Provençal heritage movement started by poet Frederic Mistral at the turn of the 20th century. Arles has its own queen, who oversees parades of hundreds of women in traditional costume. And for a little intrigue, Arles is the city where Van Gogh inexplicably cut off his ear and gave it to a prostitute.

Yet if you look closely, there's something missing that no amount of gladiator re-enactments or bull fights can fix: A city that does little but celebrate the past slowly dies. Every summer for the past 50 years, a dash of much-needed modernism has been provided by the Rencontres D'Arles International Photo Festival, which by 2015 was attracting just under 100,000 visitors. Yet, outside the tourist season, the streets of Arles still fall silent.

The Fondation Van Gogh, which opened in 2014, was a step in a new direction. The new center is forward- rather than backward-looking in that it explores the contemporary artistic response to Van Gogh's work, rather than rehashing the history of the artist's life. Now there are two more new, challenging projects on the horizon. First, there's Luma Arles, which comprises a multimillion-euro collaborative center for artists, a park, and an exhibition and performance venue. Its landmark Frank Gehry building is a skyscraper so avant-garde in design it would raise eyebrows in Manhattan. Right next door to Luma Arles, another major architectural project is just starting: France's national photography school is moving into glitzy new premises designed by Marc Barani.

Watching change as it happens, observing an entire city transform itself, is something to behold. If Arles gets it right, it will have everything: an unrivaled heritage coupled with the vibrancy of youthful creation and ideas. There's never been a more exciting time to visit.

ORIENTATION

Arles is located on the east bank of the **Rhône,** nestled into a bend in the river. The historic center, which contains most of the main sights, is small and largely pedestrian, and it can be crossed on foot in just over 15 minutes. Most people start their tour of the city from the **Boulevard des Lices,** where there is parking and a pedestrian square containing the main tourist office. Across the Boulevard des Lices from the tourist office is **Rue Jean Jaures,** which takes you to the large **Place de la République,** which in turn is bordered by the lively **Place du Forum.** Also across the Boulevard des Lices from the tourist office is the **Jardin d'Eté park.** Walk through the park, climb a small hill and some steps, and you will pass the **Roman Theatre Antique,** followed by **Les Arènes** (the Roman arena). Continuing toward the river you'll encounter other major sights, including the **Fondation Van Gogh, Thermes de Constantin** (Roman baths), and **Musée Reattu.**

Outside the center, the main sights are **Luma Arles,** the **Alyscamps,** and the **Musée Departemental Arles Antiques.** Luma Arles and Les Alyscamps are adjacent to each other. They are within walking distance of the tourist office and easy to find, just past the junction of Boulevard des Lices and Boulevard Emilie Combes. The Musée Departemental Arles Antiques is located farther out of town, near the main N113 river crossing.

SIGHTS

The most cost-effective way of discovering the sights of Arles is to buy either a Pass Avantage or a Pass Liberte. The **Pass Avantage** (€16,

€13 reduced) is valid for six months and provides entrance to all the monuments and museums of Arles with the exception of the Van Gogh Foundation. The **Pass Liberte** (€12, reduced €10) is valid for one month and provides entrance to four monuments of choice, the Reattu museum, and your choice of another museum except the Fondation Van Gogh. The passes are available from the **tourist office** (9 Boulevard des Lices, Arles, tel. 04 90 18 41 20, www.arlestourisme.com/fr).

★ LES ARÈNES (ROMAN ARENA)
Rond-point Des Arènes; tel. 04 90 49 38 20; http://Arènes-arles.com; Mar., Apr. and Oct. 9am-6pm, May-Sept. 9am-7pm, Nov.-Feb. 10 am-5pm; €9, reduced €7

For the residents of Arles, Les Arènes is part of everyday life. Throughout the year it hosts diverse events from pop concerts to bull fighting, from a rice festival to traditional-costume fashion parades. In the summer months, Camarguaise (nonlethal) bull running can be seen three nights a week. There are also frequent gladiatorial re-enactment shows. It's a working part of the city and, as such, is liable to be taken for granted. To a visitor, it's a marvel. The 20th-largest Roman arena in the world, it was built in AD 90. Modeled on the Colosseum in Rome, it could accommodate more than 20,000 spectators for a gladiatorial contest. It has 120 arches and is 136 meters (446 feet) in length. Visit just after opening time, even in the summer, and the arena will be almost deserted. The silence is easily filled by the imagination: the cries of the gladiator, the roars of the lions, the jeers and applause of the crowd. There are few places in the world where it is possible to channel the spirit of ancient Rome in such a fashion. Yet climb to the top of one of the two towers added on either end of the arena in medieval times, and you can see the future in the form of the Luma Arles building glinting in the distance. After the fall of the Roman Empire in the 5th century, the arena enjoyed a second life as a walled protective citadel. Houses were built inside—even a town square and two churches. In the 19th century a decision was made to demolish this residential neighborhood and return the arena to its Roman splendor.

ROMAN THEATER (THÉÂTRE ANTIQUE)
Rue De la Calade; tel. 04 90 49 59 05; www.arlestourisme.com/fr/monument-detail. html&code=_x0031_3T2000481&langue=fr&b ack=768; Mar., Apr., Oct. 9am-6pm, May-Sept. 9am-7pm, Nov.-Feb. 10am-5pm; €9, reduced €7

While the Roman masses packed the arena and roared at the blood being spilled, the more refined classes filled the theater a couple of minutes' walk away. There they watched Roman or Greek comedies, tragedies, mimes, and pantomimes. The theater in its pomp had three parts: the *cavea* (the semi-circular seating area for spectators), the stage and set, and an enclosing rear wall. Today, the best-preserved area is the *cavea*. Some remains of the set area do still stand, particularly two columns, nicknamed the two widows, which must have once framed the stage. The theater was built at the end of the 1st century BC during the reign of Augustus. At the time it was one of the first ever stone theaters. Nearly 3,000 years later, in the summer months the theater is still used for concerts and shows. It's possible to get a good feel for the monument by peering in from the outside, but paying the entrance fee plus the extra few euros for the audio guide provides a much more immersive experience.

PLACE DU FORUM - LES CRYPTOPORTIQUES
Place de la République, Hotel de Ville; tel. 04 90 49 59 05; www.arlestourisme.com/fr/ monument-detail.html&code=_x0031_3T2000134&l angue=fr&back=768; Mar., Apr. and Oct. 9am-6pm, May-Sept. 9am-7pm and Nov.-Feb. 10am-5pm; €4.50, reduced €3.60

The Forum was the economic and political center of Roman life in Arles. Little is known about the Forum

Arles

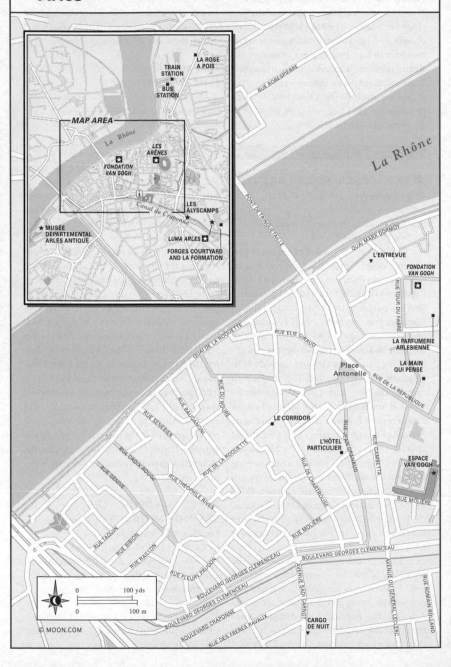

MAP AREA

La Rhône

LA ROSE A POIS

TRAIN STATION

BUS STATION

LES ARÈNES

FONDATION VAN GOGH

Canal de Craponne

LES ALYSCAMPS

MUSÉE DEPARTEMENTAL ARLES ANTIQUE

LUMA ARLES

FORGES COURTYARD AND LA FORMATION

La Rhône

QUAI MARX DORMOY

L'ENTREVUE

FONDATION VAN GOGH

RUE ROBESPIERRE

PONT DE TRINQUETAILLE

RUE TOUR DU FABRE

RUE ELIE GIRAUD

QUAI DE LA ROQUETTE

LA PARFUMERIE ARLESIENNE

LA MAIN QUI PENSE

Place Antonelle

RUE DE LA RÉPUBLIQUE

RUE DU BOURG

RUE SENEBIER

RUE BAUDANOM

LE CORRIDOR

RUE JEAN GRANAUD

L'HÔTEL PARTICULIER

RUE GAMBETTA

ESPACE VAN GOGH

RUE CROIX ROUGE

RUE DE LA ROQUETTE

RUE THÉOPHILE RIVES

RUE DE CHARTROUSE

RUE GENIVE

RUE MOLIÈRE

RUE MOLIÈRE

RUE TAQUIN

RUE BIBION

RUE RAILLON

RUE FLEUR PRUDON

BOULEVARD GEORGES CLEMENCEAU

BOULEVARD GEORGES CLEMENCEAU

AVENUE DU GÉNÉRAL LECLERC

RUE ROMAIN ROLLAND

AVENUE SADI CARNOT

BOULEVARD GEORGES CLEMENCEAU

BOULEVARD CRAPONNE

RUE DES FRÈRES RAVAUX

CARGO DE NUIT

0   100 yds

0   100 m

© MOON.COM

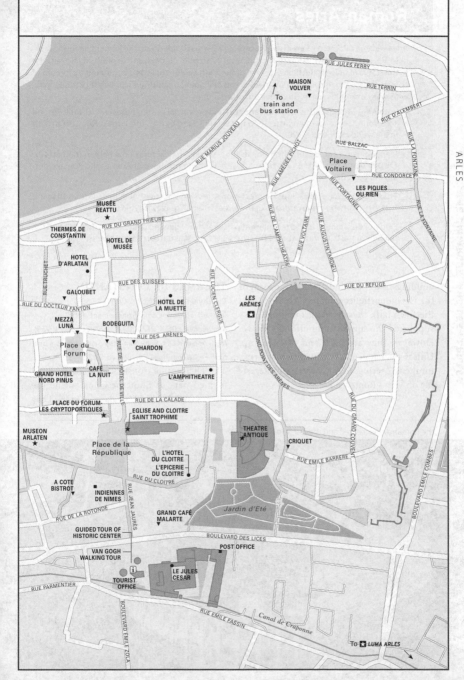

RUE JULES FERRY

MAISON VOLVER ▼

To train and bus station

RUE TERRIN

RUE D'ALEMBERT

RUE MARIUS JOUVEAU

RUE BALZAC

RUE AMÉDÉE PICHOT

Place Voltaire

RUE CONDORCET

RUE LA FONTAINE

LES PIQUES OU RIEN

RUE PORTAGNEL

RUE DE L'AMPHITHÉATRE

MUSÉE REATTU ★

RUE DU GRAND PRIEURE

RUE VOLTAIRE

RUE AUGUSTIN TARDIEU

RUE LA FONTAINE

THERMES DE CONSTANTIN ★

HOTEL DE MUSÉE

RUE DU REFUGE

HOTEL D'ARLATAN ●

RUE DES SUISSES

RUE LUCIEN CLERGUE

GALOUBET ●

RUE DU DOCTEUR FANTON

HOTEL DE LA MUETTE ●

LES ARÈNES ✪

MEZZA LUNA ■

BODEGUITA ●

RUE DES ARÈNES

RUE TRUCHET

Place du Forum

CHARDON ●

RUE DE L'HOTEL DE VILLE

ROND-POINT DES ARÈNES

CAFÉ LA NUIT ■

L'AMPHITHEATRE ●

GRAND HOTEL NORD PINUS ●

RUE DE LA CALADE

RUE DU GRAND COUVENT

PLACE DU FORUM— LES CRYPTOPORTIQUES ★

EGLISE AND CLOITRE SAINT TROPHIME ★

THEATRE ANTIQUE

MUSEON ARLATEN ★

Place de la République

CRIQUET ●

RUE EMILE BARRERE

L'HOTEL DU CLOITRE ■

L'EPICERIE DU CLOITRE ■

A COTE BISTROT ■

RUE DU CLOITRE

INDIENNES DE NIMES ■

BOULEVARD EMILE COMBES

RUE DE LA ROTONDE

RUE JEAN JAURÈS

GRAND CAFÉ MALARTE ●

Jardin d'Eté

GUIDED TOUR OF HISTORIC CENTER

BOULEVARD DES LICES

VAN GOGH WALKING TOUR

POST OFFICE

TOURIST OFFICE ℹ

LE JULES CESAR

RUE PARMENTIER

RUE EMILE FASSIN

Canal de Crâponne

BOULEVARD EMILE ZOLA

To ✪ LUMA ARLES

Roman Arles

Arles became a Roman colony in the 1st century BC when it sided with the Romans against Greek-held Marseille. The town famously built Caesar 12 ships in 30 days, and in gratitude he raised it to the status of Colonia, settling veterans of the Sixth Legion there and beginning a program of construction. Roman construction in Arles was still going on during the twilight of the Empire, with many examples still dotting the city today.

- With Arles established as an important port and provincial center, a theater was built around 1 BC during the reign of Augustus, and this was followed by the 20th-largest **Roman arena** in the world in around AD90.

- Plenty of surviving documentation, and the archaeological finds now held in the **Musée Departemental Arles Antique,** testify to the importance of Arles to the Romans during this period.

- Those looking for a quick visual appreciation Arles's significance need go no farther than the **Les Alyscamps** graveyard, one of the largest Roman graveyards in Europe.

- Emperor Constantine built a magnificent palace at the beginning of the 4th century AD, and the remains of the bathhouse **(Les Thermes de Constantine)** can still be visited.

buildings, but the foundations in the form of the Cryptoportiques remain. Accessed from the town hall, these underground galleries supported the square and buildings above. However, they are dark and often damp. Unless you happen to be a historian of structural engineering, they are the least interesting of Arles's Roman sites.

THERMES DE CONSTANTIN

Rue Dominique Maïsto; tel. 04 90 49 59 05; www.arlestourisme.com/fr/monument-detail. html&code=_x0031_3T2000297&langue=fr&back=768; Mar., Apr. and Oct. 9am-6pm, May-Sept. 9am-7pm and Nov.-Feb. 10 am-5pm; €4, reduced €3.20

The Thermes de Constantin (Roman baths) formed part of Emperor Constantine the Great's (AD 272 to 337) palace in Arles. They

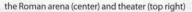

the Roman arena (center) and theater (top right)

are estimated to have covered some 40,000 square feet and included rooms for undressing, and taking cold and hot baths. There were also a warm air room and a dry resting room. Once, the baths were a social center where people met, gossiped, did business, and hatched political plots. Today only the remains of the hot air room, the hot baths, and the under-floor heating system survive. Even so, the scale is impressive and it's possible to picture the place in its operational heyday.

★ FONDATION VAN GOGH

35 rue du Dr Fanton; tel. 04 90 93 08 08; www.fondation-vincentvangogh-arles.org; Tues.-Sun. 11am- 6pm; €9, reduced €7, children 12-18 €4

Van Gogh's dream was to create an artistic commune in his yellow house in Arles. His famous fight in late 1888 with Paul Gauguin put pay to this idea. Gauguin was staying with Van Gogh at the time, and when Gauguin threatened to leave, Van Gogh severed his ear with a razor blade. The art world never forgot this incident or Van Gogh's dream of an artistic community. In the 1980s, a foundation was created to give new life to the idea of an international center of artistic exchange in Arles. Artists including Francis Bacon donated works, but it was not until the intervention of philanthropist Luc Hoffmann in 2010 that the Fondation Van Gogh finally achieved momentum, opening in a physical space four years later. The building usually hosts a few Van Gogh originals and temporary collections chosen to illustrate Van Gogh's artistic legacy. The intent is to stimulate thought through art that references the work of Van Gogh. Unless you're an art historian, the "conversation" between the modernist works on display and Van Gogh's legacy can at times be opaque. Even so the Fondation is a stimulating place to visit. An old hôtel particulier (town house), the building was extensively remodeled to host the center. Particularly striking is the entrance gate, commissioned from the artist Bertrand Lavier, which re-creates the shaky Vincent signature, surrounded by dashes of yellow and green paint.

ESPACE VAN GOGH

Place Félix Rey; daily 8am-6pm; free

Names can be misleading. From the name of this sight, you would be forgiven for expecting to find a space filled with Van Gogh's work. Instead, visitors see a pleasant courtyard filled with flowers and surrounded by shops selling postcards and prints of Van Gogh's work. Constructed in the 16th century, the Espace Van Gogh housed Arles's main hospital until the 20th century. It's notorious as the place Van Gogh was committed after the infamous episode of cutting off his left earlobe in December 1888. During his time here, Van Gogh painted the hospital. The courtyard has been restored to resemble his most famous work here, entitled *Le Jardin de L'Hotel de Dieu*. For those who enjoy matching the scene in an artwork to contemporary reality the Espace merits a visit, but with all the shops the atmosphere can feel a little too commercial.

EGLISE AND CLOITRE SAINT TROPHIME

Place de la République; tel. 04 90 18 41 20; www.provence-pays-arles.com/fr/lieux-dinteret/ eglise-et-cloitre-saint-trophime; Apr. and Oct. 9am-6pm, May-Sept. 9am-7pm, Nov.-Feb. 10am-5pm

Ducking into the Eglise and Cloitre Saint Trophime is a good way to escape the oven-like Place de la République in the heat of summer. Named after the first bishop of Arles, construction of the church began in the early 12th century. The particularly impressive Romanesque entrance was added around 1180. Some of the material used for the arched doorway was salvaged from the city's Theatre Antique. The scene depicted as you enter is the Last Judgement with the dammed heading to hell in chains and the saved floating up to heaven accompanied by angels. Inside, the church is much larger than might be expected. The interior is largely notable for Romanesque sculpture, as well as late Roman sarcophagi and baroque tapestries.

Entrance to the church is free, but to see the celebrated cloister there is a fee (€5.50,

Loving Vincent

The official story of Vincent Van Gogh's time in Provence is well-known. In February 1888 Van Gogh arrived in Arles from Paris, drawn by the clear light and bright colors. He dreamed of living in an artist's commune, and in May he rented the yellow house that was to become the subject of one of his pictures. In October fellow artist Paul Gauguin came to live with him. In December they fought and Van Gogh slashed off his ear. He was then admitted to a hospital in Arles. The people of Arles petitioned to have Van Gogh thrown out of town, and he moved to Saint-Rémy-de-Provence where he entered a mental hospital. There he spent a year before moving to Auvers-sur-Oise outside Paris, where he shot himself. During this time in Provence, Van Gogh painted 350 works.

Vincent Van Gogh self-portrait

Mere words cannot convey the pain and torment that Van Gogh's gift for painting brought to his life. His obsession with fulfilling his talent despite a lack of contemporary appreciation, his fight against epilepsy and mental illness, and the enduring beauty of his work all contributed to his story, which continues to resound through the ages. In 2016 local author Bernadette Murphy published the New York Times best-selling *Van Gogh's Ear* after new evidence was uncovered about Van Gogh's fight with Gauguin. The year 2017 saw the release of the Oscar-nominated animated feature *Loving Vincent,* calling into question the accepted version of Van Gogh's death. Then in 2018, *At Eternity's Gate,* a feature film starring Willem Dafoe as Van Gogh, attempted to capture the light and shade of the painter's time in Provence.

Though the people of Arles once kicked Van Gogh out of town, they are proud of him now. The artist's legacy can be seen all over the area:

- **Fondation Van Gogh:** Founded in the spirit of the artist's desire to create an artistic community, this old hôtel particulier usually has a few Van Gogh originals on display.

- **Espace Van Gogh:** Now filled with shops selling Van Gogh prints and postcards, this 16th century building once housed Arles' main hospital, where Van Gogh was committed after cutting off his earlobe in 1888.

- **Le Café la Nuit** (11 place du Forum, www.restaurant-cafe-van-gogh.com): This café, though not necessarily a culinary highlight of Arles, is featured in *Café Terrace at Night*.

- **Les Alyscamps:** Van Gogh and Gauguin enjoyed painting this ancient Roman graveyard.

- **Van Gogh Walking Tour:** Follow signposts throughout Arles marking the spots where 10 seminal paintings were completed.

- **Monastere St Paul de Mausole:** Van Gogh had himself voluntarily interned at this mental hospital in St.-Rémy-de-Provence.

- **The Rock with Two Holes:** The artist painted this rock, accessible by a pleasant circular walk through vineyards and the Rocky Alpilles.

- **Abbaye Montmajour:** Van Gogh visited this massive monastery more than 50 times, drawing the imposing structure from different angles.

reduced €4.50). Accessed from a separate, slightly hidden entrance, the Cloître Saint Trophime was added to the southeastern corner of the church in the same period as the entrance arch. It's a remarkable example of Romanesque architecture with arches supported by pillars surrounding a small garden. Themes from the Old and New Testament are depicted in the carvings in the stone.

MUSEON ARLATEN

31 rue de la République; tel. 04 13 31 59 99;
www.museonarlaten.fr; reopening scheduled for 2019
At the time of writing, the Museon is closed for refurbishment work. Reopening is scheduled for 2019. Its stated intention is to become a true museum of Provençal society and a space for the preservation of local resources and the memory of current events.

MUSÉE REATTU

10 rue du Grand Prieuré; tel. 04 90 49 37 58;
www.museereattu.arles.fr; Tues.- Sun. 10am-6pm;
€9, reduced €7
Located on the wind-whipped apex of a bend in the Rhône, this former Priory of the Knights of Malta, completed at the end of the 15th century, now houses Arles's arts museum. And what a museum it is, ranging from a collection of 18th century works by its former owner Jacques Réattu to a contemporary sonic art installation. The museum holds intriguing pieces of art history, such as a poignant letter from Van Gogh to Gauguin, written in January 1889, that touches on the breakup of their artistic relationship. There are also 57 sketches by Picasso donated to the museum two years before the artist's death, an impressive sculpture gallery, and as you would expect in Arles, an extensive collection of photography.

MUSÉE DEPARTEMENTAL ARLES ANTIQUE (DEPARTMENTAL MUSEUM OF ANCIENT ARLES)

Presqu'île du Cirque Romain; tel. 04 13 31 51 03;
www.arles-antique.cg13.fr; daily 10am-6pm;
€8, reduced €5. Garden open Apr. 1-Sept. 30 10am-7pm, till 5:30 out of season; free.
From a distance the big, blue modern box on the bank of the Rhône looks like a branch of Swedish furniture giant IKEA. But rather than flat-pack furniture, this blue-clad structure houses an extensive collection of archaeological artifacts found in the Arles region. Sculptures, mosaics, sarcophagi, numerous objects of everyday life, and even a 31-meter Roman barge are laid out in the spacious interior. The main theme is the Romanization of Gaul: in other words, how the Romans, came, saw, conquered, and then made the place feel like home. The arena may be the go-to monument in Arles, but to really understand the city and its history, a visit to the archaeological museum is essential. Outside the museum there is also a Roman-inspired garden.

LES ALYSCAMPS

Avenue des Alyscamps; tel. 04 90 49 59 05;
www.arlestourisme.com/fr/monument-detail.
html&code=_x0031_3T2000293&langue=fr&back=768;
Mar., Apr. and Oct. 9am-6pm,
May-Sept. 9am-7pm and Nov.-Feb. 10 am-5pm;
€4.50, reduced €3.60
Les Alyscamps was one of the most important Roman burial grounds in Europe. Its significance endured long after the Empire ended, with wealthy Christian families sending funeral barges down the Rhône to be buried in this supposedly blessed spot. The name is the Provençal Occitane derivation of Elysian Fields, a Greek perception of the afterlife where the chosen were admitted to join the gods. Looting over the years has robbed the burial ground of some of its more spectacular monuments. Today only one main alley of graves remains, leading to the Saint-Honorat 12th-century Romanesque church. Van Gogh and Gauguin enjoyed painting together here, but a 2,000-year-old graveyard is not everybody's idea of a fun outing.

★ LUMA ARLES

45 chemin des Minimes; tel. 04 90 47 76 17; www.luma-arles.org; Thurs.-Sun. 11am-6pm, opening hours and days may change when project fully finished; €15, reduced €10, under 18 free

Love it or hate it, the Luma Arles project is going to have a transformative effect on the city of Arles. Funded by philanthropist Maya Hoffmann, the site occupies an old railway repair yard. The hangars and workshops have been imaginatively transformed into exhibition centers for art shows and resident dance and theater companies. A surrounding park is due to be completed in 2020, as is the Frank Gehry building, which naysayers point to as a modernist catastrophe inflicted on the city. The jarring juxtaposition of the glinting silver tower, all jagged angles and boxes, with the symmetrical perfection of the Roman arena is hard to ignore, as are the likely gentrification and influx of tourists that will come with the site. Supporters point to the Gehry building as a symbol of hope and regeneration. When completed in 2020, the building will house artists' studios, creative spaces, and a café.

WALKING TOURS

VAN GOGH WALKING TOUR

9 Boulevard des Lices; tel. 04 90 18 41 20; www.arlestourisme.com/en/visits-of-arles.html; daily 1:30pm; €12 or free with downloadable map

Van Gogh arrived in Arles in February 1888 and in just over a year produced more than 300 paintings. *The Night Café* and *Yellow House* are just two of the works that changed the art world forever. Signposts on the walk mark where these and other seminal paintings were completed. There are 10 different spots in all, and completing the circuit, depending on how long you stop and stare, takes around 3 hours.

1: The Roman theatre staged comedies, tragedies, mimes and pantomimes. **2:** the futuristic Frank Gehry building at Luma Arles **3:** The cryptoportiques are the foundations of the Roman Forum and can still be accessed from the Place du Forum.

GUIDED TOUR OF HISTORIC CENTER

9 boulevard des Lices; www.arlestourisme.com/en/visits-of-arles.html; daily 10:30am; €12

Arles contains eight monuments listed on the UNESCO world heritage list. This guided walking tour takes in the main sights. Given by local guide Alice Vallat, an expert in history and art history, the tour lasts about 2 hours. It's a great introduction to Arles's archaeological treasure trove.

ENTERTAINMENT AND EVENTS

FERIA D'ARLES

Les Arènes; tel. 04 88 09 22 88; www.feriaarles.com; Easter weekend

The opening of the bull-fighting season is celebrated with one hell of a party in Arles. There's music, dancing, lots of drink, and crowds spilling from one bar to another. Around 500,000 people cram into the city and street bands (*peñas*) roam the city followed by streams of sangria-swilling bull-fighting fans. In the arena, there are daily bull fights.

FÊTE DES GARDIANS

Les Arènes; www.confrerie-des-gardians.com/programme; May 1; bull run €10

Some 506 years ago, the Camargue Gardians formed one of France's first *confreries* (brotherhoods). Today there are around 200 Gardians working on the *manades* (ranches) in the Camargue. Their work includes upkeep of the land and enclosures, castrating the bulls and horses, and participating in the summer course camarguaise. On May 1 the Gardians ride into Arles, celebrate a holy Mass, have a long lunch, and then stage a Course Camarguaise bull run in the arena. The proceeds of the event go to support Gardians who are injured during their work or become ill.

COURSE SATIN

Manade Mogador Petit Route de Tarascon; tel. 04 88 96 47 00; www.festivarles.com/la-course-de-satin.html; second Sunday in June; free

Dating back to 1589, this bare-back horse race

Bull Fighting and the Course Camarguaise

Camargue bulls graze at sunset

It's easy to dismiss any form of bull fighting as barbaric and inappropriate in the modern world. Before doing so, however, it's worth at least understanding the different types of bull fighting prevalent in the south of France and listening to those who defend the sport.

COURSE CAMARGUAISE

Throughout the region covered in this chapter, Course Camarguaise bull running takes place from Easter to the end of September. Participants compete in a circular arena by trying to remove ribbons pinned to the horns of a bull. Before a Course Camarguaise event, the bulls are driven through the streets of the host village or town. This often chaotic passage is known as the *abrivado*. People from the village attempt to free the bulls from the protective cordon formed by the Gardians and their horses. Other than the distress of being chased and baited, the bulls are not harmed during a Course Camarguaise. In fact, the most entertaining part is seeing the competitors fling themselves over barricades to avoid being speared.

CORRIDAS

More questionably, the arena in Arles also hosts *corridas* (runs) in which the bulls are killed. The bulls used in a *corrida* are Spanish in origin, as this form of bullfighting is a cultural import from Spain. The bulls are stronger and broader-shouldered and have shorter horns than their Camargue relatives. Spanish bulls killed in Les Arenes in Arles spend the first four years of their lives in the wilds of the Camargue. Their natural life expectancy is six years.

GARDIANS AND THE BULLS

The Gardians who look after the welfare of the bulls (both Spanish and Camarguaise) maintain that relative to animals subject to farming practices, the bulls are fortunate and live a privileged life. Such is the bond between the Gardians and their charges that brave bulls are treated to a funeral and are buried standing up facing the sea.

is as fiercly contested as ever. Only pure-bred Camarguaise horses from the best stud farms are eligible to enter. Watching the race is an exhilerating experience; winning, rather than the safety of the riders, is all that matters. The victor leaves with a gold-embroidered satin scarf, which he keeps for a year. If the same rider wins three years in a row, he keeps the scarf forever. The Course Satin caps a full day of horse races and horsemanship displays.

L'ABRIVADO DES BERNACLES

Depart Mas des Bernacles in the Camargue, arriving at Les Arènes in Arles; tel 04 88 09 22 88; www.feriaarles.com; first Monday in July

Taking place on the same day as one of the most important Course Camarguaise bull runs (Le Concorde d'Or), the *abrivado* is a display of horsemanship by the Camargue Gardians. Departing from 15 kilometers (9 miles) outside Arles, they form a phalanx of horses to drive bulls into the center of the city. As the distance to the city shrinks, so the crowd swells.

FÊTE DU COSTUME

Boulevard des Lices and Théâtre Antique; tel. 04 88 09 22 88; www.fetes-arles.com; first Sunday in July and the Friday before

Created by the poet Frederic Mistral, the Fête du Costume was instigated to preserve Provençal dress and traditions. In 1903 just 16 girls turned up for the first Arlesian costume festival. However, after this inauspicious start, the festival quickly took off, and with hundreds participating, it soon moved venue to the Roman theater. These days the festival has two parts. On the Friday night, the *pegoulado* takes place: crowds gather in traditional dress for a torch-lit procession that ends with a Farandole (Provençal dance) in the arena. On the Sunday there is a dress parade in front of the queen of Arles in the Roman Theatre. Every three years a newly elected queen is also presented to at the costume festival. The next new queen is due to be elected in 2020.

ARLES PHOTOGRAPHY FESTIVAL

Exhibitions throughout the city; tel. 04 90 96 76 06; www.rencontres-arles.com/en; July-Sept., hours depend on venue; €28 day pass, €35 unlimited pass

In the summer months Arles hosts a major photography exhibition. Thought-provoking images are displayed throughout the city. Major venues host ticketed shows by well-known photographers, but even without a pass you can partake in the atmosphere of the festival. Photos decorate windows and street corners and animate a visit to the city. The opening week is particularly busy with various VIP and press events. The festival attracts an estimated 100,000 people to the city.

FERIA DU RIZ

Boulevard des Lices and the Arena; tel. 04 88 09 22 88; www.feriaarles.com; second weekend in Sept.; free

Thanks to pump stations on the Petit Rhône and associated irrigation channels, the Camargue region produces France's entire output of rice. The harvest usually begins after this festival. Floats decorated with sheaves of rice and all sorts of other parapheulelia pass throught the streets of Arles. There's traditional dress, dance, bodegas spilling onto the streets, and of course bull fighting, in the form of a Spanish *corrida*.

The Arts
LE CORRIDOR

3 rue de la roquette; tel. 04 90 43 63 62; Wed.-Sat. 3pm-7pm; free

Annick and Michel Ray opened Le Corridor in 2016. Passionate about contemporary art, they have been collectors for 25 years and have converted part of their town house into a gallery to provide a space for artists to display and sell their work.

FORGES COURTYARD AND LA FORMATION

Luma; tel. 04 90 47 76 17; www.luma-arles.org/ fr; check website for events; prices depend on performance, open rehearsals

As part of the Luma Arles project, a residency

building with rehearsal space was created for dance groups. Performances take place throughout the summer at Luma, and rehearsals are open to the public.

SHOPPING
LA MAIN QUI PENSE
15 rue Tour de Fabre; tel. 04 90 18 24 58;
www.cecilecayrol.com/fr/accueil.html;
Mon.-Fri. 10am-noon and 2pm-6pm
In her workshop, Cecile Cayrol eschews the colorful palette that characterizes many Provençal ceramics. Instead, form and design take precedence, with collections of bowls, cups, water jugs, and plates presented in subdued grays and red.

LA PARFUMERIE ARLESIENNE
26 rue de la Liberté; tel. 04 90 97 02 07;
www.la-parfumerie-arlesienne.com;
Mon.-Sat. 10am-1pm and 2pm-6pm
Inspired by Arles and the surrounding Camargue countryside, this boutique perfumerie produces a small range of scents, candles, and soaps. Best sellers include the floral Cloud of Flamingos scent.

LA ROSE A POIS
9 rue Reattu; tel. 04 90 49 99 81; http://
lesaccessoiresdaudrey.com; Tues.-Sat. 10am-7pm
This small boutique specializes in original clothes and accessories. The clothes are either one-off creations or part of a limited line.

INDIENNES DE NIMES
14 Place de La Republique; tel. 04 90 18 21 52;
www.indiennesdenimes.fr; Mon.-Sat. 10am-12:30pm
and 2:30pm-7pm
Channel your inner cowboy or cowgirl at this clothing store selling traditional clothing for Camargue Gardians. From boots to hats and everything in between, the store can transform you into a Gardian in under 20 minutes.

FOOD
Arles has a good selection of restaurants. The city gets very busy during the tourist season from June to the middle of September, and the restaurants tend to be small with around 30 covers. To make sure you get a good table, indeed any table, it's advisable to make a reservation at the restaurants listed below. While touring the sights of Arles, look for these restaurants, poke your head in the door, and if you like what you see, reserve a table for lunch or supper. There are, of course, plenty of less memorable restaurants where you can get a table at the last moment.

Regional Cuisine
A CÔTE BISTRO
21 rue de Carmes; tel. 04 90 47 61 13;
www.bistro-acote.com; Wed.-Sun. noon-2pm and
7:30pm-9:30pm; mains €22
The sister bistro of the two-star Michelin restaurant next door has been pulling the crowds in for 10 years now. The menu is short with only three main courses on offer. Usually they are classic dishes such as roasted cod or lamb shank. Often they are served in the frying pan in which they were cooked, which adds to the rustic, no-nonsense feel. The dining room has a nice, cozy atmosphere. There is limited seating outside on the street.

★ L'EPICERIE DU CLOITRE
18 rue de Cloitre; tel. 04 88 09 10 10; www.lecloitre.
com/fr/ou-manger-a-arles; 11:30am-12:30am; €4-16
This atmospheric small courtyard restaurant bubbles with conversation and serves tapas all made from high-quality local ingredients. Seafood dominates, with squid, sardines, and sea urchin all on the menu. Vegetables are sourced from the renowned potager of the Michelin two-starred Le Chastagnette restaurant in the Camargue.

★ CRIQUET
21 rue Porte de Laure; tel. 04 90 96 80 51;
Wed.-Sun., noon-2pm and 7:15pm-9:30pm; €16-22
A local favorite, this family-run establishment offers honest, good food. The garlic prawn tagliatelli is delicious, and the tables in this small restaurant are often full. Eating outside in the narrow alleyway that leads up to the restaurant is a convivial experience. The

surrounding stone walls frame the tables, and the sound of chatting, contented diners reverbrates out into the main street.

GALOUBET

18 rue du Docteur Fanton; tel. 04 90 93 18 11;
Tues.-Sat. noon-2:30pm and 7:30pm-9:30pm; €16-22
Rain or shine, this is a popular restaurant. Inside there's a cozy bistro atmosphere with vintage furnishings; outside there's a vine-covered terrace. The cooking is an inventive take on local classics, featuring seasonal ingredients. Try the delicious medallions of pork with figs.

LES PIQUES OU RIEN

53 rue Condorcet; tel. 04 86 32 29 44;
https://les-piques-ou-rien.business.site;
Tues.-Sat. 10am-10pm, Sun. 10am-2pm, Mon. closed,
Wed. 6pm-10pm; €16-24
For an inventive concept restaurant, try Les Piques ou Rien. Here, after telling the chef about any allergies, diners simply wait to be served. What comes out of the kitchen is a surprise. There's usually a cold tapas starter, followed by a selection of hot, tasty dishes and five melt-in-the-mouth desserts.

International
CHARDON

37 rue des Arènes; tel. 09 72 86 72 04;
www.hellochardon.com; Fri.-Mon. 12:30pm-3pm and
7:30pm-11pm, Thurs. 7:30pm-11pm. closed Tues.-Wed
and Thurs. lunch; menu €39
Chardon is an ever-changing delight of a restaurant. From one season to the next, it's impossible to know who will be cooking. Leading chefs from across the world are invited to take up residency, enjoy the atmosphere of Arles, and put something special on the plates of the locals. What's served depends on the nationality and influences of the particular chef.

L'ENTREVUE

Place Nina Berberova; tel. 04 90 93 37 28;
www.lentrevue-restaurant.com; daily 8:30am-12am;
€14.50-20
Tajines are the speciality at this large popular

restaurant with a terrace overlooking the Rhône. A long menu also includes plenty of salads, burgers, and steaks.

Cafés and Light Bites
MAISON VOLVER

8 rue de La Cavaliere; tel. 04 90 96 05 88;
www.maisonvolver.com;
daily 8am-9pm
This is a nice spot for a leisurely breakfast just a couple hundred meters (650 feet) from the Roman arena. There is a large comfortable terrace, and the owners take great pride in welcoming clients. Service continues all day with more substantial dishes for lunch and supper.

MEZZA LUNA

1 Place du Forum; daily noon-7pm; €10-€15
The bustling Place du Forum is filled with cafés and restaurants. For a quick bite, Mezza Luna is a good pit stop. On the menu are salads, vegetable tarts, and bruschettas. The Place du Forum in general is a good place to find a table if you can't get into the restaurants above.

Markets
SATURDAY AND
WEDNESDAY MARKET

Boulevard des Lices and boulevard Emiles Combe;
Sat. and Wed. 8am-12:30pm
In Arles's twice-weekly market, there are clothes, linens, and gift stalls, but food dominates. In particular, look for butchers selling the locally reared bull meat, which has a richer, denser texture than normal beef, and specialty rices from the Camargue. Often these rices require lengthy cooking times (up to 25 minutes) and are specifically intended for salads. Clams fresh from the Camargue are also on sale. The Saturday market is larger and more popular.

BARS AND NIGHTLIFE
GRAND CAFÉ MALARTE

2 boulevard des Lices; tel. 04 90 54 56 74;
www.grand-cafe-malarte-restaurant-arles.com;
Mon.-Wed. noon-2:30pm, Thurs.-Sun. noon-2:30pm

and 7pm-10:30pm; drinks from €3

It's hard to miss the Grand Café; its large terrace spills out onto Arles's main street, the boulevard des Lices. There's a brasserie restaurant, but if you are not hungry or have already eaten it's a good place to stop and soak up the Arlesian atmosphere. A recent remodel includes nice touches like a wall-to-wall glass fridge filled with rosés.

CARGO DE NUIT

7 avenue Sadi Carnot; tel. 04 90 49 55 99;
www.cargodenuit.com; check website for events;
pricing depends on event

Part nightclub, part concert venue, the Cargo de Nuit is now more than 20 years old and still going strong. If there's a bigname DJ in town or a well-known artist, then chances are they'll be playing here. There's a wine and cocktail bar and restaurant on site.

BODEGUITA

49 rue des Arènes and 16 rue d'Hotel de Ville;
tel. 04 90 96 68 59; www.bodeguita.fr;
Tues.-Sat., 7:30pm-12:30am; tapas from €4

This authentic, all-singing, all-dancing tapas bar offers cocktails, shooters, imported Spanish charcuterie, and classic tapas such a *patatas bravas* (fried potatoes served with tomato sauce). It's so popular that there are now two sites open, and during weekends, each does two sittings.

ACCOMMODATIONS
€50-100
HOTEL DE LA MUETTE

15 rue des Suisses;
tel. 04 90 96 15 39;
www.hotel-muette.com; €60 d

There are 18 recently refurbished rooms in this city center hotel. Old stone walls and beams create a warm ambience. It's a perfect budget choice for families, with triples, quadraples, and even a quintuple room, all with ensuite bathrooms. There's free Wi-Fi and parking for €15.

L'AMPHITHEATRE

5-7 rue Diderot; tel. 04 90 93 98 69;
www.hotelamphitheatre.fr; €75 d

Tucked away down a side street, just minutes from the arena, this old hôtel particulier is full of character. There's a good choice of different-standard rooms, all with ensuite bathrooms, air-conditioning, and Wi-Fi, and a small outside garden. The room decor is in need of updating, and parking is 300 meters (984 feet) away on the boulevard des Lices.

HOTEL DE MUSÉE

11 rue Grand Prieure; tel. 04 90 93 88 88;
www.hoteldumusée.com; €80 d

The large interior courtyard is the main attraction of this budget city center hotel near the Roman baths and the Reattu Museum. It's a relaxing, shady place to sit and enjoy breakfast or immerse yourself in a book. The rooms are basic with old-fashioned decor, but they are all air-conditioned with ensuite bathrooms and Wi-Fi. Private parking is available for €20 per day.

€100-200
LE JULES CESAR

9 boulevard des Lices; tel. 04 90 52 52 52;
www.hotel-julescesar.fr/en; €149 d

A former Carmelite monastery that's been recently revamped by star interior decorator M Lacroix, this central hotel is full of color and moody artistic pieces. Just moments from the Roman arena and theater, the hotel offers a bar, a good restaurant with a terrace overlooking the boulevard des Lices, a swimming pool, and a spa. All rooms have air-conditioning, Wi-Fi, and ensuite bathrooms. Private parking is available for €20 per night.

★ L'HOTEL DU CLOITRE

18 rue du Cloitre; tel. 04 88 09 10 00;
www.hotelducloitre.com; €139 d

Seemingly effortlessly cool, the Hotel Cloitre has a young, vibrant vibe, with an on-site tapas restaurant, roof terrace, and funky rooms. Whimsical pieces of furniture, attentive service, and the charm of the old building work together to put a broad smile on the face of each guest. All rooms have ceiling or floor fans, Wi-Fi, and ensuite bathrooms. The public parking can be booked in advance for €11 a day.

HOTEL D'ARLATAN
26 rue Sauvage; tel. 04 90 97 20 29;
www.hotel-arlatan.fr; €155 d
A spectacular renovation of Arles's most renowned hôtel particulier has transformed this historic building a few streets from the Roman baths into the destination hotel for Arles. Everywhere you look there are works of art; the scale of the endeavor and the attention to detail make the Arlatan a unique place to stay. All rooms have air-conditioning, Wi-Fi, and ensuite bathrooms. Private parking is €18 per night.

Over €200
★ GRAND HOTEL NORD PINUS
Place du Forum; tel. 04 90 93 44 44;
www.nord-pinus.com; €210 d
The Nord Pinus is an Arlesian institution on the bustling Place du Forum, which exudes the spirit and history of the city. Fashion designer Christian Lacroix describes it best: "To me when I was a child it was the temple of every summer holiday of high society and of course bull fighting. Starting from the Place du Forum, but never leaving it, it was like a voyage of adventure toward Paris, Spain, the world. Images of...white and gold capes spring to mind, of Cocteau and Picasso in black capes...." All rooms have air-conditioning, Wi-Fi and ensuite bathrooms. Parking can be reserved in advance for €25 per day.

L'HÔTEL PARTICULIER
4 rue de La Monnaie; tel. 04 90 52 51 40;
www.hotel-particulier.com; €315 d
This small luxury haven in the middle of Arles seduces with its pristine white interiors and black-and-white photos. Every detail has been thought through and every comfort provided, including a small swimming pool and spa treatments. All rooms have air-conditioning,

Wi-Fi, and ensuite bathrooms. The hotel has its own private garage.

INFORMATION AND SERVICES
TOURIST OFFICE
Esplanade Charles de Gaulle, boulevard des Lices
13200; tel. 04 90 18 41 20;
www.arlestourisme.com;
Mon.-Sat. 9am-1pm and 2pm-5pm, Sun. 10am-1pm
Arles's central tourist office has English-speaking staff who can help with anything from finding accommodation to getting tickets for events. The office is stocked with helpful maps and brochures that cover not just Arles but also the Camargue.

HOSPITALS AND PHARMACIES
For medical services, the main **pharmacy** is on 4 rue Jean Jaures (tel. 04 90 96 16 08). The closest hospital is **Joseph Imbert** (Quartier Fourchon, tel. 04 90 49 29 29).

POST OFFICE
5 boulevard des Lices; Mon.-Fri. 8:30am-noon and
2pm-7pm; Sat. 8:30am-midday
The post office offers the usual range of services for sending letters and parcels within France and internationally. It is located half a kilometer south of the Roman theater.

GETTING THERE
By Car
Arles is easily accessible by car, although the surrounding roads can get congested, particularly at the beginning and end of the day. To reach Arles:

From Marseille: Take the A7 and then the A54 to Arles. It takes about an hour to travel the 91-kilometer (56-mile) distance.

From Aix-en-Provence: Arles is about 75 kilometers (46 miles) from Aix on the A54m. The drive takes about an hour.

From Avignon: Take the D2 for 46 kilometers (28 miles); it will take about 45 minutes.

From Saint-Rémy-de-Provence: Take the D570N. It takes about 30 minutes to cover the 30 kilometers (19 miles) between Saint-Rémy and Arles.

From Saintes-Maries-de-la-Mer: Take the D570; it will take you about 35 minutes to cover 37 kilometers (23 miles).

Parking near the center of the city can be problematic. The largest **parking lot** is on boulevard des Lices near the tourist office.

By Train

The **train station** is located a short walk from the center, next to the bus station, on avenue Paulin Talabot. Service runs from the following towns and cities.

From Marseille: Direct trains run approximately every half hour, and the journey from Marseille Saint Charles Station takes about an hour. Tickets are about €15 one way. Consult www.sudmobilite.fr for an up-to-date timetable.

From Avignon: Direct trains run from the central station every half hour or so and take less than an hour to reach Arles. Tickets cost €9 one way. Consult www.sudmobilite.fr for an up-to-date timetable

By Bus

The **bus station** is located a short walk from the center, next to the train station on Avenue Paulin Talabot. Note there is no direct bus from Aix-en-Provence to Arles. Services run from the following towns and cities.

From Marseille: Tickets on **Ouibus** (https://fr.ouibus.com) are €7, and the ride takes 1 hour and 25 minutes. Buses run five times a day.

From Avignon: LER Line 18 costs €4 and takes about one hour via Tarascon. Buses run five times a day. Info at: www.info-ler.fr/index.php?.

From Saintes-Maries-de-la-Mer: Le Pilote (www.lepilote.com) Line 20 costs €2.50 and takes 1 hour and 10 minutes to reach Arles. Buses run 10 times a day.

From Saint-Rémy-de-Provence: Take **Car Trieze** (www.lepilote.com) Line 54. Tickets cost €4 and the ride takes about an hour. Buses run three times a day.

GETTING AROUND

No matter how you arrive in Arles, the best way to see it is **on foot.** All the sights listed in this chapter are within 15 minutes' walk of each other and much of the historic city is pedestrianized. Roads that are open to traffic tend to be narrow and one-way, and they're best avoided. The only sight you will need to drive to is the Arles Archaeological Museum. **Taxis** can be booked through your hotel or **Arles Taxi Services** (tel. 04 28 31 41 06; www.arles-taxis-services.com).

Camargue Regional Nature Park

Scratch the surface of the Camargue and it may disappoint. Invest some time, though, and it seduces like few other areas of Provence. The inhabitants of this wetland delta, formed by the Rhône as it meets the sea, are fiercely proud of their way of life: rearing bulls for the Course Camarguaise and *corridas*; farming the land for rice; producing wine and some of the finest table salt in France. Away from the main roads, out in the heart of the countryside, flamboyances of flamingos fly low overhead, their bodies improbably long and pink, illuminated by the setting sun. Gardian cowboys come whooping on horseback around corners, driving bulls before them. Humans, horses, and herds change direction as one, driven by centuries-old instinct. In the bars and restaurants, the fact that life is hard here seems to have generated a reckless freedom of spirit, a desire to dance and party that is more Spanish than French. It all seems a million miles from the manicured streets of Saint-Rémy-de-Provence. For nature lovers, particularly bird-watchers, a trip to the Camargue and its nature reserves is not to be missed.

ORIENTATION

A few kilometers to the north of Arles, the Rhône splits in two as it begins to fan out toward the sea. The Petit Rhône becomes the western arm of the Camargue delta and the Rhône the eastern. The Petit Rhône meets the sea adjacent to **Saintes-Maries-de-la-Mer** and the Grand Rhône at **Plage de Piemanson.** The D570 takes you from Arles to Saintes-Maries-de-la-Mer and the D36 to Plage de Piemanson. In between, the V formed by these two roads is the **Etang de Vaccarès,** a large inland saltwater lake that effectively divides the Camargue into two peninsulas. Although it's not possible to drive along the seafront between Saintes-Maries-de-la-Mer and Plage de Piemanson, you can walk or ride along the Digue de la Mer sea wall. The **Ornithological Park of Pont de Gau** is located a few kilometers north of Saintes-Maries-de-la-Mer. **La Capelière** nature reserve, which is a popular hiking and bird-spotting area, is located off the D36 on the road to Plage Piemanson on the banks of the Etang de Vaccarès.

SAINTES-MARIES-DE-LA-MER

Saintes-Maries is an attractive port and coastal resort town. There's a long sandy beach, plenty of restaurants, and the unmissable twice-yearly gypsy pilgrimages, when the place comes alive with the legend of the Maries.

Sights
EGLISE NOTRE DAME DE LA MER
2 place de L'Eglise; tel. 04 90 97 80 25;
www.sanctuaire-des-saintesmaries.fr
It's no coincidence that Notre-Dame-de-la-Mer resembles a fortress. Built between the 8th and 12th centuries, its secondary purpose was as a refuge from pirate attacks on the port.

It's free to enter and visitors can descend into the crypt where the statue of the gypsy patron saint, Black Sarah, stands lit by flickering candles. If you look above the choir pews, you will see the Chapel of Saint Michel where the relics of Mary Salomon, Mary Jacobi, and Black Sarah are held. During the Gypsy pilgrimage (see Pelerinage de Gitans below), they are lowered from the chapel and carried out to sea. The barge that carries the statues of the Marys and Sarah is also on display in the church. Outside the church are steps leading onto the roof. For a couple of euros you can climb up and enjoy an unparalleled view of Saintes-Maries-de-la-Mer, the Mediterranean, and the Camargue.

Hiking
DIGUE WALK
Plage l'Est; €4.60 parking fee
One kilometer (0.6 miles) east of Saintes-Maries is the start of the trail that leads out onto the Digue Dyke, which stretches for 12 kilometers (7 miles) across the mouth of the Rhône. The dyke was built in the 19th century to facilitate agriculture in the southern part of the Camargue. To find the start of the walk, simply hug the coast until you reach the parking lot for Plage de l'Est. With the sea on one side, saltwater lakes on the other, and the wind inevitably blowing, the walk is a wild, invigorating experience. The track is flat but uneven, and the halfway point is the Phare de La Gacholle. Walking the length of the dyke takes around 6 hours, and with no refreshment en-route it is not surprising that most walkers retrace their steps at some point. The hardy make it all the way to Salin-de-Giraud. From there, the last bus (Pilote Line 10) back to Arles leaves around 5pm. There is no direct connection back to Saintes-Maries-de-la-Mer.

Other Sports and Recreation
BATEAU CAMARGUE
Port Gardian; tel. 06 17 95 81 96; www. bateau-camargue.com/en; €12 adult, €6 children
A good way of getting up close with the bulls and wild horses of the Camargue is to take a

Camargue Regional Nature Park

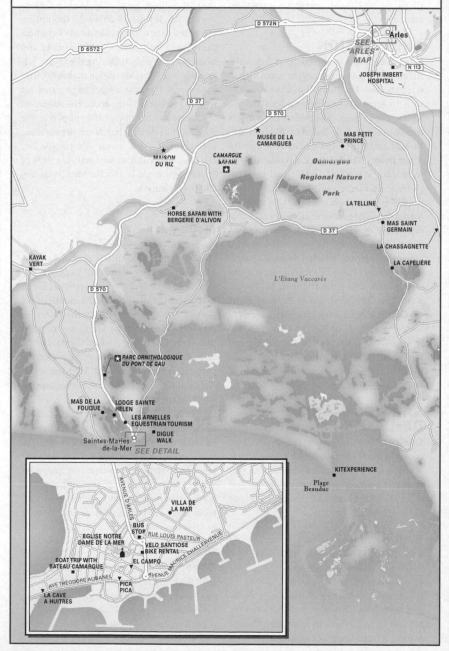

D 572N

Arles

SEE
"ARLES"
MAP

D 6572

JOSEPH IMBERT
HOSPITAL

N 113

D 37

D 570

★ MUSÉE DE LA
CAMARGUES

MAS PETIT
PRINCE

MAISON
DU RIZ

CAMARGUE
SAFARI

Camargue

Regional Nature

Park

LA TELLINE

HORSE SAFARI WITH
BERGERIE D'ALIVON

D 37

MAS SAINT
GERMAIN

LA CHASSAGNETTE

KAYAK
VERT

LA CAPELIÈRE

D 570

L'Etang Vaccarès

PARC ORNITHOLOGIQUE
DU PONT DE GAU

MAS DE LA
FOUQUE

LODGE SAINTE
HELEN

LES ARNELLES
EQUESTRIAN TOURISM

DIGUE
WALK

Saintes-Maries-
de-la-Mer

SEE DETAIL

KITEXPERIENCE

Plage
Beauduc

AVENUE D'ARLES

VILLA DE
LA MAR

BUS
STOP

RUE LOUIS PASTEUR

EGLISE NOTRE
DAME DE LA MER

VELO SANTIOSE
BIKE RENTAL

EL CAMPO

AVENUE MAURICE CHALLE

AVENUE

BOAT TRIP WITH
BATEAU CAMARGUE

AVE THÉODORE AUBANEL

PICA
PICA

LA CAVE
A HUITRES

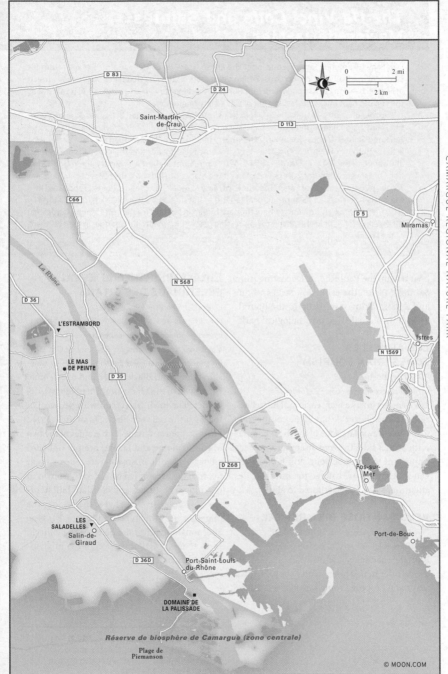

D 83

D 24

Saint-Martin-de-Crau

D 113

0   2 mi

0   2 km

C 66

D 5

Miramas

N 568

La Rhône

D 36

L'ESTRAMBORD

Istres

LE MAS DE PEINTE

N 1569

D 35

D 268

Fos-sur-Mer

LES SALADELLES

Salin-de-Giraud

Port-de-Bouc

D 36D

Port-Saint-Louis-du-Rhône

DOMAINE DE LA PALISSADE

Réserve de biosphère de Camargue (zone centrale)

Plage de Piemanson

© MOON.COM

The Da Vinci Code and Saintes-Maries-de-la-Mer

Dan Brown somehow managed to omit the Eglise Notre de la Mer in Saintes-Maries from his best-selling novel *The Da Vinci Code*. Brown's plot rests on the fact that Mary Magdalene arrived in France, bearing Christ's child, and that Christ's bloodline survived. The Holy Grail is cast not as the cup of Christ but as the last resting place of Mary Magdalene.

The role of Saintes-Maries-de-la-Mer in this story is well-established in legend. Fleeing Palestine, Mary Magdalene arrives with Mary Salomon and Mary Jacobi at the port of Ratis (later to be renamed Saintes-Maries-de-la-Mer). Their party includes a black Egyptian servant, Sarah, who is thought to be of Gypsy origin. The Marys become missionaries and their remains are eventually buried in the **Notre-Dame-de-la-Mer** church. Yet in the 15th century when Good King René of Provence exhumes the graves of the three Marys, he finds only the relics of Salomon and Jacobi, plus the remains of Sarah. The bones of Mary Magdalene, it seems, have disappeared into the mists of history, or as another local legend maintains, to **Saint-Maximin-la-Sainte-Baume** near Aix-en-Provence where they are buried in the Basilica de Santa Maria Magdalena. It's certainly more plausible than Brown's resting place: underneath the triangle in the courtyard of the Louvre.

boat trip up the Petit Rhône. Departing from Saintes-Maries, the excursion lasts an hour and a half, taking visitors up to the boundaries of the Pont de Gau ornithological park.

LES ARNELLES EQUESTRIAN TOURISM

RD570; tel. 06 86 60 15 15;
www.arnellescamargue.com; €23 for 1hr 15m

Les Arnelles offers a wide variety of horseback rides, from a short ride out in the countryside to a whole-day safari. One of the most popular is the sunset ride. To avoid disappointment it's important to describe your skill level in advance. All levels are catered for, but the rides and groups need to be tailored to ability.

VELO SANTIOSE BIKE RENTAL

19 rue de La Republique; tel. 09 40 97 74 56;
www.levelosaintois.com; €10 for half a day

Electric, road bike, and off-road bike rentals are on offer in this town-center shop. Helpful maps and proposed routes are also available.

Entertainment and Events
PÈLERINAGE DES GITANS

Eglises des Saintes-Maries;
www.avignon-et-provence.com/en/traditions/
gypsys-pilgrimage-saintes-maries-de-mer;
May 24-25, second pilgrimage Sun. nearest Oct. 22

Gypsies from all over Europe come to worship their saint, Black Sarah, and to celebrate the arrival of the Marys in Saintes-Maries-de-la-Mer. The town is overrun with people. On the 24th the relics of Black Sarah are carried down to the sea. On the 25th statues of the two Maries (Salome and Jacobi) are put onboard a boat. A flotilla of small craft follows them out to sea. Surrounded by Arlesian women in traditional costumes and Gardian bull herders, a bishop blesses the sea, the region, the pilgrims, and the gypsies. Prayers, Masses, and nonstop vigils take place in the church. In October a smaller version of the pilgrimage takes place.

1: Church of Saintes-Maries-de-la-Mer **2:** two statues of the Holy Maries (Salome and Jacobi) **3:** Ice cream offers relief on a hot afternoon in Saintes-Maries-de-la-Mer.

The Camargue Gardians

a Camargue Gardian herds horses

Whatever you do, don't call a Camargue Gardian a cowboy to his face. The bull herders of the Camargue have great respect for their cattle ranching American brethren, but in Europe the word cowboy has taken on the negative connotation of someone flying by the seat of their pants who never quite gets a job done properly. Gardians are the ultimate professionals. There are 250 or so of them remaining, and together they form a 500-year old *confrerie* (association) that is one of the oldest in France. Out in the wilds of the Camargue they look after the bulls and horses and maintain the land. During the festive summer months they drive bulls through the streets of villages, riding in a tight phalanx of white horses toward the arena where the Course Camarguaise takes place. They dress in leather boots, jeans, and checked shirts, and have a seemingly pathological aversion to riding helmets. For many, their rugged professionalism embodies the spirit of the Camargue. Their annual festival, **Fête des Gardians,** takes place on May 1 in Arles.

Food

PICA PICA

16-18 avenue Van Gogh;
tel. 06 10 30 33 49; €10-18

First things first, if you are horrified at the thought of plastic glasses and cups, this restaurant is not for you. However if you love the thought of fish as fresh as it gets and don't mind the rustic feel, then try Pica Pica. Personally I think the copious plateful of small battered fried fish and a cold beer are perfection. A reservation is usually not necessary, but in summer and during any festivals, book to avoid disappointment.

LA CAVE A HUITRES

38 rue Theodore Aubanel; tel. 04 90 97 96 60; €5-54

It's all about the spectacular seafood at this port-side restaurant. Prawns, oysters, clams, razorfish, and crab are all piled high on iced plates. Those felling less peckish can settle for a plate of mussels, topped with a Provençal gratin. A reservation is usually not necessary but in summer and during any festivals, book to avoid disappointment.

EL CAMPO

13 rue Victor Hugo; tel. 04 90 97 84 11; €12.50-21.50

Paella, flamenco guitar, and plenty of sangria send diners home happy from this lively Spanish restaurant. The menu is long, and includes salads and tapas, but what really matters is the party atmosphere. A reservation is usually not necessary, but in summer and during any festivals, book to avoid disappointment.

Accommodations

MAS DE LA FOUQUE

D38 route du Petit Rhône; tel. 04 90 97 81 02; www.masdelafouque.com/en; €225 d

A luxury treat in the heart of the Camargue awaits at Mas de la Fouque. Stay in a colorful revamped gypsy caravan right on the edge of the water, or in a suite with immaculate white furnishings. Swimming in the pool, you almost feel like you are heading out into the salt water to join the birdlife. At night, watch the sunset on the terrace of the gastronomic restaurant. All rooms have Wi-Fi, air-conditioning, and ensuite bathrooms. Parking is free.

VILLA DE LA MAR

1 bis, rue Camille Pelletan; tel. 04 90 97 06 68; www.viladelamar.com; €160 d

A perfect base for enjoying Saintes-Maries is Villa de la Mar. Little touches, such as chairs upholstered in cow hide, bring the wild spirit of the Camargue into this modern, comfortable spa hotel. There's a restaurant, bar, and small semicovered pool. All rooms have Wi-Fi and ensuite bathrooms. Free public parking is available opposite the hotel.

LODGE SAINTE HELENE

Chemin Bas des Launes; tel. 04 90 97 83 29; www.lodge-saintehelene.com/fr/hotel-saintes-maries-de-la-mer-camargue; €160 d

A couple of kilometers up the road from Saintes-Maries, the Lodge Sainte Helene overlooks the Etang des Launes. Rooms open up to unforgetable views of flocks of grazing pink flamingos. The swimming pool could not be closer to the water's edge, and neither could the breakfast terrace. It's a place where you can feel the wild spirit of the Camargue but still relax in luxury surroundings. All rooms have Wi-Fi and ensuite bathrooms. Parking is free.

Getting There and Around

BY CAR

Saintes-Maries-de-la-Mer is easily accessible by car. The access roads are usually relatively quiet, but **parking** in the summer can be difficult. Once you arrive, park as close to the center as possible and explore the old town on foot. To reach Saintes-Maries from **Arles,** take the D570, covering 37 kilometers (23 miles) in 35 minutes. From **Saint-Rémy-de-Provence,** take the D99 to Beaucaire and then the D15 to Arles followed by the D 570, covering 67 kilometers (42 miles) in 1 hour.

BY BUS

From the stop next to the train station on Avenue Paulin Talabot in **Arles,** take **Le Pilote Line A50** (www.lepilote.com, six per day, €3), with a journey time of about 1 hour to Avenue des Massoucles in the center of Saintes-Maries.

THE CAMARGUE COUNTRYSIDE

A paradise for bird-watchers, horse-riders, hikers, and bikers, the Camargue countryside is a mixture of rice fields, grazing enclosures for bulls and horses, and the occasional field of vines. The white cabins of the Gardian bull herders, which are situated to the north to provide better shelter from the wind and thatched with reeds, dot the horizon. The main sights, with the exception of Domaine de La Palissade, are to be found off the D570 road that runs between Saintes-Maries-de-la-Mer and Arles. The wilder more dramatic countryside and the large nature reserve of La Capelière is accessed by the D36, which runs between Arles and Plage Piemanson.

Sights
MUSÉE DE LA CAMARGUE

Pont de Rousty, Arles; tel. 04 90 97 10 82;
www.arlestourisme.com/en/museum-of-the-
camargue.html; daily 10am-12:30pm and 1pm-5pm

Housed in an old sheep barn, the Camargue Museum depicts daily life in the Camargue from the 19th century to the present day. Focusing on key activities such as agriculture, breeding, hunting, fishing, and annual celebrations and traditions, the museum traces the evolution of the Camargue into its modern form, explaining how the economic activities that developed over the 20th century—hydraulic works, viticulture, rice growing, and sea salt production—secured the future of the region. A visit to the museum also includes a 3.5-kilometer (2.1-mile) walk through the grounds of the Mas de Pont de Rousty, where daily life in the Camargue is illustrated through various information points and observatories.

MAISON DU RIZ

Chemin de Figares, Albaron; tel. 06 31 03 40 11;
www.maisonduriz.com; Mar.-Nov. 9:30am-12:30pm
and 2:30pm-6:30pm; €4, children under 10 free

The average French person consumes just under 6 kilos (13 pounds) of rice per year, as opposed to the whopping Chinese consumption of 37 kilos (82 pounds) a head. As ever, though, with food the French are very proud. The Camargue produces the entire rice production of France. The owners of the Maison du Riz, the Rozière family, have been farming rice in the Camargue for five generations. A visit to this center includes a small marked walk through rice fields, a demonstration of how rice is whitened, and a tasting at the end including some rice beer. Exhibits explain the year-round nature of the work in the rice fields, from planting and harvesting to continual monitoring of the water level and maintenance of the pumping equipment. There is, of course, also a shop where you can buy rice.

Hiking
LA CAPELIÈRE VISITOR CENTER

D36B, Arles; tel. 04 90 97 97;
www.parc-camargue.fr/getlibrarypublicfile.php/2d5
297d875236bd10071d0f8f5471167/parc-camargue/_/
*collection_library_fr/201500014/0001/Birdfair_*
Camargue_English.pdf; Apr.-Sept. 9am-1pm and
2pm-6pm, Oct.-Mar. 9am-1pm and 2pm-5pm,
closed Tues.; €3 visitor center

The main visitor center for the 30,000-hectare (74,131-acre) Camargue nature reserve is

Flamingos gain their distinctive color from their diet of microscopic shrimp and algae.

located on the D36B. It offers access to the 1.5-kilometer (0.9 miles) Sentier de Rainettes (Tree Frog) walking trail. Bird-watching hides for observation of the 276 species present on the reserve are also accessed from the visitor center. Sightings near the visitor center may include bittern, great egret, white stork, night herons, black-winged stilt, reed warblers, and snipe. The other reason to visit is for the plentiful information on the hiking and biking tracks that that crisscross this wetland habitat of worldwide importance. Photographers love the soft, clear light conjured by the Provence sun falling over the nearby Etang de Vaccarès, and a 50-kilometer (31-mile) two-day walking route around the *etang* departs from the visitor center. (See www.arles-tourisme.com/assets/pdf/pdfs_document/N8_vaccares_2Jours.pdf.) Allow just over an hour to visit the center and complete the Tree Frog walk.

DOMAINE DE LA PALISSADE

36 chemin Départemental, Arles;
tel. 04 42 86 21 28; www.palissade.fr; daily
9am-5pm; €3, children under 12 free

Located at the mouth of the Rhône, where the great river merges with the sea, Domaine de La Palissade is an interesting stop on the way to or back from the Plage Piemanson. Unlike most of the rest of the Camargue, the countryside is unprotected by sea dykes. This is the Camargue as nature intended it, and walks wind past inland salt lakes filled with wading birds. The stars, as always, are the flamingos, with their heads craned into the water in what seems like an eternal quest for the tiny shrimps that give them their famed pink color. It's possible to join horse rides through the domaine. Call in advance for departure times. Walkers will be given a map of the domaine upon arrival and can choose between three different circular walks of 1.5 kilometers (0.9 miles), 3 kilometers (2 miles), and 8 kilometers (5 miles), making it possible to enjoy the domaine on foot for anything from half an hour to half a day.

ETANG DU FANGASSIER

Depart rue Tournayre, next to Les Arenes,
Salin-de-Giraud, www.saintesmaries.com/assets/
downloadable/pdf/rando/N9_flamants_sel.pdf

Not for the faint-hearted, this 20-kilometer (12.4-mile) circular walk from Salin-de-Giraud will take 6 hours to complete. Take plenty of provisions and water and follow the trail around the Etang du Fangassier. You can park near the starting point at the tourist office in Salin-de-Giraud. Close encounters with wading birds are guaranteed, and if you are lucky, at some point during the walk pink flamingos will fly directly above your head. The walk begins on the road before turning off onto a dirt track, which continues around the *etang* (lake). For the energetic, there is an optional extension along a bicycle path; from the tourist office, it takes you past the salt-production facilities to Plage Piemanson. Remember to take mosquito repellant and wear a hat because shade in the Camargue is rare.

★ PARC ORNITHOLOGIQUE DU PONT DE GAU

RD 570 Lieu dit Pont de Gau, Arles;
tel. 04 90 97 87 62; www.parcornithologique.com;
daily 9am-7pm; €6, children 4-12 €4

The ornithological park is spread out over 60 hectares (148 acres) and includes more than 7 kilometers (4 miles) of nature trails that offer unrivaled proximity to the Camargue birdlife. A map of suggested walks is provided on arrival. These vary in length, but on average the marked circular trails take 1 hour and 30 minutes to walk. The management of the Parc has subtly altered the water courses and natural environment to facilitate sightings. By bringing nature closer to visitors, the Parc aims to help people appreciate it better and support conservation efforts. The birdlife varies with the time of year. From March to May many species are migrating north. Depending on the water levels in the Camargue, they will stop to rest and feed. Some species end their migration in the reserve with large colonies of herons and egrets nesting in the trees. During the winter resident species include ducks, geese, cranes, birds of prey, and a number of rarer species, such as the tiny penduline tit. Winter is also the best time to watch flamingos; the population shows off colorful new plumage during courtship displays. Guided visits in French are available and can be arranged by filling in an enquiry form on the website.

TOP EXPERIENCE

★ Camargue Safari
SAFARIS CAMARGUES ALPILLES

Pick up point outside Arles Tourist Office, 9 boulevard des Lices, Arles;
tel. 04 90 93 60 31;
www.camargue.com; €40

The Camargue covers 930 square kilometers (359 square miles), one-third of which is marshland or inland water. Unmarked, often private dirt tracks riddled with potholes crisscross the countryside between the tarmac roads. In short, you need to know where you are going to get the best out of a visit. Various companies offer educational safaris that take you in an open-topped Land Rover into the undiscovered Camargue for a couple of hours or a whole day. You'll enjoy wildlife spotting (bulls, horses, and flamingos) as well as an excellent introduction to the culture of the Camargue, from rice growing to bull herding. It is simply the best way to gain insight into the Camargue in a short amount of time. In half a day, you will see more wildlife and learn more about the culture of the Camargue than you would on your own in a week.

BERGERIE D'ALIVON

1451 route de la Trinité, Arles;
tel. 06 03 54 10 94;
from €20 per person for one hour

Join Emmanuel on a horse safari into the Camargue to see his herd of bulls and to get as close as possible to the flamingos. The horses are good-natured, and even beginners can book a ride.

Beaches and Watersports
PLAGE DE PIEMANSON

D36D, Salin-de-Giraud; www.ville-arles.fr/sports/equipements-de-loisirs/plage-equipements-de-loisirs/la-plage-de-piemanson.php

This broad sandy beach is where the Arlesians come to cool down. There's a nudist quarter, a space cordoned off for four-wheel-drive vehicles, and another for kite surfing; but don't be put of if you don't like taking your clothes off, dangling underneath a kite, or engaging in motorsports: There's an idyllic broad expanse for soaking up the sun and looking out to sea. It's also good for an early morning run. The beach is 7 kilometers (4 miles) long.

PLAGE BEAUDUC

Saintes-Maries-de-la-Mer; www.parc-camargue.fr/index.php?pagendx=app_44&actu=actu_42

Plage Beauduc is unquestionably the most deserted beach in the south of France. Sand and sea stretch for kilometers, interupted by only the odd human silhouette on the horizon. It's savage and beautiful, and difficult to reach. The access road (off the D36B, route de Fielouse) is bumpy and has been known to rip the undercarriage from standard rental cars. However, large four-wheel-drive vehicles are too large to make it down the track. Ideally, travel here with a local who knows the road and does not mind the odd scratch on his car.

KAYAK VERT

Base de Sylvereal RD202 or Base du Paty Trinite RD570, Arles; tel. 04 66 73 57 17;
www.kayakvert-camargue.fr; daily May-Oct.
9am-7pm; from €10 for 1-hour descent

Kayak Vert offers a variety of different-length trips. Boarding a canoe is an excellent way to get a different perspective on the Camargue. No particular kayaking experience is required.

KITEXPERIENCE

Place Beauduc, Saintes-Maries-de-la-Mer; tel. 06 32 41 91 86; www.kitexperience.com/nos-ecoles/ecole-de-kitesurf-de-beauduc-camargue; from €140

The Plage Beauduc, with its wide open spaces,

The Sand Wines of the Camargue

The Camargue is the only producing region of France to have a 100 percent native stock of vines. In the 19th century, French vines were ravaged by a disease called phylloxera. Across France, entire vineyards were wiped out and the industry brought to its knees. Salvation came when American and French vines were crossed to produce more resistant plants. This process happened throughout France, except in the Camargue. Here the roots of vines stretched through the narrow layer of sand in which they grew to the water table below, where the insect that carried the disease was unable to survive.

The main wine growing area in the Camargue is across the Petit Rhône estuary in the Languedoc, near the town of Aigues Mortes. Vines stretch for miles in fields of white sand, shimmering in the intense heat so they almost appear like an illusion. Smaller plantations of sand wines in the Provencal Camargue can be found near the La Capelière nature reserve. Look for extremely pale rosés, known as vin gris, or gray wines, made from the grenache gris grape variety; they are almost transparent. Beware, though, they still pack an alcoholic punch.

WHERE TO TASTE

- **Domaine Isle Saint Pierre** (Isle Saint Pierre, Mas-thibert, Arles; tel. 04 90 98 70 30): The vineyard is dramatically situated on an island in the middle of the Rhône. Rows of vines run right up to the banks of the river. After an overindulgent tasting, guests can opt to stay in one of the *gîtes*.

- **Domaine de Beaujeu** (chemin du Sambuc, Arles; tel. 09 64 18 90 33): This organic estate produces rice and cereals as well as wine. It has been in the same family for five generations, and there is immense pride in the domaine's products.

is a magical place to kite surf. There's usually no shortage of wind. The world record speed for windsurfing was set on a nearby stretch of water.

Food
★ LA CHASSAGNETTE
Chemin de Sambuc, Arles;
tel. 04 90 97 26 96; Mon.-Fri. 12:30pm-1:30pm,
Thurs.-Sat. 8:30pm-9:30pm; €69-79

This renowned restaurant draws a clientele from as far as Aix. Put simply, it's on the to do list of all locals. The chef and the gardener visit the vegetable garden first thing in the morning, adapting the menu on the spot to accommodate produce that is at its peak. No one I know has returned home disappointed. Reserving in advance is necessary.

LA TELLINE
Quartier Villeneuve, Arles; tel. 04 90 97 01 75; www. restaurantlatelline.fr; mid-Mar.-Sept. Thurs.-Mon.

noon-1:15pm (no lunch Thurs.) and 7pm-9pm,
Oct.-mid-Mar. Fri.-Sun. noon-1:15pm.; €15-28

It doesn't get any more Camarguaise than this small traditional dining room in an old *manade* (farmhouse). The name Telline means "clams," which are a speciality of the area. For meat lovers, there is also a bull steak. It's imperative to book well in advance.

L'ESTRAMBORD
7 rue l'Abrivado, Le Sambuc;
tel. 04 90 35 25 51;
www.lestrambord.fr;
Sun.-Fri. noon-2:30pm;
menus €18-31

There's been a café restaurant on this site for more than 100 years. The food is a great value, and the servings are large and reliant on local produce. Expect dishes like clams with a garlic mayonnaise and bull cheek stew. In high season, it's sensible to reserve.

LES SALADELLES

4 boulevard des Arènes, Salin-de-Giraud; tel. 04 42 86 83 87; www.hotel-restaurant-lessaladelles.fr/ restaurant; Easter to Nov. noon-2pm and 7pm-9pm, Nov.-Mar. closed Mon.; €15-19

Don't be put off by the plastic tables and chairs; the food is excellent and a good value. The stars of the menu are plates of battered fried fish, and bull steaks with Camargue rice. Pasta and salads are also offered. In high season, it is sensible to reserve.

ACCOMMODATIONS

MAS SAINT GERMAIN

Route Fielouse, Villeneuve, Arles; tel. 06 16 92 34 98; www.massaintgermain.com; €100 d

A wide choice of accomodation is available on this 200-hectare (494-acre) farm in the middle of the Camargue. Self-catering apartments, including an old pigonnier, can be rented by the week. Alternatively, there are rooms by the night. The Mas Saint Germain is especially recommended for families; kids love the farm atmosphere and on-site horse riding. All rooms have ensuite bathrooms.

MAS PETIT PRINCE

Chemin de Baynes, Gageron, Arles; tel. 06 12 16 84 60; www.maspetitprince.com; €125 d

This small bed-and-breakfast has five rooms (including a gypsy caravan in the garden). All have ensuite bathrooms. There's a pool, an expansive garden, and horse stables. Evening meals are available on request. The luxuries of a larger hotel are missing, but the Camarguaise atmosphere compensates.

LE MAS DE PEINT

Manade Jacques Bon, Le Sambuc, route de Salin-de-Giraud - RD36, Arles; tel. 04 90 97 20 62; www.masdepeint.com; €250 d

Le Mas de Peint sets the standard for luxury in the Camargue. The hotel is set in a *manade* (farmhouse). It has its own gastronomic restaurant and pool, and it is located right on the water's edge. The staff specialize in arranging unforgettable trips into the Camargue. All rooms have ensuite bathrooms, air-conditioning, and Wi-Fi.

Getting There and Around
BY CAR

If you're traveling by car, the main roads from **Arles** are the D570 toward Saintes-Maries-de-la-Mer and the D36 toward Plage Piemanson. The larger D35 to Salin-de-Giraud is a quicker road, but it runs along the eastern bank of the Rhône. A small car ferry crosses the river back into the Camargue near the mouth of the Rhône. The roads tend to be quiet, except during high season. If you plan to leave the main roads and head onto the dirt tracks that crisscross the Camargue countryside, it is advisable to drive a four-wheel-drive vehicle.

BY BUS

Buses from Arles can take you to the main nature reserves and points of interest. **Le Pilote Line** A10 runs five times a day between **Arles** and Salin-de-Giraud; it stops at Domaine La Palissade (summer only), La Capelière, and Plage Piemanson. Total journey time will depend on the stop. Fares are around €3.

Le Pilote Line A50 runs five times a day between **Arles** and Saintes-Maries-de-la Mer. It stops at the Digue de La Mer dyke, Parc Orninthologique de Pont de Gau, and Musée de La Camargue. Total journey time will depend on the stop. Fares are around €3. See www.lepilote.com for timetable details.

Les Alpilles Regional Nature Park

The Alpilles Regional Nature Park is filled with fields of olive trees and vines interspersed with jagged rocky outcrops and charming, typically Provençal villages such as Maussane-les-Alpilles and Eygalières. There are plentiful cycling, hiking, and horse-riding routes taking you into the hills where wild herbs sprout from the bases of rocks and pine trees shimmer in the blazing sun. In Saint-Rémy-de-Provence, there are the ruins of the Roman town of Glanum to visit and Van Gogh's artistic legacy from his year-long sojourn in the town to enjoy. Nearby Les Baux-de-Provence, a village perched precariously on a jagged rocky outcrop, is in danger of becoming overrun by tourists, but it's still well worth a visit for its medieval château and one-of-a-kind art projections in the Bauxite quarry. Less well-known, Fontvieille, is a sleepier place but one that still boasts a wealth of sights, such as the 10th-century Montmajour Benedictine Monastery.

ORIENTATION

The Alpilles (literally little Alps) sit just east of **Arles.** The name of the area derives from the limestone massif that runs east to west between the Durance and Rhône rivers. It is 25 kilometers (15.5 miles) long and approximately 8 kilometers (5 miles) wide. To the north of the massif sits bustling, picturesque **Saint-Rémy-de-Provence** on the D99 road between **Cavaillon** and **Beaucaire.** It's a natural base from which to explore the Alpilles. Still on the northern side of the massif is the village of **Eygalières.** Its main street is a picture-postcard image of Provence, and the village is another good base exploring the area. From Saint-Rémy the D5 winds through rocky crags to the southern side of Les Alpilles where the villages of **Maussane-les-Alpilles, Les Baux,** and **Fontvieille** are

located. Les Baux is surrounded by luxury hotels, but the medieval village itself suffers from overtourism, making Maussane and Fontvieille better places to stay.

SAINT-RÉMY-DE-PROVENCE

The town of Saint-Rémy-de-Provence dominates Les Alpilles. Its shops, restaurants, and bourgeoise atmosphere make it feel like a mini Aix-en-Provence. Days can disappear in the embrace of its small squares, bubbling fountains, and narrow cobbled streets lined with art galleries and boutiques. The pedestrianized old town is encircled by a ring road. Thankfully the traffic is slow moving and there are plentiful pedestrian crossings. Shade from centuries-old plane trees shelters café terrace after café terrace, making the ring road the main social and people-watching hub of Saint-Rémy.

Sights
MONASTERE ST PAUL DE MAUSOLE

Chemin Saint Paul; tel. 04 90 92 77 00; www.saintpauldemausole.fr; daily Apr.-Sept. 9:30am-7pm, Oct.-Mar. 10:15am-5:15pm; €4.70

In May 1889 Vincent Van Gogh had himself voluntarily interned in this mental institute. His ambitious plans for an artist's commune in the yellow house in Arles had come to nothing, and after a fight with fellow artist Paul Gauguin he lost his sanity and cut off his ear, wandering deranged through the streets. After this incident the people of Arles drove him from the town.

Van Gogh found refuge in Saint-Rémy, where he came to accept the madness induced by his epileptic fits and resumed painting. The tour includes a visit to the room where Van Gogh slept and painted, which has been restored to an approximation of its condition at the time; a walk through the gardens where

Les Alpilles Regional Nature Park

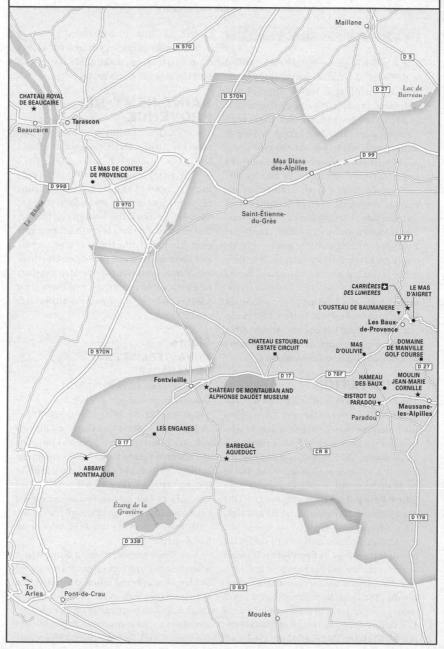

Maillane

N 570

D 5

D 570N

D 27

Lac de Barreau

CHATEAU ROYAL
DE BEAUCAIRE

Tarascon

Beaucaire

D 99

Mas Diane
des-Alpilles

LE MAS DE CONTES
DE PROVENCE

D 99B

D 970

Le Rhône

Saint-Étienne-
du-Grès

D 27

D 570N

CARRIÈRES
DES LUMIÈRES

LE MAS
D'AIGRET

L'OUSTEAU DE BAUMANIERE

Les Baux-
de-Provence

CHATEAU ESTOUBLON
ESTATE CIRCUIT

MAS
D'OULIVIE

DOMAINE
DE MANVILLE
GOLF COURSE

Fontvieille

D 17

D 78F

D 27

HAMEAU
DES BAUX

MOULIN
JEAN-MARIE
CORNILLE

CHÂTEAU DE MONTAUBAN AND
ALPHONSE DAUDET MUSEUM

BISTROT DU
PARADOU

Maussane-
les-Alpilles

Paradou

LES ENGANES

D 17

BARBEGAL
AQUEDUCT

CR 8

ABBAYE
MONTMAJOUR

Étang de la
Gravière

D 178

D 33B

To
Arles

Pont-de-Crau

D 83

Moulès

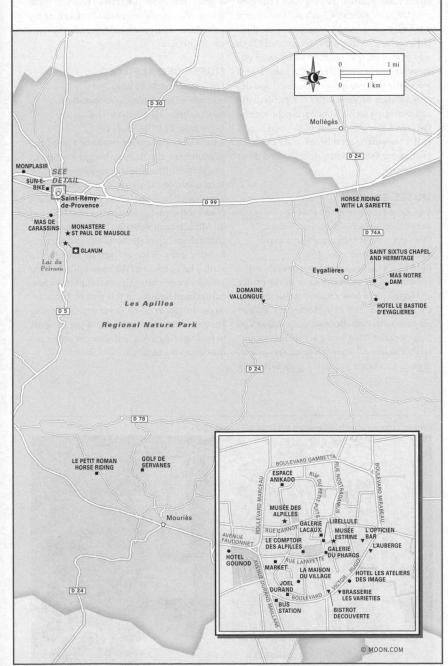

0 ____ 1 mi
0 ____ 1 km

D 30

Mollégès

D 24

MONPLAISIR

SEE DETAIL

SUN-E-BIKE ■

Saint-Rémy-de-Provence

D 99

HORSE RIDING WITH LA SARIETTE ■

MAS DE CARASSINS ■

MONASTERE ★ ST PAUL DE MAUSOLE

★ GLANUM

Lac du Peiroou

D 74A

SAINT SIXTUS CHAPEL AND HERMITAGE ★

Eygalières

● MAS NOTRE DAM

D 5

Les Apilles

Regional Nature Park

DOMAINE VALLONGUE ▼

HOTEL LE BASTIDE D'EYAGLIERES ●

D 24

D 78

LE PETIT ROMAN HORSE RIDING ■

GOLF DE SERVANES ■

Mouriès

D 24

BOULEVARD GAMBETTA

ESPACE ANIKADO ■

BOULEVARD MARCEAU

RUE DU PETIT PUITS

RUE NOSTRADAMUS

BOULEVARD MIRABEAU

MUSÉE DES ALPILLES ★

RUE CARNOT

GALERIE LACAUX ■

LIBELLULE ■

MUSÉE ESTRINE ★

L'OPTICIEN BAR ▼

LE COMPTOIR DES ALPILLES ■

GALERIE DU PHAROS ★

L'AUBERGE ▼

AVENUE FAUCONNET

HOTEL GOUNOD ●

RUE LAFAYETTE

LA MAISON DU VILLAGE ■

HOTEL LES ATELIERS DES IMAGE ●

MARKET ■

AVENUE DURAND MAILLANE

JOEL DURAND ■

VICTOR HUGO

BRASSERIE LES VARIETIES ▼

BOULEVARD

BUS STATION

BISTROT DECOUVERTE

© MOON.COM

large panels illustrate the views that Van Gogh painted; the "Roman Cloisters," considered a masterpiece of 12th-century Provençal architecture; and the baths, where Van Gogh was treated for his condition by repeated immersion in cold water. The audio guide is well worth the extra couple of euros, giving a detailed history of Van Gogh's life, particularly concentrating on his work during the year he spent in Saint-Rémy. Part of the building is still a working mental health institution, so visitors are asked to be respectful and quiet at all times.

MUSÉE ESTRINE

8 rue Lucien Estrine; tel. 04 90 92 34 72; http://Musée-estrine.fr/en; Jun.-Sept. Tues.-Sat. 10am-6pm, reduced hours out of season, closed Dec.-Feb.; €7, children under 12 free

Built in 1749, this elegant town house was the residence of the representatives of the prince of Monaco. It is now a museum that concentrates on 20th- and 21st-century art. Rather poignantly, its collections are dedicated to Van Gogh's desire "that living artists are not unjustly unknown." There's a space set aside to explain Van Gogh's artistic legacy, including a short film about the artist. However, there are no Van Gogh originals. Nonpermanent exhibitions change regularly. Check the website for details.

MUSÉE DES ALPILLES

1 place Favier; tel. 04 90 92 68 24; www.mairie-saintremydeprovence.com; May-Sept. Tues.-Sun. 10am-6pm, Oct.-Apr. Tues.-Sat. 1pm-5:30pm; €4.50, children free

Small provincial museums can be a bit of disappointment; they have no budget for the sort of glitzy multimedia displays employed by their urban counterparts, so they can seem to be stranded in the past. The Alpilles museum is an exception. Located in the Hotel Mistral de Montdragon mansion house, the architectural quality of the building, and particularly the inner courtyard, sets the tone for the visit. The purpose of the museum is to help visitors understand the current landscape, natural and human, in this part of Provence. Accordingly, exhibits cover topics ranging from the historic cultivation of poppy seeds to bull fighting. It's a well-thought-out introduction to the region.

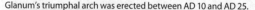

Glanum's triumphal arch was erected between AD 10 and AD 25.

The Mistral

In most of the world, high winds form part of a storm front, bringing heavy rain, thunder, and lightning. The Mistral does the opposite. It sweeps down the Rhône from its source in the Alps and chases away the clouds with gusts that frequently top 100 kilometers (62 miles) per hour. When the Mistral blows, the sky quickly becomes a piercing blue. Even in the summer the temperature plummets as the Alpine air sweeps across the Rhône delta, fanning out on either side of Avignon into the Camargue, Les Alpilles, and the Luberon. The water in swimming pools quickly turns practically glacial, and the terraces of restaurants become no-go zones, as parasols hurl across the street like javelins.

What makes the mistral even more unusual is its capricious nature. A storm will always pass in a day or so and the wind subside but not the mistral. Forecasters can usually predict its arrival; after that people rely on the old wives' tale that says it will last for 1, 3, 5, or 15 days. In the morning there is usually a lull. The morning sky is clear, the air still, and it appears as if the menace has passed. Then the trees stir, shake, and finally bend as the onslaught begins.

Like French workers, the mistral usually insists on a good lunchtime pause before resuming its mischief in the afternoon. Some years the mistral never seems to go away. It blows or threatens to blow on a daily basis, beginning to play on the mind to such an extent that it was once used as a defense in a murder case: temporary mistral-induced insanity. Other years, there's barely a whiff of wind.

★ GLANUM

Route des Baux-de-Provence; tel. 04 90 92 23 79; www.site-glanum.fr; Apr.-Aug. 10am-6:30pm, Sept. Tues.-Sun. 10am-6:30pm, Oct-Mar. Tues.-Sun. 10am-5pm; €8, reduced €6.50; €2.70 parking

If you only have a passing interest in the Romans, you can soak up a bit of culture and see a couple of the most impressive Glanum monuments for free: a triumphal arch and the Julii Mausoleum. The triumphal arch was built around AD 14 as a symbol of Roman power and authority. Study the sculptures carefully and you will see lots of Gauls in chains being lorded over by their imperial masters. The Mausoleum is one of the most impressively preserved burial monuments from the Roman era, dating to around 40 BC. The upper part consists of a circular chapel, the middle section has four arches topped by gorgon's heads, and the square base is carved with legendary scenes of battle.

Those with an appetite for more ruins can cross the road and pay the entrance fee to discover the remains of Glanum. The town was founded on the site of a sacred spring by a Celto-Ligurian tribe between the 2nd and 4th centuries BC. The tribe had regular contact with the Greek settlement at Marseille, and some of the remaining structures show a Greek influence. In 49 BC when Julius Caesar conquered Marseille and the Romanization of Gaul began, Glanum prospered. Located on the Via Domitia Roman road that linked Italy and Spain, the city even minted its own coin. As they enter, visitors can see scale models of the town in its different eras. The main ruins include the sacred well, the Hellenic fountain, the First Forum, the Second Forum, the Baths, and the Market Square.

Entertainment and Events
FÊTE DE LA TRANSHUMANCE

Saint-Rémy; www.saint-remy-de-provence.com/Fete-de-la-transhumance; seventh Sunday after Easter

For those not in the know, it can come as quite a shock to suddenly discover 5,000 or so sheep, along with some donkeys and goats, cantering gaily through the center of Saint-Rémy on Whit Sunday (the seventh Sunday after Easter). The fête commemorates the transhumance, a 10-day hike to the Alps to find fresh green pastures for Provence's sheep. These days the sheep are transported in the back of trucks, but that doesn't stop the fun part: letting animals take over the town for a few hours.

ROUTES DES PEINTRES

Saint-Rémy; www.saint-remy-de-provence.com/route-des-peintres; one Sunday each in June, Sept., and Oct., check website for dates

Both up-and-coming and established artists come from across Provence to display their work on the streets of Saint-Rémy. More than 10,000 people a day attend, and it is advised to arrive early if you want to secure a work of art.

SUMMER FERIA

Saint Rémy; around August 15

This four-day festival in the middle of summer combines music (brass bands in the day and techo at night), bull running, and traditional dress processions. Wine and pastis fortify the young men of the town to try and snatch ribbons from the horns of the bulls as they pass through the streets on the way to the arena.

The Arts
GALERIE DU PHAROS

36 rue Lafayette; 04.90.9257.90; www.lapeinture.com; Wed.-Sun. 10:30am-12:30pm and 2pm-6pm

The gallery offers permanent collections by established local artists. The works range from pop art to landscapes.

GALERIE LACAUX

14 rue Jaume Roux; tel. 04 90 26 91 33; www.galerie-lacaux.com; Tues.-Sun. 10am-1pm and 2:30pm-7pm

Denis Lacaux specializes in surrealist fantasy paintings that are full of vibrant colors. The gallery also contains permanent collections of sculpture and works by other artists.

Hiking
THE ALPILLES RIDGE AND THE ROCK WITH TWO HOLES

Depart Glanum car park; www.hikideas.com/walk-the-alpilles-ridge

This is a pleasant circular walk that takes you through vineyards into the rocky Alpilles.

The hike is 15.46 kilometers (9.6 miles) and takes 5 hours and 40 minutes. Starting from the Glanum parking lot a few kilometers to the north of Saint-Rémy, the dirt path takes you past the mental institution where Van Gogh was interned out into the hills. There are no refreshments along the route, but you can stop at the Rock with Two Holes, which was painted by Van Gogh during his time in Saint Rémy, and admire the view out across the countryside. The return loop takes you back through the vineyard to Glanum. Much of the route is on marked walking trails, but even so there are some steep points where the rocky scree can get slippery after wet weather. Only intermittent shade is provided by pine trees, so take plenty of water and wear a hat.

LAC DU PIEROOU

Access via avenue Antoine de La Salle

For a pleasant stroll and a picnic, this man-made lake is hard to beat. Surrounded by trees and rocks, it's a peaceful place to visit just a few kilometers from Saint-Rémy. The circular lake walk is 2 kilometers (1 mile) and takes 30 minutes.

Cycling

Les Alpilles is an extremely enjoyable place for cycling.

SAINT-RÉMY-EYGALIÈRES-MAUSSANE LOOP

This circular route allows you to take in some of the best scenery of Les Alpilles. Leave Saint-Rémy on the chemin La Croix des Vertus/Ancienne Voie Aurelia toward Eygalières. This is a flat road that meanders through the outskirts of the town, passing the **Domaine Milan** vineyard, a natural winery that is well worth a stop for a tasting. From Eygalières the D24 and then the D78 roads toward Maussane Les Alpilles are still relatively flat, and the countryside is a mix of pine forest, vines, and olive trees. Maussane makes a nice place for lunch before you tackle the windy climb back into the hills on the D5, which descends back to the starting point in Saint-Rémy. The entire route is about 45 kilometers (28 miles) and takes about 2.5 hours. In the summer the roads can be busy, so it is important to be aware of traffic and cycle in a single file.

SUN-E-BIKE
2 rue Camille Pelletan; tel. 04 32 62 08 39;
www.location-velo-provence.com/fr/location-de-velos_69.7.htm; daily 9am- 6pm
Sun-e-bike has a wide choice of bikes and suggests eight different circuits you can follow to explore Les Alpilles.

Shopping
MARKET
Place de La Mairie and Place de La Republique;
every Wednesday
Saint-Rémy hosts one of the biggest and best markets in Provence. You can find the usual mixture of fresh fruit and vegetables, snacks that pair perfectly with a glass of wine, and plenty of gifty products, including jewelery and textiles. There is a smaller mainly food market on Saturday.

LIBELLULE
10 rue Jaume Roux; tel. 04 90 21 19 89;
www.facebook.com/Libellule.SaintRemydeProvence;
Mon.-Sat. 10am-1pm and 3pm-7pm
The shop is full of cushions, throws, and other soft furnishings to help you get that Provençal look at home. Expert interior decorating advice is available if needed.

LE COMPTOIR DES ALPILLES
2 Place Jules Pelissier; tel. 04 90 94 86 76; www.
facebook.com/ComptoiresdesAlpilles; daily 10am-7pm
This homeware shop specializes in colorful cushions, tablecloths, and tablewear. It's hard to leave without a little something to brighten up a room back home.

ESPACE ANIKADO
1 boulevard Marceau; tel. 04 90 94. 53 52;
www.facebook.com/anikado.saintremydeprovence;
daily 10:30am-6:30pm
Located on the site of the old Saint-Rémy forge, the shop features the creations of a collection of local producers and artisans, including jewelery, furniture, shoes, and paintings

JOEL DURAND
3 boulevard Victor Hugo; tel. 04 90 92 38 25;
Mon.-Sat. 9:30am-12:30pm and 2:30pm-5:30pm;
chocolate boxes from €5
There's nothing like a chocolate fountain in the window to lure in shoppers. Joel Durand is one of France's top chocolatiers, and delicious boxes of melt-in-the-mouth chocolate creations are the specialty of this shop.

Food
BISTROT DECOUVERTE
19 boulevard Victor Hugo; tel. 04 90 92 34 49;
http://bistrotdecouverte.fr; daily noon-2:30pm and
7pm-10pm; €27 two courses, €12.90 lunch plat du jour
This ever-popular restaurant on the bustling exterior ring road serves classic French cuisine, including great steaks and a competitively priced plat du jour. The wine list is worth exploring, and the staff are helpful in matching wine with food. It's a small restaurant, and even outside the main tourist season reserving is advisable.

L'AUBERGE
12 boulevard Mirabeau; tel. 04 90 92 15 33;
www.aubergesaintremy.com/en/the-restaurant-fanny-and-jonathan.html; Mon.-Tues. and Fri.-Sat.
noon-1:30pm and 7pm-9:30pm, Sun. noon-1:30pm
and Thurs. 7pm-9:30pm; €42-69
Sample the cooking of Fanny Rey, the 2017 Michelin Female Chef of the Year, in this town institution, recently revamped and modernized. Rey's cuisine is powerful and unashamedly modern, using, for example, algae instead of oil in the cooking of some of her dishes. Reserving ahead is advisable.

BRASSERIE LES VARIETIES
32 boulevard Victor Hugo; tel. 04 90 90 37 16;
http://brasserielesvarietes.com;
daily 7:30am-12:30am; €16-23
A lively large brasserie-style restaurant with an attractive old-fashioned inside and a small

outside terrace. The menu adds a little twist to classic dishes; try, for example, the veal chop cooked in cider with truffle-infused mashed potato. Usually there is no need to reserve.

L'OPTICIEN BAR
9 boulevard Mirabeau; tel. 06 64 91 59 84;
10am-12:30am Mon.-Fri.; €10-20
This old optician's shop has been converted into a stylish bar. During the day there's a simple snack menu with salads and burgers. At night cocktails are the speciality. Order one, sip slowly, and watch the crowds pass by. Reservations during the main tourist season are advisable.

Accommodations
LA MAISON DU VILLAGE
10 rue du Huit Mai 1945; tel. 04 32 60 68 20;
www.lamaisonduvillage.com; €180 d
A village house was converted into this cozy boutique hotel with four suites. Each has a bedroom, sitting room, private bathroom, air-conditioning, and Wi-Fi. There's a peaceful and shady interior courtyard for relaxing. The nearest public parking is 200 meters (656 feet) away.

HOTEL LES ATELIERS DES IMAGE
36 boulevard Victor Hugo; tel. 04 90 92 51 50;
www.hotel-image.fr; €220 d
This large, funky hotel decorated with photo galleries and antique movie cameras is right in the center of Saint-Rémy. The large garden and pool have views out over the Alpilles. There's a good choice of rooms, all ensuite, with Wi-Fi and air-conditiong; the hotel even includes a tree house, and there's private parking.

HOTEL GOUNOD
18 Place de la République; tel. 04 90.92 06 14;
www.hotel-gounod.com; €115 d
The Gounod has a central location with comfortable rooms and a large courtyard set around a swimming pool. The decor is slightly quirky, with black and white predominating and the repeated motif of musical notes. Rooms all have ensuite bathrooms and Wi-Fi. A small spa offers beauty treatments. Public parking is available directly opposite the hotel.

★ MAS DE CARASSINS
1 chemin Gaulois; tel. 04 90 92 15 48;
www.masdescarassins.com; €152 d
Away from the summer crowds but still within walking distance of the center, the Mas des Carassins cultivates a traditional Provençal atmosphere. The old stone house has bedrooms with quilted bedspreads and a mature garden full of trickling fountains. The pool has views over the countryside toward Les Alpilles. All rooms have ensuite bathrooms and Wi-Fi, and the hotel has its own private parking.

MONPLAISIR
Chemin Monplaisir; tel. 04 90 92 22 70,
www.camping-monplaisir.fr
A short walk from the charming town of Saint-Rémy-de-Provence, this campsite has it all: professional service, swimming pool, restaurant and plenty of shady pitches. Simply a great place to stay to see Les Alpilles.

Getting There and Around
Once you have arrived at Saint-Rémy-de-Provence, the center of the town is pedestrianized and best visited **on foot.**

BY CAR
Saint-Rémy-de-Provence is easily accessible by car. Upon arrival you will be channeled onto a ring road that loops around the historic center. Parking is difficult in the peak summer months, and you can expect to have to walk for up to 10 minutes to get to the center of town. Out of the main season it is relatively easy to find a place. To reach Saint-Rémy from **Marseille,** take the A7 and then the D99; the drive takes 1 hour and 10 minutes, covering 89 kilometers (55 miles); from **Aix-en-Provence,** take the A8, A7, and the D99; the drive takes 1 hour and 5 minutes, covering 73 kilometers (45 miles).

From **Avignon,** take the D35 and then the D5; the drive takes 30 minutes, covering 24 kilometers (15 miles). If you're coming from **Arles** take the D570N; the 30-kilometer (19-mile) journey will take 30 minutes. To get to Saint-Rémy-de-Provence from **Saintes-Maries-de-la Mer,** take the D570; the journey is 65 kilometers (40 miles) and takes 1 hour 5 minutes.

BY BUS

The **bus station** (24 boulevard Marceau) is adjacent to the historic center. From **Arles,** Le Pilote **Line 54** (twice a day, €3, 1hr journey) runs to Cavaillon via Tarascon and stops in Saint-Rémy-de-Provence. From **Avignon, Line 57** (five times a day, €2, 45 minutes). The timetables can be found at www.lepilote.com.

EYGALIÈRES

Eygalières is a charming Provençal village with a small high street lined with cafés. About 1 kilometer (0.6 miles) from the center on the D24B, perched on a rocky outcrop is the 12th-century **Saint Sixtus Chapel and Hermitage.** Unfortunately, it is rarely open to visitors. Even so, it's worth parking and walking the short distance to admire the building and its location. Surrounded by cypress trees, the chapel has a simplistic perfection that lured Van Gogh from his asylum to paint.

Hiking
SAINT SIXTUS CHAPEL HIKE
Depart Avenue Léon Blum;
www.hikideas.com/walk-the-saint-sixtus-chapel-and-the-tete-du-/
This is a good circular hike that leads out into the countryside surrounding Eygalières, and offers excellent views of the old town. The route is 10 kilometers (6 miles) and will take 3 hours and 15 minutes. You will pass the 12th-century Saint Sixtus Chapel, which sits on a rocky outcrop 1 kilometer (0.6 miles) outside the village. Route markings vary; it's best to follow the precise route described online.

Horseriding
HORSE RIDING WITH LA SARIETTE
997 route du Mas des Mauniers;
tel. 04 90 95 94 50; www.lasariette.com/promenade-randonee; €40 for two hours
Ride out into the Alpilles countryside with staff from this friendly equestrian center. Routes are proposed for all skill levels. The rides pass local sights of interest such as the Saint Sixtus chapel and offer views of the Luberon, Les Alpilles, and Mont Ventoux.

Wineries
DOMAINE VALLONGUE
Route de Mouriès RD 24; tel. 04 90 95 91 70; www.lavallongue.com; daily 10am-1pm and 2pm-6:30pm
The French use the umbrella term *terroir* to describe the soil, the topography, the climate, and the wine-making philosophy of the vigneron. They insist that in every good bottle of wine you should be able to taste the *terroir.* Amateur tasters usually struggle with this concept, but one sip of the heat-baked reds of Domaine Vallongue brings the rocky perfumed hills of the Alpilles straight to mind. The tasting room/shop is also full of fantastic wine paraphernalia, like high-heeled shoes converted into bottle holders.

Food
LE CAFÉ DE LA PLACE
Place de La Mairie; tel. 04 90 26 93 60; daily 9am-10pm; €10-20
This bustling café is often full of well-heeled locals. Try the *cêpe pâté* (porcini mushrooom pâté) and in the winter book early for sea urchin evenings.

BRASSERIE LE PROGRES
6 boulevard de La Republique; tel. 09 64 13 16 88; daily 9am-10pm; €15-€25
The interior of this village café has a real wow factor. An open kitchen where you can see the chef work, a long zinc bar, and a wall lined with old French movie posters create a lively atmosphere. Signature dishes include slow-cooked lamb shank and cod with a garlic

mayonnaise (aioli). Book ahead in the summer season.

Accommodations
HOTEL LE BASTIDE D'EYAGLIERES
765 chemin de Pestelade; tel. 04 90 95 90 06; www.
hotellabastide.com/bienvenue-gb; €150 d
In this friendly 15-bedroom hotel just outside Eygalières, all rooms are ensuite and have Wi-Fi, and there are several large family rooms. The hotel has a restaurant comitted to using local organic ingredients, a large pool area, and staff happy to organize activities, including wine and olive oil tastings in the area.

MAS NOTRE DAME
995 chemin du Bagna; tel. 06 12 89 75 32; http://
location-chambres-hotes-Eygalieres.fr; €240 d
Book early in high season because there are only five rooms. All of them are immaculately decorated with ensuite bathrooms, modern conveniences including Wi-Fi, and terraces. This is a real chic retreat in Les Alpilles.

Getting There
Eygalières is a small village, and unfortunately it's not accessible via public transportation. Fortunately, **parking** is not usually a problem. To reach Eygalières from **Saint-Rémy,** take the D99 and then the D24, covering 12 kilometers (7.5 miles) in 15 minutes; from **Arles** take the N113 to Saint-Martin-de-Crau, and then the D25, covering 46 kilometers (29 miles) in 45 minutes.

FONTVIEILLE
Fontvieille is less celebrated than nearby towns and villages such as Saint-Rémy-de-Provence, Maussane Les Alpilles, and Les Baux de Provence. Yet, it has undoubted charm and there's an endearing, traditional Provençal feel. It's a perfect place to stop, stretch your legs, relax in a shady square, and

1: the imposing Benedictine monastery of Montmajour 2: an art show at Carrières de Lumières

contemplate vexing problems such as where to have lunch.

Sights
BARBEGAL AQUEDUCT
Route de Aqueduct
Roman Arles would never have survived and prospered were it not for this piece of Roman engineering. Two Roman aqueduct systems meet just outside Fontvieille, one carrying water from springs north of the Alpilles, the other from the south. In addition to supplying drinking water, this aqueduct network powered 16 overshoot watermills, providing Arles with its flour. The technology of these overflow water mills influenced the Cistercians, whose harnessing of water power was in turn an influence on the Industrial Revolution. Visitor information at the site is extremely limited. The ruins of the mill complex are about 250 meters (820 feet) south of the parking lot for the aqueduct, but the remains are not extensive and a true understanding can only really be gleaned by studying the model of the Barbegal water mill system in the Musée Departemental Arles Antique.

CHÂTEAU DE MONTAUBAN AND ALPHONSE DAUDET MUSEUM
20 chemin de Montauban; tel. 04 90 54 67 49;
http://fontvieille-provence.fr/fr/accueil-fontvieille;
July-Aug. Wed.-Sat. 10am-12:30pm and 3pm-6pm,
Tues. 3pm-6pm, Apr.-June and Sept.-Oct. Tues.-Sat.
10am-12:30pm and 3pm-5:30pm; €2.50
Before *A Year in Provence*, there was *Letters from a Windmill*. Peter Mayle may be better known in the Anglophone world for his series of novels humorously exposing the quirks of the Provençal, but Alphonse Daudet was developing the same themes more than a century earlier for a French audience. Like Mayle's, Daudet's most famous book, *Letters from a Windmill* (1869), was first published in excerpt form in newspapers. And again, like Mayle, Daudet gained success by describing rural life to a metropolitan elite audience. Whereas Mayle's Provençal base was Menerbes in the Luberon, Daudet stayed at

Château de Montauban at the invitation of his cousins. The elegant château now contains an exhibition about the author's life, a room dedicated to Provençal costumes, another to Course Camarguaise bull fighting, and a fourth room devoted to *santons* (Provençal nativity figures), as well as an exhibition on the history of Fontvieille. It's an interesting stop-off, particularly for fans of Daudet's work.

ABBAYE MONTMAJOUR

Route de Fontvieille, Arles; tel. 04 90 54 64 17; www. abbaye-montmajour.fr; daily 10am-5pm, summer till 6pm; €6, €5 reduced, free under 18

The first thing you notice about this old Benedictine Monastery is that it is very big. The building imposes itself on the landscape as if demanding attention. Van Gogh duly obliged, visiting more than 50 times and drawing Montmajour from various different angles using a reed pen. Built between the 10th and the 18th centuries, the Abbaye was, until the late Middle Ages, surrounded by marshes and only accessible by boat. There's plenty to see, most notably the rock cemetery (12 graves precisely sculpted into the rock); Chapel of the Holy Cross (built to house a piece of the crucifix cross); and the ruined Maurist Abbey. The last was constructed by a sub order of the Benedictines who started major new building work in the 18th century but never completed the building because of the French revolution. By the beginning of the 19th century, the Abbaye had been split up and sold off to more than 20 different owners. Parts were used as sheep barns and hay lofts. The Abbaye was gradually taken back into state ownership and is now one of the fewer than 100 classed national French monuments.

Hiking
SENTIER DES MOULINS DE DAUDET

Depart from Office de Tourism, avenue des Moulins; www.cheminsdesparcs.fr/pedestre/le-sentier-des-moulins-de-daudet

This walk out into the countryside passes four windmills, including the Moulin de Daudet of *Letters from a Windmill*, the only one of the four to still have its arms intact. The walk, which is 3 kilometers (2 miles) with a 48-meter (157-foot) incline, is largely flat on a dirt track with a few small uphill sections. The trail heads into the garrigue countryside, which is filled with olive trees, wildflowers, and herbs. It regularly passes from shade to sunlight and back again, and at one point runs alongside the irrigation canal for the Les Baux Valley. The best place to stop and take a break is Château de Montauban, listed in the sights section above, which is approximately at the halfway point.

CHÂTEAU ESTOUBLON ESTATE CIRCUIT

Route de Maussane; tel. 04 90 54 64 00; www.estoublon.com; free

Follow the marked walk from the château parking lot through olive groves and vines, returning to the château for a glass of wine or an olive oil tasting.

Horseback Riding
LES ENGANES

345, route de l'aqueduc Romain; tel. 04 90 54 72 10; lesenganes.ffe.com; €50 per day

Open to all levels, the Enganes equestrian center organizes rides out into the countryside. In the summer, there are activity weeks for children.

Food
CAVE LES ALPILLES

Cours Hyacinthe Bellon; tel. 04 90 54 76 81; www.cavelesalpilles.com; €12

This is a great spot to eat if you are a wine lover. The cave is principally a wine shop rather than a restaurant, so no markup is charged on the extensive wine list. A good plat du jour is served, plus cheeses and cold meats. The place is small and largely frequented by locals, but usually there is no need to book.

LE PATIO

119 Route du Nord; tel. 04 90 54 73 17; www.
lepatio-alpilles.com; Tues. noon-3pm, Thurs.-Mon.
noon-3pm and 7:30pm-11pm, closed Wed.; €29-35

Immaculate white tablecloths, a beautiful
courtyard setting, and excellent cooking using
the finest local ingredients combine to create
an unforgetable dining experience. Specials
include a rabbit thigh that is slow cooked and
then vaccuum-stored in local olive oil before
being reheated. Booking is advisable.

LA CUISINE AU PLANET

144 Grand Rue; tel. 04 90 54 63 97;
http://lacuisineauplanet.fr; Jun.-Sept. Sat.-Sun and
Tues.-Thurs. noon-2pm and 7pm-10pm, Mon. and Fri.
7pm-10pm, low season closed Sun. evening till Tues.
evening; menus €25-31

The walls of the welcoming dining room are
made from the local Fontvieille stone. Classic
dishes are given an inventive twist; try, for example, the Thai basil dip that accompanies the
grilled fish, or the peanuts with wasabi sauce.
Reservations in the tourist season are advisable.

Accommodations
VILLA REGALIDO

118 avenue Frédéric Mistral; tel. 04 90 54 60 22;
www.villa-regalido.com; €165 d

In the center of the village, this hotel is a great
base to explore Les Alpilles, Arles, and the
Camargue. Tastefully decorated rooms, all with
ensuite bathrooms and Wi-Fi, a mature garden,
in-house restaurant, and small pool help tick
all the necessary boxes for a comfortable stay.

Getting There
BY CAR

Fontvieille is a sleepy village and **parking** is
usually not a problem. To reach Fontvieille from
Arles, take the D7, covering 10 kilometers (6
miles) in 22 minutes. From **Saint-Rémy-de-
Provence,** take the D99 and the D33, covering
17 kilometers (11 miles) in 20 minutes.

BY BUS

From May 10 to the end of September, **Car
Treize Line 57** (www.lepilote.com) from
Avignon to Saint-Rémy, is extended to **Arles,**
stopping at Fontvieille. It runs five times a
day. Fares are approx. €3 for single journey.
The travel time from Avignon is 1 hour and
20 minutes.

LES BAUX-DE-PROVENCE

Les Baux-de-Provence is perhaps the only
village in Provence to suffer from the curse
of overtourism. From a distance the silhouette of the ancient ramparts, a single flag
fluttering in the wind, is a majestic sight.
Up close the narrow streets of the village are
overrun on a daily basis with coach parties.
In season, parking anywhere near the hilltop sight is increasingly difficult. Shops and
cafés sell touristy products to the hordes.
Yet, if you are willing to put up with masses,
or you can visit out of season, the sights
make the aforementioned inconveniences
seem incidental.

Sights
CHÂTEAU DES BAUX

Grande Rue; tel. 04 90 49 20 02;
www.chateau-baux-provence.com;
daily 9am-6:30pm; €8.5, reduced €6.50

Built in the 11th century by the Lords of Les
Baux and variously demolished and rebuilt
over the following centuries, the fortress is
a wonderfully evocative place to visit. In the
summer months there are daily displays of
medieval arts and crafts, and more excitingly,
for the children at least, siege re-enactments
using full-scale siege engines. The views over
the vines and olive groves of the surrounding
countryside are unsurpassed. A tour visits different parts of the château, including watch-
towers, chapels, pigeon houses, caves, and a
windmill.

★ CARRIÈRES DES LUMIÈRES

Route de Maillane; tel. 04 90 49 20 03;
www.carrieres-lumieres.com; Jan., Mar., Nov.-Dec.:
10am-6pm, Apr.-May, June, Sept.-Oct. 9:30am-7pm
daily, July-Aug. 9:30am-7:30pm, last entry one hour
before closing; adult €12.50, children 7-17 €10.50,
family ticket €40, free under 7

The old bauxite mines, from which Les Baux-de-Provence takes its name, have been converted into a venue for multimedia art displays. Each year, a new show is conceived around famous painters and their works. Paintings are projected to fill all the walls of the old mine and classical music plays in the background, guiding the mood of the experience from melancholy to cheerful.

The extensive caves with their immense walls can be disorienting at first, but soon the environment starts to feel like a cocoon in which to experience art in a different way. The most arresting parts of the show occur when a three-dimensional universe is created by the paintings, which the watching crowd walks through and explores. The ability of the creative directors to manipulate characters and images within the paintings and seemingly move them toward and away from the viewer makes viewers feel like part of the art. Ultimately, the combination of paintings and music, and the unique viewing experience, is very moving, and more than worth the price of admission. A new show debuts every January and runs throughout the year. The experience lasts 30 minutes.

MUSÉE YVES BRAYER

Place François Hérain; tel. 04 90 54 36 99; www.
yvesbrayer.com; Apr.-Sept. 10am-12:30pm and
2pm-6:30pm, Oct.-Mar. Wed.-Mon. 11am-12:30pm and
2pm-5pm, closed Jan.-Feb.; adults €8, under 18 free

Provence is so renowned for its star painters that it's easy to overlook lesser-known artists. Yves Brayer was born in 1907 and worked in the age of Picasso. Unlike Picasso, his name is not associated with any particular artistic school and many will not have heard of him before their visit to this museum. Indeed, visitors are often drawn to the museum by temporary exhibitions by more well-known artists on the third floor; recent shows have included works by Marc Chagall and Paul Signac. However, discovering a new artist is a delightful experience. The range, quality, and detail of Brayer's work surprise many visitors and often make this small museum a highlight of a trip to Les Baux.

SANTON MUSEUM

Place Louis Jou; tel. 04 90 54 34 03;
www.lesbauxdeprovence.com/fr/culture-
patrimoine/2-Musée-des-santons; Mon.-Fri.
9:30am-6pm, Sat.-Sun. 10am-5:30pm; free

One consequence of the French revolution and the establishment of a Republic was a crackdown on religion. Churches were defaced and some even destroyed. Traditional nativity services with life-size donkeys and locals playing the parts of the wise men were abandoned. In their place people celebrated the nativity in their own homes with carved wooden figures: *santons.* The anti-religious zeal soon dissipated, but the Provençal people's love of the *santon* never disappeared. This museum includes extensive collections of *santons* by the most celebrated Provençal craftsmen, as well as collections of nativity figures from around the world.

Golf
DOMAINE DE MANVILLE GOLF COURSE

Les Baux-de-Provence; tel. 04 90 54 40 20; www.
domainedemanville.fr/en/golf/course; €76 green fee

Centered around a luxury hotel and recently extended from 9 to 18 holes, this challenging course has scenic views of Les Baux.

Food
UNE TABLE AU SOLEIL

Rue du Trencat, cours des porcelet;
tel. 06 38 68 24 92; €15-20

Eating well in the historic center of Les Baux is difficult. So many tourists pass through that quality is not as high as elsewhere. Une Table au Soleil is the exception. There's a shady courtyard, welcoming staff, and good food ranging from lobster to simple pasta dishes. Reserving in advance is advisable.

L'OUSTEAU DE BAUMANIERE

D27 Les Baux-de-Provence; tel. 04 90 54 33 07; www.baumaniere.com/gastronomie/loustau-de-baumaniere/la-carte; €70-175

This is one of the best, if not the best restaurant in Provence. In a stunning setting underneath the rocks of Les Baux, the garden vibrates with cicadas and exudes the scent of wild herbs and flower blossoms. The food is delicate and complex, but the prices are high. Reserving in advance is necessary.

Accommodations
MAS D'OULIVIE

Route d'Arcole; tel. 04 90 54 35 78; www.masdeloulivie.com; €200 d

Located on the olive tree-filled planc beneath Les Baux, this hotel has a fragrant garden and a picturesque pool. The rooms are comfortably furnished with ensuite bathrooms and Wi-Fi, and there is a good choice of size. The restaurant is only open at lunchtime.

LE MAS D'AIGRET

D27A, Les Baux de Provence; tel. 04 90 54 20 20; www.masdaigret.com; €250 d

A friendly family hotel in the shadow of Château des Baux, Le Mas d'Aigret has good views over the fields of olives and vines below. Comfortable rooms with ensuite bathrooms and Wi-Fi, a good restaurant, and the opportunity to visit Les Baux before and after the crowds make this a popular choice.

Getting There and Around
BY CAR

The road network around Les Baux is good, even in high season. However, when you arrive, **parking** is extremely limited. Arrive early or visit in winter to avoid a 15-minute uphill walk to reach the town from your parking spot. To reach Les Baux from **Saint-Rémy-de-Provence** take the D5 and D27, covering 10 kilometers (6 miles) in 20 minutes.

BY BUS

From May 10 to the end of September, **Car Treize Line 57** from **Avignon** to **Saint-Rémy** is extended to **Arles,** stopping at Les Baux. It runs five times a day and the fare is about €3 for a single journey. Journey time from Avignon is 1 hour. The timetable can be found at www.lepilote.com.

MAUSSANE-LES-ALPILLES AND LE PARADOU

Maussane-les-Alpilles and Le Paradou are two separate villages, located no more than 1 kilometer (0.6 miles) apart. Maussane-les-Alpilles is prosperous and picturesque. On a daily basis it draws in well-heeled people from the villa-rich surrounding countryside for a morning coffee and a spot of food shopping. Le Paradou is smaller and is famed for the restaurant the Bistrot du Paradou, which has attracted its share of celebrities over the years. There's not a lot to see in either village, but both ooze Provençal charm.

Sights
PLACE DE L'EGLISE

D17, Maussane-les-Alpilles

Maussane-les-Alpilles's Place de l'Eglise central square is the social center of the village. It's filled with café terraces shaded by plane trees. Construction of the **Sainte-Croix church,** which overlooks the square, began in 1750. The relaxed atmosphere of the place is enhanced by the Four Seasons fountain. Built in 1860, it is unusually large for a village of Maussane's size and it bubbles away, providing the soundtrack for long Provençal lunches.

MOULIN JEAN-MARIE CORNILLE

Rue Charloun Rieu, Maussane-les-Alpilles; tel. 04 90 54 32 37; www.moulin-cornille.com; Mon.-Sat. 9:30am-12:30pm and 2:30pm-6:30pm; free

Every Tuesday and Thursday from mid-June to the end of September there are free tours of this olive oil mill. The process of harvesting the olives and then extracting the oil is explained, and there are various different oils to taste, ranging from green, thin, slightly tart offerings to my preferred style: peppery, smooth, and viscously golden.

Golf
GOLF DE SERVANES
Domaine de Servanes, Mouries; tel. 04 90 47 59 95; http://golfservanes.com; €80

This mature golf course winds through the pretty scenery of Les Alpilles. Don't get too distracted by the surroundings. There are plenty of water hazards.

Horseriding
LE PETIT ROMAN HORSE RIDING
Route du Ferigoulas, D5, Maussane-les-Alpilles; tel. 06 98 16 02 01; from €25

The stable offers horseback rides into the Alpilles countryside, including longer rides that become gourmet escapades with tastings at local producers.

BEE'S ELECTRIC BIKES
Avenue des Alpilles, Maussane-les-Alpilles; tel. 06 19 83 09 59; www.stationsbees.com; May-Sept. 9:30am-12:30pm and 2pm-5pm; from €25 half day

The countryside around Maussane is perfect for cycling. Bee's offers two different routes to hop between the local villages.

Entertainment and Events
VILLAGE FESTIVAL
Maussane-les-Alpilles, Aug. 14-15

This two-day festival includes music, dancing, a communal meal in the street, boule competitions, fireworks, and of course a bull run.

Shopping
MARKET
Place Henri Giraud, Maussane-les-Alpilles; every Thurs.

A typical Provençal market takes place every Thursday in Maussane. There's a good mixture of food, clothes, textiles, and gifts available.

Food
BISTROT DU PARADOU
57 avenue de la Vallée des Baux, Le Paradou; tel. 04 90 54 32 70; Tues.-Sat. noon- 2pm and 8pm-10pm; €49 including wine

This bistro is one of the most renowned restaurants in Provence. People come for the atmosphere as much as the food. Photos of celebrity clients hang from the walls, and the place feels a bit like a club where everybody knows each other. The menu changes daily and there's little choice; you just eat what the chef proposes. Thankfully, it's excellent. Reservations are always advisable.

MAISON DROUOT
18 impasse Michel Durand, Maussane-les-Alpilles; tel. 06 61 07 38 54; http://maisondrouot.com; Tues.-Sat. 7:30pm-10:30pm; €55 menu

Chef Julien Drouot is on the rise. In the past decade he's taken his imaginative cooking full of textures and flavors from Pernes Les Fontaine to Saint-Rémy, and now to Maussane-les-Alpilles. His latest incarnation in a village house includes outdoor dining around a pool in the summer and a cozy modern dining room for the winter. Reservations are always advisable. Lamb from Les Alpilles is usually on the menu. The rooms above the restaurant are available to rent.

CAFÉ DE LA FONTAINE
70 avenue Vallee des Baux, Maussane-les-Alpilles; tel. 04 90 54 30 15; daily noon-3pm and 7pm-10:30pm; €15-27

The heartbeat of the village, Café de La Fontaine, has tables out on the square, next to the Four Seasons Fountain. Inside there's a funky very French dining room and a bar backed by a large picture of a topless woman waving the tricolor. The café takes great pride in its food and has its own meat-aging fridge and chicken rotisserie. In summer it is advisable to reserve.

How to Taste Olive Oil

Les Alpilles is filled with olive groves and produces some of the finest olive oil in the world. It's possible to pop in and taste at many of the local mills. The flavor of an oil is determined by a number of factors, including the varietal of olive, ripeness at harvest, climate, soil type, crop maintenance, and the milling process. Oil made with unripe (green) olives contains peppery flavors, usually described as grassy. Riper olives display softer flavors that are usually described as buttery.

To taste an olive oil, first pour a small amount into a wine glass, then swirl the oil to free the aroma. Inhale deeply from the top of the glass to get an idea of the fruitiness or other characteristics of the oil. At this point, the process is still rather like tasting wine, but here's the difference: With wine you sip then gargle/swill, but with oil you slurp. Pretend you are a naughty child and make as much noise as possible. Slurping mixes the oil with air and spreads it throughout your mouth. And unlike with wine, you get to swallow. Note the burning sensation in your throat.

Once you can taste, there's a whole new vocabulary to master. The IOC (that's the International Olive Council, not the International Olympic Committee) suggests a host of descriptive terms:

- Apple/Green Apple: indicative of certain olive varietals

- Almond: nutty (fresh, not oxidized)

- Artichoke: green flavor

- Astringent: puckering sensation in the mouth created by tannins, often associated with bitter, robust oils

    And that's just the "A"s!

WHERE TO TASTE

- **Château Estoublon Estate Circuit** (Route de Maussane; tel. 04 90 54 64 00; www.estoublon.com): Enjoy a walk on the grounds of this château, then stop in for a tasting of their various olive oils.

- **Moulin Jean-Marie Cornille** (Rue Charloun Rieu, Maussane-les-Alpilles; tel. 04 90 54 32 37; www.moulin-cornille.com; Tues. and Thurs. mid-June-Sept.): This olive oil mill gives free tours and tastings Tuesdays and Thursdays in the summer. Tours cover the process of harvesting the olives and then extracting the oil. There are various different oils to taste, ranging from green, thin, slightly tart offerings to peppery, smooth, and viscously golden.

Accommodations
CASTILLON DES BAUX
10 bis Avenue de la Vallée des Baux, Maussane-les-Alpilles; tel. 04 90 54 31 93;
www.castillondesbaux.com; €115 d
Perched on a small hill on the outskirts of Maussane, this hotel is a good budget choice. It offers spacious rooms with ensuite bathrooms and Wi-Fi, decorated in Provençal style. There's a good-size pool and easy access to the restaurants of Maussane and the surrounding sights.

HAMEAU DES BAUX
285 chemin de Bourgeac, Le Paradou;
tel. 04 90 54 10 30;
www.hameaudesbaux.com; €320 d
A couple of kilometers outside of Maussane, amid olive trees, rocks, and pines, this luxury hideout offers 21 welcoming rooms and suites. All have Wi-Fi and ensuite bathrooms, and many have terraces that lead onto the gardens. There's a pool and a gastronomic restaurant, and a cute food truck serves snacks in the summer months.

Getting There and Around
BY CAR
Parking in Maussane is usually not a problem. If you can't find a spot in the center of the village, try the large parking lot a couple of minutes' walk away on avenue des Alpilles. To reach Maussane and Le Paradou from **Arles,** take the D83 and the D27, covering 24 kilometers (15 miles) in 28 minutes. From **Saint-Rémy,** take the D5, covering 10 kilometers in 15 minutes.

Around Les Alpilles: Beaucaire and Tarascon

Until Provence became part of the kingdom of France in the late 15th century, Tarascon was ruled by the Counts of Provence, and Beaucaire by the French crown. This made them rival cities, with opposing fortresses on either side of the Rhône. These days relations are more cordial and the two towns, which are linked by a bridge, pretty much merge into each other. In Beaucaire, there's a picturesque canal lined with restaurants.

SIGHTS
Château de Roi René
5 boulevard du Roi René, Tarascon;
tel. 04 90 91 01 03; http://chateau.tarascon.fr; Apr.
10am-5pm, May-Sept. 10am-6:30pm, Oct.-Mar.
Tues.-Sun. 10am-5pm; €7.50, reduced under 25
€6.50, under 18 €3.50, under 10 free

Built by the Princes of Anjou during the 15th century, this château is France's best-preserved medieval castle. Modeled on the Bastille in Paris, it was a formidable defensive presence right on the border of Provence. In 1447, King René of Provence began renovation work, creating luxurious residential apartments. Thanks to Tarascon's position off the main tourist track, the castle is a quiet place where you can escape and enjoy a little history. The rooms are largely unfurnished, but the high vaulted ceilings and occasional gargoyle evoke the past. Parts of the château were once used as a prison, and the carvings of inmates can still be read on the walls. In other rooms are exhibitions of contemporary art and collections of 18th-century medicinal pots from the infirmary. The highlight of the visit is climbing on the roof and looking back toward Arles and Les Alpilles. The château comes alive during the four-day Fêtes de la Tarasque toward the end of June, when medieval re-enactments are staged.

Sainte-Marthe Royal Collegiate Church
Place de la Concorde, Tarascon;
tel. 04 90 91 09 50; daily 8am-6pm; free

Legend has it that for centuries the people of Tarascon lived in fear of a horrible creature that lurked in the murky depths of the Rhône. The creature was called the Tarasque and resembled a giant serpent with a lion's head. It had a penchant for eating the townspeople alive. Once a dozen men set out to kill it. Only six returned. Enter Martha, a missionary from the Holy Land bent on bringing Christianity to France. With nothing but a cross and a dash of holy water, she banished the creature to the depths of the Rhône, never to return.

Built in the 12th century, the Sainte-Martha church houses her tomb, including a crypt containing the 3rd-century sarcophagus believed to contain her relics. The church itself is a pleasing piece of Provençal Romanesque architecture, but it's the legend of Martha and her fearlessness in the face of the monster that makes the visit.

Musée Souleiado
39 rue Charles-Deméry, Tarascon; tel. 04 90 91
08 80; Apr.-Sept. Mon.-Sat. 10am-7pm, Oct.- Mar.

Mon.-Sat. 10am-6:30pm; €7, reduced €5

The Provençal love affair with patterned fabrics began in the 16th century with the importation of brightly colored cotton from the Indies through the port of Marseille. Capitalizing on this rich history of "Indiennes" fabrics in the region, the Souleiado fashion house was created in 1939. Picasso quickly became a fan, sporting their vivid and wildly patterned shirts. By the turn of the millennium the brand was in crisis, but it was revived in 2009 and is once again going strong. The museum in the brand's hometown of Tarascon displays collections of clothing, as well as pottery and the works of painter Léo Lelée.

Château Royal de Beaucaire

Place Raimond VII, Beaucaire; tel. 04 66 59 26 57; Wed.-Sun. 9:30am-6pm

A small steep climb from Beaucaire takes you up to the ruins of its château. Built in the 11th century, the château was famously besieged in 1216 by Simon de Montfort as part of his war against the Cathars. More than 300 years later, wary of the strength of the fort, Cardinal Richelieu had a wall of the castle demolished, the remains of which are still visible. The gardens of the château are open to the public, and there is a small archaeology museum, but it is not possible to explore the ruins extensively.

FOOD
Le Soleil

30 Quai du Général de Gaulle, Beaucaire; tel. 04 66 59 28 52; daily noon-2pm and 6pm-11pm; €14 lunch menu

This is probably the best place to dine along the canal. There's an outside terrace with a view over the water, but you need to arrive early to secure a table. The menu has plenty of choices, from salads to meat dishes. The food is good but not sensational, and the customers are mainly passing tourists.

Bistrot La Caseta

45 rue des Halles, Tarascon; tel. 04 90 91 07 81; Mon.-Wed. noon-3pm, Thurs.-Sat. noon-3pm and 7pm-11pm; €13-20

This popular, bustling restaurant in the center of town offers a wide menu, with plenty of daily specials, such as duck breast in honey and a fresh fish of the day. A reservation is not usually necessary. The clientele is a nice mix of tourists and locals.

ACCOMMODATIONS
Le Mas de Contes de Provence

651 chemin du Mas de Provence, Tarascon; tel. 04 40 91 00 13; www.mas-provence.com; €190 d

Set in a 15th-century farmhouse less than 1 kilometer (0.6 miles) from Tarascon, this small hotel has a large garden with a pleasant swimming pool. The rooms are decorated with local antiques and there's a good restaurant on site. Rooms have ensuite bathrooms and Wi-Fi. There is on-site parking.

Hotel de Provence

7 boulevard Victor Hugo, Tarascon; tel. 04 90 91 06 43; www.hotel-provence-tarascon.com; €160 d

This 18th-century hôtel particulier built by the Marquis de Vlagny has been converted into a comfortable hotel. It offers spacious atmospheric rooms right in the center of Tarascon. All rooms have ensuite bathrooms, air-conditioning, and Wi-Fi. Parking is free.

GETTING THERE
BY CAR

Beaucaire and Tarascon are easily accessible by car. From **Arles**, take the D15 to Tarascon; the journey takes 30 minutes and covers 20 kilometers (12 miles). From **Saint-Rémy** take the D99 covering 15 kilometers (9 miles) in 25 minutes. The two towns are joined by the D999 bridge over the Rhône.

BY BUS

Le Pilote **Line 18** runs from the **Arles** train station to Tarascon; the 40-minute ride costs about €4, and buses depart four times a day. Timetable details can be found at www.lepilote.com.

The Luberon and the Lavender Fields of Haute Provence

The Luberon, with its soft-folded mountains filled with pungent pine trees and sweet-smelling wild herbs, can seem too good to true. It's almost like someone planned it as a theme park for tourists. Nearly every village has a castle, and sweeping views are commonplace. The palette of colors—red ochers, blazing purple lavender, and brittle green olive—packs an unrivaled visual punch. Hiding amid this riot for the senses are some of the best boutique hotels in the world. Nearly all the food and wine is local. Forget carbon footprints: Restaurants have their own vegetable gardens, and if they don't, they put the name of the vegetable grower on the menu. To the east, the Luberon blends into Haute Provence where, in the summer, hill villages appear to float dreamlike on seas of lavender.

Highlights

Look for ★ to find recommended sights, activities, dining, and lodging.

★ **Gordes Viewpoint:** Have your camera at the ready to capture the ultimate gravity-defying hill village of the Luberon (page 139).

★ **Village des Bories:** If only the three little pigs had learned to build bories. The mistral wind has huffed and puffed for centuries, but still these ingenious stone structures stand (page 139).

★ **Abbey Notre-Dame de Sénanque:** The Cistercians chose this remote and beautiful spot to found an Abbey in 1148. Today it still has a community of monks and is best known for the picture-postcard view when lavender is in bloom (page 139).

★ **Hot-air ballooning:** Rise at dawn and soar like one of the native Bonelli eagles over the Luberon Regional Nature Park (page 150).

★ **Ocher:** Walking amid the vibrant ocher orange cliffs of the Petit Colorado, or the Sentier des Ocres, or even underground in the caves of the Mines de Bruoux it's easy to think you have been transported to another planet (page 151).

★ **Pont Julien:** Paddle or swim in the Calavon river underneath the arches of the Roman Pont Julien bridge (page 160).

★ **Foret de Cedres:** This is a hiker's paradise in the heart of the Luberon Regional Nature Park, and it's a popular place to picnic and escape from the summer heat (page 161).

★ **Lourmarin market:** Stalls selling artisanal products and Provençal food specialties stretch through the streets in a theatrical show of color (page 169).

★ **Lavender fields of Haute Provence:** Picturesque Provençal villages and the fields of surrounding lavender compete for attention. It's best to visit during mid-July to catch the lavender in full bloom (page 179).

Perfection or near perfection like this can ultimately be off-putting, dull even. However, this region is anything but dull; its history is brutal. The castles were built for war, not tourists. The mountains might be picturesque, but they are also great for hiding. Refugees from the Protestant Vaudois during the 16th century to the Resistance during World War II took cover out in the wilds where it's harsh and remote: the perfect place to get lost. It should be no surprise that the Luberon is home to some of Europe's last remaining vultures.

To understand a place, always look to its literature. The unforgiving environment of the Luberon, with its cold winters and hot summers, has inspired multiple novels dominated by the theme of man returning to nature in search of a more basic way of life. Writer Jean Giono even tried it for real, creating a utopian community in the wilds of Haute Provence during the years between World Wars. It is this duality between the beauty of nature and its savagery that continues to make the region so appealing.

Outside the tourist season, life is still agrarian, and most of the available work is in the fields. People feel close to the land. Under a clear blue winter sky, they whisper with reverence that they are lucky enough to live in a corner of paradise. Tourists who visit for a week or so might not notice this subtle sense of profound connection between man and nature, but there is a subconscious pull that persuades many ultimately to buy homes in the region, like philosopher and writer Albert Camus for whom the Luberon was "an enormous block of silence that I listen to endlessly."

PLANNING YOUR TIME

The **Luberon Regional Nature Park** is located some 40 kilometers (25 miles) to the east of Avignon, and 40 kilometers (25 miles) north of Aix-en-Provence, right in the center of Provence. The park is divided into five different areas: the Monts de Vaucluse, the Petit Luberon, the Grand Luberon, the Southern Luberon, and the Luberon Orientale. In addition, this chapter covers the lavender fields of Haute Provence, which begin in the Luberon Orientale and wrap around to the north into a region known as the Montagne de Lure. Despite these different areas, the Luberon is easy to explore, and the most well-known villages are all within a 30-minute drive of one another. This chapter explores the Luberon from north to south, starting in the **Monts de Vaucluse,** the area that is home to iconic villages such as swanky **Gordes** and ocher-tinged **Roussillon.** Next, the areas that form the heart of the massif are grouped under the heading **Petit and Grand Luberon.** Here you will find famous hill villages such as **Bonnieux** and **Menerbes,** as well memorable hikes and rides that take you out into the depths of the nature park. Then, emerging from the mountains to the vine-filled lowlands of the **Southern Luberon,** you'll discover a string of charming villages epitomized by the unmissable **Lourmarin.** Finally the chapter swings to the east and covers the **Luberon Orientale** and the famous **lavender fields of Haute Provence.**

A car is almost essential to explore the Luberon. Public transport is very irregular. A determined and committed sightseer (with a car) can get a feel for the Luberon Regional Nature Park in just one day. The villages are rarely more than 10 kilometers (6 miles) apart, and so to hop from one to another is relatively easy. An additional day would be needed for a whistle-stop tour of Haute Provence and the Montagne de Lure. For those planning a more relaxed trip, the ideal way to visit would be to pick a base in either the Petit or Grand Luberon, or the Monts de Vaucluse, for two or three nights. The days would easily slip by as you visit many of the villages and associated sights listed below. Alternatively, as in the three-day itinerary below, you could swap

Previous: lavender in full bloom in the Luberon; washing blows in the wind outside Lourmarin; colorful village houses in Roussillon.

hotels every night. To see the lavender fields (in bloom between July and early August), a further night in the Luberon Orientale or Montagne de Lure area would be advisable.

Itinerary Ideas

TOUR OF THE LUBERON VILLAGES

Day 1

1 Start at the **Mas de La Senancole** hotel at the foot of **Gordes.** Have breakfast in the verdant garden before taking the D2 toward Gordes. One kilometer (0.6 miles) before the village, stop on the D15 to admire how the village has been hewn from the cliff face. It's reminiscent of Gondor in the *Lord of the Rings* films.

2 Tour the warren of caves underneath the **Saint-Firmin Palace** in Gordes.

3 Continue on past Gordes on the D2 toward **Roussillon** and enjoy lunch in **Restaurant David** overlooking the famous ocher-colored cliffs.

4 After lunch drop into the **Conservatoire des Ocres,** to discover all about the history of ocher mining in the area.

5 Take the D105 back toward Bonnieux, perhaps stopping on the D900 to enjoy the view of the **Pont Julien** Roman bridge. A paddle in the water is an excellent way to cool down at the end of the day.

6 Enjoy the sun setting from a room with a view in the **Le Clos du Buis** in Bonnieux.

Day 2

1 Enjoy breakfast with a view of the Monts de Vaucluse and Mont Ventoux at **Le Clos du Buis,** and then leave Bonnieux on the D3 toward **Lacoste.** This beautiful road splits the vine-filled Luberon countryside.

2 Climb through the narrow cobbled streets of Lacoste toward **Château Lacoste,** formerly owned by the Marquis de Sade.

3 Continue on the D109 toward Menerbes stopping for lunch with a view at **Bistrot le 5** restaurant.

4 Afterward, enjoy a wine tasting and tour of the corkscrew museum at **Domaine de La Citadelle.**

5 Take the D218 north toward Goult. Stop at **Café de La Poste** for a coffee.

6 Caffeinated, climb to the top of the village and take in the unsurpassed panoramic view of the Petit Luberon from the **Jerusalem windmill.**

7 Pass Bonnieux on the D36, stopping to snap photos of the **lavender fields** in June and July, before continuing to the the D943 to **Lourmarin,** staying overnight in the atmospheric **Moulin de Lourmarin.**

Itinerary Ideas

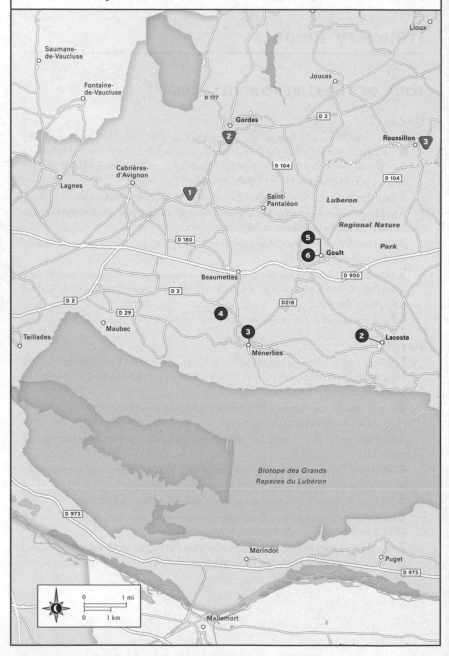

Lioux

Saumane-
de-Vaucluse

Fontaine-
de-Vaucluse

Joucas

D 177

D 2

Gordes

2

Roussillon **3**

D 104

D 104

Cabrières-
d'Avignon

Lagnes

1

Saint-
Pantaléon

Luberon

Regional Nature

D 180

5

Park

6 Goult

Beaumettes

D 900

D 3

D 218

D 2

4

D 29

Maubec

3

2 Lacoste

Taillades

Ménerbes

Biotope des Grands
Rapaces du Lubéron

D 973

Mérindol

Puget

D 973

0   1 mi

0   1 km

Mallemort

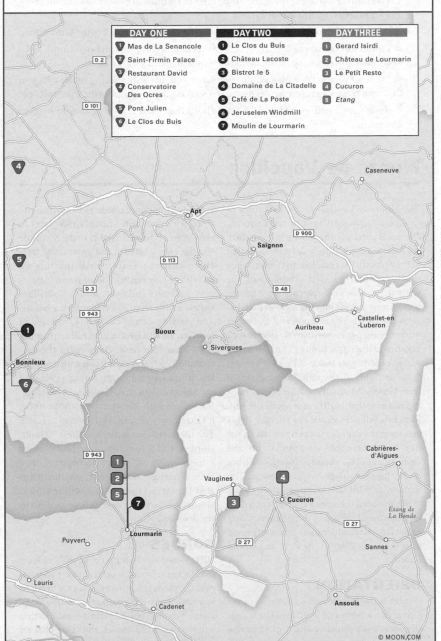

DAY ONE
1. Mas de La Senancole
2. Saint-Firmin Palace
3. Restaurant David
4. Conservatoire Des Ocres
5. Pont Julien
6. Le Clos du Buis

DAY TWO
1. Le Clos du Buis
2. Château Lacoste
3. Bistrot le 5
4. Domaine de La Citadelle
5. Café de La Poste
6. Jeruselem Windmill
7. Moulin de Lourmarin

DAY THREE
1. Gerard Isirdi
2. Château de Lourmarin
3. Le Petit Resto
4. Cucuron
5. *Etang*

Caseneuve

Apt

Saignon

D 900

D 113

D 48

D 3

D 943

Buoux

Sivergues

Auribeau

Castellet-en-Luberon

Bonnieux

D 943

Vaugines

Cucuron

Cabrières-d'Aigues

Puyvert

Lourmarin

D 27

Etang de La Bonde

D 27

Sannes

Lauris

Cadenet

Ansouis

D 2

D 101

© MOON.COM

Day 3

1 Have breakfast in one of the many sunny cafés in Lourmarin before browsing the shops and art galleries, such as **Gerard Isirdi.**

2 Take a tour of the **Château de Lourmarin,** parts of which date back to the 12th century.

3 Village hop, taking the D56 a couple of kilometers to **Vaugines** and enjoy lunch in **Le Petit Resto,** overlooking the fountain (book well ahead to secure a table).

4 Work off your lunch with a gentle, circular, 40-minute walk starting in the village of **Cucuron** (a few kilometers farther on the D56), taking in the view from the **L'Hermitage.**

5 Return for a well-earned drink by the *etang* (lake) and returning to your hotel in Lourmarin.

Monts de Vaucluse

The Monts de Vaucluse encompass some of the most famous villages in the Luberon. Gordes is certainly the most photographed. It's located on a naturally defensive site that has successfully repelled invaders since Roman times. In the hot summer sun, the walls of the precariously perched stone houses almost seem to melt into the rock, so that distinguishing where one ends and the other begins is almost impossible. Nearby there's another photo opportunity: The Cistercian Abbey of Sénanque is one of Provence's most familiar sights. A few miles along the road from Gordes is Roussillon, where ocher mining has revealed 17 different shades of soil, from pale yellow to violet. The village quickly gets overcrowded, so visit early or late in the day. Amid these show-stopping sights, the small village of Goult is often overlooked, but it's my favorite village to spend time in. The narrow, cobbled streets remain sleepy most of the year, and there are a couple of excellent restaurants. At the top of the village adjacent to the Jerusalem windmill is an unsurpassed view over the valley to the Petit and Grand Luberon.

ORIENTATION

Gordes is the largest and most well-known village in the Monts de Vaucluse. The village sits on a rocky pinnacle and it can become very crowded in the summer months. The surrounding countryside is beautiful and filled with **charming hotels** and places to stay. Most of the main sights in the Monts de Vaucluse are located in and around **Gordes.** However, distances are so small that they are all within easy reach of other possible bases such as **Goult** and **Roussillon.** Roussillon suffers a little from its extraordinary beauty. The glowing **ocher cliffs** lure busloads of tourists, and it's best to visit rather than use the village as a base. Once again the surrounding countryside is filled with good hotels. If you are planning to stay in a village in the Monts de Vaucluse, Goult is the best pick. It's replete with **Provençal atmosphere,** it's rarely too crowded, and it's easy to reach. The three villages mentioned here—Goult, Gordes, and Roussillon—are less than 10 kilometers (6 miles) apart. Together they form a triangle with Goult, which is situated the farthest south, just off the **D900.** Gordes to the northwest and Roussillon to the northeast.

GORDES

Nicknamed the lighthouse of the Luberon thanks to the way the central tower watches over the plane below, Gordes is easy to fall in love with. From its Renaissance chateau to the steep, narrow, cobbled streets (*calades*) that wind between the houses, the village has an unparalleled seductive allure.

Sights
★ GORDES VIEWPOINT

D15; www.gordes-village.com; always accessible; free

As you approach Gordes on the route de Cavaillon (D15), look out for a small slip road (chemin de Bel Air) about 1 kilometer (0.6 miles) before the town. This is the best place to stop if you want to take photos of the village. Walk around 15 meters (49 feet) up the road and you'll come to a large rock, upon which inevitably a few tourists will be standing with selfie sticks. The reason for all the fuss is the iconic view of one of Provence's most famous villages. The houses seem to defy gravity by clinging to the precipitous cliffside, and it's easy to understand why the village was so successful in repelling invaders over the centuries. There's a touch of fantasy to Gordes, as if the village was imagined for the storyboard of a science-fiction film. All that's missing is an army of orcs laying siege to the place and the image would be complete.

CHÂTEAU DE GORDES

Place du Château; tel. 04 90. 72 02 68;
www.gordes-village.com/patrimoine,musee,le-
Château,102.html; Mon.-Tues. and Thurs.-Fri.
9am-noon and 2pm-5pm, closed Wed.; about €7,
depends on exhibition

Dating back to 1031, the Château of Gordes dominates the Luberon skyline. In that time it's been used as a prison, a storehouse, and a garrison. These days, it welcomes tourists to art exhibitions within its historic walls. Be sure to take a look at the Renaissance chimney, which is remarkable for its size and the quality and beauty of its sculptures.

CAVES DU PALAIS SAINT-FIRMIN

Gordes; http://caves-saint-firmin.com; Mon.-Tues.
and Thurs.-Sat. 10am-1pm and 2pm-6pm, Sun.
2pm-6pm; €6, children 5-15 €4.50, under 5 free

Space above ground in Gordes is limited. Every spare rock has been built on and buildings hang improbably from cliff faces. With such a shortage of room, inevitably the inhabitants dug down into the rock, creating a vast network of caves under the village. Visitors can explore this subterranean world underneath the Palace of Saint-Firmin. There are 50 caves, which descend 20 meters (65 feet) underneath the palace. Together they give insight into parts of life that took place underground; there's an olive oil press and a bread oven. Build between the 11th and 18th centuries, the caves include impressive stone arches and staircases. Thankfully, breaks in the passageways allow light and fresh air to circulate.

★ VILLAGE DES BORIES

Les Savornins; tel. 04 90 72 03 48;
http://levillagedesbories.com; 9am-sunset

Bories are small huts built by stacking stones on top of each other. There's no mortar, no beams, just stones, and yet somewhat miraculously their conical roofs resist the fierce local wind and the pull of gravity. Precise weight distribution is the only thing that keeps them standing. Bories can be seen throughout France, and some examples are thought to date to the pre-Roman Ligurian era. However, the restored village of Bories near Gordes is much more recent. In the 18th and 19th centuries, field upon field in the area surrounding Gordes was reclaimed for agricultural use. The byproduct of this clearance effort was thousands of stones. These were used in the construction of bories, of which the Village des Bories is the most complete example. On the site you can learn about the construction technique and poke your head into old sheepfolds, dwellings, and kitchens. There are also exhibitions of old agricultural tools found during the restoration work.

★ ABBEY NOTRE-DAME DE SÉNANQUE

On the D177 from Gordes to Venasque; tel. 04 90 72
02 05; www.senanque.fr; Mon.-Sat. 9:30am-11:30,
last entry 11am; €7.50, children €3.50, under 6 free

It's the image that has promoted Provence around the world: the simple, near-perfect symmetry of the Sénanque Abbey with wave upon wave of lavender breaking against the stone walls. The Abbey shelters in an isolated valley, and is approached by a narrow

The Petit and Grand Luberon

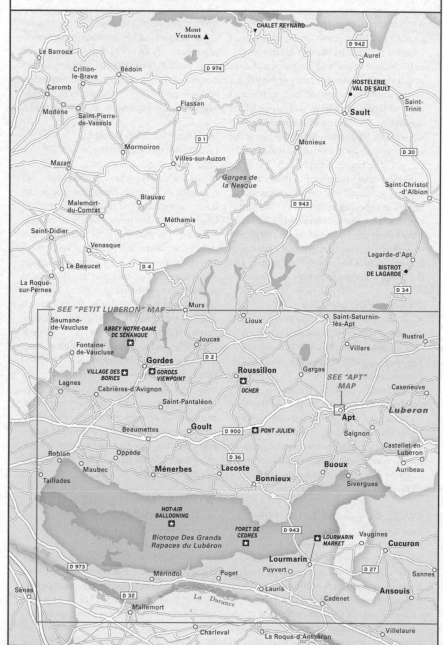

Mont Ventoux ▲

CHALET REYNARD

Le Barroux

Crillon-le-Brave

Caromb

Modène

Saint-Pierre-de-Vassols

Bédoin

D 974

Flassan

D 942

Aurel

HOSTELERIE VAL DE SAULT

Sault

Saint-Trinit

Mazan

Mormoiron

Malemort-du-Comtat

Blauvac

Villes-sur-Auzon

D 1

Méthamis

Monieux

Gorges de la Nesque

D 30

Saint-Christol-d'Albion

Saint-Didier

Venasque

Le Beaucet

La Roque-sur-Pernes

D 4

D 943

Lagarde-d'Apt

BISTROT DE LAGARDE

D 34

SEE "PETIT LUBERON" MAP

Saumane-de-Vaucluse

ABBEY NOTRE-DAME DE SÉNANQUE

Fontaine-de-Vaucluse

Lagnes

VILLAGE DES BORIES

Cabrières-d'Avignon

Gordes

GORDES VIEWPOINT

Saint-Pantaléon

D 2

Murs

Lioux

Joucas

Roussillon

OCHER

Gargas

Villars

Saint-Saturnin-lès-Apt

Rustrel

SEE "APT" MAP

Caseneuve

Luberon

Apt

Beaumettes

Goult

D 900

PONT JULIEN

Saignon

Castellet-en-Luberon

Auribeau

Roblion

Oppède

Maubec

Ménerbes

D 36

Lacoste

Bonnieux

Buoux

Sivergues

Taillades

HOT-AIR BALLOONING

Biotope Des Grands Rapaces du Lubéron

FORET DE CEDRES

D 943

LOURMARIN MARKET

Vaugines

Cucuron

D 973

Mérindol

Puget

Puyvert

Lourmarin

D 27

Sannes

Sénas

D 32

Mallemort

Lauris

La Durance

Cadenet

Ansouis

Villelaure

Charleval

La Roque-d'Anthéron

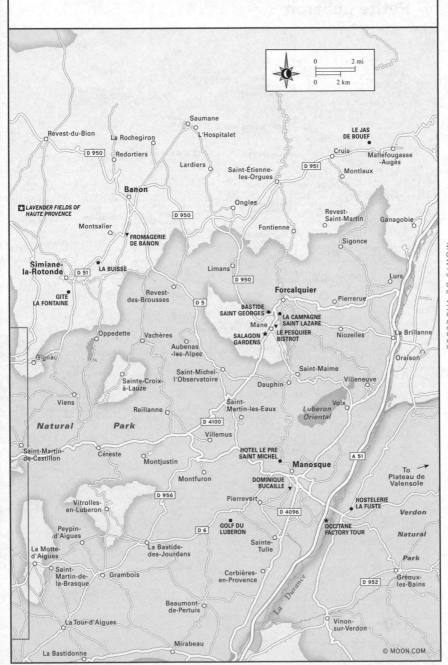

0   2 mi

0   2 km

Revest-du-Bion

La Rochegiron

Saumane

L'Hospitalet

LE JAS
DE BOUEF

D 950

Redortiers

Cruis

Mallefougasse
-Augès

Lardiers

Saint-Étienne-
les-Orgues

D 951

Montlaux

Banon

Ongles

LAVENDER FIELDS OF
HAUTE PROVENCE

D 950

Fontienne

Revest-
Saint-Martin

Ganagobie

Montsalier

FROMAGERIE
DE BANON

Sigonce

Simiane-
la-Rotonde

D 51

LA BUISSE

Limans

D 950

Forcalquier

Lurs

Pierrerue

GITE
LA FONTAINE

Revest-
des-Brousses

D 5

BASTIDE
SAINT GEORGES

LA CAMPAGNE
SAINT LAZARE

La Brillanne

Oppedette

Vachères

Mane

SALAGON
GARDENS

LE PESQUIER
BISTROT

Niozelles

Oraison

Gignac

Aubenas
-les-Alpes

Saint-Michel-
l'Observatoire

Saint-Maime

Villeneuve

Sainte-Croix-
à-Lauze

Dauphin

Luberon
Oriental

Volx

Viens

Reillanne

Saint-
Martin-les-Eaux

D 4100

Natural   Park

Villemus

Saint-Martin-
de-Castillon

Céreste

Montjustin

HOTEL LE PRÉ
SAINT MICHEL

Manosque

A 51

To
Plateau de
Valensole

Montfuron

DOMINIQUE
BUCAILLE

HOSTELERIE
LA FUSTE

Verdon

Vitrolles-
en-Luberon

D 956

Pierrevert

D 4096

OCCITANE
FACTORY TOUR

Natural

Peypin-
d'Aigues

D 6

GOLF DU
LUBERON

Sainte-
Tulle

Park

La Motte-
d'Aigues

La Bastide-
des-Jourdans

D 952

Gréoux-
les-Bains

Saint-Martin-
de-la-Brasque

Grambois

Corbières-
en-Provence

Beaumont-
de-Pertuis

La Tour-d'Aigues

Mirabeau

Vinon-
sur-Verdon

La Bastidonne

La Durance

© MOON.COM

Petite Luberon

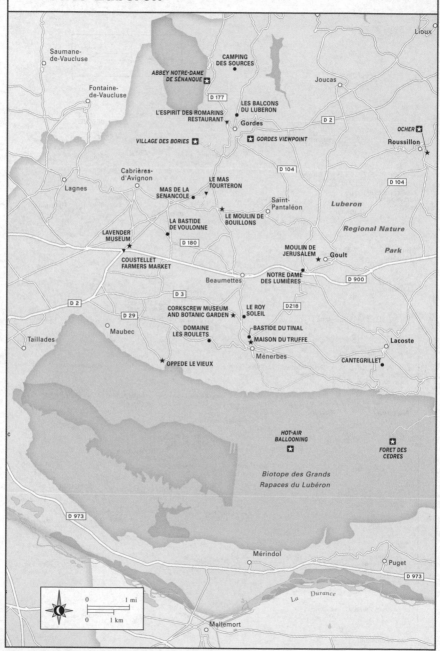

Lioux

Saumane-
de-Vaucluse

CAMPING
DES SOURCES

ABBEY NOTRE-DAME
DE SÉNANQUE ✚

Joucas

Fontaine-
de-Vaucluse

D 177

LES BALCONS
DU LUBERON

L'ESPIRIT DES ROMARINS
RESTAURANT

Gordes

D 2

OCHER ✚

VILLAGE DES BORIES ✚

★ GORDES VIEWPOINT

Roussillon

Cabrières-
d'Avignon

D 104

D 104

Lagnes

MAS DE LA
SENANCOLE

LE MAS
TOURTERON

Saint-
Pantaléon

Luberon

LE MOULIN DE
BOUILLONS

Regional Nature

LA BASTIDE
DE VOULONNE

LAVENDER
MUSEUM

D 180

MOULIN DE
JERUSALEM

Goult

Park

COUSTELLET
FARMERS MARKET

Beaumettes

NOTRE DAME
DES LUMIÈRES

D 900

D 2

D 3

CORKSCREW MUSEUM
AND BOTANIC GARDEN

LE ROY
SOLEIL

D218

D 29

DOMAINE
LES ROULETS

BASTIDE DU TINAL

Maubec

MAISON DU TRUFFE

Lacoste

Taillades

OPPEDE LE VIEUX

Ménerbes

CANTEGRILLET

HOT-AIR
BALLOONING
✚

FORET DES
CEDRES ✚

Biotope des Grands
Rapaces du Lubéron

D 973

Mérindol

Puget

D 973

La Durance

0   1 mi

0   1 km

Mallemort

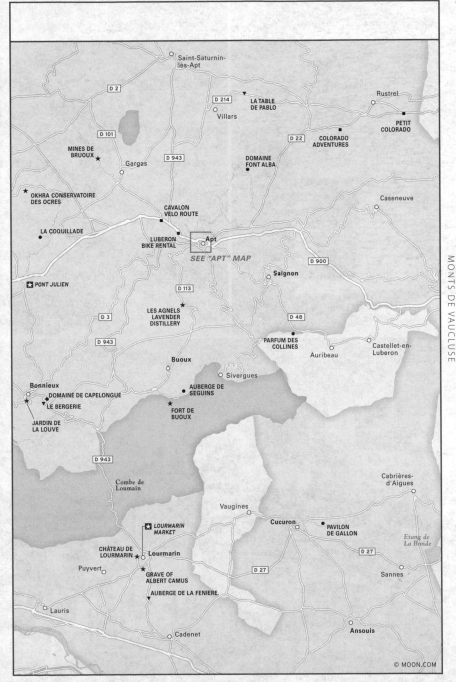

THE LUBERON AND HAUTE PROVENCE

MONTS DE VAUCLUSE

winding road, which gives visitors plenty of time to appreciate why the Cistercians chose to found a monastery there in 1148. Fed by the waters of the Senancole river and hidden from prying eyes, the location is perfect for a life of spiritual contemplation. Today, to help with the upkeep of the Abbey the monks welcome visitors. A visit takes in the church, the dormitory, the cloisters, and the chapter house. Lavender essence, honey, and even liquors produced by the monks are available to buy, with the proceeds once again funding the upkeep of the building. The truly spiritually adventurous can even sleep over, joining the monks for a day or two in their life of prayer, work, and silent contemplation. The cost of an overnight stay is €30 per night. Note that the D177 access road is one way (direction Gordes to Venasque) from the end of March to the end of September. To see the lavender in full bloom, visit before the end of July.

LAVENDER MUSEUM

276 Route de Gordes, Cabrieres d'Avignon; tel. 04 90 76 91 23; www.museedelalavande.com/en; May-Sept. 9am-6pm, Feb.-Apr. and Oct.-Dec. 9am-12:15pm and 2pm-6pm, closed Jan.; €6.80, under 15 free

Lovers of lavender can discover all they need to know about the harvesting and uses of lavender at this ever popular museum. There's an interesting collection of old equipment used to distill lavender, an informative film, and themed events throughout the summer, including special kids' days and tastings of lavender teas.

LE MOULIN DE BOUILLONS

Route de Saint Pantaléon; tel. 04 90 72 22 11; Apr.-Oct. 10am-noon and 2pm-6pm, closed Tues.; €5, children €3.50

Located on a site that dates back 2,000 years to the Roman occupation of Provence, this museum contains some of the oldest examples of olive oil presses in the world. As always,

Roman ingenuity is evident both in the system of capturing water for the site and the location of the Roman press set into the rocks. There are also various other ancient presses on display, the most notable of which is a 7-ton, 16th-century Greek-style press. The neighboring stained-glass window museum is also worth a visit.

Hiking
LES GORGES DU VÉRONCLE HIKE

Depart from parking lot on the D2 between Gordes and Joucas, after the Chapo Gallery

There are not one, not two, but six mills on this hike up the Véroncle valley. The oldest dates back to the 16th century, and panels along the route explain how each mill functioned. Late spring is the best time to see the Véroncle river in full flow together with its picturesque waterfall. At other times of year, the water can dry up. In places the walk can be slippery and the gorge narrow, so wear good walking shoes. A map is available from the Gordes tourist office, and here: www.luberoncoeurdeprovence.com/bouger/pied/balade-dans-les-gorges-de-veroncle. The walk is 4 kilometers (2.5 miles) there and back, with a 430-meter (1,410-foot) incline. Look for the yellow signposting. The hike will take about 2 hours and 30 minutes.

Festivals and Events
FESTIVAL LES SOIRÉES D'ÉTÉ

Theatre des Terrasses; tel. 04 90 72 65 05; www.festival-gordes.com; first week in August; from €35 per performance

The performances are varied at the festival de Gordes (jazz, piano, acoustic guitar), but one thing never changes: The intimate 500-seat theater overlooking the Luberon amplifies the effect of the music, sweeping the audience away on an unforgettable emotional journey just as the stars blink into light overhead.

1: Village des Bories is an open-air museum of dry stone huts. 2: Abbey Notre-Dame de Sénanque 3: the village of Gordes

Food

L'ESPIRIT DES ROMARINS RESTAURANT

Route de Sénanque; tel. 04 90 72 12 13;
www.masromarins.com/fr/restaurant-gordes.html;
Tues.-Sat. 12:30-2:30pm and 7:30pm-9:30pm; €17-26

It's the image that has graced many a magazine cover: the village of Gordes rising from the rocky mountainside. For a couple of hours over lunch or supper, it feels like it belongs exclusively to the diners on the terrace of the L'Espirit de Romarins. A menu signed by Michelin-starred Mark Passorio delivers flavor and attention to detail, right down to the sugar cubes for the coffee, which arrive on a picturesque prong.

LA TRINQUETTE

Rue des Trapacelles; tel. 04 90 72 11 62; www.
facebook.com/LaTrinquette; noon-9:45pm; €16-20

Honeymooners should book well in advance to secure the most romantic table in the Luberon, and possibly the whole of Provence. La Trinquette boasts a single table on a Romeo-and-Juliet balcony that juts out onto a vista of the whole of the Luberon. For unlucky couples who can't secure the table with the view, the excellent food is ample consolation.

LE MAS TOURTERON

Chemin Sainte Blaise; tel. 04 90 72 00 16;
www.mastourteron.com; Wed.-Sat. 7:30pm-9:30pm,
Thurs.-Sun. 12:30pm-2pm, closed Oct. 30-Mar. 1; €65

This is a no-nonsense family restaurant that celebrates the strong and vibrant flavors of Provençal cuisine. Expect hearty fare with plenty of garlic, tomatoes, and eggplant, served on a beautiful sweet-scented wisteria-covered terrace. The restaurant is located a couple of kilometers outside Gordes in a bucolic environment.

COUSTELLET FARMERS MARKET

Place du Marché, Maubec 84660;
www.marchepaysandecoustellet.com; Wed.
5pm-7:30pm and Sun. 7:30am-12:30pm

Indisputably, the best fresh produce market in the Luberon takes place every Sunday morning at the Coustellet crossroads just a couple of kilometers from Gordes. The Wednesday evening affair is a smaller more intimate version of the main event, a mere dress rehearsal for Sunday, when every farmer worth his bulb of garlic pitches up and sells his best fresh vegetables. To complement it all, there's sourdough bread, fresh fish from the Mediterranean, and organic free-range rotisserie chicken. In the summer there's a party atmosphere with an oyster bar in the ticket office of the former train station.

Accommodations

LA BASTIDE DE VOULONNE

2213 route des Beaumettes; tel. 04 90 76 77 55,
www.bastide-voulonne.com, €129 d

Surrounded by ancient plane trees, this old Provençal bastide has been converted into a welcoming hotel. The rooms are spacious, and many have balconies overlooking an interior courtyard. In the garden there's a pool and the restaurant serves meals outside weather permitting.

LES BALCONS DU LUBERON

Route de Murs; tel. 04 90 72 17 50;
http://lesbalconsduluberon.fr; €170 d

A lovely old house built from the local stone is the setting for a five-bedroom bed-and-breakfast just five minutes from the center of Gordes. There's a beautiful garden with a pool overlooking the Luberon. Rooms are simply decorated, and delicious dinners composed from locally sourced seasonal ingredients are offered.

MAS DE LA SENANCOLE

Hameau Les Imberts; tel. 04 90 76 76 55;
www.mas-de-la-senancole.com; €140 d

At first glance this hotel set on the plane beneath Gordes seems nondescript. However, walk through the entrance hall and you come upon a ravishing swimming pool set in a beautiful mature garden. There's a good choice of size of room, and some have little terraces that open onto the garden. Right next door there's a well-regarded restaurant.

CAMPING DES SOURCES

Route de Murs, Gordes, 84220; tel. 04 90 72 12 48;
www.campingdessources.com

Just outside of Gordes in the heart of the Luberon Regional Nature Park, this campsite has pitches, chalets, and mobile homes. There's a pool and restaurant, and in the summer, live music. It's a beautiful place to stay.

Getting There and Around

Once in Gordes, the Château and the Saint-Firmin caves are in the center of the village and can be visited **on foot.** For the other sights listed you will need a car.

BY CAR

Gordes, Roussillon, and **Goult** are roughly 10 kilometers (6 miles) apart. Together, they form a triangle with Gordes at the most northerly point. To reach Gordes by car, take the D2 from **Saint-Saturnin-les-Apt;** the D15 from **Murs;** the D56 from **Goult;** and the D177 from **Venasque.** Once you arrive, park in the village **parking lot,** which is a short two-minute walk from the center. There is a €5 parking charge.

Travelling from **Avignon,** the village is reached by taking the A7 south and then the D900. The journey of 50 kilometers (31 miles) takes around 50 minutes.

BY BUS

From Apt, there are four buses a day to Gordes. **Line 17** departs from outside the tourist office in **Apt** (788 avenue Victor Hugo), arriving at the square in front of the Chateau in Gordes. The journey takes 50 minutes and costs €2.10 (www.apt.fr/Les-transports.html).

GOULT

Goult is noticeably quieter than neighboring Roussillon and Gordes. While no village in the Luberon can be described as undiscovered, Goult is at least understated. Year-round the village feels calm, and in summer it's good a good place to keep in mind if you want to escape from the summer bustle. The pedestrian streets encourage a slow, joyful meandering, and all paths eventually lead to the windmill that crowns the village.

Sights
MOULIN DE JERUSALEM

Goult; tel. 04 90 72 38 58;
*www.goult.fr/images2011/Visite/Visite%20village_*
GB.pdf; sunrise to sunset daily; free

No one is quite sure how the windmill, which dates back to the end of the 17th century, was given its name. One theory is that it was named after the nobles from the Goult area who headed off to the Crusades centuries earlier. Although you can't actually see inside the windmill, it's easy to visualize how the mistral wind (which frequently nears 100 kilometers per hour/62 miles per hour) could power the milling process. The view of the Luberon from adjacent to the windmill is one of the best and worth the climb up through the picturesque village streets. Starting at the windmill, it is possible to follow a marked trail back through the medieval streets of Goult, past the ramparts, the old gate, and the château. This quiet, shady walk takes about 45 minutes to complete, arriving back at the parking lot at the entrance to the village. See the website listed above for details.

CONSERVATOIRE TERRASSES DE CULTURE

Goult; tel. 04 90 72 38 58;
www.goult.fr/images2011/terrasses_eng_2015.pdf;
open sunrise to sunset daily; free

Next to the Jerusalem windmill are signs indicating the way to the Conservatoire Terrasses de Culture. Maintained as a link to the region's agricultural past, these ancient terraces demonstrate how man tamed the harsh Provençal landscape through the use of abundantly available stone. Dating the terraces is difficult. The Romans used terracing to cultivate olive trees and vines, and some of the terraces might date back a couple of thousand years. However, it is likely that they fell in and out of use over the centuries as demand for land changed. Stones bearing dates show that

The Wines of the Luberon

The statistics: Some 3,410 hectares (8,430 acres) of vines enjoy 130 days of sunshine, hot days, and cold nights, as well as the drying effect of the mistral wind and a clay limestone soil that is ideal for viticulture. The main grape varieties are syrah and grenache for the reds, and rosé and grenache blanc and vermentino for the whites.

As wine has morphed from an agricultural industry into a tourist activity, upmarket tasting rooms have sprung up over the region, offering tours, tastings, and courses. The other trend has been a shift toward organic production and a continued concentration on rosé, which remains the region's best seller (89 percent of the wine produced is rosé). The quality of the wine produced has definitely improved, as well, but with this improvement prices have risen. For a decent bottle of rosé, prices now hover around €10. Whites and reds can easily reach €15.

THE FIVE-STAR TREATMENT

· **Aureto winery** (www.aureto.fr) on the road between Apt and Cavaillon.

· **Domaine de La Fontenille** (www.domainedefontenille.com) in the southern Luberon, just outside Lourmarin.

· The extravagant tasting room of **Domaine de La Cavale** (www.domaine-lacavale.com/en) just outside Lourmarin.

SMALLER DOMAINES AND ORGANIC PRODUCTION

· **Château Canorgue** (http://châteaulacanorgue.com) in Bonnieux formed the dreamy backdrop to the Ridley Scott and Russell Crowe adaptation of Peter Mayle's novel *A Good Year*.

· **Domaine de La Verrière** (www.domainedelaverriere.fr) outside Goult makes an excellent viognier for less than €10.

· One of the region's rare natural wine producers, **Les Tuiles Bleus** (www.lestuilesbleues.fr), is just outside Cucuron.

the terraces were rebuilt right up until the end of the 19th century. In addition to preventing soil erosion, the rock walls were ingeniously used to house beehives, with the extra warmth retained by the stones increasing the productivity of the bees. These days the stone terraces provide a pleasant and educational walk amid olive and almond trees.

Food and Accommodations
CAFÉ DE LA POSTE
Rue de La Republique; Mon.-Sun. 9am-6pm; €12-18
This café was made famous by Peter Mayle in his best-selling memoir *A Year in Provence*. The tables are now filled with tourists rather than Mayle's celebrated *paysanne* (local farmers). The food is simple but good, and the

ambiance convivial. The terrace is the unofficial social heart of the village, and if you speak French it's a great place to eavesdrop on the latest gossip.

LA BARTAVELLE
29 rue Cheval Blanc; 04 90 72 33 72; https://labartavellegoult.com; Thurs.-Mon. 7:30pm-8:30pm; reservations required; €39
La Bartavelle has been a runaway success of a restaurant, and you need to book a couple of days in advance to be sure of getting a table. The setting is idyllic in the back streets of Goult, and the food resolutely seasonal and local. Visit in spring for delectable fresh asparagus dressed with parmesan shavings.

LE CARRILLON

Avenue du Luberon; tel. 04 90 72 15 09;
www.restaurant-goult.com; Thurs.-Mon. 12:15pm-2pm
and 7:15pm-8:30pm for latest reservation or start of
service; €22-31

On the main square in Goult, the Carillon is a favorite with villagers. The menu is eclectic, with local ingredients complemented by the occasional more exotic dish such as slow cooked cod in a ginger and coconut vinaigrette, served with sweet potatoes and caramelized banana chips.

NOTRE-DAME DES LUMIÈRES

Lumières; tel. 04 90 72 22 18;
www.notredamedelumieres.com; €101 d

A couple of minutes' drive from the village of Goult in the hamlet of Lumières, this former convent is a good base for exploring the Luberon villages. There's a large pool overlooked by a restaurant. Because there are 54 rooms, booking can be done at the last minute, making it a good emergency choice, although because of its size, it lacks a little charm and intimacy.

Getting There and Around

Once in Goult, the village is almost entirely **pedestrianized.**

BY CAR

Goult is located off the D900, which runs between **Apt** and **Coustellet.** There is a large **parking** area opposite Café de La Poste.

Travelling from **Avignon,** the village is reached by taking the A7 south and then the D900. The journey of 50 kilometers (31 miles) takes around 50 minutes.

BY BUS

Transvaucluse bus **Line 15** (www.apt.fr/Les-transports.html) runs seven times a day between **Avignon** and **Apt,** stopping at Goult. The bus stops at the **Lumières hamlet** beneath Goult. Allow at least 30 minutes to walk to the village up the hill.

ROUSSILLON

The red-orange cliffs of Roussillon are a sensational sight. A great shard of color plunges away from the villages into a deep canyon, which visitors can explore by taking the Sentier des Ocres. The village itself is a pleasing collection of vibrant colored houses. The streets are pedestrianized and filled with art galleries and shops that cater largely to tourists. The best time to experience Roussillon is either at daybreak or sunset. During the day there are often too many people, and the

Moulin de Jerusalem in Goult

sunlight is too strong to appreciate the range of color on the cliffs. An overnight stay in this village hotel offers the chance to chart the subtly changing shades of the rock as the light fades or gathers strength.

Sights
OKHRA CONSERVATOIRE DES OCRES
D104; tel. 04 90 05 66 69; http://okhra.com; Jan. by appointment, Apr.-June 10am-1pm and 2pm-5pm, July-Aug. 10am-7pm, Sept.-Oct. 10am-6pm, Nov.-Dec. 2pm-5pm; €7, under 18 €5.50, under 10 free

A cooperative society dedicated to preserving and sharing know-how relating to the use of color could not have chosen a better base than Provence. A visit to this old ocher factory is just the start of a journey into the world of color. Year-round presentations and workshops offer opportunities to delve into a creative artistic world.

SENTIER DES OCRES
Parking des Ocres; tel. 04 90 05 60 25; http://otroussillon.pagesperso-orange.fr/sentier.html; daily from 9am-one hour before sunset in the summer, 10am-one hour before sunset out of season, hours may fluctuate with number of visitors; €2.50, under 15 €1.50, under 10 free

According to local legend, a lovesick noblewoman fell to her death from the cliffs of Roussillon and as her corpse bled, the soil around her turned red. From that day onward the soil of the village has stayed red in her memory. The scientific explanation of how sand and clay combined with iron oxide deposits to create ocher is, of course, more probable, but this being France, the story of an old love affair still survives in the popular imagination. The walk, which starts adjacent to the main village car park (Parking des Ocres) is a pleasant one and winds through the cliffs and rocky crags, which at certain times of day glow a vibrant orange, calling to mind Mars as imagined in movies. Allow 30 or 60 minutes to complete the visit, depending on whether you choose the 2 kilometer (1 mile) or 4 kilometer (2 mile) route. If you have time, opt for the longer walk, which is more spectacular. There's a gift shop selling postcards and cold drinks at the start of the walk. Finally, if you take children, make sure they are wearing old clothes, because ocher stains!

★ Hot-Air Ballooning
Simply the most sensational way to enjoy the Luberon is by hot-air balloon, floating silently from perched village to perched village, rising and falling with the birds. Flights depart at dawn, entering the park at the moment when nature rather than man dominates. In summer the land below looks like an impressionist painting, with deep swathes of purple competing with vibrant splashes of yellow, as the balloon drifts over lavender and sunflower fields. In spring, expanses of red poppies carpet the land and white blossoms from almond and cherry trees blow in the air. In autumn a rich gold and red coat dresses the fields of vines as the Luberon experiences a fall to rival New England. Whatever time of year you choose to fly, it's a majestic once-in-a-lifetime experience.

MONTGOLFIERE LUBERON VOL-TERRE
1066 routes de Gaillanes; tel. 06 03 54 10 92; www.montgolfiere-luberon.com; flights by reservation; from €230 per person

This company offers hot-air balloon rides out of Roussillon. Guests help to prepare the balloon for flight. The average altitude during the trip is 1,000 meters (3,280 feet), and the flight time is one hour. Group sizes vary between four and 15 people. After the ride, enjoy a glass of champagne.

Food and Accommodations
RESTAURANT DAVID
Place de La Poste; tel. 04 90 05 60 13; www.luberon-hotel.fr; Thurs.-Mon. 12:15pm-1:30pm and 7:15pm-8.45pm (last reservation), closed Sunday dinner; €25-34

Nearly every table in the elegant light-filled dining room has a captivating view of the ocher cliffs of Roussillon. Dishes might

☆ Ocher

walking on the moon, or rather Mars, the Petit Colorado ocher mine near Apt

When science can't explain a phenomenon, myth and religion step in. For centuries, the inhabitants of Apt, Gargas, Roussillon, and Rustrel couldn't understand why the landscape around them glowed almost blood red and so they invented fanciful stories. There's the one about the forlorn lover casting herself off the cliffs and another about the Archangel Gabriel slaying a battalion of fallen angels and their blood staining the ground red.

Buy a local a pastis and he or she will probably indulge you with a different tall tale. Of course, you may get lucky and hit upon an amateur geologist who'll explain that more than 100 million years ago Provence was covered by a sea. The retreat of the water left sandy deposits and clay, both of which had absorbed iron from the sea water. Over the millennia, they combined to produce ocher, the unique color of which is derived from the high concentration of iron. (Personally I prefer the biblical version with angels swarming in combat over the Luberon Hills.)

In any event, extraction of ocher began in 1780 in Roussillon, and by 1925 there were 22 mines in the area, sending the finished pigment in more than 20 different shades worldwide for use in paints and industrial products. The introduction of synthetic coloring agents after the second world war led to a drastic decline in the industry. However some ingenious and very Gallic uses were still found for ocher and its industrial legacy. Until mushroom cultivation in the otherwise abandoned mines of Bruoux was discontinued, it was possible to find an ocher-inspired menu of goat's cheese (with an ocher rind) and Bruoux Mine mushrooms on toast. Local rumor has it that an overindulgent diner's stomach once glowed in the dark.

WHERE TO SEE OCHER

- **Okhra Conservatoire des Ocres:** A society dedicated to sharing knowledge about using and preserving color, including ocher.

- **Sentier des Ochres:** Beware of ocher stains on this fascinating walk through an ocher-dominated landscape.

- **Restaurant David:** Eat dinner with a view of Rousillon's ocher cliffs.

- **Mines de Bruoux:** Not for the claustrophobic, a visit to this former ocher mine is a testament to what man can create without machines.

- **Petit Colorado:** Two signposted walks take you through the site of an old open-air ocher mine.

include Guinea fowl served with a crunchy honey-and-saffron polenta, or monk fish with a ravioli of artichoke and chorizo. It's the best restaurant for a serious meal in Roussillon.

CAFÉ LES COULEURS

Place de La Mairie; tel. 04 90 06 12 83;
Tues.-Sun. 10am-10pm; €16-22
Right in the heart of Roussillon this café is a convenient place to stop. On the menu are well-prepared French bistro classics, such as *coq au vin* (chicken in wine) with fresh tagliatelle. The service can be a little brusque in the high season, as the staff struggle to keep up with the influx of tourists.

CLOS DE LA GLYCINE

Place de La Poste; tel. 04 90 05 60 13;
www.luberon-hotel.fr; €190 d
Clos de La Glycine is a charming village center hotel. Rooms are well-furnished and comfortable. All have Wi-Fi, air-conditioning, and ensuite bathrooms. If available, opt for a room overlooking the cliffs.

LA COQUILLADE

Hameau Le Perrotet, Gargas; tel. 04 90 74 71 71;
www.coquillade.fr; €450
Five minutes away by car from Roussillon

this luxury hotel has been created out of an old Provençal hamlet. Most of the rooms are located in their own individual stone buildings with accompanying terraces. Bike hire, three restaurants, a pool, a vineyard, extensive views, and a spa add to the reasons to stay, though the prices are high.

Getting There and Around

BY CAR

Roussillon is reached by taking the D104 from **Goult,** the D169 from **Joucas,** or the D227 from **Saint-Saturnin-les-Apt. Parking** can be difficult in high season. Be prepared to walk for up to 10 minutes from the parking lot to the village. The village is pedestrianized.

Travelling from **Avignon,** the village is reached by taking the A7 south and then the D900. The journey of 50 kilometers (31 miles) takes around 50 minutes.

BY BUS

Transvaucluse Line 17 (www.apt.fr/Les-transports.html) departs four times a day from **Apt** to Roussillon. The journey takes 25 minutes and costs €2.10.

The Petit and Grand Luberon

TOP EXPERIENCE

Without exception, all the villages in the Petit and Grand Luberon in this guidebook merit a lengthy visit. Many visitors will never find time to see sights such as the Pont Julien Roman bridge let alone the Fort de Buoux, marooned as it is the depths of the Grand Luberon. Instead they will wander contently along cobbled village streets lined with art galleries and small boutiques. Sightseeing here often consists of no more than a leisurely

lunch and a look at the view over an old stone wall.

Everyone, of course, has a favorite village. Some are drawn to Lacoste by the mystique of the Marquis de Sade, others to Menerbes by the late Peter Mayle's descriptions in *A Year in Provence*, others still to Bonnieux by the views of Mont Ventoux. The fun of visiting the Luberon is to explore and fall in love with one of the villages yourself. For those who can tear themselves away from the pleasures of village hopping, then biking and walking trails crisscross the mountains.

ORIENTATION

The **Combe de Lourmarin** is a canyon between rocky cliffs through which passes the **D943** road dividing the Petit and Grand Luberon. At the northern entrance to the Combe sits the bustling market town of **Apt,** which is the transport hub for the region. To the east of the Combe, the Grand Luberon is wilder and the villages, such as **Buoux** and **Saignon,** are more spaced out. There are fewer sights and fewer people, and the scenery is savage and inspiring. To the west of the Combe, the Petit Luberon is gentler. Renowned **picturesque villages,** such as **Bonnieux, Lacoste,** and **Menerbes,** are all located within 10 kilometers (6 miles) of each other. All three are built on hills and can be challenging for the less mobile to fully navigate on foot. Bonnieux and Menerbes are both large prosperous villages and make good bases from which to explore. Lacoste is much quieter and now has many empty houses. Out of season you'll often just have the village cats for company as you stroll the narrow streets.

Just outside the village of Bonnieux is the **Foret de Cedres,** which is a hiking and cycling center. For wine lovers the Petit Luberon is home to many of the nature park's best **vineyards.**

APT

The town of Apt, is not as instantly appealing as many of the neighboring villages, but it is pleasant enough with a long pedestrianized shopping street and plenty of cafés with large terraces shaded by plane trees. It comes alive on Saturday mornings for one of the most vibrant, and least touristy, of the region's markets.

As a base to explore the whole region, it's geographically ideal, as it is adjacent to the main roads heading in every direction. It is also home to the region's main tourist office (788 avenue Victor Hugo 84400, Apt) as well as the Maison du Parc information center. A few kilometers out of town near Rustrel, the major sight is the Colorado Provençal, where open-air ocher mining has created a luminous red/orange landscape filled with seemingly alien rock formations.

Sights
LA MAISON DU PARC
60 Place Jean Jaures;
www.parcduluberon.fr; Mon.-Fri. 1:30pm-6pm; free
All sorts of great information related to the Luberon is available at the Maison du Parc, including an introduction to the region's most famous bird, the Egyptian vulture, and an explanation of the region's geology, which is closely linked with the retreat of the Aptian sea from the area 120 million years ago.

CATHEDRAL SAINTE-ANNE
187 rue des Marchands; tel: 06 88 47 23 42;
open daily, guided visits by appointment June-Oct.
Mon.-Fri. at 10am, 11am, 3pm and 4pm; €5
The domed roof of the Sainte-Anne Cathedral stands out from afar, its golden cross glinting in the sunshine. Like Saint-Sauveur Cathedral in Aix, the building is a mix of styles. The earliest evidence of construction dates back to the 5th century, when a church was built on the old Roman Forum. A side nave was added in 1200, and the chapel of Sainte-Anne in 1660. Perhaps the most exceptional feature is the 14th-century stained glass in the apse depicting Mary with the infant Jesus and Anne.

LES AGNELS LAVENDER DISTILLERY
Route de Buoux; tel. 04 90 04 77 00;
www.lesagnels.com; daily Apr.-Aug., Sept.-Mar.
closed Sun., tours in English available with
appointment; €6 distillery visit, €15 lavender field
and distillery visit (June-early Aug. only)
One of several providers offering lavender-themed experiences in the region, Les Agnels distinguishes itself by distilling lavender year-round, allowing visitors to observe the process of extracting the essential oil from the flowers. The tour of the distillery is preceded by a short film on the history of lavender in the region, and there is a shop where you can purchase all things lavender, from soap to honey, and from bath salts to the essential oil itself.

Apt

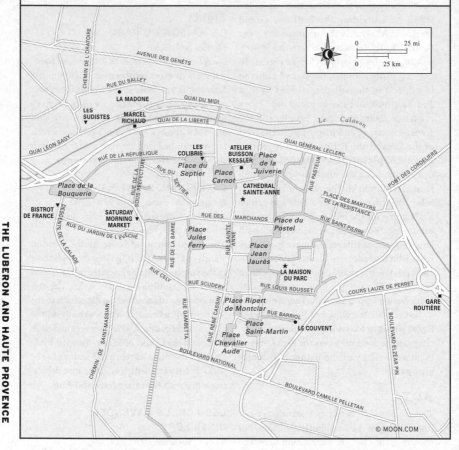

MINES DE BRUOUX

1434 route de Croagnes, Gargas;
tel. 04 90 06 22 59; www.minesdebruoux.fr;
open daily Mar.-Nov. 10am-6pm, 10am-7pm Jul.-Aug.,
all visits are guided and depart every half hour in
season, less frequently out of season; €8.90, under 22
€7.50, under 12 €6.50, under 6 €2.50

The Bruoux mine is the place to appreciate the industrial scale of ocher mining in the area. It's almost impossible to imagine how man could have created this immense underground network of caves. In all there are 40 kilometers (25 miles) of hollowed out galleries.

Men worked four hours a day, six days a week, using only pick-axes to carve the route. So intensive was the work that one man would typically change pick-axe three or four times a day. In places the ceilings are 15 meters (49 feet) high and reminiscent of an underground cathedral. Somewhat incongruously, when the mine closed in 1940, the caves were used for the cultivation of mushrooms before finally opening as a tourist destination in 2009. It is a humbling experience to see what man was able to achieve without machines. It's certainly not for the claustrophobic.

Sports and Recreation

PETIT COLORADO

D22, Rustrel; tel. 04 90 75 04 87;
https://coloradoprovencal.fr; open daily, hours vary
according to seasonal daylight, closed January;
€5 parking charge

Taking a walk in the Colorado Provençal can be disorienting. From the verdant green of the Luberon, you enter a landscape of vibrant reds and oranges. The two signposted walks take you through the site of an old open-air ocher mine. The first walk is 2 kilometers (1 mile) and takes 40 minutes, and the second walk is 4 kilometers (2 miles) and takes 1 hour and 45 minutes. There are strange rock formations aplenty, reminiscent (on a much of smaller scale) of Colorado in the United States, and there's even a stretch of bare sand called the Mini Sahara. Beware: The soles of visitors' shoes glow red on their return. Information about the two trails, both of which begin and end at the parking lot, is available on arrival.

CAVALON VELO ROUTE

From Coustellet to Castellet; www.veloloisirprovence.
com/en/luberon/circuit/la-veloroute-vole verte du
calavon

This ride is billed by the tourist office as the ultimate family cycling outing: no cars, no gradient. Even if you are not a cycling enthusiast, the appeal is obvious. The path runs for some 37 kilometers (23 miles) from Coustellet to the foot of Castellet, along the route of an old railway track. It splits the valley between the Monts de Vaucluse and the Petit and Grand Luberon. If you pick up the route at Apt, there is a choice of heading east into wilder and less inhabited countryside, or west toward Coustellet. On a spring or autumn Sunday, I can imagine few better activities than to set off from Apt along the veloroute toward Coustellet, stopping at the farmers market to buy lunch for a picnic at the Roman Pont Julien bridge on the way back. There is a 1-kilometer (0.6-mile) section on the way to Coustellet that runs alongside a small road. The ride takes about two hours to complete. You can park and pick up the route

in Apt adjacent to the tourist office at 788 avenue Victor Hugo.

LUBERON BIKE RENTAL

669 avenue Victor Hugo; tel. 06 48 72 16 13;
www.luberonbikeshop; Mon.-Sat. 9am-7pm,
bike rental from €20 per day

Located next to the tourist office and the cycle route, the shop has its own parking, making it the ideal place to start your ride. Electric as well as a wide range of road and all terrain bikes are available.

COLORADO ADVENTURES

Quartier Nôtres Dames des Anges, Rustrel;
tel. 06 78 26 68 91; www.coloradoaventures.com;
July-Aug. 9:30am-7:30pm, last entrance 5pm, out of
season phone in advance

For those who are tired of lazing by the swimming pool, Colorado Adventures offers the opportunity to spend a few hours swinging from branches and hanging from ropes. There's a range of color-coded routes through the treetops, with security assured by a metal guide rope, harness, and climbing clips. It's great fun for all of the family. There's even a new reverse bungy jump where people are catapulted skyward.

Shopping

ATELIER BUISSON KESSLER

17 place du Septier; tel. 04 90 04 89 61;
www.atelierbuisson-kessler.com; July-Aug. Mon.-Sat.
10am-6pm, Sept.-June Mon.-Tues. and Thurs.-Fri.
8:30am-6:30pm

This is a charming family-run ceramics shop inspired by the natural palette of the Luberon. Plates and bowls are multicolored and often dotted with wild patterns. The ceramics are guaranteed to liven up any table setting, and they make great mementos of a holiday in Provence.

MARCEL RICHAUD

112 Quai de la Liberté; tel. 04 90 74 43 50;
Tues.-Sat. 9:45am-12:15pm and 2:30pm-7pm

Apt is a world leader in the production of candied fruit (fruit confit). The process of preserving fruit by extracting the water and injecting a sugar solution that covers and conserves it was discovered in the late Middle Ages, and the town hasn't looked back since. This well-established shop sells everything from small bags to nibble on, to beautifully arranged displays on trays, perfect for taking to a dinner party. All of them are prepared by hand.

Food
LA TABLE DE PABLO
Les Petits Clements, Villars;
tel. 04 90 75 45 18;
www.latabledepablo.com;
Thurs.-Tues. noon-1:30pm and 7:30pm-9pm,
closed Sat. lunch; €35

La Table de Pablo nestles a few kilometers into the countryside outside Apt. There's a pleasant shady terrace bordered by greenery, and summer dining is accompanied by a chorus of cicadas. The food is excellent, with a seasonal menu nicely balanced between meat and fish; accompanying sauces are rich and intense.

LES SUDISTES
17 Quai Léon Sagy; tel. 06 42 81 00 33;
www.facebook.com/LesSudistes84400;
Mon.-Sat. 6pm-10pm; €5-15

A popular new edition to the Apt restaurant scene is Les Sudistes tapas bar. There's a nice outside terrace, a comprehensive list of wines by the glass, and a wide selection of tapas, including the freshest local goat's cheese, and ice cream from artisan producer Scaramouche in neighboring Cereste.

BISTROT DE FRANCE
67 place la Bouquerie; tel. 04 90 74 22 01;
Mon.-Sat. noon-2pm and 7:30pm-10pm; €15-25

An ever-popular favorite serving classic French bistro dishes. Look out for anything served with cèpes (porcini) or girolle mushrooms in the autumn, particularly a couple of days after a heavy rain shower. Rustic interior decoration adds to the atmosphere, as do the hunters in the winter time, stopping in for a restorative drink.

BISTROT DE LAGARDE
RD34 Lagarde d'Apt, Lagarde d'Apt;
tel. 04 90 74 57 23; http://lebistrotdelagarde.free.fr;
Wed.-Sun. 12:30pm-1:30pm and 7:30pm-9:30pm; €35

For years, this bistro hidden amid fields of lavender outside Apt has been a word-of-mouth success. People think nothing of traveling an hour or so to taste the inventive cuisine of Lloyd Tropeano. Dishes include a medley of heirloom tomatoes presented in various mouth-watering ways.

LES COLIBRIS
16 Place du Septier; tel. 04 86 69 53 98;
Tues.-Sat.; €5-10

If it is just a cup of tea, a slice of cake, and a warm welcome that you are after, then Les Colibris is the solution. The home-made biscuits and chocolate concoctions are beautifully presented and taste delectable.

Markets
SATURDAY MORNING MARKET
Place Gabriel Péri; tel. 04 90 74 00 13;
www.apt.fr/Les-marchA-c-s.html; Sat. 8am-12:30pm

Apt market is busy, bustling, and authentic. Excellent fresh fruit and vegetables draw the locals from miles around. In the winter, the earthy scent of truffles drifts in the cold frosty air. In the summer, arrive early or parking will be scarce.

Accommodations
LE COUVENT
36 rue Louis Rousset; tel. 04 90 04 55 36,
www.loucouvent.com; €99 d

As the name suggests this bed-and-breakfast occupies the building of an old convent in Apt. Arched ceilings and ornate rugs create a warm ambiance. There's a lovely pool set in a walled courtyard. All in all, it's the perfect antidote to dull chain hotels.

DOMAINE FONT ALBA
Chemin des Coulets; tel. 04 90 06 12 83;
www.Châteaufontalba.com; €125 d

Vineyard hotels in France can be a little over the top. If they've got a few vines and a château, the owners too often think they can charge a fortune. Domaine Font Alba's ethos is the opposite. There are five rooms, each named after a grape variety, and one suite in the converted old sheep fold. The views back over the Luberon are wonderful, and the vineyard's own rosé is the perfect accompaniment to the setting sun.

LA MADONE
66 Faubourg du Ballet;
tel. 06 86 73 39 32;
www.lamadone.net; €300 d for 2 nights
There are five apartments in this old hôtel particulier (see Aix-en-Provence chapter for more information on hôtel particuliers). Each apartment overflows with charm, atmosphere, and luxury touches. Chandeliers catch the light, frescoes adorn the ceiling, and Roman busts sit atop stone fireplaces. Note there is a two-night minimum stay.

Getting There and Around
Apt is a small town, and the easiest way to get around is **on foot.** Walking from one side of the town to the other takes no more than 15 minutes.

BY CAR
Apt is an important transport hub. It can be reached in under 20 minutes by car on the following roads: the D3 from **Bonnieux,** the D22 from **Rustrel,** the D48 from **Saignon,** the D900 from **Coustellet,** the D113 from **Buoux,** and the D943 from **Saint-Saturnin-les-Apt. Aix-en-Provence** is 55 kilometers (34 miles) away, and **Avignon** 53 kilometers (33 miles). Both journeys take just over an hour.

BY BUS
There are regular buses to Apt from **Aix-en-Provence** (three times a day), **Avignon** (eight times a day), **L'Isle-sur-la-Sorgue** (five times a day). The buses arrive at the **Gare Routière,** avenue de la Liberation. The lines run in both directions and the timetables can be downloaded at www.apt.fr/Les-transports.html.

BUOUX

Buoux is a small hamlet in the heart of the Grand Luberon. There are no cafés or shops, and it is easy to drive through without realizing. Its best-known landmark is the Fort de Buoux, which sits on an isolated hilltop. For hikers, the Auberge de Seguins is a much-loved place to stop for refreshment.

Sights
FORT DE BUOUX
Buoux; tel. 04 90 74 25 75;
http://lefortdebuoux.e-monsite.com; Feb.-Nov.
Wed.-Mon. 10am-5pm, Dec. and Jan. by appointment
Isolated is not quite the word; this fort is in the middle of nowhere set high on a hill in the middle of the nature park. You might see one of the four pairs of rare Egyptian vultures that are known to be resident in the Luberon circling overhead as you climb the hill. The oldest parts of the fort date back to the pre-Roman Celto-Ligurian period and the place is full of mystery and historical debate: Who made the strange silo-like circles in the rock? What was the hidden staircase cut into the rocks used for? The walk up to the fort from the parking area in the nearby Auberge des Seguins takes about 30 minutes.

Food and Accommodations
AUBERGE DE SEGUINS
Signposted from the D113; tel. 04 90 74 16 37;
daily noon-2pm and 7:30pm- 9pm, closed Nov.-Mar.;
€118 half board, €25 evening menu, lunch €15
The Auberge is a true retreat. It's situated in a hidden valley; the surrounding cliffs reach vertiginously toward the sky, and some of the rooms are carved into the rock. There's a freshwater swimming pool, which is icy cold, and a feeling of being a million miles from anywhere. The rooms are not luxurious, but they are comfortable. There are 27 rooms ranging from doubles to a large dormitory that sleeps 20. There's a restaurant serving filling food to fuel the many hikers who pass through, and a snack bar offering sandwiches. Cell phone signal is at best patchy, and Wi-Fi is only available in the main bar area.

Getting There and Around

There is no public transportation to Buoux, which is a small hamlet. Take the D113 from **Apt**. The fort is located a few kilometers away from the village on the same road. **Parking** to visit the fort is at the Auberge des Seguins.

SAIGNON

The coat of arms of Saignon bears the image of three châteaux, and their remains can be seen clinging to a 30-meter (98-foot) high rock that overlooks the village. Around the base of the rock, visitors can walk amid the old **ramparts,** along a narrow cobbled stone path that leads up to rocky terrace with an orientation table granting a 360-degree view of the Luberon and Monts de Vaucluse. It's an easy place from which to appreciate the origin of the name of the village, believed to come from the word "signal." Saignon was constructed to provide early warming of the approach of enemies to the town of Apt in the valley below. The village is quintessentially Provençal: all narrow, cobbled streets, shade, light, and trickling water.

Food

BISTRO L'ATELIER

Place Horloge; tel. 04 90 75 01 58;
Wed.-Sun. noon-2pm; €10-20

On a sunny day it's hard to beat this spot right in the center of a picturesque Luberon village. The bistro has outside tables overlooked by the 17th-century clock tower. The menu includes simple dishes, such as steak-frites (steak and fries), and there's a popular buffet bar.

Accommodations

LE RIMAYON

Route de Jas; tel. 06 09 67 41 33; le-rimayon-hotel-de-charme.business.site; €110 d

This is another bijou hotel with just five rooms that requires early booking to secure a room. On the outskirts of Saignon, it has a small pool with a view, a delightful garden, and a restaurant that serves dishes based around fresh produce from the vegetable garden. All rooms have ensuite bathrooms, and there is one larger apartment suitable for a family.

CHAMBRE AVEC VUE

28 rue des Bourgades; tel. 04 90 04 85 01;
http://chambreavecvue.com; €110 d

Based upon a unique concept, Chambre avec Vue offers residencies to artists and writers, displaying and selling their work to guests in the associated bed-and-breakfast. As you might expect, there is a bohemian feel to the decoration.

PARFUM DES COLLINES

RD 48 Route d'Auribeau; tel. 04 32 52 93 46;
www.parfum-collines.com; €230 d

The name means perfume of the hills. This little guest house is surrounded by lavender fields and the pungent smell of the wild herbs of the Provençal garrigue. Luxurious decor, spacious rooms, and a pool with a view make it one of the region's best kept secrets. Evening meals, often truffle-based, are available on request. All rooms have Wi-Fi, air-conditioning and ensuite bathrooms.

Getting There and Around

The village is largely **pedestrianized,** with a **parking lot** located two minutes' walk from the center.

BY CAR

Take the D48 east from **Apt** for 5 kilometers (3 miles). The journey time in 9 minutes.

BY BUS

Line number 16 (www.apt.fr/Les-transports.html) runs on Saturdays between **Apt** and Saignon once a day. The ride takes 15 minutes and costs €2.10.

BONNIEUX

Bonnieux is all about the views and forgetting about the inconvenience of building a village on the side of a cliff face. Approached from

---

1: Bonnieux silhoutted against the blue sky **2:** The Roman Pont Julien bridge is a perfect place to cool down in the summer.

the south on the D36, the silhouette of the village dominates the skyline. The cypress trees, church spire, and Luberon hills in the background are the perfect subjects for painters' canvasses. Another highlight is the view to the north from the upper level of Bonnieux out toward Mont Ventoux. Navigating around Bonnieux, though, is difficult. There is a cluster of shops and restaurants at the top of the village. The central level hosts the supermarket and the popular Fournil restaurant. Farther down the hillside is the boulangerie and more shops and restaurants. Steps and narrow roads link the levels, so a certain degree of physical fitness is a prerequisite for fully exploring the village.

Sights

★ PONT JULIEN ROMAN BRIDGE

Route de Pont Julien; free

Compared to other Roman sites in Provence, the Pont Julien can seem insignificant. Its three arches span a miserly 50 or so meters (164 feet) of the Cavalon river and its presence is heralded only by a small parking area and minimal tourist information.

Yet, it remains well worth a visit for two reasons: In spring and autumn when the waters of the Cavalon are running and the weather is warm, it's an idyllic spot to dip your feet in the water and enjoy a picnic. The bridge sits on the Cavalon cycle route, which bisects the Luberon valley and is a popular stopping off point. Children jump from the stone arches into the river below and hop between the exposed rocks while their parents enjoy a glass of wine on the banks. Second, if you visit early in the morning, you will often find yourself alone and able to contemplate in solitude an evocative monument of Roman Provence. The bridge was built in 3 BC on the Via Domitia, a key road that connected Roman territories in France with Italy. In the shadow of the Petit Luberon and the Monts de Vaucluse, without a single visible building, it's momentarily easy to step back in time and imagine horses and carts rolling over the arches (built purposefully large to accommodate flood water). Over

the years, the horses morphed into cars and quite incredibly the bridge still carried traffic up until 2005, amounting to over 2,000 years of continuous use.

MUSÉE DE LA BOULANGERIE

*12 rue de la République; tel. 04 90 75 88. 34;
www.avignon-et-provence.com/en/museum/bakery-museum-Bonnieux; Apr.-Oct. 1pm-6pm; €3.50*

It's impossible to understand the French obsession with bread without living in France. The Bonnieux bakery museum traces the history of bread making from when itinerant bakers used to travel between villages with the live yeast, to the present day. For those unaccustomed to the centrality of bread, and particularly the iconic baguette, to French life, the collection of old prints and bread making memorabilia on display at this small museum offers important insight.

JARDIN DE LA LOUVE

*Chemin de Saint Gervais; www.lalouve.eu;
visits by reservation only, use the monthly calendar on the website; €10 per person, children under 13 free*

Provençal gardens used to be haphazard affairs given over to growing vegetables and maximizing shade, but these days if you poke your head over the boundary wall of an old *mas* (farmhouse), more often than not you'll encounter a garden of geometric precision. There will be lavender laid out in lines, rosemary falling artfully from walls, cypress trees spearing the skyline straight as arrows, and countless varieties of bushes clipped into perfect circles. The Jardin de la Louve is one of the first formal gardens in a private home in Provence and perhaps still the finest, created by Nicole de Vésian, a Hermes stylist, in 1986. Year by year, she created a unique garden filled with color and rare varieties of plants, interspersed with clear spaces from which to contemplate the view of the Luberon. Such was the local renown of the garden that Nicole enjoyed a second career creating gardens in the area for celebrities such as Ridley Scott. Visits are by reservation only and are made with the current owner of the property through the website.

L'ÉGLISE LOUISE BOURGEOIS

Rue Aristride Briand, Bonnieux 84480;
tel. 04 90 75 80 54; www.egliselouisebourgeois.com;
July or Sept. 1-10 10am-1pm and 3pm-5pm; free

Louise Bourgeois was a surrealist artist working during the 20th century. Her output was frequently provocative and linked with the feminist movement. In 1998 toward the end of her career she installed various works in this deserted chapel in the hills above Bonnieux. Among them is a cage-like confessional, an iron cross that grows hands, and a mother suckling her child in an air-tight container. The power of the art to shock is augmented by the religious setting, and viewing the works can be disconcerting. A visit is a thought-provoking experience, and questions as to the symbolic meaning of the art remain long after one has departed. Note the church can only be visited in July and September.

Sports and Recreation
★ FORET DE CEDRES

Chemin de La Foret, Bonnieux 84480;
daily 9am-5pm; free

The cedar forest that covers some 250 hectares (617 acres) at the summit of the Petit Luberon (727 meters/2,385 feet) has become a year-round mecca for cyclists and hikers, and a popular refuge from the summer heat. The first cedar seeds (taken from the Atlas Mountains in Algeria) were sown in 1861 by botanists. The trees reached maturity in 1920 and have been reproducing ever since. Entering the forest, there is an immediate feeling of separation from the traditional Provençal landscape. Pine and rock, and sunshine and shade, give way to towering cedar trees and heavy shadow. Paths wind deep into the forest, occasionally breaking out to offer panoramas of the Provençal landscape below. The sharp-eyed claim to be able to see all the way to the Mediterranean. Popular walks include a 2-hour descent to the village of Lauris

in the southern Luberon. For the less active, the forest is a pleasant place to picnic, and the drive up offers one of the best views of the hilltop village of Bonnieux. There is no visitor center, but in the summer staff from the Luberon Regional Nature Park are often on hand to give advice at the entry point to the forest. Information panels along the main route indicate trails that you can follow and the way to the main viewpoints.

SUN-E-BIKE

1 avenue Clovis Hugues, Bonnieux 84480;
tel. 04 90 74 09 96;
www.location-velo-provence.com/fr;
daily 9am-5:30pm; from €28 for a day rental.

Bonnieux is an ideal place to locate an electric bike business. In all directions, there are some pretty serious gradients. Only experienced cyclists dream of taking these hills on, and even the riders of the Tour de France looked spent in 2017 when they swept out of the Combe de Lourmarin. But strap a battery to a bike and suddenly the endeavor seems a lot less daunting. Villages such as Menerbes and Lacoste are within easy reach of Bonnieux, and the quiet country lanes of the Luberon are perfect for a relaxing morning in the saddle.

Shopping
L'ATELIER DUO

11 rue Voltaire; tel. 04 90 74 17 13;
daily 10am-7pm, closed Jan.-Mar.

This is a charming boutique selling a clothing collection designed by its owner, Éléonore Magnani, as well as a collection of jewelry by Gérard Seror. Cotton skirts, wool sweaters, and silver bracelets are the must-have pieces.

BOUTIQUE POETIC

2 rue de La Republique; tel. 06 40 92 87 78;
daily Apr.-Oct. 10am-1pm and 3pm-7pm

Colorful ceramics and sculptures draw customers back again and again to the shop of Thimothée Humbert. It's rather cramped inside, so best to leave pets and children on the street.

Wildlife of Luberon Regional Nature Park

Hikers (particularly quiet ones) might come across a wide variety of wildlife when exploring Luberon Regional Nature Park. Some encounters are thrilling; others may require caution.

Egyptian vulture

MAMMALS

- Most well-known and ever more frequently seen in and around villages are the **wild boar.** They tend to be nocturnal, so sightings are most usual at dusk and dawn. In the **Foret de Cedres,** boars snuffle underneath the trees. Boars travel in family troops and can be dangerous to humans, particularly if there are young. It's best to steer clear if at all possible.

- Less threatening is an encounter with the largest species of **beaver** in Europe, weighing between 20 and 40 kilos (44 to 88 pounds). You'll know these beavers are present if you see claw markings on trees and branches sharpened to a point like pencils.

BIRDLIFE

- Birdlife is abundant. The stars of the show are the four pairs of **Egyptian vultures** known to nest in the steep rock cliffs of the Grand Luberon. In flight the vultures are recognizable by the contrast between their pure white plumage and black wing tips. From September to February the vultures migrate to the Sahara.

- Other exciting sightings could include the **bonelli eagle** and the **eagle owl.** Pheasants and guinea fowl roam wild, and as dusks falls the song of nightingale pairs fill the treetops. Around the **Fort de Buoux,** birds of prey soar above the intimidating cliff face.

INSECTS AND REPTILES

- The diverse flora is a refuge for more than 265 species of insects, as well as the **ocelle lizard,** the largest lizard in Europe.

- Turning over too many rocks is not advisable, because the Luberon has two species of **scorpion.** The sting of the dark brown almost black one (*euscorpius flavicaudis*) is relatively harmless, but if you get stung by the lighter, yellowy orange scorpion (*buthus occitanus*) it's best to hurry to the hospital.

POTTERY MARKET

Le Village; Easter weekend

Every Easter the winding narrow streets of Bonnieux are filled with local artisans selling pottery in a rainbow of colors. Some designs are innovative, some traditional, and some wildly eccentric. You can buy everything from salad bowls to serving plates, and from vases to great garden pots; each piece is unique and created by hand rather than in a factory.

Food

LES TERRACES

Cours Elzear Pin; tel. 04 90 75 99 77;
www.brasserielesterrasses.com; daily 10am-midnight;
€12.50-22

Indisputably the café with the best view in Bonnieux is Les Terrasses. On one side of the small road is the kitchen, and on the other there's a long, narrow wooden parquet terrace that commands a view over the whole valley up to the Monts de Vaucluse and Mont Ventoux behind. A long menu caters for all without sacrificing quality.

LE FOURNIL

5 Place Carnot; tel. 04 90 75 83 62;
www.lefournil-bonnieux.com; Tues.-Sun. noon-2pm
and 7:30pm-9:30pm; €17.50-27

People travel from throughout the Luberon for lunch on the Fournil's shady terrace. Tables are set next to a trickling fountain. Unlike in some restaurants in overly picturesque spots, the food commands as much attention as the setting. Slow-cooked rabbit with eggplant is a specialty.

L'AROME

2 rue Lucien Blanc; tel. 04 90 75 88 62;
www.laromerestaurant.com; Thurs. evening-Tues.
noon-3pm and 7pm-11pm; €34

Even without an outside space, talented chef Jean Michel Page keeps drawing the crowds with an eclectic menu marrying fresh ingredients from the Provençal markets with exotic spices from around the world. The menu is slightly tilted toward fish dishes, the chef's specialty.

LE BERGERIE

Chemin des Cabanes; tel. 04 90 75 89 78;
www.capelongue.com/carte-bergerie; daily
noon-1:30pm and 7pm-9:30pm; €22-34

Set in an old sheep fold, this bistro is famous for one dish: truffle pizza. It's like no other pizza you have ever tasted: a light base, a cream sauce that the cheese is on the point of dissolving into, and a generous shaving of truffle. After eating this pizza, people have been known to dream about it, only to wake up in the morning questioning whether such a delicious dish could really exist.

Accommodations

DOMAINE DE CAPELONGUE

Chemin des Cabanes, Bonnieux 84480;
tel. 04 90 75 89 78; www.capelongue.com; €260 d

Two-star Michelin chef Edouard Loubet reigns in this gastronomic hotel. Rooms are competitively priced, perhaps to entice diners to splash out on the menu in the restaurant. La Bergerie is across the road for those whose pockets or stomachs aren't deep enough for the full dining experience. Comfortable rooms and a pool with a picture-postcard view of Bonnieux complete the offering.

LE CLOS DU BUIS

Rue Victor Hugo, Bonnieux 84480;
tel. 04 90 75 88 48; www.leclosdubuis.fr; €125 d

Light, spacious rooms are attractively decorated, and many have views out across the valley. The garden is mature and well-kept with a small swimming pool surrounded by shady trees and bushes. A summer kitchen where guests can prepare picnics is a welcome touch.

Getting There and Around

Once you're in Bonnieux, be aware that the village can be challenging to negotiate. Steps carved into the stone between the houses link the various levels of the village. It's best to wear sturdy walking shoes.

BY CAR

From **Avignon,** take the D900 and then the D36. The journey of 54 kilometers (34 miles) takes around 50 minutes. From **Apt,** take the D3. The journey of 15 kilometers (9 miles) takes 20 minutes. From **Lourmarin,** take the D943 and then the D36. The journey of 13 kilometers (8 miles) takes 20 minutes.

BY BUS

The **Transvaucluse Line 15** bus runs five times a day from **Avignon** to **Apt,** stopping at the Pont Julien bridge at the foot of the village. The journey takes 1 hour. It's a long uphill walk of at least an hour to the village from the stop. **Line 9** runs three times a day between Apt and **Aix-en-Provence,** taking 2 hours and stopping in the center of Bonnieux. Full timetables can be found here at www.sudmobilite.fr. **Transvaucluse Line 18,** between Apt and **Cavaillon,** runs three times a day and stops at Bonnieux. It costs €2.60 and takes 20 minutes. Consult www.apt.fr/Les-transports.html for the latest timetable.

LACOSTE

Lacoste provokes controversy in the Luberon. Fashion designer Pierre Cardin has fallen in love with this alluring hillside stone village and has purchased multiple houses. Families who have lived in the village for generations have moved out, and Cardin is accused of creating a ghost village that exists as little more than a tourist attraction. The village remains an enjoyable place to visit, but be aware that there is a backstory of local anger.

Sights
CHÂTEAU LACOSTE
Lacoste; tel. 04 90 75 93 12;
www.festivaldelacoste.com; summer opening to
view Pierre Cardin's art and the Marquis de Sade's
apartments; telephone in advance for a visit; €12

The 18th century's Christian Grey, the Marquis de Sade, kept this château in the Luberon as his bolt-hole from the authorities. His behavior during his stays gave rise to the term "sadism." Scandals included a woman employed as a maid being strapped to a bed, whipped, and having hot wax tipped in her wounds. She escaped to tell the story by jumping from a window. These days, the castle, and many of the village houses, belong to fashion designer Pierre Cardin. Some rooms of the château are open to visits during the summer months, but those hoping for surviving evidence of the marquis's sexual deviancy will be disappointed. However, the views over the Luberon are beguiling and sinuous cobbled streets lead up to the château. Seen from afar the château's ruined silhouette still conveys a sense of past Gothic horrors.

Entertainment and Events
FESTIVAL DE LACOSTE
Château Lacoste, Lacoste 84480;
tel. 04 90 75 93 12; www.festivaldelacoste.com;
program available on website; from €50

Lacoste is now famed for its weeklong summer dance, opera, and theater festival. The château provides a hauntingly atmospheric backdrop, and the festival specializes in identifying and giving opportunities to talented young artists. An extra frisson is provided by the knowledge that the Marquis had a taste for amateur dramatics. He frequently put on performances but was so hard pressed to find an audience that he often forced his servants to watch. These days it's best to book tickets well in advance.

Food and Accommodations
CAFÉ DE FRANCE
Le Village D106; tel. 04 90 75 82 25;
Mon.-Sun. 9am-10:30pm; €12-20

Quiches, omelets, and other simple dishes make up the menu in this pleasant café located on the outskirts of Lacoste. There's a nice view back toward Bonnieux and local wine served by the glass and carafe.

CAFÉ DE SADE
Place L'Eglise; tel. 04 90 75 82. 29;
Mon.-Sun. 9am-10:30pm; €14-20

The choice of restaurants in Lacoste is not extensive. In addition to the Café de France is the Café de Sade. It lacks the views of the former over the countryside but still has a nice terrace facing the village streets. The food is slightly more ambitious, with staple local dishes and the increasingly ubiquitous hamburger, which is said now to appear on more menus in France than the once staple ham and butter baguette.

CANTEGRILLET
Quartier Contard; tel. 04 90 75 84 25;
cantegrillet.com; €75 d

Sometimes simplicity is all that you need. The Cantegrillet is a small guesthouse with five bedrooms, all lovingly maintained. Each room has a private bathroom, and there's a shared outside terrace and a pretty garden.

Getting There and Around
The village is **pedestrianized** and built on a hillside. Once again, walking shoes are advisable.

BY CAR

From **Avignon,** take the D900 and then the D106, covering 50 kilometers (31 miles) in 50 minutes. From **Menerbes,** take the D1109, covering 6 kilometers (4 miles) in 11minutes.

BY BUS

Transvaucluse Line 18 between **Apt** and **Cavaillon** runs three times a day and stops at Lacoste. It costs €2.60 and takes 30 minutes. Consult www.apt.fr/Les-transports.html for the latest timetable.

MENERBES

Menerbes is a hilltop village without the associated inconveniences. Compared with, say, Bonnieux, there are no steeply sloping streets or sets of steps that seem to go on forever. The village is built on a plateau, and the central streets have gentle inclines, making it a popular place to visit. There's plenty of Provençal charm: Stone houses line the streets, fountains trickle, and in the tourist season, cafés and restaurants do a vibrant trade.

Sights
CORKSCREW MUSEUM AND BOTANIC GARDEN

Domaine de La Citadelle; tel. 04 90 75 93 12;
http://museedutirebouchon.com; May-Oct. daily
10am-5:30pm, Nov.-Apr. Mon.-Fri. same hours;
€5, €3.50

An unusual way to work up a thirst for a wine tasting is to spend half an hour or so touring this fabulous collection of corkscrews. There are more than 1,200 of them divided into various categories, which include pocket, precious, and mechanisms. Many also have a double purpose; one even incorporates a pistol. Before sampling the wine in the adjacent tasting room, it's worth visiting the aromatic herb garden.

MAISON DU TRUFFE

Place L'Horloge; tel. 04 90 72 38 37;
www.vin-truffe-luberon.com; daily 10am-6:30pm; free
Part shop, part restaurant, part activity center, the Maison du Truffe is a temple to the tuber

melanosporum, the famed black diamond of Provence. Groups can organize truffle hunting demonstrations and truffle-themed cooking classes. There are also frequent wine-tasting seminars. For a quicker visit, the shop is replete with gifts for gourmands, such as olive oil infused with truffles.

MAISON JANE EAKIN

Rue Sainte Barbe; tel. 06 14 75 50 33;
www.jane-eakin.com;
May 10-June 22 Thurs.-Sat. 2:30pm-6pm,
July 3-Sept. 1 Wed.-Sat. 3pm-6:30pm
Jane Eakin was an American artist who came to Europe after the World War II. After many years in Paris and an itinerant period voyaging with world-renowned violinist Isaac Stern, she settled in Menerbes. A selection of her paintings is presented in this small museum thanks to a foundation created on her death to promote her life and memory.

OPPÈDE LE VIEUX
Oppède
Once a deserted village, Oppède le Vieux is being slowly re-inhabited by a largely artistic community. The village can only be visited on foot. It's just a few minutes along the road from Menerbes above the nondescript modern village of Oppède. Visitors park at the foot of the hill and make their way through lush vegetation up a windy path (steep in places), before eventually arriving at Oppède le Vieux. There's a broad open square, a couple of cafés, a château, old workshops, washhouses and plenty of medieval and Renaissance houses to admire.

Shopping
PETITS POINTS DE PROVENCE

5 Place Albert Roure; tel. 04 90 72 08 77;
www.petitspointsdeprovence.com; Mon.- Fri.
10am-6pm, Sat. 11am-6pm, Sun. 2pm-6pm
The perfect shop for those who dream of setting an immaculate, elegant table. Linen is available in a wide range of colors and is of the highest quality. There are even tiny table ornaments, such as ceramic fruit, to—forgive

the pun—put the cherry on top of any table dressing.

GALERIE PASCAL LAINE

15 rue Sainte Barbe; tel. 04 90 72 48 30; http://galerie-pascal-laine.com; Mon.-Sat. 10:30am-12:30pm and 3:30pm-7:30pm

One of the most well-regarded art galleries in the Luberon is that of Pascal Lainé. Pascal started his gallery in Gordes, where he showed work by, among others, Victor Vasarely, before moving first to Avignon, and then in 2007 to Menerbes. Exhibitions of art and sculpture change regularly.

Food
BISTROT LE 5

5 place Albert Roure; tel. 04 90 72 31 84; www.bistrotle5.fr; daily 10am-midnight; €19-34

In the summer months this restaurant with a large terrace overlooking the Luberon has the vibe of a Riviera beach club. Chill out music plays in the background, and clients lounge around ordering ever larger bottles of rosé. The menu is extensive, ranging from French classics such as steak tartare to a prawn *tajine* (stew).

RESTAURANT LES SAVEURS GOURMAND

51 rue Kléber Guendon; tel. 04 32 50 20 53; www.restaurantlessaveursgourmandes.com; Mon.-Sat. 7pm-9:30pm; €36 evening menu

Meticulously sourced ingredients shine through with every mouthful in this atmospheric restaurant. Specials include medallions of free-range local Monteux pork in a honey and rosemary glaze. For aficionados of Provence's "black diamond," there's a special truffle menu, including a delectable truffle infused brie.

CHEZ AUZET

52 rue du Portail Neuf; tel. 04 90 72 37 53; www. facebook.com/ChezAuzet; Tues.-Sat. 9am-7pm; €5-12

A charming small café serving simple food on a stone terrace, Chez Auzet offers biscuits, cakes, teas, and coffees, supplemented by larger dishes such as omelets. Try the renowned biscotti (almond biscuits). There are few better places to stop for a restorative nibble.

Accommodations
LE ROY SOLEIL

D103; tel. 04 90 72 25 61; www.roy-soleil.com; €155 d

Basking in the warm Provençal sunshine on the plane beneath Menerbes, the Roy Soleil is a good base for exploring the Luberon hill villages. Luxurious but not in an over the top way, this discreet hotel is small enough (20 rooms) to offer personal service. All rooms have Wi-Fi, air-conditioning, and ensuite bathrooms, and many have terraces that open onto the garden. There is a good range of choice, from standard rooms to large suites.

BASTIDE DU TINAL

660 Chemin Neuf; tel. 04 90 72 18 07; www.bastide-du-tinal.com; €270 d

Book early to secure one of the five bedrooms (all with Wi-Fi, air-conditioning, and ensuite bathrooms) in this intimate guesthouse located on the outskirts of Menerbes. Sumptuously furnished rooms, two pools with panoramic views, a cozy lounge, and an extensive terrace can tempt guests to spend whole days cocooned away. There's a snack bar but no restaurant.

DOMAINE LES ROULETS

305A Chemin de Fondreche, Oppede; tel. 04 90 71 21 88; www.lesroullets.com; €330d

This boutique bed-and-breakfast is set in the grounds of a vineyard. The rooms are large, light, and big on detail; they are even all equipped with blue-tooth speakers. Breakfast is indulgent, and plates of charcuterie are available to sate hunger pangs. There's also a heated pool and a summer kitchen where guests can prepare their own food.

Getting There and Around

Upon arrival, Menerbes is best visited **on foot.** There is parking on the access road (Rue de La Fontaine).

BY CAR

The D3 runs from **Bonnieux** to Menerbes. The journey of 10 kilometers (6 miles) takes 16 minutes. The D109 runs from **Lacoste** to Menerbes. The journey of 7 kilometers (4 miles) takes 11 minutes. From the town of **Apt,** take the D900. The journey of 21 kilometers (13 miles) takes 26 minutes.

BY BUS

Line 18 between **Apt** and **Cavaillon** runs three times a day and stops at Menerbes. The full timetable can be found online at www.apt.fr/Les-transports.html.

The Southern Luberon

Once upon a time, the villages of the Southern Luberon were the poor neighbors of their more illustrious northern cousins. Second-home owners and tourists flocked to the giddy delights of the northern hill villages with their sweeping views and treated the southern Luberon very much as an afterthought. These days, led by Lourmarin, the southern Luberon has more than caught up in terms of desirability. The climate is noticeably less harsh than on the northern slopes of the Luberon. Rather than the oak of the north, evergreen pine predominates, giving the area a more Mediterranean feel. Plus, as pretty as hill villages can be, they are distinctly inconvenient to walk around and live in. Countless steps and sinuous narrow streets complicate everyday life in a northern Luberon village. Although they're not without the odd incline, the villages of the southern Luberon are noticeably easier to navigate.

ORIENTATION

It's only a small exaggeration to say that daily life in the southern Luberon begins and ends with **Lourmarin.** Sitting on the D943 at the southern entrance to the **Combe de Lourmarin,** the village is the jewel in the region's crown and exerts a disproportionate pull on the tourist masses. Yet, despite its popularity, the village copes well. Parking is rarely problem (except on market day on

Château de Lourmarin

Friday), and the maze of narrow streets lined with **art galleries** and **boutiques** disperses the crowds. To the east of Lourmarin, **Cucuron** and **Ansouis** are charming villages that are all too often overlooked. In the center of Cucuron you will find a stunningly attractive water basin, lined by centuries-old plane trees. It's one of a kind and a must-see. Ansouis oozes Provençal atmosphere and is capped by a 10th-century château and 11th-century church. These three villages are the most well-known in the southern Luberon, but exploring east from Lourmarin, there are numerous other small villages dotted among the vine- and olive-filled landscape. Distances between these villages are short. To drive from Lourmarin, through Cucuron to Ansouis takes 20 minutes at a leisurely pace.

LOURMARIN

It's hard not to fall in love with Lourmarin. The village seems to have everything: It boasts a rich literary history, an imposing 12th-century chateau, and streets lined with cafés, restaurants, shops, and art galleries. The ultimate test is to mention the village to Parisians. The French urban elite tend not to get overexcited about much, but take a token Parisian, drop Lourmarin into the conversation, and a smile will inevitably comes over his or her face. "J'adore Lourmarin," they will confess.

Sights
GRAVE OF ALBERT CAMUS
Off the D27, Cimetière, Lourmarin
Visiting the grave of Albert Camus is a poignant pilgrimage for fans of his philosophy and books. In works such as *The Stranger* and *The Fall,* Camus tackled fundamental questions about the meaning, or rather the lack of meaning, in life, arguing that man should live by embracing the absurd rather than searching for explanations through faith. Religious and political systems, Camus believed, overcomplicated life for their own purposes. Part of the appeal of his point of view is that,

although he accepted the absurdity of life, he also rejected nihilism. Solidarity between humans could be found in the act of rebellion, or more mundanely playing together in a soccer team. (Camus excelled as a goalkeeper.)

Camus died in a car accident aged 46 in 1960 and was buried in the cemetery in Lourmarin, where he lived. His grave is a simple stone marked with his name. To find it, head south out of the center of the village on rue Henri de Savornin until you reach the D27, turn right, and continue for 500 meters (547 yards). Cross the road away from the village and you will see a sign for the cemetery. Go to the back of the first section of the cemetery and walk left along the wall, turn left at the end of the path, walk past five graves, and you will come upon the small stone right next to the path.

CHÂTEAU DE LOURMARIN
24 avenue Laurent Vibert; tel. 04 90 68 15 23; www.Château-de-lourmarin.com/home; July-Aug. daily 10am-6pm, Feb.-Oct. daily 10am-12:30pm and 2:30pm-6pm, Nov.-Jan. 10am-12:30pm and 2:30pm-4:30pm; €6,80, children 6-16 €3, under 6 free
Unbelievably, this 12th-century castle was nearly knocked down at the beginning of the 20th century. It had descended into ruins and was saved by Robert Laurent Vivert, a cosmetics businessman. Together with architect Henri Pacon, Vivert set about restoring the château. In 1926 Vivert died and the castle was given to a trust, which runs it today. Visiting is a rewarding experience. The entrance terraces afford the best available view over the Luberon and the village of Lourmarin. Inside, the visitors explore the 12th-century fortress, the 15th-century château, and the 16th-century château neuf. There's a fine art collection, an impressive double-spiral staircase, a collection of 16th- to 19th-century furniture, and the largest fireplace you are ever likely to see. The château is a center for classical music concerts and variety of festivals.

Entertainment and Events

YEAH FESTIVAL

*Château de Lourmarin, 24 avenue Laurent Vibert,
Lourmarin 84160; festivalyeah.fr; first weekend in
June, see website for details; €30 day pass,
€75 weekend*

One of the best small dance music festivals
in Europe takes place in the first weekend of
June in Lourmarin. The main stage is high up
on the terrace of the Château de Lourmarin
where 500 or so ticket holders party the nights
away to a collection of DJs headed by local resident Laurent Garnier. The real appeal of the
festival, though, is the way it takes the party
out into the streets of the village. Throughout
the weekend, DJs play sets outside the village
cafés, at the tennis club, and even within the
walls of the primary school.

CLASSICAL MUSIC

*Château de Lourmarin, 24 Avenue Laurent Vibert;
tel. 04 90 68 15 23; www.Château-de-lourmarin.com;
July-Aug., see website for details; €28 adults,
€22 reduced, €25 under 25*

Throughout the summer the château hosts
classical music recitals. In addition to the
pleasure of hearing renowned musicians perform, guests enjoy the ability to picnic on the
terrace of the château before performances.

Markets

★ LOURMARIN MARKET

Boulevard du Rayol; May-Sept. every Fri. 8am-1pm

From May to the end of September, Friday
morning is party time in Lourmarin. Buskers
fill the streets, the café terraces overflow, and
the main boulevard becomes busier than a
toy shop on Christmas Eve, as people try to
squeeze through the narrow spaces between
the traders' stalls. There's plenty of fresh fruit
and vegetables, and takeaway food in the form
of spit-roasted chickens, couscous, and even
Chinese noodles. The other stands offer an
eclectic mix of goods from sweet-smelling
lavender sachets to creams guaranteed to remove the scratches from a car's paintwork.
Shopping amid the crowds can be difficult
and the best advice for people intending to

visit in high season is to come either early
(before 10am) or late (after 12:30pm). From
October to May the market is a quieter affair,
parking is easier and browsing amid the stalls
a more enjoyable experience. A market tour
followed by a rosé wine tasting is available in
English every Friday in season (€50 per head,
call 06 98 06 68 99, www.provenceguru.com/
winetasting for reservations).

SUNDAY ARTISAN MARKET

Place Henri Barthélémy; May-Sept. Sun. 8am-6pm

The premise is simple. In order to take a stand
at this market you have to make what you sell.
The result is, the market hosts an interesting
group of artisans, including painters, sculptors, jewelers, and even furniture makers.
Items for sale include storage baskets made
in the traditional fashion from dried twigs,
and iron fish sculptures perfect for decorating a bathroom or hanging beside a swimming pool.

Art Galleries

GERARD ISIRDI

*4 rue Henri de Savornin; tel. 04 90 08 50 96;
www.isirdi.com; daily 10:30am-12:30pm and 3pm-6pm*

Enter anyone's second home in Provence
and there's a good chance that you will see a
framed picture of a man sitting in a café with a
glass of pastis reading *La Provence* newspaper.
This iconic image is part of painter Gerard
Isirdi's back catalog, and prints, posters,
and paintings of this and other humorously
Provençal images are on sale in his gallery.

DAN ADEL

6 rue du Temple; tel. 06 84 59 82 80; daily 2pm-7pm

Illustrator, photographer, portrait artist, and
painter, multitalented American Dan Adel is a
central figure of the Lourmarin Art Scene. His
work has graced the cover of magazines such
as *The New Yorker, Vanity Fair,* and *Rolling
Stone.* Dan's latest series of paintings employs
a revolutionary technique known as dimen-
sional abstraction. The resulting canvases are
mesmerizing.

Behind the Scenes of a Provençal Market

Visit the mayor's office (*mairie*) in any Provençal village and enquire about the possibility of a place in the weekly market, and the response is always the same: The market is full and has been for years. Out of season this is clearly not true, and on a weekly basis the local policeman (*placier*) decides who should be allowed free places according to an informal hierarchy. At the top are the local traders who've been frequenting the market for years but still never got themselves onto the official list at the *mairie*. With a nod to the *placier* these traders set up where they want. Second, there are start-up traders with local connections. They usually easily find a place.

Finally there is a third group, composed of outsiders who are new arrivals in the region. During the winter, members of this third group of traders make sure they are ever present in the markets. They endure the howling mistral and the fierce hail and snowstorms. They persevere, because they know that to make any money they need to secure a place for the summer season. As the days lengthen and the first stirrings of spring creep into the air, anxiety creeps into the traders' demeanors as week by week the available space is eroded by returnees from generations of market traders. Their right to a space is officially recorded at the *mairie*. Many winter traders give up, their dream shattered. Some persevere, and week by week, inch by inch, they enlarge their stalls. Almost without anyone noticing they join the privileged list of summer traders.

LUBERON MARKET DAYS

- **Monday:** Cadenet, Cavaillon, Goult, Lauris
- **Tuesday:** Lacoste, Gordes, Cucuron, La Tour d'Aigues
- **Wednesday:** Gargas, Merindol
- **Thursday:** Goult, Menerbes
- **Friday:** Bonnieux, Lourmarin, Lagnes
- **Saturday:** Apt, Pertuis
- **Sunday:** Ansouis, Coustellet.

Sports and Recreation
STATION BEE'S
Station Bee, D27 opposite the tennis club; tel. 06 50 69 49 53; www.stationsbees.com; €25 per half day
A great way to see the southern Luberon is to hire an e-bike. Take the D56 toward Vaugines, stop beside the *etang* in Cucuron for lunch and return via the D27 to Lourmarin, taking a break at Domaine de la Cavale for a wine tasting.

Food
TUESDAY FARMERS MARKET
Fruitière Numerique, avenue du 8 Mai; mid-Mar.-Dec. 5:30pm-9pm
In the space of a few years the weekly farmers market that runs every Tuesday evening from mid-March until December, has become a village institution. Residents and tourists mingle, and many buy cheese and bread and sit down for an impromptu supper with wine purchased from the adjacent bar run by the village wine cooperative. The atmosphere is convivial, and at around 7pm a local chef gives a cookery demonstration.

NUMERO 9
Rue du Temple; tel. 04 90 79 00 46; http://numero9-lourmarin.com; noon-2pm and 7:30pm-10pm, closed all day Thurs. and Sun. night; €28
Undoubtedly the best restaurant in Lourmarin, this small bistro has a terrace set in an idyllic courtyard with a central fountain. The lunchtime menu in particular is an excellent value at €26 for two courses. The cooking is consistent and occasionally quite inventive.

MAISON REYNAUD

2 avenue Philippe Girard; tel. 04 90 09 77 18;
https://maison-reynaud.business.site; Thurs.-Mon.
noon-2pm and 7:30pm-9:30pm; €12-25

For a couple of years, this small restaurant has been building a reputation for its French take on tapas. Diners order three or four dishes to make a meal for two, combining simple offerings of cured ham and melon with more exotic dishes such as char-grilled squid with garlic and parsley.

AUBERGE DE LA FENIERE

Route du Cadenet; tel. 04 90 68 11 79;
www.aubergelafeniere.com; daily noon-2pm and
7:30pm-10pm; €40-140

Michelin-starred chef Reine Sammut is slowly handing over the reigns to her daughter Nadia, whose specialty is gluten-free cooking. There's a formal gastronomic restaurant and a more casual bistro. Both work on the ethos of using the best locally sourced ingredients. The hotel/restaurant is located on the D943 road between Lourmarin and Cadenet.

LE PETIT RESTO

33 place de La Mairie, Vaugines; tel. 04 90 77 11 08;
www.leptitrestovaugines.com; Wed.-Sat. noon-2pm
and 7pm-9:30pm; €24 lunch menu, €35 evening menu

Right or wrong, locals are quite dismissive of the restaurant scene in Lourmarin, particularly the prices. For an excellent meal that does not break the budget they all head to the Petit Resto, 2 kilometers (1 miles) up the road, in the neighboring village of Vaugines. The fountain in the square as you enter sets the scene for a wonderfully Provençal experience.

Accommodations
LE MOULIN DE LOURMARIN

Rue du Temple; tel. 04 90 68 06 69;
www.moulindelourmarin.com; €180 d

The village-center location of the Moulin is its greatest draw. On the doorstep are cafés, restaurants, art galleries, and shops. The rooms are comfortable, and the hotel restaurant good but not exceptional; perhaps the only thing missing is a pool.

BASTIDE DE LOURMARIN

Route de Cucuron; 04 90 07 00 70;
www.hotelbastide.com/en; €132

The decor is slightly edgy and challenging, and the restaurant is only open in the summer months. However, the big plus for this hotel is that it has a small pool and is a one-minute walk from the village. There's a spa offering a range of well-priced beauty treatments. All rooms have Wi-Fi, air-conditioning, and en-suite bathrooms.

CÔTÉ LOURMARIN

Impasse du Pont de Temple; tel. 06 09 16 91 80;
www.cotelourmarin.fr; €195

This is an upmarket bed-and-breakfast on the picturesque main street. The soft furnishings and bed linens are as fine as you will find in any five-star hotel. There's no need for a restaurant, because there's a good brasserie and three cafés just 15 meters (49 feet) away across the road. For a romantic stay in the Luberon this is a top choice.

AJOUCADOU

9 rue Juiverie; tel. 06 98 83 93 16;
www.ajoucadou.com; €80

The Ajoucadou apartments are a real labor of love. Pascal Aussud the owner renovated this old town house by hand, creating three bright, light, and spacious apartments. Two have three bedrooms, and one is a studio. There is a minimum three-night stay during peak season. All the apartments are air-conditioned.

LES HAUTES PRAIRIES

Route de Vaugines, Lourmarin, tel. 04 90 68 02 89;
www.campasun-lourmarin.eu

Just outside Lourmarin, this campsite has a large pool and a separate water slide area. There's also a play area for children and a snack bar. As well as pitches for tents, it has cabins for rent. The campsite is a five-minute walk from the village.

Getting There and Around

The village is largely pedestrianized. There is plenty of parking near the center.

BY CAR

Take the D27 from **Lauris** (8 minutes, 5 kilometers/3 miles) or **Cucuron** (11 minutes, 8 kilometers/5 miles); the D56 from **Vaugines** (8 minutes, 5 kilometers/3 miles); or the D943 from **Cadenet** (8 minutes, 4 kilometers/2 miles) or **Bonnieux** (22 minutes, 13 kilometers/8 miles).

BY BUS

There is a twice-daily bus (**Line 9,** www.apt.fr/Les-transports.html) that runs between **Apt** and **Aix-en-Provence,** stopping at Lourmarin. There is also a bus (**Line 19,** www.sudmobilite.fr) to and from the neighboring villages of **Vaugines** and **Cucuron,** which runs seven times a day; it takes 25 minutes to reach Cucuron.

CUCURON

There's much more to Cucuron than its enchanting plane-tree ringed water basin (*etang*). Visitors can easily lose half a day meandering the charming narrow streets. Although not on the same scale as Lourmarin, there are still plenty of shops and artists' ateliers to dip your head into. It's perfect for those who wish to escape the crowds that can beset more well-known Luberon villages.

Sights

L'ETANG

Place de L'Etang, Cucuron

The *etang* (water basin) in Cucuron is one of the best-kept secret sights in Provence. It's roughly the size of an Olympic swimming pool and surrounded by hefty chunks of old stone that residents use as benches. As on the Cours Mirabeau in Aix, the unique atmosphere is thanks to the centuries-old plane trees that line the *etang,* which was once a watering point for animals. Over the years the trees have been pruned so that the uppermost branches stretch toward the heavens like the arms of supplicants. The light beneath these trees is a dappled mixture of sunshine and shade, perfect for sitting in a café and enjoying a glass of rosé. Every Tuesday morning one of the most appealing markets in Provence takes place around the *etang,* and throughout the year there are various events, including a model boat festival in the last weekend of August, and in spring a boat jousting festival.

Sports and Recreation

ETANG DE LA BONDE

intersection of D9 and D27, Cucuron

Just outside the village, this large man-made lake surrounded by views of the Luberon

The beautiful *etang* in Cucuron is not to be missed.

mountains is one of the best places to swim in the region. In summer the pebbly beach can get very busy. Out of season, people take their paddleboards and can be seen making serene progress over the still waters. It's also a popular spot with dog walkers. There's a beachside café that serves the local campsite, and halfway up the southern side of the lake, there are two nice spots to stop and eat: Le Loup Bleu (for more formal dining) and the Café du Lac (good simple food).

CIRCUIT L'ERMITAGE HIKE

Depart from Cucuron tourist office 11 Cours Pourrières; www.luberoncotesud.com/page/rando-:-circuit-de-l-ermitage+1283.html

This relatively gentle 6.7-kilometer (4.1-mile) walk with a 207-meter (679-foot) incline climbs slowly into the Luberon hills. The landscape is dominated by pine trees, rock, and the smell of wild herbs. Halfway around the loop, the 13th-century church of Notre Dame de Bellevoir, also known as the Ermitage, is the main sight. It sits on a rocky promontory overlooking the valley of the Aigue River and the chapel includes a small habitable part. A map and information are available from the Cucuron tourist office.

Festivals
LA FETE DU MAI

Rue de l'Eglise; first Sat. after May 21

After the great plague of 1720, the people of Cucuron agreed to cut down a poplar tree as high as the church as an offering to Saint Tulle in return for being saved from the pestilence. Every year since the people of the village have kept their side of the bargain. The festival is an opportunity for the people of the village to dress in traditional costumes and remember the history of the village.

Food and Accommodations
LA PETITE MAISON DE CUCURON

Place de l'Etang; tel. 04 90 68 21 99; www.lapetitemaisondecucuron.com; Wed.-Sun. noon-2pm and 8pm-10pm; €60 menu

An evergreen stalwart of the village, this one-star Michelin restaurant run by well-loved chef Eric Sapet has a loyal clientele. The menu changes on a weekly basis; dishes might include beef cheeks slow cooked in red wine. There are also very popular cookery courses on offer.

BAR LE CERCLE

D56; tel. 04 90 77 27 17; Mon.-Fri. noon-2pm and 7pm-9pm, Sun. noon-2pm; €12-20

Twenty meters across the road from the *etang*, up a small side street, is the Cercle restaurant. There is a vine-covered terrace and a wide choice of well-prepared food including pasta dishes starting at just over €10. The clientele is largely locals enjoying the plat du jour before draining a *pichet* of wine.

★ PAVILON DE GALLON

Chemin de Gallon; tel. 04 90 77 24 15; https://pavillondegalon.com; €230 d

This old hunting lodge has been converted into a luxury bed-and-breakfast. There are three immaculately furnished suites, a remarkable formal garden, and an infinity pool. It's an expensive choice but this property offers seclusion, total privacy, and pampering within walking distance of Cucuron. The rooms all have Wi-Fi and ensuite bathrooms. There are large fans but no air-conditioning.

HOTEL DE L'ETANG

Place de L'Etang; tel. 04 90 77 21 25; www.hoteldeletang.com; €81 d

It is hard to imagine a more quintessentially Provençal spot for a hotel than overlooking the *etang* in Cucuron. It's so scenic that photos of the hotel grace the local postcards. Rooms are clean but simply furnished, and most have terraces giving onto the *etang* where guests can often be seen lost in peaceful contemplation. All have Wi-Fi, air-conditioning, and ensuite bathrooms.

Getting There and Around
Cucuron is a small village best visited **on foot.**

BY CAR

Take the D27 from **Lourmarin** (11minutes, 8 kilometers/5 miles) or **Sannes** (6 minutes, 5 kilometers/3 miles), or the D56 from **Vaugines** (5 minutes, 2.5 kilometers/1.5 miles) or **Ansouis** (7 minutes, 5 kilometers/3 miles).

BY BUS

Bus **Line 19** (www.sudmobilite.fr) runs to and from the neighboring villages of **Vaugines** and **Lourmarin** seven times a day. The journey from Lourmarin takes 25 minutes.

ANSOUIS

Like Cucuron, Ansouis is a little off the beaten tourist track. If it were located anywhere but in the Luberon, the village would be a star attraction. However, with so much competition from neighboring tourist gems, it can be overlooked. This makes it more enjoyable to visit, and it's a pleasant place to use as a base for exploring the region and also south to Aix-en-Provence. The village is built on a relatively steep hill, so reaching the château and church at the summit requires a little effort.

Sights
CHÂTEAU D'ANSOUIS

Rue de Cartel; tel. 04 90 77 23 26;
www.chateauansouis.fr;
June 15-Sept. 15 3pm and 4:30pm, Thurs.-Mon.
guided 1-hour 15-minute visit in French,
reserve in advance, and Apr. 1-June 15 and Sept.
15-mid-Oct. at 3pm only; €10,
€8 children under 15

The owners who conduct the tour (only in French) share details of their daily lives as custodians of the castle and collectors of antiques. The château began life in the 10th century as a military fortress guarding the Aigue River. The 12th- and 13th century saw further building work before, in the 17th century, it was transformed into an elegant family home surrounded by formal gardens. Of particular interest is the richly decorated Provençal interior.

EGLISE D'ANSOUIS

5114F Grande Rue

Continue to climb on past the château another 100 meters (109 yards) or so to the highest point of Ansouis: the village church. The records of the cathedral in Aix point to a date of establishment around the 11th century, although it is unlikely that any of the current building predates the 13th century. Relatively small in size, the church is a peaceful place to visit. The courtyard at the foot of the steps affords an expansive view out over the Luberon.

Food and Accommodations
LA CLOSERIE

Boulevard des Platanes; tel. 04 90 09 90 54;
www.lacloserieansouis.com; Fri.-Tues. noon-1:30pm
and 7:30pm-9pm, closed Sun. evening;
€35 lunch menu, €53 evening

Located halfway up the hill at the entrance to Ansouis, this restaurant has earned a reputation as one of the best in the southern Luberon. It serves refined, perfectly executed dishes based on the freshest local ingredients. There's a small terrace, and tables outside need to be reserved well in advance.

LE GRAIN DE SEL

Grand Rue; tel. 04 90 09 85 90;
June-Sept. Wed.-Mon. noon-10pm,
Oct.-May noon- 7pm; €12-20

This simple restaurant is perched at the top of Ansouis. There are plates of charcuterie, tapas, and antipasti, as well as a fish and meat dish of the day. All can be enjoyed on the small terrace overlooking the Luberon. The restaurant is excellent value, given the idyllic location, and it's loved by locals and tourists alike.

UN PATIO EN LUBERON

Route du Grand Four; tel. 04 90 09 94 25;
https://info611076.wixsite.com/patioenluberon;
€100 d

Ansouis is a great place to stay for those wishing to escape the crowds that can overwhelm some Luberon villages. This two-bedroom bed-and-breakfast has bright, well-decorated rooms and a small terrace. Dating back to the 17th century, it's full of characterful stone arches and old wooden beams. There's even a small fountain in the courtyard.

Getting There and Around

The village is **pedestrianized.** There is a small **parking lot** halfway up the hill where the village is built, and there's more parking at the foot of the hill.

BY CAR

Take the D56 from **Cucuron** (8 minutes, 5 kilometers/3 miles) or **Pertuis** (14 minutes, 8 kilometers/5 miles), or the D135 from **Lourmarin** (14 minutes, 10 kilometers/6 miles).

BY BUS

From **Pertuis, Line 8** (www.sudmobilite.fr) runs nine times a day. The journey takes 25 minutes.

The Luberon Orientale into Haute Provence

More remote than the rest of the Luberon, the villages and towns of this region have a gentler feel. In tourist terms, they are as yet relatively undiscovered: not asleep, just gently slumbering; welcoming to visitors, but not overrun by them. The star of the region is Forcalquier, which is crowned by the Notre Dame Chapel built on the ruins of the old citadel. It has a bohemian vibe, and artists spill from their studios to paint on the street. The houses are a little run-down but in a shabby-chic way. Manosque is more workman-like with a pleasant center. It boasts the literary heritage of Jean Giono, and the famed *Apocalypse* painting by Carzou.

Out in the countryside, it's the lavender that draws the crowds. From June to the beginning of August the landscape becomes a patchwork of purple. The higher you go, the later the lavender blooms. Then on the August 15, a crowd that would fill a sports stadium converges on the town of Sault for harvesting competitions and the celebration of all things purple. For gourmands, the town of Banon and its world-famous melt-in-the-mouth goat's cheese is also not to be missed.

ORIENTATION

The town of **Manosque** is situated at the eastern extremity of the Luberon Regional Nature Park and at the southern end of **Haute Provence.** Twenty-three kilometers (14 miles) northwest of Manosque is the town of **Forcalquier,** and farther northwest again are the Lure mountain and the villages of **Banon, Sault,** and **Simiane-la-Rotonde.** To the south of these villages is the town of **Apt** and the Grand and Petit Luberon.

Out in the countryside, the roads are narrow, windy, and often hilly. It can take some time to travel from place to place, particularly if you get stuck behind a tractor or camper van. Sault and Forcalquier are the pick of the places to choose as a base for your stay. Forcalquier is a small town with a vibrant artistic community, and Sault is a large village that has grown prosperous thanks to lavender tourism.

MANOSQUE

Workmanlike and without any immediate visual allure, Manosque can be off-putting. However, it is worth persevering. The center of the town is attractive and there are some interesting sights.

Sights
LA VIERGE NOIR

Notre Dame de Romigier; www.ville-manosque.fr/la-ville/lhistoire-de-ville/vierge-noire-de-dame-de-romigier

According to legend, this wooden statue of the Virgin Mary and her child was uncovered by a workman in the 10th century. Clearing away brambles, he uncovered a sarcophagus containing the wooden statue that had been hidden away to protect it from the Sarrasins. A more likely date for La Vierge Noir is the 12th century. It is now housed in the church of Notre-Dame de Romigier and is venerated by the residents of Manosque for protecting the town, and particularly mothers in childbirth.

FONDATION CARZOU

7-9 boulevard Elemir Bourges; tel. 04 92 87 40 49; www.fondationcarzou.fr; Apr.-Oct. Tues.-Sat. 9:30pm-noon and 2pm-6pm, Nov.-Mar. Wed.-Sat. 2pm-6pm; €3, children under 12 free

Completed in 1991 on the walls of the Chapelle de la Presentation in Manosque, Syrian born artist Carzou's *Apocalypse* painting represents a fear of the year 2000, the danger of rising sea levels, and the disappearance of animal species. Covering more than 666 square meters (7,168 square feet), the work depicts major historical genocides and the four horsemen of the apocalypse in the form of fighter jets. Out of this chaos emerges a symbol of the rebirth of the land: a figure of a woman sprouting branches and leaves. Throughout the painting, the sky remains blue and serene, suggesting that all the human disorder beneath might just be a nightmare. In addition to being a place to view and reflect on the Apocalypse painting, the Carzou Center hosts art and photo exhibitions.

CENTRE JEAN GIONO

3 boulevard Élémir Bourges; tel. 04 92 70 54 54; http://centrejeangiono.com/en; Oct.-Mar. Tues.-Sat. 2pm-6pm, closed school holidays, Apr.-Sept. Tues.-Sat. 10am-noon and 2pm-6pm; €2, under 18 free

Manosque's best known literary son is Jean Giono. He was born in 1895 in Manosque and died there in 1970. His best-known works include *Colline*, *The Horseman on the Roof*, and *The Man Who Planted Trees*. In 1992, to safeguard his legacy, the municipal council established this cultural and exhibition center in an old hôtel particulier. Visitors can view a permanent exhibition, and films and videos that outline the principle stages of the author's life and works. For true aficionados, there's an archive of Giono's papers, as well as a program of cultural events related to the author.

OCCITANE FACTORY TOUR

Chemin Saint-Maurice; tel. 04 92 72 17 19; https://fr.loccitane.com/l-occitane-invites-you-to-manosque,74,1,87870,1107744.htm; June-Sept. daily 9:30am-12:30pm and 2:30pm-7pm; Oct.-May Mon.-Sat. 9:30am-12:30pm and 2:30pm-7pm, reserve in advance for a tour of the museum, factory, or garden; all free

The location of the factory in an industrial zone outside Manosque can be a disappointment, as can the fact that the products on sale in the shop are at high street rather than factory prices. However, for lovers of the brand it's interesting to take a tour of the factory and discover the provenance and restorative qualities of the ingredients in the thousands of face creams, shower gels, and moisturizing creams produced here. There's also a museum charting the history of the company and a garden filled with many of the plants used in the products.

Sports and Recreation
GOLF DU LUBERON

Chemin du Golf, Pierrevert; tel. 04 92 72 17 14; seasonal tee times depend on daylight hours; 18 holes from €58

This picturesque, undulating course isn't long, but subtle slopes and challenging approach shots make up for it. Views to the north of the snow-capped Alps frequently distract golfers from their scorecards.

Food
DOMINIQUE BUCAILLE

715 Avenue des Savels; tel. 04 92 77 59 37; www.restaurant-bucaille.com; Tues. and Thurs.-Sat. 12:30pm-1:30pm and 7:30pm-9pm, Sunday

12:30pm-1:30pm; closed Mon., Wed., and Sun. night (open Sun. night July and Aug.); €38

It's always nice to eat in a restaurant where the chef takes the trouble to tell you the name of grower who provides the restaurant's vegetables. In the case of the carrots that accompany the rack of lamb in a parsley crust, the grower is Monsieur Rabanin. Colorful, flavorful food is served outside on the garden terrace, weather permitting.

L'AROMAVIN

9 Place Marcel Pagnol; tel. 04 13 37 09 17; www.laromavin-restaurant-manosque.com; Wed.-Sun. 9:30am-3pm and 6:30pm-9:30pm, closed Mon. and Tues.; €14-25

Located on the picturesque Marcel Pagnol square, L'Aromavin offers a blackboard of daily specials, a good local wine list, and small à la carte menu. Seared tuna served with Camargue rice is a popular choice. The atmosphere is convivial and the service swift (for Provence!).

L'ANTIDOTE

34 rue Soubreyas; tel. 04 92 76 51 81; Tues. and Thurs.-Sat. 12:30-1:30pm and 7:30pm-9pm, Sun. 12:30pm-1:30pm; closed Mon., Wed., and Sun. night; €21-34

A pleasant terrace, a warm welcome, and relaxed service combine to make l'Antidote a popular restaurant. There's a good selection of competitively priced local wines, and classic dishes are given a local twist, such as king prawns with garlic pesto. The clientele is a good mix of locals and tourists.

SENS ET SAUVEURS

43 boulevard des Tilleuls; tel. 04 92 75 00 00; www.sensetsaveurs.com; Tues.-Wed. and Fri.-Sat. 12:30-1:30pm and 7:30pm-9pm, closed Mon., Thurs. and Sun. night; €18-32

The arches of the old convent building lend a nice theatricality to dining in this semi-gastronomic restaurant. Expect delicious, beautifully presented food, such as steak topped with fried *foie gras*. Make sure you treat your food with due reverence; the

regulars like nothing better than discussing the food with the gravity usually afforded to politics.

Accommodations

HOTEL LE PRE SAINT MICHEL

425 Montee de La Mont Imbert; tel. 04 92 72 14 27; www.presaintmichel.com; €80 d

This simple, small hotel is a good base for exploring the town of Manosque and visiting the Valensole lavender fields. There's a heated pool and a good restaurant, and guests are only a few minutes' drive from the center of Manosque. All rooms have ensuite bathrooms, Wi-Fi, and air-conditioning.

HOSTELERIE LA FUSTE

La Fuste, Valensole; tel. 04 92 72 05 95; www.lafuste.com; €130 d

La Fuste is a 17th-century post house, perfectly situated for visiting the Valensole lavender fields. There's a well-regarded restaurant serving grilled fish and meat, 300-year-old plane trees shade the terrace, and a mature garden surrounds the pool. The 10 rooms are comfortable, but the decor is a little old fashioned. All rooms are ensuite and have air-conditioning.

Getting There and Around

The old center of Manosque is **pedestrianized.** A local bus network is provided by **Manobus** (www.manobus.fr).

BY CAR

The main access road is the A51 motorway heading north from **Aix-en-Provence** toward Sisteron. It takes 50 minutes to cover the 60 kilometers (37 miles) between Aix and Manosque.

BY TRAIN

SCNF trains (www.ter.sncf.com/paca/horaires/recherche) run every couple of hours between Manosque, **Aix-en-Provence,** and **Marseille.** Ticket prices are around €15 euros, and the journey time is 40 minutes from Aix and 1 hour from Marseille.

The **train station** in Manosque is located on Place Frédéric Mistral.

BY BUS

Zou bus **lines 25** and **29** (www.info-ler. fr/465-Fiches-Horaires.html) run nearly every hour between Manosque and **Aix**. The journey takes 1 hour and costs €4.50. The main **bus station** is on Boulevard Charles de Gaulle.

FORCALQUIER

Home to one of Provence's largest and most famous markets, Forcalquier is one of the must-visit towns of Haute Provence. It has a thriving artistic community and a plethora of restaurants, bars, cafés, and appealing squares. Any visit is not complete without a lung-busting climb to La Citadelle.

Sights

LA CITADELLE/NOTRE-DAME DE PROVENCE

The Chapel of Notre-Dame de Provence, built in the 19th century on the ruins of the old citadel, exerts a siren song on visitors. The gold statue of the Virgin Mary glints in the sunshine, challenging all comers to join her near the heavens. The walk up through Forcalquier old town, through charming squares, past restaurant terraces and fountains, becomes progressively more difficult. The last five minutes of the 20-minute climb is up an uneven cobbled path. In a way it's like a mini-pilgrimage; the journey itself is as important as the end destination. Upon arrival there's a feeling of satisfaction and a wonderful panoramic terrace. It was from here in the 12th century that the Counts of Forcalquier exerted dominion over lands stretching in a 100-kilometer (62-mile) radius around them. The striking carillon of the chapel houses 15 bells and rings out at 11:30 every Sunday morning. It is one of the very few remaining manual carillon in Provence. The main route to the citadel is up rue Saint Mary from the Old Town, but it's possible to just discard the map and head upward.

ARTEMESIA

Couvent des Cordeliers;
tel. 04 92 97 50 68;
https://artemisia-museum.fr; Mon.-Fri.,
9:30am-12:30pm and 1:30pm-7pm; €6,
children 10-15 €4, under 10 free

This museum of the senses provides real insight into the history of the Pays de Forcalquier. The botanic richness of the neighboring Montagne de Lure gave rise to

the picturesque streets of Forcalquier

☆ Lavender

the lavender peaks in late July

It's the purple plant with superpowers. Hollywood hasn't made the blockbuster yet but perhaps they might consider it. A dab of the essential oil is said to cure arthritis, and a few squirts on the pillow at night will turn the occupant of a bed into Sleeping Beauty. Sprayed around the entrance to a house, the essence will send scorpions scuttling in the opposite direction; applied just above children's ears before school, it keeps away the head lice. The list is endless. What is more, the star of the show is not shy or retiring; these flowers can be seen out and about all summer. Here's where:

- **Abbey Notre-Dame de Sénanque, Luberon:** Picture-perfect rows of lavender chase up to the walls of the Cistercian Abbey. Leave Gordes on the D177 (page 139).

- **Plateau de Valensole, Manosque:** Just off the D6 from Manosque, direction Valensole, are some of the most extensive fields of lavender in Provence. Continue on past Valensole on the D8 for more sightings.

- **Simiane-la-Rotonde:** Fields of lavender lap at the base of this medieval village and line the D51 road to Banon (page 181).

- **Sault:** There is a 5-kilometer (3.1-mile) lavender walking trail around the base of the village. It takes around 1 hour and 40 minutes to complete. Stop at the car park after the Vallon Distillery between Sault and Aurel. From Sault, take the D164 and almost immediately turn off for Les Michouilles (page 182).

Lavender blooms from **late June to early August.** Phone local tourist offices during your stay to discover where the color is at its peak. A useful rule of thumb is that the higher the altitude, the later it blooms.

a burgeoning pharmaceutical industry in the region, and subsequently to alcoholic distilleries. To make the experience fun as well as interesting, there are sensory games to play for both adults and children based around touch, sense, and hearing.

SALAGON GARDENS

La Prieure, Mane; tel. 04 92 75 70 50; www. musee-de-salagon.com/accueil.html; Wed.-Sun. 10am-6pm, July-Aug. late hours Thurs. until 10pm; €8, €6 children, under 6 free

Human occupation of the site at Salagon

dates back 2000 years. There are traces of Neolithic huts and a Roman villa, succeeded by a Christian site and finally the church that was built in the 11th century. Construction of additional buildings continued until the 19th century. As well as admiring the architectural heritage and enjoying the museum, the principle reason to visit is the gardens. There are four different themed zones: village garden, medieval garden, contemporary garden, and the garden of the senses. Approximately 1,700 species of plants grow on the 6-hectare (15-acre) site. As well as providing a botanic paradise for people to visit, the purpose of the gardens is to study the relationship between humans and plants, from how plants are used in medicines to folklore and foretelling the future.

Shopping
FORCALQUIER MARKET
Place Bourguet

Every Monday morning, Forcalquier hosts one of the largest and most famous markets in Provence. Place de Bourguet and the parking area off rue des Écoles are adorned with the multicolored parasols of the traders. The smell of spit-roasted chicken, bundles of freshly harvested lavender, earthy mounds of dried mushrooms, and steaming plates of couscous and paella are more than enough to justify the town's reputation as a center of the flavors and the senses. as Along with the food, there are bedspreads, tablecloths, artisan leather goods, and plenty of clothes.

DISTILLERIES ET DOMAINES DE PROVENCE
9 avenue Saint Promasse; tel. 04 92 75 15 41; www.distilleries-provence.com; Apr.-Dec. Mon. and Wed.-Sat. 10am-12:30pm and 2pm-6pm

Forcalquier, with its tradition of distilling alcohol from plants harvested on the Mur mountains, is a great place to sample some of the more exotic Provençal alcohols, from absinthe to rinquinquin (peach liqueur) from the Durance valley. The dominant pastis brand is, of course, Ricard, but for something more floral and with more subtlety of flavor, connoisseurs might opt for the Henri Bardouin variety, prepared using a balance of 65 plants and spices.

Food
LE BISTROT PESQUIER
Chemin des Jeux de Mai, Mane; tel. 04 92 74 77 77; www.couventdesminimes-hotelspa.com; daily noon-2pm and 7:30pm-9:30pm; €27-30

Book ahead to secure a table at this bistro restaurant linked with the luxury Couvent de Minimes hotel. The food is delectable, visually stunning, and adventurous. Dishes include grilled cuttlefish, candied egg yolk, and a ginger-infused ratatouille. The setting is magnificent.

AIGO BLANCO
5 Place Vieille; tel. 04 92 75 27 23; daily noon-2pm and 7pm-10pm; €12-24

Tucked away in a side street of Forcalquier's old town, this popular bistro has a large shady terrace and serves classics such as 7-hour cooked Sisteron lamb shank. It's a favorite with locals and tourists alike, and has been pulling in the crowds for years thanks to its eclectic menu.

★ BISTROT HOME
Boulevard des Martyrs; tel. 04 92 77 06 64; noon-3pm and 7pm-10:30pm, closed Wed.; €16-20

Owner Maryame Kuhn surveys every plate that comes from the kitchen to make sure it meets her exacting standards. The menu is small and seasonal. When I visited, Maryame had just been up to the Lure Mountains to pick chanterelle mushrooms to accompany the steak.

Accommodations
BASTIDE SAINT GEORGES
Route de Banon; tel. 04 92 75 72 80; www.bastidesaintgeorges.com; €185 d

Located just outside Forcalquier on the road to Banon, this luxury hotel and spa is a great base from which to explore the town and the Lure mountains. Sumptuous furnishings, spacious rooms, a large pool, and a good restaurant sometimes mean that guests don't travel too far afield. All rooms have air-conditioning, Wi-Fi, and ensuite bathrooms.

LE JAS DE BOUEF
Route de Mallefougasse, Cruis; tel. 04 92 79 01 05; www.lejasduboeuf.fr; €115 d

Book early to get a room at this word-of-mouth success a 30-minute drive north of Forcalquier. It's an off-the-beaten track, out-in-the-middle-of-nature chic retreat that hosts a maximum of 10 guests a night. Rooms overlook an infinity pool, and the summit of the Mountagne de Lure is a hike away. All rooms have ensuite bathrooms. Wi-Fi is not available in all rooms; check when booking.

LA CAMPAGNE SAINT LAZARE
La Louette; tel. 06 80 40 73 58; www.stlazare.net; €140 d

This small, welcoming bed-and-breakfast has a relaxed atmosphere. The garden is verdant and fed by its own water source. Rooms are comfortable rather than ultra-luxurious, and during weekends there's an excellent restaurant on the terrace. All rooms have ensuite. Check when booking for Wi-Fi.

Getting There and Around
The old town is **pedestrianized.**

BY CAR
From **Apt** take the D900, which becomes the D4100. The journey of 43 kilometers (27 miles) takes 40 minutes. From **Manosque** take the D5, which joins the D4100. The 22-kilometer (14-mile) journey takes 30 minutes.

BY BUS
Zou bus **line 25** (www.info-ler.fr/465-Fiches-Horaires.html) runs nearly every hour between Forcalquier and **Aix**. The journey takes 90 minutes and costs €7.50. The main **bus station** is on Boulevard Charles de Gaulle.

SIMIANE-LA-ROTONDE

If there was a prize for having the narrowest streets in Provence, Simiane-La-Rotonde would be one of the top contenders. Although visitors arriving in cars can follow signs to the parking lot next to the château at the top of Simiane, it's much more fun to walk up through the old streets, soaking up the sleepy atmosphere of this remote hill village.

Sights
THE CHÂTEAU AND ITS ROTONDE
Le Village; tel. 04 92 73 11 34; www.simiane-la-rotonde.fr/visite-historique.htm; Mar. 15-Apr. 30 and Sept. 1-Nov. 11 1:30pm-6pm closed Tues., May 1-June 30 10:30am-1pm and 2pm-7pm, July-Aug. 9am-7:30pm; €5.50, €3.50 children, under 12 free

Built around the 11th century on the site of a former Roman settlement, the château gives its name to the village. It was built by Simiane Agoult and features a round keep (rotonde) that can be seen for miles around. Recent restoration work allows visitors to appreciate the living space of the inhabitants during the Middle Ages. There's an exhibition setting out the history of the château and, of course, the architectural perfection of the rotonde's magnificent vaulted ceiling. Visitors can drive to the top of the village and park next to the château; another option is to park next to the entrance to the old village and climb through the atmospheric cobbled streets to the château at the summit.

Festivals
ANCIENT MUSIC FESTIVAL
La Rotonde; tel. 04 84 54 95 10 for tickets; www.festival-simiane.com/accueil.php; first two weeks in Aug.; €30 adult, €10 children, free under 12

Each year there's a different theme. For the 2018 edition, the festival concentrated on the importance of dance in medieval music. Renowned musicians and the unique setting of La Rotonde result in memorable evenings.

Food and Accommodations
RESTAURANT CREPERIE FLEUR DE CACTUS

Rue Ponson du Terrail; tel. 04 92 75 94 65;
Thurs.-Tues. 10am-8pm; €5-15

Located on a typically narrow street in the center of the village, this café is a welcome place to stop on the way up to La Rotonde. There are three tables out on the street, and another five inside. Sweet and savory pancakes are the specialty. Even if you are not hungry, you can just stop for a drink.

GITE LA FONTAINE

La Fontaine; tel. 04 92 73 13 79;
www.gitelafontaine.fr; €79 d

Horses, guinea fowl, cats, dogs, and even a goldfish living in the old fountain, make this is a great place to stay with kids. Clean rooms, a nice pool, and great pizzas prepared by the owner on the weekend complete the offering for nature lovers. Rooms have ensuite bathrooms. Not all have Wi-Fi; check when booking.

LA BUISSE

La Buisse; tel. 04 92 79 10 59;
www.domainelabuisse.com; €110 d

Almost equidistant between Simiane-la-Rotonde and Banon, La Buisse is situated in an idyllic spot in the middle of the countryside. Guests rave about the breakfast and then work off the extra calories on the tennis court and in the pool. There's a barbecue corner at the disposal of clients. All rooms have ensuite bathrooms. Not all have Wi-Fi; check when booking.

Getting There and Around

The old village is **pedestrianized.**

BY CAR

Take the D30 from **Apt** (26 minutes, 23 kilometers/14 miles) or the D201 from **Banon** (11 minutes, 10 kilometers/6 miles).

BY BUS

Line 16 (www.apt.fr/Les-transports.html) runs once a day from either **Banon** (30 minutes) or **Apt** (1h and 30 minutes). The price is €2.60.

SAULT

Although plenty of other villages would like the title, Sault can rightfully claim to be the center of the Provençal lavender industry. It is surrounded by field upon field of the purple bloom, and the tourist office has taken the trouble to mark out an enjoyable circular walk (see below). In the village there are, of course, plenty of shops selling lavender-related products, and on August 15, the village goes lavender crazy when its hosts nearly 30,000 people for the annual lavender festival.

Sights
THE BOYER NOUGAT FACTORY

Place de l'Europe; tel. 04 90 64 00;
www.nougat-boyer.fr; daily 7:30am-7pm; free

The Boyer family have been making nougat in Sault since 1887. Their shop is the oldest of its kind in the Vaucluse, and their nougat some of the tastiest around. Ingredients include lavender honey from the slopes of Mont Ventoux and almonds from trees across the region. Those with a sweet tooth might decide to skip a visit to the small museum outlining the history of nougat production in the region, and plunge straight into the enticing shop.

HISTORIC WALK

Avenue de La Promenade; tel. 04 90 64 01 21

Pick up a brochure at the tourist office and follow the arrows through Sault old town that lead passed the ruins of the château and the Notre Dame de La Tour church.

1: Salagon Gardens 2: Banon is famed for its cheese, which is protected in a wrapping of dried chestnut leaves. 3: Lavender fields surround Simiane-la-Rotonde.

1

2

3

Festivals
LAVENDER FESTIVAL

Sault; tel. 04 90 64 00 23;
www.fetedelalavande.fr; Aug. 15; free

It's hard to imagine, but every August 15 the village of Sault welcomes around 30,000 people to its Lavender Festival. It's the size of crowd more commonly associated with sporting events or pop concerts, not Provençal festivals. At the event there is, of course, plenty of lavender and lavender products, including soap, honey, essential oil, scented candles, and more. What makes the festival unique is its attempt to explore the broader cultural associations with lavender. Musicians play old folk songs, authors sign books, and lavender-harvesting races are held using modern and ancient tools. The races have amateur and professional categories, with the latter attracting entrants from around the world.

Food and Accommodations
LE PROVENÇAL

Rue Porte des Aires;
tel. 04 90 64 09 09;
www.restaurant-le-provencal-sault.fr;
Wed-Sun. noon-2pm and 7pm-9pm, closed Mon. evening and all day Tues.; €18, €22, or €27 menu

Le Provençal is a popular stop in the center of Sault. It offers full-flavored, hearty food that is perhaps a little lacking in finesse. The menus in particular are an excellent value at €22 for three courses. This being Sault, expect lavender to crop up somewhere on the menu.

CHALET REYNARD

Route de Mont Ventoux, Bedoin;
tel. 04 90 61 84 55;
www.chalet-reynard.fr;
Wed.-Mon. noon-3pm; €15-30

Halfway up Mont Ventoux, Chalet Reynard is a Provençal institution. Cyclists stop here for an omelet and fries in the café, while gourmands head upstairs for truffle-inspired dishes. In the winter there is even an adjacent ski-lift and an equipment rental shop.

HOSTELERIE VAL DE SAULT

Ancien Chemin D'Aurel; tel. 04 90 64 01 41;
www.valdesault.com; €165 d

High in the hills next to Sault, overlooking the lavender fields, is this regional stalwart. It's known for its friendly staff, and restaurant offering good local produce. Rooms have been nicely updated over the years, and there's a pool, tennis court, and— somewhat incongruously—a resident peacock. All rooms have Wi-Fi and ensuite bathrooms.

Getting There and Around
BY CAR

Pick up the D30 outside **Simiane-la-Rotonde** and head north for 20 kilometers (12 miles), which takes 23 minutes. From **Apt** follow the D34 for 30 km taking 38 minutes.

BY BUS

The **Line 16** bus from **Apt** (www.apt.fr/Les-transports.html for timetables) runs three times a day, and the trip takes just over an hour.

BANON

Banon is famed throughout France for its goat cheese. Even the finest Parisian restaurants will find space on their crowded cheeseboards for a ripe Banon. The village's other claim to fame is Le Bluet, the 11th-largest bookshop in France. Cheese and book shop aside, Banon is a bustling place during the tourist season, when the main cafés fill up with cyclists and hikers. There's not a lot to see, but even so, it's a pleasant place to stop when touring Haute Provence.

Sights
LE BLEUET

Rue Saint Just; tel. 04 92 73 25 85;
www.lebleuet.fr; daily 10am-7pm

Out in the middle of the wilds of Provence, it is something of a wonder that this shop has survived in the internet age. The stock is mainly French language, but it is still interesting to browse and gain an appreciation of the French publishing industry, which remains resolutely high-brow.

Food and Accommodations

FROMAGERIE DE BANON
*Route Carniol; tel. 04 92 73 25 03;
www.fromagerie-banon.fr; Mon.-Fri. 2:30pm-5:30pm;
€3.50 for a Banon cheese*

This is fast food Provençal style and probably the greatest, simplest takeaway available in the world. Buy a Banon goat's cheese from the village fromagerie, grab a baguette, and you are away. Rather than the greasy paper wrapping of a burger, you gently unfold dried chestnut leaves that are secured around the cheese with a raffia tie. Note, these are not just any chestnut leaves; they have been soaked in wine to impregnate the cheese with flavor. Eaten at perfect ripeness, a Banon goat's cheese hovers on the dividing line between solid and liquid, and can simply be mopped up with the end of a baguette. The good news is that with each cheese measuring 75 to 85 millimeters (3 to 3.5 inches) in diameter and between 20 and 30 millimeters (0.7 and 1.1 inches) high, there should be enough for two to share—unless you are hungry!

CHARCUTERIE LA BRINDILLE MELCHIO
*Place de La Republique; tel. 04 92 73 23 04;
Apr.-Sept. Wed.-Mon. 8:30am-12:30pm and
2:30pm-6pm, Oct.-Mar. Wed.-Sun.; €5 for a brindille*

Banon is also known for its *brindilles*, which are an elongated versions of the more familiar *saucisson*. The Brindille Melchio charcuterie shop is the place to taste this delicacy. Typically, they are a couple of centimeters thick and nearly half a meter long. They are so popular, the shop ships them around the world. Other delights include Provence's answer to Nutella, a chestnut cream that's a perfect filling for pancakes.

LES VOYAGEURS
*Rue de la Bourgade; tel. 04 92 73 21 02;
daily noon-2.30pm and 7.30pm-9.30pm; €12-20*

The most well-known café restaurant in town is the Voyageurs. Its name sums up the clientele: cyclists and tourists who need to be well fed before embarking on the next stage of their journey. The food is good, but by no means gastronomic, and the large terrace a fun bustling place to eat lunch or supper.

LA PARENTHESE
*Route de Forcalquier; tel. 09 50 79 45 71;
https://laparenthese-banon.com; €86 d*

This simple no-fuss bed-and-breakfast is a short walk from the center of Banon, offering clean modern decor, a small garden, and a couple of family rooms that sleep up to four. There are good views out over the surrounding countryside, and everything you need for an enjoyable stay is provided. It's excellent value. All rooms have Wi-Fi and ensuite bathrooms.

Getting There and Around
Banon is a small village and is best explored **on foot.**

BY CAR
Take the D201 and D51 from **Simian La Rotonde** (12 minutes, 10 kilometers/6 miles). From **Forcalquier,** take the D950 (25 minutes, 25 kilometers/16 miles).

BY BUS
Line 16 (www.apt.fr/Les-transports.html) runs once a day from either **Banon** (30 minutes) or **Apt** (60 minutes). The price is €2.60. The **B1** bus runs twice a day to and from **Manosque;** the trip takes 80 minutes.

Aix-en-Provence

Most cities have their detractors. It's human nature. Give people the slightest opportunity to complain and they will find something to complain about. Yet, in 12 years living just north of Aix-en-Provence, I have never heard a bad word said about the place. Mention Aix (pronounced "X") and people smile, almost involuntarily. The city seems to have an inherent positive energy. It makes people happy.

There are obvious reasons to visit Aix, including: Cézanne's artistic legacy, the world-class Musée Granet, picturesque daily markets, eclectic shops, and numerous excellent restaurants. What is less apparent from the pages of most guidebooks and what surprises people about Aix is how time slips pleasantly away in the embrace of her streets.

Highlights

Look for ★ to find recommended sights, activities, dining, and lodging.

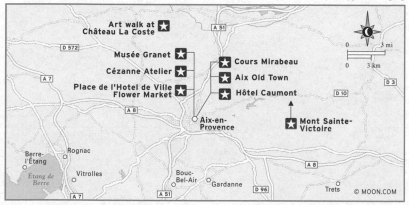

★ **Cours Mirabeau:** The year-round heart of Aix-en-Provence, the Cours is shady in the summer and a sun trap in the winter—the epitome of café society at its southern best (page 194).

★ **Aix Old Town (La Vieille Ville):** With squares, fountains, narrow streets, eclectic shops, plentiful cafés and restaurants, this area is simply a joy to wander around (page 194).

★ **Hôtel Caumont:** This recently renovated hôtel particulier in the Mazarin district offers a garden restaurant and holds major art exhibitions (page 199).

★ **Musée Granet:** The Granet museum hosts an extensive collection of modern art, including works by Picasso, Matisse, Monet, and Klee, as well as 10 Cézanne originals (page 200).

★ **Cézanne Atelier:** Cézanne's last studio has been re-created to mirror its condition at the time of his death (page 200).

★ **Place de l'Hotel de Ville flower market:** Every day the Place de l'Hotel de Ville is transformed into a botanic paradise centered around an imposing 18th-century fountain (page 208).

★ **Mont Sainte-Victoire:** Much-painted by Cézanne, this mountain to the east of Aix offers great hiking and/or a driving tour, taking in chic Le Tholonet and Vauvenargues, where Picasso is buried (page 221).

★ **Art walk at Château La Coste:** This vineyard, hotel, and modern art destination—including a famed Louise Bourgeois spider installation—is located 20 minutes north of Aix (page 223).

Aix-en-Provence

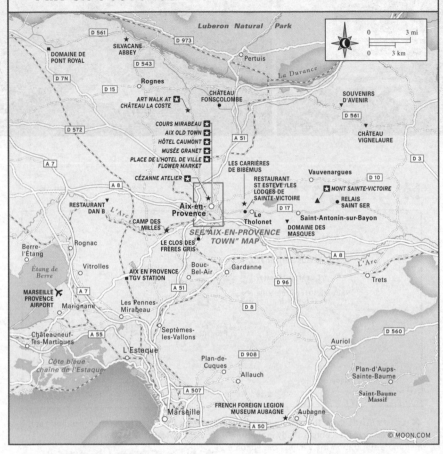

Luberon Natural Park

D 561
SILVACANE ABBEY
D 973
DOMAINE DE PONT ROYAL
D 543
Pertuis
La Durance
D 7N
Rognes
D 15
CHÂTEAU FONSCOLOMBE
ART WALK AT CHÂTEAU LA COSTE
SOUVENIRS D'AVENIR
D 572
COURS MIRABEAU
AIX OLD TOWN
HÔTEL CAUMONT
MUSÉE GRANET
PLACE DE L'HOTEL DE VILLE
FLOWER MARKET
CÉZANNE ATELIER
A 51
D 561
CHÂTEAU VIGNELAURE
D 3
A 7
LES CARRIÈRES DE BIBEMUS
Vauvenargues
D 10
RESTAURANT ST ESTEVE /LES LODGES DE SAINTE-VICTOIRE
MONT SAINTE-VICTOIRE
RELAIS SAINT SER
A 8
Aix-en-Provence
D 17
Saint-Antonin-sur-Bayon
RESTAURANT DAN B
L'Arc
CAMP DES MILLES
Le Tholonet
DOMAINE DES MASQUES
SEE "AIX-EN-PROVENCE TOWN" MAP
Rognac
LE CLOS DES FRÈRES GRIS
A 8
L'Arc
Berre-l'Étang
Vitrolles
Bouc-Bel-Air
Gardanne
Trets
Étang de Berre
AIX EN PROVENCE TGV STATION
A 51
D 96
MARSEILLE PROVENCE AIRPORT
A 7
Les Pennes-Mirabeau
D 8
Marignane
Châteauneuf-les-Martigues
A 55
Septèmes-les-Vallons
Auriol
D 560
L'Estaque
Plan-de-Cuques
D 908
Plan-d'Aups-Sainte-Baume
Côte bleue chaîne de l'Estaque
Allauch
Saint-Baume Massif
A 507
Marseille
FRENCH FOREIGN LEGION MUSEUM AUBAGNE
Aubagne
A 50
0   3 mi
0   3 km
© MOON.COM

For a city there is very little traffic noise, as the old town is pedestrianized, as is most of the main street, the Cours Mirabeau. In the Mazarin Quarter, filled with its hôtel particuliers, people stroll happily on the roads, rarely disturbed by cars but lulled instead by the sound of trickling fountains. This is the unnoticed song of the city. There are some 43 fountains altogether. Turn a few corners in the old town, and you'll quickly find yourself in a picturesque small square, next to an ancient moss-covered fountain. People congregate around them, and they sit and chat on the surrounding walls, treating them like pieces of furniture. The fountains are identifiable meeting points in what can otherwise be a confusing maze of streets. They are places to cool down when the summer sun gets too hot. They are the hub of everyday life.

Aix's other secret is that, from April to the end of September, a park emerges leaf by leaf in its heart. The Cours Mirabeau appears on

Previous: A novel way to cool rosé is in the fountain at Place des 3 Ormeaux in Aix-en-Provence; the daily flower market at Aix; visiting the Cézanne Atelier takes you into the personal universe of the painter.

maps as a road, but it really shouldn't. On either side of this grand avenue, running the entire 440 meters (1,443 feet) of its length, stand giant, centuries-old plane trees. They transform the strong Provençal light into soft dappled shadow, creating a natural amphitheater with their arching branches and verdant greenery. The senses of inhabitants and visitors are fooled by this conjuring trick of nature: People walk more slowly, they feel less threatened by work deadlines, and they are more inclined to pause for a chat and a drink on the terrace of one of the many cafés. There are benches and buskers, and of course more fountains, four of them in total on the Cours, gurgling away, persuading urban life to retreat.

Much of the city's beauty is owed to the Counts of Provence, who ruled between the 12th and the 16th centuries. Aix-en-Provence was declared the capital of the region, and peace promoted construction, including the Cistercian Abbey at Silvacane to the north of Aix, and the Cathedral of Saint-Sauveur in the heart of the city. The most cherished of the Counts was the penultimate, Good King René (1430-1480), who was a great promoter of the arts in the city, and whose rule is commemorated by a statue on the Cours Mirabeau. When Provence became part of France after René's death, a regional parliament made the city a playground for France's nobility, and their grand houses (hôtel particuliers), which today give Aix so much of its architectural character.

The development continues today. The center of the city is being revitalized with the creation of a high-speed bus route and the pedestrianization of three squares in the old town. A new Picasso museum will open in 2021, housing the private collection of Catherine Hutin, the daughter of Jacqueline, Pablo Picasso's last wife.

The end result is that Aix ends up feeling more like a village than a metropolis, a place to return to again and again. It's a city like no other.

ORIENTATION

Aix slopes gently from north to south toward the **Arc river.** To the east, the rocky peak of **Mont Sainte-Victoire** pierces the skyline. The historic center is relatively small and can be crossed on foot in a little more than 20 minutes. It is divided into three main neighborhoods, the Cours Mirabeau, Aix old town, and Quartier Mazarin. These central neighborhoods are surrounded by a ring road that delineates the outskirts of Aix.

Cours Mirabeau is a large tree-lined avenue that divides the other two central neighborhoods of Aix Old Town from Quartier Mazarin. It begins in a cascade of water at the imposing **Rotonde fountain** in the West, and ends with a pleasing trickle near the **Fountain of King Roi René** in the East. The Cours is the center for people watching; it is lined with **cafés** with large terraces on the north side, and with **banks, offices,** and **shops** on the south side.

Aix Old Town (Vieux Vieille), to the north of the Cours Mirabeau, consists of a maze of small streets filled with **shops** and plentiful **restaurants.** At times it feels like it might be sensible to trail a ball of string behind you so that you find your way back to where you started. The tight, confusing layout of this neighborhood is broken up by several large **market squares** and **open spaces.** In particular, there's **Place de l'Hotel de Ville** in the heart of the old town, and **Places Verdun, Prêcheurs,** and **Madeleine** to the east.

The **Mazarin quarter** south of the Cours Mirabeau has a block layout and is relatively easy to navigate. The quarter is characterized by numerous imposing town houses (**hôtel particuliers**) built in the 17th and 18th centuries by the nobility. The neighborhood is now a mix of **historic sites, museums, apartments, offices,** and the occasional restaurant and shop. The main sights are the **Musée Granet** and **Hôtel Caumont.**

The **ring road** that surrounds the center changes its name as it loops around the city, from **boulevard de Roi René** as it leaves

Aix-en-Provence Itinerary Ideas

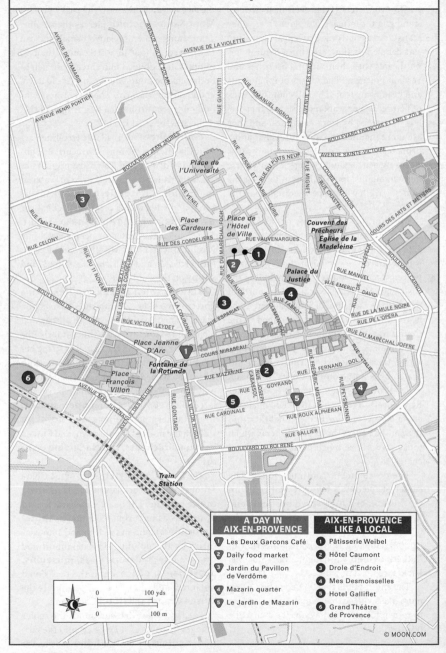

AVENUE DE LA VIOLETTE
AVENUE DES TAMARIS
AVENUE PHILIPPE SOCARD
AVENUE HENRI PONTIER
RUE GIANOTTI
RUE EMMANUEL SIGNORET
AVENUE JULES ISAAC
BOULEVARD FRANÇOIS ET EMILE ZOLA
AVENUE SAINTE-VICTOIRE
BOULEVARD JEAN JAURÈS
Place de l'Université
RUE PIERRE ET MARIE CURIE
RUE DU PUITS NEUF
RUE MIGNET
COURS SAINT-LOUIS
RUE CHASTEL
COURS DES ARTS ET MÉTIERS
RUE ÉMILE TAVAN
3
Place des Cardeurs
RUE VENEL
Place de l'Hôtel de Ville
Couvent des Prêcheurs
Église de la Madeleine
RUE CELONY
RUE DU MARÉCHAL FOCH
RUE DES CORDELIERS
RUE VAUVENARGUES
LACÉPÈDE
BOULEVARD CARNOT
RUE DU 11 NOVEMBRE
COURS SEXTIUS
RUE LISSE DES CORDELIERS
RUE DE LA COURONNE
2 **1**
RUE ALUDE
Palace du Justice
RUE MANUEL
RUE EMERIC DAVID
3
RUE FABROT
4
RUE CLÉMENCEAU
RUE DE LA MULE NOIRE
RUE DE L'OPÉRA
BOULEVARD DE LA RÉPUBLIQUE
RUE VICTOR LEYDET
RUE ESPARIAT
RUE DU MARÉCHAL JOFFRE
Place Jeanne D'Arc
1
COURS MIRABEAU
RUE FRÉDÉRIC MISTRAL
RUE D'ITALIE
6
Place François Villon
Fontaine de la Rotunde
RUE MAZARINE
2
RUE FERNAND DOL
4
AVENUE MAX JUVÉNAL
AVENUE DES BELGES
AVENUE VICTOR HUGO
RUE GONTARD
RUE JOSEPH CABASSOL
GOYRAND
RUE PEYSSONNEL
RUE DE
5
RUE CARDINALE
5
RUE ROUX ALPHÉRAN
RUE SALLIER
BOULEVARD DU ROI RENÉ
Train Station

A DAY IN AIX-EN-PROVENCE

1. Les Deux Garcons Café
2. Daily food market
3. Jardin du Pavillon de Verdôme
4. Mazarin quarter
5. Le Jardin de Mazarin

AIX-EN-PROVENCE LIKE A LOCAL

1. Pâtisserie Weibel
2. Hôtel Caumont
3. Drole d'Endroit
4. Mes Desmoisselles
5. Hotel Galliflet
6. Grand Théâtre de Provence

0   100 yds
0   100 m

© MOON.COM

the Rotonde fountain, to **Cours Saint Louis, boulevard Aristride Briand,** and finally **Cours Sextius** as it returns to La Rotonde. The city's main parks—**Jourdan** to the south, **Rambot** to the east, and **Vendôme** to the northwest—are located just off this ring road, in the **Aix Outskirts. Cézanne's atelier** and the main view point from which he painted Mont Sainte-Victoire are a short distance to the north.

PLANNING YOUR TIME

Aix-en-Provence is a small city. Although historic sites and museums are plentiful, most people will feel that two days is long enough to explore the center of Aix. Another day could easily be added to explore the outskirts of the city. If you plan to stay longer than this, use Aix as a base to head into the surrounding countryside (**Pays d'Aix-en-Provence**); perhaps schedule a couple of wine tastings and consider hiking and biking options. In the evening you can return to the city to enjoy the excellent choice of restaurants, cultural events, and city vibe.

When you're trying to decide what to visit, bear in mind that the tourist office offers a **City Pass,** which includes visits to 25 cultural sites and a further 30 for a reduced price, plus access to Aix-en-Bus. The adult prices are €25 for 24 hours, €34 for 48 hours, and €43 for 72 hrs. There are reduced prices for children under 13; under 3 years free.

Itinerary Ideas

A DAY IN AIX-EN-PROVENCE

1 Have breakfast at **Les Deux Garcons Café** on Cours Mirabeau. Sit in the dappled shade across from a trickling fountain, and enjoy a café crème and a croissant while watching the city slowly come to life.

2 Leave the café and walk down rue Fabrot. Browse the **boutiques** of the old town before heading for the vibrant **daily food market** in Place Richelme. There's plenty to make a picnic: olives, tapenade, goat's cheese, *saucisson*, and seasonal fruit.

3 A short walk to the northwest at the top of the Cours Sextius, enjoy a shady picnic in the verdant **Jardin du Pavillon de Vendôme.**

4 Return to the Cours Mirabeau, cross the road and head into the **Mazarin quarter.** Immerse yourself in the enriching art collection of the **Musée Granet.**

5 Enjoy a romantic meal on the secluded terrace of **Le Jardin de Mazarin** restaurant.

AIX-EN-PROVENCE LIKE A LOCAL

1 Pick up a croissant or pain au chocolat, and something more sugary for later in the day at **Pâtisserie Weibel** in the old town. Wash it down with an espresso.

2 Explore the grandeur of one of Aix's most celebrated town houses, the **Hôtel Caumont.** Tour the latest art exhibition and stop for a pre-lunch drink in the formal gardens.

3 Avoid the crowds and eat inside at **Drole d'Endroit,** a hidden gem of a restaurant.

4 Enjoy a little light **shopping** in the old town, perhaps picking up a new piece for your wardrobe from the on-trend **Mes Desmoisselles.**

5 Have a sundown drink in the gardens of **Hotel Galliflet** in the Mazarin quarter.

6 Take in opera or classical music at the **Grand Théâtre de Provence.**

THE PAYS D'AIX

1 Leave Aix and drive into the surrounding countryside. Enjoy a wine tasting at picturesque **Domaine des Masques,** the only vineyard on the rocky ridge that surrounds the base of Mont Sainte-Victoire.

2 Eat lunch at the **Relais de Saint Ser** on the terrace, with a stunning view of vines, olive groves, and in the distance the Massif de la Sainte-Baume.

3 Loop around to the north face of Mont Sainte-Victoire, and head north toward the Durance, stopping for a tour of the 12th-century Cistercian, **Silvacane Abbey.**

4 On your way back to Aix, stop and enjoy the art walk at **Château La Coste.** Afterward, have a bite to eat in one of the vineyard's four restaurants.

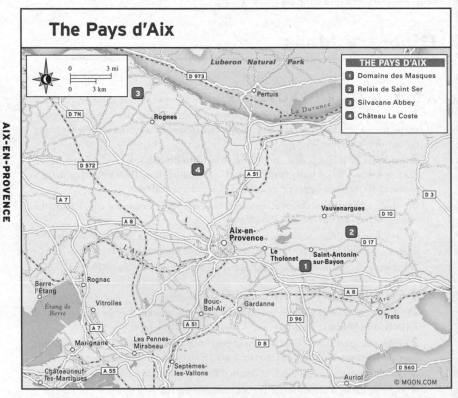

The Pays d'Aix

THE PAYS D'AIX
1 Domaine des Masques
2 Relais de Saint Ser
3 Silvacane Abbey
4 Château La Coste

© MOON.COM

Aix-en-Provence Town

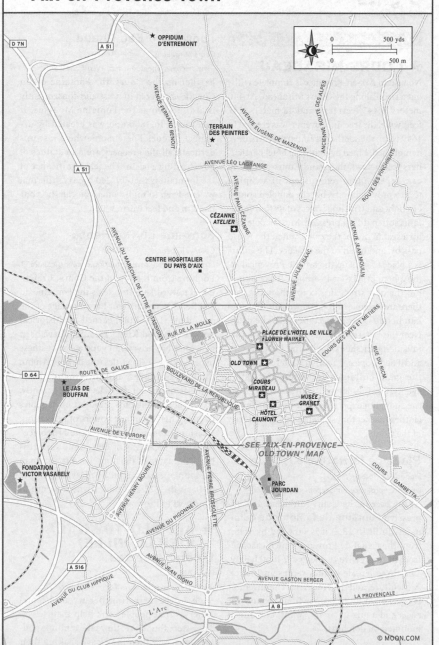

D 7N

A 51

★ OPPIDUM
D'ENTREMONT

A 51

AVENUE FERNAND BENOIT

AVENUE EUGÈNE DE MAZENOD

ANCIENNE ROUTE DES ALPES

ROUTE DES PINCHINATS

0   500 yds

0   500 m

★ TERRAIN
DES PEINTRES

AVENUE LÉO LAGRANGE

AVENUE PAUL CÉZANNE

CÉZANNE
ATELIER ★

CENTRE HOSPITALIER
DU PAYS D'AIX ■

AVENUE DU MARÉCHAL DE LATTRE DE TASSIGNY

AVENUE JULES ISAAC

AVENUE JEAN MOULIN

RUE DE LA MOLLE

PLACE DE L'HÔTEL DE VILLE
FLOWER MARKET ★

COURS DES ARTS ET MÉTIERS

RUE DU RIOM

D 64

ROUTE DE GALICE

LE JAS DE
BOUFFAN ★

BOULEVARD DE LA RÉPUBLIQUE

OLD TOWN ★

COURS
MIRABEAU
★

MUSÉE
GRANET
★

HÔTEL
CAUMONT ★

AVENUE DE L'EUROPE

SEE "AIX-EN-PROVENCE
OLD TOWN" MAP

FONDATION
VICTOR VASARELY ★

AVENUE HENRY MOURET

AVENUE PIERRE BROSSOLETTE

PARC
JOURDAN ■

COURS GAMBETTA

AVENUE DU PIGONNET

AVENUE JEAN GIONO

A 516

AVENUE DU CLUB HIPPIQUE

AVENUE GASTON BERGER

LA PROVENÇALE

A 8

L'Arc

© MOON.COM

Sights

★ COURS MIRABEAU

No visit to Aix-en-Provence is complete without a stroll along the Cours Mirabeau. At 440 meters (1,443 feet) long and 48 meters (147 feet) wide, the tree lined avenue was created in 1649 when the southern ramparts of Aix were demolished. Lined by imposing hôtel particuliers (see below), the grand Cours Mirabeau can appear more reminiscent of a capital than a provincial city, but the dappled southern light and trickling waters of its four fountains soften this impression. Most people pull up a seat in one of the cafés, watch the world pass by, and listen to the buskers. The Cours is a place to soak up the unique Provençal atmosphere of Aix-en-Provence. It's certainly not the best street in Aix for shopping, but there are a couple of good paper, painting, and handicraft stores wedged between the cafés. Near the eastern end of the road there are various designer shops, including Longchamps and The Kooples, but other than restaurants, the main buildings are banks and estate agents. On Tuesday and Thursday mornings, the shopping experience is transformed by a clothes market that stretches up the majority of the Cours.

Place de la Rotonde

Place de La Rotonde;

www.aixenprovencetourism.com/en/fiche/2677

At the base of the Cours Mirabeau, the impressive **Fontaine de la Rotonde** dominates. Built in 1860 it is now fed by water from the Canal de Provence which cascades from its impressive 18-meter (59-foot) height. The three female statues represent Justice, Agriculture, and the Fine Arts. The ensemble is completed by 12 bronze lions around the base, and a mix of sirens, swans, and angels mounted on dolphins.

Fontaine d'Eau Chaud

Cours Mirabeau;

www.aixenprovencetourism.com/en/fiche/2612

Farther up the Cours, the Fontaine d'Eau Chaude is covered in moss and consequently is also known as the Fontaine Moussue. It dates back to 1866 and was created by architect Jacques Fossé. Somewhere lost underneath all the greenery are four statues of boys holding a basin. The real significance of the fountain is that it is fed by Aix's thermal waters. Even in mid-winter you can dip your hand in and feel warm water.

Fontaine du Roi René

Cours Mirabeau;

http://www.aixenprovencetourism.com/en/fiche/2673

Looking from the top of the Cours, straight down toward La Rotonde, is the Fontaine du Roi René. Renowned for his patronage of the arts, René (1430-1480) earned the historical honorific "Good King." He might have been generous, but he was not good at the business of being king, losing titles (the duke of Anjou, the king of Naples, and the king of Sicily) with seemingly carefree alacrity. Apparently, he was able to take his mind off his troubles by using his legendary powers of relaxation: "warming yourself on King René's fireplace" is a still a local way of describing sunbathing. The statue of the king that sits on top of the fountain was sculpted by David D'Angers in Paris in 1822 and took a whole month to transport to Provence.

★ AIX OLD TOWN (LA VIEILLE VILLE)
L'Hôtel Albertas

Place Albertas;

www.aixenprovencetourism.com/en/fiche/2626

Such is the arresting beauty of L'Hôtel Albertas that people can't help themselves: They stop, they stare, they take multiple photographs, and then they leave shaking their heads in wonder. The hotel takes its name from a family of parliamentarians from the Italian town of Alba. Its current form dates back to 1745, when the family acquired the houses surrounding the hotel and with the help of architect George Vallon, demolished them to create a look reminiscent of the royal squares in Paris. The architecture of the façade is regency with a nod to the baroque. The central fountain was added in 1912 and was designed by students of the Aix art school. The hotel is now divided into offices and private residences, and so, although Casanova once visited, the public now can't.

Cathédrale Saint-Sauveur

34 Place des Martyrs-de-la-Résistance;
04 42 23 47 40; www.aixenprovencetourism.com/en/
fiche/2713; open daily 8am-7:30pm; free

As you look down on Aix from afar, the bell tower of the Saint-Sauveur Cathedral dwarfs all the other buildings. However, once you enter the warren of narrow streets in the old town, the cathedral disappears from view. Many visit by chance, stumbling upon the building as they meander between shops. There's no imposing forecourt. Instead, the 16th-century entrance, carved from walnut, is set just meters back from the main thoroughfare. Inside it's cool and peaceful. The cathedral is said to be built on the site of an old Roman temple to Apollo. Christian construction started around 500, and continued intermittently until the 18th century. Some find the cathedral a confusing mishmash of Romanesque, baroque, and Gothic architecture. Victorian art critic John Rushkin called it, "ugly enough" and described the interior as "corrupt Roman." Others, like me, find it a delightful fusion of styles. Enjoyable elements include the carved Romanesque pillars of the cloisters, depicting the beast of the revelation: man, lion, eagle and bull.

Art lovers are lured to Saint-Sauveur by the chance to see the *Burning Bush Triptych* by the Renaissance painter Nicolas Froment. In the center of the painting, the Virgin Mary is depicted with her child, sitting on a burning bush. At her feet, Moses is shown, amazed by the vision before him. On either side are portraits of King René and his wife Jeanne de Laval. The painting was commissioned by King René in 1475.

Les 3 Places

Place Precheurs/Verdun/Madeleine, Aix-en-Provence

By the fall of 2019, Place de Prêcheurs, Place de Verdun, and Place de la Madeleine will

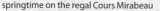
springtime on the regal Cours Mirabeau

Aix-en-Provence Old Town

0   100 yds

0   100 m

GALERIE IMBERT

BOULEVARD JEAN JAURÈS

Place de l'Université

RUE DE LA MOLLE

RUE DU BON PASTEUR

HÔTEL MAYNIER D'OPPÈDE

JARDIN DU PAVILLON DE VENDÔME

THERMES SEXTUS

RUE ÉMILE TAVAN

RUE GAUFFREDY

RUE DU CANCEL

RUE MÉRINDOL

Place des Cardeurs

RUE CELONY

RUE DES CORDELIERS

LA VIDA LOCA

RUE DU 11 NOVEMBRE 1918

RUE LIEUTAUD

LE ZINC DE HUGO

EL BOLERO

LA CITA

RUE DES CHARTREUX

COURS SEXTIUS

RUE LISSE DES CORDELIERS

RUE FERMÉE

LA BOUCHE À OREILLE

RUE DES TANNEURS

RUE DU DOCTEUR JEAN D'ARGELOS

BOULEVARD DE LA RÉPUBLIQUE

RUE BRUEYS

RUE IRMA MOREAU

RUE DES BERNARDINES

LES VIEILLES CANAILLES

RUE DE L'ENTREPÔT

RUE VICTOR LEYDET

HOTEL DE FRANCE

TRAVERSE DE L'AIGLE D'OR

RUE DU BRAS D'OR

LA ROTONDE

Place Jeanne D'Arc

L'ESTELLO

DARIUS CAFÉ

Fontaine de la Rotonde

AVENUE MAX JUVENAL

GRAND THÉÂTRE DE PROVENCE

TOURIST OFFICE

PLACE DE LA ROTONDE

Place François Villon

DARIUS MILHAUD CONSERVATOIRE

LE PAVILLON-NOIR

AVENUE MAX JUVENAL

AVENUE DES BELGES

HOTEL SAINT CHRISTOPHE

AVENUE VICTOR HUGO

RUE GONTARD

AVENUE MAX JUVENAL

POLICE STATION

HOTEL CÉZANNE

AIX CENTER BUS STATION

RUE VICTOR HUGO

Train Station

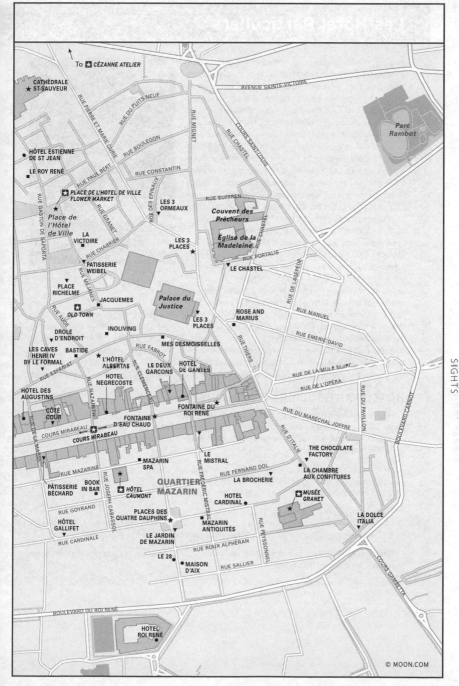

AIX-EN-PROVENCE

SIGHTS

Les Hôtel Particuliers

Also responsible for the unique atmosphere of the Cours Mirabeau are the many hôtel particuliers that line either side. Don't let the name fool you: Hôtel particuliers are townhouses—not hotels— that were built largely during the 17th and 18th centuries and were the main residences of nobles. Thanks to its parliament and university Aix attracted the upper classes of French society in unparalleled numbers. At the beginning of the 17th century, it is estimated 13 percent of the city's population was composed of nobility. Of course they all needed somewhere to live, and so began a construction boom of lavish town houses. Today the concentration of hôtel particuliers on the Cours Mirabeau lends the road its unique charm, even if many are now used for mundane purposes such as supermarkets and insurance brokers.

Hôtel Albertas's current form dates back to 1745.

Of particular note is number 20, Hotel Forbin. In 1701, from the balcony of this building, the Duke of Burgundy watched 300 people fight each other with oranges for his entertainment. In the same building in 1807, Napoleon's sister Pauline Borghese received guests from the old French nobility, taking the advice of her brother that in the "good town of Aix ... people and especially the fair sex do not like the classes to mix." This theme was picked up by the writer Émile Zola who, in the later half of the 19th century, used to sit in the Deux Garcons café on the Cours Mirabeau and observe Aix society. The fictional town of Plassans that Zola created in his *Les Rougon-Macquart* novel series is loosely based on Aix, where the nobility strolled up the south side of the Cours backed by a quarter filled with hôtel particuliers and the people frequented the cafés on the north side. The two sections of society never met.

HÔTEL PARTICULIERS WORTH VISITING

- **Hôtel Estienne de St Jean,** 17 rue Gaston de Saporta, used to be called the "musée du vieil Aix," and houses a collection of objects (furniture, clothes, santons, and pottery), which together tell the story of the history of Aix-en-Provence. Open Wednesday to Monday 10am-12:30pm and 1:30-5pm.

- **Hôtel Caumont Art Center,** 3 rue Joseph Cabassol, is a restored hôtel particulier and the best place to gain an appreciation of the lifestyle of the nobility in the 18th century. See the Quartier Mazarin sights section below for hours.

- **Hôtel Maynier d'Oppède,** 21 rue Gaston de Saporta, now houses the institute of French studies for foreign students. There are also summer concerts in the courtyard. There are no specific opening hours but you can usually poke your head in and look around.

- **Hôtel Gallifet,** 52 rue Cardinale, is an art center, café, and venue for jazz concerts. It's open noon-6pm Tuesday to Sunday.

have been transformed into the second-largest pedestrianized space in Aix. During the excavation, the ruins of the Palace of the Counts of Provence dating back to the 12th century were uncovered. These are located at the bottom of the stairs that lead up to the Palais du Justice and will be visible through glass pavement slabs. The finished area promises to be a great addition to Aix-en-Provence.

QUARTIER MAZARIN
★ Hôtel Caumont

3 rue Joseph Cabassol; tel. 04 42 20 70 01; www.caumont-centredart.com; May-Sept. 10am-7pm, late hours Fri. until 8:30pm, Oct.-Apr. 10am-6pm; €14 adults, €10 7-17, free under 7, audio guide €3

Built between 1715 and 1742 by the architect Robert de Cotte for the Marquess of Cabannes, the Hôtel Caumont has been largely restored to its original state. It presents a unique opportunity to experience the grandeur and luxury in which the French nobility lived in the 18th century.

A visit begins with the exploration of the restored part of the hôtel particulier, starting in the large courtyard, where ample space was provided for the carriages of guests. The façade, in classical French style with plentiful horizontal and vertical lines, was completed by both Aixoise and Parisian artisans, creating a pleasing mix of styles. Inside, the entrance hall wows with its intricate high staircase, considered a showstopper even at the time of construction. The fountain in the corner of the entrance hall is testament to the wealth of the occupants; in the 18th century water was precious, and to have an interior fountain was the ultimate luxury. Climbing the staircase, the bedroom of the young Pauline de Caumont has been re-created, its intimate nature reflecting the fashion of the Louis XV era. Next door, the music room is illustrative of the aspirations of the owners. Typically, only princely palaces had rooms dedicated to specific pursuits, but in the 18th century wealthy nobles began to copy the idea.

The second part of the visit takes in an art exhibition in the east wing of the hotel (the former servant's quarters). The exhibition changes twice a year, typically focusing on individual painters with strong links to the region.

Finally the visit ends in the gardens of the hotel. These have been restored to the original design of Robert de Cotte. The layout is geometric and formal, and the plants are representative of those used at the time the hotel was constructed. There is a café-restaurant

Fontaine des Quatre-Dauphins, the heart of the Mazarin Quarter

overlooking the gardens, and in summer jazz evenings take place every Saturday.

Places des Quatre Dauphins

Place des Quatre Dauphins;
www.aixenprovencetourism.com/en/fiche/2631

In 1646 Archbishop Mazarin of Aix, brother of the famed Cardinal, was authorized by Louis XIV of France to begin construction of a new residential quarter of Aix. At its heart he placed the Places des Quatre Dauphins. Installed at the center is a fountain by sculptor Jean Claude Rambot. Four dolphins surround a pyramid, on top of which initially stood a statue of Saint Michel, later replaced by the Maltese Cross, and finally a pinecone. Writing in the Revue des Deux Mondes in 1932, Louis Gillet likened the fountain to a musical toy "that sends the idle hours to sleep and charms the silence of this quiet provincial place." While ambient noise may intrude more these days, the square, encircled as it is by a hôtel particulier, is still a place to stop, pause, and reflect.

★ Musée Granet

Place Saint-Jean de Malte; tel. 04 42 52 88 32;
www.museegranet-aixenprovence.fr/nc/accueil.html;
June 9-Sept. 23 Tues.-Sun., 10am-7pm, Sept. 24-June
8 Tues.-Sun. noon-6pm; €10 peak season, €5,50 out
of season, free under 18

Cézanne's artistic legacy can be truly appreciated at the Musée Granet and the associated Planque collection. The collection at the Granet anchors Cézanne's work in the history of art by surrounding the 10 original canvasses held there with work by his artistic predecessors and successors. In this environment Cézanne's daring use of color to create perspective and challenge artistic norms becomes clear.

The museum is housed in the former Priory of the Knights of Malta, which was turned into a museum in 1828. It was renamed the Musée Granet in 1949 after Francois Marius Granet, a 19th-century Provençal painter who donated a large number of his works to the museum. In addition to the permanent collections of paintings spanning the 14th to the 20th centuries, there is an impressive sculpture gallery, and a display of archaeological finds from the pre-Roman Celto-Ligurian Entremont settlement located just to the North of Aix.

The Planque collection, housed in La Chappelle des Penitents Blancs a short two-minute walk from the main museum, showcases 300 paintings lent to the Granet Museum by the Fondation Jean Planque in 2010. Planque was an artist and art dealer with an unusually keen eye. During his life he amassed works from the impressionists, post-impressionists, and 20th-century masters. A visit to the collection is included in the entry price to the main museum, and it is well worth the small detour to see works by Monet, Van Gogh, Cézanne, Picasso, de Stael, and Klee.

AIX OUTSKIRTS
★ Cézanne Atelier

9 avenue Paul Cézanne; tel. 04 42 21 06 53;
www.Cézanne-en-provence.com/en;
Apr.-May daily 10am-12:30pm and 2pm-6pm,
June-Sept. daily 10am-6pm, Oct.-Mar. daily
10am-12:30pm and 2pm-5pm, closed Jan. 1-9,
May 1, Dec. 25, and every Sun. Dec.-Feb.; €6,50,
13-25 €3.50, under 13 free

In 1886 Cézanne's father died, freeing the painter from financial reliance. The family house at Jas de Bouffan was sold in 1899 and Cézanne purchased a site in the hills above Aix, in the Lauves neighborhood. Here he began construction of a villa with an atelier in which he could work. Today the first-floor atelier has been restored to mirror its condition during the years before Cézanne died. Many of the original objects remain. For example, the olive jar sitting on the table in the middle of the room appeared in Cézanne's paintings no less than 22 times.

The atelier is 50 square meters (538 square feet), and Cézanne spared no expense in creating the perfect environment for painting. The northern wall is almost entirely filled by one window that lets in as much natural light as possible. Still not satisfied with

Cézanne's Provence

Objects from Cézanne's paintings are dotted throughout his atelier.

Paul Cézanne was born in Aix-en-Provence in 1839 and died there in 1906. After an early unsuccessful career as a banker, he left Aix for Paris to begin training as a painter. His subsequent work changed the way painters interpret the world around them, but like many outliers, he was scorned by the contemporary establishment. Rejected by the École des Beaux-Arts in Paris, he worked in the Académie Suisse where he encountered painters from the emerging impressionist school. Even for impressionists, themselves no strangers to causing outrage, Cézanne's work was a bridge too far. Claude Monet dismissively said that Cézanne "paints with his trowel."

Classifying Cézanne's work is difficult; calling it post-impressionism probably gets the closest. He painted landscapes, still lives, and nudes using a range of different techniques, notably favoring revolutionary color rather than a linear perspective.

Cézanne's early paintings were rejected from prestigious Parisian shows, and every time he left the capital to return to Provence, laughter echoed in his wake. Lack of success forced him into a double life. He met his wife-to-be, Hortense Fiquet, in Paris, where she modeled for him. They kept her existence secret from his father, for fear he would lose his allowance (and with it his ability to paint the other love of his life, Provence).

Cézanne died a painter's death, working on a canvas in a rainstorm and catching pneumonia as a result. It was only after his death that Cézanne's work became widely recognized. Picasso famously called him "the father of us all," referring to how the cubist school built upon Cézanne's paintings of Bibémus quarry.

FOLLOWING CÉZANNE'S FOOTSTEPS

- A visit to Cézanne's atelier or his family home, the Jas de Bouffan, helps foster more understanding of his life and work.
- His particular obsession was Mont Sainte-Victoire, painting it 87 times from various observation points.
- Other favored places to paint included the quarry at Bibémus just outside Aix and the fishing port of L'Estaque just outside Marseille.

the quality of the light, Cézanne also ordered that the original floor tiles be pulled up and replaced with a wooden parquet that was less reflective. To the right of the large window is another reminder of Cézanne's determined nature: A narrow alcove stretching the height of the wall was open to the elements. Cézanne had the hole made so that he could slide his larger canvasses in and out of the room.

Visiting the atelier should be an intimate experience, a chance to sit and contemplate the life of the painter. However 70,000 people climb the steps to the studio every year, with around 15 people admitted at a time. For many it is just an opportunity to pose for a photo using long selfie sticks. The best way to feel the spirit of the painter is to pay the extra €3 for an audio guide and sit on one of the benches, slowly soaking up the atmosphere as you listen to the narrative.

It takes approximately 20 minutes to walk from the center of Aix-en-Provence, up avenue Cézanne to the atelier. Alternatively, take bus Line 5 or Line 10 from the Rotonde Poste stop next to the Apple store. Upon arrival, there is a small shady park in which to relax before entering the atelier.

Terrain des Peintres

49 avenue Paul Cézanne;
http://terrain-des-peintres-aix-en-provence.fr/index.
php/fr/le-terrain-des-peintres

A short distance uphill from the Cézanne Atelier is the "Land of the Painters" view point. It was from here that Cézanne painted the obsession of his artistic life: Mont Sainte-Victoire. In all, Cézanne painted the mountain 87 times, with the most famous paintings created at this, the Sainte Marguerite view point. Reproductions of some of these works are available to view on-site, enabling visitors to make the link between the landscape before them and Cézanne's paintings. The walk from the atelier to the Land of the Painters takes about 15 minutes.

Les Carrières de Bibémus

3090 Chemin de Bibémus; tel. 04 42 16 11 61;
www.cezanne-en-provence.com/en; open for 1-hour tours
only Apr.-Oct. Mon.-Sat., 10am tours in French with
printed info in English; €7.70, 13-25 €4.70, under 13 free

Cézanne's ability to cross between artistic styles is illustrated by the work he did at the Bibémus quarry west of Aix-en-Provence. In his renderings of the rocks at the quarry, Cézanne laid the foundation for the cubist movement of the early 20th century. Cubist painters, such as Picasso, often present multiple views of the same subject at the same time. The beginning of this technique can be discerned in the blurring of perspectives in Cézanne's paintings at Bibémus, such as *The Red Rock* (1797).

The sight is only open to pre-booked tours. These are reserved at the tourist office. The bus to the meeting point at the Les 3 Bons Dieux parking departs from the Gare Routiere (6 boulevard Coq, Depart Belge, Line 6); the ride costs €1.20 and takes about 45 minutes. Timetable information can be found here: www.aixenbus.fr. Alternatively, you can drive to Les 3 Bon Dieux parking, which is located on the D10 5 kilometers (3 miles) from the center of Aix. From here, a special shuttle takes you to the quarry. The site is located in the middle of countryside, and there are steep paths requiring a good level of mobility. Walking shoes are recommended.

Le Jas de Bouffan

17 route de Galice; tel. 04 42 16 11 61;
www.cezanne-en-provence.com/en; at the time of
writing this sight was closed for repairs until 2020,
see website for hours and pricing

Le Jas de Bouffan was the home of the Cézanne family. Between 1859 and 1899, Cézanne completed 39 oil paintings and 17 watercolors here, inspired by the garden, the line of chestnut trees, and the surrounding woods. Major renovation work is under way, designed to make Le Jas de Bouffan the main center for Cézanne-related tourism and study in Aix.

Fondation Victor Vasarely

1 avenue Marcel Pagnol; tel. 04 42 20 01 09;
www.fondationvasarely.org; 10am-6pm daily; adults
€9, children 5-15 €4, audio guide €3, under 5 free

Arriving at the Fondation Victor Vasarely is like stepping onto the set of a science-fiction movie. First there is the building itself, a concoction of giant black and white squares that resemble one face of a half-finished Rubik's cube. Step inside and everywhere there are walls of color, geometric shapes, and odd angles. It's truly an alien world, a place that challenges the senses, constantly fooling the eye by playing with perceptions of space.

Vasarely is a unique figure in the history of 20th-century art, the creator of an entirely new movement: optical art. While painting at Gordes, an hour to the north of Aix, Vasarely had a revelation: In the intense summer light, he noticed a contradictory perspective to the linear one he had been using. "Never can the eye identify to what a given shadow or strip of wall belongs, solids and voids merge into one another, forms and backgrounds alternate. Thus identifiable things are transmuted into abstractions," he said of Gordes. Construction of the center began in 1973, with Vasarely writing a personal message in the cement foundations. He shared only the first few words: "From Cézanne to Vasarely, we will be worthy."

Camp des Milles

40 chemin de la Badesse; tel. 04 42 39 17 11;
www.campdesmilles.org; daily 10am-7pm; adults
€9.50, reduced (students under 25, disabled people)
€7.50, under 9 free

Less than 10 kilometers (6 miles) from the leafy shade and joyously bubbling fountains of the Cours Mirabeau, in the Provençal landscape that was a crucible of 20th-century artistic creativity, lies, almost inconceivably, the site of a former concentration camp. Between 1940 and 1942 Camp des Milles was a detention center for "undesirables" and eventually became the base from which more than 2,000 Jews were deported to Auschwitz. If much of a visit to Aix is about celebrating the unlimited potential of the human imagination, then Camp des Milles is an important reminder of the dangers of xenophobia and racism The building (an old tile factory) and the rooms within stand as a memorial to the people who passed through the camp. The exhibits in the museum attempt to explain how "free" Vichy, France, agreed to deliver 10,000 Jews to the Germans, including children under 16. Ultimately the purpose of this site is to teach lessons of the past that we can apply to today's society.

Oppidum d'Entremont

960 avenue Fernand Benoît; tel. 04 42 21 97 33;
www.entremont.culture.gouv.fr/fr; June-Sept.
9am-noon and 2pm-6pm, closed Tues. and three
weekends per month out of season; free

Located on a hill north of Aix, L'Oppidum D'Entremont was a stronghold of the Celto-Ligurian civilization that dominated Provence before the Romans. It was built around 175 AD. The settlement was divided into two distinct areas: one for inhabitants and trade, and the other for the warriors. The ruins of the two are still clearly distinguishable today. The settlement should be visited in conjunction with the collection of archaeological finds that were discovered here and are held at the Musée Granet. Views of Mont Sainte-Victoire and Aix are spectacular.

Sports and Recreation

For most people, recreation in Aix consists of finding a shady spot on a café terrace, ordering an espresso, and watching the world pass by. This makes people watching officially the most popular sport in Aix. Sunbathing in the parks comes a close second. Fortunately, for those with itchy feet there are popular walking tours offered by the tourist office. It is also still possible to take the thermal waters that first attracted the Romans to this area, but modern spas proliferate and are a better choice for beauty treatments and pampering.

GUIDED TOURS

FOOTSTEPS OF CÉZANNE WALK

Tourist office, 300 avenue Giuseppe Verdi;
tel. 04 42 16 11 61; www.aixenprovencetourism.com/
en/fiche/3305; Thurs. 10am-noon; from €6

Either join the weekly guided group or pick up a map at the tourist office and follow the route yourself. Starting next to the statue of Cézanne outside the tourist office, the walk takes you up into the Mazarin Quarter before crossing the Cours Mirabeau and looping around the old town. There are embossed "C"s set into the paving stones to help you find the way. The trail includes Cézanne's school, various apartments he lived in, the café he frequented, and the church where he was married to Hortense Fiquet and where his funeral was held. For Cézanne fans, it's a window into the artist's daily life. It's also a good circular walk taking about 1 hour and 30 minutes to complete and encompassing all the main districts of Aix.

VISIT AIX OLD TOWN

Tourist office, 300 Av. Giuseppe Verdi;
tel. 04 42 16 11 61; www.aixenprovencetourism.com/
en/fiche/3305; Apr.-Sept. Tues. and Sat. 10am-noon,
Oct.-Mar. Sat. only; from €6.

This fascinating tour is full of historical anecdotes and it's a great way to explore the old town for the first time, allowing you to get your bearings and discover the best hidden squares. Highlights include the hôtel particulier at Place d'Albertas and the Cathedral Saint-Sauveur.

FOUNTAINS AND GARDENS

Tourist office, 300 avenue Giuseppe Verdi;
tel. 04 42 16 11 61; www.aixenprovencetourism.com/
en/fiche/3305; Wed. 10am-noon; from €6

This tour explores the history of the city through its fountains and gardens. Understanding how and why they came into being gives unique insight into the city, plus gives you a list of some of the most pleasant place in Aix to revisit.

PARKS

PARC JOURDAN

Main entrance rue Anatole France; tel. 04 42 16 11 61;
www.aixenprovence.fr/Parc-Jourdan; June-Aug. daily
9am-8pm, out of season usually closes around sunset

The Aixoise have been enjoying spending their leisure time in this park since the 1930s. It's one of the largest parks in the city and has plenty of shady, grassy areas. There's a good children's play area and a boulodrome for fans of Provence's favorite sport, petanque. During the summer months the park hosts large exhibitions and concerts.

JARDIN DU PAVILLON DE VENDÔME

Entrance 32 rue Celony or rue de La Molle;
www.aixenprovence.fr/Jardin-du-Pavillon-Vendome;
June-Aug. daily 9am-8pm, out of season usually
closes around sunset

A real hidden treasure of Aix-en-Provence, the gardens are 9,000 square meters (2.2 acres) and are designed in a formal French style. Bushes, plants, and trees are all trimmed with geometric precision to be as aesthetically pleasing as possible. The rose garden is in bloom in early summer, and you'll often see a bride and groom having their wedding photos snapped. In the Pavillon overlooking the garden, there's a fine art museum (Pavillon de Vendone, Jardin du Pavillon de Vendome; www.aixenprovence.fr/Presentation-du-Pavillon-de-Vendome; Tues.-Mon. 10am-12:30pm and 1:30pm-5pm, till 6pm Apr. 15-Oct.; €3.70), which has a permanent collection of 17th- and 18th-century portraits and hosts regular modern art exhibitions.

SPAS
MAZARIN SPA
27 rue Mazarine; tel. 04 42 50 27 27; www.srmazarine.fr; closed Sun.
Probably the pick of the many spas in Aix-en-Provence, this spa is located on the genteel rue Mazarine. Clients enter through a boutique selling luxury candles and cosmetic products. There's a small indoor swimming pool, hammam, and the full range of massages and treatments.

THERMES SEXTIUS
55 avenue des Thermes, Aix-en-Provence 13100; www.thermes-sextius.com; Mon.-Sat. 8am-8pm, closed Sun.; from €100
The architecture may be modern, but the thermal waters have been used as a cure since Roman times. The range of spa treatments available at the Sextius spa relies heavily on the in-house source for the thermal water, filtered by Mont Sainte-Victoire, which bubbles up beneath Aix at a perfect 33° Celsius (91.4°F). Full pricing information can be found on the spa's website.

Entertainment and Events

Entertainment is all around you in Aix-en-Provence. Street performers with tubs of soapy liquid blow bubbles the size of small children, entire groups of buskers jazz up the atmosphere on the Cours Mirabeau, and the ubiquitous human street statues doff their caps in return for a coin or two.

Aix is also a world capital for opera and classical music. From Easter until the end of summer, concerts and performances draw

the Pavillon de Vendôme

top stars and large audiences to venues across the city.

THE ARTS
GRAND THÉÂTRE DE PROVENCE

*380 avenue Max Juvénal; tel. 04 42 91 69 70; www.
lestheatres.net; hours depend on performance; from €8*

Designed by Milanese architect Vittorio Gregotti and inaugurated in 2007, the Grand Théâtre is one of a trio of modernist cultural buildings. Together they form a distinct contemporary district of Aix. The stones chosen for the construction of the building were selected in a variety of shades to mirror the way light plays on the rocky faces of Mont Sainte-Victoire. With 1,370 seats, the Grand Théâtre can host all but the largest events and there's a lovely roof terrace where the public can look over Aix. Performances are varied, with the venue playing a key role in the city's opera and classical music festivals, but also offering the stage to up-and-coming bands, jazz musicians, and magicians to appeal to a younger audience.

LE PAVILLON NOIR

*530 avenue Wolfgang Amadeus Mozart;
tel. 04 42 93 48 14; www.preljocaj.org; hours depend
on performance; from €25*

Le Pavillon Noir has been the home of the Preljocaf ballet since 2006. When the company is not in residence, other dance companies from around the world are invited to perform. Once again the building is architecturally arresting, designed as a cube by Rudy Ricciotti; there are four rehearsal rooms and one stage.

DARIUS MILHAUD CONSERVATOIRE

*380 avenue Wolfgang Amadeus Mozart;
tel. 04 88 71 84 20; www.aixenprovence.fr/
Conservatoire; open for performances and Mon.-Fri.
7:30pm-10pm, Sat. 8am-7pm*

Part music school, part performance center, the Conservatoire has 62 classrooms, 4 dance studios, and a 500-seat auditorium. The arresting design using sheet-metal folds is by

architect Kengo Kuma. The Conservatoire plays a full role in the two major Aix music festivals: the Festival de Paques and the Festival d'Aix. Of particular interest are music masterclasses from well-known musicians.

FESTIVALS
FESTIVAL DE PAQUES

*Various locations, including Grand Théâtre de
Provence, 380 avenue Max Juvénal; tel. 08 20 13
20 13; www.festivalpaques.com; two weeks around
Easter; €25-105*

This classical music festival runs for two weeks over the Easter period. It attracts some of the best orchestras in the world, including in recent years, the London Symphony Orchestra. Expect performances of works by the big names of the classical music world: Bach, Vivaldi, Brahms, Mozart, as well as some lesser known composers.

LE SMA'ART

*Parc Jourdan; tel. 04 42 49 97 52;
www.salonsmart-aix.com; mid-May; €10, free under 10*

Never has a stroll in the park been so much fun. Thousands of paintings, mostly by young up-and-coming artists, are displayed in Parc Jourdan. If something catches your eye, prices tend to be reasonable and shipping costs low.

FESTIVAL D'AIX-EN-PROVENCE

*Various locations; tel. 08 20 92 29 23;
www.festival-aix.com; July; from €20*

Whether you are an afficionado or an amateur Aix-en-Provence is the place to experience opera. The festival tends to feature five major operas and a host of subsidiary events, including performances of everything from classical music to flamenco guitar. Now over 70 years old, the Festival d'Aix even has an offshoot event, Aix-in-June, offering plays, masterclasses and classical music performances across the city and out into the countryside, taking place in venues such as Silvacane Abbey. A €20 pass for all the events in June is available. For the main festival's operas and events, ticket sales open in February and booking is essential.

Shopping

Aix-en-Provence is often called the Paris of the South. The reputation comes partly from the attention to detail with which the residents dress. Big brands such as Hermes, Longchamps, and Agnes B are on display, and there are plenty of jewelers where locals can source that finishing touch of bling. For on-trend purchases, there's Zadig et Voltaire, Comptoir des Cotonniers, and Sandro. The main shopping area is the old town, where there are plenty of owner-operated boutiques selling original collections mixed in with national brands. Les Allées Provençal is a modern development on the opposite side of La Rotonde fountain from the Cours Mirabeau. It is largely filled by national chain stores such as H&M and Zara. The Mazarin quarter also has a few boutiques, but it is not a shopping destination.

BEAUTY
BASTIDE
14 rue Espariat; tel. 04 84 47 00 29; https://bastide.com; Mon.-Thurs. 10am-7pm, Fri.-Sat. 10am-7:30pm, Sun. 11am-6pm
Bastide specializes in simple, clean, natural skin and hair-care products made from Provençal ingredients. Examples include, lavender honey body wash, summer fig hand cream, and rose and olive tree *eau de toilette*. The shop, located in the heart of the old town, is a joy to visit. The scents of Provence waft out of the door, enticing shoppers to enter.

★ ROSE AND MARIUS
3 rue Thiers; tel. 09 82 59 35 35; www.roseetmarius.com/fr; Tues.-Sat. 10:30am-1pm and 2pm-7pm, closed Sun.
Rose and Marius sells fragranced candles in beautiful Limoges porcelain holders, with intricate colored geometric patterns inspired by the tiled floor of the family bastide where the owner grew up. Look for the unique rosé *eau de toilette*. Once again the emphasis is on

natural products created from Provençal ingredients. By appointment, the shop also offers smell workshops to help you recognize scents and find the perfect fragrances for you and your house.

CLOTHING AND TEXTILES
MES DESMOISSELLES
12 rue Marius Reynaud; tel. 04 42 29 67 46; www.mesdemoisellesparis.com/fr; Mon.-Sat. 10am-7:30pm, closed Sun.
Mes Desmoisselles is a Parisian fashion house now open in Aix. It specializes in the chic, stylish womenswear that makes French women seem so effortlessly graceful. One joke about the local women is that they always look beautiful but have nothing in the fridge back at home. Apparently shops such as Mes Desmoisselles are responsible for their limited grocery budgets.

LA VICTOIRE
34 rue Vauvenargues; tel. 04 42 23 14 36; www.instagram.com/lavictoirefabricshop; Tues.-Sat. 9:30am-12:30pm, 2pm-6:45pm, closed Mon.
During the 17th century, Provence was the undisputed center of the bedspread trade. Factories turned out thousands of quilted bedcovers and established a reputation for fabrics that endures today. This shop in the center of Aix, offers a wide range of colors, patterns, and materials. It's the place to pick up something small (like napkins or place mats) or large (like a bedspread) as a souvenir.

SPECIALITY FOOD AND WINE
JACQUEMES
9 rue Mejanes; tel. 04 42 23 48 64; www.jacquemes. fr; Tues.-Sat. 9:15am-12:15pm and 2:30pm-7pm
Jacquemes is something of an Aix institution, selling the finest Provençal food and wine for three generations. Regulars stock up on

truffles, high-quality olive oil, and *foie gras*. There's an excellent range of wines and spirits, featuring the top local vineyards and big-name wines from across France.

LE ROY RENÉ

11 rue Gaston de Saporta; tel. 04 42 26 67 86; www.calisson.com; Mon.-Sat. 10am-1pm and 2pm-7pm, Sun. 10am-1pm

Calissons are small almond-shaped treats, not much larger than a mint candy, made from a paste of preserved melons and almonds, and topped with icing. They have been produced in Aix since the 15th century. These days Le Roy René is the self-declared king of the *calisson* business. While small bakeries turn out hand-crafted sweets, this large enterprise ships Aix's specialty worldwide. At its out of town factory there's even a *calisson* museum. The choice, flavors, and colors, combined with the attractive packaging, make the shop a good choice to pick up a gift. There's also a range of artisan syrups and nougat.

LA CHAMBRE AUX CONFITURES

16bis rue d'Italie; tel. 04 42 24 07 74; https:// lachambreauxconfitures.com/en; Mon.-Fri, 10am-2pm and 3pm-7pm, Sat. 10am-7pm, Sun. 10am-1pm

The humble pot of jam has been given a 21st-century makeover by La Chambre aux Confitures. Rows and rows of conserves line the walls. There's a jam for every occasion: spreading on toast, eating with cheese, accompanying *foie gras*. Such is the overwhelming range, it's best to ask for guidance to find your perfect jam and food combination.

BOOKSTORES

BOOK IN BAR

4 rue Joseph Cabassol; tel. 04 42 26 60 07; www.bookinbar.com; Mon.- Sat. 9am-7pm, closed Sun.

Book in Bar is so much more than a bookshop. It's the center for Anglophones in Aix-en-Provence. There are book clubs, book signings, and talks by authors. Like all good bookshops, it has a slightly cluttered feel,

as if there are too many books to fit within its walls. Bestsellers are prominent. There's also a good travel literature section, and of course a selection of the great and the good of Provençal literature. If browsing gets tiring, Coffee and cake are served from a hole-in-the-wall kitchen, and you can relax on sofas and various tables and chairs.

MARKETS

Scarcely a day passes in Aix without a market of some form or other.

COURS MIRABEAU

Cours Mirabeau; Tues.-Thurs. 8:30am-1pm

On Tuesday and Thursday, the Cours Mirabeau is lined with a clothes market. There's a good range of items including coats, shoes, gloves, underwear, and fashion wear, and prices are much lower than in the Aix boutiques. The backdrop of course is gorgeous: the long view down to the tumbling waters of La Rotonde, the imperious rows of hôtel particuliers, and the watchful plane trees. It's hard to imagine a more scenic place to shop.

LES 3 PLACES

Place des Prêcheurs, place de Verdun, place de la Madeleine (squares intersect with rue Portalis); Tues., Thurs., Sat. 8:30am-1pm

There really is something for everyone in this market, from rare books and *brocante* to fruit, vegetables, and spit-roasted chickens, to artisan-made leather wallets, belts, and handbags. It's a joy to lose yourself amid the stalls and see what you emerge with at the end. Be sure to take a look at the remains of the old palace of the Counts of Provence under the glass paving stones near the Palais de Justice.

★ PLACE DE L'HOTEL DE VILLE FLOWER MARKET

Intersects with rue Vauvenargues; daily, except first Sun. of the month, 8:30am-12:30pm

Even if you have no interest in

buying flowers, this market is a delight to see. Seasonal flowers and plants are laid out around an 18th-century fountain, capped with a column salvaged from the ruins of the Palace of the Counts of Provence. One side of the square is dominated by the imposing town hall buildings, and on the other three sides, café terraces spill into the square. It's a great place to sit and enjoy a drink and the visual theater of city life. Visit in March and there will be stalls filled with bright yellow mimosa, and in the summer there will be neatly piled bunches of freshly cut lavender. Of course the best day of the year is Valentine's Day when an abundance of red roses envelops the square, and the sky is normally a crystal clear blue; the colors are so sharp, the moment so perfect, that even the most hard-hearted will be moved to make a romantic gesture.

BROCANTE ART AND ANTIQUES

GALERIE IMBERT

7 rue Jacques de la Roque; tel. 09 72 58 37 30; https://galerieimbert.com; Mon.-Sat. 10:30am-1pm and 3pm-7pm, closed Sun.

Galerie Imbert opened nearly 20 years ago near the cathedral in Aix. Landscapes and still life paintings line the walls of the narrow space. The gallery represents around 20 local artists, and prices range from the hundreds to the thousands of euros. The gallery is run by Canadian Kathleen Imbert, and she is happy to offer her advice on the local art world.

MAZARIN ANTIQUITÉS

8 rue Frédéric Mistral; tel. 04 42 27 16 06; www.aixenprovencetourism.com/fr/fiche/3385; 10am-12:30pm and 3pm-7pm, closed Sun.

Here, you'll find a haphazard treasure trove of items from the Provençal past. Finds might include chandeliers, grandfather clocks, coffee grinders, plates, and paintings. Don't be afraid to negotiate on price.

The daily flower market is an Aix institution.

Calissons

Here's a simple recipe for a moment of bliss during a visit to Aix-en-Provence:

- Stop at favorite local bakery **Patisserie Béchard** on the Cours Mirabeau and treat yourself to a box of Aix's signature sweet treat, the *calisson*. They are small and almond-shaped, and they're made from a paste of preserved melons and almonds, topped with icing. Some chefs add a dash of orange blossom, some lemon zest or even a little vanilla, but tinkering more than this is frowned upon.

- With your box of *calissons* in hand, cross the road and settle into a table with a view at the iconic **Deux Garcons** café. Depending on the time of day and your mood, order any one of the following: a glass of champagne, a glass of sweet wine, a coffee, or a tea. Take a sip of your drink and then a bite of *calisson,* and then repeat until a broad smile inevitably spreads across your face.

Enjoy some delicious *calissons,* the signature pastry of Aix.

Calissons have been delivering these little moments of pleasure since the 15th century. They were famously served at the marriage of King Roi René to his second wife, Jeanne de Laval, in Aix. Rumor has it they owe their name to a hug (*calin*) bestowed at this event. True or not, they are deliciously indulgent and the perfect gift to take home for friends and relatives.

Food

The best way to eat out in Aix is to start thinking about your ideal meal early in the day. As a rule of thumb, when you eat outside on a terrace in one of the more touristy areas, you have to sacrifice a little on value for money. Weather is crucial: The midday sun in summer turns some restaurant terraces into furnaces, but for the rest of the year, the same terraces are pleasant. If you go to one of the many more local restaurants hidden in side streets, you may not be able to sit outside, but you'll pay less and often eat better. Above all, enjoy the experience of window-shopping and salivating over the varied menus. If you spot an ideal table, perhaps next to a trickling fountain, be sure to reserve. Restaurant menus will often contain the odd Provençal specialty such as *pieds paquets* (stuffed pig's feet), but mainly the food is modern French.

COURS MIRABEAU
Regional Cuisine
★ LE DEUX GARCONS

53 Cours Mirabeau; 04 42 26 00 51; www.lesdeuxgarcons.fr; open daily 7am-12:59am; main courses €23-32

The most famous café brasserie in Aix, Les Deux Garcons still pulls in the occasional celebrity. Cézanne and Zola were old patrons. White tablecloths, formally dressed waiters, and diners digging into towering platters of iced shellfish all help to create a sense of spectacle. The outside terrace is large and usually packed. A more intimate dining experience is available inside, in the gold-gilded dining room. Daily specials such as *daube de boeuf* (beef stew with red wine) complement a traditional French brasserie menu.

CÔTÉ COUR

19 Cours Mirabeau; tel. 04 42 93 12 51; www.restaurantcotecour.fr; Mon.-Sat. noon-2pm and 7pm-10pm; mains €24-36

Probably the best restaurant on the Cours Mirabeau is Côté Cour. The restaurant is nestled in a courtyard behind one of the street's grand old buildings. There's a retractable roof and pleasing modern decor. The service is slick and the food excellent. Try the pungent truffle risotto around Christmas time.

L'ESTELLO

1 Cours Mirabeau; tel. 04 42 50 03 69; https://m.facebook.com/Estello-152869058087269; daily 7am-2am; mains €18-28

For the same brasserie feel as Les Deux Garcons, but with lower prices, L'Estello is a popular choice with locals and tourists. Inventive salads, such as a deconstructed salad Nicoise and Buddha bowls are popular. The lunchtime dish of the day usually has a Provençal twist.

LA ROTONDE

2A place Jeanne d'Arc; tel. 04 42 91 61 70; www.larotonde-aix.com; daily 7:30am-1:30am; mains €21-29

Newly refurbished La Rotonde is the best place to sit and enjoy the cascading waters of its namesake fountain. The atmosphere is vibrant and young. The food—a mixture of Provençal (*pied pacquets*), Italian (pizzas), and American (burgers)—is good but a little overpriced.

Bakeries and Cafés
PÂTISSERIE BÉCHARD

12 Cours Mirabeau; tel. 04 42 26 06 78; www.facebook.com/maisonbechard; Tues.-Sat. 8am-7:30pm; snacks from €2.50

Beloved by the Aixois for generations, thanks to its sweet concoctions, this pastry shop also offers plentiful savory snacks. Try the *feuilleté*

à la saucisse, a hotdog encased in crumbling pastry. Depending on your view, the serving system is either charming or antiquated: You line up for one person to take your order. This is then written on a slip of paper. You then queue again to pay before finally being given your goodies. Fortunately, the wait is worth it.

AIX OLD TOWN (LA VIEILLE VILLE)
Regional Cuisine
LES CAVES HENRI IV BY LE FORMAL

32 rue Espariat; tel. 04 42 27 08 31; www.restaurant-lescaveshenri4-byleformal.com; Tues.-Fri. noon-1:30pm and 7:30pm-9:30pm, Sat. 7:30pm-9:30pm, closed Sun. and Mon.; mains from €27

Les Caves Henri IV by Le Formal is popular with locals hiding from the summer sun or sheltering on rare rainy days. It's also supposedly a great place for a romantic tryst. Diners are hidden away from prying eyes down a flight of stairs in an arched cellar. The food is exemplary, and the menu is based on local ingredients, such as Sisteron lamb with a basil crust.

LES VIEILLES CANAILLES

7 rue Isolette; tel. 04 42 91 41 75; www.vieilles-canailles.fr; Tues.-Sat., noon-2pm and 7pm-9:45pm, Wed. theme nights by reservation only; mains €14-23

It's hard to find a more atmospheric dining experience in Aix than Les Vieilles Canailles. Over the sound system Serge Gainsborough croons away and bottles of wine, personally chosen by owner Pierre Hochart, line the walls. Dishes might include Corsican charcuterie and a roast rack of lamb *en croute* (in a pastry crust) with purple mustard.

LE ZINC DE HUGO

22 rue Lieutaud; tel. 04 42 27 69 69; www.zinc-hugo.com; Tues.-Sun. noon-2:30pm and 7pm-10:30pm, closed Mon.; mains €20-36

Meat lovers should look no further than Zinc de Hugo, a cozy brasserie with an open-fire grill. Meat is sourced from across the world, including steaks from Argentina, Ireland, Spain, and France. Generous portions, traditional decor, an excellent wine list, and a convivial atmosphere make the Zinc enduringly popular.

LA BOUCHE À'OREILLE

1 rue Aumone Vieille; tel. 09 72 89 19 19; www.facebook.com/leboucheaoreilleaix; Mon.-Sun. noon-2pm and 7:30pm-10pm, closed Mon.; two-course menu €26

Tucked away in a quiet little square, Le Bouche à Oreille is a rustic brasserie with a small menu chalked up on a blackboard. Inside the decor is simple but charming, and outside there's a small shady terrace. The salted pig's knuckle is delicious.

DROLE D'ENDROIT

1 rue Annonerie Vieille; tel. 04 42 38 95 54; http://droledesite.fr; Thurs.-Sun. noon-2pm and 7pm-10pm, Tues. noon-2pm and 7pm-10pm, Wed. 7pm-10pm, closed Mon.; €13.60-19

Drole d'Endroit is a hard place to find, which makes good sense, as the name means "funny location." It's tucked down a side alley, and thousands of people must walk past every week not knowing it's there. The interior is spacious with the quirky industrial decor

offset by temporary art exhibitions. The menu changes every week and attracts a loyal following of in-the-know locals, returning for dishes such as spiced cod with ratatouille.

★ LES 3 ORMEAUX

Place des 3 Ormeaux; tel. 04 42 21 59 95; www.facebook.com/les3ormeaux; Tues.-Sat. noon-2pm and 7pm-10pm, closed Sun. and Mon.; mains €22-32

One of the best places for a shady lunch in the heat of summer is Les 3 Ormeaux, which is located next to a trickling fountain in an attractive square. Salads and pizzas predominate on the menu, but they are a cut above the average. Particularly worth trying is the house special: truffle pizza.

LE CHASTEL

18 place des Prêcheurs; tel. 04 42 29 70 64; www.lechastel.com; Mon.-Sat. noon-2:30pm and 7pm-10pm, closed Sun.; mains €15-34

On the Place des Prêcheurs, Le Chastel and Le Mado tussle with each other for the title of the square's best brasserie. Bragging rights probably go to Le Chastel, which has a smaller more intimate feel, and is always crowded. It offers excellent French food plus a few Italian classics, such as spaghetti *vongole* (with

Place des 3 Ormeaux is a charming place for lunch in the shade.

clams) and veal Milanaise (breaded and fried) thrown in for good measure.

Bakeries and Cafés
PATISSERIE WEIBEL
2 rue Chabrier; tel. 04 42 23 33 21;
www.maisonweibel.com;
daily 7:30am-7pm; €5-12
Established in 1954, the Maison Weibel serves delicious cakes and pastries. It is also a good stop for breakfast, lunch, or a light supper. There's a row of tables outside on the street, and seating inside as well. On the menu are sandwiches, *croque monsieur* (grilled ham and cheese sandwich), and salads. The quality is very high and the service professional. For a quick snack it is hard to beat.

Food Markets
PLACE RICHELME
Between rue Vauvenargue and rue Marechal Foch;
www.aixenprovencetourism.com/fr/fiche/19107;
daily 8am-1pm
Many Aixoise buy all their food in this one market. In spring and summer, there's plentiful fresh fruit and vegetables, and autumn brings the first mushrooms and winter truffles. There's a fishmonger with a wide variety of seafood straight from the Mediterranean. The market is also a great place to pick up something to nibble on, including olives and local goat's cheese.

LES 3 PLACES
Place de Verdun, place des Prêcheurs,
and place Madeleine;
www.aixenprovencetourism.com/fr/fiche/19107; Tues.,
Thurs., Sat. 9am-1pm
During the renovation of these squares the tri-weekly food market was shifted to the bottom of Cours Mirabeau and the Cours Sextius. Work is scheduled to end in 2019 with the market resuming its traditional location. There's a slightly better selection than the market on Place Richelme with, for example one trader selling freshly made Italian ravioli and another oriental specialties.

QUARTIER MAZARIN
Regional Cuisine
LE JARDIN DE MAZARIN
15 rue du 4 Septembre; tel. 04 28 31 08 36;
www.jardinmazarin.com; Mon.-Sat. noon-3pm and
7:30pm-10:30pm, closed Sun.; mains from €22
Le Jardin de Mazarin is a refined, discreet restaurant, and the perfect bolt hole for the residents of this expensive quarter of Aix. Hidden behind an unassuming façade are a warmly furnished dining room and a long terrace opening onto a small garden. It's a great place to escape the crowds and eat well-executed dishes such as roasted fillet of beef with truffles.

LA BROCHERIE
5 rue Fernand Dol; tel. 04 42 38 33 21;
www.labrocherieaix.com; Mon.-Sat. noon-3pm and
7pm-10pm closed Sun.; mains €12-25
The emphasis here is very much on meat and fish grilled on an open fire. The prices are very competitive for Aix, and as well as the various grills, there are plenty of pasta dishes and other options.

LA DOLCE ITALIA
67 rue d'Italie; tel. 04 88 14 60 18;
http://la-dolce-italia.fr; Tues.-Sat. noon-3pm and
6pm-10pm, closed Sun. and Mon.; mains €17-25
As the name suggests, the focus is on Italian cuisine. Start with a plate of antipasti, including peppers stuffed with tuna, sun-dried tomatoes, grilled artichoke, grilled eggplant, sliced meats, and Italian cheeses; then follow with one of the restaurant's specialty fresh pastas. There is a blackboard menu of daily specials, including dishes such as veal Milanaise.

Bakeries and Cafés
HÔTEL GALLIFET
52 rue Cardinale; tel. 09 53 84 37 61;
http://hoteldegallifet.com; June-early Sept.
Tues.-Sun. noon-6pm; mains €14-16
This is a great summer pop-up restaurant/café in the garden of a hôtel particulier. At lunch there's a small menu with dishes such

as breaded chicken, or salmon filet. After 3pm the restaurant transforms into a tea/coffee shop. The garden is a lovely shady place to sit with the hôtel particulier forming a beautiful backdrop. There are occasional jazz concerts in the garden, and an art exhibition in the hotel.

THE CHOCOLATE FACTORY

23 rue D'Italie; www.facebook.com/ chocolatefactoryaix; Mon.-Sat. 10am-7pm, closed Sun.; snacks from €3

This is the place for an extremely sugary snack. The main offering is donuts, with all sorts of different toppings, from basic chocolate to salted caramel. They are absolutely delicious but best shared (half is plenty). There are also brownies, cookies, and various other chocolate concoctions. There are tables inside where you can sit with a coffee or drink.

AIX OUTSKIRTS
Bakeries and Cafés
DARIUS CAFÉ

115 avenue Giuseppe Verdi; tel. 04 42 27 98 97; Mon.-Sat. 6am-midnight; daily specials from €14

This very popular café in Les Allées Provençal shopping area, just outside the center of Aix, is a two-minute walk from the tourist office. There's a big terrace, and an atmospheric interior that bubbles with conversation. This is a good place to stop for a break and mix with the locals. At lunchtime, there is a full menu on offer, with a well-priced daily special such as beef fillet with morels and creamy potatoes.

Bars and Nightlife

The city is one of the campuses of Aix Marseille university, which, with approximately 74,000 students, is the largest university in the French-speaking world. Cafés and bars are filled during the day with youngsters trying to look both hip and studious at the same time. In the evening they drop the pretense of studiousness and head for Irish bars and tapas restaurants. Given its student population, the club scene in the city is surprisingly understated.

LA CITA

16 rue Félibre Gaut; tel. 04 86 31 52 43; http://lacita.fr; Mon.-Sat. 7pm-12:30am; beer or sangria €3.50 a glass or €12 a liter, tapas from €4.50

This traditional Spanish tapas bar gets rowdier and rowdier as the evening progresses. Jugs rather than glasses of alcohol are the norm, and the tapas are an essential way to soak up the booze.

EL BOLERO

14 rue Félibre Gaut; tel. 04 86 31 16 70; www.restaurant-elbolero.fr; Tues.-Sat. 7pm-1am; cocktails from €9, tapas from €5.50

El Bolero is right next door to La Cita, and the crowds on the street outside happily spill into each other. The vibe here is more South American, with a rum bar, cocktails, and ceviche serving as the alcohol sponge.

LA VIDA LOCA

11 rue Félibre Gaut; tel. 06 24 40 78 70; www.facebook.com/profile. php?id=100016784325910; Tues.-Sat. 7pm-2am; drinks from €4

Completing the trio on this popular street is La Vida Loca. As the name suggests this is not the place to go for a quiet drink and intimate conversation, but to dance with students and locals. Expect to have to shout to be heard.

LE MISTRAL

3 rue Frédéric Mistral; tel. 06 20 38 50 25; http://mistralclub.fr; Tues.-Sat. 11:55pm-6am

The grand dame of Aix nightclubs, Le Mistral is 65 years old and still drawing the crowds. A great central location, big name DJs, and a revamped interior by designer Gianni Fasciani make Le Mistral the place to see and be seen.

Accommodations

The center of Aix has a good choice of hotels, but room prices are expensive compared to the rest of France and space can be limited. Hotels with a more spacious feel can be found in the Aix outskirts. Most hotels here are a few minutes' walk from the center and have air-conditioned rooms available. A few have their own parking.

COURS MIRABEAU
€100-200
HOTEL NEGRECOSTE
33 Cours Mirabeau; tel. 44 22 77 42 22; https://hotel-negre-coste.com/en; €150 d
Hotel Negre Coste has a central location halfway up the Cours Mirabeau with a large terrace bar and restaurant. Rooms are modern and nicely designed with air-conditioning, Wi-Fi and ensuite bathrooms. A Nuxe spa offers some much-needed pampering after a day's sightseeing. Private parking is available for €20 a day.

AIX OLD TOWN (LA VIEILLE VILLE)
€100-200
HOTEL DE FRANCE
63 rue Espariat; tel. 04 42 27 90 15; https://hoteldefrance-aixenprovence.com/en; €120 d
Hotel de France is located on the bustling pedestrian rue Espariat, which runs parallel to the Cours Mirabeau. The breakfast room is large, airy, and a charming mix of old and new. Bedrooms are decorated in a clean, minimalist style; rooms with windows onto the rue Espariat may experience some nighttime noise. All rooms are ensuite and have Wi-Fi and air-conditioning. The closest parking is La Rotonde.

★ HOTEL DES AUGUSTINS
3 rue de La Masse; tel. 04 42 27 28 59; https://hotel-augustins.com/en; €109 d
For a sense of history, try the Hotel des Augustins, a converted chapel with links to the 12th-century Augustins Convent, which once stood in the area. In particular, the reception area has a wonderful ecclesiastical feel. Some rooms still have a touch of historic character, with the occasional exposed stone arch and views of the bell tower of the Augustins church. All rooms are ensuite and have Wi-Fi and air-conditioning. The closest parking is La Rotonde.

Over €200
HOTEL DE GANTES
1 rue Fabrot;
tel. 04 42 90 31 60;
http://hoteldegantes.fr/en; €220 d
Hotel des Gante is housed in an old hôtel particulier. The vibe these days is modern and there is no real sense of the history of the building. Luxury double rooms and junior suites overlook the Cours Mirabeau, and the top-floor suite has a terrace facing the Cours. Unfortunately, there's no restaurant but the Deux Garcons café is right underneath. All rooms are ensuite and have Wi-Fi and air-conditioning. The closest parking is La Rotonde.

QUARTIER MAZARIN
Under €100
HOTEL CARDINAL
24 rue Cardinale;
tel. 04 42 38 32 30;
www.hotel-cardinal-aix.com; €80 d
Hotel Cardinal is a good budget option right next door to the Musée Granet. The decor is a little dated with an overuse of chintzy florals and old-fashioned paintings, but the rooms are comfortable. Suites with kitchenettes and small terraces are available for those planning a longer stay in Aix. All rooms are ensuite and have Wi-Fi and air-conditioning. The closest parking is Mignet.

Over €200
★ MAISON D'AIX

25 rue du 4 Septembre; tel. 04 42 53 78 95;
www.lamaisondaix.com; €420 d

Maison d'Aix plays on the reputation of its former owner Henriette Reboule, a "priestess of love" who purchased the 18th-century hôtel particulier in 1903. Guests now sleep in the rooms where Henriette once entertained her lovers and there is still an underlying erotic feel to the place. The four rooms are named Corset, Secret Garden, Le Chambre d'Henriette, and the Love Suite, which might explain why *The Parisian* newspaper declared it the most romantic hotel in France in 2016. Materials used throughout, from the wooden floors to the bed linens, are all very high end. There's a small spa and red room for late-night chats. All rooms are ensuite and have Wi-Fi and air-conditioning. The nearest parking is located at Mignet.

LE 28

28 rue du 4 Septembre; tel. 07.83.15.75.92;
www.hotelparticulier-le28.com; €300 d

Le 28 is a close neighbor of Maison D'Aix but it's a touch more flamboyant in its interior decor. This is another hôtel particulier converted into a boutique hotel. The hotel offers access to the pool and spa at the nearby Spa Mazarin. Couples traveling with a child should consider The Suite Sensazione, which has a small single bedroom off the main double bedroom. All rooms are ensuite and have Wi-Fi and air-conditioning. There are seven rooms in total, so early booking is recommended.

AIX OUTSKIRTS
Under €100
HOTEL SAINT CHRISTOPHE

2 avenue Victor Hugo; tel. 04 42 26 01 24;
www.hotel-saintchristophe.com; €80 d

Hotel Saint Christophe has a charming bar and a restaurant-brasserie reminiscent of many in Paris. The hotel has 67 rooms and is well-located next to the tourist office and Rotonde fountain. At the budget end, the rooms can be a little cramped and it's best to upgrade if possible. All rooms are ensuite and have Wi-Fi and air-conditioning. Private parking is available at €14 per day.

€100-200
HOTEL CÉZANNE

40 avenue Victor Hugo; tel. 04 42 91 11 11;
www.hotelaix.com/en; €150 d

Hotel Cézanne has 57 rooms and is a popular choice with families, thanks to plenty of interconnecting rooms. There are nice practicalities such as an honesty bar and a buffet breakfast (including truffle omelets) that is served until 11am. Although this property is not central, the walk to the Cours Mirabeau takes only a couple of minutes. Ask about free airport transfers if you book direct rather than booking on the website. All rooms are ensuite and have Wi-Fi and air-conditioning. For those with a car, the closest parking is either La Rotonde or Mignet.

LE CLOS DES FRÈRES GRIS

2240 avenue Fortuné Ferrini; tel. 04 42 24 13 37;
http://freres.gris.free.fr; €130 d

Le Clos des Frères Gris is a small bed-and-breakfast run by the Lecomte family. Caroline is English, her husband Hubert, French. Together they have been welcoming visitors to their home just outside Aix for 14 years. There are five bedrooms (only two with air-conditioning), all with ensuite bathrooms and a large garden with a swimming pool. Aix feels a long way away in this peaceful retreat, yet in reality it's just five minutes by car.

Over €200
HOTEL ROI RENÉ

24 boulevard du Roi René; tel. 04 42 37 61 00;
www.accorhotels.com/gb/hotel-1169-grand-hotel-roi-rene-aix-en-provence-centre-mgallery-by-sofitel/index.shtml; €260 d

Hotel Roi René, is part of the Accor Sofitel chain, and what it lacks in individual charm it makes up for in convenience. The lobby is large and perfect for a relaxing drink or coffee, and there's a good restaurant and a sizeable

Christmas in Aix-en-Provence

At any time of year, the Cours Mirabeau is enchanting to visit. At Christmas time it delivers memories to last for life. The smell of roasting chestnuts drifts in the air. Stretching up the road for as far as the eye can see, silver lights loop from centuries-old plane trees. All along one side of the road are pop-up shops housed in little wooden cabins. There's something for every member of the family: a delicate crystal ballerina encased in glass, cashmere gloves, wooden puzzles, and for the gourmand, truffle oils.

Cross the road and the terraces of the cafés are aglow with heaters and rosy faces. Stroll into the old town and the enchanting cobbled streets take on a magical dimension. Christmas trees glitter in windows and shoppers walk hand-in-hand, clutching bags of presents. Restaurants put on festive menus, vying with each other to discover the most inventive use for the "black diamond" of Provence, the truffle.

Christmas *santons*

At the base of the Cours Mirabeau, next to the bubbling waters of the Rotonde fountain is a santon fair. When these traditional nativity scenes were banned after the French revolution, the Provençaux took their faith underground. Locals began carving small wooden figures for their own crèches, and soon the new *santon* industry was born. Now it's possible to buy not only the Virgin Mary, baby Jesus, and accompanying animals, but also entire villages of people: There are fishmongers, chimney sweeps, knife grinders, even snail vendors. Another Provençal tradition not to be missed is the 13 desserts, which are traditionally eaten after midnight Mass on Christmas Eve. Thankfully, most of the 13 consist of fruits and nuts, so there's still room for a big meal the next day.

Make sure you pack a warm coat. Provence can get very cold in the winter. Snow in Aix is not uncommon.

open-air pool. It's two minutes' walk from the center and backs onto the open spaces of Park Jourdan. The rooms, as one would expect of the Sofitel chain, are standardized and comfortable. All are ensuite and have Wi-Fi and air-conditioning. Private parking is available.

Information and Services

TOURIST INFORMATION

Aix-en-Provence has a large, well-staffed **tourist office** (300 avenue Giuseppe Verdi; tel. 04 42 16 11 61; www.aixenprovencetourism.com). It is the departure point for many walking tours and the best place to pick up maps and information. It is located at the bottom of the Cours Mirabeau, at the entrance to Les Allées Provençal shopping center.

Book in Bar (4 rue Joseph Cabassol; www.bookinbar.com) bookshop and coffee shop is an excellent place to get in touch with the local expat network. They have a notice board full of postings for events and clubs for English speakers.

POST OFFICES

There are numerous post offices in Aix-en-Provence. The main office near La Rotonde fountain is on 2 rue Lapierre. It is open Mon.-Fri. 9am-6:30pm and Sat. 9am-noon and 2pm-5pm. More centrally, in the old town there is a post office in Place de l'Hôtel de Ville. It is open Mon.-Fri. 9am-noon and 1pm-6pm and Sat. 9am-noon.

HEALTH AND SAFETY
Police

The **police station** is located at Hotel de Police, avenue de l'Europe, Aix-en-Provence; tel. 04 42 93 97 00. To phone the police dial 17 or European emergency number 112.

Hospitals and Pharmacies

For health care, the **Centre Hospitalier du Pays d'Aix** (avenue des Tamaris, Aix-en-Provence; tel. 04 42 33 50 00) offers emergency services, including an excellent children's emergency department. There are numerous pharmacies in Aix-en-Provence. They all display a prominent green cross jutting out into the street. The pharmacy on the Cours Mirabeau is located at 17 bis Cours Mirabeau, and it is open Mon.-Sat. 8am-8pm.

COMMUNICATIONS
Wi-Fi

Many, but by no means all, cafés offer free Wi-Fi. Ask before sitting down. The Les Allees Provençale shopping center (95 avenue Giuseppe Verdi) offers free Wi-Fi.

Transportation

GETTING THERE
By Air
MARSEILLE PROVENCE AIRPORT

Marignane

Marseille Provence Airport is 32 kilometers (20 miles) from Aix and offers 152 regular flight routes. The drive to Aix-en-Provence takes about 30 minutes. Traffic in the morning and evening is bad, so allow an hour at these times of day. It has a dedicated low-cost flight terminal, offering budget flights with carriers such as **Ryan Air** and **Easyjet** to many European capitals. A **shuttle bus** runs every half hour from the airport to the center of Aix, also stopping at the Aix **TGV train station.** The journey takes 1 hour and costs €8.60.

By Train
AIX-EN-PROVENCE TGV STATION

9 route Départementale, Aix-en-Provence;
www.voyages.sncf.com

The TGV station is located a short distance outside the city center. It offers high-speed connections to major European destinations (Paris 3 hours, Barcelona 4 hours). A **shuttle bus** runs every half hour to the center of town, taking 30 minutes and costing €4.30. All TGV train tickets need to be booked in advance, either online or from a ticket office at a train station.

LOCAL TRAINS

Local trains, including ones from Marseille, stop at the **central train station** on rue Gustave Desplaces.

By Bus
AIX CENTER BUS STATION

Boulevard Victor Coq, tel. 08 09 40 04 15,
www.lepilote.com

The bus station, Aix Center, is located 500 meters (0.3 miles) from the town center. Buses run every 30 minutes to **Marseille airport** and the **TGV station** (taking 60 minutes and 30 minutes, respectively), and frequently to **Marseille, Avignon,** and **Arles.** There is an extensive network of local destinations.

By Car

At the heart of the autoroute network of Provence, Aix-en-Provence is easy to get to and it makes an ideal base for exploring the rest of the region.

From Marseille Provence Airport: Take the D9 for 28 kilometers (17 miles), about 29 minutes.

From Avignon: Take the A7 for 88 kilometers (55 miles), about 60 minutes.

From Lyon: Take the A7 for 300 kilometers (186 miles), about 3 hours.

From Paris: Take the A6 and the A7, covering 760 kilometers (472 miles), about 7 hours 30 minutes.

From Arles: Take the A54 for 77 kilometers (48 miles), about 1 hour.

From Cannes/Nice: Take the A8 for 175 kilometers (109 miles), about 2 hours.

From Barcelona: Take the Ap-7 and the A9, covering 500 kilometers (311 miles), about 5 hours.

GETTING AROUND

Once visitors have arrived in the center of Aix en Provence, there is little need for public transportation. The old town is largely pedestrian. It takes a little over 15 minutes **on foot** to cross from one side of the old town to the other. Probably because of this, there is no pickup and drop-off cycle scheme in Aix, and in central Aix cycling is not a popular method of transportation. For the less mobile, the Diabline electric vehicles are a good way of getting around. The bus network is not heavily used by tourists.

Bus and Diablines

The local bus network is provided by **Aix en Bus** (www.aixenbus.fr). It is a good option for visits to Cezanne's atelier, which is about a 20-minute walk up a hill from the center of town. Routes number 5 and 10 depart from the **La Rotonde stop** next to the Apple Store and take you to the atelier.

A new express bus route is under construction.

The historic center of Aix-en-Provence is served by small electric vehicles called **Diablines.** They follow three routes and have access to the otherwise pedestrianized old town area. Tickets cost €060 and are purchased directly from the driver. There are no specified stops; a Diabline will stop when hailed.

Taxi/Uber

The main **taxi rank** is at the bottom of the Cours Mirabeau near La Rotonde fountain. Taxis can also be booked through **Taxi Radio Aixois** (tel. 04 42 27 71 11) or by using the **Uber** app or asking at your hotel. Licensed taxi journeys are metered. Note taxis are not needed to travel around Aix. It is much easier to walk, although visitors may consider taking one to Cezanne's atelier, which is about a 20-minute walk up a hill from the center of town.

Pays d'Aix-en-Provence

To the east of Aix is some of the most beautiful countryside in Provence. Mont Sainte-Victoire is, of course, the star of the show, drawing the eye with the ever-changing interplay of light and rock that so entranced Cézanne. In summer the surrounding landscape is a patchwork of different shades of green. The brittle almost gray olive groves, the lush light vineyards, and the darker pine forests blur together in the indeterminate lines of an impressionist painting. Hiking, biking, and wine tasting are the main activities, although in July and August many people choose just to sit by a pool and listen to the chorus of cicadas.

Heading to the north toward the Durance and to the west toward Arles, there are pleasant towns and villages that serve as commuter settlements for people working in and around Aix, as well as on the nuclear research project, ITER, to the north near Manosque. The stand-out sight to visit is one of the most architecturally ambitious vineyards in the world, Château La Coste, where an afternoon or even a day can be lost in artistic and epicurean pleasures.

South of Aix-en-Provence, the countryside is choked by a necklace of motorways and various out-of-town shopping centers that all eventually blend into the outskirts of Marseille.

ORIENTATION

Le Tholonet and **Saint-Antonin-sur-Bayon** are the main bases for exploring **Mont Sainte-Victoire** from the south, and **Vauvenargues** is the main base from the north. These villages can be easily reached by car from the center of Aix. The **D17** runs through Le Tholonet (15 minutes from the center of Aix) and Saint-Antonin-sur-Bayon (20 minutes from the center of Aix). The **D10** from the center of Aix takes you to Vauvenargues in 30 minutes. It's possible to drive the entire circuit of Mont Victoire: The D17 and the D10 are linked just to the east of the village of Puyloubier by the D23.

Other key points of orientation around Aix are the town of **Rognes,** 30 minutes north of Aix, which hosts a famous piano festival in the summer and is the home of a much-loved truffle market before Christmas. And the **Cistercian Silvacane Abbey** is just north of Rognes outside the village of La Roque-d'Anthéron. Also of interest, **Chateau La Coste** vineyard and art center is to the south of Rognes on the way back toward Aix, near the village of Le-Puy-Sainte-Réparade. South of Aix on the way toward Marseille is the town of **Aubagne,** which is nestled west of the **Sainte-Baume Massif,** a rock formation that divides the Var and Bouches-du-Rhone departements. Aubagne is also home to the French Foreign Legion Museum.

SIGHTS
Silvacane Abbey

RD561, La Roque-d'Anthéron; tel. 04 42 50 41 69; www.abbaye-silvacane.com/fr/infos-pratiques; May-Sept. daily 10am-5:15pm, Oct.-Apr. closed Mon.; €7.50, free under 12

One of three Cistercian Abbeys in Provence, Silvacane was built in the 12th century. The Abbey's bare Gothic- and Roman-influenced architecture still conveys a sense of the life of devotion led by the monks. The Cistercians—known as the white monks because their robes were left undyed—divided their days between devotion, manual work, and intellectual improvement. The visit takes in the Abbey's various rooms, such as the *salle des monies* where the monks copied manuscripts and the *salle capitulaire* for hearing confessions, as well as its gardens and the *vivier* (fishpond), which supplied the monks with food. Silvacane now stages art exhibitions, piano recitals, even acrobatic shows

French Foreign Legion Museum Aubagne

Chemin de la Thuilière, Aubagne; tel. 04 42 18 10 96; https://musee.legion-etrangere.com; Sat.-Sun. 10am-noon and 2pm-6pm; free

Since 1831 many of the most forlorn, lovesick young men in the world have joined the French Foreign Legion to forget their troubles and spill their blood for France. At least that's how joining has often been portrayed in film and literature. A more accurate history of the Legion can be enjoyed at its Museum. Men of any nationality can still join the Legion today. The Legion is renowned for fostering a sense of belonging; recruits swear allegiance not to the French state but to the Legion itself. The purpose of the museum is to remember and honor the legionnaires of the past and to integrate and educate new recruits. The museum features temporary exhibitions as well as permanent exhibits dating back to the heroic age of the legion in the 19th century, recalling its most desperate battles.

HIKING
★ Mont Sainte-Victoire

Pays d'Aix-en-Provence; tel. 04 42 26 67 37; www.grandsitesaintevictoire.com.

Thousands of people live their daily lives in the shadow of this white and gray limestone massif, and thousands more drive past on the motorways that circle around its base. Mont Sainte-Victoire dominates the landscape of the Pays d'Aix-en-Provence, yet many locals and tourists are ignorant of the secrets of the mountain. Like Cézanne, they regard it from afar.

The mountain is rich in biodiversity. The garrigue, or scrubland, which to the untrained eye appears uniform, contains numerous species of plant, including rosemary, thyme, gorse, and wild-flowers, all of which explode into color in spring, draping the bare rock in pinks, whites and yellows. Pines, oaks, olives, almond, mulberry, and cypress trees complete a landscape in which birdlife proliferates. Unsurprisingly, the mountain is a center for outdoor sports, from hiking and biking to parascending, climbing, and horseback riding. For *Jurassic Park* enthusiasts, there's always the chance of stepping on a dinosaur egg, left from the 1950s when a spate of archaeological discoveries led to Aix being rechristened "Eggs en Provence." Just below the Mont's 1,011-meter (3,316-foot) peak is the 19-meter (62-foot) iron cross of Provence. It was installed in 1877 to give thanks to God that France had been saved from the Prussians.

Particularly during the summer, access can be restricted because of the fire risk. Always check with the information centers or on the website for the latest information.

CHAPEL HIKE

Trailhead: *Vauvenargues Information Center (Maison du Grande Site Sainte-Victoire), Place de Verdun, Vauvenargues*

Distance: *12 km (7 mi)*

Hiking Time: *4 hours*

Information: *Vauvenargues Information Center, tel. 08 92 68 72 70; www.grandsitesaintevictoire. com; Apr. 6-Sept. 30 10am-1pm and 2pm-6pm*

After consulting at Vauvenargues Information Center opposite the church in Vauvenargues, the fit and adventurous can scale the heights and visit a former hermit's refuge that has been converted into a small chapel. The route takes you from the Vauvenargues valley on a marked trail (GR9, white and red markers) up to 986 meters (3,234 feet) where the chapel is located.

spring poppies beneath Mont Sainte-Victoire

SENTIER IMOUCHA

Trailhead: *Parking du barrage Bimont, Saint-Marc Jaumegarde*

Distance: *9 km (6 mi)*

Hiking Time: *3-4 hours*

Information: *Barrage Bimont Information Center, www.grandsitesaintevictoire.com; June 1-Sept. 30 9:30am-12:30pm and 3pm-6pm*

Departing from the car park for the Bimont dam, where there is an information kiosk (Barrage Bimont Information Center) with route information, the Sentier Imoucha is the most popular hike onto Sainte-Victoire. From the kiosk, cross the dam and pick up the trail posts on the far side. As with most hikes in Provence it passes from sunshine to shade, climbing gently toward the Iron Cross of Provence at the summit of Sainte-Victoire. From the cross you will need to retrace your route for 1 kilometer (0.6 miles) before the trail splits, offering you an alternate route back to the parking to complete a circle. Along the way, you will be treated to many different perspectives of Mont Sainte-Victoire, many of which are featured in Cézanne's paintings. You'll need good walking shoes and to be prepared for the occasional steep ascent/descent.

SUMMIT SENTIERS

Trailhead: *Saint Antonin Sur Bayon Maison Sainte-Victoire Visitor Center parking lot, 17 chemin départemental, Saint Antonin Sur Bayon*

Distance: *Varies by route*

Hiking Time: *4 hours*

Information: *Saint Antonin Sur Bayon Maison Sainte-Victoire Visitor Center; 04 13 31 94 70; www.departement13.fr/le-13-en-action/environnement/les-lieux-daccueil/la-maison-sainte-victoire; Mon.-Fri. 10am-6pm, Sat.-Sun 10am-7pm.*

From the visitors center parking lot, follow the signs for the Mont Sainte-Victoire sentiers. It's possible to follow four different routes, marked as yellow, red, green, and black, to the Iron Cross at the top of the mountain. Yellow is the hardest and is occasionally closed because of falling rocks. Always ask for route information at the visitors center before starting

out. Allow at least 4 hours for the climb and descent. For those who do not wish to reach the summit, the brown sentier offers great views of Mont Sainte-Victoire, taking you east 8 kilometers (5 miles) to Puyloubier. It is an easy hike, but it's not circular. Enquire at the visitors center about guided walks.

SAINT-SER CHAPEL HIKE/ BOTANIC WALK

Trailhead: *Parking Saint-Ser, D13 Avenue Cezanne, 1.5km east of Puyloubier*

Distance: *3 km (2 mi)/1 km (0.6 mi)*

Hiking Time: *1.25 hours/1 hour*

For an easier climb, head to the parking Saint-Ser in Puyloubier and follow the trail shown by the red markers to the Saint-Ser Chapel. From the chapel, there is an excellent view of the vineyards of Puyloubier, the valley of the River Arc, which runs into Aix, and the Sainte-Baume Massif that marks the boundary between the Bouches-du-Rhone departement and the Var.

Another option from the same parking area is to follow a botanic walk, which takes around 1 hour, covers 1 kilometer (0.6 miles), and introduces you to the main species of plant on the mountain.

OTHER SPORTS AND RECREATION
Cycling

On a spring or autumn day there are few more scenic bike routes than looping around Mont Sainte-Victoire, stopping at vineyards for a wine tasting, or at one of the many restaurants for lunch. The road, which you will have to share with cars, is gentle and passes from sun to shade, and there are plenty of places to stop and admire the view. Follow the D17 on the southern side and the D10 on the northern side. The road that links north and south is the D23.

STATION BEES

Le Tholonet: parking Paysager des Infernets, 3333 Route Cezanne, tel. 07 81 64 47 34; Vauvenargues:

boulevard du Moraliste, 06 50 55 90 51;
www.stationsbees.com; July-Aug. daily
8:30am-11:30am and 4pm-7:30, check website out of
season; from €25

This outfit rents e-bike at two locations, Le Tholonet or Vauvenargues, for access to Mont Sainte-Victoire.

Golf
DOMAINE DE PONT ROYAL
Mallemort; tel. 04 90 57 40 79;
www.golf-pontroyal.com; daily
€65-85 green fee

This is one of the best golf courses in Provence, designed by the late Severiano Ballesteros. To succeed here you will need some of the designer's legendary powers of escape. There are numerous water hazards and the occasional rocky chasm to negotiate. Views from certain points on the course are spectacular. For a more casual game, there is also a 6-hole par 3 course, which is interesting even for those with a low handicap.

WINERIES
★ ART WALK AT CHÂTEAU LA COSTE
2750 route de la Cride, Le Puy Ste Reparade;
tel. 04 42 61 92 92; https://Chateau-la-coste.com/en;
Mon.-Fri 10am-5pm, Sat.-Sun. 10am-7pm; cave visit
€12, art walk €15, tasting free

Arriving at Château La Coste is visually shocking. First there's the winery, an elongated silver dome glinting in the sun that looks more suited to housing fighter jets than making wine. Next there's the sculpture of a *Lord of the Rings*-size spider, created by Louis Bourgeois, skating on a thin film of water. In the distance, an elliptic silver pod rotates, appearing as if it has just landed from outer space. The château is a modern art and architecture destination as much as a vineyard. After contemplating the often challenging works—simultaneously alien and totally at home in their environment—you can taste the domaine's wines take a full tour of the wine-making facilities, and enjoy a meal in one of the estate's four restaurants.

CHÂTEAU VIGNELAURE
Route de Jouques, Rians; tel. 04 94 37 21 10;
www.vignelaure.com; March-Dec., daily 10am-5pm;
visit to cave and art gallery €7, tasting free

The famed American wine critic Robert Parker calls Château Vignelaure "one of the showpiece properties not only of Provence, but of France." Cabernet sauvignon from the vines of Château La Lagune in Bordeaux was planted here in 1966, making this the first winery to use this Bordeaux grape varietal in Provence. There are now five subterranean levels to age the wine, each holding its own secrets, including an art gallery filled with photos by Henri Cartier Bresson and more recent works of modern art, and a rock wall into which wine cuvées have been built. At each turn in the underground maze there are iron grills that have to be unlocked and slid back to provide access to the precious wine of a particular vintage. The garden is a Provençal dream, filled with works of art, with a terrace abutted by two basins, giving way to a row of plane trees running down to the gates.

DOMAINE DES MASQUES
Chemin Maurely, Saint-Antonin-sur-Bayon;
www.domainedesmasques.com;
tel. 04 42 12 38 30; telephone in advance; tasting
free, cellar tour on request

The road to Domaines des Masques can be off-putting. There are signs prohibiting access to all but fire vehicles, and there are bumps that will destroy the undercarriage of a sports car. But even if you have no interest in wine, it is worth the ride. When descending there's a sensational view of Mont Sainte-Victoire and you'll have the wonderful feeling of being totally alone in the Provençal countryside. For the last few hundred meters, the track bumps along the edge of the Plateau du Cengle, the belt-like rock formation that runs around the foot of Mont Sainte-Victoire. The vineyard, when it comes into view, is a delight. Rows of lavender chase up to the door of an old *mas* (farmhouse), and cypress trees pierce the sky outside the cave. The tasting room is to one side of the ultramodern wine-making facilities.

FESTIVALS AND EVENTS

ROGNES TRUFFLE MARKET

Cours Saint Etienne, Rognes; www.festivites-rognes. fr/fete-de-la-truffe; all day the Sun. before Christmas

Since 1988, year after year, the Rognes Truffle Market has grown in size. A variety of Christmas culinary treats are on sale, but the star of the show is undoubtedly the truffle. The deep earthy smell of the black diamond of Provence hangs in the cold winter air. The traders are always ready with cooking instructions, suggesting, for example, a last-minute shaving of truffle over the traditional Christmas bird of Provence, the capon. For those in want of an immediate hit there are stands selling scrambled eggs seasoned with truffle shavings, which is absolutely delicious. If you purchase a truffle, expect to pay around €90 per 100 grams (3.5 ounces).

LA ROQUE D'ANTHÉRON INTERNATIONAL PIANO FESTIVAL

Château de Florans, La Roque d'Anthéron; tel. 04 42 50 51 15; www.festival-piano.com/en/homepage/welcome.html; mid-July-mid-Aug.; tickets €39-55

Lovers of classical music will already have heard of La Roque D'Anthéron International Piano Festival. Nearly 80,000 tickets are sold every year. Most recitals take place in the enchanting outdoor arena in the grounds of the Château de Florans or in the nearby Cistercian Abbey of Silvacane. In recent years the festival has also spread its wings, staging concerts as far afield as the Théâtre Antique in Arles. However, the mainstay of the festival and the reason for its continued success remains the unique atmosphere offered by the nighttime concerts at Château de Florans.

FOOD

★ RESTAURANT DAN B

1 rue Frédéric Mistral, Ventabren; tel. 04 42 28 79 33; www.danb.fr/en; Apr.-Sept. noon-1:15pm and 7:45pm-9:15pm, closed Mon., Tues.,

and Sat. lunch, Oct.-Mar. closed Mon., Tues. lunch, and Sun. evening; two-course lunch €48, evening tasting menu €77

Architecture and fine dining meet in perfect harmony in Restaurant Dan B. A small stone Provençal terrace with a view over the surrounding countryside has been transformed into a modern temple to gastronomy. An entire glass wall slides away, opening the restaurant to the countryside. On summer nights the sound of cicadas is like a concert. Acoustics, chairs, tables, knives and forks—every detail has been analyzed and planned with the aim of perfecting the dining experience. The menu is imaginative and playful. The food is joyous and delicious, full of color, texture, and flavor, relying on seasonal vegetables, locally caught fish, and carefully sourced meat.

★ RESTAURANT SAINT ESTEVE

2250 route Cézanne, Le Tholonet; www.leslodgessaintevictoire.com/fr/restaurant-le-st-esteve.html; tel. 04 42 27 10 14; daily noon-2pm and 7:30pm-10pm; mains €69-89

There's an additional presence at every table in the Restaurant Saint Esteve, a dining partner who says little but surveys all. This inescapable "third person" is Mont Sainte-Victoire. So perfect is the view of the mountain that it almost feels like you are dining inside a painter's canvass. The food more than matches the environment with classical French dishes such as guinea fowl with girolle mushrooms executed to perfection.

SOUVENIRS D'AVENIR

Val de Campoumal, Jouques; tel. 04 42 63 70 26; daily noon-2pm and 6:45pm-10:45pm, closed Mon.-Tues. and Sat.; €12.50 three-course lunch with wine

Lunch at Souvenirs d'Avenir is simply a fantastic value. The locals are not ones to pass up a deal, and they come from afar to fill up this hilltop restaurant. There's a garden for children to play in, a shady terrace, and a cheerful feeling that comes from eating good food at a great price. Portions are large, and the cooking rustic; expect salads that spill off their plates, and grilled meat with sauces.

ACCOMMODATIONS
€100-200
★ RELAIS SAINT-SER

Avenue Cézanne, Puyloubier, Pays d'Aix-en-Provence;
tel. 04 42 66 37 26;
www.relaisdesaintser.com; €125 d

The Relais is a recently renovated old farmhouse just outside of Puyloubier. There are eight spacious rooms, five with terraces, and all with ensuite bathrooms and Wi-Fi. Guests can walk the 100 or so meters (328 feet) and touch the base of Mont Sainte-Victoire. In the clear skies above, paragliders swirl on thermals before swooping to their landing point adjacent to the hotel. Best of all is the sensational panorama from the terrace. Fields of vines and olive trees sweep away toward the Massif de Sainte-Baume. It's a view to revel in. There's an excellent restaurant and a pool with the same scenic view.

Over €200
CHÂTEAU FONSCOLOMBE

Route de Saint-Canadet, Le Puy-Sainte-Réparade,
Pays d'Aix-en-Provence;
tel. 04 42 21 13 13;
https://fonscolombe.fr; €240 d

Château Fonscolombe, is a great choice for those wishing to explore both the Luberon and Aix-en-Provence. Almost equidistant between the two, this renovated 18th-century château has retained all the grandeur and imperiousness of its heyday. Guests get to glimpse the past as they move between the various formal reception rooms. The bedrooms are tastefully decorated to echo the history of the château. All have air-conditioning, ensuite bathrooms, and Wi-Fi. The estate produces its own excellent wines; there's also a spa and a swimming pool, and extensive grounds to explore.

LES LODGES DE SAINTE-VICTOIRE

2250 route Cézanne, Le Tholonet, Pays d'Aix-en-Provence; tel. 04 42 50 51 15;
www.leslodgessaintevictoire.com; €360 d

Staying at Les Lodges de Sainte-Victoire is one of the most relaxing ways to see Aix and the surrounding countryside. The location is wonderful: a hotel set in a mature park with views of Mont Sainte-Victoire. Centuries-old plane trees shade the terrace, and there are two restaurants to choose from. There are seven different room types in all, ranging from a standard room to a luxury suite. All have air-conditioning, ensuite bathrooms, and Wi-Fi. A short hop in a car along the route de Cézanne takes you to the center of the city. It's easy to pop in for a morning or a couple of hours and then return to the poolside. Hiking and biking are on the doorstep.

GETTING THERE AND AROUND

Once you have arrived, the villages listed in this section are best explored **on foot.** Walking between villages and sights, though, is not advisable; the distances tend to be long and the roads busy. The exception is when following a marked sentier, such as the brown sentier between Saint-Antonin-sur-Bayon and Puyloubier to the south of Mont Sainte-Victoire.

By Car

From the center of **Aix,** the **D7** takes you out toward Le Tholonet and the southern face of Mont Sainte-Victoire, and the **D10** leads to Vauvenargues and the northern face of the mountain. The two roads meet at the village of Pourrières where the **D23** takes you around to the opposite face of the mountain. Jouques and the River Durance can be reached by taking the **D11** from near Vauvenargues. These roads are small and picturesque, and in places they wind up and down hills.

To head north from Aix toward Silvacane Abbey, Rognes, and Château La Coste, take the **D14.** Again, this is a small, picturesque road. The main autoroute north is the **A7.**

The **A52** motorway takes you south out of Aix toward Aubagne and the French Foreign Legion Museum.

By Bus

Bus is the only way to explore the Pays d'Aix-en-Provence without a car. Buses run from the **central bus station** on boulevard Victor Coq in Aix (tel. 08 09 40 04 15). The main routes you may want to use are: **Line 140,** to Vauvenargues, approximately one bus every hour 7am-8pm; **Line 110,** Le Tholonet, approximately one bus every hour 7am-7pm; and **No. 250 Rognes** and **Le Roque D'Antheron,** approximately one bus every hour 6am-9pm. You can find precise times and maps for these routes online at www.lepilote.com.

Marseille, Les Calanques, and the Côte Bleue

Marseille: You either love it or you hate it. The city, which began life as a small Greek trading settlement in 600BC, is today a big, brash, multicultural, graffiti-splattered metropolis and port. It's a sensory whirlwind that's part African, part Arab, part European, and as much Mediterranean as it is French. For country bumpkins, the shock of arrival can be an unexpected slap to the face. When visitors recover, they discover a city rich in culture and blessed by some of the most inspiring architecture in Provence. Hidden amid the cars, the trams, and the crowds are neighborhoods so picturesque it's difficult to believe they belong to the same city.

At the turn of the 21st century, Marseille had developed a reputation for organized crime and drugs and was considered to be only for

Highlights

Look for ★ to find recommended sights, activities, dining, and lodging.

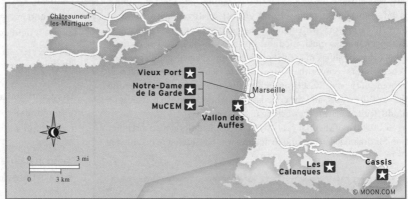

★ **Vieux Port:** Overlooked by Notre-Dame de la Garde, this is the heart of the city, where man, metropolis, and the Mediterranean meet, and where any tour of the city should begin (page 236).

★ **Notre-Dame de la Garde:** High on a hill, Notre-Dame de la Garde is more than just a church; the Marseillais believe a whispered prayer to the huge statue of the Virgin Mary crowning the dome will save them. Wherever you are in Marseille, you can sense the statue glinting in the sun (page 237).

★ **MuCEM:** Architect Rudi Riciotti's MuCEM hosts a permanent exhibition about Mediterranean culture, but the star is the building itself. It's a work of futuristic fantasy that enlivens anybody's day (page 241).

★ **Vallon des Auffes:** The port of this city is nestled in a rocky coastal inlet. Fishermen mend nets and small waves ripple into the harbor. The feel is very much Greek island rather than big city.

Yet the old port is only a five-minute drive away (page 246).

★ **Bouillabaisse:** This fish soup is synonymous with the city, and eating a bowl is a theatrical dining experience, with waiters tending to the bubbling pot with a maternal level of care (page 254).

★ **Cassis:** Sitting at the foot of the highest cliff in Europe, surrounded by vineyards producing the best white wine in Provence, within walking distance of the first of the Calanques, and with arguably the most beautiful harbor in the south of France, Cassis is simply a must-visit (page 265).

★ **Les Calanques:** This area offers the opportunity to travel back in time and experience France's Mediterranean coast, free from the curse of mass tourism. Largely inaccessible to cars, this dreamy stretch of pine-fringed seaside is reached on foot or by boat (page 271).

the adventurous tourist. Recent years, however, have thankfully transformed the city. In 2001 it was finally connected to Paris by the high-speed TGV train, which brought much-needed business investment. Major sports tournaments followed, such as the Rugby World Cup in 2007. Marseille was even voted the most welcoming city of the tournament, a title that would have been unthinkable just 10 years earlier.

The good times kept rolling. In 2013 it was designated by the European Union as the European Capital of Culture—a distinction that is marked with a series of multicultural events. In the years leading up to the big occasion, money poured into the city, financing major urban-renewal work, including the Euroméditerranée project, which redeveloped the quays nearest the old port. The ripple effect still hasn't finished. Opening in 2021 is a multimillion-euro re-creation of the nearby (but inaccessible) Grotte Cosquer, a coastal cave filled with 29,000-year-old prehistoric paintings.

And so, in the space of under 20 years, the city has opened itself up to the world. It now offers visitors an eclectic mix of major sights, vibrant neighborhoods, and picturesque seaside spots. The MuCEM building, the center-piece of the Euroméditerranée project, links past and future with its modernist bridge crossings to Fort Saint-Jean and the old port. The Cathédrale de la Major and Notre-Dame de La Garde are avant-garde ecclesiastical constructions that bring a smile to the face. The Palais Longchamp is the site of the biggest fountain most people are likely to see in their lives, and a reminder of Marseille's prosperity in the 19th century.

Then there are simpler joys, like walking around the old port and visiting its fish market, or discovering neighborhoods like Le Panier and the Cours Julien, which are incubators for youthful artisan talent and creativity. Remarkably, it's also possible to slip away

from the bustle of the city into seaside inlets, such as Vallon des Auffes, that call to mind the fishing villages of small Mediterranean islands. To swim from the rocks at Malmousque in the Endoume neighborhood first thing in the morning is to experience a freedom every bit as delicious as the bouillabaisse soup for which the city is famous.

The discoveries continue to either side of Marseille, where there are two of the most scenic stretches of coast in the South of France. For beauty and crystalline waters, they easily surpass the more celebrated French Riviera. One area, Les Calanques to the east of Marseille heading toward Cassis, is a much-feted national park. Mostly accessible on foot or by boat, the coastline transports visitors back to the Mediterranean of the past, free from traffic jams and crowds, allowing the unalloyed beauty of nature to shine through. To the west of Marseille is the lesser known but still impressive Côte Bleue, where the main resorts are linked by a vertiginously beautiful railway line

Many tourists simply ignore Marseille and head to these coastal areas, but those ready for the challenges presented by a big city are likely to be seduced by its undoubted inner beauty.

ORIENTATION

Marseille is a big city. Whereas the centers of other cities in this book—Aix, Arles, Avignon, and Toulon—can be crossed on foot in little more than 20 minutes, it can easily take an hour or more to walk between different neighborhoods in Marseille.

The city is divided into **16 arrondissements.** To simplify matters, this guidebook divides them into five areas:

Vieux Port

Head to the old port and the adjacent hill to the south, upon which sits the church of **Notre-Dame de la Garde,** to get an instant feel for the atmosphere of the city. It's where

---

Previous: boats line the harbor in Marseille's old port; the sparkling waters of the Calanques are a magical place to swim; the unforgettable MuCEM building in Marseille.

Marseille, Les Calanques, and the Côte Bleue

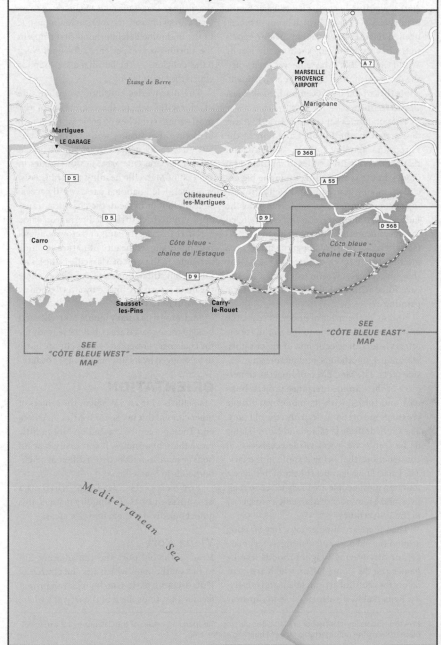

Étang de Berre

MARSEILLE PROVENCE AIRPORT

A 7

Marignane

Martigues
LE GARAGE

D 368

D 5

A 55

Châteauneuf-
les-Martigues

D 5

D 9

D 568

Carro

Côte bleue -
chaine de l'Estaque

Côte bleue -
chaine de l'Estaque

D 9

Sausset-
les-Pins

Carry-
le-Rouet

SEE
"CÔTE BLEUE EAST"
MAP

SEE
"CÔTE BLEUE WEST"
MAP

Mediterranean Sea

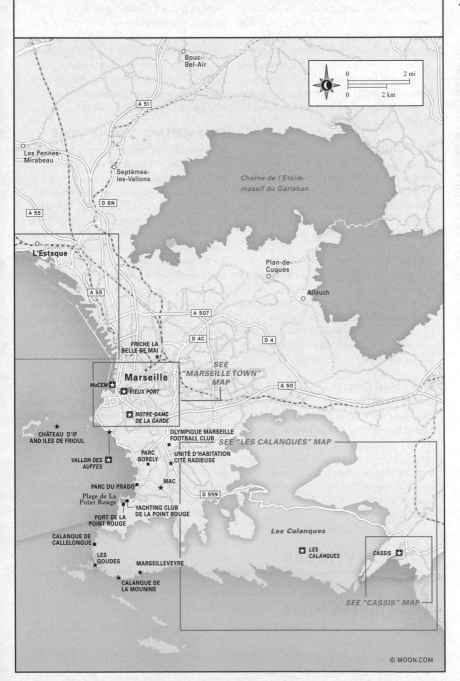

old meets new, as fishermen unload their catch in centuries-old fashion in the shadow of the daring modernist **L'Ombrière,** designed by Norman Foster. Climb away from the port toward Notre-Dame de la Garde, and the streets of the city immediately clasp you in their multicultural embrace, with ethic supermarkets and Provençal *brocante* shops sharing the sidewalks.

Le Panier

The oldest residential district of Marseille is adjacent to the old port facing Notre-Dame de la Garde. Le Panier is a warren of narrow cobbled streets that climb up toward the impressive **Vieille Charité** building. Head here for boho boutiques and colorful street art.

Euroméditerranée Project

The quays adjacent to the **Fort Saint-Jean** at the entrance to the old port were redeveloped as part of the Marseille 2013 Capital of Culture celebrations. This neighborhood is dominated by the **MuCEM** building. The grand public spaces are the perfect antidote to the tight streets of the rest of the city.

Marseille Center

The **La Canebière** shopping street heads east, away from the old port toward **Palais Longchamp.** This is the least touristy of the five areas; here you encounter the city at work, with presses of people boarding trams and hurrying (as much as the Provençal can) from meeting to meeting. The stand-out sight is the Palais Longchamp, and for shopping the **Cours Julien.**

Toward Les Calanques

Heading south into the outskirts of Marseille along the coast, you really begin to appreciate the two faces of Marseille. The big smoke fades, giving way to long beaches and parks, and unforgettable inlets like **Vallon des Auffes,** a seaside port that would not feel out of place on a remote Greek island.

PLANNING YOUR TIME

If you decide you want to dive into Marseille, as distinct as it is from the rest of Provence, even a stay of a week is not long enough to explore it properly. Before you arrive, prioritize what you want to see and plan how to get from one sight to another. Buy the **City Pass** from the tourist office (an adult pass costs €26 for 24 hours, €33 for 48 hours, and €41 for 72 hours, www.marseille-tourisme.com/fileadmin/user_upload/CityPassAvril2018_FicheGB.pdf). Not only do you get free access to all the city's museums, but also it serves as a transit pass on the public transport network. If spending some time in a big city appeals to you, then allocate at least a couple of nights to Marseille. However, if you are attracted by some of the world-class sights but don't want the associated hassles of urban life, then it's possible to dip into Marseille for a day, say, before or after your flight from **Marseille Provence Airport.** You can easily get a feel of the place by visiting the **old port** and **MuCEM,** and enjoying a lunch by the seaside. Try to allow a day to visit **Cassis** and **Les Calanques** as well, and, if possible, a third day to enjoy the **Côte Bleue,** which can be visited by train.

Itinerary Ideas

A DAY IN MARSEILLE

1 Begin the day with a riot of wonderful color wandering through the **Panier** district and admiring the street art.

2 Stop at **Cup of Tea** for a light breakfast.

3 Continue the climb up through the neighborhood to enjoy the architectural splendor of **Vieille Charité.**

4 Make your way down out of the Panier toward the **Euroméditerranée project.**

5 Tour the architectually impressive **MuCEM.** Make sure to exit the MuCEM on the fourth floor, taking the futuristic, vertigo-inducing pedestrian bridge to Fort Saint-Jean.

6 Stop for lunch on the old port at **Au Bout du Quai.**

7 Walk around the **old port** and see what you think of Norman Foster's architectural fantasy **L'Ombrière.**

8 Catch a tram up the **Canebière** to see the cascading waters of the **Palais Longchamp.**

9 Finish the day with a walk in the **Jardin du Pharo.**

10 Have supper in the **Chalet du Pharo** restaurant overlooking the glinting lights of the old port.

MARSEILLE LIKE A LOCAL

1 Begin the day in style: Swim off the rocks at **Malmousque.** Follow this exertion with two of the blackest coffees you can find.

2 Head up to **Notre-Dame de la Garde** and pin an ex-voto to the wall, giving thanks for your continued existence. Have another black coffee.

3 Lunch on seafood at **Maison Calambo** while reading about the fortunes of the Olympique Marseille soccer team in *La Provence.*

4 Head to the **Parc du Prado** for either a siesta on a shady bench or a game of boule.

5 As the heat drains from the day, enjoy a pastis overlooking the old port at **Café de L'Abbaye.** Tell your friends an exaggerated story about how you narrowly escaped colliding with a cruise ship on your early morning swim.

6 Finish the day dancing away to Corsican folk music in the **Son des Guitares.**

A DAY IN CASSIS

1 Begin the day with a gentle walk. Take the avenue des Calanques, until you arrive at the large parking for the Presqu'il. Follow the circular **Sentier de Petit Prince** around the shady, pine tree-covered headland, enjoying the vertiginous views of Calanque de Port-Miou.

2 Browse the shops of Cassis and then enjoy a leisurely lunch on the port at **Chez Gilbert,** making sure to sample the excellent local white wine.

3 Arrange a **boat tour** with Les Calanques en Bateau to take you along the coast to see the more inaccessible **calanques.** Bring your bathing suit for a dip along the way.

4 Finish the day by driving along the **Route des Crêtes** to the top of the Cap Canaille and admiring the view out to sea from the highest cliff in Europe.

Marseille Itinerary Ideas

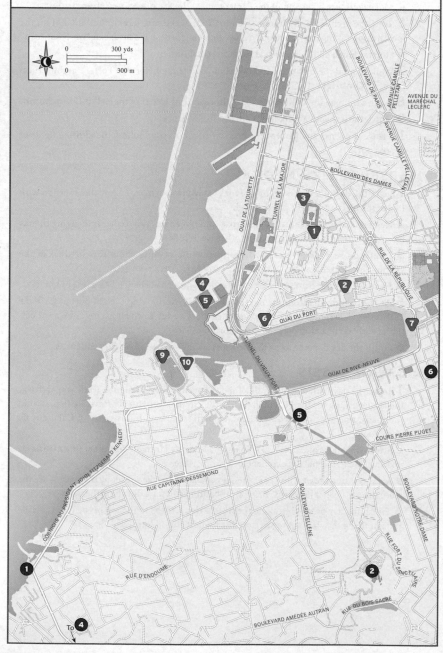

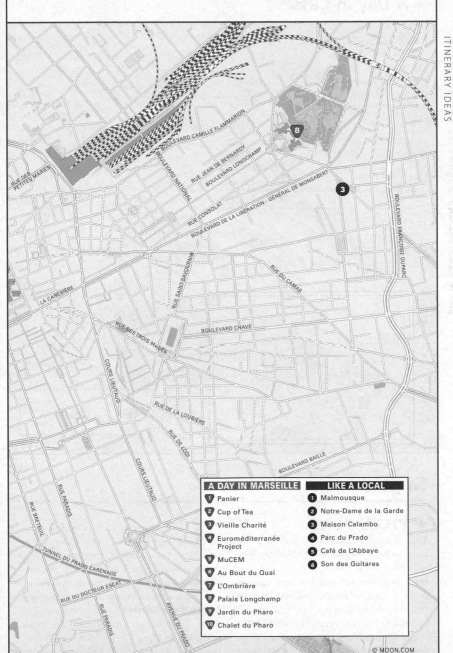

© MOON.COM

A Day in Cassis

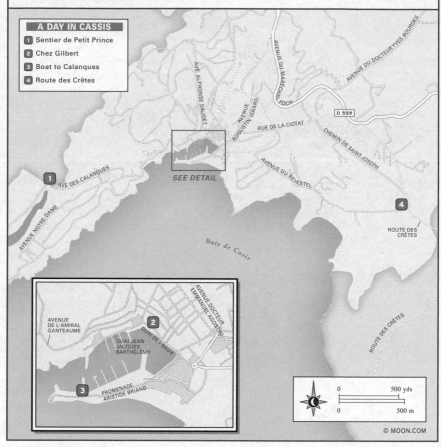

A DAY IN CASSIS
1. Sentier de Petit Prince
2. Chez Gilbert
3. Boat to Calanques
4. Route des Crêtes

© MOON.COM

Sights

★ VIEUX PORT

The entrance to the old port is guarded by two forts, **Saint-Jean** and **Saint-Nicolas.** These were built in the 17th century as symbols of royal authority. Tellingly, the forts' cannons faced inward toward the notoriously rebellious city rather than out to sea, where four islands can be seen, including **Château D'If,** where the fictional Edmund Dantes was imprisoned in Alexandre Dumas's *The Count of Monte Cristo.* Boats for visits to the Frioul islands and tours of the Calanques, along with several bus routes, depart from the old port.

On the hill, south of the port, are the **Abbaye Saint-Victor,** one of the oldest Christian sites in France, and the **Notre-Dame de la Garde** church with its iconic dome crowned with a majestic golden statue of the Virgin Mary. The port is ringed by restaurants and cafés, and it's a pleasant place to stroll. In the summer there's a popular market selling gifts and local products to the throngs of cruise ship passengers.

The 16th-century **Hôtel de Ville,** office of the mayor of Marseille, is on the northern side of the port on quai du Port, directly facing Notre-Dame de la Garde. The imposing building, constructed in the style of Genoese Palaces, twice escaped destruction: once during the French revolution when the building was thought to be housing opponents of the revolution, and then during World War II, when the Nazis destroyed the quarter. Miraculously, the building survived and is now a working administrative center.

Norman Foster's **L'Ombrière** has added a touch of glinting modernism to Quai de Rive Neuve on the old port and is a symbol of the city's forward-facing nature. The parasol-cum-pavilion, whose name literally means the shade giver, was installed as part of the 2013 City of Culture urban-renewal program. The old port area was pedestrianized to create more of a connection between the city and the sea. It's an arresting installation, 48 meters (157 feet) long and 22 meters (72 feet) wide, composed of mirrored sheets that have the effect of inverting the surrounding world. In the summer it provides plenty of shade.

Any visit to Marseille should include a moment to stop and contemplate the Vieux Port. After all, it was here that the Greeks landed in 600 BC, and it's been the center of the city ever since.

Château d'If and Iles de Frioul

Depart from 1 quai de la Fraternité, Vieux Port; tel. 04 96 11 03 50; www.frioul-if-express.com/ en; June-Aug. half hourly 6:30am-8:30pm, out of season hourly 6:30am-8:30pm; €10.80 one island stop, €16.20 two island stops, reduced €12 and €8, Château d'If €5 supplement

The most famous of the four Iles de Frioul, thanks to Alexandre Dumas's story of *The Count of Monte Cristo,* is the Isle of If. Dumas's fictional hero Edmond Dantes was imprisoned for 14 years in the Château d'If before escaping and taking revenge for his imprisonment. The château was built by Francis I

in 1524 for primarily defensive purposes, enabling the monarch to guard the new Royal Fleet at anchor outside Marseille and to keep an eye on the city. It quickly became a prison, with Protestants and Republicans topping the list of inmates. For literature enthusiasts, the tour of the château contains plenty of information and allusions to Dumas's book. Note that the château shuts at 6pm and walking shoes are advisable. The ferry boat also stops at Port Frioul, which gives access to the other islands of the Frioul archipelago. It's a pleasant harbor surrounded by restaurants and cafés. Allow at least half a day to visit the prison, including a stop-off at Port Frioul for refreshment and a stroll.

Abbaye Saint-Victor

Place Saint Victor; tel. 04 96. 11 2 .60; www.saintvictor.net; daily 9am-9pm; €2

Climbing the hill to the Abbaye Saint-Victor is another way of enjoying a good view over the old port. The abbey dates back to the 11th century, and the crypts beneath go back to the 5th century. The interior of the displays a mix of Roman (the main nave) and Gothic (choir and transepts) architectural styles. The four chapels in the crypts are particularly atmospheric. The cool air, enveloping stone walls, and ancient carvings transport visitors back through the centuries.

★ Notre-Dame de la Garde

Rue Fort du Sanctuaire; tel. 04 91 13 40 80; www.notredamedelagarde.com; church: Apr.-Sept. 7am-7:15pm, Oct.-Mar. 7am-6:15pm, museum: Tues.-Sun. 10am-1pm and 2pm-5:30pm

Sitting proudly on top of the highest point in Marseille, Notre-Dame de la Garde is the most recognizable symbol of the city. The 11.2-meter (37-foot) golden statue of the Virgin Mary and child that caps the dome of the church is a visible reminder to the Marseillais that someone is always watching over them. The church, like the city's inhabitants, is brash and colorful. Built in 1852, it incorporates pink and red marble columns, mosaic domes, and gold cornices, inlaid with glinting stones. Everywhere there are small

Marseille Town

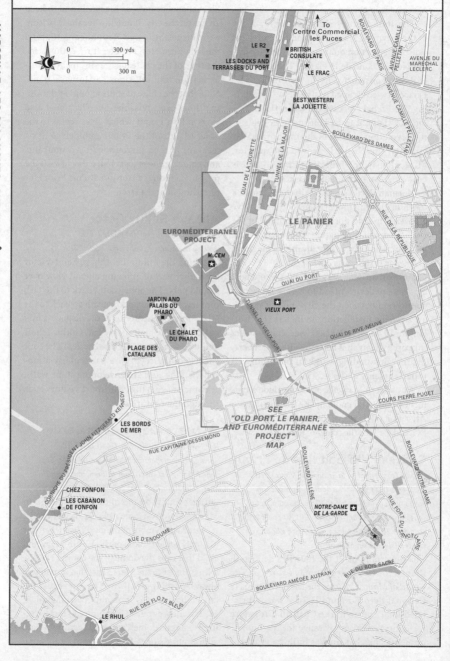

↑ To
Centre Commercial
les Puces

LE R2

LES DOCKS AND
TERRASSES DU PORT

BRITISH
CONSULATE

LE FRAC

BEST WESTERN
LA JOLIETTE

BOULEVARD DE PARIS

AVENUE CAMILLE PELLETAN

AVENUE DU
MARECHAL
LECLERC

BOULEVARD DES DAMES

QUAI DE LA TOURETTE

TUNNEL DE LA MAJOR

RUE DE LA REPUBLIQUE

LE PANIER

EUROMÉDITERRANÉE
PROJECT

MuCEM

QUAI DU PORT

JARDIN AND
PALAIS DU
PHARO

TUNNEL DU VIEUX PORT

VIEUX PORT

LE CHALET
DU PHARO

PLAGE DES
CATALANS

QUAI DE RIVE-NEUVE

CORNICHE DU PRESIDENT JOHN FITZGERALD KENNEDY

LES BORDS
DE MER

COURS PIERRE PUGET

SEE
"OLD PORT, LE PANIER,
AND EUROMÉDITERRANÉE
PROJECT"
MAP

RUE CAPITAINE DESSEMOND

BOULEVARD TELLENE

BOULEVARD NOTRE-DAME

CHEZ FONFON

LES CABANON
DE FONFON

NOTRE-DAME
DE LA GARDE

RUE FORT DU SANCTUAIRE

RUE D'ENDOUME

BOULEVARD AMÉDÉE AUTRAN

RUE DU BOIS SACRÉ

LE RHUL

RUE DES FLOTS BLEUS

0   300 yds

0   300 m

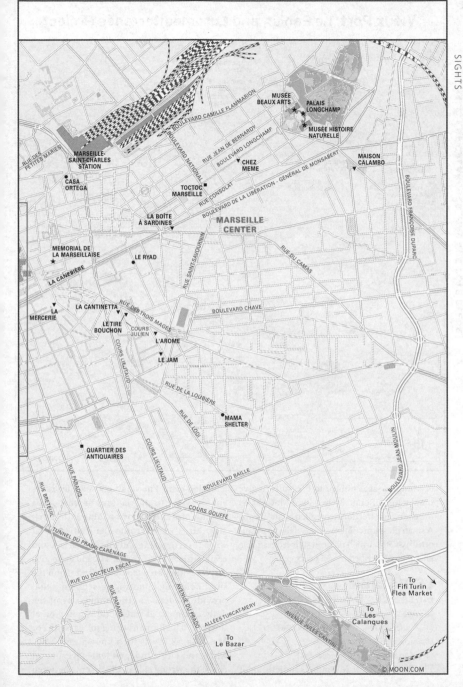

MUSÉE
BEAUX ARTS
PALAIS
LONGCHAMP
MUSÉE HISTOIRE
NATURELLE

BOULEVARD CAMILLE FLAMMARION

RUE JEAN DE BERNARDY
BOULEVARD LONGCHAMP

BOULEVARD NATIONAL

MAISON
CALAMBO

CHEZ
MEME

MARSEILLE-
SAINT-CHARLES
STATION

RUE DES
PETITES MARIES

CASA
ORTEGA

TOCTOC
MARSEILLE

RUE CONSOLAT

BOULEVARD DE LA LIBÉRATION - GÉNÉRAL DE MONSABERT

BOULEVARD FRANÇOISE DUPARC

LA BOÎTE
À SARDINES

MARSEILLE
CENTER

RUE SAINT-SAVOURNIN

RUE DU CAMAS

MÉMORIAL DE
LA MARSEILLAISE

LE RYAD

LA CANEBIÈRE

LA CANTINETTA

RUE DES TROIS MAGES

BOULEVARD CHAVE

LA
MERCERIE

LE TIRE
BOUCHON

COURS
JULIEN

L'AROME

LE JAM

COURS JULIEN

RUE DE LA LOUBIÈRE

RUE DE LODI

MAMA
SHELTER

QUARTIER DES
ANTIQUAIRES

COURS LIEUTAUD

RUE PARADIS

RUE BRETEUIL

BOULEVARD BAILLE

BOULEVARD JEAN MOULIN

COURS GOUFFÉ

To
Fifi Turin
Flea Market

TUNNEL DU PRADO CARÉNAGE

RUE DU DOCTEUR ESCAT

RUE PARADIS

AVENUE DU PRADO

ALLÉES TURCAT-MERY

AVENUE JULES CANTINI

To
Les
Calanques

To
Le Bazar

© MOON.COM

Vieux Port, Le Panier, and Euroméditerranée Project

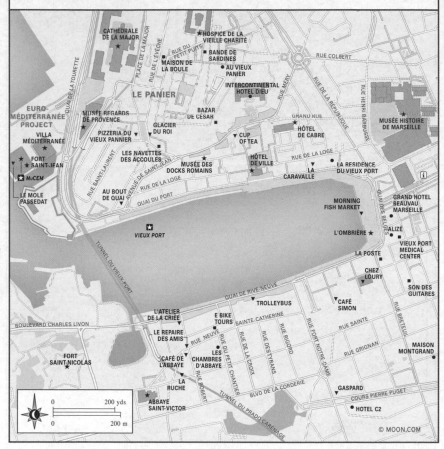

© MOON.COM

ex-voto messages pinned to the walls to give thanks to La Bonne Mere (Good Mother), as the church is affectionately called by the locals. A small museum contains some of the most colorful ex-votos, which range in style from simple plaques to enscribed model boats.

LE PANIER
Musée des Docks Romains
28 Place Vivaux; tel. 04 91 91 24 62;
www.musées-Méditerranée.org/portail/Musée_fiche.php?menu=1&num_Musée=85;
Tues.-Sun. 10am-6pm; €3, reduced €2

The Roman Docks Museum is something of a hidden gem. The small entrance fee takes you quayside to the remains of what was a Roman storage depot on Marseille port. Huge urns were set into the walls, so that ships carrying wine and oil could arrive and easily unload their cargo. The museum also displays other archaeological finds from the site, including counting instruments that provide evidence of the complexity of the daily commercial transactions going on at the port. The Romans came to Marseille, or Massalia, as it was then known, in 49 BC, when the city's independent government chose the wrong side in the dispute between

Ex-Voto Suspecto

Translated from Latin, *ex-voto suspecto* means the consequence of a vow made. To understand how an ex-voto works, imagine a seaman clinging to the mast as his ship sinks. The waves crash around him and he promises to repent and be a good Christian. There will be no more drinking or womanizing, and he'll attend church every Sunday, if only someone will save him. He calls to mind the image of the golden statue of the Virgin Mary who watches over all Marseillais and says his silent prayer. Miraculously a giant wave plucks him from the wreckage and sends him tumbling toward the shore. He's washed up alive on the rocks. As soon as he can, he heads to **Notre-Dame de la Garde** and pins an ex-voto to the walls of the church as evidence of keeping his vow. The ex-voto could simply be the words of his promise written on a piece of paper, or something more complex like a model of his ship that sunk. At Notre-Dame de la Garde you will see ex-votos relating to almost every aspect of life, from escaping a car crash to getting promoted at work.

Notre-Dame de la Garde

Caesar and Pompey. An enraged Caesar invaded and captured the city.

Hospice de la Vieille Charité

2 rue de la Charité; tel. 04 91 14 58 80; http://culture.marseille.fr/node/949; Tues.-Sun. 10am-6pm; €6, reduced €3, or City Pass

It's something of a climb up to La Vieille Charité hospice, but the building and associated museums merit the effort. The hospice was built between 1671-1749 to treat the poor. At various stages during its history, it became a children's hospital, senior citizens' home, and army barracks. Incredibly, after World War II this architecturally harmonious and arresting building was scheduled for demolition before being saved at the last minute. It now houses two excellent museums: one of Mediterranean archaeology that contains the largest Egyptology collection in France outside Paris, and the other of African, Oceanic, and American arts.

EUROMÉDITERRANÉE PROJECT

TOP EXPERIENCE

★ MuCEM

7 promenade Robert Laffont; www.mucem.org; Wed.-Mon. 11am-6pm; €9.50 or City Pass

The MuCEM is as much an architectural statement as a museum. It's a futuristic glass box, clad in a web-like concrete skin that the architect (Rudi Riciotti) claims was inspired by the ocean floor. Minimalist concrete bridges connect the box to Fort Saint-Jean and on from there to the the Vieux Port. It's undeniably mesmerizing to look at and walk around. Gangplanks snake round the exterior of the building in the space between the glass and the concrete skin. The roof has a terrace café that feels connected to both sky and sea. In the words of the architect, "Culture is an element of peace making," and MuCEM is Marseille's attempt to make peace with and welcome the world. It's possible to visit without paying the entrance fee to the exhibitions, which, almost inevitably, fail to live up the spectacle of the building that houses them. On the ground floor, the permanent "Ruralities" exhibition, charts the rise of agriculture in the Mediterranean basin. On the second floor is a temporary exhibition with a Mediterranean theme, and on the third another temporary exhibition with a broader non-Mediterranean concept. Technology is well used, with walls of television screens showing documentaries and graphics. Even so, the memorable part of the visit is the building rather than the artifacts it houses.

Fort Saint-Jean

Vieux Port or MuCEM; Wed.-Mon. 11am-6pm; free, or exhibitions with MuCEM pass (€9.50) or City Pass

Built in 1660 by Louis XIV, at the same time as Fort Saint-Nicolas on the other side of the harbor, the two forts are notable for the direction of fire of their cannons. Rather than facing out to sea toward a possible threat from an enemy vessel, the guns were turned inward on the people of Marseille. After an uprising against the governor of Marseille, Louis XIV commented with a healthy dose of royal sarcasm: "We noticed the people of Marseille are rather fond of fortresses. We wanted to have our own at the entrance to this great port." The entrance to the fort is across sleek, concrete, modernist pedestrian bridges, either from the MuCEM building or from the old port. Once inside the fort, visitors are free to wander around the battlements, duck through low tunnels in the rock, and climb up to guard posts and lookout points. The Mediterranean Garden of Migration, which is filled with herbs from Jewish, Islamic, and Christian medical traditions and planted with olive trees, is a pleasant place to picnic. Be aware that out on the ramparts there are head-spinning drops to the Mediterranean below. The entrance to MuCEM includes a themed five-stage walk through the history of the fort beginning in the Galerie des Officiers. This exhibition is scheduled to end in July 2021. Temporary exhibitions are also staged in the George Henri Rivière building. Fort Saint-Nicolas, across the harbor, can only be visited once a year on special cultural days; a renovation project is much talked about but has yet to get underway.

Villa Méditerranée

Promenade Robert Lafont; opens summer 2021

Constructed as part of the 2013 European City of Culture celebrations, the Villa Méditerranée is a striking building that never quite found its purpose. To look at, it resembles the bridge of the *Starship Enterprise* from *Star Trek*. There's a top-heavy wedge of concrete stretching out to sea on top of a thinner neck. The impression is that the whole edifice could, at any moment, tumble forward into the sea. In 2021 it will re-open to visitors as **Musée de La Grotte Cosquer,** showcasing the reconstruction of a subterranean grotto (La Grotte Cosquer) located in the nearby Calanque de Morgiou. In this cave, the earliest evidence of Stone Age humans in Provence was found, along with paintings dating back to 27,000 years BC. Until 2021, visitors can only stop and admire the architecture.

Musée Regards de Provence

Avenue Vaudoyer; tel. 04 96 17 40 40; www.museeregardsdeprovence.com/en; Tues.-Sun. 10am-6pm; €8.50, reduced €7.50 or City Pass

The aim of the Regards de Provence foundation is to assemble and make available to the public the artistic heritage of Marseille and the Mediterranean. Works in the permanent collection are displayed on two floors and span a period from the 18th century to the present day. Artists include Pierre Ambrogiani, Louis Audibert, Auguste Chabaud, and Raoul Dufy. Temporary exhibitions change frequently and are often photographic. Facing the sea, opposite the MuCEM, the old sanitary station building which houses the collection is flooded by the Mediterranean light that stars in so many of the artworks. Viewing the collection is an uplifting experience.

Hôtel de Cabre

Some houses live a charmed life. The Hôtel Cabre (27 Grand Rue), constructed in the early part of the 16th century, is the oldest building still standing in Marseille. In January 1943, it had a close shave. The Nazis considered the narrow warren of streets surrounding the old port as a haven for the Resistance and a no-go zone for Nazi troops, so they set about demolishing the entire quarter. However, they left the Hôtel Cabre untouched. Then in 1954 when the area was being reconstructed after the war, Hôtel Cabre stood right in the way of a proposed enlargement of the adjacent Grand Rue. The planners hit upon an ingenious solution and moved the entire building 15 meters (49 feet) and 90 degrees. The building is not open to the public, but you can still stop and admire a real historical survivor.

Le Frac

20 boulevard de Dunkerque; tel. 04 91 91 27 55;
www.fracpaca.org; Tues.-Sat. noon-7pm, Sun.
2pm-6pm; €5, reduced €2.50, free Sun.
Provence's modern art foundation has a collection of 1,200 works by 560 artists. It's a treasure trove of contemporary art. Exhibitions change frequently and its best to consult the website for details about what's on display.

Cathédrale de La Major

Place de la Major; Wed.-Mon. 10am-7pm
The only cathedral in France to be constructed in the 19th century, Cathédrale de la Major is a wonder of byzantine architecture. Large ecclesiastical buildings typically inspire awe and, ultimately, seem forbidding. Here the playful stripes on the exterior, created by alternating stone from Cassis and green Florentine marble, convey a sense of welcome. Inside there are yet more stripes, alternating a warmer colored marble with stone. The cathedral is, in fact, two buildings; the 19th-century construction was superimposed on a 12th-century Romanesque church, of which only the choir and one bay of the nave survive. The cathedral is one of the largest in the world, 140 meters (459 feet) long with 60-meter (197-foot) high towers, seating 3,000 people.

MARSEILLE CENTER
Friche La Belle de Mai

41 rue Jobin; tel. 04 95 04 95 95;
www.lafriche.org/fr;

exhibitions Wed.-Fri. 2pm-7pm, Sat.-Sun. 1pm-7pm,
La Friche public spaces always open;
€5 exhibitions, €3 reduced
La Friche is constantly evolving and changing its identity. For the moment it's a cultural center where artists, dancers, and performers create; it's also a neighborhood center where children come to play and go to the cinema; it's a social housing project; it's an exhibition and event center; it's a place to hang out, drink a coffee, meet friends, and eat; above all it's a place of tremendous positive energy of which Marseille is rightly proud.

Musée Histoire de Marseille

2 rue Henri Barbusse; tel. 04 91 55 36 00;
http://Musée-histoire-marseille-voie-historique.fr;
Tues.-Sun. 10am-6pm; €6, €3 reduced,
and free with City Pass
The museum delves into Marseille's rich past, telling the story of France's oldest city from its first prehistorique origins to contemporary urban developments, with a focus on the personal stories of its inhabitants. The marquee exhibit is the remains of an old Roman trading boat dating back to the 2nd century AD; the museum states that it is the best preserved example of a vessel from this period in the world. There are also two older, less pristine examples of Greek trading vessels. The exhibits are brought to life through technology, with more than 100 multimedia displays and 3D reconstructions of the city during various periods of its development. These modern

1

2

3

"La Marseillaise"

"La Marseillaise" is the French National anthem. The stirring marching song was written in 1792 by Claude Rouget de Lisle after France declared war on Austria. He named the composition "War Song of the Armies of the Rhine." The anthem acquired its name and popularity thanks to a unit of Fédérés soldiers from Marseille, who sung the song as they entered Paris later the same year. The first rendition of the song by the unit took place before their departure in a real tennis court in Marseille that now hosts a memorial museum. During the visit to the memorial, various different versions of the anthem are played and the story of the march of the Marseille volunteers is told. The lyrics are blood curdling, reflecting the French fear of a foreign invasion. The first verse ends with this salvo of unpleasantness: "Do you hear, in the countryside, the roar of those ferocious soldiers, they're coming right into your arms, to cut the throat of your sons, your women." The song was officially adopted as the national anthem in 1795, but Napoleon I replaced it with a more imperial number, "Veillons au

Sing along to "La Marseillaise"!

Salut d'Empire," and "La Marseillaise" was banned outright by the restored French monarchs Louis XVIII and Charles X. Only in 1879 was the song reinstated as the national anthem.

You can visit the **Marseillaise Memorial** (23 rue Thubaneau; tel. 04 91 55 36 00; http://culture.marseille.fr/musees-et-patrimoine/les-musees-de-marseille; Tues.-Fri. 10:30am-3pm) as a part of your visit to the **Musée Histoire de Marseille.**

additions accompany 4,000 or so exhibits, many of which include artifacts that were found when the museum site was excavated in 1967. The museum opens onto a large courtyard garden containing even more archaeological finds, including port buildings and the city walls, which were stormed by the armies of Julius Caesar in 49 BC.

Palais Longchamp

Boulevard Jardin Zoologique; http://environnement. marseille.fr/node/782; 8am-8pm; free
The Palais was opened in 1869 to celebrate the arrival of the Durance canal, which brought running water to the city. Water cascades from a decorative fountain at the summit of the immense monument known as the Chateau

d'Eau, or water castle, into a middle basin, and then an artificial lake at the base. Given the size and magnificence of the builidng, it's clear the Marseillais were overjoyed at the arrival of the canal. Climbing to the top of the ornamental staircase takes you to a pleasant parkland square. Descending another set of steps takes you into a formal garden that used to be a zoo. Some of the old gilded cages for the animals are still on display as well as a collection of animal statues. To either side of the Chateau d'Eau two wings of the Palais Longchamp house the Musée des Beaux Arts and the Muséum d'Histoire Naturelle.

Musée des Beaux Arts

9 rue Edouard Stephan; tel. 04 91 14 59 30; www.marseille.fr/node/639;
Tues.-Sun. 10am-6pm; €6, €3 reduced or City Pass
The collection of the museum, which is located in the north wing of the Palais de

1: a typical narrow street in Marseille's oldest district, Le Panier 2: Fort Saint-Jean in the Vieux Port 3: Night descends over Vallon des Auffes.

Longchamps, comes from works of art seized from churches and the wealthy during the French Revolution. Paintings by the old masters, such as Rubens's *The Wild Boar Hunt*, are on view.

Muséum d'Histoire Naturelle

Palais Longchamp, rue Espérandieu; tel. 04 91 14 59 50; http://culture.marseille.fr/musees-et-patrimoine/les-musees-de-marseille; Tues.-Sun. 10am-6pm; €6, €3 reduced or City Pass

In the opposite wing of the Longchamp Palace from the Musée des Beaux Arts is France's most visited natural history museum. However, unless you are a particular fan of stuffed animals and the natural world, the visit is the least rewarding out of the two Longchamp museums.

TOWARD LES CALANQUES

Mac

69 avenue d'Haifa; tel. 04 91 25 01 07; http://culture.marseille.fr/node/637; Tues.-Sun. 10am-6pm; €6, reduced €3

Modern art needs a minimalist setting, and the pure white walls of Mac, Marseille's showpiece for contemporary art, certainly deliver. Works by local southern French sculptors and artists, such as César Baldaccini and Benjamin Vautier (known as Ben), mix with better-known names such as Warhol.

★ Vallon des Auffes (Endoume)

Corniche Kennedy, Endoume

Follow the Corniche Kennedy as it hugs the coast on the way out of Marseille toward the Calanques National Park, passing through the Endoume neighborhood. Park adjacent to the World War I memorial (dedicated to soliders and sailors who died in the East) and descend a set of steps that winds between buildings down to the Vallon des Auffes fishing port. It's like stepping back in time, or even entering another world. The little port is surrounded by the pastel-colored houses of fishermen.

Small boats are pulled up at anchor, and workers sit mending nets while the Mediterranean gently laps around their feet. This face of Marseille couldn't be more different from the graffiti-marked streets of some areas. There are a couple of good restaurants where you can kick back, relax, and wonder whether the otherworldly big city will still be there when you climb back up the steps. In addition to Vallon des Auffes, Endoume itself has plenty more to offer. The neighborhood is a curious mixture of old fishing huts and mansion houses. There are three rocky inlets/calanques in Malmousque (Calanque du Cuivre, Anse de Maldormé, Anse de la Fausse Monnaie), and there's a coastal peninsula just past Vallon des Auffes where you can swim off the rocks and wash the big-city feel from your hair.

Unité d'Habitation Cité Radieuse

280 boulevard Michelet; tel. 08 26 50 05 00; www.marseille-citeradieuse.org; daily 9am-6pm

After World War II, France faced a desperate shortage of affordable housing. The state asked renowned French/Swiss architect Le Corbusier to come up with a new way of building to solve the problem. Notorious for a 1925 plan to demolish much of central Paris and replace it with 60 skyscrapers surrounded by landing areas for planes, he'd also developed less contentious proposals for the construction of uniform appartment buildings using modern materials. Marseille gave him his first public commission, and his response was a brutalist concrete block divided up into modular housing. A total of 337 apartments were built to house 1,600 people. The exterior was so shocking that the Marseillais quickly christened the building the Maison de Fada, which roughly translates as the "nuthouse." Whether this refers to the appearance of the building itself or the people mad enough to live there has never been clear. There's now a hotel and restaurant, as well as guided tours organized by the Marseille Tourist board. Tours can be booked by phone.

Les Goudes

Chemin des Goudes

Les Goudes sits on the boundary between Marseille and Les Calanques. Technically still part of the city—it belongs to the 8th arrondissement—the small fishing port set back amid the rocks has a much more relaxed vibe. The Marseillais like to joke that the port exists at the end of the world, perhaps revealing a fear of what lies beyond their urban environment. Depending on whether you share the Marseillais attitude, Les Goudes is either as far as you are willing to venture, or a staging post for a hike out into the wilds of Les Calanques. Whatever conclusion you come to, it's a nice place for a long lunch. Note that Les Goudes' proximity to Marseille means the road there and back often becomes overcrowded. It's best to visit mid-morning, after the rush hour has finished but before people's tummies start rumbling.

Sports and Recreation

PARKS

JARDIN AND PALAIS DU PHARO

58 boulevard Charles Livon; Mon.-Fri. 8:30am-6pm

Perhaps the best way to appreciate the geography of the old port is to climb the adjacent hill to the Jardin du Pharo. High on the headland, this magnificent garden houses the Palais du Pharo, which was intended as a residence for Napoleon Bonaparte. Construction of the Palais started in 1852, but unfortunately for Napoleon he fell from power before he could take up residence. The building now has a more prosaic use as a conference center. On the lawn in front of the Palais is a moving monument to sailors lost at sea in World War I. Looking back from the gardens toward Marseille you can see the two forts (Saint-Jean and Saint-Nicolas) on either side of the harbor entrance and MuCEM development. The Chalet du Pharo restaurant is a good spot to stop and enjoy the view.

PARC DU PRADO

Avenue Pierre Mendes

Right next to the sea, this park is a great spot to take some time out from the busy city. It's heavily used for festivals and events, including a kite festival, fireworks, and a beach volleyball festival. The park is particularly good for kids, with three play areas and a skate park for bikes, scooters, and skateboards.

PARC BORELY

Avenue du Parc Borely; tel. 04 91 76 59 38;
http://monumentsdemarseille.com/parc-borely;
daily 6am-8:45pm

This park consists of a series of formal gardens: Chinese, rose, botanical, and English. There's a pleasant lake, and for those who are not yet sated by Marseille culture, the 18th-century Château Borely houses a museum of decorative arts. The park is adjacent to the Plage de La Pointe Rouge.

BEACHES

The Marseillais are a sun-loving lot. From early spring to late autumn, they hit the beaches. Expect skimpy swimwear, bling sunglasses, and crowds of youngsters playing beach volleyball with rap music booming in the background. Head away from the public beaches and take to the rocks of Endoume if you are looking for a more peaceful experience.

PLAGE DES CATALANS

Opposite 6 rue de Catalans

Almost in the city center, in the Pharo neighborhood to the south of the old port, this small sandy beach fills up quickly in the summer. Even in mid-winter, you'll find some brave locals soaking up the sun in a sheltered spot before an icy dip. The beach is served by bus Line 4.

1

2

3

Plus Belle La Vie, French TV's Longest-Running Soap Opera

Since 2004, for five nights a week, a half-hour slice of Marseille has been beamed into French living rooms. *Plus Belle la Vie*, France's longest-running soap opera, is set in the fictional Marseille district of Le Mistral. More than 3,000 episodes of the trials and tribulations of the main characters have been broadcast. In 2008 the nightly audience reached its peak at some 6 million viewers. These days each episode draws an audience of around 5 million viewers, and the series competes with *Game of Thrones* for the top of the streaming charts. Keeping the viewers hooked is a mix of the daily trials and tribulations of the characters, their illnesses and love lives, and a healthy dose of crime. At times the plotlines can stray too close to the unbelievable. Cliff-hanger follows cliff-hanger in an all too obvious attempt to bring the audience back the next day. The episodes are filmed on location in Marseille and at the *Plus Belle la Vie* studios in La Belle de Mai in Marseille's 3rd arrondissement (37 Rue Guibal).

PLAGES DU PRADO

Intersection of promenade Georges Pompidou and avenue du Prado

This series of artificial sandy beaches, located to the south of the city center in the 8th arrondissement, was created in the 1970s to offer the Marseillais better access to the sea. They are now very popular and back onto a large park (Park Balneaire du Prado). There are more than 1,000 parking spaces, plus the beaches are served by bus Lines 19 and 83.

PLAGE DE LA POINT ROUGE

Opposite 39 avenue de Montredon

Farther south along the coast from the Prado beaches, La Pointe Rouge is another busy beach. It's bordered by cafés and restaurants, and is seemingly always lively. There's a yachting and kite surfing school.

YACHTING CLUB DE LA POINT ROUGE

Port de La Pointe Rouge; tel. 04 91 73 06 75; www.ycpr.net; Tues., Wed. and Fri. 9am-12.30pm and 2pm-6.30pm, Thurs. 8am-noon, Sat. 9am-12.30pm and 2pm-6pm

This welcoming club offers a range of sporting activities, including sailing, diving, paddleboarding, and wind surfing. There's an on-site restaurant and courses for kids in the summer, including a five-day morning sailing school for €200.

MARSEILLE KITE KLUB

Entre no 3, Digue Ouest, Port de la Pointe Rouge; tel. 06 18 73 29 93; www.marseillekiteclub.com; daily with reservation; €130 for a half day

On the other side of the port from the yachting club, this kite surfing school offers courses for all levels.

TOURS

TOCTOC MARSEILLE

28 boulevard Longchamps; tel. 06 26 89 24 78; www.toctoc-marseille.com/fr; prices from €45

Marseille is a large, busy city, and it is often overwhelming. For those short on time, the easiest way to explore all the best parts of the city is with a guide. Laurianne Collange is a charming local who tailors her tours to her clients and knows Marseille as well as anyone. The maximum group size is nine.

PÉTANQUE (BOULE)

MONDIAL LA MARSEILLAISE

Throughout Marseille; www.mondiallamarseillaiseapetanque.com; second week in July

The Mondial Marseillaise is the pétanque equivalent of the soccer World Cup. Teams

1: Les Goudes sits at the edge of Marseille. 2: formal gardens at Parc Borely 3: Palais Longchamps was built to celebrate the arrival of water from the Durance canal in Marseille.

travel from all over the world to take part. There's one important difference though: Anyone can enter. Sign up on the website and you'll be allocated a pitch number somewhere in Marseille (there are more than 1,000 pitches). Then turn up at the appointed time, and you're off. The competition is a knock-out. After four days of intense competition, the surviving players meet in the televised final, which takes place in Marseille's old port.

MAISON DE LA BOULE

4 Place des 13 Cantons; tel. 04 88 44 39 44;
http://maison-de-la-boule.com; daily 10am-6pm
Part shop, part museum, part sports club, the Maison de La Boule is the place to go if you are interested in pétanque. There's an indoor pitch if you can't wait to test your new purchases.

SPECTATOR SPORTS

OLYMPIQUE MARSEILLE FOOTBALL CLUB

The Velodrome, 3 boulevard Michelet;
www.om.net/en; package tickets include an overnight
hotel from €55 per person
In Provence you'll see a plethora of little patches of blue, gold, and orange adorning tracksuits, hats, and car stickers. These are the colors of Olympique Marseille football (soccer) club. In the press, there's a daily mention of the club. Often embroiled in a scandal, financial or otherwise, the team remains the beating heart of Provence. On the pitch, the 11 men who represent Marseille are expected to defeat all comers, particularly the Parisian aristocrats of Paris Saint-Germain.

The fervor with which OM is supported

is stoked by an unusual method of ticket allocation. The club has multiple supporters' clubs, and these clubs are allocated tickets at the beginning of each season based on the number of members. Competition between the supporters' clubs to recruit new members is fierce, and chants in the stadium are often aimed at opposing supporters' clubs rather than opposing fans. Whatever the score, the rivalry between the supporters' clubs makes attending a match in the Velodrome an entertaining night. The French football season begins in the blistering heat of August and runs until May. Olympique Marseille play at home every other weekend and may have a mid-week match as well, depending on their success in cup competitions.

CYCLING

LE VELO

Stations throughout Marseille;
http://en.levelo-mpm.fr; €1 subscription cost covers
first 30 minutes, plus €1 every additional 30 minutes
Marseille operates a pickup and drop-off bike system, with various stations spaced throughout the city. It's easy and quick to sign up on the website.

E BIKE TOURS

Meeting point: La Criée/Café des Arts, 30 quai de
Rive Neuve; tel. 07 82 00 73 47; www.ebiketours.fr;
Mar.-Oct. year-round for groups; from €29 per person
E-bikes are a great way to take in a lot of Marseille in just one day. This company offers various guide-led tours, including all the main sights of the city, as well as longer trips out to Les Calanques and Cassis.

Entertainment and Events

JAZZ DES CINQ CONTINENTS

Various locations, Marseille;
www.marseillejazz.com; mid-July; from €20
For just over a week in July, the city celebrates jazz music with large open-air concerts in

spectacular venues such as outside the Palais Longchamp, or at the entrance to MuCEM. The festival builds on a long tradition of jazz in Marseille. At the end of World War II, *Jazz*

A History of *Pétanque* and How to Play

HISTORY

Back at the turn of the 20th century, in the seaside town of La Ciotat, which neighbors Marseille, poor Jules Lenoir was so afflicted by rheumatism that he could no longer play his favorite game: *jeu provençal*. The three leaps required before throwing his boule toward the target were too much for him. A local café owner took pity and suggested a version of the game where players plant their feet before throwing. Because leaping around in the hot sun is rather tiring, the new game, which was named *pétanque* (meaning "stuck feet" in Provençal), quickly took off.

pétanque boules

RULES

The rules are simple: A formal match has four players, two on each side. Play begins with the drawing of a circle in the gravel from which the target ball (*cochonette*) is thrown. The teams then try and get their boule the closest to the *cochonette*. A team continues to throw until they manage to get a boule closer than the opposing team. Play then switches to the opposing team, until they get closer. An end is reached when all players have thrown all their boules (customarily three each). One point is awarded for each boule that is closer to the *cochonette* than any of the boule from the opposing side. The circle is redrawn in the gravel and the *cochonette* thrown once again. A match is won when one side gets to 13 points.

Beware, if you lose 13-0 at *pétanque* (also often simply called "boule") you are required to "Kiss the Fanny." This tradition is believed to have originated in the same café in La Ciotat where the game was invented. Fanny was a notably fetching barmaid with a penchant for wearing sexy stockings. As recompense to whitewashed losers, she lifted her skirt and allowed them to kiss her bottom. There is usually a statue of Fanny in a boule club, with an amply pert posterior to kiss.

WHERE TO PLAY

There are plenty of spots across Marseille to play boule. The rule of thumb is that if you find a suitable area of gravel where there aren't too many pedestrians, then you're fine to start playing. One such scenic spot is immediately to the right of the **Cathédrale la Major** as you stand facing it.

Hot magazine christened the city the new capital of French Jazz.

LA FÊTE DU VENT

Parc du Prado; www.facebook.com/F%C3%AAte-du-vent-Marseille-Festival-International-du-Cerf-volant-167488229932278; mid-Sept.; free

Seventy to 100,000 people come to this increasingly popular kite festival. The sky fills with color as extraordinarily shaped kites soar over the sea. Fish chase dragons, octopuses dance with sea lions, and of course there's the odd Donald Trump kite.

MARSATAC

Parc Chanot; www.marsatac.com; mid-June; one night €35, three nights €55

Marsatac is an electronic, indie, and hip-hop music festival with a particular focus of giving exposure to local and emerging artists.

FESTIVAL DE MARSEILLE
Various locations, Marseille; tel. 04 91 99 00 20; www.festivaldemarseille.com; mid-June-early July; from €15
Like the city, this festival is open to the world, celebrating all cultures and all forms of expression. Dance, music, opera, mime—the shows make the most of Marseille's dramatic cityscape as a backdrop to performances.

Shopping

SHOPPING DISTRICTS AND STREETS

LE PANIER
www.lepanierdemarseille.com/shopping
Le Panier is Marseille's oldest quarter. It's an atmospheric area to shop with its mix of cobbled narrow streets and walls covered in street art. The shops are small and tend to be owner-run. They offer individual creations, including works of art, ceramics, clothes, *santons* (nativity figures), and soaps.

LA CANEBIÈRE
Marseille's high street is a broad, tree-lined avenue running away from the coast. It's a little run-down, and the shops are now a mixture of chain stores and ethnic grocery stores. Its purpose is more to serve the practical needs of the population, rather than tourists.

COURS JULIEN
Once an edgy neighborhood, the Cours Julien is now one of the trendiest in Marseille. Walls are, of course, covered in graffiti, but that's Marseille. As in Le Panier, there are lots of small boutiques offering artisan clothes, jewelry, and handbags. If you are looking for an original piece, it's the perfect place to shop.

LES DOCKS AND TERRASSES DU PORT
Quai du Lazaret; www.lesterrassesduport.com and www.lesterrassesduport.com
These two new shopping centers near the Euroméditerranée project are filled with all the high-end brands. There's nothing original here, but it's all very practical and air-conditioned.

a small neighborhood bar in Le Panier district

ANTIQUES AND BROCANTE

FIFI TURIN FLEA MARKET

20 boulevard Fifi Turin; tel. 06 64 30 51 54; www. facebook.com/lespucesdefifi; Mon.-Sat. 9am-12:30pm and 2pm-6pm, first Sun. of the month 10am-6pm

A group of nine antique dealers have created a little go-to hot spot for vintage furniture and collectibles.

QUARTIER DES ANTIQUAIRES

Rue Edmond Rostand; www.antiquairesmarseille.com/fr/les-boutiques; hours of shops vary, most are closed Sun.

Since the 1950s this quarter of Marseille has been known for its antiques. The eclectic range of shops offers everything from guitars to paintings, oriental antiques, and Provençal furniture. In the South of France, this quarter of Marseille is second only to L'Isle-sur-la-Sorgue for the range of items available.

CENTRE COMMERCIAL LES PUCES

130 chemin de la Madrague de la Ville; www.centrecommerciallespuces.com; Tues.-Sun. 8:30am-7:30pm

If you love shopping and don't mind crowds, this 20-year-old flea market is a must-visit. Part indoor, part outdoor, the center is filled with objects and furniture from house clearance sales. It's the place to pick up a real bargain.

CRAFT

CRUISE PASSENGER MARKET

Vieux Port; May-Oct. 3pm-midnight

Although it's not the most auspicious name for a market, the Cruise Passenger Market is quite enjoyable. Stroll along the quayside in the warm summer air, browsing artisan-made local products. Expect plenty of bundles of lavender, jewelry, olive-wood boards, salad bowls, etc.

MARSEILLE SPECIALTIES

BAZAR DE CÉSAR

4 Montée des Accoules; tel. 06 19 70 95 76; www.lebazardecesar.com; daily 9:30am-7pm

Soap making began in Marseille in 1307, and the city is still famous for it today. By law, Marseille soap must contain 72 percent oil, making it exceptionally pure and kind to sensitive skin. The Bazar de Cesar in Le Panier district is a good place to pick up a bar or two.

BANDE DE SARDINES

8 quai de Rive Neuve; https://bandedesardines-shop.com; daily 10am-7pm

Did you hear the one about the giant sardine that blocked the old port? Ask a Marseillais today and they'll insist it happened. In fact, it was a boat called the Sartine that blocked the port. It's just that the residents of the city seem to have sardines on their mind: grilled, marinated, even turned into a logo and stamped on clothing, as at the Bande De Sardines. The shop sells funky sardine-themed T-shirts, which make a nice momento of a visit to the city.

LES NAVETTES DES ACCOULES

68, rue Caisserie; tel. 04 91 90 99 42; www.les-navettes-des-accoules.com; Mon.-Sat. 9:30am-7pm, Sun. 10am-6pm

You'll find *navettes* across Provence. They are biscuits prepared with a dash of *fleur d'oranger* and other spices. The city that gave birth to them was Marseille in 1781. Their boat-like shape was supposedly designed to recall the landing of Mary Magdalene in the Camargue. This shop prepares some of the best *navettes* in the city.

☆ Bouillabaisse

The Marseillais are known for exaggerating to the very limit of credibility, and so it's no surprise that it was this city that transformed a humble fish soup into a dish famed around the world. The story begins with the local fishermen perfecting a dish from the unsellable leftovers of their catch. Bony, practically fleshless rockfish were added to boiling water, and from the resulting stock is made the most intense fish soup imaginable.

Local restauranteurs got hold of the recipe and popped in some more delectable morsels of fish at the last moment. Croutons were another addition, toasted and then spread with a powerful garlic, pepper, and saffron sauce. What had once been a dish for the poor was re-christened the reason God invented fish. In 1980 a group of Marseillais chefs created an official charter stipulating the ingredients and method of cooking.

Eating bouillabaisse is expensive. It usually costs more than €50 per person, but the experience is dramatic and tasty. Waiters parade the raw fish on a silver platter for

fresh bouillabaisse, a signature Marseille dish

customers to check the freshness. Each ladle is carefully measured into the bowl with solemn reverence. Delicate, perfumed filets are then doused—again reverentially—with even more soup. As you would expect, the flavor is intensely fishy. For some it is incomparably delicious, but it's not to everyone's liking.

WHERE TO FIND BOUILLABAISSE

- **Chez Loury** in the Old Port (page 255).
- **Chez Fonfon** near the Vallon des Auffes (page 257).
- **L'Esplai du Grand Bar des Goudes** in Goudes Harbor (page 257).
- **Le Rhul** has a reputation for some of the best bouillabaisse in Marseille (page 261).

Food

Marseille is the most exciting place to eat out in Provence. There is a huge variety of restaurants to choose from and a constantly evolving scene with young chefs opening innovative concept restaurants. The biggest buzz at the moment centers around AM by Alexandre Mazzia, named chef of the year in 2018 by prestigious French restaurant guide Gault & Millau. Seafood is, of course, big in Marseille; look out for towering plates of shellfish (*fruits de mer*) on ice, any dish with sardines in it (the fish is the unofficial symbol of the city), and, of course, the king of fish soups: bouillabaisse.

VIEUX PORT
Seafood
L'ATELIER DE LA CRIÉE

42 quai de la Rive Neuve; tel. 09 73 24 22 88; daily 8:30am-2am; €15-25

Few restaurants around the old port in Marseille are worth bothering with, but right next to the celebrated Marseille Theatre, L'Atelier de La Criée offers fresh fish and shellfish with attentive and friendly service. A reservation is normally not neccessary.

CAFÉ SIMON
28 cours Honoré d'Estienne d'Orves;
tel. 04 91 33 05 14; Mon.-Sat. 8am-10:15pm; €14-22
A little back from the old port, Café Simon is another spot for fish and shellfish. The prices are competitive, and the service is welcoming. It's probably the best restaurant on the attractive Place Estienne d'Orves.

LE CHALET DU PHARO
58 boulevard Charles Livon; tel. 04 91 52 80 11;
www.le-chalet-du-pharo.com; Mon.-Sat.
noon-2:30pm and 7pm-10:30pm; €19-34
Located on the hillside park above the old port, this restaurant affords beautiful views across the harbor. It's particularly atmospheric at night when the city lights wink back. Cod fillet with a crab bisque is excellent.

CHEZ LOURY
3 rue Fortia; tel. 04 91 33 09 73;
www.loury.com/fr; Mon.-Sat. noon-2:30pm and
7:30pm-10:30pm; €19-48
A traditional-style restaurant with 35 covers and white tablecloths, Chez Loury is known for its excellent bouillabaisse, served either in the traditional way over three courses, or for those with less time, as a simple one-course soup.

Markets
★ MORNING FISH MARKET
Quai du Port; daily 8am-1pm
Get up early and greet the fisherman as they return to port to ensure you get the best of the day's catch. Fish simply does not get any fresher, going straight from the boat to the shopping bag. The market is daily, but it's biggest on Friday.

LE PANIER
Seafood
LA BOÎTE À SARDINES
2 rue de la Libération; tel. 04 91 50 95 95;
www.laboiteasardine.com; Tues.-Sat. noon-5pm,
Thurs.-Fri. 7:30pm-10:30pm; €20-30
There's no doubt about the speciality of the house: sardines. If you're not in the mood, then there's fresh fish of the day and shellfish on ice. The nets and starfish hanging from the ceiling play up the nautical vibe of this Le Panier institution.

Pizza
PIZZERIA DU VIEUX PANNIER
14 Place Lenche; tel. 04 95 09 21 30;
daily noon-3:30pm and 7:30pm-11:30pm; €12-18
Located on a small square with a view of Notre-Dame de la Garde, this buzzy restaurant produces high-quality pizzas and accompanying salads and desserts.

Cafés and Light Bites
CUP OF TEA
1 rue Caisserie;
tel. 04 91 90 84 02;
www.facebook.com/Cup-of-Tea-168429123172778/;
Mon.-Sat. 9:30am-7pm; cakes €3.50
A popular stop on the way up the hill to the Vieux Charité, this combination café and bookshop has a shady terrace and an interior overflowing with books to buy.

GLACIER DU ROI
4 Place Lenche; tel. 04 91 91 01 16; http://leglacierduroi.
com; Wed.-Mon. 9am-7pm; cones from €3.50
According to staff working on *Plus Belle la Vie,* France's longest-running soap opera, which is filmed in Marseille, the Glacier du Roi is undoubtedly the best ice cream parlor in the city. Try the *calissons d'Aix* ice cream and the *navette de Marseille* ice cream. You might even bump into a star of the show having a quick fix of something sweet.

EUROMÉDITERRANÉE PROJECT

Regional Cuisine

LE MOLE PASSEDAT

1 esplanade du J4; tel. 04 91 19 17 80; www.passedat.fr; Wed.-Mon. 12:15pm-2:30pm and 7:30pm-10:30pm; €38

Gerald Passedat won three Michelin stars for his other Marseille restaurant, Le Petit Nice, in 2008. Consequently, when MuCEM opened and a star chef was needed as a name to open the rooftop restaurant, he was the obvious choice. There's both a gourmet restaurant and a more casual outside bistro/bar. The gourmet restaurant is slick and the food impeccable. Diners have good views out over the Bay of Marseille. However, the atmosphere feels manufactured and lacks soul, even if dishes such as roasted pigeon served in its own cooking juices are memorable. Reserve to be sure of a table.

Seafood

AU BOUT DU QUAI

1 avenue Saint-Jean; tel. 04 91 99 53 36; Wed.-Mon. noon-2:30pm and 7:30pm-10:30pm, Sun. noon-2:30pm; €15-30

Another exception to the "don't eat on the old port" rule, this restaurant, right at the tip of the port next to Fort Saint-Jean, serves good fresh fish. The service is welcoming and the crowd is a mixture of locals and tourists. Reservations are usually not necessary.

MARSEILLE CENTER

Seafood

★ MAISON CALAMBO

2 avenue Maréchal Foch; tel. 04 91 34 56 85; www.maison-calambo.fr; Mon.-Fri. noon-8pm, Sat.-Sun. noon-10pm; €5.50-30

Outside this family-run seafood institution, icy trays of oysters, mussels, and prawns sit ready for takeway orders. Inside, the vibe is relaxed as locals and tourists enjoy seafood platters, licking their fingers as they go. Reserve to be sure of a table.

International

★ LA CANTINETTA

24 Cours Julien; tel. 04 91 48 10 48; www.restaurantlacantinetta.fr; Mon.-Sat. noon-2pm and 7:30pm-10:30pm; €15-19

Located on the popular Cours Julien shopping street, La Catinetta offers authentic Italian food at competitive prices. There's a leafy courtyard where you can sample dishes such as *linguine alle vongole* (pasta with clams). A reservation is advisable.

satisfied sidewalk diners in Marseille

Regional Cuisine
LA MERCERIE

9 Cours Saint Louis; tel. 04 91 06 18 44;
www.lamerceriemarseille.com;
Wed.-Sat. noon-2:30pm and 7:30pm-10pm, Sun.
noon-2:30pm; lunch menu €23, evening menu €45

Harry Cummins, an itinerant London chef responsible for the Le Chardon restaurant in Arles, has also opened up a restaurant in the old textile center of Marseille. A frequently changing menu focuses on seasonal produce, such as char-grilled asparagus, and always includes touches of inspiration from Harry's travels. The crowd is local, and the wine list is excellent and competitively priced. Reservations are advisable.

L'AROME

9 rue des 3 Rois; tel. 04 91 42 88 80;
Mon.-Sat. 7:30pm-11pm; €28 three-course menu

L'Arome offers inventive, great-value cooking in a small city-center restaurant. This spot has a bistro look, with wooden tables and chairs and no tablecloths. Contemporary art brings a welcome edge to the dining room. Reserve ahead to try dishes such as hake ravioli with a seafood broth.

CHEZ MEME

84 boulevard Longchamps; tel. 07 81 02 21 47;
Tues.-Sat. noon-2pm and 7:30pm-10:30pm, Mon.
7:30pm-10:30pm; lunch menu from €19

This is the place to stop if you are feeling peckish after visiting the Palais Longchamp. The short menu changes daily, and during the week the restaurant pulls in the local business community with dishes such as tagliatelle with squid. You can usually get a table, but reserve to be sure.

LE TIRE BOUCHON

11 Cours Julien; tel. 04 13 25 36 78; www.facebook.
com/letirebouchons; Tues.-Sat. 3pm-2am; €5-12

This very French tapas restaurant offers taster plates of snails, pigs' ears, and sausages made from intestines. It's perfect for the epicurious. For the less adventurous, there are simpler plates of cured ham, cheese, and seafood. Reserve to be sure of a table.

TOWARD LES CALANQUES
Seafood
★ CHEZ FONFON

140 rue du Vallon des Auffes; tel. 04 91 52 14 38;
www.chez-fonfon.com/restaurant; daily noon-2pm
and 7pm-10pm; €25-28, bouillabaisse €53 per person

Since 1952 Chez Fonfon has been offering what is widely considered one of the best bouillabaisses in Marseille. Against the idyllic backdrop of Vallon des Auffes, the king of fish soups is served to diners by a coterie of waiters with the pomp and ceremony usually reserved for visiting dignataries. Reservation is necessary.

L'ESPLAI DU GRAND BAR DES GOUDES

29 rue Désiré Pelaprat; tel. 04 91 73 43 69;
Thurs.-Tues. noon-2pm and 8pm-10pm; €15-32,
bouillabaisse €48 per person

Three generations of the same family have run this restaurant in the heart of the Goudes harbor. It's buzzy, full of locals, and great for fish lovers. Reserve ahead; it's very popular.

Regional Cuisine
L'AUBERGE DU CORSAIRE CHEZ PAUL

35 rue Désiré Pelaprat; tel. 04 91 73 19 26;
www.facebook.com/chezpaul.lesgoudes; daily
noon-2pm and 8pm-10pm; €18-€35

The restaurant is so close to the sea that diners who swing on their chairs while admiring the great view of Marseille have been known to tumble into the water. As always in Marseille, fish stars, but for carnivores there's a good rib of beef. Reserve in advance.

AM PAR ALEXANDRE MAZZIA

9 rue François Rocca; tel. 04 91 24 83 63;
www.alexandremazzia.com; Tues.-Sat. noon-2pm and
8pm- 9:30pm; menu €57-170

This is the place to eat in Marseille at the moment. Chef Alexandre Mazzia received a Michelin star just six months after opening and was named chef of the year in 2018 by the prestigious Gault & Millau French restaurant guide. His food is passionate, inventive, and full of surprising flavors. Alexandre's skill in smoking the local fish is legendary. Reserve at least a week or even a month ahead of your visit.

Cafes and Light Bites

LE TROPICANA

46 avenue de Montredon, La Pointe Rouge; tel. 04 91 73 03 14; http://tropicana.free.fr; daily noon-4pm and 7:30pm-11pm; €12-25

Le Tropicana is a popular beach club on the Pointe Rouge beach. Hire a sunlounger, chill out with the locals with your feet in the sand, and then have a long lunch. The menu has everything from pizzas to steaks to seafood. Reserve in advance.

Bars and Nightlife

Whether it is dancing the night away in a rooftop bar, swaying by a pool, shivering by an ice bar, or sipping cocktails in a chic club, the Marseillais love a good night out. Big-name DJs get the crowds going, and girls and boys drip with gold chains and rings. Wearing sunglasses late into the night is encouraged. Perhaps it is to protect sensitive eyes from stray rays of strobe light.

BEACH BARS AND CLUBS

APEROBOAT

Qui d'Honneur de la Mairie; www.sortiramarseille. fr/agenda/les-aperos-du-bateau; every Sun. June 9-Sept. 1, 7pm-10:30pm; €21.80

Head out to sea and watch the sunset over Marseille, sipping on a cocktail and swaying to the vibes of top local DJs. Budget extra for drinks and food.

SPORT BEACH CAFÉ

138 avenue Pierre Mendès; tel. 04 28 31 24 56; www.sportbeach.fr; Tues.-Thurs. 7pm-11pm, Fri.-Sat. 7pm-2am; drinks from €6

This beach club is a popular spot for an evening drink during the week, but it really gets going on Friday and Saturday nights, with a glamorous crowd drinking and dancing around the pool.

LE R2

Les Terrasses du Port, 9 quai du Lazaret; tel. 04 91 91 79 39; www.airdemarseille.com/le-rooftop; nightly 7pm-2am; admission from €10, depends on event

Dance the night away or simply chill out on a sofa overlooking the sea. The R2 is a rooftop bar/nightclub that draws in the crowds during the summer with a different theme every night of the week.

BARS

GASPARD

7 boulevard Notre Dame; tel. 06 88 23 86 66; www.facebook.com/bargaspard; Mon.-Sat. 7pm-1am; cocktails €10-12

One of Marseille's best-known cocktail bars is Gaspard. It has a lively ambiance, with the bartenders indulging in plenty of showy throwing of cocktail shakers. Taking a stool at the wood-panelled bar is a great start to an evening out on the town.

CAFÉ DE L'ABBAYE

3 rue d'Endoume; tel. 04 91 66 87 57; www.facebook. com/lecafedelabbaye; Mon.-Fri. 8:30am-10:30pm, Sat.-Sun. 3:30pm-10:30pm; drinks from €3.50

Just along the road from L'Abbaye Saint-Victor, this bar has a popular terrace overlooking the old port. It's got a lively local vibe and is an atmospheric place for a sundowner.

LA RUCHE

128 rue Sainte; tel. 04 91 21 62 03;
www.laruche-marseille.fr; Tues.-Sat. 6pm-2am;
tapas and cocktails €6-12

This tapas bar is always packed with a hip twenty-something Marseillais crowd. The food ranges from plates of cheese and cold meats to more serious nibbles like prawns flambeed in pastis.

LE REPAIRE DES AMIS

1 rue d'Endoume; tel. 06 09 52 99 33;
www.facebook.com/lerepairedelapoissonnerie;
Tues.-Sat. 5pm-midnight; oysters €16-19

This small bar on the hill above the old port has a great reputation for fresh platters of oysters and other shellfish. Arrive early to grab a table and stay late, as the evenings get lively.

NIGHTCLUBS

TROLLEYBUS

24 quai de Rive Neuve; tel. 04 91 54 30 45; http://letrolley.com; Thurs.-Sat. midnight-6am; €10 entry

Located in an old arsenal, this nightclub consists of three separate rooms: dance club, whisky bar, and private club. The old brick ceilings and long narrow rooms give an intimate feel.

LE BAZAR

90 boulevard Rabatau; tel. 05 68 52 15 15; www.bazarmarseille.com; Fri.-Sat. midnight-6pm; €25 entry

It's all going on at Le Bazar. In the summer there's an open-air club, and in the winter an ice bar. Dress smart because the bouncers working the door are known to be very picky.

LIVE MUSIC

SON DES GUITARES

16 rue Corneille; tel. 04 91 33 11 47;
https://m.facebook.com/pages/Au-Son-Des-Guitares/160204710675811; Wed.-Sat. 11pm-5am;
drinks from €10

Be warned, you might need a good word from a contact to get past the doorman. Try asking the hotel concierge, or a tour guide. Once you're in, the atmosphere is unique, with Corsican musicians playing live. Historically, Corsica is an island stoked by a sense of the injustice at French rule and marked by feuds between rival families. Consequently, Corsican music is about as passionate as any you will encounter.

LA CARAVALLE

34 quai du Port; tel. 04 91 90 36 64;
www.lacaravelle-marseille.com; daily 7am-2am;
€3 on music nights

Twice a week there's live music at this old port bar. Performances range from flamenco to jazz. There's a small terrace where you can enjoy a view out over the boats to Notre-Dame de la Garde.

LE JAM

42 rue des Trois Rois; tel. 06 09 53 40 41;
http://lejam.unblog.fr; see website for details, doors 7:30pm, show 8:30pm; €13

An intimate bar that attracts top jazz artists. The tables and chairs are pushed right up close to the performers. It's best to reserve by text message in advance.

Accommodations

VIEUX PORT

€100-200

MAISON MONTGRAND

35 rue Montgrand; tel. 04 91 00 35 20;
www.maison-montgrand.com; €100 d

A good choice for families, the Montgrand has a wide selection of rooms, including two that sleep four and one that sleeps six. It's a few streets back from the old port, with a modern boutique-hotel vibe. There's a funky bar and even a concept store. All rooms have en-suite bathrooms, Wi-Fi, and air-conditioning. Public parking is nearby.

ALIZÉ
35 quai des Belges;
tel. 04 91 33 66.97;
www.alize-hotel.com; €120 d
A 2019 remodel has given this portside stalwart a more contemporary feel. Rooms, all with Wi-Fi, air-conditioning, and ensuite bathrooms, open onto the old port and have lovely views straight out to sea. Private parking is available.

★ LES CHAMBRES D'ABBAYE
8 rue Petit Chantier; tel. 06 09 75 87 12;
www.leschambresdelabbaye.fr; €120 d
If you are looking for something a little bit different, consider this three-bedroom bed-and-breakfast just a one minute's walk from the old port. The rooms are large, all with ensuite bathrooms, Wi-Fi, and air-conditioning. My favorite room is the Chambre Ninon, which opens onto the small courtyard garden. Booking well in advance is advisable. There is a garage available for parking.

GRAND HOTEL BEAUVAU MARSEILLE
4 rue Beauvau; tel. 04 91 54 91 00;
www.grandhotelbeauvaumarseille.com; €170 d
Part of the Sofitel chain, the Grand Hotel sits almost directly opposite Norman Foster's L'Ombrière and faces directly out to sea. It offers comfortable, contemporary rooms, all with Wi-Fi, ensuite bathrooms, and air-conditioning. The clientele is a mix of well-heeled tourists and businessmen.

LA RESIDENCE DU VIEUX PORT
18 quai du Port; tel. 04 91 91 91 22;
www.hotel-residence-marseille.com; €180 d
Book into a color-filled room with a terrace overlooking the old port and Notre-Dame de la Garde. The suites are particularly large (up to 60 square meters/645 square feet) with stunning picture windows. All rooms have Wi-Fi, ensuite bathrooms, and air-conditioning. There's an excellent on-site restaurant to enjoy when your feet just can't carry you any farther. Private parking is available on request.

Over €200
HOTEL C2
48 rue Roux de Brignoles; tel. 04 95 05 13 13;
www.c2-hotel.com; €270 d
The C2 is a 20-bedroom luxury boutique hotel with a focus on interior design. Rooms have furniture by luminaries such as Le Corbusier as well as Wi-Fi, ensuite bathrooms, and air-conditioning. A boat transfer to the hotel's private beach club on an island is a glam optional extra. Private parking is available.

LE PANIER
€100-200
AU VIEUX PANIER
13 rue du Panier; tel. 04 91 91 23 72;
www.auvieuxpanier.com; €100 d
This is a good place to stay to experience the unique atmosphere of the Panier quarter of Marseille. Rooms come in three sizes: small, medium, and large. They all have air-conditioning, Wi-Fi, and ensuite bathrooms, and are redecorated every year by an upcoming artist. The public parking on the old port is the closest.

Over €200
INTERCONTINENTAL HOTEL DIEU
1 Place Daviel; tel. 04 13 42 42 42;
www.intercontinental.com/marseille; €300 d
Facing Notre-Dame de la Garde, the palace-like building dominates one side of the Vieux Port at the entrance to Le Panier district. Even if you don't stay, drinks on the imperious terrace are a must. All rooms have air-conditioning, ensuite bathrooms, and Wi-Fi. Private parking is available.

EUROMÉDITERRANÉE PROJECT
€100-200
BEST WESTERN LA JOLIETTE
49 avenue Robert Schuman; tel. 04 96 11 49 49; www.bestwestern.fr; €120 d

This location is perfect for those wishing to dip into Marseille for a visit to the Euroméditerranée project. It's on the main street that runs parallel to the quayside. Rooms all have Wi-Fi, air-conditioning, and ensuite bathrooms, and are decorated in a contemporary style. Private parking is available on request.

MARSEILLE CENTER
Under €100
CASA ORTEGA
46 rue des Petites Maries; tel. 06 80 62 53 21; www.casa-ortega.com/en; €90 d

Caroline Contoz is a welcoming host. Full of local knowledge, she's always available to help you get the very best out of your stay in Marseille. The Casa has five rooms, all with ensuite bathrooms. It's decorated with an eclectic mix of furniture from *brocantes*. Visit the website to pick the room that suits your needs best; sizes and beds vary, although all have ensuite bathrooms and Wi-Fi.

€100-200
★ LE RYAD
16 rue Sénac de Meilhan; tel. 04 91 47 74 54; www.leryad.fr; €120 d

Le Ryad is an oasis of calm just off Marseille's bustling main shopping street, La Canebière. As the name suggests, it has a Moroccan feel. Rooms have delightful arched recesses, and the courtyard garden is the perfect to place to relax to the sound of water bubbling away in the fountain. Art exhibitions line the walls, and there are occasional musical evenings. All rooms have Wi-Fi and ensuite bathrooms.

TOWARD LES CALANQUES
Under €100
MAMA SHELTER
64 rue de La Loubière; tel. 04 84 35 20 00; www.mamashelter.com; €80 d

Conceived by renowned interior designer Philippe Starck, Mama Shelter is hip and low-cost, but also fun, luxurious, and a little naughty. All rooms have Wi-Fi, ensuite bathrooms, and free movie streaming (including adult films).

€100-200
LE RHUL
269 Corniche John Fitzgerald Kennedy; tel. 04 91 52 01 77; www.hotel-restaurant-le-rhul.com; €100 d

Perched on a rock, Le Rhul has a romantic terrace looking out to sea and a reputation for some of the best bouillabaisse in Marseille. Rooms have nice period touches, and all have Wi-Fi, air-conditioning, and ensuite bathrooms. There is private parking, and guests are a 10-minute drive from the old port.

LES CABANON DE FONFON
140 rue du Vallon des Auffes; tel. 04 91 52 43 37; www.chez-fonfon.com/nos-chambres-cabanons; €130 d

Four small apartments in the fishing port of Vallon des Auffes have been created by the Chez Fonfon restaurant. They are spacious, equipped with Wi-Fi and air-conditioning, and located in what is probably the most picturesque part of Marseille. Public parking nearby is limited.

HOTEL 96
Chemin de La Soude; tel. 04 91 71 90 22; www.hotel96.com; €140 d

This is a great base from which to explore Marseille and Les Calanques. Spacious luxury rooms, all with ensuite bathrooms, Wi-Fi, and air-conditioning, open onto a large garden with a pool. There is parking on-site.

★ **LES BORDS DE MER**

52 Corniche Président John Fitzgerald Kennedy; tel. 04 13 94 34 00; www.lesbordsdemer.com/fr; €200 d

Five minutes from the first Calanque, and five minutes from the Old Port, Les Bords de Mer has an unequalled location, right on the Plage des Catalans. All rooms have sea views, Wi-Fi, air-conditioning, and ensuite bathrooms. In the morning, a restorative dip in the sea before the crowds arrive is just outside the door. The hotel has five parking spaces that are a short walk away; parking must be reserved well in advance.

Information and Services

VISITOR INFORMATION
MARSEILLE TOURIST OFFICE

11 La Canebière; tel. 08 26 50 05 00; www.marseille-tourisme.com

This is the best place for maps, tickets (including the City Pass), and general advice. The **City Pass** can be purchased for 24, 48, or 72 hours (€26, €33, and €41, respectively). It entitles holders to free use of the city's transport system (buses, trams, ferries, metro), free entry into the city museums, reduced entry prices into events and exhibitions, and many other benefits. Full details can be found here: www.marseille-tourisme.com/fileadmin/user_upload/CityPassAvril2018_FicheGB.pdf.

Post Office

The **La Poste** nearest the old port is located at 50 Rue de Rome. It's open Mon.-Fri. 8:30am-6:30pm and Sat. 8:30am-12:30pm. There are numerous other post offices throughout the city.

HEALTH AND SAFETY
Police

Police headquarters are located on Marseille's busy central shopping street at 66 La Canebière; tel. 04 88 77 58 00.

Hospitals and Pharmacies

For medical attention, go to **Vieux Port Medical Center** (48 rue de la Republique; tel. 04 91 90 65 64; 9am-6pm daily). Pharmacies are plentiful in Marseille. They all display a green cross symbol, which usually juts out into the street. On the old port, the pharmacy is located at 4 quai du Port. It is open Mon.-Sat 9am-8pm.

Foreign Consulates

The **British Consulate** is located at 10.3 rue des Docks, 1st floor; tel. 04 91 15 72 10. The **U.S. consulate** is located at 12 boulevard Paul Peytral; tel. 01 43 12 48 85. Consulates for other countries are located in Paris only.

COMMUNICATIONS
Wi-Fi

Large public spaces such as the Gare de Marseille-Saint-Charles and Marseille airport offer free Wi-Fi. The city is committed to offering free Wi-Fi on public transport, but it is not universally available yet. When taking public transport, check your phone for available networks. Restaurants, bars, and cafés in Marseille may offer their customers free Wi-Fi. Ask before you order.

Newspapers

The regional paper *La Provence* publishes a Marseille edition, concentrating on news from the city and across Provence.

Transportation

GETTING THERE

By Air

MARSEILLE PROVENCE AIRPORT

Marseille Provence airport is located 20 minutes out of town. It serves more than 100 destinations with scheduled direct flights, and 40 European destinations with flights from its low-cost terminal. **Air Transat** and **Air Canada** fly from Montreal to Marseille airport, but most North Americans will have to fly to a European hub and connect with a flight to Marseille. There are 20 daily connections between Paris and Marseille. There are also plentiful connections between Marseille and the UK as follows: **EasyJet** flies from London Gatwick, Manchester, Bristol, and Glasgow to Marseille; **Ryan Air** flies from London Stansted, Manchester, and Edinburgh to Marseille; **British Airways** flies from London Heathrow to Marseille.

A **shuttle bus** runs from the airport to the city center every 15 minutes between 4:30am and 12:10am, costing €8 for a one-way trip and and €12 for a round trip. A **taxi** from the airport to the center of Marseille costs €55.

By Train

MARSEILLE-SAINT-CHARLES STATION

Marseille-Saint-Charles Station is just over 3 hours from **Paris** by TGV (bullet train). There is service nearly every hour, and most TGVs also stop at both **Avignon** and **Aix-en-Provence.** In the main tourist season, it is also possible to travel direct to **London** by TGV. The journey time is 6 hours and 30 minutes, and there are four trains each week. The price of TGV tickets varies hugely depending on the day, time of travel, and how far in advance you book. A TGV ticket to Paris can be purchased for as little as €25 or can cost over €200. Ouigo tickets are the cheapest; these are basic, low-cost TGV trains without buffet cars.

By Bus

The Marseille **bus station** is located at rue Jacques Bory, next to the Marseille-Saint-Charles train station.

From Aix: Bus Line 50 (www.lepilote.com) runs every 5 minutes between the Aix and Marseille bus stations. The journey time is 30 minutes and the cost €6.

From Avignon: Three buses a day run between Avignon and Marseille (www.ouibus.com), taking 1 hour and 15 minutes and costing €9.

From Nice: Ouibus (fr.ouibus.com) runs a service four times a day from the Nice airport to Marseille-Saint-Charles. The journey takes 2 hours 30 minutes. Last-minute prices are as low as €5. Zou line 20 runs from central Nice (Gare Routière Vauban) to Marseille bus station, taking 3 hours and costing €30 euros (www.info-ler.fr).

From Cannes: Ouibus (www.ouibus.com) runs a service four times a day from Place Benidorm, 73 avenue du Campon Le Cannet, taking 2 hours with last-minute prices as low as €5.

From Barcelona: Ouibus (www.ouibus.com) runs a service once a day from Barcelona Nord - Gare routièr Carrer d'Ali-Bei, costing around €17 taking 7 hours.

By Car

From Marseille Provence Airport: Take the A55, covering 24 kilometers (15 miles) in 20 minutes.

From Aix: Take the A51 and A7, covering 32 kilometers (20 miles) in 35 minutes.

From Nice: Take the A8 for 200 kilometers (124 miles) in 2 hours and 15 minutes.

From Cannes: Take the A8 for 180 kilometers (112 miles) in 2 hours 5 minutes.

From Barcelona: Take the AP-7 and A9, covering 500 kilometers (311 miles) in 4 hours and 45 minutes.

GETTING AROUND

Marseille is famous for its heavy traffic and for the eccentric—or dangerous, depending on your point of view—driving of its inhabitants. Avoid driving in Marseille if possible. It's also better to avoid the bus network, because you will inevitably become snarled in traffic. Check distances before walking between the sights listed in this book. Marseille is a big city, and walking from place to place takes a long time. Fortunately, there are excellent metro, tram, and ferry services. All information about public transport can be found here: www.rtm.fr.

Transit Passes

By purchasing a **City Pass** (www.rtm.fr) to the city's museums and sights, tourists visiting Marseille can use public transport for free. Visitors without a City Pass should purchase a **Carte 1 voyage** (solo) for €1.70 from tickets offices in tram and metro stations. This carte allows multiple journeys across the network (except ferries) within a one-hour time period. It is best to ask for a Transtick, which can be charged again if necessary. There are also ticketing options for groups.

Visitors planning a long stay should consider applying for a **Carte de Transport** by bringing a piece of identity and a passport photo to any of the network's ticket offices. The carte is validated every journey and can be charged again in metro and tram stations.

By Metro

The Marseille Metro (www.rtm.fr/sites/default/files/planaxeslourds.pdf) has two lines. **M1** almost—but not quite—completes a circle of central Marseille. **M2** runs north to south roughly parallel with the coast.

By Tram

Marseille has three tram lines. They are modern, efficient, and do not get held up by the terrible traffic. **T1** runs diagonally across the center of the city from east to west. **T2** and **T3** depart just to the north of the Euroméditerranée project and run through the city center. T2 turns east toward the Palais Longchamps, whereas T3 continues to the south, ending just to the east of Notre Dame de La Garde.

By Bicycle

Marseille operates a pickup-and-drop bike system, with various stations spaced throughout the city. It's easy and quick to sign up on the website (http://en.levelo-mpm.fr; €1 subscription cost, then €1 per 30 minutes after first 30 minutes). Be aware of the aforementioned eccentric driving habits of the Marseillais when cycling.

By Taxi/Uber

Les Taxis Marseillais can be booked by calling (tel. 04 91 92 92 92) or by downloading their app from your app store. Rides are metered. Uber operates also within Marseille.

By Boat Shuttle
LA NAVETTE

Ferries run in both directions between:

The **Vieux Port** and **Pointe Rouge,** Apr. 27-Sept. 29, every hour 8am-7pm.

The **Vieux Port** and **L'Estaque,** Apr. 27-Sept. 29, every hour 8:30am-7:30pm.

Pointe Rouge and **Les Goudes,** June 1-Sept. 1 every hour 8:50am-7:30pm.

Tickets are purchased on board and cost €5. Check for timetable updates here: www.rtm.fr/guide-voyageur/se-deplacer/navettes-maritimes.

THE FERRY BOAT

By far the best way to get across the old port is taking the legendary Ferry Boat. The Ferry made its first crossing in 1880 from the Place aux Huiles (quai de Rive-Neuve) on the south side to the Mairie on the north side. Today the ferry runs every 10 minutes in both directions from 7:30am to 8:30pm. The journey costs 50 cents (free with City Pass) and takes 10 minutes.

Les Calanques National Park

Christianity tells us that one is supposed to ascend into heaven and descend into hell. God must have forgotten this small nuance when he created Les Calanques. Access by road is restricted, and most visitors hike down mountain paths to visit the string of rocky inlets that punctuate the limestone cliffs between Marseille and Cassis. The deserted beaches and turquoise waters that await resemble many people's vision of Paradise. Only the larger calanques, such as Sormiou and Morgiou, are developed with services and restaurants; the rest of the National Park is a wilderness of pine, rock, immense skies, and shimmering sea. Cassis, the seaside town that sits at the easterly limit of Les Calanques, is one of the most attractive resorts in the South of France.

ORIENTATION

Cassis is located 25 kilometers (16 miles) to the east of Marseille. The coast between the seaside resort and the city constitutes **Les Calanques National Park.** The inland limit of the national park is delineated by the **D559** road, which runs between Cassis and Marseille. The largest calanques of **Morgiou** and **Sormiou** are accessed off this road, as it runs into the suburbs of Marseille. The other calanques are accessed either by boat or on foot by taking the **GR98-51** walking trail that runs between the Calanque of **Callelongue** (which is a few kilometers to the east of the **Port des Goudes** in Marseille) to Calanque of **Port-Miou,** 1 kilometer (0.6 miles) to the west of Cassis.

★ CASSIS

The pastel-colored houses that surround the half-moon harbor of Cassis are reminiscent of Saint-Tropez. From here, boat trips depart regularly into Les Calanques. The more active can follow in kayaks. However, many travelers find Cassis, with its beaches and narrow cobbled shopping streets, captivating enough, particularly since the two nearest calanques—Port-Miou and Port Pin—are easily accessible on foot from a parking area adjoining the town.

Sights
CAP CANAILLE
Routes des Crêtes, Cassis
A good pitstop on the way into or out of Cassis is Cap Canaille, France's highest sea cliff. Follow the Route des Crêtes (D141) from Cassis to the parking area at the top of the cliff. From here, there is a marvelous sweeping view of the Mediterranean, the cliffs of Les Calanques, and the Bay of Cassis.

CALANQUE DE PORT-MIOU
50 avenue des Calanques, Cassis
Calanque de Port-Miou is a long, narrow calanque that is accessible on foot or by car from Cassis by following the avenue des Calanques. The calanque, which is bordered by limestone cliffs that were once mined for lime, is lined by small yachts. As you near the entrance to the open sea, the yachts peter out and the landscape becomes more rugged. If you are in Cassis and don't have the time for a full excursion into Les Calanques, then visiting Calanque de Port-Miou at least gives you a taste. The Sentier de Petit Prince is a marked trail around the headland. The trail runs parallel to Port-Miou for half of its 2-kilometer (1-mile) length. It takes about 60 minutes to complete.

Wineries
DOMAINE PATERNEL
1 route Pierre Imbert, Cassis;
tel. 04 42 01 77 03; www.domainedupaternel.com;
Mon.-Sat. 9:30am-noon and 2:30pm-6pm;
free tasting
Provence is not well-known for its white wines. The one exception is Cassis. The steep hillsides around the port produce

Les Calanques

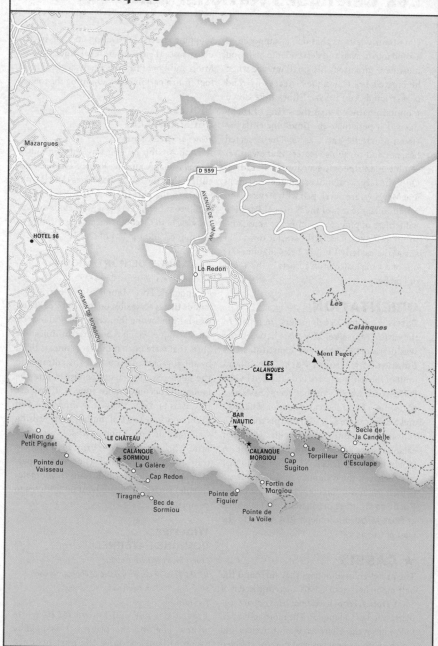

Mazargues

D 559

AVENUE DE LUMINY

HOTEL 96

CHEMIN DE MORGIOU

Le Redon

Les

Calanques

Mont Puget

LES CALANQUES

BAR NAUTIC

Socle de la Candelle

Vallon du Petit Pignet

LE CHÂTEAU

CALANQUE SORMIOU

Le Torpilleur

Cirque d'Esculape

Pointe du Vaisseau

La Galère

CALANQUE MORGIOU

Cap Sugiton

Cap Redon

Fortin de Morgiou

Tiragne

Bec de Sormiou

Pointe du Figuier

Pointe de la Voile

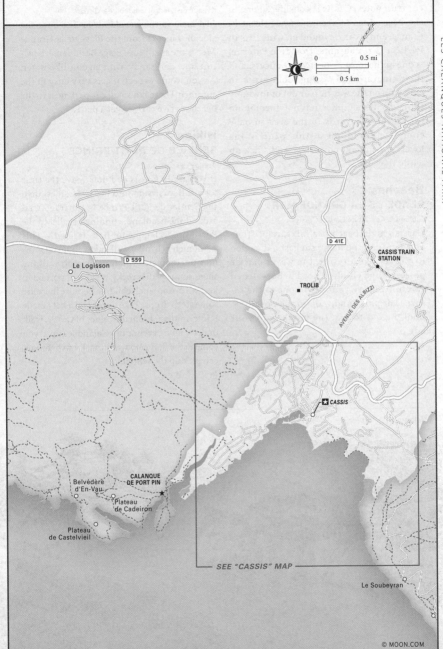

0   0.5 mi

0   0.5 km

Le Logisson

D 559

D 41E

CASSIS TRAIN
STATION

TROLIB

AVENUE DES ALBIZZI

CASSIS

Belvédère
d'En-Vau

Plateau
de Cadeiron

CALANQUE
DE PORT PIN

Plateau
de Castelvieil

SEE "CASSIS" MAP

Le Soubeyran

© MOON.COM

the region's best white. Thanks to its citrus fruit notes, Cassis is considered one of the best wines to accompany seafood in France, and it can be found on wine lists in Paris's top restaurants. Domaine Paternel is one of the most respected producers, and their vineyard and tasting room make an easy stop on the way into or out of town. By the end of the summer, it is not uncommon for all the vineyards in the area to have completely sold out of this wine. Wine lovers should take advantage and stock up while they can.

Beaches
PLAGE DE LA GRANDE MER
Esplanade Charles de Gaulle, Cassis

Cassis's main beach is a mixture of stone and sand. As the name suggests, it's open to the sea. As a result, the waves can be powerful and children need to be watched carefully. Leave your car in one of the resort's car parks and walk to the port area. Looking out to sea, the beach is to your left.

PLAGE BESTOUAN
Avenue de l'Amiral Gauteaume, Cassis

Just around the headland, on the opposite side of the port from the Plage de la Grande Mer, is the small cove Plage Bestouan. It's picturesque and sandy, with lagoon-like water. As you would expect, it gets very busy in the summer. There is a small car park next to the beach. Arrive early to get a place.

Hiking
SENTIER DE PETIT PRINCE
Avenue des Calanques, Cassis

If you are in Cassis and don't have the time for a full excursion into Les Calanques, then the Sentier de Petit Prince is a marked trail around the headland, running parallel to the Port-Miou calanque for half its length. This 2-kilometer (1-mile) walk takes about 60 minutes to complete. You'll need good walking shoes, as the path is rocky. It's also important to keep an eye on small children because there are some steep drops. Take water and a hat. Shade is intermittent. From the center of Cassis, walk or drive along avenue des Calanques until you come to the Port Miou parking. From here, you can pick up the sentier.

Calanque de Port Pin

Cassis

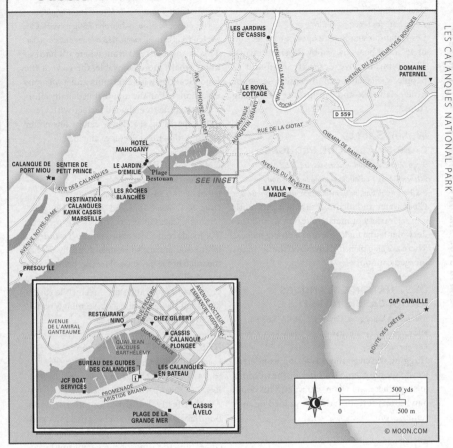

© MOON.COM

BUREAU DES GUIDES DES CALANQUES

Rue Séverin Icard, Cassis; tel. 06 61 50 38 48; www. guides-calanques.com; €19 per person for a half-day hike

These experienced local guides help you get the best out of Les Calanques. They are experts in the local flora, fauna, and wildlife, and they know the hidden routes off the main hiking trails. Excursions can be for a couple of hours or a whole day. They also offer climbing classes for beginners.

Cycling
CASSIS À VELO

Place Montmorin, Cassis; tel. 06 26 04 05 28; https://cassisavelo.fr; daily 10am-7pm; from €40

Maylis and Pascale are the enthusiastic founders of Cassis a Velo. They propose six imaginative circuits, including one through the vines and one up to the heights of Cap Canaille to watch the sun go down. Some tours are guided, while others rely on maps to follow.

Sailing and Boat Tours
LES CALANQUES EN BATEAU

Quai Saint-Pierre, Cassis; www.cassis-calanques.com;
see website for times; from €16

Les Calanques en Bateau operate a collection of 15 small boats owned by Cassis residents. They typically have a capacity of around 12 people. Visits can be to three, five, seven, or nine calanques, and can include swimming stops.

Water Sports
CASSIS CALANQUE PLONGEE

3 rue Michel Arnaud, Cassis; tel. 06 71 52 60
20; www.cassis-calanques-plongee.com; daily
8:30am-noon and 2:30pm-6.30pm; dives from €60

Clear water and plentiful diving sights, with a great variety of marine life, coral, and underwater fauna make the area a diving mecca. There are also plentiful caves and the odd submerged cannon.

DESTINATION CALANQUES KAYAK CASSIS MARSEILLE

Avenue des Calanques, Cassis; tel. 06 07 15 63 86;
https://cassis-kayak-marseille.fr/fr; daily 9am-6pm;
€30 for half a day

Hugging the coast in a kayak is a wonderful way to see the calanques, offering the freedom to stop where and when you want. This company offers full- or half-day, guided or solo rentals from Cassis.

Food
LA VILLA MADIE

Avenue de Revestel-anse de Corton, Cassis;
tel. 04 96 18 00 00; http://lavillamadie.com;
Thurs.-Mon. noon-1:15pm and 7pm-9:15pm; €72-86

One of the top gastronomic restaurants in Provence, the Villa Madie's food manages somehow to outshine it's idyllic location perched on a rock cliff jutting out into the Mediterranean. Sublimely skillful cooking plays with surprising flavors such as roasted lobster with kumquat. There's an adjacent brasserie with a more competitively priced menu. Reservations are necessary.

★ PRESQU'ÎLE

Quartier Port-Miou, Cassis; tel. 04 42 01 15 40;
www.restaurant-la-presquile.fr/restaurant-la-plage-
Bleuee-cassis; daily noon-3pm and 7:30pm-10pm; €65
weekend and evening menu, €38 midweek lunch menu

This is another restaurant where it's hard to know what's more enjoyable, the view or the food. Scallops with chestnuts and a *foie gras* emulsion melt in the mouth, but equally alluring is the pine tree-shaded terrace with views of the sparkling sea. There can be few better settings for a meal. Reserve ahead.

CHEZ GILBERT

19 quai des Baux, Cassis;
tel. 04 42 01 71 36; www.chezgilbert.net;
Thurs.-Tues. noon-2:30pm and 7pm-10pm; €30-50

Dining at Chez Gilbert is a theatrical experience. The locals come here to be seen. Fish is ordered by the 100 grams, so waiters dutifully proffer the catch of the day on a silver tray before cooking. Shellfish arrives on icy platters, and portside promenaders stop and stare. Meanwhile, diners keep their shades on and look, seemingly oblivious to the attention, out to sea.

RESTAURANT NINO

1 quai Barthélemy, Cassis;
tel. 04 42 01 74 32; http://nino-cassis.com;
Tues.-Sun. noon-2pm and 7pm-10pm; €20-35

Another festival of fish is on offer at Nino. Bouillabaisse, oysters, sea bass in a salt crust, the list goes on. The seafood is a fresh as it comes, and the atmosphere is enjoyably buzzy. Reservations in season are advisable.

Accommodations
LE JARDIN D'EMILIE

23 avenue de l'Amiral Ganteaume, Cassis;
tel. 04 42 01 80.55; www.lejardindemile.fr; €115 d

This charming small hotel is nestled under pine trees, a short walk from the Plage Bestouan. The room furnishings are just a little old-fashioned, but given the competitive prices and sea views, it's hard to quibble. All rooms have air-conditioning, Wi-Fi, and en-suite bathrooms. Private parking is available.

LES JARDINS DE CASSIS

Avenue Auguste Favier, Cassis; tel. 04 42 01 84 85;
www.hotel-lesjardinsde-cassis.com; €150 d

It's about a 20-minute walk down to the port from Les Jardins de Cassis, and given the steepness of the hill, you might want to consider taking a taxi back. The flipside of being out of town is a large verdant garden with a pool and quick access to neighboring seaside towns, such as Bandol. Rooms are nicely furnished and spacious, with ensuite bathrooms, air-conditioning, and Wi-Fi.

LE ROYAL COTTAGE

6 avenue du 11 Novembre 1918, Cassis;
tel. 04 42 01 33 34; www.royal-cottage.com/fr/hotel-
charme-cassis; €220 d

Up the hill from the old port, this modern hotel has 25 spacious rooms with Wi-Fi, air-conditioning, and ensuite bathrooms. The pool is set in a small garden. Views across the bay at sunset are delightful. Private parking is available.

★ LES ROCHES BLANCHES

9 avenue des Calanques, Cassis;
tel. 04 42 01 09 30;
https://roches-blanches-cassis.com; €270 d

A short walk from the center of town, out on the headland leading to the Calanques, Les Roches Blanches is the standard-bearer for Cassis hotels. Recently redecorated with an eye toward the hotel's art deco 1930s origins, Les Roches Blanches is a dreamy romantic getaway with all the services you would imagine from a luxury small hotel. All rooms have Wi-Fi, ensuite bathrooms, and air-conditioning. Private parking is available.

HOTEL MAHOGANY

Plage du Bestouan, 19 avenue de l'Amiral Ganteaum,
Cassis; tel. 04 42 01 34 82;
www.hotelmahogany.com; €240 d

On the same headland as Les Roches Blanches, Hotel Mahogany overlooks the Bestouan beach. It's an idyllic spot, looking straight out to sea but only a few minutes' walk from the port. There are only six rooms so book ahead. One of the suites even has its own private pool. All have Wi-Fi, air-conditioning, and ensuite bathrooms. Private parking is available and needs to be reserved.

Information and Services

The Cassis **tourist office** is located at Place Baragnon; tel. 08 92 39 01 03; www.ot-cassis. com. It offers information on where to stay and what to do in Cassis, as well as maps and advice on how best to access Les Calanques.

Getting There
BY TRAIN

Cassis **train station** is located at Quartier de La Gare. Trains run almost every hour from **Marseille Saint-Charles Station.** The walk to the harbor takes about 30 minutes. Luckily, it is downhill. One-way tickets are €2.70 and up.

BY CAR

From **Aix-en-Provence,** take the A52. The journey is 50 kilometers (31 miles) and takes 55 minutes. From **Marseille,** take the A7 and A51, covering 30 kilometers (19 miles) in 40 minutes.

★ LES CALANQUES
Sights
CALANQUE DE PORT PIN

Access from Port-Miou,
50 avenue des Calanques, Cassis

Continuing on from the ancient quarry at Port-Miou on the GR98-51 for 2 kilometers (1 mile) on foot takes you to Port Pin. Once Port Pin comes into sight, it's worth a detour out to the open sea (about 150 meters/500 feet). Here you can listen for the whistling hole, where waves crash through an underground hole in the rock, sending air and spray shooting upward. Port Pin is named after the pine trees that cling to the cliffs on all sides. There's a small sandy beach, and plenty of rocks where you can spread out your towel and relax.

CALANQUE MORGIOU

Les Baumettes, Marseille

Morgiou is one of the larger calanques. The attractive pastel-colored houses that nestle behind the port area are testament to its past as a busy fishing village. Outside the summer season, it's possible to drive all the way into the calanque. In summer when the fire risk is high, the path to the calanque departs from two residential districts of Marseille: Luminy and Les Baumettes. The 6.5-kilometer (4-mile) walk into the calanque takes about 90 minutes. Allow a little more time for the return trip. Morgiou is famous for the Grotte de Cosquer, a coastal cave reached through a submerged passage containing prehistoric drawings of more than 100 different animals; the cave drawings are estimated to date back to 27,000 BC. The interior of the cave is being re-created at the **Villa Méditerranée Musée** in Marseille and is scheduled to open in 2021.

CALANQUE SORMIOU

Les Baumettes, Marseille

Neighboring Morgiou and joined to it by a coastal path, Sormiou is another of the larger calanques. It has a port, small village, and a restaurant. A small sandy beach gives access to crystal-clear waters that are frequented by scuba divers. Outside the summer season, it's possible to drive all the way into the calanque. But in summer, when the fire risk is high, visitors have to park at Les Baumettes. The 4.5-kilometer (2.8-mile) walk takes 1 hour. If you reserve at the Château restaurant, you will be given an access code that allows you to drive into the calanque at all times of year.

MARSEILLEVEYRE

Callelongue, Marseille

Gone are the pine trees that characterize the calanques closest to Cassis. Instead, there's bare rock, grass, and the odd fig tree that can cope with the arid climate. Park at the Calanque de Callelongue on the outskirts of the Les Goudes district of Marseille, and then walk 4 kilometers (2 miles) (50 minutes

GR98-51) or catch a boat. When you arrive, there's a small sand and stone beach, and a restaurant that recieves all its deliveries by sea.

CALANQUE DE LA MOUNINE

Callelongue, Marseille

A shorter 2-kilometer (1-mile) 30-minute walk along the GR98-51 from Calanque de Callelongue, Mounine is one of the smallest callanques. There's no beach, but you can stand on the rocks and watch the schools of fish in the clear water below.

Hiking

MARSEILLE TO CASSIS HIKE

Depart Callelongue, Marseille

If you are fit and determined, it's possible to walk the 35-kilometer (22-mile) GR 98-51 coastal path between Cassis and Marseille in a day. Pick up the IGN Map of the Calanques from either the Marseille or Cassis tourist office, and wear sturdy walking shoes and a hat, taking plenty of water with you. The route climbs 400 meters (1,300 feet) total and is marked, but it is rocky and sometimes slippery. Along the way there are good lunch spots at Calanques Morgiou and Sormiou, and there are plenty of places for a swim. At the Marseille end of the walk, there is no shade, but nearer Cassis the rocks are covered with pine trees.

Cycling

E BIKE TOURS

Meeting point: A Criée / Café des Arts, 30 quai de rive neuve, Marseille; tel. 07 82 00 73 47; www. ebiketours.fr; Mar.-Oct., year round for groups; €45 for a half day tour per person and €99 for a day tour

A day trip from Marseille takes in some of the city's main sights, such as Notre-Dame de la Garde, and then heads along the coast to Les Goudes and the Callanque de Callelongue. Some tours finish with a ride as far as Cassis. The trips give you a taste of Les Calanques but do not really take you out into the wilds. For this, you'll need to put on your walking boots.

TROLIB

3 chemin des Gorguettes, Cassis; tel. 06 72 50 47 26;
www.trolib.com; daily 9am-7pm; €40 per person.
Trolib offers trips to see two or three calanques (Port-Miou, Port Pin, and Calanque d'en Vau). Visiting the two Ports, Miou and Pin, takes about two hours and is relatively easy. The terrain gets a little rougher as you head out to Calanque d'en Vau, which adds more than an hour to the round-trip (including a pause for a swim).

Sailing and Boat Tours
BLEUE EVASION

Port de La Pointe Rouge, Marseille;
tel. 04 91 06 18 87; www.bleueevasion.com; see
website for times, or private booking; from €65
Bleue Evasion operates small motorboats and a catamaran, both departing from Marseille (Port de La Pointe Rouge). They can be booked privately or you can join a scheduled trip to visit the calanques closest to Marseille. The motorboats also offer activities such as wakeboarding. Swim stops are part of the experience, and cold drinks are included in the price.

Food
★ LE CHÂTEAU

Route du Feu de la Calanque de Sormiou, Marseille;
tel. 04 91 25 08 69; www.leChâteau sormiou.fr;
Mon.-Sat. noon-2:30pm and 7:30pm-9:30pm,
Sun. noon-2:30pm; €21-26
Probably the best known and most serious restaurant in Les Calanques, the Château has an unparalleled position, looking straight out over the Calanque Sormiou to the open sea. In season, when the road to the port is closed you can phone ahead to the restaurant and be given a password to allow you through. The food is good but relatively simple, with dishes such as grilled swordfish or king prawns and parsley on offer.

BAR NAUTIC

Calanque Morgiou, Marseille; tel. 04 91 40 06 37;
Tues.-Sun. 10am-10pm; €15-25
Bar Nautic boasts a large terrace overlooking the sea. It provides fresh grilled seafood and salads to weary hikers. The experience is as much about the location as the food, which although good is not that sophisticated.

CHEZ LES BELGES

Marseilleveyre, Marseille; June-Oct. noon-2:30pm and
7pm-10pm, low season Fri.-Mon. noon-2:30pm; €15-20
What could be more Provençal than a restaurant that does not have a phone, and whose opening hours have been known to be so irregular, the owners put up information at the hike departure point in Calanque de Callelongue. There's no terrace, the tables and chairs are on the beach, and the water laps at the feet of diners. The food is simple (the restaurant gets its supplies by boat), with plenty of fresh fish, as well as a hearty Provençal stew served with a baked potato.

Accommodations

The Calanques are a national park with restricted access at certain times of year. It is possible to rent holiday apartments in some of the larger calanques but there are no hotels. The closest places to stay are listed in the Cassis and Marseille accommodations calansections.

Information and Services

The best places for information on the Calanques are the Cassis and Marseille tourist offices.

The **Cassis tourist office** (Place Baragnon; tel. 08 92 39 01 03; www.ot-cassis. com) offers maps and advice on how best to access Les Calanques. The **Marseille Tourist Office** (11 La Canebière; tel. 08 26 50 05 00; www.marseille-tourisme.com) has maps, tickets (including the City Pass), and general advice.

Getting There and Around

The main access points to Les Calanques are from **Port-Miou** in Cassis and **Calanque de Callelongue** in Marseille. From these points visitors must continue **on foot** or **bike.** Port Miou can be reached by following **Avenues**

des **Calanques** (either on foot or in a car) out of Cassis. The road leads to the Port Miou parking. Calanque de Callelongue can be reached by following **Boulevard Alexandre Delabre** (either on foot or in a car) out of the **Les Goudes** neighborhood of Marseille.

BY CAR

It's possible to reach the larger calanques of **Sormiou** (Chemin de Sormiou) and **Morgiou** (route du Feu de la Calanque de Morgiou), but note that access is closed in the summer due to the fire risk. To find both these roads, turn off the **D559** at the Mazargues

roundabout; there is an obelisk in the middle. Follow signs to Sormiou and Morgiou.

BY BOAT

Boats to the calanques depart frequently from Cassis and from Port de La Point Rouge in **Marseille.** Try the following operators: **Les Calanques en Bateau** (quai St Pierre, Cassis; www.cassis-calanques.com; see website for departure times; from €16 for a visit to three calanques) and **Bleue Evasion** (Port de La Pointe Rouge, Marseille; tel. 04 91 06 18 87; www.Bleuevasion.com; see website for times, or private booking; from €65 for half a day in the Calanques).

Côte Bleue

Stretching from Marseille's 16th arrondissement along the coast to the town of Martigues is one of Provence's best-kept secrets: La Côte Bleue. Hundreds of thousands of tourists arrive in Marseille Provence airport every year and head inland without realizing they are 20 minutes' drive from hidden creeks and coves where they can lunch with their feet practically in the Mediterranean. It's the perfect way to begin or end a holiday in style. The Côte Bleue has its own series of calanques, equally as beautiful as the national park to the south. For snorkelers, there's a marine reserve easily accessible from the beaches of the seaside town of Carry-le-Rouet. For wind and kite surfers, the town of Carro offers some of the best waves in Provence. A scenic train line runs the length of the coast, making the return leg of a seaside hike a relaxing pleasure.

ORIENTATION

L'Estaque is technically still part of Marseille. It forms part of the western 16th arrondissement of the city. However, in

spirit, this is where the Côte Bleue begins. Immediately to the west are the small seaside villages of **Niolon** and **Mejean.** Both have picturesque calanques. Farther west are the two larger, more traditional seaside resorts of **Carry-le-Rouet** and **Sausset-les-Pins.** The final resort on this stretch of coast is **Carro.**

L'ESTAQUE

Famous painter after famous painter found Provence's renowned artistic light to be at its purest in L'Estaque. Renoir, Dufy, Braque, and Cézanne all made a pilgrimage at some stage in their careers to this small fishing village on the outskirts of Marseille. Information points offer details about the views they painted and the associated impressionist, post-impressionist, fauvist, and cubist art movements. Aside from its artistic links, L'Estaque is simply a pleasant place to visit. From the port, the narrow streets that lead up the hillside are worth exploring. The Chaîne de l'Estaque limestone hills start here and continue along the coast of the Côte Bleue.

1: view of Cassis town, Cap Canaille rock, and the Mediterranean Sea from the Route des Crêtes mountain road **2:** A railway line runs the length of the Côte Bleue.

Côte Bleue

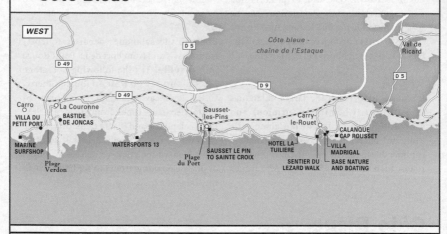

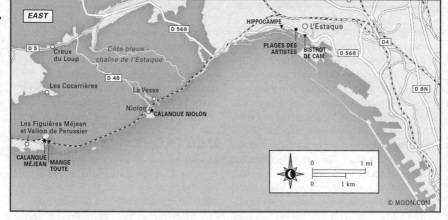

© MOON.COM

Beaches
PLAGES DES ARTISTES

L'Estaque, Marseille

Head out of L'Estaque for about 1 kilometer (0.6 miles) on the D568 toward the Côte Bleue, and on your left are three small, sandy beaches known collectively as the Plages des Artistes. The water is very calm, and as a result the beaches are popular with children. The beaches also offer a panoramic view back toward Marseille.

Food
BISTROT DE CAM

1 Plage L'Estaque, Marseille; tel. 09 83 75 48 66; www.lebistrotducam.com; Wed.-Thurs. noon-2pm and 8pm-10pm, Fri.-Sun. noon-2pm and 8pm-10pm; €25 two-course menu

With a terrace jutting out into the port, it feels like you are dining on the deck of your own yacht. The restaurant draws a crowd of Marseillais foodies keen to escape the smoke of the big city. Try cod with a pumpkin confit and a beetroot reduction. Reserving is sensible in the summer season.

The Birth of Modern Painting

In July 1876, Paul Cézanne wrote to Camille Pissarro: "The sun is so terrifying that it seems as though the objects are silhouetted, not only in black and white, but also in blue, red, brown, and violet." The place he was describing was **L'Estaque,** and it was here that Cézanne began experimenting with a revolutionary technique to let color give a painting its perspective. Where Cézanne went others followed, particularly Georges Braque, whose works are associated with the fauvist school, which has become known for using bright colors to provoke emotional response. Braque famously represented the houses of L'Estaque in geometric cubes, yet shaded them to look both flat and three-dimensional. He went on to work with Picasso, who had been developing a similar proto-cubist style of painting. While Braque and Cézanne are the most renowned names, between 1860 and 1920 L'Estaque's sublime light also lured the following painters: Derain, Dufy, Marquet, Friesz, Macke, Renoir, Guigou, and Monticelli. The port is rightly considered to be the birthplace of modern painting. Famous works created there include:

- *Houses at L'Estaque* by Georges Braque (1908)

- *L'Estaque Melting Snow* by Paul Cézanne (1871)

- *Rochers a L'Estaque* by Auguste Renoir (1882)

HIPPOCAMPE

151 Plage L'Estaque, Marseille;
tel. 04 91 03 83 78; Tues.-Sat. noon-2pm and
7:45pm-9:30pm, Sun.-Mon. noon-2pm; €15-25
From the road the Hippocampe restaurant looks like a smugglers' hideout, hunched against the cliffs and accessed by a set of steep steps descending to the water's edge. There are 10 or so tables on the terrace, all of which are so close to the sea that the accepted sport for diners is to throw bread rolls into the Mediterranean to see if the fish are biting. On the menu are fresh grilled fish and copious salads. The clientele is largely day-trippers from Marseille and the odd tourist. Reserve ahead to be sure of a table on the terrace.

CALANQUE NIOLON

Located between L'Estaque and Carry-le-Rouet, Calanque Niolon is accessed by a sinous road (the D48 accessed by the D5) that winds down the cliff face. It's next to impossible to park in the small fishing village, so you might as well abandon your car with the others by the roadside and walk down. The views of the sparkling Mediterranean, and the colorful cacti by the roadside make it an enjoyable walk. Niolon has a small port, which young boys mistake for the municipal swimming pool, and a couple of restaurants.

Food
THE PERGOLA

13 chemin de la Pergola, Le Rove;
tel. 04 91 46 90 26;
www.restaurantlapergola.fr;
daily noon-2pm and 7pm-10pm; €22-29
To find this 20-table restaurant, you'll walk through a stone arch and onto a vine-covered terrace. The shade is heavy and deep. Gaze out from here, past the yachts and pleasure boats to the other side of the bay, and you see Marseille. The food is simple, focusing on seafood. In particular try the moorish *petite friture* (small battered fish).

Accommodations
AUBERGE DE MEROU

3 chemin du Port, Le Rove; tel. 04 91 46 98 69;
www.aubergedumerou.fr; €105 d
This Auberge and restaurant in the Calanque de Niolon offers five rooms decorated in a nautical style. The accommodations are basic, but the rooms do have ensuite bathrooms and wonderful seaviews. They offer a rare opportunity to experience a calanque at sunrise and sunset.

CALANQUE MÉJEAN

The Calanque de Méjean is divided into two parts: Petit and Grand. The access road (from the D5, take the avenue du Vallon de Graffiane and follow signs) takes you through the Petit Calanque first. You'll see a restaurant and port, but it's best to continue on the roller coaster of a road to the Grand Méjean. Here the railway passes on a majestic high bridge across the valley, and there's an excellent restaurant. A small path leads from the edge of the port past the boule pitch (it's usually empty and perfect for a scenic game) out onto the headland where there is access to a pretty inlet.

Food

MANGE TOUTE

8 chemin du Tire Cul, Calanque Méjean, Ensuès La Redonne; tel. 04 42 45 91 68;

daily 10am-noon; €12-18

Next to the restaurant, boats float at anchor, fishermen mend their nets, and scuba divers prepare for their next dive. The light is clear, and the air is scented with pine and salt. The Mange Tout serves mainly fish, but for those averse to seafood there are a couple of salads as well.

CARRY-LE-ROUET

Look out to sea from portside at Carry-le-Rouet and the view is magnificent. Fishing and pleasure boats bob at anchor, high, pine-fringed cliffs rise on either side, and the famous Provençal light dances on the sea. Walk out toward the beginning of the Sentier de Lezard and look back, though, and the view is less alluring. Modern, ill-conceived buildings have ruined what might have otherwise been another jewel in the crown of the French Mediterranean coast. Nevertheless, the resort pulls in big crowds in the summer months.

Beaches and Watersports

CALANQUE CAP ROUSSET

Avenue Gerard Montus

Around the headland from Carry-le-Rouet, this small picturesque pebble beach draws the crowds in the summer. There's a small parking area opposite, which is almost inevitably full, and a café restaurant.

PARC MARIN

Parc Marine de La Côte Bleue; www.
parcmarincotebleue.fr; price depends on activity

Created in 1982 and running along most of the Côte Bleue, the Parc Marin is dedicated

The incredible light and wild scenery of L'Estaque have informed generations of modern art.

to preserving the rich sealife of the coast. The Parc Marin is easily accessible from Cap Rousset or the Les Bouchons beach, both in Carry-le-Rouet. Simply pull on a mask and snorkle and head out to sea. Guided tours are available in the summer; ask at the Carry-le-Rouet tourist office (11-13 route Bleue, Carry-le-Rouet; tel. 04 91 13 20 36; www.ot-carrylerouet.fr/en).

BASE NATURE AND BOATING
Quai du Professeur Vayssière; tel. 06 22 01 10 93; www.loisirsprovence.fr; June-Sept. 9:30am-12:30pm and 1:30pm-6:30pm; price depends on activity
On offer are kayaking into the calanques of the Côte Bleue, paddleboarding, and snorkling. To go snorkeling, you can rent a mask, snorkel, and flippers and arrange a guided tour of the marine reserve.

Hiking
SENTIER DU LEZARD WALK
Le Port; www.baladeenprovence.com/Carry-le-Rouet
Departing from the port of Carry-le-Rouet, this marked 2-kilometer (1-mile) trail takes you along the cliffs of the Côte Bleue. Particularly at the beginning, the path is narrow and the steps are sometimes uneven and slippery, but any difficulty is more than made up for by the scenery, with azur waters and hidden coves. The small lighthouse on the outskirts of Carry-le-Rouet makes a nice spot for a photo. This walk takes about an hour and 15 minutes to complete.

Food
VILLA MADRIGAL
4 avenue Docteur Gérard Montus; tel. 04 28 31 23 32; www.lavillamadrigal.fr; Wed.-Sat. noon-2pm and 7:30pm-10pm. Sun. and Tues. noon-2pm; €24-33
Inside Le Madrigal, new and old money clash. There's plenty of bling, short skirts, and large sunglasses (according to the guest book, Le Madrigal is popular with the Olympique Marseille football team), but there are also tables full of sedate and sated locals. Le Madrigal is all about the terrace, which is vertiginous and shaded by ancient pines. The

secret ingredient in every dish served is the majesty of the view. Reserving in season is advisable, and the turbot with morel mushrooms is not to be missed.

Accomodations
HOTEL LA TUILIERE
34 avenue Draio de la Mar; tel. 04 42 44 79 79; www.hotel-tuiliere.com; €100 d
The hotel offers 22 functional, clean, modern rooms, all with Wi-Fi, air-conditioning, and ensuite bathrooms. There's not a lot of Provençal atmosphere, but it's a practical base, with sea views, a pool, and private parking.

Information and Services
The Carry-le-Rouet **Tourist Office** is located at 11-13 route Bleue, Carry-le-Rouet; tel. 04 42 13 20 36; www.otcarrylerouet.fr. It offers information on accommodation in the region, maps, information for hikers, and advice on the best ways to enjoy the coast.

SAUSSET-LES-PINS
Smaller than its neighbor Carry-le-Rouet, Sausset has a more relaxed air. Out of season, it's a good place to head to for a bracing walk up the coast. In July and August, there's easy access to beaches for a quick dip.

Beaches
PLAGE DU PORT
Route de La Couronne
A short walk from the center of town (head west on Route de La Couronne) is this long pebble beach. It's not the prettiest on the coast, but it's convenient and good for a walk after lunch in one of the portside cafés.

PLAGE FOUR À CHAUX
Route de La Couronne
In between Sausset-les-Pins and La Couronne, this small creek-like beach with turquoise waters is accessed by steps. It's very popular in the summer, so arrive early. On a hot day in spring or autumn, it's idyllic. To find the beach, leave Sauset le Pin and take the Route de La Couronne (D49) for 2 kilometers (1 mile). On

your left you will see a small road that leads to the parking for the beach.

Hiking
SAUSSET-LES-PINS TO SAINTE CROIX
Le Port; www.baladeenprovence.com/Sausset-les-Pins
Departing from Sausset-les-Pins, this 12-kilometer (8-mile) hike takes about 3 hours to complete. The trail hugs the coast and offers plenty of opportunities for swimming. It's relatively flat with the odd climb, but there is very little shade, so make sure you take a hat, and in the summer set off early with plenty of water. Along the way, you will encounter the Sausset-les-Pins lighthouse, Tamaris port, and the Chapelle de Sainte Croix. It's possible to get the train back from Sainte Croix to Sausset-les-Pins.

Information and Services
The Sausset-les-Pins **Tourist Office** is located at 14 avenue du Port, Sausset-les-Pins; tel. 04 42 45 60 65; www.ville-sausset-les-pins.fr. It offers information on accommodation, restauraunts, and what to see and do along this stretch of the coast.

CARRO AND MARTIGUES
Every morning, Carro's busy little port hosts a market, with the fish loaded straight from the boats onto the stalls. Once the morning hubbub has died away, Carro is a sleepy but attractive port. Along with Martigues, it is known for the "caviar martegal" delicacy, made by drying the eggs of mullet in their own pockets. Martigues sits on the canal that links the Etang de La Berre inland salt lake to the sea. Pretty pastel-colored houses and moored boats line the banks of the canal. However, note that Martigues is quite industrial, and the picturesque part is small and centered around the island in the middle of the canal, where there are several cafés and restaurants.

Beaches and Watersports
PLAGE VERDON
Chemin du Verdon, La Couronne, Martigues
Plage Verdon is a wide sandy cove, naturally sheltered from the wind, and it gets very busy in the summer. There are toilets and showers, a lifeguard in summer, paddleboats for rent, and plenty of beach restaurants. It is located around the headland just off the D948 to the east of the Port of Carro.

KITE AND WINDSURFING D49B
Rue des Ragues, Carro
Carro is acknowledged as one of the best spots for wind surfing and kite surfing in Provence. High winds tempt the very best riders onto the water. Getting afloat can be difficult as the entrance to the water is over slippery rocks.

MARINE SURFSHOP
Quai Jean Vérandy, Carro; www.marinsurfshop.com; Tues.-Thurs. 10am-12:30pm and 2pm-6pm, Sat.-Sun. 2pm-7pm
In this local surf shop, you can pick up the latest gear and get information on the best spots to catch the day's biggest waves.

WATERSPORTS 13
Chemin des Paluds, Martigues; tel. 06 62 03 29 91; www.water-sports-13.com; June-Sept. 9:30am-12:30pm and 1:30pm-6:30pm; price depends on activity
Jet Skis, Flyboard, jet packs, kayaks, paddleboarding, and being dragged behind a boat on an inflatable: You name it, this company offers it.

Food
LE GARAGE
20 avenue Frédéric Mistral, Martigues; tel. 04 42 44 09 51; http://restaurantmartigues.com; Tues.-Sat. noon-1:30pm and 7:30pm-9pm; €37 two-course menu
As the name suggests, the restaurant occupies an old garage. The building lends an industrial atmosphere but the cooking is

precise and modern, drawing gourmands from Marseille and Aix. Try the signature scallops with a butternut cream. A reservation is advisable in season.

Accommodations
VILLA DU PETIT PORT
20 avenue du Caro; tel. 06 68 15 30 67;
www.lavilladupetitport.com; €95 d
This small friendly bed-and-breakfast includes an apartment that sleeps five and a double bedroom, both with ensuite facilities. It's five minutes' walk from the beach and the port and has a small outdoor pool.

BASTIDE DE JONCAS
7 chemin du Petit Mas, La Couronne;
tel. 04 42 80 72 34; www.lesjoncas.com; €90d
This holiday village complex is set in a wooded area, five minutes' walk from the beaches of La Couronne. There's a relaxed familial atmosphere, and storage space for water sports equipement. Also on-site are water sports gear-rental facilities and tennis courts. Rooms are basic but have ensuite bathrooms and Wi-Fi.

INFORMATION AND SERVICES
The main tourist offices are in **Carry-le-Rouet** and **Sausset-les-Pins.**

GETTING THERE AND AROUND
By Train
The **Train de La Côte Bleue** (daily twice per hour; €10.80; www.ter.sncf.com/paca/loisirs/lignes-touristiques/train-cote-bleue) is one of the best ways to see the Côte Bleue. The line runs right along the coast and crosses over a series of high bridges. Along the way, there are plenty of opportunities to get off and explore the resorts and calanques. The 1-hour and 20-minute ride is one of the most beautiful in Provence. If you're hiking the coast, remember you can usually catch the train back for the return leg.

The train runs from **Marseille-Saint-Charles** to Miramas twice an hour, stopping at **L'Estaque** (avenue Caronte, Marseille), **Niolon** (Chemin des Poseurs), **Ensues La Redonne** (Chemin de La Gare), **Carry-le-Rouet** (avenue Pierre Semard), **Sausset-les-Pins** (avenue de La Gare), **La Couronne** (avenue de La Gare de Couroone), and **Sainte Croix** (Route de La Gare de Sainte Croix). A one-way ticket travelling the length of the line costs €10.

By Car
The A55 motorway runs from **Marseille** to Martigues. **Calanque de Niolon** is reached by exiting the A55 and taking the D568 through La Rove. The rest of the coast is accessed by exiting the A55 and taking the D9.

By Bus
There are regular bus services between the resorts of the Côte Bleue (www.lepilote.com). The line numbers are: **C3 Carry-le-Rouet; C8 Marseille, C10 Carry Marignane; 55 Martigues.** Tickets cost 90 cents.

The Var and the Verdon Regional Nature Park

Provence does not come to an end with a line on a map. Instead somewhere in the Var the sense of being in Provence ebbs subtly away. There is a feeling of changing geography, light, and people. Sitting in the quintessentially Provençal village of Cotignac, shaded by a majestic avenue of plane trees, this seems like nonsense, particularly because the surrounding villages of the Var have a similar vibe. Interspersed between vines and pine forests, they boast somnolent squares and trickling fountains. As elsewhere in Provence, there's always the clack of boule as the sun goes down.

Yet just to the north, the landscape in unrecognizable. The Gorges du Verdon (Verdon Gorge) is a 700-meter (2,300-foot) high, 25-kilometer (16-mile) long chasm cut into limestone cliffs. It is a natural wonder, a one-off, an area that resembles nowhere else in France. Yes, lavender

Highlights

Look for ★ to find recommended sights, activities, dining, and lodging.

★ **Corniche Sublime and Route des Crêtes:** Take a drive along either of these sinuous cliffside roads to appreciate the true majesty of the Gorges du Verdon (page 294 and 291).

★ **Lac de Sainte-Croix:** This beautiful man-made lake at the foot of the Gorges is renowned for its clear blue and emerald waters and the chance to take a boat into the Gorges (page 299).

★ **Musée de Préhistoire des Gorges du Verdon:** This Norman Foster-designed museum showcases the rich archaeological finds of the region from the Stone to the Bronze Age. There's also a chance to visit the Grotte de la Baume Bonne, where evidence of humans dating back 400,000 years has been found (page 303).

★ **Abbaye du Thoronet:** Thought to the oldest of the three Cistercian Abbeys in Provence, the Abbaye du Thoronet is renowned for its rare architectural unity (page 309).

★ **Plage Anse de Renécros, Bandol:** This beach is an almost perfect half moon of sand located on the opposite side of the headland to Bandol's port and main shopping drag (page 321).

★ **Wine tasting in Bandol:** Experienced tasters note truffles, black cherries, and cinnamon as common characteristics of Bandol's world-renowned reds. The rosés are also among the best in France (page 321).

★ **Musée National de La Marine, Toulon:** Toulon's wonderfully evocative naval museum is located in the port's old armory (page 327).

© MOON.COM

still clings to high plateaus, but the turquoise waters of Lac de Sainte-Croix are almost otherworldly. Rather than sit in cafés admiring the view, tourists seek adrenalin, flinging themselves on bungee ropes from bridges, or shooting in special wetsuits down canyons in the rock. The most sedentary activity is hiring a paddleboat. To the north of the Gorge, the landscape becomes increasingly Alpine. The scent of pine and wild herbs fades. Summer nights are cool. As winter falls, snow and ice quickly coat the slopes. Provence ends.

Heading south from Cotignac, you encounter the Var coast. Resorts such as Saint-Cyr Les Lecques, Bandol, and Sanary-sur-Mer are mostly ignored by foreign tourists in favor of their more famous cousins on the Riviera. Yet they are a delight and retain a Provençal character. Boule was invented on this coast, so was the Pastis brand by Paul Ricard. Regional specialties such as *pieds paquets* (a local favorite of sheep's feet and tripe) are still served in restaurants.

But the farther east you go, the more Provence slips away. The town and French naval base of Toulon acts as an appropriate full stop. Like Marseille, it is emerging from a troubled past to take advantage of its rich history and the beauty of its beaches. On the outskirts there are hidden coves with beachside restaurants where it remains rare to hear English spoken. But after Toulon people start referring to the coast as the Côte d'Azur. Although still technically in the Var, resorts such as Saint-Tropez share a glitzy, decadent spirit with Nice and Cannes. Super yachts with their own military-grade defense systems hover in bays. Waiters, by default, speak English and Russian. Provence ends.

PLANNING YOUR TIME

The area covered in this chapter is delineated in the north by the **Gorges du Verdon** and in the south by the stretch of Var coast between the resort of **Saint-Cyr Les Lecques** and the city of **Toulon.** The town of **Saint-Maximin-la-Sainte-Baume** marks the western boundary of the Var with the Bouches-du-Rhône département. To the east, the **Inland Var** section of this chapter stretches as far as the village of **Lorgues,** just before the town of **Draguignan.** Farther east into the Var, Provence ends and the famous resorts and beaches of the **Côte d'Azur** begin.

The area covered by this chapter, particularly the Inland Var, has a very poor public transport network. A car is highly advisable. The main autoroutes are the **A50,** which runs along the coast from Marseille to Toulon, the **A8,** which runs through the center of the Inland Var toward the Cote d'Azur, and **A51,** which runs north from Aix-en-Provence to Manosque, giving access to the Gorges du Verdon from the west.

Adventure/water sports enthusiasts and keen hikers could easily spend a week or more in the Gorges du Verdon. However, if you plan to visit just to get a feel for the remarkable landscape, then one or two nights will suffice. Villages in the Gorges, although bustling in the summer, have a remote, slightly Alpine feel. Out of season, they fall very quiet. The main villages of the inland Var are quintessentially Provençal and can be toured in just over a day, with perhaps an overnight stay in **Cotignac.** Plan for a two- or three-night stay on the coast to explore resorts such as **Saint-Cyr-sur-Mer, Sanary-sur-Mer,** and **Bandol;** to hike and bike; and to visit the city of Toulon.

Previous: look out for vultures from viewpoints on the Corniche Sublime; castle and vinyards at Lac de Sainte-Croix; view of Moustiers-Sainte-Marie from Notre Dame de Beauvoir chapel.

The Var and the Verdon

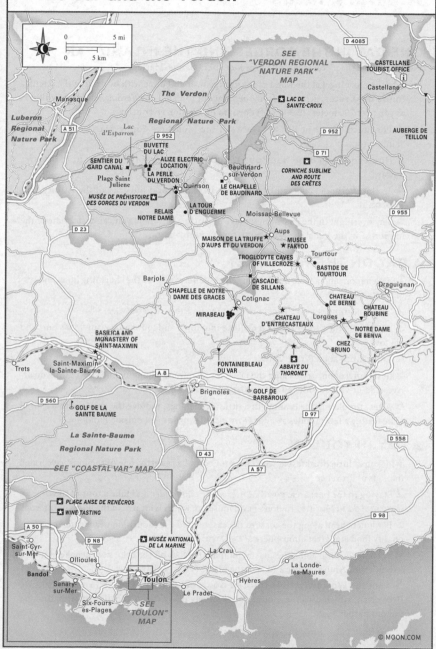

SEE "VERDON REGIONAL NATURE PARK" MAP

CASTELLANE TOURIST OFFICE

Castellane

D 4085

AUBERGE DE TEILLON

★ LAC DE SAINTE-CROIX

The Verdon

Manosque

Luberon Regional Nature Park

A 51

Regional Nature Park

Lac d'Esparron

D 952

BUVETTE DU LAC

ALIZE ELECTRIC LOCATION

SENTIER DU GARD CANAL

LA PERLE DU VERDON

Plage Saint Juliene

MUSÉE DE PRÉHISTOIRE DES GORGES DU VERDON

Quinson

RELAIS NOTRE DAME

LA TOUR D'ENGUERME

Baudinard-sur-Verdon

LE CHAPELLE DE BAUDINARD

Moissac-Bellevue

D 952

D 71

CORNICHE SUBLIME AND ROUTE DES CRÊTES

D 955

D 23

Aups

MAISON DE LA TRUFFE D'AUPS ET DU VERDON

MUSÉE FAKYOD

Tourtour

TROGLODYTE CAVES OF VILLECROZE

BASTIDE DE TOURTOUR

Draguignan

Barjols

CHAPELLE DE NOTRE DAME DES GRACES

CASCADE DE SILLANS

Cotignac

MIRABEAU

CHATEAU D'ENTRECASTEAUX

CHATEAU DE BERNE

CHATEAU ROUBINE

Lorgues

NOTRE DAME DE BENVA

CHEZ BRUNO

BASILICA AND MONASTERY OF SAINT-MAXIMIN

Trets

Saint-Maximin-la-Sainte-Baume

A 8

FONTAINEBLEAU DU VAR

ABBAYE DU THORONET

D 560

GOLF DE LA SAINTE BAUME

Brignoles

GOLF DE BARBAROUX

D 97

D 558

La Sainte-Baume Regional Nature Park

D 43

A 57

D 98

SEE "COASTAL VAR" MAP

PLAGE ANSE DE RENÉCROS

WINE TASTING

A 50

D N8

MUSÉE NATIONAL DE LA MARINE

La Crau

Saint-Cyr-sur-Mer

Bandol

Ollioules

Sanary-sur-Mer

Six-Fours-es-Plages

Toulon

SEE "TOULON" MAP

Le Pradet

Hyères

La Londe-les-Maures

0   5 mi
0   5 km

© MOON.COM

Itinerary Ideas

ONE DAY IN THE GORGES AND THE INLAND VAR

Wake up in the the picturesque village of Moustiers-Sainte-Marie.

1 In the morning, get the worst of the vertigo over and done with by driving the circular **Route des Crêtes,** departing from the village of La Palud-sur-Verdon. Spot some vultures as you peer 700 meters (2,300 feet) down to the Verdon river below.

2 For lunch, picnic at **Pont Galetas** at the Moustiers-Sainte-Marie end of Lac de Sainte-Croix.

3 Hire a boat from **Base Nautique l'Etoile** to view the gorge, looking from the river upward.

4 In the afternoon, contemplate the grand architectural integrity of the **Abbaye du Thoronet.**

5 Stay overnight in the charming village of **Cotignac,** where you can taste some of the finest rosé in the Var at the **Mirabeau en Provence shop.**

A DAY ON THE VAR COAST

1 Book a room and a table overlooking the Mediterranean at the charming hotel and restaurant **O Petit Monde.**

2 In the morning, spend a few hours relaxing on **Plage Portissol**.

3 Walk along the **Chemin de La Colline** into town and tour Sanary-sur-Mer's port and old town.

4 Enjoy lunch at **La P'tite Cour.**

5 In the afternoon, drive along the D599 for 20 minutes, hugging the coast until you arrive at Saint-Cyr-sur-Mer's **Tauroentum Roman Villa.**

6 After stimulating the brain with a little archaeology, indulge the palate with a spot of wine tasting a few minutes away at **Domaine Tempier** just outside Bandol.

A DAY IN TOULON

1 Pick up a little breakfast at **Marché du Cours Lafayette,** one of the most celebrated markets of Provence.

2 Staying in the port area, go all *Master and Commander* and take a tour of the **Musée National de la Marine,** Toulon's naval museum, which is located in the port's old arsenal.

3 For lunch, head along the coast to the east toward the Mourillon beach and enjoy top-quality food and great atmosphere at **Le Local bistro.**

4 Afterward, stroll along the coastal footpath to work off the calories. Then, head inland to boulevard Amiral Vence and take the **Mont Faron cable car.**

5 Visit the **World War II Mémorial du débarquement et de la libération de Provence,** which caps the mountain, or simply enjoy the unequalled view of Toulon's famous harbor.

One Day in the Gorges and the Inland Var

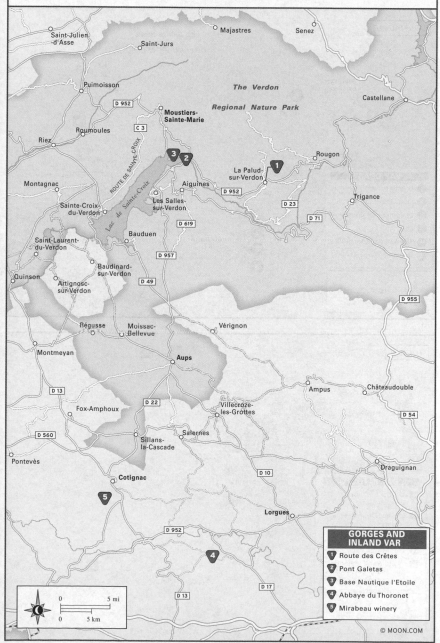

Saint-Julien
-d'Asse

Majastres

Senez

Saint-Jurs

Puimoisson

The Verdon
Regional Nature Park

Castellane

D 952

Moustiers-
Sainte-Marie

Roumoules

C 3

Riez

ROUTE DE SAINTE-CROIX

3 2

Rougon

Montagnac

Aiguines

La Palud-
sur-Verdon

1

Sainte-Croix-
du-Verdon

Lac de Sainte-Croix

Les Salles-
sur-Verdon

D 952

D 23

Trigance

Saint-Laurent-
du-Verdon

Bauduen

D 619

D 71

Quinson

Baudinard-
sur-Verdon

D 957

D 49

Artignosc-
sur-Verdon

Régusse

Moissac-
Bellevue

Vérignon

D 955

Montmeyan

Aups

D 13

Ampus

Châteaudouble

Fox-Amphoux

D 22

Villecroze-
les-Grottes

D 54

D 560

Sillans-
la-Cascade

Salernes

Pontevès

Draguignan

Cotignac

D 10

5

Lorgues

D 952

4

D 17

D 13

0   5 mi

0   5 km

GORGES AND INLAND VAR

1 Route des Crêtes
2 Pont Galetas
3 Base Nautique l'Etoile
4 Abbaye du Thoronet
5 Mirabeau winery

© MOON.COM

The Var Coast and Toulon

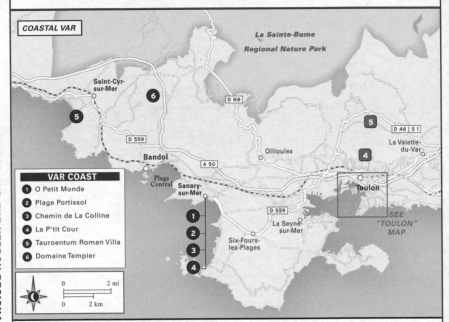

COASTAL VAR

La Sainte-Bume
Regional Nature Park

Saint-Cyr-sur-Mer

6

5

D N8

D 559

Bandol

Plage Central

Sanary-sur-Mer

Ollioules

5

D 46 | S 1

La Valette-du-Var

4

Toulon

A 50

D 559

La Seyne-sur-Mer

Six-Fours-les-Plages

SEE "TOULON" MAP

VAR COAST

1 O Petit Monde
2 Plage Portissol
3 Chemin de La Colline
4 La P'tit Cour
5 Tauroentum Roman Villa
6 Domaine Tempier

0 — 2 mi
0 — 2 km

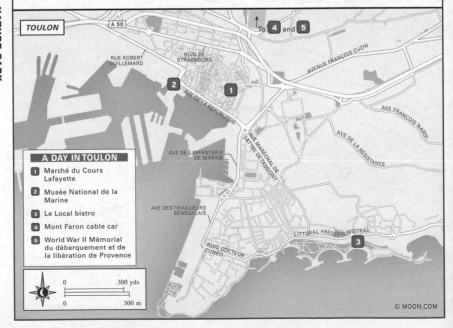

TOULON

A 50

To 4 and 5

RUE ROBERT GUILLEMARD

BLVD DE STRASBOURG

2

1

AVENUE FRANÇOIS CUZIN

AVE DE LA RÉPUBLIQUE

AVE FRANÇOIS NARDI

AVE DE L'INFANTERIE DE MARINE

AVE MARECHAL DE LATTRE DE PASSION

AVE DE LA RESISTANCE

AVE DES TIRAILLEURS SÉNÉGALAIS

LITTORAL FRÉDÉRIC MISTRAL

3

BLVD DOCTEUR CUNÉO

A DAY IN TOULON

1 Marché du Cours Lafayette
2 Musée National de la Marine
3 Le Local bistro
4 Mont Faron cable car
5 World War II Mémorial du débarquement et de la libération de Provence

0 — 300 yds
0 — 300 m

© MOON.COM

Verdon Regional Nature Park

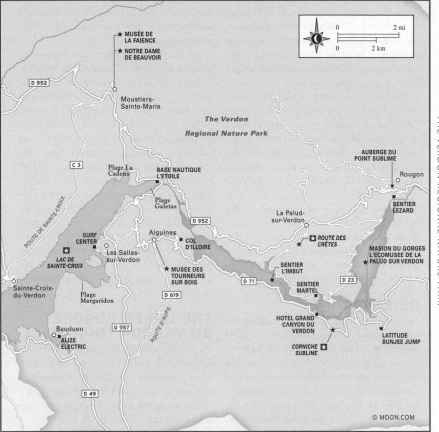

The Verdon Regional Nature Park

TOP EXPERIENCE

You've seen the photos, you've planned the trip, you know what to expect, and yet the Gorges du Verdon still delivers a visceral thrill, a stomach churning, head spinning surge of excitement that slowly gives way to silent awe and head scratching. The 700-meter (2,300-foot) deep, 25-kilometer (16-mile) long gorge cut by the Verdon river in the limestone cliffs seems to defy logic. How could such a small river cut through so much rock? At this point, geologists might like to note that the limestone rock deposits laid down by a prehistoric sea in the Jurassic period were heavily weakened by large-scale tectonic activity during the Cretaceous period. Non-geologists will probably just continue shaking their heads at the improbability of it all.

In any event, nature has created the most

wonderful playground for tourists of all persuasions. Motorists, e-bikers, and hikers can soak up the vertiginous views from either the Route des Crêtes on the north side of the gorge or the Corniche Sublime on the south side. Nature lovers taking the same routes will hope to see one of three species of vultures that inhabit the gorge. Adrenalin junkies can bungee jump, climb, canyon, and white-water raft.

Farther downstream man has lent nature a helping hand. The construction of the Sainte-Croix dam in the early 1970s created France's third-biggest lake. Bordered by pretty villages with beaches and boat hire facilities, the lake now draws just as many crowds as the gorge. The best place to hire a boat is probably the Pont du Galetas (Galetas Bridge). From here it's possible to head up the gorge, enjoy a dip in the clear waters, and stare up in wonder at the cliffs. Farther downstream, a similar experience is available at a second lake, Lac d'Esparron, although here the Gorges du Verdon is of a more moderate size.

ORIENTATION

The park is split into three main regions: the **upper gorge,** where the cliffs are at their highest; the human-made **Lac de Sainte-Croix,** the main base for water sports; and the **lower gorge,** which is scenic but less spectacular. **Castellane** and **La Palud-sur-Verdon** are the main entry points for the northern side of the upper gorge; **Moustiers-Sainte-Marie** and **Aiguines** are good bases from which to explore Lac de Sainte-Croix and the southern side of the upper gorge. The entire circuit of the upper gorge in a car is 130 kilometers (80 miles) and because of the narrow and windy roads takes a day. Most visitors choose to take either the **Route des Crêtes** on the north side or the **Corniche Sublime** on the south side, both of which offer spectacular view points. **Quinson** and **Esparron** are the main bases for the lower gorge.

Moustiers-Sainte-Marie is the liveliest and most attractive village and the best base for the majority of people. However, if you love nature and hiking, then pick either Aiguines

or La Palud-sur-Verdon as your place to stay. In summer they both bustle with the coming and going of tourists; out of season they quickly fall quiet. In the winter often the only sound is the footfalls of intrepid groups of hikers returning from the Gorges.

Public transportation in the region is very limited. **Bus Line 27** (www.info-ler.fr/53-Fiches-horaires.html) runs from Marseille and Aix-en-Provence to La Palud and Castellane once a day Monday to Saturday in July and August, and on Monday and Saturday out of season. There is also a small bus (www.castellane-verdontourisme.com/infos-pratiques-en-live/venir-a-castellane/en-bus) that runs three times a day between Castellane and La Palud. Most visitors will be traveling by car, in which case the main access road from Marseille, Aix, and Avignon is the **A51** motorway to Saint-Paul-lez-Durance and then the **D952.** Allow two hours to drive from Aix to the Gorges du Verdon, and just under three hours to get there from Marseille or Avignon.

THE UPPER GORGES DU VERDON (NORTH)

On the north side of the Gorges du Verdon, the main base and departure point for activities is La Palud-sur-Verdon. It's an attractive village with a mountain feel, and a good place to stop overnight, or just to stretch your legs after a drive around the Route des Crêtes. La Palud offers a wide range of sports and activities to set your adrenalin surging, including canyoning where you don a wetsuit and throw yourself down narrow cascades between rocks. Aquaphobes can opt for traditional climbing or a roped course across the rocks, featuring zip lines and other heart-thumping challenges. Finally, for a real bird's-eye view there's paragliding. An alternative larger base for the north side of the upper gorge is the town of Castellane to the east of La Palud on the D952. Here you will find more life in the evenings with a bigger choice of restaurants. Castellane is also the place to stop for tourist information, with two visitors centers offering

Wildlife of the Gorges du Verdon

- The griffon vulture was reintroduced into the gorge in 1999, and numbers have risen from 24 to more than 300 in a short time, making it the vulture you are most likely to see. They are tawny in color except for their flight and tail feathers, which are nearly black, and the head is a creamy white. If you are lucky enough to see one of these birds at eye level, you can hear the wind rushing through their feathers.

- Sightings of the black vulture, which is bigger than the griffon, with a nearly 3-meter (10-foot) wingspan are less common.

- Rarer still are sightings of the Egyptian vulture, which is nearly half the size of the black.

- By far the rarest bird to see is the golden eagle, but when they do appear, their courtship displays in mid-autumn are an unforgettable spectacle of giddying dives.

short-toed snake eagle

- Bird-watchers can also look forward to sightings of the short-toed snake eagle, eagle owl, hoopoe, Alpine swifts, ravens, choughs, and crag martins.

- Hikers frequently come across the chamois, a horned animal that looks like a cross between a goat and an antelope.

- Wolves have also recently been making a return to the area, although they are almost never encountered.

THE VAR AND THE VERDON REGIONAL NATURE PARK
THE VERDON REGIONAL NATURE PARK

maps, and guidance on everything from activities to accommodations.

Sights
★ ROUTE DES CRÊTES

Route des Crêtes, off the D952,
departing La Palud-sur-Verdon

This 24-kilometer (15-mile) circular route from La Palud runs alongside the gorge for much of its length. At places the drop is a head-spinning 700 meters (2,300 feet) to the valley below. There are 14 different points where you can park, admire the views, and perhaps spot vultures and eagles. Thanks to the altitude of the road, it's possible to enjoy some real eye-to-eye encounters. It's important to follow the Route des Crêtes in a clockwise direction, as indicated in the village of La Palud-sur-Verdon; a small part of the road

is one way, and you'll have to turn back if you set off in a counterclockwise direction. If you are in a car, don't expect to complete the circuit quickly, because bikes and buses will slow your progress.

MAISON DU GORGES L'ECOMUSEE DE LA PALUD-SUR-VERDON

Le Chateau, La Palud-sur-Verdon;
tel. 04 92 77 38 02; www.lapalud-verdontourisme.
com/visiter_bouger/maison-des-gorges-du-
verdon-598370; Apr.-end of Oct. Tues.-Sat.
9am-noon and 2pm-6pm, July-Aug. daily; €4

This pleasant small museum concentrates on man's changing relationship with nature in the Gorges du Verdon, starting from prehistoric times. There's plenty of information on the flora and fauna of the region and the unique geology that gave rise to the gorge.

Adventure Sports
MAISON DES GUIDES DU VERDON

Rue Grande, La Palud-sur-Verdon;
tel. 04 92 77 30 50; www.escalade-verdon.fr;
book in advance

Offers canyoning, climbing, roped climbing courses, and hiking. The business has been running since 1984 and caters for all levels from beginners to experts. Excursions can last anything from a couple of hours to the entire day. Prices depend on the activity but are generally about €45 per person per half day.

AVENTURES ET NATURE

La Palud-sur-Verdon; tel. 04 92 77 30 43;
www.provenceweb.fr/04/faudou/index.htm; daily
9am-7:45pm; half day from €40

In addition to canyoning, climbing, and roped climbing courses, Aventures et Nature also offers aqua rando, hikes with lots of dips in the water along the way.

DES GUIDES POUR L'AVENTURE

Auberges des Crêtes meeting point, La
Palud-sur-Verdon; tel. 06 85 94 46 61;
www.guidesaventure.com; May-Sept. daily 9am-6pm;
half day from €40

Check out Des Guides Pour L'Aventure for white-water rafting. They also offer canyoning, climbing, roped climbing courses, and hiking

ROC N VOL

Las Alaves, La Palud-sur-Verdon;
tel. 04 92 72 54 08; www.rocnvol.com; May-Sept.
daily 9am-6pm; half-day activity from €40

Roc n Vol offers paragliding, in addition to canyoning, climbing, roped climbing courses, and hiking.

Hiking
SENTIER LEZARD

Depart Parking, Point Sublime, Rougon

Pick up the leaflet that accompanies this walk from the **Maison du Gorges L'Ecomusee de La Palud-sur-Verdon** (Le Chateau, La Palud-sur-Verdon; tel. 04 92 77 38 02) for a detailed description of the flora and fauna you will encounter on this 5-kilometer (3-mile) circular walk. The gravel trail is signposted from the parking lot, and unusually for the Gorges du Verdon, the walk is not too hilly. The path passes between the cliffs from sun to shade and offers spectacular views. Allow two hours to complete the circuit. When you return, Rougon is a pleasant village that has a couple of cafés where you can relax and enjoy the view.

SENTIER MARTEL

Depart from D23 Chalet de La Maline, La
Palud-sur-Verdon

For more experienced hikers, the Sentier Martel is a 14-kilometer (9-mile) trail that leads down into the gorge. There's a celebrated descent of 200 meters (660 feet) or so down a rickety old staircase, as well as, at one point, a wobbly bridge over the river. Both keep minds focused. The route is rocky and difficult at times, and passes through the odd small cave, so keep a flashlight handy. Picnic spots are scarce, and the best is a large beach you will encounter beside the river. To avoid having to wait for a bus when you finish the walk, park your car at **Point Sublime** in Rougon and take the navette (www.castellane-verdontourisme.com/infos-pratiques-en-live/venir-a-castellane/en-bus) to the start point at **Chalet de la Maline,** which is a small stone refuge for hikers and climbers (https://chaletlamaline.ffcam.fr).

Cycling
VERDON E BIKE

1 Route de Moustiers, La Palud-sur-Verdon;
tel. 06 88 10 91 73; http://verdonebike.
pagesperso-orange.fr; daily May-Sept. 30 9am-5pm; €22

The Gorges du Verdon is just too hilly for all but superhuman cyclists. However, hiring an e-bike is an excellent way to enjoy the 23-kilometer (14-mile) Route des Crêtes.

Food
AUBERGE DE TEILLON

Route Napoleon, La Garde; tel. 04 92 83 60 88;
Tues. evening-Sun. noon-2pm and 7pm-10pm; €22
lunchtime menu, €28 evening menu

This unapologetically traditional restaurant

offers dishes such as veal sweetbreads in a port-wine sauce. The clientele is largely foodie French tourists, but the atmosphere is relaxed and friendly. Reserve in season to be sure of a table.

AUBERGE DU POINT SUBLIME

D952, Rougon; tel. 04 92 83 69 15;
www.auberge-pointsublime.com; daily May-Sept. 30
noon-2pm and 7pm-10pm; €19-24.50
Simple, locally sourced food is served on a large terrace overlooking the Gorges du Verdon. The clientele is a mixture of cyclists and hikers taking a well-earned break. Hearty portions include grilled rosemary-crusted lamb cutlets. A reservation is not normally necessary, but if you are planning to eat here after a long hike, it's best to be sure.

LE MUR DES ABEILLES

Rougon; tel. 04 92 83 76 33;
daily May-Sept. 30 noon-10pm; €8-€15
Inventive sweet and savory crepes are served on a spectacular terrace overlooking the Gorges du Verdon. Try goat's cheese and honey or eggplant. There are only six or seven tables outside, so it is sensible to reserve.

Accommodations
★ HOTEL AND SPA DES
GORGES DU VERDON

Route de La Maline, La Palud-sur-Verdon;
tel. 04 92 77 38 26;
www.hotel-des-gorges-du-verdon.fr; €260 d
This beautiful luxury retreat sits at an altitude of just under 1,000 meters (3,280 feet). There are 30 rooms, all with ensuite bathrooms and Wi-Fi. Families will like the suite, which sleeps six. The hotel is committed to the environment and is one of two French pilot hotels for the European Union's Nearly Zero Energy Hotels (neZEH) initiative. There's onsite parking, a spa, and a heated outdoor pool.

LE PERROQUET VERT

Rue Grande, La Palud-sur-Verdon;
tel. 04 92 77 33 39; www.leperroquetvert.com; €60 d
Book early to get a room in this popular four-bedroom guesthouse in the center of the Gorges du Verdon gateway village of La Palud. Rooms are simple but they do all have Wi-Fi and ensuite bathrooms. The breakfast is particularly good and really sets you up for the day.

NOUVEL HOTEL DU COMMERCE

Place Marcel Sauvaire, Castellane; tel. 04 92 83 61 00;
www.hotel-du-commerce-verdon.com; €100
This is a comfortable 30-bedroom hotel with an outdoor swimming pool and welcoming relaxed atmosphere. The former coaching inn is located in the heart of the picturesque town of Castellane, and there are plenty of local restaurants to choose from in the evening. It's ideal for those who want to visit the Gorges du Verdon, but also like the busier scene offered by a town in the evenings. Rooms all have Wi-Fi and ensuite bathrooms. Private parking is available.

Information and Services
There are two visitors centers in Castellane, the **Maison Nature & Patrimoines** (Relais du Parc; Place Marcel Sauvaire, Castellane; tel. 04 92 83 19 23; www.maison-nature-patrimoines.com; Apr. 19-Sept. 15 weekends, Wed., public holidays 10am-1pm and 3pm-6:30pm, July-Aug. daily) and the **Verdon Tourist Office** (rue National, Castellane; tel. 04 92 83 61 14; www.verdontourisme.com; May-June and Sept. Mon.-Fri. 9am-noon and 2pm-6pm Sun. 10am-1pm, July-Aug. 9am-noon and 2pm-7.30pm). The Verdon Tourist Office offers a broad range of services, with information on everything including hotels, restaurants, activities, and hikes. The Maison Nature has a narrower focus on providing information about accessing the Gorges and its flora and fauna.

Getting There and Around
BY CAR
From Marseille: Take the A51 to Saint-Paul-lez-Durance and then the D952, covering 144 kilometers (89 miles) in 2 hours 20 minutes.
From Aix: Take the A51 to

Saint-Paul-lez-Durance and then the D952, covering 108 kilometers (67 miles) in 1 hours 50 minutes.

From Avignon: Take the A51 to Saint-Paul-lez-Durance and then the D952, covering 183 kilometers (114 miles) in 2 hours 34 minutes.

From Nice and Cannes: Take the A8 and then the D54 from Le Muy and the D955, covering 147 kilometers (91 miles) in 2 hours 20 minutes.

BY BUS
LER Bus Line 27 (www.info-ler.fr/affichage.php?id=465&visu=1) runs from **Marseille** (Rue Jacques Bory) and **Aix** (boulevard Victor Cog) to La Palud (Route de Moustiers) and Castellane (Place M Sauvaire), once a day Monday to Saturday in July and August, and on Monday and Saturday out of season. From Marseille the price is €27. There is a **local bus** (www.castellane-verdontourisme.com/infos-pratiques-en-live/venir-a-castellane/en-bus) that runs three times a day between Castellane and La Palud. Prices from €2 to €6 depending on length of the journey.

THE UPPER GORGES DU VERDON (SOUTH)

On the southern side of the Gorges du Verdon, perched above Lac de Sainte-Croix, the village of Aiguines is the main base to explore the southern gorge. It offers easy access to the beaches of the lake, the Corniche Sublime, and some of the best hiking and climbing in the region, including the challenging Sentier Imbert, which takes walkers into the depths of the gorge. Like most of the villages in the region, Aiguines is vibrant in the summer months but quickly becomes sleepy out of season. It's a good place to stop and pick up maps, and advice on activities and accommodation, thanks to its welcoming tourist office.

Sights
MUSEE DES TOURNEURS SUR BOIS
Place de La Resistance, Aiguines; tel. 04 94 70 99 17; https://museedestourneurssurbois.com; July-Aug.

daily 10:30am-6:30pm; May-June and Sept.-Oct. Mon.-Fri. 10am-6pm; €3.50, under 12 free

This is a small but interesting museum that charts the changing craft of wood-turning in the village since the 16th century. Beginning with the use of old-fashioned tools to create wooden pieces for games, the museum shows how wood turning has evolved to the methods that artisans now use to create sculptures and designer furniture. In summer on Sunday and Tuesday mornings, a guided walking tour called "In the Footsteps of the Woodcutters" is offered for €12, including admission to the museum. For the tour, contact Jean-Michel Novaro (tel. 06 79 33 72 10).

★ CORNICHE SUBLIME
D71, Aiguines to Comps-sur-Artuby
Constructed in 1947 to open up the Gorges du Verdon to motorists, the Corniche Sublime is the glamorous name for the stretch of the D71 between Aiguines and Comps-sur-Artuby. Along the way, there are plenty of places to stop and admire the imposing topography of the gorge. As with the Route des Crêtes, there's the chance of spotting vultures and eagles. Progress can be slow in the summer with cars and cyclists traveling at about the same speed. The most picturesque spot is approximatley 10 kilometers (6 miles) from Aiguines. Here the road becomes increasingly sinous and the drops ever more vertiginous. Among the best viewpoints to stop at are the Belvedere du Plan, the Belvedere Aiguines, and the Balcon de La Mescla.

Climbing
The southern side of the upper gorge offers a variety of climbs for people with the gear and know-how to make their way up on their own. A list of available climbs, including difficulty levels, can be found on the **Aiguines**

1: Set off from La Palud-sur-Verdon on the Route des Crêtes for spectacular views of the Gorge. 2: a flower-clad doorway in the village of Quinson 3: one of many head-spinning view points on the Corniche Sublime

Tourism Office website (www.aiguines.fr/ en/a-faire-a-aiguines/sensations-fortes).

LA CORDITELLE

Chemin de La Pinede, Aiguines; tel. 06 10 49 51 92; www.lacorditelle.com; from €20

La Corditelle offers a range of climbing activities for all levels and all ages (starting as young as 5). There are roped courses across the cliffs, and climbing initiation classes.

Adventure Sports
LATITUDE BUNGEE JUMP

D71, Artuby Bridge; tel. 04 91 09 04 10; www.latitude-challenge.fr; weekends 9am-noon, mandatory online reservation 24 hours in advance; €130 a jump

Among the highest bungee jumps in Europe at 182 meters (597 feet), the Artuby bridge is not for the faint-hearted. It's on the south side of the gorge so it is best accessed from either Castellane or Aiguines.

Hiking
SENTIER DE L'IMBUT

Depart Parking Cavaliers D71, Aiguines; www. cheminsdesparcs.fr/pedestre/le-sentier-de-limbut

Probably the most beautiful walk in the whole of the Verdon region departs about 15 kilometers (9 miles) from Aiguines near the Grand Canyon hotel. Plunging you straight down into the gorges, the path is uneven with some drops of over 100 meters (330 feet) on either side. Other obstacles include slippery rocks and river crossings. The hike is not for the inexperienced and is certainly not for children under 12. Covering 9 kilometers (6 miles) and taking 4-5 hours to complete, this walk does offer lots of shade, thanks to the high cliffs and plentiful vegetation.

COL D'ILLOIRE

Aiguines; www.aiguines.fr/wp-content/ uploads/2016/02/Col-dIlloire-EN-2.pdf

This 2-kilometer (1-mile) unmarked trail takes about two hours (there and back) to complete. The departure is from the center of the village, and the trail crosses the Corniche

Sublime to the spectacular Col D'Illoire viewpoint at 967 meters (3,172 feet). The tourist office website (www.aiguines.fr) has a full and accurate English description of the walk.

Food and Accommodations
HOTEL VIEUX CHÂTEAU

Place de La Fontaine, Aiguines; tel. 04 94 70 22 95; http://hotelvieuxchateau.fr; €104 d

A good base to explore the region, the Hotel de Vieux Château has 10 simply furnished rooms, all with ensuite bathrooms and Wi-Fi. The terrace of the hotel spills out onto the pretty Place de La Fontaine. The hotel's restaurant has a good reputation for regional food. The soup *au pistou* (with garlic and basil) is particularly restorative after a day of adventure sports.

HOTEL GRAND CANYON DU VERDON

Falaise des Cavaliers, Aiguines; tel. 04 94 76 91 31; www.hotel-canyon-verdon.com; €130 d

Seemingly clinging to the edge of the cliff face, this hotel is not for anyone who suffers from vertigo. Terraces from some of the rooms look directly out over the canyon. All are simply decorated and come with Wi-Fi and ensuite bathrooms. The restaurant offers an affordable three-course menu for €25, and there are panoramic views from the dining room. Hikers will love the nearby Col d'Illoire walk.

Information and Services

The **Aiguines Tourism Office** is located at Allée des Tilleuls, Aiguines (tel. 04 94 70 21 64; www.lacs-gorges-verdon.fr; Apr.-Sept. Mon.-Fri. 9am-12:30pm and 2pm-5:30pm July-Aug. daily same hours, Oct.-Mar. Mon.-Fri. 9am-12:30pm). It offers information about restaurants, accommodation, and all activities available in the Gorges.

Getting There and Around
BY CAR

Aiguines is accessed by the **D71** road, which runs from Lac Sainte-Croix through Aiguines to Comps sur Artuby. Moustiers-Sainte-Marie is 15 kilometers (9 miles) away. The drive takes 30 minutes.

BY BUS

Public transportation is poor in this area. **Zou Bus Line 1005** (www.varlib.fr) connects the Pont du Galetas at the foot of Aiguines with Moustiers, running four times a day from July 7 to Aug. 31; the journey takes 20 minutes and costs €3. The bus does not run outside the high tourist season. The latest timetable is available here: www.varlib.fr/ftp/FR_lignes/1005.pdf.

MOUSTIERS-SAINTE-MARIE

The most prosperous village in the area is Moustiers-Sainte-Marie. built on either side of a mountain stream, it has charm to spare with its arching bridges and winding boutique-lined streets. It's certainly the place to go for a gastronomic meal in the region, with an Alain Ducasse hotel and restaurant on the outskirts and plentiful options for foodies in the village. Maps and friendly advice are available from two helpful tourist offices.

Sights
MUSÉE DE LA FAIENCE

Rue du Seigneur de la Clue, Moustiers-Sainte-Marie; tel. 04 92 74 61 64; www.moustiers.fr/fr/musee-faience; Apr.-end of Oct. Wed.-Mon. 10am-12:30pm and 2pm-5pm, Nov.-Mar. Sat.-Sun. 10am-12:30pm and 2pm-5pm; €3, under 16 free

Thanks to the quality of the local clay and the abundance of water Moustiers-Sainte-Marie has a long tradition of making fine glazed ceramic pottery (*faience*). The museum includes pottery dating back to the 17th century, and as you proceed through the different rooms the decorative fashion of the plates changes dramatically with the decades.

NOTRE DAME DE BEAUVOIR

7136 Place Pomey, Moustiers-Sainte-Marie

It takes about 15 minutes to climb the 262 steps that lead out of the eastern side of the village up to the chapel of Notre Dame de Beauvoir. The church itself is dark and bare, but the climb is worth it for the view back down over Moustiers and the surrounding countryside. A little farther on up the trail, at some 300 meters (1,000 feet) above the village, a star is suspended between the two cliff faces that frame the village. Now in its 17th incarnation, the star is said to have been initially hung by the Knight Blacas to give thanks for his safe return from the crusades in the 13th century.

Sports and Recreation
DES GUIDES POUR L'AVENTURE

Magnans, Avenue de Lérins, Moustiers-Sainte-Marie; tel. 06 85 94 46 61; www.guidesaventure.com; May-Sept. daily 9am-6pm; €40 half-day walk

The company offers 3- to 6-hour walks out into some of the lesser known trails of the gorge. They're also planning to begin offering walks with llamas, as well as a whole range of other adventure activities from climbing to rafting.

VERDON PASSION

Rue de Courtil, Moustiers-Sainte-Marie; tel. 06 08 63 97 16; www.verdon-passion.com; in season daily 9am-7pm; from €40

Paragliding is the specialty of Verdon Passion, with flights for all levels departing from nearby Hamel de Vincel. The instructors will take you soaring over Lac de Sainte-Croix, and during July and August, there are sensational views of lavender fields. Canyoning, white-water rafting, and white-water kayaking are also offered.

EQUIVERDON

Hameau de Vincel, Moustiers-Sainte-Marie; tel. 06 10 91 31 72; daily in season 9am-7pm; 2-hour trek €50

Equiverdon offers horseback riding for all levels in the countryside surrounding Moustiers-Sainte-Marie. Pony tours are also available for small children.

Shopping

L'ATELIER BONDIL

Place de l'Eglise and Rue Bourgade, Moustiers-Sainte-Marie; tel. 04 92 74 67 02; www.faiencebondil.fr; daily 10am-7pm

Supplied exclusively by the local Bondil Faience atelier, these two shops offer both traditional ceramics with decorative blue motifs and more contemporary colorful pieces. They are both right in the center of Moustiers-Sainte-Marie.

Food and Accommodations

LA FERME DE SAINTE CECILE

Route des Gorges du Verdon, Moustiers-Sainte-Marie; tel. 04 92 74 64 18; www.ferme-ste-cecile. com; Tues.-Sat. noon-1:30pm and 7pm-8:30pm, Sun. noon-1:30pm; €30 lunch menu, €39 evening menu

Enjoy top-quality regional produce in this peaceful, spacious restaurant with a large terrace overlooking verdant gardens. Dishes are beautifully presented and full of flavor. Try the fish of the day dressed with a distinctive algae cream.

LES SANTONS

Place Pomey, Moustiers-Sainte-Marie; tel. 04 92 74 66 48; www.lessantons.com; daily noon-2:30pm and 7pm-9:30pm; menus from €37

The relaxed ambience and contemporary designer furniture create the perfect setting for some of the best cooking in the village. The clientele are foodies settling in for a long meal rather than a casual passing trade. Dishes include slow-cooked lamb shoulder *tajine* (stew) and bream with girolles. Reserve in season.

LA TREILLE MUSCATE

Rue de L'Eglise, Moustiers-Sainte-Marie; tel. 04 92 74 64 31; www.restaurant-latreillemuscate. fr; daily noon-2pm and 7pm-9pm; menus from €28, rooms from €100 d

This is not a place for a quick meal; the cheapest bistro menu runs to five courses. However, if you have had a long day out in the wilds and need refueling, it's ideal. Refined dishes include a *vol au vent* (puff pastry bowl) of mussels with curried leeks, mushrooms, and fried king prawns. Reserve in season. The restaurant also has two simple rooms with ensuite bathrooms and Wi-Fi.

★ LA BASTIDE DE MOUSTIERS

Chemin de Quinson, Moustiers-Sainte-Marie; tel. 04 92 70 47 47; www.bastide-moustiers.com; restaurant daily 12:30pm-1:45pm and 7:30pm-8:45pm; restaurant menu from €65, rooms from €360 d

One of the best known addresses in Provence, La Bastide de Moustiers, formerly the home of a local ceramicist, was bought in 1994 by chef and hotelier Alain Ducasse. The bastide was transformed into a 13-bedroom luxury retreat with one of the finest restaurants in the South of France. Each morning, the gardener picks the freshest vegetables from the hotel potager and leaves them at the kitchen door. The chef then creates the menu. Expect delicate flavors that let the ingredients shine through.

HOTEL LE COLOMBIER

Quartier Saint Michel, Moustiers-Sainte-Marie; tel. 04 92 74 66 02; www.le-colombier.com; €100 d

Located on the outskirts of Moustiers, this simple hotel has large grounds, a tennis court, and small swimming pool. The rooms can be on the small side, but all have air-conditioning, ensuite bathrooms, and Wi-Fi. It's a good base to explore the Gorges du Verdon and Moustiers-Sainte-Marie.

Information and Services

Moustiers-Sainte-Marie boasts two excellent visitors centers: the **Parc Naturel Régional du Verdon office** (Maison du Parc, Domaine de Valx, Moustiers-Sainte-Marie; tel. 04 92 74 88 00; www.parcduverdon.fr; Mon.-Fri. 9am-12:30pm and 2pm-5:30pm) and the main village **tourist office** (Maison Lucie, Place de l'Eglise, Moustiers-Sainte-Marie; tel. 04 92 74 67 84; www.moustiers.fr/fr; daily 10am-12:30pm and 2pm-5:30pm). The tourist office has the broader range of services, offering advice on restaurants and accommodations as well as how to best access the nature park.

Getting There and Around

BY CAR

From Aix, Avignon, and **Marseille,** the main motorway is the A51. Exit at Manosque and then follow the signs to Valensole, and subsequently Moustiers-Sainte-Marie. From Marseille, the journey is 120 kilometers (75 miles) and takes just under 2 hours; from Aix the journey is 90 kilometers (56 miles) and takes 90 minutes. From Avignon the journey is 150 kilometers (93 miles) and takes 2 hours and 20 minutes.

BY BUS

Public transportation in the region is very limited. **LER Bus Line 27** (www.info-ler.fr/465-Fiches-Horaires.html) runs from Marseille and Aix to Moustiers-Sainte-Marie and costs about €20. The route takes 3 hours from Aix and 3 hours 40 minutes from Marseille, with buses running once a day July and Aug. Mon.-Sat., and on Mon. and Sat. out of season. A local bus, **Zou Line 1005** (www.varlib.fr), runs four times a day between Aiguines and Moustiers-Sainte-Marie. The latest timetable is available at www.varlib.fr/ftp/FR_lignes/1005.pdf. The journey takes 20 minutes and costs €3.

ON FOOT OR BY BIKE

A **cycle and walking route** links Moustiers-Sainte-Marie with Lac de Sainte-Croix. The route is 5 kilometers (3 miles) long and takes either 40 minutes or 90 minutes, depending on whether you are riding or walking.

★ LAC DE SAINTE-CROIX

Lac de Sainte-Croix is France's third-biggest lake. It is 10 kilometers (6 miles) long and 2 kilometers (1 mile) wide and was created in 1973 by the construction of the Sainte-Croix Dam. This glittering expanse of turquoise water has white sand and stone beaches that call to mind the Caribbean, but the three villages that give onto the lake—Les Salles-sur-Verdon, Bauduen, and Sainte-Croix-du-Verdon—are typically French, with plentiful outdoor cafés.

The lake draws water sports enthusiasts from across France, and on the beaches you'll find multiple providers renting out boats and other recreation equipment. Petrol (gasoline) motors are forbidden, however, so all watercraft must be powered by by wind, oars, or electricity. To drive around the lake in a car takes about 1 hour. The best place to rent paddleboat and head up into the gorges is at the easternmost point of the lake at Pont du Galetas.

Plage Galetas

Pont du Galetas, Moustiers-Sainte-Marie

Immediately adjacent to the Pont du Galetas, near Moustiers-Sainte-Marie on the southern side of the lake, this beach is very busy in the summer months. It marks the point where the gorge opens up into the Lac de Sainte-Croix. The small beach is a pleasant place to relax after a paddleboat ride up the gorge.

BASE NAUTIQUE L'ETOILE

Pont du Galetas, Moustiers-Sainte-Marie;
tel. 07 68 94 17 87; Apr.-Sept. daily 10am-6pm; from
€8 per hour for a kayak

This is the best spot to help you explore the gorge by boat. On offer are canoes, kayaks, paddleboats, and electric boats. It is not possible to reserve in advance. Gazing up at the cliffs can be mesmerizing and leads to the odd gentle collision!

Plage La Cadeno

Route du Lac, Saint-Saturnin, Moustiers-Sainte-Marie

Just off the D957 on the northern side of the lake on Route du Lac in Saint-Saturnin, there is a beach next to the Base Nautique La Cadeno. The pebble beach is close to Moustiers and is convenient for a quick swim.

BASE NAUTIQUE LA CADENO

Route du Lac, Saint-Saturnin, Moustiers-Sainte-Marie; tel. 07 82 10 67 03; Apr.-Sept. daily 10am-6pm; from €14 an hour for a paddleboat

Located on a pretty, sandy beach, the Base Nautique rents out sailboats, paddleboards and windsurfing equipment, as well as the usual paddleboats, canoes, and electric boats.

Plage Margaridon

Route Margaridon, Les Salles-sur-Verdon

Numerous little beaches line the shore off Route Margaridan near the village of Les Salles-sur-Verdon. Fringed by oak trees, with sand and pebbles glowing in the sun, each beach is fit for a postcard. However, Plage Margaridon is the pick of the bunch. Boat hire facilities are available, and there is a large parking area.

SURF CENTER

Plage Margaridon, Les Salles-sur-Verdon; tel. 04 94 84 23 22; www.facebook.com/ surfcenterlessallessurverdon; from €8 a day

Kayaks, paddleboats, and small sailing boats can be rented on this picturesque beach. A paddleboat with a slide keeps the kids amused for hours.

Bauduen

The pretty village of Bauduen sits on a rocky outcrop. At its base, a long sandy beach curves out into the lake. To find a more secluded spot away from the crowds and the boats, climb a few rocks and head around the bend. Parking can sometimes be difficult because the beach is so close to the center of the village.

ALIZE ELECTRIC LOCATION

Bauduen; tel. 04 92 75 44 69; www.location-bateau-verdon.fr; daily Apr.-end of Sept.; from €35 an hour

This provider specializes in electric boats that seat up to eight and have batteries that last up to 8 hours. Alize allows reservations to be made 48 hours in advance; it's a service worth taking an advantage of, because the wait for a boat in high season can be annoyingly long.

Sainte-Croix-du-Verdon

Coming around the corner as you descend into Sainte-Croix-du-Verdon, the beach appears shimmering in the hot sunshine, curving sinuously away to one side of the town. Unsurprisingly the pebble and sand beach is very popular in the summer. There's a large parking lot, boat hire, and a lifeguard on hand during the main tourist season.

LAC LOC

La Plage, Sainte-Croix-du-Verdon; tel. 04 92 77 77 62; www.lacloc-saintecroix-verdon.com; Apr.-end of Sept. daily 10am-6pm; paddleboats from €8 per half hour

Kayaks, canoes, electric boats, and paddleboats are all available. There's also a small snack bar for a refreshing drink after all the pedaling.

LE PETIT PORT

Plage de La Fontaine, Sainte-Croix-du-Verdon; tel. 04 92 74 82 53; www.lepetitport04.com; Apr.-Sept. daily 10am-6pm; paddleboats from €8 for half an hour

Electric boats and paddleboats are available next to a small beach. There's a snack bar for a nibble and to quench your thirst.

Hiking

SENTIER DES MULETIERS

Depart La Plage, Sainte-Croix-du-Verdon; www.cheminsdesparcs.fr/api/fr/treks/54240/ le-sentier-des-muletiers.pdf

This 5-kilometer (3-mile) walk, marked with yellow trail markers, starts from the Sainte-Croix-du-Verdon beach. Facing the lake, turn left and follow the dirt track. The circular walk takes 2 hours, during which the gradient rises by 200 meters (660 feet). At times the path is uneven and you'll need good walking shoes. The track passes through lavender fields (which will be in bloom between the end of June and early August) and offers good views back over the lake. Shade is not plentiful, so wear a hat and take plenty of water.

LE CHAPELLE DE BAUDINARD

Baudinard sur Verdon

Families will enjoy this 3-kilometer (2-mile), 30-minute walk along a dirt track with a climb of 100 meters (330 feet) to a viewpoint over the lake. Park at the entry to the village of Baudinard and take the track that passes the tennis courts. After 300 meters (980 feet), take the left-hand track, which climbs up to

---

1: Try one of the highest bungee jumps in Europe from the Artuby Bridge. **2:** Sainte-Croix-du-Verdon **3:** The village of Moustiers-Sainte-Marie nestles against huge cliffs.

the chapel and a viewpoint with an orientation table. Afterward, there is a small café (L'Auberge, 37 Grand Rue) in picturesque Baudinard where you can pause and enjoy a drink and light meal.

MOUSTIERS-SAINTE-MARIE TO LAC DE SAINTE-CROIX

A 5-kilometer (3-mile) walk from Moustiers takes you down to the lake in approximately 1 hour and 15 minutes. Take chemin de La Maladrerie, cross the road, and follow the path to Quinson. At the end of the path, cross the stream and follow the signs to the Lac. The trail comes out at Pont du Galetas, and the return trip can be done by bus (Line 1005).

Food and Accommodations
CAFÉ DU MIDI
Rue du Cours, Bauduen; tel. 04 94 70 08 94; daily 9am-10pm; €12.50-22
Bauduen is a great spot for lunch when touring the lake. This is a simple, kid-friendly restaurant with good food and a terrace overlooking the lake. Try king prawns fried in pastis or one of the copious salads.

★ L'ACTUEL
Le Cours, Sainte-Croix-du-Verdon; tel. 04 92 77 87 95; Wed.-Sat. noon-1:30pm and 7pm-8:30pm; €25-35
In the heart of Sainte-Croix-du-Verdon, L'Actuel welcomes a crowd of in-the-know tourists. The food is excellent. Even so, the views (particularly from the small terrace) frequently distract from the plate in front of you. Try beef filet topped with *foie gras* and a truffle gravy. Reservations are necessary in the summer season.

AUBERGE DU LAC
Bauduen; tel. 04 94 70 08 04; www.logishotels.com/fr/hotel/auberge-du-lac-2058?partid=661; €90 d
This attractive small hotel overlooking the lake also has a restaurant. All rooms have Wi-Fi and ensuite bathrooms. Note that in July and August, there is a minimum six-night stay. The atmosphere is welcoming and informal.

LES CAVALETS
D71 Route du Barrage, Bauduen; tel. 04 98 10 62 40; www.lescavalets.com; €100 d
The rooms, all with ensuite bathrooms, need a little updating, but the setting is idyllic with a garden and small swimming pool overlooking the lake. The restaurant has a large panoramic terrace and offers good-value menus for around €21 as well as à la carte mains (€17-28).

Getting There and Around
BY CAR
From Marseille: Take the A51 to Manosque and then the D6 and D8, following directions for Moustiers-Sainte-Marie and then Lac Sainte-Croix, covering 150 kilometers (92 miles) in 2 hours 18 minutes.

From Aix: Take the A51 to Manosque and then the D6 and D8, following directions for Moustiers-Sainte-Marie and then Lac Sainte-Croix, covering 110 kilometers (68 miles) in 1 hours 50 minutes.

From Avignon: Take the A7 and then A51 to Manosque and then the D6 and D8, following directions for Moustiers-Sainte-Marie and then Lac Sainte-Croix, covering 182 kilometers (113 miles) in 2 hours 40 minutes.

From Nice and Cannes: Take the A8 and then the D1555 from Le Muy to Draguignan and then the D955, covering 136 kilometers (85 miles) in 2 hours 20 minutes.

BY BUS
Public transportation is very limited. Sainte-Croix-du-Verdon can be reached by taking the bus from **Manosque** to Riez and then taking a taxi. **Transagglo bus Line 132** (www.autocars-sumian.fr/LIGNES/pdf/L132.pdf) runs four times a day from Manosque station and costs €1; the trip takes 1 hour. A **taxi** from Manosque to Sainte-Croix-du-Verdon costs an additional €20. **Zou bus Line 1005** (www.varlib.fr) runs four times a day from **Moustiers** to Pont du Galetas.

THE LOWER GORGES DU VERDON

Traveling into the heart of the Gorges du Verdon can be time consuming. An alternative is to visit the lower gorge area. The cliffs are not as spectacular and Lac d'Esparron is smaller than Lac de Sainte-Croix, but a visit to the Musée de Préhistoire des Gorges du Verdon followed by an afternoon on a boat exploring the lower gorge, is a great way to spend a day in Provence. The main entry point for the lower gorge is the village of Quinson, and from there Lac d'Esparron is a short 20-minute drive.

Sights
★ MUSÉE DE PRÉHISTOIRE DES GORGES DU VERDON

Route de Montmeyan, Quinson; tel. 04 92 74 0959; www.museeprehistoire.com/accueil.html; July-Aug. 10am-8pm, May-June and Sept. 10am-7pm, Oct.-Apr. 10am-6pm; €8, child €6

This Norman Foster-designed museum showcases the rich archaeological finds of the region from the Stone Age to the Bronze Age. The long entrance ramp creates a nice sense of theater as you enter the permanent exhibition of the museum. There are displays of tools and jewelry, and re-creations of families in their home environments. Also on offer are two walking excursions from the museum: The first, just over 1 kilometer away (0.6 miles), takes you to the re-creation of a prehistoric village on the banks of the Verdon river. The second is a longer (3.5-kilometer/2-mile) hike to the Grotte de Baume Bonne. Here, evidence of man dating back 400,000 years has been found. Trips to the grotto have to be booked in advance with the museum. The walk takes 1 hour and 15 minutes, and the visit, including the walk there and back, lasts about 3 hours and 30 minutes. It is not suitable for children under 7.

Beaches
PLAGE SAINT-JULIEN

Lac d'Esparron, Esparron de Verdon

Lac d'Esparron is the region's second man-made lake. Created in 1967, it's another center for boat hire and water sports. The main point of access for the lac is the small village of Esparron de Verdon. Plage Saint-Julien, which is located next to the boat rental facilities in port area of Esparron de Verdon, is a great place to spend a summer day. The water is clean and cold, and the beach a combination of sand and pebbles. At the back of the beach, there's plenty of shade for a picnic. The view out across the lake is enchanting.

Boat Hire
ALIZE ELECTRIC LOCATION

Le Port, Esparron de Verdon, Lac D'Esparron; tel. 04 92 75 44 69; www.location-bateau-verdon. fr; Apr.-end of Sept. daily 9am-7pm; from €35 for one hour

This provider specializes in electric boats that seat up to eight and have batteries that last up to eight hours. Alize allows reservations 48 hours in advance. This service is worth taking advantage of, because the wait for a boat in high season can be annoyingly long.

LA PERLE DU VERDON

Le Port, Esparron de Verdon, Lac d'Esparron; tel. 04 92 77 10 74; www.laperleduverdon.fr; Apr.-end of Sept. daily 9am-7pm; from €7 for half an hour

It's a good idea to head down to the office of La Perle du Verdon upon arrival at Lac d'Esparron. Waiting times for electric boats, in particular, can be long and it pays to get your name down early. The paddleboats with slides are a fun option for kids. There's also a pleasure boat that tours the lake.

Hiking
SENTIER DU GARD CANAL

Depart Plage Julien, Esparron de Verdon, Lac d'Esparron; www.rando-alpes-haute-provence.fr/ randonnee-pedestre/lac-desparron-de-verdon-sentier-du-garde-canal

This gentle 3-hour, 9-kilometer (6-mile) walk offers panoramic views over the lake and is relatively flat. From the beach, climb the steps to the canal and follow the path that runs alongside it. The walk is marked by yellow and red markers for the outward loop, and red for the return. Sunshine and shade alternate; take water and a hat.

Food and Accommodations
BUVETTE DU LAC
Hameau du Port, Lac D'Esparron;
tel. 04 92 77 80 99;
www.instagram.com/buvettedulac04;
Thurs.-Tues. 10am-6pm; €10-18
Nestled on a hilltop overlooking the lake, this picturesque café gets busy quickly with day-trippers. A small terrace wraps around the building, and inside there's a relaxed casual vibe. The pizzas are good and the salads generous.

LA TOUR D'ENGUERME
Route de Quinson, Montmeyan;
tel. 04 94 80 93 42;
www.latourdenguerne.com; €190
Luxury stays near the Gorges du Verdon are rare. This bed-and-breakfast has five immaculately and creatively decorated rooms, all with ensuite bathrooms. They form part of a 100-hectare (247-acre) estate dotted with private shady places where you can relax. The pool is a little on the small side, and Wi-Fi coverage in the rooms can be patchy, but these are minor quibbles.

RELAIS NOTRE DAME
D11 Route de Montmeyan, Quinson;
tel. 04 92 74 40 01;
http://relaisnotredame04.com; €90
The Relais offers 13 simply decorated rooms and is located just down the road from the Musée de Préhistoire des Gorges du Verdon. All rooms have ensuite bathrooms and Wi-Fi. The main draws are the mature garden with pool and the excellent restaurant, offering menus from €22.

Getting There and Around
BY CAR
Quinson and Esparron de Verdon are joined by the **D15.** The route is 10 kilometers (6 miles) and takes 20 minutes.

From Marseille: Take the A51 to take the Vinon-sur-Verdon turnoff from the autoroute, and then follow the D952 for Gréoux-les-Bains and then Esparron de Verdon, or if heading for Quinson, take the Vinon-sur-Verdon turnoff and follow the D554 for Ginasservis and then Quinson.

The journey to Esparron de Veron is 105 kilometers (65 miles), taking 1hour 35 minutes.

The journey to Quinson is 119 kilometers (4 miles), taking 1 hour 38 minutes

From Aix: Take the A51 to the Vinon-sur-Verdon turnoff from the autoroute, and then follow the D952 for Gréoux-les-Bains and then Esparron de Verdon, or if heading for Quinson take the Vinon-sur-Verdon turnoff and follow the D554 for Ginasservis and then Quinson.

The journey to Esparron de Veron is 68 kilometers (42 miles), taking 1 hour 10 minutes

The journey to Quinson is 88 kilometers (55 miles), taking 1 hour 19minutes

From Avignon: Take the A7 and then A51 to take the Vinon-sur-Verdon turnoff from the autoroute, and then follow the D952 for Gréoux-les-Bains and then Esparron de Verdon, or if heading for Quinson, take the Vinon-sur-Verdon turnoff and follow the D554 for Ginasservis and then Quinson.

The journey to Esparron de Veron is 157 kilometers (98 miles), taking 2 hours

The journey to Quinson is 145 kilometers (90 miles), taking 2 hours

From Nice and Cannes: Take the A8 and then the D1555 from Le Muy to Draguignan and then the D557 to Salernes, followed by the D13 to Quinson. The journey to Quinson is 138 kilometers (86 miles), taking 2 hours. For Esparron de Verdon continue another 10 kilometers (6 miles) for 20 minutes on the D15.

BY BUS
A bus (**Line 136,** https://mobilite.dlva.fr/ligne/136/) runs once a day from **Manosque** to Lac d'Esparron in July and August; in May, June, and September the service only runs on weekends. The journey takes an hour and costs €1.

Inland Var

Provence spoils people for choice. Be it architecture, history, or natural wonders, seemingly every region, city, town, and village has something unique to offer. The inland Var is different; here is perhaps only one show stopping sight: the Abbaye du Thoronet, thought by many to be the perfect expression of minimalist Cistercian architecture. Otherwise, the Var has no compelling must-see monument, no one-of-a-kind vestige of the Roman empire or stunning piece of modernist architecture. Perhaps this is a relief to some. The rest of Provence can be left to the culture vultures. The Var is for the more laid-back types who simply wish to sit, relax, and soak up the joys of life in the sun-kissed south.

Villages such as Aups, Cotignac, Tourtour, and Lorgues are not as well-known as their more celebrated contemporaries in, say, the Luberon or Les Alpilles, but they're every bit as enjoyable. Plus, rosé, that arbiter of the good life in Provence, is arguably better here. The countryside surrounding these villages is a pungent mix of pine forest and vineyards. Be warned, traveling without a car is difficult, with public transport sporadic at best. Barjols, Brignoles, Draguignan, and Saint-Maximin-la-Sainte-Baume are the main transport hubs but, other than Saint-Maximin, those towns offer little else.

ORIENTATION

The **A8** autoroute, which runs between **Saint-Maximin-la-Sainte-Baume** in the west and **Draguignan** in the east, forms the southern boundary of the area covered by this section. The northern limit is the villages of **Aups** and **Tourtour,** which sit just off the **D560.** This road runs between **Barjols** in the west and **Draguignan** in the east. **Cotignac, Lorgues,** and the **Cistercian Le Thoronet Abbey** are located in the countryside between the **A8** and the **D560.**

AUPS

Aups was once thought to be where the Alps began. The Romans called the village Castrum de Alpibus (Fortress of the Alps). It's busy particularly on market days (Wednesday and Saturday) and has become a regional center for truffles, with a truffle visitors center and a truffle market every Thursday from November to February.

Sights
OBELISK
Place Martin Bidouré
This monument, surrounded by plane trees, is a moving memorial to the French spirit of resistance. Erected in 1881 it commemorates the Battle of Aups, which took place in 1851. Local forces loyal to the republic met with those of Louis Napoleon, the instigator of a coup d'État. The loyalists lost and a massacre of the local villagers ensued. The obelisk also commemorates members of the French Resistance who fell during World War II.

MAISON DE LA TRUFFE D'AUPS ET DU VERDON
1 Place Martin Bidoure; tel. 04 94 84 00 69; http://maisondelatruffe-verdon.fr; Sept.-June Mon.-Fri. 9am-12:30pm and 2pm-5:30pm, Sat. 9am-12:30pm, July-Aug. daily, hours to be determined; €9 gourmet visit, €2.50 visit
Truffles don't just taste good, they are also have a rich associated folklore. Rain in spring, an early frost, and a full moon are just some of the climatic conditions thought to encourage their growth. Truffle hunters rely on secrets passed from generation to generation and an expert dog, rather than science, to find the "black diamonds" of Provence. The Maison de La Truffe lifts the veil on this undercover world, explaining where and how truffles grow, and examining the lives of the truffle hunters who spend their winters poking around in the forests of the Var. The various

exhibits are informative and multisensory. There's even a dedicated children's truffle discovery game.

Food and Accommodations

AUPS MARKET

Place Frederic Mistral; Nov.-Mar. Wed. and Sat. morning, and Thurs. morning truffle market

Aups market is wonderful for fresh fruit and vegetables throughout the year. It has retained a traditional ambiance, and is less touristy than markets in the Provençal heartlands, such as the Luberon and Les Alpilles. In August, the Wednesday morning market has stands selling white truffles. These summer truffles are less pungent than their dark winter cousins, but they can still be used to impart a delicate flavor to rice and egg dishes. In the winter there is a Thursday morning market entirely dedicated to black truffles. If you purchase a truffle, make sure it is nice and clean. At nearly €1,000 a kilo (2.2 pounds), you don't want to pay for the weight of a coating of mud.

RESTAURANT TRUFFE

10 rue Maréchal Foch;

tel. 04 94 67 02 41;

www.restaurantlatruffe.com;

Tues.-Thurs. and Sun. noon-2pm; Fri.-Sat. noon-2pm and 7:30pm-9:30pm; €20-30

You don't have to like truffles to eat here, but it certainly helps. Ninety percent of the dishes are based around the black diamond of Provence, and there's a special tasting menu as well. Plates such as chicken supreme with a truffle velouté show off the richness and depth that judicious use of truffles can bring to food. The clientele is a mix of local truffle addicts, and novice tourists poking their noses deep into dishes, in search of the allusive aroma of truffles. Book in season to be sure of a table.

BASTIDE DU CALALOU

Route de Baudinard, Moissac-Bellevue;

tel. 04 94 70 17 91;

www.bastide-du-calalou.com; €190 d

This 32-bedroom luxury hotel is perfectly situated a few kilometers from Aups at the entrance to the Gorges du Verdon. Guests can divide their time between visiting the gorge and the inland Var villages, and lazing in the garden by the pool. Rooms are sumptuously decorated and all have Wi-Fi and en-suite bathrooms. The hotel has one of the best restaurants in the area.

Getting There and Around

Once you have arrived, the village is best explored **on foot.**

BY CAR

Aups sits at the intersection of the D9, the D957, and the D557.

From Cotignac: Take the D22, covering 16 kilometers (10 miles) in 22 minutes.

From Lorgues: Take the D10 and the D557, covering 21 kilometers (13 miles) in 25 minutes.

From Tourtour: Take D77 the covering 10 kilometers (6 miles) in 17 minutes.

From Saint-Maximin-la-Sainte-Baume: Take the D560, covering 47 kilometers (29 miles) in 56 minutes.

From Tourtour: Take the D77, covering 10 kilometers (6 miles) in 17 minutes.

BY BUS

Buses run four times a day from Moustiers-Sainte-Marie (**Line 1005**). The trip takes just over an hour.

TOURTOUR

Tourtour is nicknamed the "Village in the Sky," because from its highest point next to the Romanesque church Saint Denis, the views across the Var toward the Mediterranean are magnificent. It has a more affluent feel than Aups, and like Cotignac and Lorgues to the south, it invites at least a gentle few hours of exploration. The village boasts a medieval castle and ramparts. Next to the castle are two sculptures by French expressionist painter Bernard Buffet, who died in 1999 in the village. Tourtour is now home to a vibrant artistic community, and galleries are plentiful.

Sights

TROGLODYTE CAVES OF VILLECROZE

Boulevard Charles Bernard, Villecroze;
tel. 04 94 67 50 00; www.villecroze-tourisme.com;
July-Aug. daily, 10am-noon and 4pm-6pm, Sept.
daily 10am-noon and 2pm-4pm, Apr.-May Wed.-Sun.
2pm-5pm, June Wed.-Sun. 10am-1pm and 2pm-5pm,
Oct. Wed.-Sun. 1pm-6pm; €4, under 12 free

Formed 700,000 years ago at the end of an Ice Age, the caves were created by the large waterfall that used to tumble down the entire cliff face. A somewhat shrunken version of the cascade can still be admired. Back in the 10th century, Benedictine monks used the caves created by the waterfall as a refuge from the Sarrasin invaders. In the 16th century the caves were fortified by Nicolas d'Albertas to take advantage of their seemingly impregnable position in the event of a siege. The defenses were never tested, and the caves were never permanently occupied. They are now bordered by a pleasant municipal park and the waterfall (cascade) which gives the neighboring village its name.

MUSEE FAKYOD

3366 Route de Tourtour, Aups; tel. 04 94 70 03 94;
www.musee-de-faykod.com; Oct.-Apr. Wed. and
Sat.-Sun. 2pm-6pm, May-June and Sept. Wed.-Mon.
2pm-6pm, July-Aug. daily 3pm-7pm; €5

Visiting this sculpture garden located in a wood between Aups and Tourtour is a slightly surreal experience. It feels like you have entered Narnia's realm of the White Witch, the sorceress who turned all her enemies to stone. Instead, the museum is the creation of Maria Fakyod, a renowned French sculptor, who was born in Hungary to a Swedish father and Hungarian mother. The sculptures are unusual in the sense of movement that seems to inhabit them. Notable subjects include Princess Diana and Mozart. Observe the opening times carefully; you'll be admitted after ringing a bell at the gate.

Food and Accommodations

LA TABLE

Les Ribas, Tourtour; tel. 04 94 70 95 55;
www.latable.fr; Wed.-Mon. 12:15pm-1pm and
7:30pm-8:30pm; €32-47, menus from €36

This is an absolute gem of a restaurant in the heart of Tourtour. Surprisingly, given the hilltop location, there's no view. The outside terrace is large and shady, and the dining room intimate, but the real star is the showstopping food. A clientele of foodies lap up dishes such as grilled kangaroo steak, and pumpkin and chorizo mash with a balsamic sauce.

LA FARIGOULETTE

Place des Ormeaux, Tourtour; tel. 04 94 70 57 37;
daily 8am-10pm; €16-21

La Farigoulette is a popular village stalwart with a panoramic terrace overlooking the countryside. The crowd is a mixture of tourists and locals enjoying dishes from a bistro-style menu. There's the odd flash of invention like duck in a raspberry sauce, but mainly it's the quality of the ingredients and the fair prices that keep drawing people back. Reserve in season to guarantee a good table on the terrace.

★ BASTIDE DE TOURTOUR

Route de Flayosc, Tourtour; tel. 04 98 10 54 20;
www.bastidedetourtour.com/en; €200 d

Located just outside Tourtour, the Bastide de Tourtour is one of the best-known luxury hotels in Provence. It offers 360-degree views of the Provençal countryside, and at night in the summer, its hilltop position brings a refreshing coolness to the air. As you would expect, the hotel has an excellent restaurant, a pool with a view, and spa facilities. Rooms are richly furnished and all have Wi-Fi, air-conditioning, and ensuite bathrooms.

Getting There and Around

Tourtour has no bus service. Once you have arrived, the village is best explored **on foot.**

BY CAR
From Lorgues: Take the D10 and the D77, covering 20 kilometers (12 miles) in 20 minutes.

From Cotignac: Take the D560 and the D51, covering 24 kilometers (15 miles) in 30minutes.

From Aups: Take D77, covering 10 kilometers (6 miles) in 17 minutes.

From Saint-Maximin-la-Sainte-Baume: Take the D560, covering 55 kilometers (34 miles) in 1 hour 3 minutes.

LORGUES
Lorgues boasts plentiful cafés and restaurants, and on Tuesday morning hosts one of the largest markets in the Var.

Sights
NOTRE-DAME DE BENVA
Route de Saint Antonin; tel. 04 94 73 92 37;
visits by appointment with Lorgues tourist office,
12 rue 8 Mai; €5
Located on a pilgrimage route, the chapel is famous for its well-preserved medieval frescoes, which are believed to date to the beginning of the 16th century. No artist has been identified, but the frescoes are particularly important because they depict the only representation of purgatory ever discovered in medieval Provence. Angels are shown offering refreshment to imprisoned souls to tide them over before their ascension to heaven.

★ ABBAYE DU THORONET
Le Thoronet; tel. 04 94 60 43 90; www.le-thoronet.
fr/en; Jan. 2-Mar. 31 daily 10am-1pm and 2pm-5pm,
Apr. 1-Sept. 30 10am-6:30pm, Oct. 1-Dec. 31
10am-1pm and 2pm-5pm; €8, reduced €6.50
Thought to be the oldest of the three Cistercian Abbeys in Provence (the other two are Sénanque and Silvacane), the Abbaye du Thoronet nestles in the heart of La Daboussière

Forest. Construction began around 1176. The church and the rest of the abbey buildings were finished early in the following century. The speed of construction means the abbey boasts a rare architectural unity. The monks used only basic and pure elements in the design, concentrating on rock, light, and water, to achieve a simplicity envied by modern architects. When famed French/Swiss architect Le Corbusier was asked to build a convent near Lyon in the 1950s, he came to Le Thoronet for inspiration. After his visit he commented, "The light and shadows are the loudspeakers of this architecture of truth." Visitors today tour the church and the monks' buildings, including the dormitory, the sacristy, the library, and the chapter house, as well as the cloisters. In the summer, there are themed days with a special focus on subjects such as the music of the Middle Ages and Romanesque symobols. Consult the website for up-to-date details. Even abbeys such as Le Thoronet haven't escaped our commercial times; expect the now-ubiquitous gift shop as you exit.

Sports and Recreation
NATURE EVASION
Pardigon, Entrecasteaux; tel. 06 79 60 94 94;
https://naturevasion.com; June-Aug. daily 9am-6pm,
Apr.-May and Sept.-Oct. by reservation only; from
€15, depending on activity
This is a multisports activity base on the River Argens that offers kayaking, paddleboarding, bike rentals, and accrobranching over the water. Various different courses are laid out for each activity. It's possible to put together whole weekends combining the various sports.

Wineries
CHATEAU ROUBINE
4216 Route de Draguignan; tel. 04 94 85 94 94; www.
chateauroubine.com/fr; June 15-Sept. 15 Mon.-Fri.
9am-6pm and Sat.-Sun. 10am-6pm, Sept. 15-June 15
Mon.-Fri. 9am-6pm and Sat. 10am-6pm, cellar tours
by appointment; free tasting, €12 tour of cellar
An excellent local producer, the vineyard has a walking trail laid out through the vines

---

1: Arguably the Var makes the best rosé in Provence—try some at the Mirabeau wine shop. **2:** village square in Tourtour **3:** Formed by an ice age waterfall, the Villecroze caves were once inhabited by Benedictine monks.

explaining the different grape varieties and soil types. The vineyard also frequently hosts art exhibitions. The cru classé rosé, in particular, is a delight, with night harvesting and quick pressing of the grapes leading to a delicate pale pink wine that is the expression of Provence in a bottle.

Food and Accommodations
LORGUES MARKET
Center Village; Apr.-Oct. every Tues.
8:30am-12:30pm
More than 100 traders crowd the streets of Lorgues every Tuesday morning, making this one of the largest markets in the Var. On sale are the usual array of Provençal delicacies, including olives, *saucissons,* tapenades, pestos, honeys, and rotisserie meat. It's a joy to wander around and pick up something delicious for lunch.

LA TABLE DE POL
18 boulevard Georges Clémenceau;
tel. 04 94 47 08 41; Sun. and Tues.-Wed. noon-3pm,
Thurs.-Sat. noon-3pm and 6pm-11pm; plat du jour €15
This is a casual, welcoming restaurant in the center of Lorgues, with a focus on using local seasonal ingredients. The relationship between the quality of food and price means

that the place is frequently packed. The menu is small and mixes local favorites such as aioli and *tartare de boeuf* (raw beef) with more simple grilled fish and meat. It is sensible to reserve ahead in the summer.

CHEZ BRUNO
2350 route des Arcs; tel. 04 94 85 93 93;
www.restaurantbruno.com; Tues.-Sat. noon-3pm and
7pm-10pm, Sun. noon-3pm; menus from €78
If you have ever wondered why people make such a fuss about truffles, then a lunch or dinner at Chez Bruno will reveal all. A wood-paneled dining room attracts gourmands from around the world, with menus constructed entirely around truffles. The signature dish of the restaurant—a baked potato served with a truffle cream—has been known to make diners swoon with pleasure. For diners too replete to move after their meal, the restaurant has six rooms and a pool. Advance reservations for the restaurant are required.

CHATEAU DE BERNE
Chemin des Imberts, Flayosc; tel. 04 94 60 43 60;
www.chateauberne.com; €550 d
This luxury vineyard hotel is right at the top of the price range for the region, with standard rooms costing more than €500 in the

Abbaye du Thoronet

summer. As you would expect, the location is stunning and the rooms are immaculate and well-equipped. The grounds are extensive and include two swimming pools (one indoor one outdoor), and walking and cycling routes. There's a spa and gym, plus two restaurants and a cooking school.

Getting There and Around

Lorgues has extremely poor public transport connections. Buses to the other local towns and villages run only during school terms and are filled with schoolchildren. Once you have arrived, the village is best explored on foot.

BY CAR
From Cotignac: Take the D13 and D562, covering 25 kilometers (16 miles) in 30 minutes.

From Aups: Take the D557 and D10, covering 23 kilometers (14 miles) in 27 minutes.

From Tourtour: Take the D77 and D10, covering 17 kilometers (11 miles) in 22 minutes.

From Saint-Maximin-la Sainte-Baume: Take the D28 and D562, covering 47 kilometers (29 miles) in 53 minutes.

COTIGNAC

Cotignac has star quality. The plane-tree-lined Cours Gambetta is reminiscent of the Cours Mirabeau in Aix, just a little sleepier. For those who tire of people watching, there are plentiful small boutiques and art galleries, as well as a walk along the cliff face that looms over the village.

Sights
CHAPELLE DE NOTRE-DAME DES GRACES
Chemin Notre Dame;
tel. 04 94 69 64 92;
www.nd-de-graces.com; daily 7am-7pm; free

On August 10-11, 1519, the Virgin Mary appeared to Jean de La Baume and instructed him to ask the people of Cotignac to build a church in her honor. Just one month later the first stone was laid. The Virgin reappeared in Cotignac in 1637. At the time, after 20 years

of marriage, King Louis XIII was still without an heir. Speaking to Frere Fiacre, the Virgin promised a child would be born if prayers were said for nine days in the church. An heir to the throne was duly conceived, and so it was that in 1660 Louis XIV made a pilgrimage to Cotignac to give thanks for his son's birth. These days, the church is a place of contemplation run by a small community of monks. Surrounded by pine trees, the chapel is located on a hill outside Cotignac, affording views over the surrounding countryside. The building is modest, and the most remarkable feature is perhaps the vaulted ceiling, painted a brilliant blue. There's a café and gift shop.

CHATEAU D'ENTRECASTEAUX
2 rue le Courtil, Entrecasteaux;
tel. 04 94 04 43 95;
www.chateau-entrecasteaux.com/fr; July-Sept. daily guided tour 4pm, Aug. additional guided tour 11:30pm, Easter-June Sun. and public holidays guided tour 4pm; €10, €5 children

Construction of this fortress started in the 11th century and continued up until the 18th century. Surrounded by formal gardens, it is one of the most impressive castles in the Var. The interior has been restored with period furniture and the guided visits take in the dining rooms, bedrooms, and guard rooms.

Wineries
MIRABEAU
5 Cours Gambetta;
tel. 04 94 37 40 02;
www.mirabeauwine.com; Tues. 10am-5pm, Wed. 10am-12:30pm, Thurs.-Sat. 10am-5pm; free tasting

When Stephen and Jeanny Cronk moved to Provence in 2008, they had one simple aim: to make the best rosé possible. They scoured Provence for the top growers and the most talented wine makers before putting together a team to produce Mirabeau, now recognised internationally as one of Provence's signature rosés. Taste any of their five different cuvées in the village center shop. Rumor has it, a Provençal gin is soon going to hit the shelves too.

FONTAINEBLEAU DU VAR

Route de Montfort sur Argens, Le Val;
tel. 04 94 59 59 09; http://
chateaufontainebleauduvar.com; Tues.-Sat.
11am-6pm; cellar visits €7; horse-drawn cart ride €11

Vineyards these days have to do so much more than produce wine. Fontainebleau enjoys an enviable locaton in the heart of the Var countryside. As well as cellar visits, Fontainebleau also offers yoga classes, horse-drawn cart rides, musical and aperitif evenings, and a bistro. The red wines are full of the aromas of red fruits, soft spices, and exotic wood.

Hiking
CASCADE DE SILLANS

Sillans La Cascade

A 44-meter (144-foot) waterfall tumbles into an azure-blue pool cut by the river Bresque, just outside the village of Sillans. Park in the village car park and follow the signs to the cascade. The walk takes about 20 minutes. Upon arrival there's a viewing platform from which to watch the crashing waters. Swimming is not allowed, although farther downstream, plenty of people ignore the prohibition and jump in.

CLIFFSIDE TRAIL

Cotignac

Cotignac sits under an 80-meter (260-foot) high cliff. At the top stand two sentinel towers that have been watching over the village since the Middle Ages. The cliff itself has been hollowed out in places to create caves that were used as refuges from invaders. Over time, the villagers added walls and windows to make the caves more habitable during times of crisis. The trail up the cliffside starts from the town hall. From there, pick up the path that leads toward the cliff. The route is a little precipitous, but there is an iron railing for protection. During the walk you can observe the caves close-up and enjoy the view of the village below. You'll need sturdy walking shoes. Note the trail is not suitable for small children. Allow around 1 hour, including the return leg, and be aware that there are a lot of steps to negotiate. If you wish to go inside the troglodyte caves, there is a fee of €2.

Food
CAFÉ DU COURS

23 Cours Gambetta;
tel. 04 94 04 60 14;
daily 7am-10pm; €15-28

Too often, cafés in the center of tourist villages dish up lowest-common-denominator food to the summer masses, confident that the next day will bring a fresh wave of unsuspecting customers. Café du Cours is an exception. The large menu offers everything from pizzas to noodles, but the quality is good and the large terrace is perfect for a glass of the local rosé.

LA TARENTE

15 Cours Gambetta; tel. 04 94 04 75 31;
daily noon-3pm and 7pm-10pm; €10-24

La Tarente is a buzy pizzeria in the heart of Cotignac. It's a good value and does an excellent plat du jour.

TABLE DE FANETTE

298 Chemin des Pouvets, Fox Amphoux;
tel. 04 94 80 72 03; Tues.-Sat. noon-2pm and
7:30pm-8:30pm, Sun. noon-2pm; menus from €32

A little way out into the countryside, this excellent restaurant also has three rooms for overnight stays. The cooking is inventive and makes the best of seasonal local ingredients. In the summer, eating outside on the large terrace beneath foliage throbbing with cicadas is a delight. The truffle menu in the winter months is not to be missed.

Accommodations
MAS DE COTIGNAC

2930 route de Carcès; tel. 06 80 30 36 55;
www.lemasdecotignac.fr/?lang=en; €120 d

In this welcoming small hotel just outside Cotignac, rooms have all the modern conveniencess: air-conditioning, Wi-Fi, and ensuite bathrooms. Bedrooms open onto a garden filled with olive trees. A heated pool and spa add to the allure.

LA LICORNE

1 rue des Pas Perdu; tel. 04 94 04 31 37;
www.lalicorne-cotignac.com; €90 d

Expect a warm welcome at this five-bedroom bed and breakfast in Cotignac. The rooms are cosy and decorated in pastel shades. They have ensuite bathrooms and Wi-Fi but no air-conditiong, so in the summer it can get a little hot. Breakfasts are excellent, and there's a small pool to relax around.

Getting There and Around

Cotignac has very poor public transport connections. Once you arrive at Cotignac, it is best to **walk.**

BY CAR

From Aups: Take the D22, covering 17 kilometers (11 miles) in 21minutes.

From Lorgues: Take the D562 and D13, covering 23 kilometers (14 miles) in 28minutes.

From Tourtour: Take the D51 and D560, covering 34 kilometers (21 miles) in 25 minutes.

From Saint-Maximin-la-Sainte-Baume: Take the D28 and D22, covering 35 kilometers (22 miles) in 40 minutes.

SAINT-MAXIMIN-LA-SAINTE-BAUME

Saint-Maximin is a busy market town with an enjoyable medieval center and a basilica that holds the relics of Mary Magdalene. Beware: The traffic coming in and out of town in the summer can be bad.

Sights

BASILICA AND MONASTERY OF SAINT-MAXIMIN

10 Place de L Hotel de Ville; tel. 04 94 78 00 19; www.
paroissesaintmaximin.fr; Daily 7:30am-7:30pm; free

According to legend, Mary Magdalene, Jesus' partner, fled the holy land and arrived by boat at Saintes-Maries-de-la-Mer in the Camargue. She headed inland and ended her life in a cave in the Sainte-Baume mountains. In the 13th century, her remains were discovered

in Saint-Maximin and the basilica was constructed. Construction continued for the next 300 years, giving the basilica the slightly mismatched architectural feel that is so common in Provence. In the crypt it is still possible to see the relics of Mary Magdalene encased in a 4th-century sarcophagi. The skull in its glass casing is not for the squeamish. Art lovers visit the basilica for the extravagant decorations and Ronzen's *Retable de la Passion* painting (1520). The medieval streets surrounding the basilica are enjoyable explore after the visit.

Golf

GOLF DE LA SAINTE BAUME

2664 route de Brignoles, Nans les Pins; tel. 04 94 78
60 12; www.golfsaintebaume.com; open daily during
daylight hours; €78 green fee

This attractive 18-hole, par 72 park-land golf course offers good views of Mont Sainte-Victoire.

GOLF DE BARBAROUX

Route de Cabasse, Brignoles; tel. 04 94 69 63 63;
www.barbaroux.com/fr; open daily during daylight
hours; €79

Created by renowned American golf course architect Pete Dye, Barbaroux has been rated among the top 50 courses in Europe by *Golf World*. It is certainly among the best, if not the best course in Provence. Every one of the 18 holes is a challenge to the imagination and nerve of players. There is an associated hotel where you can stay.

Food

LA TABLE DE BRUNO

2 avenue Maréchal Foch; tel. 04 94 80 50 39; www.
la-table-de-bruno.com; Tues.-Sat. noon-2pm and
7:30pm-8:30pm, Sun. noon-2pm; menus from €28

Considered by most to be the best restaurant in Saint-Maximin, the Table de Bruno has a small, cozy interior with modern decor. The menu is limited, with four main courses to choose from, but it reflects modern Provençal cooking at its best. Dishes include crayfish with girolle mushrooms and peaches roasted with lavender. Reserve ahead in season.

RENAISSANCE

2 Place Malherbe; tel. 04 69 00 12 35;
www.facebook.com/cafédelarenaissance;
daily 7am-10pm; €12-20

On the main crossroads in the center of town, this café is always bustling and full. The interior is light and the decoration funky with a long wooden bar, wooden tables and chairs, a bright red wall, and an antique phone hanging from the wall. The food is standard French bistro fare, with a long menu offering salads, steaks, and the now ubiquitous hamburger.

CASA CORSA

26 Boulevard du Dr Bonfils; tel. 04 89 36 58 65;
Tues.-Thurs. and Sun. noon-2:30pm, Fri. noon-2:30pm
and 6pm-10:30pm; €15-20

For those unfamiliar with Corsica, the French island shares many similarities with Provence. It is wild and mountainous with a sensationally beautiful coastline, and its scrubland, known as the maquis, is filled with an abundance of wild herbs. Corsican cuisine echoes Provençal cooking, but the flavors of the food and wine are noticeably more intense. The island is renowned for making some of the best dried meats in France. Casa Corsa is an authentic restaurant where you can sample plates of Corsican cheese and charcuterie, which are accompanied with wine by the glass. Normally there is no need to book.

Accommodations

HOTEL LE COUVENT ROYALE

Traverse Saint-Jean; tel. 04 94 86 55 66;
www.hotel-lecouventroyal.fr; €100 d

Phrases like "steeped in history" can be overused. However in the case of this 67-bedroom hotel in the 13th-century cloisters of the basilica of Saint-Maximin-la-Sainte-Baume, the phrase is apt. Hotel guests have access to the cloisters and the gardens. Eating in the restaurant under ecclesiastical arches, it is easy to let your mind drift to the monks who once occupied the building. All rooms have Wi-Fi and ensuite bathrooms. Private parking is available.

LES TERRES DE SAINT HILAIRE

RD3, Ollières;
tel. 04 98 05 40 10;
www.terresdesainthilaire.com; €70 d

This wine estate has an Auberge with low-cost- rooms with shared bathrooms, plus more upmarket rooms in separate buildings across the estate. Some but not all of the rooms have access to a pool. They all have Wi-Fi. Guests have the opportunity to taste the estate's wines, and there is a horseback riding school on-site.

Getting There and Around

Once you arrive, **walking** is the best way to get around.

BY CAR

From Aix en Provence: Take the A8, covering 45 kilometers (28 miles) in 35 minutes.

From Aups: Take the D560, covering 47 kilometers (29 miles) in 56 minutes.

From Cotignac: Take the D22 and D28, covering 35 kilometers (22 miles) in 40 minutes.

From Lorgues: Take the D562 and D28, covering 47 kilometers (29 miles) in 53 minutes.

From Tourtour: Take the D560, covering 55 kilometers (34 miles) in 1 hour 3 minutes.

BY BUS

Bus connections to Saint-Maximin-la-Sainte-Baume are good. **Zou Bus Line 36** (www.varlib.fr), which runs between **Saint-Tropez,** the **Aix TGV,** and **Marseille airport,** stopping at Saint-Maximin, has one bus a day on weekends, and three on weekdays. **Line 20** between **Nice, Aix,** and **Marseille** also stops at Saint-Maximin twice a day. Travelling from the Nice airport and Marseille airport to Saint-Maximin costs €40, and from Saint Tropez it costs €20.

Coastal Var

The resorts of Saint-Cyr Les Lecques, Bandol, and Sanary-sur-Mer are part of a succession of seaside resorts that stretch east along the Var coast toward Toulon. For sun worshippers, all three have beach clubs where you can rent a sun lounger, sip on a drink of choice, and soak up the rays while the Mediterranean laps at your feet. Sporty types can indulge in a full range of water sports, including sailing, diving, and windsurfing. Coastal paths connect the resorts, and the railway network is good. Outside of the worst heat of the peak summer season, it's a joy to take a cliff-top hike followed by lunch and then the train back home. The resorts are largely unknown outside France and retain a Provençal atmosphere. Beaches like Anse de Renécros in Bandol can rightly claim to be among the prettiest in the whole of the South of France. Adding to the pleasures of this stretch of the coast is a hinterland filled with vineyards producing some of the finest wines in Provence and attractive villages such as La Cadière d'Azur, and Le Castellet.

ORIENTATION

Saint-Cyr-sur-Mer is located 40 kilometers (25 miles) east of **Marseille.** The resorts listed in this section of this chapter continue eastward toward **Toulon,** which is 66 kilometers (41 miles) from Marseille. They are all accessible off the **A50** autoroute, which runs parallel to the coast. Heading eastward from Saint-Cyr, visitors will encounter the resorts in the following order: **La Cadière-d'Azur, Le Castellet** (both slightly inland), **Bandol, Sanary-sur-Mer,** before arriving at the city of Toulon.

SAINT-CYR LES LECQUES

Saint-Cyr and Les Lecques are actually two different places that are commonly referred to as one. Saint-Cyr is an inland town, a couple of kilometers from the sea. Its palm-tree-fringed suburbs stretch all the way to the wide sandy bay of Les Lecques. Here, there's a port with water sports activities, a long promenade for a seaside stroll, and a child-friendly beach.

Sights
MUSÉE TAUROENTUM
131 route de la Madrague; tel. 04 94 26 30 46; https://museedetauroentumsaintcyrsurmer.fr; Wed.-Mon. 3pm-7pm; €5, reduced €2.50

Legend has it that in the 5th century BC, Greek sailors landed in the bay of Les Lecques. On the prow of their boat was the symbol of a bull, after which they named their new settlement. The Greek Taurois was later Romanized to Tauroentum. The site was designated a historic monument in 1926, and an associated museum opened in 1966. Housed in the remains of a former Roman villa, the museum displays archaeological finds from the Roman period, including mosaics, urns, and tools. Some of the paths around the surrounding site are a little steep, but Roman enthusiasts who enjoy traipsing around rocky ruins shouldn't be put off.

Beaches
PLAGE DES LECQUES
Boulevard de La Plage

Stretching for several kilometers, this sandy, shallow bay is ideal for children. There's a pedestrian promenade where you can walk and gaze out at the sparkling sea. Out of season, the promenade is heavily used for for Rollerblading and jogging. There are a couple of private beach clubs with sun loungers for hire. Try the Plage de Sophie (www.laplagedesophie.com).

PLAGE DE LA MADRAGUE
Saint-Cyr Les Lecques

This small, sheltered beach is next to the fishing port of La Madrague at the end of Les

Coastal Var

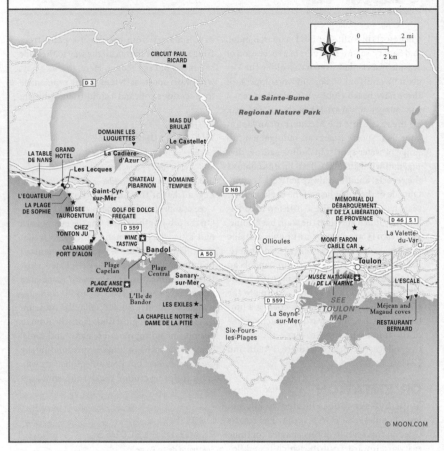

CIRCUIT PAUL RICARD

D 3

La Sainte-Bume
Regional Nature Park

MAS DU BRULAT

DOMAINE LES LUQUETTES

Le Castellet

LA TABLE DE NANS

GRAND HOTEL

La Cadière-d'Azur

Les Lecques

CHATEAU PIBARNON

DOMAINE TEMPIER

L'EQUATEUR

Saint-Cyr-sur-Mer

D N8

MÉMORIAL DU DÉBARQUEMENT ET DE LA LIBÉRATION DE PROVENCE

D 46 | S 1

La Plage DE SOPHIE

GOLF DE DOLCE FREGATE

La Valette-du-Var

MUSÉE TAUROENTUM

D 559

Ollioules

MONT FARON CABLE CAR

CHEZ TONTON JU

WINE TASTING

Bandol

A 50

Toulon

CALANQUE PORT D'ALON

Plage Capelan

Plage Central

Sanary-sur-Mer

MUSÉE NATIONAL DE LA MARINE

L'ESCALE

PLAGE ANSE DE RENÉCROS

L'Ile de Bandor

LES EXILES

SEE "TOULON" MAP

Méjean and Magaud coves

LA CHAPELLE NOTRE DAME DE LA PITIÉ

La Seyne-sur-Mer

RESTAURANT BERNARD

Six-Fours-les-Plages

0   2 mi
0   2 km

© MOON.COM

Lecques bay. This is another beach that is excellent for children.

CALANQUE PORT D'ALON

Route de La Calanque

This stone beach is only 60 meters long but remains popular because of its clear waters and idyllic setting, fringed by pine trees. Parking is a five-minute walk from the beach. There's a small bar/restaurant (Chez Tonton Ju) for refreshments.

Water Sports
LEC SURF CLUB

Promenade Rose; tel. 06 64 61 58 57;
www.lecsurfclub.com; year-round activities; open
daily during school holidays 9:30am-5pm, Sat. and
Sun. outside of school holidays 9:30am-5pm; from
€15 for board rental

The largest paddleboard and surfing club in Provence takes advantage of the ideal conditions offered by the Bay of Les Lecques. During school holidays, there are weeklong courses available for children of all ages.

WAKE SENSATION

Vieux Port des Lecques; tel. 06 63 46 10 71; http://wakesensation.fr; May-Oct.; waterskiing and wakeboarding from €30 for 10 minutes

Wake Sensation runs courses for all skill levels, and in the summer offers weeklong programs for children. The main activities are wakeboarding and waterskiing. There's also the option of sitting on an inflatable ring and bouncing around on the surf behind a speedboat.

LECQUES AQUANAUT

Nouveau Port des Lecques; tel. 04 94 26 35 35; www.lecquesaquanaut.fr/PALANQUEE_WEB/FR/Accueil.awp; year-round activities; €60 beginners session

This established diving school offers equipment rental and dives for all skill levels.

Hiking
SENTIER DU VIGNES

Saint-Cyr Les Lecques; www.saintcyrsurmer.com/sites/saintcyrsurmer/files/content/files/the_vineyard_walk_2018_1.pdf

This walk takes you through the Bandol vineyards from the La Madrague Port in Les Lecques to the Port d'Alon Calanque. The 4-kilometer (2-mile) walk takes just over an hour on a marked path. As always, wear a hat and take plenty of water. Consider also booking a table for lunch at Chez Tonton Ju situated on the beach of the Port D'Alon Calanque. A restorative lunch with a few glasses of wine make the return leg (another 4 kilometers/2 miles) much easier. Alternatively, from the Port d'Alon Calanque you can continue on the Sentier du Littoral to Bandol, and take the bus back to Saint-Cyr.

Golf
GOLF DE DOLCE FREGATE

Lieu dit Fregate; tel. 04 94 29 38 00; daily during daylight hours; green fees from €69

The Dolce Fregate is a picturesque parkland course with several holes offering spectacular sea views.

Food and Accommodations
LA TABLE DE NANS

126 Corniche du Liouquet, La Ciotat; tel. 04 42 83 11 06; www.latabledenans.com; Mon.-Sun. 12:15pm-2pm and 7:30pm-10pm, closed Sun. evening; €35-55

Be prepared for a memorable meal on the terrace of La Table de Nans. The restaurant, which is perched high on the cliffs between Saint-Cyr and La Ciotat, serves exceptional food in an exceptional setting. The menu is well balanced between fish and meat; try

the port at Les Lecques

seared scallops with a cauliflower and nut cream. Reserve in advance.

CHEZ TONTON JU

Saint-Cyr Les Lecques;
tel. 04 94 26 20 08;
Apr.-Oct. noon-3pm; €10-18

This relaxed beach bar comes with a view over the sparkling waters of the Calanque d'Alon. Salads and plates of prawns and oysters dominate the menu. It's a place to kick your shoes off and relax with your feet in the sand.

LA PLAGE DE SOPHIE

Plage des Lecques;
tel. 06 82 57 89 57;
www.laplagedesophie.com;
daily Apr.-Oct. 9am-8pm; €17-22

A friendly beach bar with sun loungers to rent and a decent restaurant serving salads, seafood, and burgers. In summer a reservation is imperative.

L'EQUATEUR

9 avenue du Port; tel. 04 94 26 20 02;
daily 8:30am-7:30pm; €15-20

Right in the center of Les Lecques' bay, on the promenade behind the beach, this bar/restaurant is filled with a mix of old sea dogs sipping pastis at the bar, and tourists enjoying the food. The service is friendly, the vibe relaxed, and the portions copious. *Moules frites* (mussels with fries) overlooking the Mediterranean has rarely tasted better.

★ GRAND HOTEL

24 avenue du Port; tel. 04 94 26 23 01;
https://grand-hotel-les-lecques.com/en; €120 d

This 60-bedroom hotel with large gardens is just a minute's walk from the seafront. The decor is a nice mix of period glamour and modern style. It has two restaurants, one poolside and the other on a terrace overlooking the sea. All rooms have Wi-Fi, air-conditioning, and ensuite bathrooms. Book well in advance for the busy summer months of August and September.

Getting There and Around

Once you have arrived at Saint-Cyr, it is best explored **on foot.**

BY CAR

Saint-Cyr Les Lecques is off the A50 coastal autoroute that runs between **Toulon** and Aubagne. From **Aix-en-Provence,** take the A52 and then the A50, covering 62 kilometers (39 miles) in 50 minutes.

BY BUS

Zou Bus Line 8001 (www.varlib.fr) connects the coastal villages and towns of Bandol, Saint-Cyr, Le Castellet, La Cadière d'Azur, and La Ciotat. It runs three times a day. In Saint-Cyr, it stops at the train station and also the beach. A single ticket is €3. Travelling the whole length of the line takes 1 hour. It is no more than 20 minutes between adjacent resorts.

BY TRAIN

Trains run hourly from Saint-Cyr to **Marseille** and **Toulon.** Note that the **train station** (avenue de La Gare) is inland, approximately 2.5 kilometers (1.6 miles) from the beach. The journey from Marseille costs €8 euros and takes 30 minutes. Consult the timetable here: www.oui.sncf.

LA CADIÈRE D'AZUR AND LE CASTELLET

These two villages face each other across a valley blanketed with the vineyards of the Bandol appellation. Of the two, La Cadière is the more immediately appealing. Perched on a hillside and with a main street lined with cafés and boutiques, it resembles a chic Luberon village transplanted to the seaside. Le Castellet, a fortified village with buildings dating back to the 12th century, has plenty of craft stalls and shops. However, it feels a little like a standalone tourist attraction rather than a thriving village. Le Castellet is also famous for hosting the French Formula 1 Grand Prix at the Circuit Paul Ricard.

Paul Ricard and the Origins of Pastis

On March 17, 1915, the French government banned absinthe, a drink whose key ingredient is the wormwood plant, once thought to be an addictive hallucinogenic. One of the main manufacturers of absinthe was **Jules Pernod** in Avignon. Faced with the prospect of going out of business, he switched to the production of anis, an aniseed-based concoction. The drink caught on immediately. However, for over a decade there was no recognizable brand name. In 1932, in a moment of inspiration, **Paul Ricard**—the son of a Marseille-based wine merchant—christened his version of the anis drink "pastis," meaning in the local patois either "cloudy" or "a troubled situation." Ricard sold millions of bottles a year, earning himself enough money to buy a couple of islands of the coast of Bandol. In 1974, after years of competition, Ricard and Pernod merged to create the dominant pastis brand, **Pernod Ricard.** The French consume an unbelievable 20 million glasses of pastis a day. Be careful if you feel like adding to this statistic because pastis is notoriously easy to drink, but it's not so easy to stand up after a few glasses. A great place to drink it is **L'Equateur** in Saint-Cyr Les Leques. If you're feeling adventurous, absinthe is now legal in both France and the United States.

a glass of pastis with one of its ingredients, star anise

Sights

CIRCUIT PAUL RICARD

2760 route des Hauts du Camp, Le Castellet;
www.circuitpaulricard.com

The circuit Paul Ricard is the home of the French Formula 1 Grand Prix and various other motor racing events throughout the year. When there are no races, the circuit offers customers the chance to drive sports cars around the track. It also has its own Xtrem Park center for thrill seekers, which offers karting (€20 for 10 minutes) and other activities. The Grand Prix usually takes place around June 20.

Cycling

VAR OUEST E-BIKE

12 rue de La Republique, La Cadière d'Azur;
tel. 06 61 92 83 63; www.location-velo-var.fr;
Apr.-Oct., reserve in advance; from €15 for half a day

There's a selection of routes to suit everyone, from a ride down to the Calanque d'Alon to a visit to the nearby medieval village of Le Castellet. It's possible to go on guided trips or head off alone for a morning or even a couple of days.

Food and Accommodations

LA PETITE CAVE

11 rue Gabriel Péri, La Cadière d'Azur;
tel. 04 93 57 66 23; Tues.-Sun. noon-2pm; €12-18

The owners of La Petite Cave keep things simple: a small menu, a welcoming terrace, and a wine list encompassing the best Bandol has to offer. A shrimp and leek risotto is the perfect match for a glass of Bandol pink, a wine so delicate in color it seems to wink back at you in the sunshine.

LA FARIGOULE

2 Place du Jeu de Paume, Le Castellet; t
el. 04 94 32 64 58; www.lafarigoule-restau.fr;
June-Sept. daily noon-2pm and 7:30pm-9:30pm, out of season Fri.-Tues. same hours; €23-26

Inside La Farigoule, there is a cosy bistro

feel with an open fire and wooden tables and chairs. Outside, the shady terrace is perfect for long summer lunches. A short menu of classics with a twist keeps the locals coming back. Try pork chops cooked over an open fire with a chorizo cream. Reserve in the peak summer months.

HOSTELLERIE BERARD

6 rue Gabriel Péri, La Cadière d'Azur 83740; tel. 04 94 90 11 43; www.hotel-berard.com/en; €150 d

This 30-bedroom boutique hotel in the heart of the village of La Cadière d'Azur overlooks the vines of the surrounding Bandol vineyards. It has a small pool located on a sunny terrace. The hotel specializes in cooking courses, which are held in a nearby bastide. All rooms have air-conditioning, Wi-Fi, and ensuite bathrooms.

MAS DU BRULAT

47 route du Grand Vallat Le Brulat, Le Castellet; tel. 04 94 05 06 00; http://olivesandvines.eu; €200 d

A new seven-bedroom hotel set amid the vines of the Bandol vineyards, Mas du Brulat is a relaxing, intimate place for a holiday in the region. It has a pool, and its own restaurant and bar area. Rooms are decorated in typical Provençal style and benefit from air-conditioning, Wi-Fi, and ensuite bathrooms.

Getting There and Around

Upon arrival, the villages are best explored **by foot.**

BY CAR

La Cadière d'Azue and Le Castellet are both off the A50 coastal autoroute, which runs between Toulon and Aubagne. From **Aix-en-Provence** take the A52 and then the A50, covering 65 kilometers (40 miles) in 52 minutes.

BY BUS

Zou Bus line 8001 (www.varlib.fr) connects the coastal villages and towns of Bandol, Saint-Cyr, Le Castellet (stop Real Martin), La Cadière d'Azur (stops Chemin des Baumes and La Mal), and La Ciotat. It runs three times a day. A single ticket is €3. Travelling the whole length of the line takes 1 hour. It is no more than 20 minutes between adjacent resorts.

BY TRAIN

The nearest **station** is **Saint-Cyr-sur-Mer** (avenue de La Gare). Trains run hourly from Saint-Cyr to Marseille and Toulon. Note the train station is inland, approximately 2.5 kilometers (1.6 miles) from the beach. The journey from Marseille costs €8 and takes 30 minutes. Consult the timetable at www.oui.sncf.com. Bus 8001 stops at the station and can be used to travel onward.

BANDOL

Bandol is a busy, bustling resort filled with shops and restaurants. It's large enough to have its own Casino and has several different beaches. Undoubtedly, the best of them is Plage de Renécros. But it's wine that has made Bandol famous. The rosés are among the best in France.

Sights

L'ILE DE BENDOR

Departs from Le Port; www.lesilespaulricard.com/ acces-ile-bendor; boats daily, every 15 minutes; adults €15, children 3-12 €9

Until the 1950s L'Ile de Bendor was a true desert island just off the coast of the south of France. It was then bought by the pastis entrepreneur Paul Ricard and turned into a tourist attraction with an art gallery and zoo. The zoo has since been closed, but the gallery, with a collection of works dominated by Ricard, still exists. The artistic theme is continued by sculptures positioned across the small island. There's a hotel, shops, and five restaurants. Visiting can be a slightly surreal experience; the island is a little too clean and a little too perfect, almost like an amusement park. However, the circular path that follows the shoreline affords wonderful views of the open sea and back toward the mainland. Many come for the small sandy beaches, which are much quieter than those back in

Bandol. The island is also pedestrianized, making it an ideal place to enjoy a stress-free time with small children.

Beaches
★ PLAGE ANSE DE RENÉCROS
Corniche Bonaparte
One of the most attractive beaches on the Var coast, Plage Anse de Renécros is an almost perfect half moon of sand located on the opposite side of the headland from Bandol's port and main shopping drag. A couple of hotels and beach clubs line one side of the bay, and on the far side, dreamy villas peek from beneath pine trees. The sea is sheltered and shallow for a good 15 meters (49 feet). Schools of fish and even the odd squid dart amid the occasional rocks. On a windy day when the mistral is blowing, the beach is remarkably sheltered.

PLAGE CENTRAL
Quai Charles de Gaule
If you are visiting Bandol and only have time for a quick dip or a stroll along the beach, then the Plage Central is a sandy stretch right next to the port and the main parking. This beach is popular with locals, but it lacks the charm of Plage Anse de Renécros.

PLAGE CAPELAN
Presqu'Il de Capelan
Around the headland from Plage Anse de Renécros, this small beach is the place to go to escape the crowds. There are two small parking areas, and the beach is accessed by a set of steps. The waters are clear, the surrounding rocks perfect to lounge on, and pine trees filter the summer sun. It's ideal for nature lovers yet just a couple of kilometers from the center of Bandol.

Water Sports
NATUR'EVASION
Parking du Stade Deferrari;
tel. 04 94 29 52 48; https://naturevasion.com;
July-Aug. daily 9:30am-1:30pm and 4:30pm-7:30pm;
from €20 for a half-day rental
Rent a kayak or an electric bike and head around the coast to discover hidden coves and beaches. The staff are helpful and can provide advice on times and itineraries. Guided trips are available.

BANDOL PLONGEE
Quai de la Consigne, Place n°6; tel. 06 07 45 2781;
www.bandol-plongee.com; initiation dive €60
This established scuba diving school offers dives along the coast for all levels.

Hiking
SENTIER DU LITTORAL
Depart avenue Albert 1er, Anse de Renecros;
*www.bandoltourisme.fr/fileadmin/user_upload/Itineraire_*
Le_Sentier_du_Littoral_sentier_des_Vignes.pdf
This coastal path between Bandol and Saint-Cyr Les Lecques is closed at one section due to instability. Thankfully, it's still possible to walk along much of the coast, but at Port d'Alon you need to cut inland and take the 4-kilometer (2-mile) Sentier du Vignes, to Saint-Cyr. See the listing above for Saint-Cyr. At times the Sentier detours through residential areas, but most of the time it follows the coast, offering delightful views out to sea. Expect the odd rocky section, and consider lunch and a swim at the Calanque Port d'Alon. The walk to the calanque and back is approximately 9 kilometers (6 miles) and takes around 3 hours.

★ Wine Tasting
DOMAINE TEMPIER
1082 chemin des Fanges; tel. 04 94 98 70 21;
http://domainetempier.com; Mon.-Fri. 9am-noon and
2pm-6pm; from €18
The reference domaine for Bandol wine, Domaine Tempier still operates out of a small tasting room at the back of the family home. For serious tasters, it's all about the reds; an aged tempier has an aroma of fine cigar, and swirls of rich long-lasting flavor hit the back of the throat. Tempier reds age extremely well for up to 10 years or more. Getting your hands on an older bottle, though, is difficult, so you will need to have the facilities to store the wine yourself.

CHATEAU PIBARNON

410 chemin de la Croix des Signaux, La Cadière d'Azur; tel. 04 94 90 12 73; www.pibarnon.com/fr; Mon.-Sat. 9am-noon and 2pm-6pm; from €18

The circle of vines that surround the tasting room and rise in steps up the hillside are reminiscent of a Roman theater. It's certainly a spectacular setting to taste wine. The rosé is one of the best in Provence: complex with plenty of fruit flavors and full of delicate aromas. It is distinguished by its minerality and structure, making it an ideal accompaniment for food.

DOMAINE LES LUQUETTES

Chemin des Luquettes, La Cadière d'Azur; tel. 04 94 90 02 59; www.les-luquettes.com; Mon.-Sat. 8:30am-7pm; from €16

This small family domaine of only 12 hectares (30 acres) offers an intimate tasting experience. The range of wines is much smaller than you'll find at the larger estates, but the tasting room opens onto a shady garden where you can sit and sample magnificent mourvedre-based reds and a delicate mourvedre and cinsault rosé.

Food

LA CHIPOTE

12 Corniche Bonaparte; tel. 04 94 29 41 62; www.restaurant-lachipote.com; Tues.-Sun. noon-3pm; €14-28

The Var coast is full of restaurants on idyllic beaches; however, La Chipote with its sweeping view over the Renécros beach is up there with the best. The food is a cut above the average with inventive salads and fresh seafood dishes. The garlic and parsley squid could not be fresher.

LA GOÉLETTE

Plage Anse de Renecros; tel. 04 94 29 33 17; www.thalazur.fr/bandol/hotel/restaurant-plage; daily noon-3:30pm; July and Aug. additional evening service 7:30pm-10pm; €26-48

Set on a shaded deck just meters from the sea, La Goelette serves food that is as about as good at it gets on the beach. The staff are

charming, and the clientele a mix of passing trade and well-heeled residents at the associated spa hotel. Fresh lobster from the tank is a specialty. Reserve in season.

BENDOR PLAGE

Ile de Bendor; tel. 04 94 05 54 68; www.lesilespaulricard.com/restaurants/bendor-plage; daily in season 10am-7pm, check website for evening hours; €12-28

Bendor Plage, the main restaurant on Ile de Bendor, enjoys a beautiful setting looking back over the sandy beach toward the mainland. The food is decent but not spectacular; many will find themselves choosing the reassuring security of a burger.

L'AMIRAL

Allée Jean Moulin; tel. 04 94 29 40 61; Tues.-Sun. 8am-7pm; €12-20

Located on the corner of a church square facing the port, L'Amiral is a large café-restaurant with a bustling atmosphere. It's great for people watching, particularly on market days. The food is good seaside fare. The moules frites (mussels with fries), which come with a choice of sauces, are hard to beat.

L'ESPÉRANCE

21 rue du Dr-Louis-Marçon; tel. 04 94 05 85 29; www.lesperance-bandol.com; Wed.-Sun. noon-1:15pm and 7:15pm-9:15pm; menus from €33

This is an address for foodies, for whom sublime food is more important than a sublime view. Kick off the flip-flops and dress up to enjoy dishes like roasted half pigeon with cêpes and a port sauce. Reserve in the summer season to be sure of a table.

Accommodations

HOTEL DU GOLF

10 Corniche Bonaparte; tel. 04 94 29 45 83; www.golfhotel.fr; €115 d

A 24-bedroom family hotel on Bandol's best beach, Anse de Renécros, the Hotel Du Golf is a good budget option for a few days on the Mediterranean. Rooms are simply furnished but have air-conditioning, Wi-Fi, and ensuite

Viticulture in Bandol

Vines were first cultivated in the Bandol area around 600 BC. Several centuries later, none other than Julius Cesar mentions the port of Tauroentum (now Saint-Cyr-sur-Mer), where large quantities of amphorae have been unearthed from the seabed. Historical documents through the subsequent centuries continue to refer to wines shipped out of the port of Bandol, a fishing village that eventually gave its name to the wine. The contemporary success of Bandol wines can be attributed to the cultivation of the mourvedre grape. Young red Bandol can be a little aggressive on the palate, but taste an aged wine (five years or more) and a remarkable transformation has taken place. The flavors have mellowed and softened, and experienced tasters note truffles, black cherries, and cinnamon as common characteristics. At a more accessible price point are the rosés, which are made from a combination of mourvedre, grenache, and cinsault; they rightly lay claim to being among the best in France.

grapes at harvest time

BANDOL WINERIES TO VISIT

- **Domaine Tempier** (1082 chemin des Fanges; http://domainetempier.com): Domaine Tempier, which still operates out of a small tasting room at the back of the family home, is known for its reds. A serious taster will appreciate the swirls of rich, long-lasting flavor.

- **Chateau Pibarnon** (410 chemin de la Croix des Signaux, La Cadière d'Azur; www.pibarnon.com/fr): Chateau Pibarnon's rosé is one of the best in Provence: complex with plenty of fruit flavors and full of delicate aromas.

- **Domaine les Luquettes** (Chemin des Luquettes, La Cadière d'Azur; www.les-luquettes.com): This small family domaine offers an intimate tasting experience where you can sample mourvedre-based reds and a delicate mourvedre and cinsault rosé.

bathrooms. Opt for a room with a terrace overlooking the sea if at all possible. Private parking adjacent to the hotel is included in the price.

HOTEL DELOS

L'Ile de Bendor;

tel. 04 94 05 90 90;

www.lesilespaulricard.com/hebergement/hotel-delos;

€200 d

If you enjoy the magic of being on a Mediterranean island and watching the sunset over the beach after the crowds have left by the last ferry, then Hotel Delos is for you. Simple comfortable rooms with air-conditioning, Wi-Fi and ensuite bathrooms are, of course,

part of the package, but the real joy is the tranquility of the Ile de Bendor at night and first thing in the morning.

★ HOTEL ILE ROUSSE

25 boulevard Louis Lumière;

tel. 04 94 29 33 00;

www.thalazur.fr/bandol/hotel; €280 d

A budget buster, with even the simplest rooms coming at nearly €300, the Hotel Ile Rousse has a spectacular infinity pool overlooking the Anse de Renécros Plage. The rooms are modern with terraces overlooking the sea. Many clients come for the spa treatments and wander around cosseted in fluffy white bathrobes.

HOTEL DE LA BAIE

62 rue du Dr Louis Marçon; tel. 04 94 29 40 48;
www.hoteldelabaie.pro; €100 d

The Hotel de Baie offers 14 modern, simply decorated rooms with Wi-Fi, air-conditioning, and ensuite bathrooms. Most of the rooms have sea views and small terraces, so check when you book. The nearest beach is just across the road. For a few days in Bandol this is a good basic base.

Getting There and Around

Upon arrival the best way to get around is **on foot.**

BY CAR

Bandol is located off the A50 coastal autoroute, which runs between Toulon and Aubagne. From **Aix-en-Provence,** take the A52 and then the A50, covering 75 kilometers (47 miles) in 58 minutes.

BY BUS

Bus Line 8001 (www.varlib.fr) connects the coastal villages and towns of Bandol, Saint-Cyr, Le Castellet, La Cadière d'Azur, and La Ciotat. It runs three times a day. Bus **Line 8005** connects the coastal towns of Bandol and Sanary to Toulon. It runs 10 times a day Monday to Friday, taking approximately 30 minutes to Sanary and an hour to Toulon. Single tickets on both lines cost €3.

BY TRAIN

Trains run hourly from Marseille (45 minutes) and Toulon (30 minutes) to Bandol (Avenue de La Gare). Note the **train station** (www.oui.sncf.com) is inland, approximately 2 kilometers (1 mile) from the beach. Single tickets cost around €10.

SANARY-SUR-MER

You can drive through Sanary-sur-Mer and think there's not much to it. The port area is wide and attractive, but the real charm of the town lies hidden. The narrow streets and squares of the old town are tucked away, And the resort's best beaches are not immediately accessible from the center of town. Consequently, Sanary reveals its beauty slowly and only to determined visitors. The cliff-side path from port side to Plage Portissol is a delight.

Sights
LA CHAPELLE NOTRE-DAME DE PITIÉ

Chemin de La Colline;
summer daily 8:30am-8pm, winter 9am-6pm

Take the steps on the western side of the port and climb onto a pedestrian path that leads around the headland. High on the hill you encounter the Chapel Notre-Dame de Pitié. The building started life in the 18th century as a lookout point during storms and for spotting enemy boats. Over the years, it was used to house plague victims and the injured from the Franco-Prussian war. Restored in 2008, it is now a peaceful small chapel with a magnificent view out to sea. Juxtaposed with the simplicity of the chapel, the beauty of the location conjures a sense of divinity.

LES EXILES

1 quai du Levant;
tel. 04 94 74 01 04;
Mon.-Fri. 9am-6pm, Sat. 9am-1pm and 2pm-5pm

From the early 1930s, Sanary-sur-Mer became a place of refuge for German intellectuals fleeing the Nazi regime. Philosophers, writers, poets, and politicians frequented the town's cafés, playing chess while they waited for their papers to be approved. During this period, Sanary became known as the world capital of German literature. Pick up a map from the tourist office and follow in the footsteps of the exiles around the town.

Beaches
PLAGE PORTISSOL

1-131 boulevard Frédéric Mistral

This popular half-moon bay is linked to the Port of Sanary by the chemin de la Colline. There are a couple of beach clubs and a hotel-restaurant. The beach itself is stony, but the waters are clear and it's a lovely place to swim.

PLAGE DU LEVANT

Parking l'Esplanade

This small sandy beach near the center of town is a good spot for a quick swim, but to spend a day on the beach, Plage Portissol is preferable.

Water Sports
SANARY LOCATION

Quai Levant;
tel. 06 29 47 41 02;
www.sanary-location-bateau.fr; daily 9am-6pm;
from €140 for a half day

Sanary Location is a great boat-rental service that offers speedboats with and without boating permits, giving visitors the opportunity to explore up and down the coast. Water sports equipment is also available to rent, including wakeboards, water skis, and inflatables to tow. For those wishing to stick to dry land, there are also e-bikes to rent.

SANARY JET SKI

Parc de l'Esplanade; tel. 06 80 61 59 57;
www.sanary-jetski.fr; June-Sept. 10 daily 9am-6pm,
May weekends only; from €20 for a 15-minute ride

Chose between getting towed round the bay on an inflatable donut and a Jet Ski lesson. Experienced riders can head out to sea and discover the coast by themselves. Advice on places to go and timing of trips is available.

Food and Accommodations
KIMA PLAGE

Plage Portissol; tel. 04 94 74 50 90;
www.kima-plage.com;
June-Sept. daily 11am-11pm; €15-25

With a location like this it's hard to quibble. On the odd occasion the relaxed vibe leads to slow service, but generally a meal at Kima gets close to beachside perfection. The restaurant, which perches on the rocks shaded by an old pine tree, serves simple grilled fish and salads. In the evening as the sun descends over the sea, it's an incredibly romantic spot for a dinner.

LA P'TITE COUR

6 rue Barthélémy-de-Don; tel. 04 94 88 08 05;
www.laptitecour.com; Thurs.-Mon. noon-1:30pm and
7:30pm-9:30pm, July- Aug. daily 7:30pm-9:30pm,
closed Wed. evening; menus from €30

This is an extremely popular small courtyard restaurant in the heart of Sanary. It has a loyal clientele of locals and tourists who return year after year. The food is light and delicate, and it's an excellent value. In early spring, the terrace is covered in purple wisteria blooms. Dishes might include fish of the day served

Plage Portissol, Sanary-Sur-Mer

with a leek tart and a lemon sauce. A reservation is advisable.

★ O PETIT MONDE

Plage Portissol; tel. 04 94 34 39 59; www. opetitmonde.com; restaurant €24-29; rooms €180 d

O Petit Monde on the Portissol Plage in Sanary-sur-Mer is a restaurant with rooms. The restaurant is located on the ground floor, with tables close enough to the sea that you can feel the spray. The five rooms, all with ensuite bathrooms, are on the upstairs terrace. They are spacious and each has outside space with sun loungers and tables. Guests wake up to an empty beach, breakfasting with the priceless sensation of having the Mediterranean to themselves. Bookings for the summer season need to be made several months in advance.

HOTEL L'ATMOSPHÈRE

13, rue Gabriel Péri; tel. 04 94 88 10 29; www.hotelatmosphere.com; €100 d

A block back from Sanary's colorful port, the hotel was renovated in 2018 and offers comfortable modern rooms with Wi-Fi, air-conditioning, and ensuite bathrooms. There's a small shady courtyard for breakfast, and the restaurants and beaches of Sanary are just a few hundred meters away. The nearest parking is Parking de L'Esplanade. In season, Sanary is a buzzy place, and L'Atmosphère lives up to its name by putting you in the heart of the festivities.

Getting There and Around

Upon arrival, Sanary is best explored **on foot.**

BY CAR

Sanary is off the A50 coastal autoroute, which runs between Toulon and Aubagne. From **Aix-en-Provence,** take the A52 and then the A50, covering 77 kilometers (48 miles) in 1 hour.

BY BUS

Zou Bus Line 8005 (www.varlib.fr) connects the coastal towns of Bandol and Sanary to Toulon. It runs 10 times a day Monday to Friday, taking approximately 30 minutes from Toulon to Sanary. A single journey costs €3.

BY TRAIN

Trains run hourly from **Sanary Ollioules** (around 3 kilometers/2 miles from the center of Sanary) to **Marseille** (45 minutes) and **Toulon** (15 minutes). Timetable details can be found at www.oui.sncf.com. The cost of a single journey from Marseille is €12, and €2 from Toulon.

TOULON

Toulon is a city that, like Marseille, is in the process of rediscovering itself. Twenty years ago, the old town (roughly the area between avenue de la République and boulevard Strasbourg) was deserted with abandoned public spaces and crumbling buildings and streets. Thanks to a major renewal program aimed at restoring Toulon's status as the capital of the Var, the center has been revitalized. Landmark buildings such as the opera house on Place Victor Hugo have been renovated, and major squares and roads (Place de la Liberté and Place de la République) have been transformed. New fountains have been built, and associations of shop keepers (see the rue des Arts listing below) created. From the museums to the beaches, the municipal government has been bent on transforming the city and celebrating its proud naval tradition as the home of France's Mediterranean fleet since the 16th century. There is still some work to do though. Compared to the rest of Provence, Toulon has a slightly run-down air.

However, sightseers, particularly those with an interest in history, should not be put off. Catching the cable car and looking down at the Rade (Toulon's harbor) from the heights of Mont Faron is the best way to appreciate the size of the harbor and its importance to the city. There's also a fascinating exhibition and memorial commemorating the World War II allied landings in Provence. Alternatively, hop on a boat and tour the bay's docks and naval

Toulon

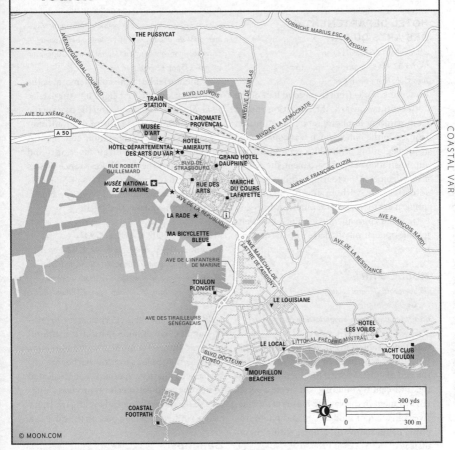

installations. There's usually a warship or two to marvel at.

Sights
★ MUSÉE NATIONAL DE LA MARINE

Place Monsenergue, quai de Norfolk; tel. 04 22 42 02 01; www.musee-marine.fr/toulon; July-Aug. daily 10am-6pm, June and Sept. Wed.-Mon. 10am-6pm; €6.50, reduced €5.50

Founded in 1814, Toulon's naval museum is located in the port's old arsenal. Visitors enter through a monumental arch that dates back to 1738. The building and the adjacent clock tower are rare historical survivors of World War II. Inside the museum, exhibits illustrate Toulon's key importance to French naval power. Model ships are plentiful, including some large many-meters-long examples that were used to train sailors in the 18th century. Other objects of interest include navigational aids and weapons. Up the stairs on the first floor, the museum moves on to the history of Toulon in the 20th century, depicting key events, such as the scuttling of the French fleet during World War II to prevent the ships falling into German hands. It's a wonderfully evocative museum to visit, particularly in relation to Anglo-French naval rivalry over the centuries.

HÔTEL DÉPARTEMENTAL DES ARTS DU VAR

236 boulevard Général Leclerc;
tel. 04 83 95 18 40; https://hda.var.fr/;
Tues.-Sun. 10am-6pm; free

Presenting works from the second half of the 20th century onward, the collection ranges from painting to photography to sculpture. Housed in the hotel, which was constructed at the beginning of the 20th century for the administration of the département, the gallery also welcomes major touring exhibitions from across France, with an aim of opening up modern art to the general public. Admission is free, and consequently it's a great and enjoyable opportunity to delve into the creative universe.

MUSÉE D'ART

113 boulevard Général Leclerc;
tel. 04 94 36 81 01;
https://toulon.fr/envie-bouger/article/musee-d-art;
admission prices to be determined

Currrently subject to a major renovation, this museum is scheduled to reopen its doors at the end of 2019. Architectural remodeling of the 19th-century building will create a better environment to display the museum's extensive collection of modern art and photography. The museum will reopen with a major display of the works of Picasso.

LA RADE

Toulon; tel. 04 94 46 29 89;
www.visitedelaradedetoulon.com; daily tours, see
website for timetable; €13, children 4-10 €8

La Rade is the name given to Toulon's large deep-water harbor. Boat tours take visitors around the bay past Toulon's naval base, where battleships and aircraft carriers are frequently moored, to the commercial port and the old naval docks. The boat then sweeps around the entrance to the harbor, taking in a mussel farm, the fortifications, and the long outer seawall. The trip takes about an hour.

MÉMORIAL DU DÉBARQUEMENT ET DE LA LIBÉRATION DE PROVENCE

8488 route du Faron; tel. 04 94 88 08 09;
www.onac-vg.fr/hauts-lieux-memoire-necropoles/
memorial-du-debarquement-et-de-la-liberation-de-
provence-mont-faron; Wed.-Mon. 10am-12:30pm and
1:15pm-5:15pm; €5, reduced €2

This memorial building commemorates the moment when, at first light on August 15, 1944, allied soldiers landed on the coast of the South of France. Inside there is a multimedia explanation of the liberation, code-named Operation Dragoon. With air superiority and the support of the French Resistance, it was only a few days before the cities of Marseille and Toulon were liberated from the Nazis. German units quickly fled north.

MONT FARON CABLE CAR

2 boulevard Amiral Vence; tel. 04 94 92 68 25;
July-Aug. daily 10am-7:45pm, May-June and Sept.
10am-7pm, Feb. and Nov. 10am-5:30pm, Apr. and
Oct. 10am-6:30pm, Mar. 10am-6pm; €7 adults, free
under 4

Built in 1958, the cable car runs every 10 minutes and takes 6 minutes to reach the summit of Mont Faron. From the top at 584 meters (1,916 feet), the views over the harbor are unsurpassed. There's a specialist zoo dedicated to helping wild cat species reproduce, a nature park, and walking and cycling trails. It's also permitted to bring a bike on the cable car.

Beaches

MOURILLON BEACHES

Littoral Frederic Mistral, Toulon

Just east of the port area is a series of four sandy coves. Behind them is a park and kids amusement center. The beaches have lifeguards, restaurants, and boat-rental facilities, and are very popular with families in the summer. They are reached by bus Lines 3 and 23 of the Mistral network (www.reseaumistral.com/en).

MÉJEAN AND MAGAUD COVES

Chemin du Fort du Cap and chemin de La Mer

These two adjacent coves set at the foot of

Naval Power and the Napoleonic Wars

At the beginning of the 19th century, Britain ruled the waves. However, the French, under Emperor Napoleon, were the undisputed military land power of continental Europe. To keep French plans to invade Britain at bay, the Royal Navy blockaded the French ports of Brest and Toulon. Early in 1805, Admiral Nelson gave the order for the British ships under his command to loosen the blockade of Toulon, hoping to lure the French ships under the command of Villeneuve out into battle. The strategy backfired, and Villeneuve and the French Mediterranean fleet escaped. The French commander's orders were to link up with the Spanish fleet in the Caribbean; raise the British blockade of the French Atlantic fleet at Brest; and head to the English Channel to clear the waters of British ships. Nelson ordered his fleet off their station outside Toulon and gave chase. He finally caught up with Villeneuve months later at Cape of Trafalgar on the coast of Spain. The French commander had successfully linked up with his Spanish counterpart, stacking the numeri-

Pierre Charles Villeneuve

cal odds against the British—33 to 27 ships—but Nelson made a revolutionary tactical decision. Rather than attack in a formation parallel with the French line, he cut across the line of the enemy boats, instantly creating a melee that the superior seamanship of the English could exploit. The French and Spanish fleets lost 22 ships, the British none.

pine-fringed cliffs and lined with fishermen's cottages are blessed with clear lagoon-like water that's ideal for snorkeling. Here you'll find pebble beaches bordered by rocks. They can be reached by taking bus Line 23 of the Mistral network (www.reseaumistral.com/en) or by walking the coastal footpath.

Sports and Recreation
COASTAL FOOTPATH

Depart Tour Royale, Toulon

Running from the Tour Royal tower all the way to the Magaud cove, the coastal footpath skirts the Mourillon beaches. Here it is bordered by parks, and it's good for cycling and Rollerblading as well as walking. The trail becomes wilder and more rugged as it heads out of town. Unsurprisingly, it was once used by smugglers. The walk to the cove and back is 11 kilometers (7 miles) and takes approximately 4 hours. You can also return from the cove by bus; use Line 23 of the Mistral network (www.reseaumistral.com/en).

MA BICYCLETTE BLEUE

Quai du Président Pierre Fournel;
tel. 06 28 58 60 13;
www.mabicyclettebleue.com; Mon.-Sat.
8:30am-6:30pm; from €15 a day

Toulon offers plenty of interesting rides for cyclists. Try taking a bike up the Mont Faron cable car and following the marked trails, or riding the beginning of the coastal path as it leaves the harbor and passes the Mourillon beaches. Ma Bicyclette Bleue offers city bikes and electric bikes, and will even deliver to your door for orders over €50.

TOULON PLONGEE

Le Drakkar, quai des Sous/Mariniers;
tel. 06 09 43 16 23; www.toulonplongee.com;
open year-round by reservation;
beginning course from €65

The coast around Toulon is rich in dive sites. This friendly diving club organizes dives for all levels and will help you discover the best the Var coast has to offer.

YACHT CLUB TOULON

Plage du Mourillon, Lieu Dit Anse Tabarly;
tel. 04 94 46 63 18;
daily 9am-noon and 1:30pm-5pm;
from €13 per hour

Yacht Club Toulon rents kayaks and stand-up paddleboards, and offers helpful advice on where to explore.

Shopping

RUE DES ARTS

Rue Pierre Semard; www.ruedesarts.fr

An association comprising artists and designers has helped revitalize rue Pierre Semard in the heart of Toulon's old town. Boutiques selling individual creations, including underwear, pottery, and works of art, now line this funky narrow road.

MARCHÉ DU COURS LAFAYETTE

Cours Lafayette;
Tues.-Sun. 7:30am-12:30pm

One of the most celebrated markets of Provence takes place every morning (except Monday) on the Cours Lafayette, which stretches away to the northeast from the Port. In addition to fruit and vegetables, there are textiles, flowers, and artisan products, such as locally made soap and olive-wood boards.

Festivals and Events

FORT SAINT LOUIS FIREWORK DISPLAY

Toulon; July 14 and Aug. 15

One of the largest fireworks displays in Provence is held every August in Toulon. The Mourrillon beaches and parks fill with crowds keen to secure a good spot to see the fireworks over the bay at around 11pm. There's a musical accompaniment synchronized with each bang, and the reflections of the cascading sulphorous explosions in the water give the display double the normal impact. A smaller display takes place on the July 14 in celebration of Bastille Day.

Food

L'ESCALE

4 Sentier des Douaniers, Anse de Méjean; tel. 04 94 36 06 64; daily noon-2pm and 7pm-9:30pm; €23-25

It's like you've jumped back a few decades in time at L'Escale. Surrounded by the rickety houses of fishermen, the restaurant sits on a terrace right on the water's edge. The tables and chairs are plastic, and the place feels both temporary and like it has been there forever. The overall experience is charming, munching on squid fried in parsley, sipping a local white, and gazing out at the sparkling sea.

Toulon's naval museum is located in the port's old arsenal.

RESTAURANT BERNARD

367 chemin de la Mer, Anse Magaud;
tel. 04 94 27 20 62;
Tues.-Sat. noon-2pm and 7pm-9pm.,
Sun. noon-2pm; €26-59

Restaurant Bernard is a slightly more serious restaurant than L'Escale in the neighboring bay. Even so, there's nothing to stop you from taking a dip, dusting off the sand, pulling on a T-shirt, and sitting down for lunch. The joy, once again, is the combination of freshly caught seafood and an uninterupted sea view. True seafood lovers should order the bouillabaisse 24 hours in advance. Booking is sensible in the summer months.

LE LOCAL

455 Littoral Frédéric Mistral;
tel. 04 94 20 61 32;
www.restaurant-lelocal.fr;
Wed.-Sat. noon-1:30pm and 8pm-9:30pm, Tues.
8pm-9:30pm; €31 menu, mains €18

The tables may be wooden and there may not be any tablecloths, but Le Local is a cut above your average bistro. The food is staggeringly good for the prices charged. Ingredients are sourced locally and seasonally, and colorful plate after colorful plate emerges from the kitchen, to the sound of the bubbling conversation of contented diners. Try fish of the day served with a sauce made from a stock of its own bones, infused with fennel.

L'AROMATE PROVENÇAL

32 rue Gimelli;
tel. 04 94 29 73 87;
www.aromate-Provençal.fr;
Tues.-Sat. noon-1:30pm and 7:30pm-9pm; €18-20

This small restaurant, located a couple of blocks from the station, is run by local graduates of Toulon's hotel school. The pride in their region and in everything that comes out of the kitchen is evident. The crowd is mainly locals with the odd tourist off the train who got lucky by accident. Try the melt-in-the-mouth roast baby chicken with fried *foie gras* and buttered new potatoes.

Bars and Nightlife
THE PUSSYCAT

655 avenue de Clarat; tel. 04 94 92 76 91;
Thurs.-Sun. 11pm-5am; free

The Pussycat is a good place to dance the night away. The clientele is a mixture of locals and tourists from the cruise boats. The atmosphere is friendly and the music is mainly dance classics.

LE LOUISIANE

12 rue Montauban; tel. 04 94 41 16 60;
Wed.-Sun. 6:30pm-2am; drinks from €5

This lively karaoke and piano bar is a little kitsch, but who cares? The place welcomes wannabe popstars of all ability.

Accommodations
HOTEL LES VOILES

124 rue Gubler; tel. 04 94 41 36 23;
www.hotels-toulon-mer.com; €100 d

A short walk from the Mourillon beaches, this hotel is clean and comfortable, and offers rooms with sea views and balconies. Each room has free Wi-Fi, ensuite bathrooms, and air-conditioning. Parking is available but needs to be booked ahead.

GRAND HOTEL DAUPHINE

10 rue Berthelot; tel. 04 94 92 20 28;
www.grandhoteldauphine.com; €70 d

The walls of the Grand Hotel—a family-run 55-bedroom hotel in the center of Toulon—are filled with the work of local artists, which adds a colorful splash to the walls. All rooms have ensuite bathrooms, Wi-Fi, and air-conditioning. The nearest secure parking is 50 meters (160 feet) away. Book in advance with the hotel for a special daily rate.

HOTEL AMIRAUTE

4 rue Adolphe Guiol; tel. 04 94 22 19 67;
www.hotel-toulon-amiraute.com; €60 d

This 50-bedroom hotel has clean modern rooms, all with air-conditioning, ensuite bathrooms, and Wi-Fi. It's particularly child-friendly, with board games on offer at reception, and the ability to have a child under 12

Into the Côte d'Azur and the Riviera

Saint-Tropez harbor is thick with well-to-do tourists.

To the east of Toulon begins one of the most famous stretches of coast in the world: the Côte d'Azur, or the French Riviera. To begin with there is little noticeable difference from the rest of the Var coast. The pick of the resorts to the immediate east of Toulon are **Le Lavandou Saint-Clair, Rayol-Canadel-sur-Mer,** and **Cavalaire-sur-Mer.** Slowly, though things begin to change. The farther east you go, the more Ferraris and Porsches begin to clog the roads. As you near the legendary bay of **Saint-Tropez,** helicopters buzz repeatedly overhead. From Saint-Tropez onward the big-name resorts continue—**Cannes, Nice, Monaco**—all the way to the Italian border. Apart from a protected area between **Saint-Raphael** and Cannes, the coast is heavily built up with villa after villa clinging to the cliff face. Even so, and despite the traffic and the in-your-face wealth, there's still something incredibly alluring about the region. Partly, this is because the climate is subtly different from the rest of Provence. Lemon and orange trees sprout, mimosa blooms in February, and verdant bougainvillea drapes terraces. If winter ever comes, then it only visits for a few days. It's best to visit any time other than during the summer months, when the overcrowding is almost unbearable. Out of season, daytime temperatures can still soar into the high 20s and low 30s Celsius (82°F to 90°F), but the crowds disappear, leaving gorgeous resorts like **Villefranche-sur-Mer** to the fortunate few.

stay in your room for free. The nearest parking is 100 meters (330 feet) from the hotel. Book in advance with the hotel for a special rate

Information and Services

The Toulon **tourist office** is located at 12 Place Louis Blanc. It offers advice and information on hotels, restaurants, and local activities. It is open Monday-Saturday 9am-5pm and Sunday 9am-1pm.

The **hospital,** Sainte Musse, is located at 54 rue Henri Sainte-Claire Deville in Toulon. It offers an emergency service.

Pharmacies are located throughout the town. Pharmacie de La Marine on 7 Place Gambetta is centrally located and open

Monday-Friday 8:30am-7pm and Saturday 8:30am-12:30pm.

Getting There

BY CAR

From Marseille: Toulon is 67 kilometers (41 miles) on the A50 motorway. The journey takes around 1 hour.

From Aix en Provence: Toulon is 86 kilometers (53 miles) away on the A52 and A50 motorway. The journey takes around 1 hour.

From Avignon: Toulon is 167 kilometers (104 miles) away on the A7 and A50 motorway. The journey takes around 1 hour and 47 minutes.

From Nice/Cannes: Toulon is 150 kilometers (93 miles) away on the A8 and A57 motorway. The journey takes around 1 hour and 50 minutes.

BY BUS

Zou Bus Line 8005 (www.varlib.fr) connects the coastal towns of Bandol and Sanary to Toulon. It runs 10 times a day Monday to Friday, taking approximately 30 minutes to get to Toulon from Bandol or Sanary. The **bus station** is at 331 boulevard Tessé. A single journey costs €3.

BY TRAIN

The **train station** is located on Place de l'Europe. Trains run every 15 minutes from Marseille, taking 1 hour costing €12. Trains also run hourly along the coast from Bandol, Sanary-sur-Mer, and Saint-Cyr Les Lecques. Consult the timetable at www.oui.sncf.

BY FERRY

Corsica Ferries (www.corsicaferries.com) operates daily ferries between Corsica and Toulon. The **port** is located at 2 avenue de l'Infanterie de Marine in Toulon. Prices vary according to the time and date of crossing. Including taking your car, a crossing can usually be found for €150. The length of the journey depends on the destination port in Corsica, and the time of crossing. The shortest journey time is 9 hours.

Getting Around

Upon arrival, Toulon is best explored **on foot.**

Reseau Mistral (www.reseaumistral.com) runs the Toulon **bus system** as well as ferries across the bay. Books of tickets can be bought in *tabacs* (tobacco shops) and cost €10 for 10 trips, or €3.90 a day. The bus system is largely used by local residents/commuters rather than tourists.

THE VAR AND THE VERDON REGIONAL NATURE PARK

Background

The Landscape

GEOGRAPHY

Provence is bordered to the east by the Côte d'Azur and the Maritime Alps, and to the west by the Rhône river. Its geography is varied, encompassing mountains, river deltas, fertile planes, and coastal areas.

The mountainous areas (Mont Ventoux, the Luberon Nature Park, Les Alpilles Nature Park, the Dentelles de Montmirail, Mont Sainte-Victoire, and the Gorges du Verdon) were created by the same tectonic lifting that gave rise to the Alps and the Pyrenees. The highest peak is Mont Ventoux at 1,912 meters (6,273 feet).

Provence's three main rivers are the Rhône, the Verdon (a tributary of the Durance), and the Durance, (a tributary of the Rhône). The flood plain of the Durance is the center for fruit growing in Provence. Farther south where the Rhône delta meets the sea in a wild, wet marshland known as the Camargue, rice is the principal agricultural product.

To the east of the Camargue, beginning on a stretch of coast known as the Côte Bleu and continuing again to the east of Marseille, there is a series of deep gorges cut into limestone cliffs. These gorges are known as calanques, a derivation from the word calanco which means "to fall" in Provençal. The calanques are renowned for their unspoiled clear blue waters. Heading farther east toward Toulon, the coast is characterized by a succession of seaside resorts with broad sandy bays.

CLIMATE

Provence has three climatic zones: continental, Mediterranean, and alpine.

The continental zone, referring broadly to inland Provence below the tree line, experiences significant annual variations in temperature, with temperatures in July and August regularly nudging 40 degrees and in winter frequently falling below zero.

The alpine climate is concentrated in the northwestern Vaucluse and in Haute Provence above 1,000 meters (3,280 feet). Once again, there are large variations in temperature. Warm Mediterranean air means summer temperatures reach the upper 20s to low 30s Celsius (low 80s to 90°F) during the day. However, in the winter the temperature can easily plummet to -20°C (-4°F). Snow is common.

Finally, there's the Mediterranean zone, which is situated along the coast and the inland areas bordering the coast. Here, winter temperatures remain mild with frosts uncommon.

The good news for visitors is that Provence is blessed with an inordinate amount of sunshine. Toulon gets nearly 3,000 hours of sun a year, making it the sunniest city in mainland France. The bad news is that it rains as much, if not more, in Provence than it does in Paris or London. Luckily, the rain usually comes in heavy bursts rather than a dull drizzle. The skies soon clear again.

No discussion of the climate of Provence is complete without a mention of the mistral wind. Sweeping down the Rhône valley from the Alps, the wind brings cold mountain air to Provence. Gusts frequently surpass 80 kilometers (50 miles) an hour, and the mistral can blow for up to 15 consecutive days. More commonly, it lasts one or two days. It can blow at all times of year and is notoriously unpredictable. Months can pass without a whiff of wind, and then suddenly the branches of trees stir and then their trunks bend. The mistral is at its strongest in the Rhône delta around Arles, Avignon, and the Camargue. It is also a fearsome force in Les Alpilles and the Luberon, but it fades away as you enter the Var.

ENVIRONMENTAL ISSUES

Climatic data, as always, is open to debate. A recent high temperature of 44 degrees was recorded in the Vaucluse département in 2019. However, a similar high of 44 degrees was recorded in the Var in 1982. Anecdotal evidence from farmers does suggest that weather patterns are becoming more extreme. Bee keepers in particular have been hit by reduced yields of honey, which they blame on global warming. Twenty years ago they expected 20 kilos (44 pounds) per hive of honey; that figure is now 10 kilos (22 pounds). Longer, hotter, dryer summers and warmer winters, mean that bees are active for more of the year. Consequently, they suffer from exhaustion and struggle to find flowers to pollinate.

Plants and Animals

PLANTS

Much of the landscape of Provence is taken up by the garrigue, a scrubland typically found on limestone soils where wild herbs such as lavender, thyme, sage, rosemary, and artemisia thrive.

Pine trees flourish throughout Provence. The main varieties are aleppo, maritime, stone, and northern. Oak trees are also prevalent in three main varieties: holm, kermes and cork oak. The kermes oak is the principal tree of the garrigue. Its leaves have a special protective layer that slows evaporation. Other species of tree include chestnut and olive trees. The latter grow wild as well as in farmed plantations.

ANIMALS

Mammals

The most frequently spotted large wild mammals are wild boar. They are nocturnal, so sightings are most common at dusk and dawn. Boars travel in family troops and can be dangerous to humans, particularly if there are young. It's best to steer clear if possible. There are also rare wolf sightings, largely in Haute Provence, but as recently as 2015, pairs were believed to have attacked livestock around Aix-en-Provence. Less threatening is an encounter with the largest species of beaver in Europe, which weighs between 20 to 40 kilos (44 to 88 pounds) and lives in the Luberon. You'll know these animals have been present if you spot claw markings on trees and branches sharpened to a point like pencils. Wild hare, chamois, and deer are also commonly seen throughout Provence.

Birds

Birdlife is abundant in Provence. The Luberon and the Gorges du Verdon are home to rare birds of prey, including three species of vulture and three eagle species. Pheasants and guinea fowl roam wild throughout Provence. Nightingales are also common. The Camargue delta is a center for migratory birds. Some species end their migration in the nature reserve, with large colonies of herons and Egrets nesting in the trees. During the winter, resident species include ducks, geese, cranes, birds of

a wild chamois in spring

prey, and several rarer species, such as the tiny penduline tit. Winter is also the best time to watch flamingos in the Camargue, when the population shows off their colorful new plumage during courtship displays.

Reptiles, Arachnids, and Insects

The diverse flora and fauna of the garrigue host nearly 300 species of insect. Lizards are common, including in the Luberon, the ocelle lizard, the largest lizard in Europe. Turning over too many rocks is not advisable, because Provence has two species of scorpion. The sting of the dark brown almost black one (*euscorpius flavicaudis*) is relatively harmless, but if you get stung by the lighter, yellowy orange scorpion (*buthus occitanus*) it's best to hurry to the hospital.

History

PREHISTORY

The earliest sign of humans in Provence is found in the Grotte Baume Bonne near Quinson in the Gorges du Verdon. Here, marks on the walls suggest the presence of men some 400,000 years ago. In the Cosquer Cave, in Les Calanques just outside Marseille, the walls of the cave (now accessed by an underwater passage) contain drawings dating between 27,000 BC and 19,000 BC. It is assumed that Provence was home to Stone Age populations well before this, but, other than the Grotte Baume Bonne, there have been no significant finds. An archaeological dig at Châteauneuf-les-Martigues suggests that around 6,500 BC the Castelnovian people who lived on the wetlands outside what is now Marseille were one of the first groups in Europe to abandon a migratory existence in favor of the domestication of sheep. From 10 BC on there is evidence of the arrival of the Ligurian people eastward into Provence. It is thought the Ligurians were responsible for the earliest bories (conical shaped stone buildings that you can still see all over Provence today). Shortly afterward, the Celts arrived from the north and the combined Celto-Ligurian civilization constructed fortified towns, or *oppida,* an example of which is the Oppidum d'Entremont built around 200 BC outside Aix-en-Provence.

EARLY HISTORY

The Greek trading post of Massalia (Marseille) was established around 600 BC by traders from Phoccea. When Phoccea was destroyed by the Persians around 550 BC, Massalia became a refuge for its citizens. The settling Greeks were not conquerors but traders. Massalia became an independent republic governed by its 600 wealthiest citizens. The Greeks introduced money, wine, the olive tree, and fruit trees such as cherry and fig into Provence. They were responsible for its first inland towns at Glanum near Saint-Rémy-de-Provence and Mastrabala (Saint-Blaise) on the Étang de Berre. By 3 BC the Roman Empire was becoming an increasing force. Its initial efforts were concentrated on the conquest of Spain. The Greeks supported this effort and were allies of the Romans in the Roman Empire's war against the Carthaginian Empire. In return, the Romans supported Greek efforts to suppress the Celto-Ligurian tribes of Provence.

After the defeat of Spain, the republic of Massalia in 125 BC invited Roman forces into Provence to help with the fight against the Celto-Ligurians. The Romans won notable victories, including a battle in 123 BC at the Oppidum d'Entremont under general Gaius Sextius, which led to the establishment of Aix (Aqua Sextius). The Romans remained in Provence to keep the land route open between

Historical Timeline

about 400,000 years ago	The first evidence of humans in Provence, some 400,000 years ago, is in the Grotte Baume Bonne.
27,000 BC to 19,000 BC	Cave drawings in the Cosquer Cave provide further evidence of Stone Age humans in Provence.
6,500 BC	Castelnovian people abandon their migratory existence and settle near Châteauneuf-les-Martigues.
10 BC onward	Provence sees the arrival of Ligurians from the east and Celts from the north.
600 BC	The Greek trading port of Massalia (Marseille) is established.
125 BC	Massalia invites Roman armies into Provence to help fight the Celto-Ligurians.
49 BC	Julius Caesar lays siege to and enters Massalia.
49 BC to 3rd century AD	Provence is "Romanized" with the construction of arenas, theaters, and forums.
5th century	The Roman Empire falls.
8th century	The Frankish Caroligian dynasty rules Provence.
879	Charles Boso breaks from the Caroligian dynasty and becomes King of Burgundy and Provence.

Rome and the empire in Spain, but they held back from full-scale conquest.

Things changed in 49 BC when Massalia chose to support Pompey in his dispute with Caesar. Caesar laid siege to and defeated Massalia, and over the next few centuries the Romanization of Provence began in earnest. Cities such as Apt, Arles, Avignon, and Vaison were established to give homes to former Roman legionaries. A major program of public works was established, resulting in the construction of theaters, arenas, baths, and aqueducts. Just as the power of the Roman Empire was fading in the 3rd and 4th centuries, Christianity began to take hold in Provence. Early churches were built on the sites of Roman forums and churches. A synod of bishops took place in Arles in 314. However, around the same time German tribes attacked and began to make progress into Provence. These invasions continued, and by the 5th century and the fall of Rome, the Visigoths had captured Arles.

THE FRANKS

Between the 5th and the 9th centuries Provence was not the safest place to live. Facing the dual threat of warring Germanic tribes from the north and the Muslim Saracens from the south, hill villages sprung up to provide at least some protection to inhabitants. By the 8th century Provence, at least in theory, was part of the Frankish empire. There were, however, many virtually autonomous local rulers; the Saracens controlled much of the Mediterranean coast and frequently sent armies inland. In 732 the Saracens challenged Frankish authority at the Battle of Tours near Poitiers in the center of France. Subsequently, Frankish power was consolidated under Charlemagne and the Carolingian dynasty. However, dynastic infighting in the 9th century once again opened

11th to 13th century	Provence is ruled by competing counts. This is the construction period for many Romanesque ecclesiastical buildings
1348	The Black Death strikes Provence.
1434 to 1480	Good King Rene of Provence rules.
1483	Provence passes to the French crown.
1536	Army of Holy Roman Emperor Charles V enters Provence.
1545	Massacre of Vaudois Protestants in Merindol.
1789	Rioting in Marseille in spring signals the beginning of the French revolution in Provence.
1790	Provence is divided into four départements.
1849	The Avignon-Marseille railway opens.
1942	November, Provence occupied by the Germans.
1944	August, Operation Dragoon is successful, and Provence is liberated.
1962	Algerian independence starts a wave of mass immigration to Provence.
1995	National Front wins control of Orange, Toulon, and Marignane.
2013	Marseille is declared the year's European Capital of Culture.

the door to the Saracens. Marseille was pillaged and Arles sacked. In 879 Charles Boso (known as Charles the Bald) broke away from the Carolingian kingdom of his brother-in-law Louis III and was elected King of Provence and Burgundy. The title was a hollow one, with Provence being controlled by rival local counts.

THE COUNTS OF PROVENCE

By the 12th century, control of Provence had passed to the Counts of Toulouse and the Counts of Barcelona. To the northeast, the land around Forcalquier formed an independent fiefdom. During this period, Provence enjoyed relative prosperity. Major Romanesque ecclesiastical buildings were constructed, including the Cistercian Abbeys of Thoronet, Silvacane, and Sénanque.

The Counts of Toulouse lost much of their land in the 13th century as a consequence of supporting the Cathars during their war with the French King. During the same century the Catalan count Raymond Béranger made his capital Aix-en-Provence and succeeded in creating a Provençal ministate that stretched as far north as Barcelonnette. After Béranger's death, control of Provence passed to the House of Anjou.

The 14th century was less than pleasant, as Provence faced twin menaces: The Black Death decimated the population, and returning mercenaries from the 100 Years' War pillaged what they could find.

Prosperity returned in the 15th century under Good King René (1434-1480), who established his court in Aix-en-Provence and was a notable patron of the arts. Control of Provence passed to the French crown when René's son died just one year after his succession to the crown.

THE FRENCH KINGS

Any feeling that the Provençaux had of lingering independence was swiftly crushed by French King Louis XI and his successor Charles VIII. Local officials were removed from their posts and replaced by royal appointees. The castles at Les Baux and Toulon were deemed too threatening and promptly destroyed. Jews, who until now had enjoyed religious freedom in Provence, were massacred in Arles and Manosque, and a policy of convert or leave was instigated.

In the early 16th century Provence was drawn into the conflict between King Francois I of France and the Holy Roman Emperor Charles V. The French succeeded in taking but not keeping Milan; in response Charles sent armies into Provence; they arrived at the gates of Aix-en-Provence and Marseille but never succeeded in entering the cities. The French army eventually drove the Emperors out, earning the King at least a modicum of loyalty from the Provençaux.

The second half of the 16th century was just as difficult. The Wars of Religion tore French society apart. Provence was split between the two faiths. For example, Avignon was staunchly Catholic, whereas Orange allowed Protestants to practice freely. Tension turned to action when in 1545 the parliament of Aix ordered the massacre of Vaudois Protestants in the Luberon town of Merindol.

Religious confusion reached its peak in 1584 when the European Catholic League seized Paris and drove out the King. The new Parisian government appointed their own alternative governor to Provence and named their own alternative capital of the region. The mess was only resolved when Henri IV converted to Protestantism.

Over the following centuries, royal power in Provence, as in the rest of France, became ever more firmly entrenched. The almost obsessive bureaucracy that still characterizes France today was born under Louix XIV, France's "Sun King" (1614-1715). Plague, famine, and taxes kept the countryside and small towns impoverished. Only Aix, Avignon, Arles, and Marseille prospered. In the run up to the 1789 revolution, Provence was hit by twin economic shocks: a fall in the price of wine, and a severe winter that killed off thousands of olive trees.

REVOLUTIONS

The French Revolution has been so popularized in literature and film that anglophones sometimes believe the dramatic version of events. It's as if, in one swoop in 1789, France rejected monarchy and became a republic. In fact there were successive revolutions and restorations. The French Revolution, the first one, began in 1789 and ended in 1799 with a coup d'état that installed Napoleon Bonaparte as First Consul. In 1814 with Napoleon supposedly defeated and exiled on Elba, Louis XVIII was restored to the throne of France. His reign was briefly interrupted by the return and subsequent defeat of Napoleon in 1815 at the Battle of Waterloo. Royal authority did not last long. In 1830 rioting over three days in Paris, led to the second revolution, the abdication of Louis XVIII's successor Charles X, and the creation of a new constitutional monarchy under Louis Philippe, Duke of Orleans. The big idea was to substitute the principle of hereditary right to throne with popular sovereignty. In fact, this proved about as successful as a Microsoft search engine, and Louis was overthrown in 1848 by more rioting in Paris. The second revolution installed Louis Napoleon Bonaparte as president of the Second French Republic.

Events in Provence need to be set against this broader context. During this 50-year period there were revolutionaries, royalists, and forces with local rather national loyalties, and the allegiances of cities, towns, and villages shifted between the three positions. The beginning of the first revolution in Provence can be traced to the Spring of 1789 when the population of Marseille revolted against the nobility and magistrates. From Marseille, Republicanism spread throughout Provence, and it was in Marseille that the new French national anthem, "La Marseillaise," was born and taken north to Paris by the city's Féderés guard. In inland Provence, counter-revolutionary forces organized and Royalism remained a dominant force up until the 1830s and the restitution of Louis Philippe to the throne. As with the rest of France there are horror stories from Provence of excessive revolutionary zeal, of arrest without charge, and even cannons being shot into cells as an expeditious method of execution. For a time, chaos reigned. Retrospectively one of the notable consequences of the revolution in Provence, was the creation of four cohesive government départements (Var, Vaucluse, Bouches-du-Rhône, and Basses Alpes) including the incorporation of papal territories of Avignon and the Comtat Venaissin.

Just as significant as the political upheavals was the Industrial Revolution, with a railway opening between Marseille and Avignon in 1849. Agricultural areas found it easy to get their produce to market, particularly with the expansion of the rail network to Paris. The same rail network gave birth to the tourist industry, with the beaches of Provence and the Côte d'Azur becoming popular meeting spots for high society.

WORLD WAR I

The battlefields of the first world war were a long way from Provence, and so the countryside and towns of the region were spared destruction. However, villages in particular suffered depopulation, losing entire generations of their young, who were sent to fight. To provide soldiers with their ration of wine, field upon field was planted with vines. The low-quality crop proved unprofitable after the war, and many vines were ultimately ripped up to make way for housing.

WORLD WAR II

France fell to the Germans in June 1940 and was divided into occupied and unoccupied zones. Provence was in the unoccupied zone until November 1942 when the Germans annexed the rest of France. The French Mediterranean fleet at Toulon destroyed its ships rather than let them fall into Nazi hands. Resistance fighters found refuge in the mountainous areas of Provence. Urban resistance in Marseille, in particular, was particularly difficult for the Germans do deal with. Parts of the city were no-go areas for German troops. To solve this problem, the Germans demolished Le Panier in 1943. Further destruction was caused by Axis bombing ahead of the planned landings. Marseille, Toulon, and Avignon were badly damaged. On August 15, 1944, Operation Dragoon was launched with landings across the south of France. The allied forces were assisted by local resistance fighters and a demoralized German army quickly fled north.

POST WAR

Algerian independence in 1962 led to an influx of hundreds of thousands of so-called *pieds noir* refugees. The *pieds noir* were mostly ethnic French, born in Algeria during the period of French rule from the 1830s onwards. A second wave of immigration from North Africa was encouraged by the government, stoking anti-immigration sentiment. By the late 20th century, the far-right Front National had become a major force in Provence. In the 1995 elections, the party under Jean-Marie Le Pen won control of Toulon, Orange, and Marignane. In 2002 Le Pen entered the Presidential race and enjoyed victories in five out of the six départements, which constituted the Provence-Alpes-Côte d'Azur (PACA) region. The onward march of a more sanitized version of the Front National continued in the 21st century. Le Pen's granddaughter Marion Maréchal Le Pen was elected from the Vaucluse to the National Assembly in 2012, while his daughter Marine Le Pen made it to final round of the Presidential campaign in 2017, finally losing to Emmanuel Macron.

The Provençal Language

Provençal is an Occitan dialect that was widely spoken throughout the south of France in medieval times. It was the base language of the lyric medieval poetry used by troubadours, who traveled from town to town performing their works. The troubadour tradition spread from the south of France throughout much of Europe. The beginning of the decline of the Provençal language was a royal decree of 1539 requiring all new laws made in Provence to be translated into French, not Provençal. At the end of the 19th century, the language was revived by a group of poets led by Frederic Mistral. Intent on preserving traditional Provençal culture, Mistral created a dictionary and transcribed the works of the troubadours. He also organized a traditional dress parade that still takes place in Arles. Today it is rare to hear Provençal spoken, although place names and business names are sometimes given in Provençal. For example, *lou pebre d'ai* is Provençal for the summer savory herb *sarriette,* a favorite of local donkeys, and is also the name of a restaurant in the Luberon village of Lauris.

Government and Economy

ORGANIZATION

The head of state in France is the president. He is directly elected for a five-year term. At the same time the electorate votes for candidates in the National Assembly, the legislative arm of the French government. The president appoints a prime minister and additional ministers who can call on the support of the majority of the members of the National Assembly. Because the Presidential election and the National Assembly election take place at the same time, the president is usually able to control policy making. A second less powerful political force is the Senate. Members of the Senate are elected by local officials, and in the event of a dispute between the Senate and the National Assembly, the National Assembly takes precedence.

On a local level, France is split into 96 départements, with each département controlled by a prefect appointed by central government. Since 1986 Regional Councils have been elected to discuss and pass laws relevant to each individual département. The Regional Councils take responsibility for matters such as housing, transportation, and schools. This book covers four départements: the Vaucluse, the Bouches-du-Rhône, the Var, and part of the Alpes d'Haute Provence.

POLITICAL PARTIES

The main political parties in France are as follows:

- **En Marche:** the new centrist party created by President Emmanuel Macron to contest the 2017 election.

- **The Republicans:** a right of center, socially conservative, pro-European party that holds the second-largest number of seats in the National Assembly.

- **The Socialists:** a center-left social democratic, pro-European party.

- **National Rally:** formerly the Front National, the party has a strong presence at a local level controlling 22 of the 74 regional councils.

ELECTIONS

During the final round of the 2017 presidential campaign, Emmanuel Macron of En Marche faced off against Marine Le Pen, the daughter of the founder of the Front National. The overall share of the vote was 66.1 percent to Macron and 22.9 percent to Marine Le Pen. The départements of Provence voted as follows: Var: 50.9 percent to Macron and 49.1 percent to Le Pen; Vaucluse: 53.5 percent to Macron and 46.5 percent to Le Pen; Bouche du Rhône: 57.8 percent to Macron and 42.2 percent to Le Pen; Alpes de Haute Provence: 58.5 percent to Macron and 41.5 percent to Le Pen. Therefore, compared to the national average, the far right performed much better in Provence than in the rest of France. Such results are attributable to concerns over immigration and a loss of identity. The next French presidential election will take place in 2022. Emmanuel Macron is eligible to stand again. All French citizens over age 18 are eligible to vote.

AGRICULTURE

Provence is a rich agricultural region, thanks to a varied landscape including both coastal and mountainous areas. Wine dominates employment with 20,340 vignerons in the PACA region. Fruit is the next biggest employer with 4,530 farmers, and then livestock (sheep and goats) with 1,550 farmers. Taken together, the number of farmers in Provence accounts for 4.5 percent of French agriculture.

Geographically, production is spread as follows: sheep, and goats tend to be raised in the mountainous areas and their foothills. On the plateau of Valensole, mixed grains and lavender are grown. Fruit cultivation is centered on a small area in the Rhône Valley and the river valley of the Durance. Vineyards can be found throughout Provence, although they are particularly predominant in the Var.

INDUSTRY

Industry tends to be concentrated around the major cities of Provence. Important sectors are alimentary products for agriculture, steel, energy, and chemicals. Major industrial sites include the Eurocopter helicopter-manufacturing business located adjacent to Marseille Marignane airport; petrochemical refineries at Fos; the Agroparc outside Avignon; and the ITER experimental fusion reactor near Manosque.

DISTRIBUTION OF WEALTH

The PACA region displays the second-highest level of inequality in France. The top 10 percent have a disposable income of more than €3,000 per month, while the bottom 10 percent have less than €800. Urban areas are the worst, with an estimated 31 percent of the population of Avignon and 26 percent of the population of Marseille living below the poverty line. Carpentras (30 percent), Cavaillon (28 percent), and Orange (23 percent) also have notable high levels of poverty. Part of the problem is lack of jobs; Provence has a high unemployment rate compared to the rest of France: 3.4 percent compared with the national rate of 3.2 percent.

TOURISM

Tourism is an essential part of the economy in Provence. International visitors account for approximately 6 million out of 18 million tourist arrivals. Major new tourist infrastructure projects are underway, including a new Picasso museum in Aix-en-Provence, a reconstruction of the Cosquer Cave in the Villa Mediterranée in Marseille, and the blockbusting Luma Arles project. At the same time there is a growing awareness of the dangers of overtourism. Villages such as Les Baux-de-Provence have become overrun by tourists and are no longer as enjoyable to visit as they once were. Directors of tourism across the regions covered in this book indicate that there is a real desire to promote the new and the undiscovered, whether this be a sight, village, or experience. This broadening of what Provence has to offer has successfully driven visitor numbers higher; tourism experienced 6 percent growth between 2016 and 2017.

People and Culture

DEMOGRAPHY AND DIVERSITY

The Provençaux are descended from the Celt, Ligurian, Italic, Greek, and Germanic peoples, as well as Moors and Saracens. Modern data on the ethnicity of the population is hard to come by. A law dating back to 1872 prevents the national census from collecting this information. However, surveys and polls are free to ask such questions, so a demographic pattern can be built up. Italians make up the most numerous non-indigenous population; around 8 percent of residents are at least partly of Italian origin if their lineage is traced back over three generations. Provence also has a disproportionately large North African population due to waves of migration after the end of World War II.

RELIGION

Provence like the rest of France is predominantly Roman Catholic. Secularism is spreading, and church attendance figures are not high. A survey of the whole of France in 2003 found that 65.3 percent of people considered themselves Roman Catholic, 27 percent atheist, and 12.7 percent belonged to a religion other than Catholicism. It is estimated that 5 million Muslims live in France. Precise figures are not available for Provence or the whole of France because of a law preventing the national census from collecting religious data.

LANGUAGE

The official language of Provence is French. It is a romance language and belongs to the Indo-European grouping of languages. Very rarely in Provence, you may hear Provençal being spoken. Provençal is not taught in schools. It was codified by poet Frederic Mistral at the turn of the 20th century. It is an Occitan language once used by medieval troubadours in their lyric poetry. Some place and business names are still given in Provençal form.

LITERATURE

Although he was not a native Provençal writer, or adoptive resident, Alexandre Dumas wrote some of the most memorable accounts of Provence in the middle of the 19th century. In *The Count of Monte Cristo* (1844) the description of Château d'If prison off the coast of Marseille is so evocative that it has transcended the boundary of fiction. Today many visitors to the island believe that Edmond Dantès, the hero of the book, was actually imprisoned there. Another classic of French literature, Victor Hugo's *Les Misérables* (1862), features Toulon prison, where the character Jean Valjean is incarcerated for stealing a loaf of bread.

A Parisian who frequently visited Provence, Alphonse Daudet wrote *Letters from a Windmill* (1869), which was first published in excerpt form in newspapers. Daudet's success was based upon describing rural life in Les Alpilles to a metropolitan elite audience. The book is, in fact, a collection of short stories. "Old Cornille's Secret" is typical. It tells the story of the last windmill in the region: Once the hills of Les Alpilles were filled with turning windmills, but the invention of the steam-driven mill put them out of business; the only exception is Old Cornille's, which, inexplicably, keeps turning. Nobody knows how he manages it. Day after day, he leaves the mill with his donkey laden with sacks of what everybody assumes must be flour. One day Cornille leaves the door to his windmill open and the locals discover there's no grain inside. Instead, the sacks on the donkey's back are filled with plaster from neighboring windmills that have been pulled down. Pride has driven Old Cornille to this pretense. From that day, the locals bring him grain to keep his mill turning.

Perhaps Provence's most famous literary son is Jean Giono. Born in 1895 in Manosque, Giono is the writer of works including *Colline* (1929), *The Horseman on the Roof* (1951) and *The Man who Planted Trees* (1953). After military service during World War I, Giono became a pacifist. In his work he returned again and again to the theme of man returning to nature in search of a more basic way of life. He even tried it for real, creating a Utopian community in the wilds of Haute Provence during the interwar years. As an introduction to Giono, *The Man who Planted Trees* is an inspiring short story that has achieved worldwide fame.

Henri Bosco's *Mas Théotime* (1945) is another deliberation on man's relationship with nature. An epic family story, it concerns the daily lives of peasant farmers. The narrative is centered around a farmhouse, just outside the Luberon village of Lourmarin. It's a gentle, slow, subtle book.

Born in Aubagne just outside Marseille, playwright, filmmaker, and novelist Marcel Pagnol is best known for his novels *Manon of the Spring* and *Jean de Florette* (1962). Filled with black humor and acutely observed detail, the novels are part morality tale, part tragedy, part love story. They are also a meditation on a great literary theme, explored most famously in Robinson Crusoe: whether living in a state of nature, stripped of all the trappings of civilization, is beneficial to the soul.

Pagnol's narrative centers around the attempt of Provençal peasant Ugolin to make his fortune from growing carnations. To do so he needs water, which is in abundant supply on his neighbor's land. After a couple of murders, the land in question is eventually inherited by Jean de Florette, a tax clerk. Jean decides to quit work and move to the countryside to make his fortune raising rabbits. Before his arrival, Ugolin blocks the spring, rendering Jean's land worthless and unsuitable for the rabbits. Ugolin sits back and waits for, what he assumes is, Jean's inevitable departure, when he will have an opportunity to buy the land. Jean refuses to leave and a generational saga ensues.

Never has an author provoked as much unjustified criticism and jealousy as Peter Mayle. Mayle was an advertising executive in London when he ditched the day job and started a new life in Provence. His weekly musings about the idiosyncrasies of the locals became first a newspaper column, and then a multimillion-selling series of books, beginning with *A Year in Provence* in 1989. The success of the series was such that it created a whole new literary genre, the "good life abroad" book. The books attracted tens of thousands of wanna-be Mayles to the Luberon. Ex-pats who already lived in the region turned on Mayle for ruining the area they loved. Without a hint of self-awareness, they complained that farmhouses were being converted into second homes at such a rate that the traditional character of the region was being lost. Literary critics attacked Mayle's portrayal of the locals as patronizing and disparaged his books. The French, however, took Mayle to their heart, recognizing what a great service he had done promoting Provence. He was awarded the government's most prestigious award and made a knight of the Legion d'Honneur in 2002. He was still writing right up until his death in 2018. Reading his work today, it's clear that Mayle was great storyteller with a gentle and generous sense of humor.

VISUAL ARTS

In the late 19th century an artistic revolution began in the South of France. In Arles and Saint-Rémy-de-Provence, Vincent Van Gogh was painting with aggressive, wild swirls of color. For a stormy nine-week period of intense painting, he was joined by Paul Gauguin, before the two men fell out. Meanwhile in Aix-en-Provence and L'Estaque, Paul Cézanne was throwing artistic norms out of the window. Painting in a wide variety of different styles, he played with perspective using first color to create it and then geometry at Bibémus quarry outside Aix, to flatten it.

Film Locations in Provence

Cinema's origins were in Provence. In 1895 the Lumière brothers directed a short black-and-white film entitled *A Train Arriving at La Ciotat Station*. It was one of the first ever moving picture films, and in 1896 when it was shown, the audience were reportedly so horrified at the image of the train steaming toward them that they screamed and ran to the back of the room. Fast-forward a century and Provence was rarely out of cinemas. Famous films included *Manon of the Spring* (1986) starring Emmanuel Beart, shot mainly in the southern Luberon and in the countryside outside Aubagne, and *Horseman on the Roof* (1995), which starred Juliette Binoche and was shot on location throughout Provence. Also released in 1995 *French Kiss*, starring Meg Ryan and Kevin Kline, was shot in the southern Luberon.

Visiting Provence, it's easy to stumble accidentally upon film locations. Stop for a drink at Bar de La Marine on Marseille's old port and you might recognize the place from the final scenes of *Love Actually* (2003); it's where Colin Firth's character proposes to his cleaning lady. Pause for a wine tasting at Château Canorgue outside Bonnieux and you'll be transported to the 2006 Ridley Scott adaptation of Peter Mayle's *A Good Year*. The film is a cinematographic tour de force, full of golden light and rolling hills. The vineyard is the main location, but other scenes were filmed around the *étang* in Cucuron and opposite the château in Gordes.

Most recently, *At Eternity's Gate* (2018) starring Willem Dafoe as Vincent Van Gogh is the latest attempt to explore the troubled life of the famous painter. Filmed on location outside Arles and Saint-Rémy de Provence, the rich Provençal light and countryside are again at the fore.

Both Van Gogh and Cézanne were outliers who struggled for success during their careers. Van Gogh famously committed suicide and Cézanne only achieved a sense of financial security at the end of his life, when the death of his father left him with enough money to build his own atelier. Both artists broke with the prevailing impressionist school that was associated with painters such as Monet, Renoir, and Sisley. Their use of color and distortion of the people and places before them paved the way for artistic movements to follow: fauvism, expressionism and cubism.

For want of a better name, Van Gogh and Cézanne were labelled post-impressionists. The name was first used by Roger Fry, who in London in 1910 put on an exhibition entitled "Manet and the Post Impressionists," which included work by Cézanne, Van Gogh, and Gauguin.

Around the same time as Fry's exhibition Georges Braque and Pablo Picasso were working together in the South of France developing ideas around the multiple uses of perspective. Braque was heavily influenced by Cézanne and in 1906 followed in his footsteps to L'Estaque, where Cézanne had marveled at the unique quality of the light. Braque and Picasso deconstructed objects and turned them into geometric pieces before putting them back together again. Unlike their predecessors, they produced work that was very much of their time and commercially successful. Picasso, who had a showman's personality to match his artistic skill, made a fortune. In 1958 he bought Château de Vauvenargues, outside Aix-en-Provence, where he was buried in 1973.

Even after the death of Picasso, the light of Provence continued to work its magic. Victor Vasarely (1906-1997) is a unique figure in the history of 20th-century art, the creator of an entirely new movement: optical art. While painting at Gordes, 1 hour to the north of Aix, Vasarely had a revelation. In the intense summer light, he noticed a contradictory perspective to the linear one he had been using: "Never can the eye identify to what a given shadow or strip of wall belongs, solids and voids merge into one another, forms and backgrounds alternate. Thus, identifiable things are transmuted into abstractions," he said of Gordes. A center dedicated to his work was constructed outside Aix in 1973, with Vasarely writing a personal message in the cement foundations. He shared only the first few words: "From Cézanne to Vasarely, we will be worthy."

MUSIC AND DANCE

The traditional dance of Provence is the farandole. It is a line dance performed to a flute or a drum. The dancers skip with every beat, alternating lead feet. To see it performed in traditional dress, head to the Roman Arena in Arles on the first Sunday in July.

Essentials

Transportation

GETTING THERE
From North America

Marseille airport offers direct flights via **Air Canada** (www.aircanada.com) and **Air Transat** (www.airtransat.com) from Montreal. Visitors coming from other North American destinations must fly first to major hubs such as Paris, Amsterdam, and London, and then take a connecting flight to Marseille.

Alternatively, North Americans can fly from New York direct to Nice, which is approximately 1 hour's drive from the area covered in

Marseille-Saint-Charles train station

this book. Flights are offered by **Delta** airways (www.delta.com/fr/en) and newcomer **La Compagnie** (lacompagnie.com).

From Europe
BY AIR
Easyjet, Ryan Air, and British Airways fly from London Gatwick, Manchester, Bristol, and Glasgow to **Marseille.**

Ryan Air (www.ryanair.com) flies from London Stansted, Manchester, and Edinburgh to Marseille.

British Airways (www.britishairways.com) flies from London Heathrow to Marseille.

Direct flights are available to Marseille from most major European capitals.

Avignon airport is a low-cost hub that has flights to and from Birmingham and Southampton with **Flybe.**

Similarly, **Nîmes airport,** which is a 45-minute drive from Avignon, is a low-cost hub, with Ryan Air flights from Stansted and Luton airports near London, as well as flights from Brussels.

Easyjet (www.easyjet.com) flies from London Gatwick, London Luton, and Bristol to Montpellier, which is a 1-hour drive from the nearest region covered in this book. There

are also flights to Montpellier from Paris, Berlin, Copenhagen, and Dublin.

BY TRAIN
The easiest way to get to Provence by train is to connect with France's **TGV** (high-speed train) network (www.oui.sncf). The main connection is out of Paris. There are TGVs from the Gare du Nord every hour to Marseille, which takes about 3.5 hours; most stop both at Avignon and Aix-en-Provence. There are also now daily trains (Spring to Autumn) from Barcelona to Avignon, Aix-en-Provence, and Marseille.

Eurostar (www.eurostar.com) operates a weekend service from May to mid-October from London to Avignon. The outward journey is nonstop, but the return trip involves getting off the train at Lille for passport control.

BY BUS
Oui Bus (ouibus.com) operated by the French railway service, offers connections from major cities such as Lyon and Paris to Aix, Avignon, and Marseille. **Flixbus** (flixbus.com) offers similar services. If you're booking on short notice, the prices tend to be much cheaper than the trains.

Previous: Country road outside Aix-en-Provence

BY FERRY

Corsica Ferries (www.corsica-ferries.fr) operates services from Corsica and Sardinia to Toulon. **Corsica Linea** and **La Meridionale** operate services from Corsica to Marseille. La Meridionale also operates a service from Sardinia to Marseille.

BY CAR

The main route from the north to Provence is the A7 autoroute which runs between Lyon, Avignon, and Aix-en-Provence. It is nicknamed the Autoroute du Soleil. At weekends in the summer months of July and August it is advisable to find alternative routes because the stretch between Avignon and Lyon becomes one long traffic jam.

The A8 autoroute runs from the Italian border near Nice to Aix-en-Provence, and the A9 runs from just outside Avignon to the Spanish border near Barcelona.

From Australia and New Zealand

The quickest way to get to the south of France is a flight to Dubai. From Dubai **Emirates** (emirates.com) flies direct to Nice. Alternatively, there are direct flights to Nice from Hong Kong.

South Africa

There are no direct flights to the South of France from South Africa. South Africans should fly to either London, Amsterdam or Paris and pick up a connecting flight.

GETTING AROUND

The best way to get around is by hiring a car. Major car hire companies such as **Hertz** (hertz.com), **Eurocar** (eurocar.com), and **Avis** (avis.com) have offices at the airports and TGV stations, as well as city center offices. In high season a small rental car will cost around €400 per week. Non-EU residents can also take advantage of low rates on long leases. Note that the Autoroutes (motorways/highways) operate a toll system. Take a ticket

as you enter and then pay as you progress/leave the autoroute at a *péage* (pay station). The cost varies from €0.03 to €0.16 per kilometer (0.6 mile), depending on the stretch of road. The autoroute network in the immediate vicinity of large cities is free to use. The speed limit on autoroutes is 130 kilometers (80 miles) per hour and 110 kilometers (68 miles) per hour in the rain. Route Nationale (RN) roads often run parallel to autoroutes. They are free to use and a good alternative, particularly when the autoroute is busy. The speed limit on Route Nationale roads has recently been reduced to 80 kilometers (50 miles) per hour.

The bus network across Provence is patchy. The various regional bus companies are being grouped together under one brand: **Zou.** Confusingly, the websites for the various regional companies still exist, although some have been branded Zou. For intercity bus routes, the best website is: www.info-ler.fr. For services in the Vaucluse the best website for information is www.sudmobilite.fr; in the Bouches-du-Rhône, the best website is www.lepilote.com; and in the Var, use www.varlib.fr.

The local train network connects the major cities and towns of Provence but not the villages. Along the coast, trains can be an option. The Côte Bleue coast can be seen by train. There is a picturesque route that runs from Marseille to Martigues, stopping at all the major seaside resorts. Similarly, the railway runs from Marseille to Toulon, stopping at resorts along the way. The best website for local train journeys is www.oui.sncf.

When planning a trip and deciding between transport methods the best website is: www.sudmobilite.fr. This site provides both train and bus timetables.

For short sightseeing trips, e-bikes are proving increasingly popular. Throughout this guide there are listings of e-bike providers. One of the largest in the region with bases in multiple villages is Station Bees: www.stationsbees.com.

Visas and Officialdom

PASSPORTS AND VISAS

The very latest visa requirements can be quickly checked at www.diplomatie.gouv. fr/en/coming-to-france. There is a "Visa Wizard" that will quickly tell you your requirements. A summary of the current regulations are found below.

United States, Canada, Australia, and New Zealand

Nationals of these countries can enter France and stay for up to 90 days without a visa. Stays of more than 90 days require a visa, and proof of income and medical insurance.

European Union/Schengen

Nationals of EU-member countries who have a valid passport and national identity card can travel freely to France. At the time of writing, the situation of British nationals remains unclear due to the process of the United Kingdom exiting the European Union.

South Africa

South African nationals require a short-stay visa for stays of up to 90 days, and a long-stay visa for more than 90 days.

VACCINATIONS

There are no specific requirements, although health bodies recommend that visitors be vaccinated for hepatitis A and B, and yellow fever. In addition, a rabies shot is recommended for those likely to come into contact with animals.

Recreation

There's so much to do in Provence. Here's a round-up of ways you might spend your time.

RELAXING

This is practically an art form in Provence. The region is famed for its slow pace of life. Nobody seems in a hurry to do anything. Entire afternoons can be passed on the beach or sitting in the shade of an ancient plane tree, sharing a bottle of wine and chatting away. The most energetic thing many locals contemplate is a game of petanque as the sun goes down.

WINE TASTING

Wine-focused tourism is booming in Provence. Private companies offer daylong tours of the most famous wine-producing areas, such as Châteauneuf-du-Pape, Gigondas, and Vacqueyras. On a more basic level, local vineyards and wine shops offer tastings and here the drink of choice is rosé. There is simply no better place to drink pink wine in the world. The pale rosé produced by Provençal vineyards is a perfect match for the blue sky and is typically drunk in copious amounts.

CULTURE

Aix, Arles, and Avignon are all major attractions. Their promise is similar: picturesque streets, good restaurants and hotels, and major museums and historic sights. On offer are cherished moments such as seeing a Van Gogh original, visiting Cézanne's workplace, channeling Russell Crowe and having a Gladiator moment inside a Roman arena, and marveling at the majesty of the Palais des Papes.

Shopping and Souvenirs

ANTIQUES

Brocante (antiques fairs) are plentiful during the summer months. Restored tables, chairs, clocks, garden furniture, and statues are all on sale at sometimes inflated prices. Bargain hunters should head for *vide-greniers* (the garage sales of Provence), where similar items are on sale for half the price. Popular purchases include old irons that are used as doorstops, and antique coffee grinders.

BEDSPREADS

Quilted bedspreads have been produced for centuries in Provence. In the late 17th century, Marseille was the world capital of bedspread production. Shoppers these days have a choice either to opt for a cheaper mass-produced imitation available in nearly every Provençal market, or to pay the price commanded for a hand-sewn original.

Aix-en-Provence hosts outdoor markets nearly every day.

LAVENDER

Cut, dried, and bundled when in full color, dried lavender makes an attractive table decoration as well as making the room smell sweet. Easier to transport are linen bags filled with lavender petals, which can be used to line clothes drawers to help ward off moths. Lavender essential oil has a multitude of medicinal uses from preventing migraines to alleviating rheumatism. A dab is also commonly used to protect local children from head lice.

MARKETS

Provence is famous for its weekly markets, and most tourists will visit at least one of them during their trip. Fresh fruit and vegetables are a major lure, as are artisan-made products.

OUTDOOR ACTIVITIES

Outdoor enthusiasts tend to visit in Spring or Autumn when average temperatures are lower. Hiking Les Calanques is a popular activity, and for cyclists there is no greater challenge than the ascent of Mont Ventoux, one of the most punishing climbs on the Tour de France.

Festivals and Events

It's hard for a visitor to Provence not to happen upon a festival. Nearly every food type—from the Pertuis potato to the Cavaillon Melon and the Strawberries of Carpentras—has its own festival. People will gather in the streets and taste themed menus. There are numerous wine festivals, and each village has its own *fete votive* (village fair) with rides and music. The nearer you get to the Camargue, the more likely you are to encounter bull running. The events that draw the largest crowds are:

SPRING

Easter Feria
ARLES

This festival is a bull-fighting spectacle with street parties and live music (page 93). It is one of the largest events in Provence. Expect crowded streets, dancing, drinking, and plenty of noise. Arles is transformed during the Feria into the party capital of Provence.

Antiques Fair
L'ISLE-SUR-LA-SORGUE

Traders from across France display their goods along the picturesque banks of the River Sorgue (page 72) in one of the biggest antiques fairs in Europe. The choice and variety of goods on sale is staggering. Even if you have only a passing interest in antiques, the fair is one-of-a-kind experience.

Fête de la Transhumance
SAINT-RÉMY-DE-PROVENCE

On Whit Sunday (the seventh Sunday after Easter), herds of sheep are driven through the streets of Saint-Rémy en route for the mountains where they spend the summer (page 117). It's a crazy affair. The traffic is halted, and for a half a day, animals takes over the town. Along with the sheep come donkeys, goats, and, of course, shepherds.

Pèlerinage des Gitans
SAINTE-MARIES-DE-LA-MER, MAY 24-25

This gypsy festival celebrates the landing of the three Marys (Magdalene, Salome, and Jacobe) in France. Fleeing the Holy Land in a small boat, they were, so the story goes, washed ashore in Sainte-Maries. For years gypsies have flocked to the town to celebrate. Then, Dan Brown boosted the already large crowds by suggesting in his novel *The Da Vinci Code* that Mary Magdalene was carrying the child of Christ when she disembarked (page 104). Conspiracy theorists as well as gypsies now love the festival. There's plenty of religious symbolism, and at least some of the festival takes place out at sea, as statues of the Marys are carried into the water. Locals with boats have the best view.

SUMMER

Fête de La Musique
ACROSS FRANCE, JUNE 21

During this annual festival, there is live music in the streets of every village. Many restaurants and cafés put on special menus for the evening. Tables and chairs spill into the middle of streets, stages are erected on street corners, and everybody has a party. Best of all, it's all free.

Arles Photography Festival
ARLES, JULY TO SEPTEMBER

Now nearing its 50th year, this festival includes photography exhibitions in venues across the town (page 95). Major venues host ticketed shows by well-known photographers, but even without a pass you can partake in the atmosphere of the festival. Photos decorate windows and street corners and animate a visit to the city. The opening week is particularly busy with various VIP and press events. The festival attracts an estimated 100,000 people to the city.

Festival d'Aix-en-Provence
AIX-EN-PROVENCE, JULY

Every year, Aix hosts an internationally renowned opera festival with performances throughout the month (page 206). The festival tends to feature five major operas and a host of subsidiary events, including performances of everything from classical music to flamenco guitar.

Avignon Festival
AVIGNON, JULY

This annual theater festival (page 46) presents 60 shows spread across 40 venues, attracting an audience of 155,000 people. Shows range from dance, theatre, and comedy, to mime, readings, and films. Thankfully many events, such as dance, don't require any language skills and are often performed in unforgettable venues such as the courtyard of the Palais des Papes.

International Piano Festival
LA ROQUE D'ANTHÉRON, LATE JULY TO EARLY AUGUST
This festival attracts some of the best pianists in the world (page 224). Nearly 80,000 tickets are sold every year. Most recitals take place in the enchanting outdoor arena in the grounds of the Château de Florans or in the nearby Cistercian Abbey of Silvacane.

Jazz des Cinq Continents
MARSEILLE, MID-JULY
Now into its 14th year, this festival continues to attract large crowds and top musicians (page 250). There are large open-air concerts in spectacular venues such as outside the Palais Longchamp, or at the entrance to MuCEM. If you are in Marseille, it's great fun to attend.

Floating Market
L'ISLE-SUR-LA-SORGUE, FIRST SUNDAY IN AUGUST
Market traders forsake dry land and board long, narrow boats to sell their goods (page 75). Making a purchase is not easy: first there are the crowds to negotiate, and then the large drop down to the boats. Overeager shoppers have been known to tumble in. Due to these hazards, the floating market is more of a spectacle than a serious opportunity to shop. Arrive early to avoid the crowds and see the boats pulled up by the banks filled with their goods.

AUTUMN

Luberon Marathon
BEGINNING OF OCTOBER
The marathon is a picturesque run through the vineyards, with wine tastings for runners and spectators. The date and route varies every year. Check the website for details on where best to spectate: www.marathon-luberon.com.

Richerenches Truffle Festival
RICHERENCHES, NOVEMBER
This festival marks the opening of the town's truffle market. The event includes a truffle-based Holy Mass (page 60) and all sorts of delicious truffle-based delicacies to try. Check the village website for the date of the celebration: www.richerenches.fr.

Rognes Truffle Market
ROGNES, LAST SUNDAY BEFORE CHRISTMAS
This village's ever-more-popular truffle market is the perfect occasion to stock the fridge with delicacies for the big day, and to taste truffle dishes such as scrambled eggs laced with truffles (page 224).

Food and Drink

EATING IN
Provence has a rich food and drink culture. Markets are the best places to shop for fruit, vegetables, cheeses, dried meats, and aperitif snacks. Villages usually have one market each week, although some may have two: a farmers market and a more traditional weekly market. Markets open early around 8am, and the stall holders pack up between 12:30pm and 1pm.

Among the largest markets in Provence, selling everything from fruit and vegetables, to jewelry and clothes, are: Apt (Saturday), Saint-Rémy-de-Provence (Wednesday), Lourmarin (Friday), and Forcalquier (Monday).

EATING OUT

Most restaurants start serving lunch at noon. The locals tend to get hungry early, and so tables fill up quickly and it's not unusual for a restaurant to sell out of its plat du jour before 1pm. At lunchtime, restaurants will often offer a fixed-price menu in addition to á la carte items. Service usually lasts until 2pm, but try to be seated by 1:45pm. In the summer, serving hours tend to be extended.

In the evening, restaurants open around 7:30pm. There is not usually a plat du jour, although a fixed-price menu may still be offered. At night, restaurants will often not accept new customers after 10pm.

When making a reservation make sure you specify where you want to eat—on the terrace or inside. If at all possible, make a reservation in person. By doing this you can select your table and pick one with a view or one that is nicely shaded. In the winter, be aware that a lot of restaurants cover their terraces with a plastic awning. For the purposes of smoking laws, the terrace (with plastic cover) is still considered to be outside and smoking is therefore permitted. If you object to smoking, it is best to eat inside.

WINE

Most vineyards offer free tastings. However, there is an implicit understanding that visitors have an intention of buying at least one bottle of wine. It's considered rude to turn up, taste multiple wines, and leave empty handed. Larger, more commercial vineyards have started charging for tasting. In this case, it is entirely at your discretion whether you choose to purchase wine or not.

SPECIALTIES

Look for the following regional products while traveling in Provence.

Rosé

The world is experiencing a boom in rosé consumption. Pale, coral-colored pink wines that glint in the sun are all the rage. These wines were first made in Provence and now the region offers the finest range of rosés in the world, including oaked rosés, rosés *d'une nuit* (where the vinification is completed in one night), and a rosé so pale and light in color it is called a *gris* (gray).

Châteauneuf-du-Pape

The dream of many oenophiles is to enjoy a tasting in the cellar of a Châteauneuf-du-Pape vineyard: to pour the deep ruby liquid into a glass and inhale as the heady scents of ripe fruits are released; to close their eyes and sip, counting the seconds as the flavors reach a crescendo in the mouth before receding gently like a tide. Note though that Châteauneuf-du-Pape is a wine that needs to age. A young Châteauneuf (under five years) can be a disappointment. Also, beware of buying Châteauneuf-du-Pape in a supermarket; the quality is unlikely to be good.

Pastis

The French drink a mind-boggling 20 million glasses of this aniseed-flavored liquor a day. Depending on whom you believe, it was invented by either a hermit in the Luberon or Jules Pernod, who decided to capitalize on the banning of absinthe manufacture in 1715. Either way, pastis is synonymous with Provence and it's a perfect slow drink to enjoy with the setting sun.

Bouillabaisse

The famous fish soup of Marseille was originally cooked by fishermen using the rock fish they were unable to sell to restaurants. The word bouillabaisse refers to the cooking method of reducing the fish to a stock using boiling water. Restaurants now sign an official charter to cook the dish. They use agreed-upon ingredients and serve it in the traditional way. Bouillabaisse is accompanied by a feisty garlic-infused rouille paste that is spread on croutons, adding an extra punch to the already intensely flavored soup. As memorable as the dish is the pomp and ceremony that accompany its serving.

Daube de Boeuf

This hearty winter beef stew became so popular that it is now served year-round. Cooks need to be patient; the meat is marinated for three days, cooked for 4 hours and then rested for another day. The result is rich, pungent, melt-in-the-mouth, deeply satisfying comfort food.

Soupe au Pistou

This is a traditional vegetable soup finished off with a large dollop of basil-garlic pesto. It's more common to find this on menus during the winter. Beware, it can be quite garlicky.

Banon Goat's Cheese

This is fast food Provençal style and probably the greatest, simplest takeaway available in the world. Buy a Banon goat's cheese from a market trader, grab a baguette, and you are away. Rather than the greasy paper wrapping of a burger, you gently unfold dried chestnut leaves that are secured around the cheese by a raffia tie. Note, these are not just any chestnut leaves; they have been soaked in wine to impart flavor into the cheese. Eaten at perfect ripeness, a Banon goat's cheese hovers on the dividing line between solid and liquid, and can simply be mopped up with the end of a baguette.

Truffles

Between late November and early February, Provence goes truffle mad. Nicknamed "black diamonds," truffles are a fungus that grows underground, attached by a gossamer thin thread to the roots of oak trees. Prices for truffles commonly reach nearly €1,000 euros a kilo (2.2 pounds). The good news is that they are best eaten as a complement to basic ingredients. Eggs, cheese, even the common baked potato are elevated to almost ethereal levels by the judicious addition of truffle shavings.

Accommodations

HOTELS AND GUESTHOUSES

Booking accommodations in advance is essential during the summer months. In May, June, and September, it is still advisable to reserve ahead. From October to April, it is possible to wait until the last minute before deciding on accommodations.

Hotels

The hotels featured in this book range from two- to five-star properties. Prices for a standard double room in a two-star hotel in high season in the less touristy areas of Provence start around €70 per night, rising to €100 in the more touristy areas. Rooms at this price point have ensuite bathrooms and usually have Wi-Fi. Hotel services are limited, and there is not always a bar or restaurant.

Paying a little more for a three-star hotel usually means rooms will have air-conditioning. The hotel will often have a bar/restaurant and a nice outside area with a pool.

Prices for four- and five-star hotels start around €200 a night and rise to over €500. The region is graced by some of the most magnificent hotels in the world, combining spectacular locations with luxurious furnishings and high-end services.

Guesthouses

Guesthouses in Provence are referred to as *chambre d'hote*. They all offer bed-and-breakfast and may also offer an evening meal. They tend to be small with no more than five rooms. Some are as luxurious as the top hotels and have prices to match. Typically, they offer a much more intimate experience than a hotel with the host offering advice on what to do and where to eat.

CAMPING

Nearly all villages, towns, and cities in Provence have camping nearby. Between July 14 and August 14, booking is advisable. Outside this period (which coincides with the main French summer holiday), it is not normally necessary to book. Campsites tend to open around May and close at the end of September. Campsites are not generally listed in this book, but information is available on all the tourist office websites under the accommodation heading.

Conduct and Customs

The French tend to be more soft-spoken than Anglophones. Apart from students, they rarely eat or drink when walking about in the street. They tend to dress smartly and take care with their appearance. Taking a shirt off in public, other than on the beach, is not done. Wine is consumed slowly and in moderation.

Both French men and French women greet each other with a kiss on both cheeks. In some Provence villages, two kisses rise to three or even four kisses. Unless visitors become close friends with a local, they are not expected to kiss when saying hello; a handshake suffices.

Most waiters, hotel staff, and people working in the tourist industry will speak enough English to enable them to perform their jobs. Speaking just a little bit of French will endear a visitor to locals, even if it is as simple as saying "Merci beaucoup" rather than "Thank you."

Health and Safety

Provence is a very safe place to travel. Petty crime such as mobile phone or wallet theft occurs infrequently in crowded places such as the weekly markets. When visiting any large city in the world travelers are always advised to keep an eye on the neighborhoods they are exploring and not to wander too far from the established trail. This remains true in Provence, although violent crime is extremely rare.

There are no specific health risks associated with traveling to Provence. Perhaps the greatest threat is the summer heat. Visitors should take sensible precautions such as wearing a hat, applying plenty of sunscreen, and staying in the shade or indoors during the hottest hours of the day between 2pm and 5pm. Insect bites and stings are common, and it is wise to pack repellent sprays and calming lotions.

The French health care service is excellent. It has a basic principle of universal access. In emergencies, treatment is given first and questions about insurance asked later. European Union nationals should always travel with their European Health Insurance card. This entitles them to the same level of treatment as French nationals. Non-EU nationals should travel with appropriate medical insurance. It is usually relatively easy and quick to get a doctor's appointment. To get the phone number of the nearest practitioner near you, go to the local pharmacy and ask. If you have problems making an appointment, you can also ask in the pharmacy for help. An appointment with a doctor costs around €30. You will be expected to pay up front and will be given a form that you can use to claim back the money from your insurer.

In the event of an emergency, dial 112, the European emergency number, which is staffed by English-speaking operators. To be connected directly to a French operator, dial 15 for an ambulance, 17 for the gendarmerie (police), or 18 for emergency medical help from the fire service.

Practical Details

WHAT TO PACK

In the summer, light dresses, shorts, and T-shirts should make up the majority of what you pack. However, it is always worth packing a long pair of trousers and a warm sweater because the evenings can get cold, particularly if the mistral wind is blowing, or if you are staying at altitude. It's also sensible to pack a light raincoat.

In spring and autumn, shorts, T-shirts, and light summer dresses should be supplemented by more warm clothing, and again a light raincoat.

In the winter, sweaters, jeans, and long trousers should take up most of your suitcase. A warm coat is also advisable. It's still worthwhile packing some shorts/light dresses because temperatures can occasionally rise into the mid-20s Celsius (high 70s Fahrenheit).

If you are planning to engage in outdoor sports, it's best to bring as many appropriate clothes as possible. Items such as bike and riding helmets can be rented from the activity center. However, buying specialist clothing like hiking boots will entail spending precious holiday time hunting down items in out-of-town shopping centers.

BUDGETING

Provence is a relatively expensive travel destination. The cheapest room rates start around €70 a night in high season, rising to over €500 for luxury hotels.

For transportation bookings (train, bus, flights) and hotel rooms, the further ahead you book, the better the price. Outside of the main summer season, it is sometimes possible to negotiate down the prices of hotel rooms at the last minute.

To save money, if you are going to eat out, do so at lunchtime when most restaurants offer a competitively priced plat du jour and two- or three-course menus. When eating in restaurants, ask for a jug of water (carafe d'eau) rather than bottled water. If you drink wine and want so save money, order a *pichet* (pitcher). These jugs can be ordered in 250-milliliter (half pint) and 500-milliliter (pint) sizes. The quality of the wine is usually reasonable, and it is much cheaper than ordering by the bottle. Make sure you arrive in restaurants at or shortly after midday. The plat du jour often runs out quickly. Expect to pay around €12-15 for a plat du jour and €18-28 for a three-course menu. A half-liter *pichet* of wine should cost around €6.

Rather than eating breakfast in a hotel, which usually cost around €15, go to the nearest boulangerie and pick up a couple of croissants. It's then perfectly acceptable to go to the nearest café, order a coffee and eat your croissants. The only exception to this rule is when you see a café that is heavily promoting its own breakfast. If in doubt, ask.

When visiting cities with multiple sights such as Aix-en-Provence, Avignon, Arles, and Marseille, visit the main tourist office and purchase a pass that includes admission to all sights for a fixed price. Transportation is often included in these tickets. Check the relevant chapters for details.

MONEY

The currency of France is the euro. Notes that are commonly in circulation are 500, 100, 50, 10, and 5. Some businesses may not wish to take notes anything larger than €50.

Cash points (ATMs) are readily available throughout France. Even small villages have them. In general, you should not need to carry much cash. Nearly all restaurants and businesses accept credit cards.

Places where you can exchange foreign

currency are ever rarer and are limited to the main airports and large train stations. The rates of exchange do not tend to be favorable, and more often than not it is best to take money out from a cash machine rather than to bring cash from home and exchange it for euros. Check with your bank before leaving about charges.

COMMUNICATIONS
Cell Phones
The international dialing code for France is 0033. When using a foreign cell phone to dial a number in France, you will need to use this prefix, and drop the first 0 at the beginning of the French number. Since 2016, roaming charges across the European Economic Area and the EU have been restricted. This means that most Europeans should be able to use their mobile phones without incurring extra charges. Non-Europeans should consider changing their SIM cards. All the main French operators (Orange, SFr, Bouygues, and Free) offer prepaid SIM cards that can be swapped into your phone.

Internet Access
Internet access is available in nearly all hotels, restaurants, and cafés. Provided you are a customer, you just need to ask for the password.

Shipping and Postal Service
Even small villages have post offices. The postal service is quick and reliable. Shipping packages abroad is easy, and prepaid boxes can be picked up at the post office. To courier items, the post office offers a service called Chronopost, which guarantees next-day delivery in France. Details can be found online: www.chronopost.fr/en#/step-home.

OPENING HOURS
Most businesses are open Tuesday to Saturday from 9am to noon and from 3pm to 6pm. Restaurants and shops in touristy locations will open seven days a week during the busy summer season. Many shopkeepers also choose not to shut for lunch in the summer months.

PUBLIC HOLIDAYS
There are 11 public holidays in France:

- January 1: New Year's Day (Jour de l'An)
- Easter Monday (Lundi de Pâques)
- May 1: Labor Day (Fête du Travail)
- May 8: VE Day (Fête de la Victoire 1945)
- Ascension Day: 39 days after Easter Sunday (l'Ascension)
- Whit Monday: 50 days after Easter, 10 days after Ascension Day (Lundi de Pentecôte)
- July 14: Bastille Day (Fête Nationale)
- August 15: Assumption of the Blessed Virgin Mary (l'Assomption)
- November 1: All Saints' Day (La Toussaint)
- November 11: Armistice Day (Armistice 1918)
- December 25: Christmas Day (Noël)

When a public holiday falls on a Thursday or Tuesday, it is common for the French to take an extra day off and create a long weekend. This is known as a *pont* or bridge.

WEIGHTS AND MEASURES
France uses the metric system. All distances are given in kilometers and all weights in grams and kilograms. Drinks are served by the centiliter. A beer is 25 centileters (half pint) and a bottle of wine 75 centiliters (a pint and a half).

TOURIST INFORMATION
Tourist Offices
There are tourist offices in most villages, and in all towns and cities in Provence. They usually open from Monday to Friday outside of the main season, and Monday to Saturday in the summer. Main tourist offices in cities will be open seven days a week in the summer season. They are excellent places to pick up information on everything from accommodations to tours, experiences, and hikes. They also offer free local maps.

The main tourist office websites are as follows:

- **Aix-en-Provence:**
  www.aixenprovencetourism.com/en
- **Avignon:** www.avignon-tourisme.com
- **Arles** and the **Camargue:**
  www.arlestourisme.com/en
- **Marseille** and **Les Calanques:**
  www.marseille-tourisme.com/en

- **Toulon:** https://toulontourisme.com/en
- **The Luberon:**
  www.luberoncoeurdeprovence.com
- **Northern Vaucluse:**
  www.ventouxprovence.fr/accueil.html
- **Gorge du Verdon:**
  www.verdontourisme.com
- **The Var:** www.visitvar.fr

Traveler Advice

OPPORTUNITIES FOR STUDY AND EMPLOYMENT

Nationals of EU-member states are free to move to and work in Provence. Nationals of other countries will need a visa and authorization to work.

In the summer season, bars and restaurants are always looking for bilingual staff. In cities, there is high demand from businesses for English language lessons. A good resource for vacancies is the Teaching English as a Foreign Language website (www.tefl.com).

French universities welcome applications from foreign students. Opportunities can also be found on the AFS intercultural program website (https://afs.org) and the American Institute for Foreign Study (www.aifsabroad.com).

For more detailed advice on working or studying in France, see *Moon Living Abroad France*.

ACCESS FOR TRAVELERS WITH DISABILITIES

Most public transportation in Provence is adapted for passengers with disabilities. Stations have special access points, and trains have carriages with ramps. Buses, particularly in cities, are adapted for wheelchairs.

Museums and art galleries have almost universally been adapted to accommodate disabled access. Historical sights are not always easy to access, and their websites should be checked for information.

TRAVELING WITH CHILDREN

Provence is a family-friendly holiday destination. Most restaurants welcome children and offer children's menus (*menu enfant*). Hotels rarely have interconnecting rooms, but they often have large rooms that can accommodate up to six people. They will also put an additional bed or a cot into a room for a small extra charge.

Public transportation is free for children under 4. Museums are usually free for children under 12 and offer reduced rates up to the age of 18.

Tourist offices have plenty of suggested activities for children. It is also always worth enquiring whether there are any "stage" holiday activities being run in the near vicinity. For example, horse riding and tennis clubs frequently have weeklong courses for children during holidays.

LGBTQ TRAVELERS

France has a liberal attitude toward sexuality, and LGBTQ travelers should not normally encounter any discrimination. The main website for LGBTQ travel in Provence is www.gay-provence.org/en.

TRAVELERS OF COLOR

The face of Provence has changed dramatically since the end of World War II. Algerian independence in 1962 was the start of large-scale immigration. Since then, Provence has become increasingly diversified with communities of Eastern Europeans, Arabs, Asians, South Americans, and Africans contributing to the cultural mix. Ethnic minorities no longer turn heads, and if any French are surprised to find you in their bar, hotel, or restaurant, they certainly won't show it. Blatant discrimination is rare, but if you think you've been refused service based on race, report the incident to the local police (gendarmerie), who treat all acts of racism seriously.

Resources

Glossary

aioli: a garlic mayonnaise, commonly served with salt cod and boiled vegetables on a Friday

Appellation D'origine Contrôlée: geographic and production certification given to products such as wine and cheese

autoroute: a French motorway/highway that operates a toll system

baroque: a style of art, music, and architecture, often with a complicated design, that originated in 17th-century Italy

bouillabaisse: fish soup served in Marseille and the surrounding coastal area

boulangerie: bakery

calanque: a gorge-like inlet cut in rocky sea cliffs

chambre d'hote: bed-and-breakfast/guesthouse.

château: a castle, or the name given to a wine estate based around a large historic house

Course Camarguaise: nonlethal bullfighting spectacle where competitors try to remove ribbons/garlands from the bull's ears

corrida: Spanish bull-fighting spectacle where the bull is killed

daube: a slow-cooked stew, usually made with beef, but sometimes wild boar is substituted

département: governmental regions. Provence is split into four départements: The Vaucluse, the Var, the Bouches-du-Rhône, and the Alpes de Haute Provence.

domaine: a name given to a wine estate

fête votive: annual village or town festival with carnival rides

Fêria: bull running and bull fighting festival in Arles.

gendarmerie: the French police. Gendarmes belong to a branch of the French army and live in barracks. They are armed.

jardin des enfants: playground.

mairie: the mayor's office, which can be found in every village, town, and city. If you need an official piece of paper/permit it is a good place to start.

mas: provençal farmhouse

office de tourisme: tourist information point

pharmacie: drug store or chemist where you can get basic medical advice and purchase medicines

place: a square in a village, town, or city

plat du jour: daily special of a restaurant, usually competitively priced

police (municipal): the level of law enforcement below the gendarmerie. Each village will normally have one police municipal. It is his/her job to deal with small civic crime and parking/traffic issues. Towns and cities have a larger Police Municipal force. They are armed.

poste: post office

prefecture: an administrative center responsible for driving licenses, resident permits, etc.

Romanesque: a style of architecture that prevailed in Europe from 900 to 1200, taking inspiration from the Romans

sentier: a marked hiking/biking trail

soupe au pistou: clear vegetable soup dressed with a dollop of garlicky pesto

stade: a sports stadium/municipal sports facility

tabac/presse: shop where you can buy newspapers, magazines, and cigarettes

tuber melanosporum: the official Latin name for the Provençal "black diamond" truffle

Urgence: Emergency department of a hospital.

vendange: grape harvest

vigneron: a winemaker

French Phrasebook

PRONUNCIATION

French is not an easy language to master. The mouth shapes and tongue position are alien to anglophones. In addition, the local Provençal accent distorts many words. For example, "vin" sounds like "ving," which is very hard to distinguish from the number twenty ("vingt").

Vowels

a   like *ah* in *father*

à   as above, the accent is used for spelling purposes to avoid confusion between identical words.

e   with a few exceptions, such as the word "le" (the), e is silent at the end of a word. When it is pronounced, as is the case with "le," the sound is akin to the English "er." In the middle of a word, "e" sounds like *ai* in *fair*. For example, "mer," meaning sea.

é   like short *e* in *hey*

è   like the *e* in *bet*

i   like *ee* in *feet*

o   like the short *o* in *hot*

ô   like the long *o* in *oh*

œ   like the *u* in *upset*

u   like a long *u* sound, but more emphasized: *uuu*

ù   only used in the word *où* to distinguish it from *ou*. The former means "where" or "when," and the u sound is even more emphasized and comes from farther back in the mouth. The later means "or."

Consonants

B D F K L M N P T U X V Z: These French consonants are pronounced the same or nearly the same as English ones:

C G : These consonants have both hard and soft ways of being pronounced, depending on the letters that follow: soft when followed by E, I, or Y (e.g., cerise), hard when followed by A, O, or U (e.g., cadeau).

Ç   always pronounced S (i.e., soft c).

S   at the end of a word, S is almost always silent.

The following consonants are different from English:

J   pronounced like a soft G

Q   pronounced like a K

R   This sound is extremely difficult for foreigners to master. It is a strong rolled R sound, produced by positioning the tongue in the same place as if saying the word "get."

W   Rare in France. Usually occurs in an imported German or English word. If the word is of German origin, pronounce with a V sound. If English, pronounce the English W.

H   always silent.

ESSENTIAL PHRASES

Hello   Bonjour

Hello (to a friend)   Salut

What's your name?   Comment vous appellez-vous?

Mrs./Mr./Miss   Madame/Monsieur/Mademoiselle

Nice to meet you   Enchanté

How are you?   Comment ça va?

Cheers   Sante

Excuse me   Pardon, excusez-moi

Do you speak English?   Parlez-vous anglais?

I do not speak French.   Je ne parle pas français.

I do not understand.   Je ne comprends pas.

See you later À tout à l'heure
Thank you/Thank you very much Merci/ Merci beaucoup
Goodbye Au revoir
See you soon À bientot
You are welcome De rien
Yes Oui
No Non
Where are the restrooms? Où sont les toilettes?
Can you take my/our photo? Pouvez-vous prendre ma photo/notre photo?
Can you help me? Pouvez-vous m'aider?
Speak slowly, please. Pouvez vous parler lentement, s'il vous plait.

TRANSPORTATION/ DIRECTIONS

Where is…? Où se trouve…?
How far is…? À quelle distance est…?
Is there a bus to…? Y a-t-il un bus pour…?
Does this bus go to…? Est-ce que ce bus va à…?
Where do I get off? Où est-ce-que je désends?
What time does the bus/train leave/ arrive? A quelle heure part/arrive le bus/ train?
Where is the nearest subway station? Où est la station de métro la plus proche?
Where can I buy a ticket? Où puis-je acheter un billet?
Where are the toilets? Où sont les toilettes?
Where is a good restaurant? Où est un bon restaurant?
Where is the beach/city center? Où est la plage/le centre-ville?
I am searching for the train station/ airport. Je cherche le gare/l'aéroport.
I am searching for the hotel/hospital/ bank. Je cherche l'hôtel/l'hôpital/la banque.
Is it far/close? C'est loin/proche?
To the left? C'est à gauche?
To the right? C'est à droite?
Straight ahead? C'est tout droit?

Where is the ticket window? Où est le guichet?
I would like to look at the timetable. Je voudrais regarder l'horaire.
I would like to reserve a ticket. Je voudrais réserver un billet.
I would like to purchase a one-way ticket/a return ticket to… Je voudrais acheter un billet aller simple/aller-retour pour…
What time should it arrive? À quelle heure faut-il arriver?

HOTELS

I would like a double room. Je voudrais une chambre pour deux.
I would like to cancel my reservation. Je voudrais annuler ma réservation.
At what time should we check out? À quelle heure est-ce qu'il faut partir?
air-conditioning climatisation
bathroom salle de bain
balcony balcon
parking parking
breakfast petit dejeuner

SHOPPING

money argent
Where are the shops? Où sont les magasins?
Can I pay with a credit card? Est-ce que je peux payer avec une carte de crédit?
At what time is it open? À quelle heure est-il ouvert?
At what time is it closed? À quelle heure est-il fermé?
I am searching for a supermarket. Je cherche un supermarché.
How much does it cost? Combien ça coûte?
It's too expensive. C'est trop cher.
I'm just looking for now. Je regarde pour l'instant.

RESTAURANTS

Do you have a menu in English? Avez vous la carte en anglais?

The menu, please. La carte, s'il vous plaît.
I would like a coffee. Je voudrais un café.
I would like a glass of wine. Je voudrais un verre de vin.
I would like some water. Je voudrais de l'eau.
We are two. Nous sommes deux.
What is the daily special? Quel est le plat du jour?
The bill, please. L'addition, s'il vous plaît.
I'm going to have… Je vais prendre…
I'm a vegetarian. Je suis végétarien.
salad la salade
soup la soupe
beef le bœuf
lamb l'agneau
chicken le poulet
pork le porc
fish le poisson
vegetable le légume
pasta les pâtes
fruit le fruit
cake le gâteau
pie la tarte
ice cream la glace
beer bière
bread pain
breakfast petit déjeuner
cash en espèces
coffee café
dinner le dîner
glass verre
lunch le dejeuner
sandwich(es) sandwich/des sandwichs
snack grignoter
waiter servur
wine vin

HEALTH
drugstore pharmacie
pain douleur
fever fièvre
headache mal à la tête
stomachache mal au ventre
toothache mal au dents
burn la brûlure
cramp la crampe
nausea la nausée

vomiting vomissement
medicine médicament
antibiotic antibiotique
pill/tablet le comprimé
aspirin aspirine
I need to see a doctor. J'ai besoin de voir un médecin.
I need to go to the hospital. J'ai besoin d'aller à l'hôpital.
I have a pain here… J'ai mal ici…
She/he has been stung/bitten. Il/elle a été piquée.
I am diabetic/pregnant. Je suis diabétique/enceinte.
I am allergic to penicillin/cortisone. Je suis allergique à la pénicilline/la cortisone.
My blood group is…positive/ negative. On groupe sanguin est… positif/négatif.

NUMBERS
0 zéro
1 un
2 deux
3 trois
4 quatre
5 cinq
6 six
7 sept
8 huit
9 neuf
10 dix
11 onze
12 douze
13 treize
14 quatorze
15 quinze
16 seize
17 dix-sept
18 dix-huit
19 dix-neuf
20 vingt
30 trente
40 quarante
50 cinquante
60 soixante
70 soixante-dix
80 quatre-vingts

90 quatre-vingt-dix
100 cent
101 cent un
200 deux cent
500 cinq cent
1,000 mille
10,000 dix mille
100,000 cent mille
1,000,000 un million

To write numbers from 20 to 69 in French, you add the single number to the tens number.

- vingt (20) + trois (3) = vingt-trois (23)
- trente (30) + sept (7) = trente-sept (37)
- quarante (40) + deux (2) = quarante-deux (42)
- cinquante (50) + neuf (9) = cinquante-neuf (59)
- soixante (60) + six (6) = soixante-six (66)

TIME

What time is it? Quelle heure est-il?
It's one/three o'clock. Il est une/trois heure.
midday midi
midnight minuit
morning matin
afternoon après-midi
evening soir
night nuit
yesterday hier
today aujourd'hui
tomorrow demain

DAYS AND MONTHS

week semaine
month mois
Monday lundi
Tuesday mardi
Wednesday mercredi
Thursday jeudi
Friday vendredi
Saturday samedi
Sunday dimanche
January janvier
February fevrier
March mars
April avril
May mai
June juin
July juillet
August aôut
September septembre
October octobre
November novembre
December decembre

VERBS

to have avoir
to be être
to go aller
to come venir
to want vouloir
to eat manger
to drink boir
to buy acheter
to need avoir besoin
to read lire
to write ecrire
to stop arrêter
to get off descendre
to arrive arriver
to return revenir
to stay rester
to leave partir
to look at regarder
to look for chercher
to give donner
to take prendre

Suggested Reading

FICTION

La Conquette de Plassans by Emile Zola is part of his 20-book *Rougon-Macquart* series, which tells the story of a family between 1851 and 1871. Most of the books center on Paris, but four are concerned with Plassans, Zola's fiction-alized version of Aix-en-Provence. Of these, *La Conquette de Plassans* is the most accessible.

The Count of Monte Cristo by Alexandre Dumas is the story of Edmund Dantès, a man wrongly imprisoned in the Château d'If island prison off the coast of Marseille. While held captive, Dantès plots his brilliant revenge. It's an epic, world-famous story.

The Fly Truffler by Gustaf Sobin is a moving, poetic book. The title refers to the practice of looking for truffles by searching for the flies which lay their eggs in the soil next to where the tuber grows. The lead character, a university lecturer called Cabassac, dis-covers that when he eats a truffle he enters a state of receptivity where he is able to dream clearly about his dead wife: Julieta. This re-alization drives him to an obsession with the "black diamond," and we follow him through the countryside, stick twitching ahead of him, shadow always behind to avoid disturbing the flies.

Horseman on the Roof by Jean Giono tells the story of Angelo Piardi, an Italian hussar sol-dier who arrives in Provence in the summer of 1838 in the middle of a cholera epidemic. To escape a mob in the town of Manosque he climbs on to the roofs of houses and watches as cholera kills the inhabitants of the town.

The Man who Planted Trees by Jean Giono, is an award-winning short story about a shepherd who over the space of four decades reforests a valley in the Alpes de Haute Provence.

Manon of the Spring and *Jean de Florette* by Marcel Pagnol center around the attempt of Provençal peasant Ugolin to make his fortune from growing carnations. To do so he needs water, which is in abundant sup-ply on his neighbor's land. After a couple of murders, the land in question is eventually inherited by Jean de Florette, a tax clerk. Jean decides to quit work and move to the countryside to make his fortune raising rabbits. Before his arrival Ugolin blocks the spring, rendering Jean's land worthless and unsuitable for the rabbits. Ugolin sits back and waits for, what he assumes is, Jean's inevitable departure, when he will have an opportunity to buy the land. Jean refuses to leave and a generational saga ensues.

Le Mas Théotime by Henri Bosco is another deliberation on man's relationship with na-ture. An epic family story, it concerns the daily lives of peasant farmers. The narrative is centered around a farmhouse, just out-side the Luberon village of Lourmarin. It's a quiet, slow, subtle book.

NONFICTION
Lifestyle

A Year in Provence, Toujours Provence, and *Encore Provence* by Peter Mayle are the books that popularized Provence as a holi-day destination. They consist of collections of humorous anecdotes about Mayle's life in the Luberon.

The A to Z of Provence by Peter Mayle. A col-lection of facts and anecdotes compiled by Mayle in encyclopedia form to reflect his love of Provence.

Letters from a Windmill by Alphonse Daudet was first published in excerpt form in news-papers and can perhaps best be described as faction. Daudet's success was based upon describing rural life in Les Alpilles to a met-ropolitan elite audience.

Put Me Back on My Bike by William Foth-eringham tells the story of British cyclist's

Tom Simpson's death while racing to the summit of Mont Ventoux.

Rosé en Marché by Jamie Ivey tells the story of the year he spent working in the Provençal markets selling rosé.

Art

Van Gogh's Ear by Bernadette Murphy recounts the author's attempts to find out the truth about the night when Van Gogh sliced off his ear after a fight with fellow artist Paul Gauguin.

The Yellow House by Martin Gayford is a similar attempt to dig behind the myth and tell the story of the artist's commune that Van Gogh hoped to establish in Arles.

History

France, A Modern History from the Revolution to the War with Terror by Jonathan Fenby provides a sweeping account of the last 200 years of French history. Although not specifically focused on Provence, it's full of useful background information.

Provence, A Cultural History by Martin Garrett is a fascinating literary history of Provence's main cities and regions.

Internet Resources and Apps

PROVENCE BLOGS

http://provenceguru.com
An excellent online magazine about all things Provençal.

www.provencepost.com
A popular Saint-Rémy-de-Provence-based blog with updates on daily life, new businesses and events.

http://shuttersandsunflowers.com
A Lourmarin-based blogger writes about her favorite places in Provence.

www.provencewinezine.com
A site focused on food and wine pairings from Provence.

https://curiousprovence.com
Based in Les Alpilles, Ashley Tinker blogs about all things Provençal, particularly house renovation.

HOLIDAY RENTALS

www.onlyprovence.com

A luxury villa rental business with an excellent selection of houses.

www.theluberon.com
Luberon-based villa, cottage, and apartment-rental business.

https://provence.emotional-escapes.com
More luxury villas for rental in Provence.

www.homeaway.com
Offers the largest selection of villas, many of them rented from the owner.

SPORTS AND RECREATION

www.hikideas.com/walk-provence-alpes-cote-d-azur.html
Has a good selection of hikes with maps, directions, distances, all downloadable in pdf form.

Visorando
A useful app to help keep track of your location during hikes.

www.provence-a-velo.fr
All the information you need to plan a great cycling holiday in Provence is available on this site.

WEATHER
www.lachainemeteo.com
Check the weather before you arrive on this excellent French site. There is also a downloadable app.

NEWS
www.thelocal.fr
The French news in English.

TRAVEL
www.autoroutes.fr/fr/trafic-en-temps-reel.htm
The latest live information on traffic on the autoroutes.

Waze
A route planning app with up to date information on traffic conditions.

www.marseille.aeroport.fr
Flight arrival and departure information for Marseille airport

www.avignon.aeroport.fr
Flight arrival and departure information for Avignon airport

www.sudmobilite.fr
A good travel planning site that gives you access to both train and bus timetables at the same time.

www.oui.sncf
For train bookings and timetables.

ouibus.com
Operated by the French railway service, offers connections from major cities such as Lyon and Paris to Aix, Avignon, and Marseille.

flixbus.com
Offers similar services. If you're booking on short notice, the prices tend to be much cheaper than the trains.

www.lepilote.com
Bus information in the Bouche du Rhone department

www.infor-ler.fr
Information on bus services between major destination.

www.varlib.fr
Information on bus services in the Var.

SHOPPING
www.leboncoin.fr
A treasure trove for second-hand goods, selling everything from stone fireplaces to cars. There is also a downloadable app.

Index

List of Maps

Photo Credits

(bottom) Philippe Murtas, photographe; page 310 © Gilles Barattini | Dreamstime.com; page 317 © Tanya Ivey; page 319 © Eziogutzemberg - Dreamstime.com; page 323 © Barmalini - Dreamstime.com; page 325 © Tanya Ivey; page 329 © By: Morphart Creation; page 330 © Kovalenkov Petr | Dreamstime.com; page 332 © Madrabothair - Dreamstime.com; page 334 © Sam74100 | Dreamstime.com; page 336 © Patrice Correia - Dreamstime.com; page 348 © Ryhor Bruyeu | Dreamstime.com; page 349 © Jiri Vondrous | Dreamstime.com; page 352 © Susan Kanfer, Adeliepenguin | Dreamstime.com

Trips to Remember

ANGKOR WAT

TRIP OF A LIFETIME

GALÁPAGOS
ISLANDS

JAPAN

JONATHAN DEHART

TRIP OF A LIFETIME

MACHU
PICCHU

MOROCCO

NEW
ZEALAND

JAMIE CHRISTIAN DESPLACES

NORWAY

TRIP OF A LIFETIME

PATAGONIA

WAYNE BERNHARDSON

VIETNAM

DANA FILEK-GIBSON

YELLOWSTONE
& GRAND TETON

INCLUDING JACKSON HOLE

BECKY LOMAX

ZION &
BRYCE

INCLUDING ARCHES, CANYONLANDS,
CAPITOL REEF, GRAND STAIRCASE-
ESCALANTE & MORE

W. C. McRAE & JUDY JEWELL

Epic Adventure

Drive & Hike

APPALACHIAN
TRAIL

THE BEST TRAIL TOWNS, DAY HIKES,
AND ROAD TRIPS IN BETWEEN

TIMOTHY MALCOLM

ROUTE 66

Road Trip

JESSICA DUNHAM

YELLOWSTONE TO
GLACIER NATIONAL
PARK

Road Trip

JACKSON HOLE, CODY, THE GRAND TETONS
& THE ROCKY MOUNTAIN FRONT

CARTER G. WALKER

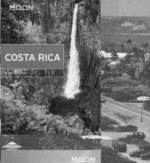

MOON

CAMINO DE SANTIAGO

SACRED SITES,
HISTORIC VILLAGES,
LOCAL FOOD & WINE

BEEBE BAHRAMI

Embark on an epic journey along the historic Camino de Santiago, stroll the most popular European cities, or chase the northern lights in Norway with Moon Travel Guides!

MOON
AMALFI COAST
Irish Coast, Naples & Pompeii
LAURA THAYER

MOON
BARCELONA & MADRID
JESSICA JONES

MOON
CROATIA & SLOVENIA
SHANN FOUNTAIN ALIPOUR

MOON
EDINBURGH, GLASGOW & THE ISLE OF SKYE
SALLY COFFEY

MOON
ICELAND
JENNA GOTTLIEB

MOON
IRELAND
CAMILLE SMANGELO

MOON
NORMANDY & BRITTANY
With Mont-Saint-Michel
CHRIS NEWENS

MOON
NORWAY
DAVID NIKEL

MOON
PORTUGAL
CAROLINE ZOE BEATLEY

MOON
PRAGUE, VIENNA & BUDAPEST
JENNIFER D WALKER, AUERN LINDELAUF

MOON
PROVENCE
JAMIE IVEY

MOON
ROME, FLORENCE & VENICE
ALEXEI J COHEN

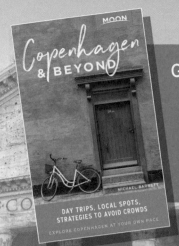

GO BIG AND GO BEYOND!

These savvy city guides include strategies to help you see the top sights and find adventure beyond the tourist crowds.

OR TAKE THINGS ONE STEP AT A TIME

MOON

PACIFIC NORTHWEST
Road Trip

SEATTLE, VANCOUVER, VICTORIA,
THE OLYMPIC PENINSULA, PORTLAND,
THE OREGON COAST & MOUNT RAINIER

ALLISON WILLIAMS

MOON

ROUTE 66
Road Trip

JESSICA DUNHAM

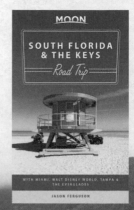

MOON

SOUTH FLORIDA & THE KEYS
Road Trip

WITH MIAMI, WALT DISNEY WORLD, TAMPA &
THE EVERGLADES

JASON FERGUSON

MOON

SOUTHWEST
Road Trip

LAS VEGAS, ZION & BRYCE, MONUMENT VALLEY
SANTA FE & TAOS, AND THE GRAND CANYON

TIM HULL

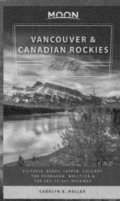

MOON

VANCOUVER & CANADIAN ROCKIES
Road Trip

VICTORIA, BANFF, JASPER, CALGARY,
THE OKANAGAN, WHISTLER &
THE SEA-TO-SKY HIGHWAY

CAROLYN B. HELLER

MOON

YELLOWSTONE TO GLACIER NATIONAL PARK
Road Trip

JACKSON HOLE, CODY, THE GRAND TETONS
& THE ROCKY MOUNTAIN FRONT

CARTER G. WALKER

MOON

Road Trip
USA

CROSS-COUNTRY ADVENTURES ON
AMERICA'S TWO-LANE HIGHWAYS

Jamie Jensen

Road Trip USA

Covering more than 35,000 miles of blacktop stretching from east to west and north to south, *Road Trip USA* takes you deep into the heart of America.

This colorful guide covers the top road trips including historic Route 66 and is packed with maps, photos, illustrations, mile-by-mile highlights, and more!

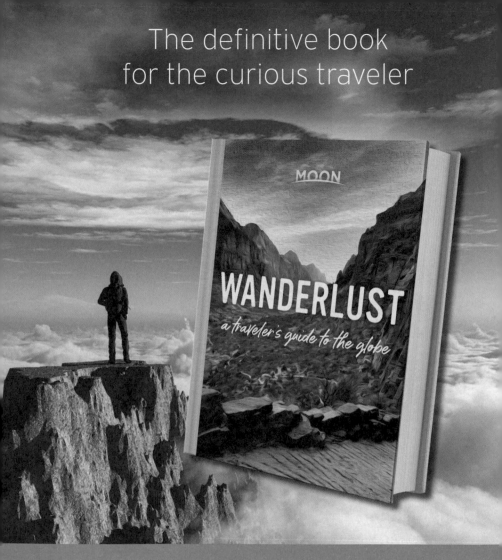

MAP SYMBOLS

═══	Expressway	○	City/Town	✈	Airport	⌡	Golf Course
═══	Primary Road	◉	State Capital	✗	Airfield	🅿	Parking Area
═══	Secondary Road	⊛	National Capital	▲	Mountain	▅	Archaeological Site
------	Unpaved Road	★	Point of Interest	✦	Unique Natural Feature	⛪	Church
───	Feature Trail	•	Accommodation			🛢	Gas Station
-----	Other Trail	▼	Restaurant/Bar	🌊	Waterfall		Glacier
·········	Ferry	■	Other Location	▲	Park		Mangrove
═══	Pedestrian Walkway	△	Campground	🚩	Trailhead		Reef
▩▩▩	Stairs			⛷	Skiing Area		Swamp

CONVERSION TABLES

°C = (°F − 32) / 1.8
°F = (°C x 1.8) + 32
1 inch = 2.54 centimeters (cm)
1 foot = 0.304 meters (m)
1 yard = 0.914 meters
1 mile = 1.6093 kilometers (km)
1 km = 0.6214 miles
1 fathom = 1.8288 m
1 chain = 20.1168 m
1 furlong = 201.168 m
1 acre = 0.4047 hectares
1 sq km = 100 hectares
1 sq mile = 2.59 square km
1 ounce = 28.35 grams
1 pound = 0.4536 kilograms
1 short ton = 0.90718 metric ton
1 short ton = 2,000 pounds
1 long ton = 1.016 metric tons
1 long ton = 2,240 pounds
1 metric ton = 1,000 kilograms
1 quart = 0.94635 liters
1 US gallon = 3.7854 liters
1 Imperial gallon = 4.5459 liters
1 nautical mile = 1.852 km

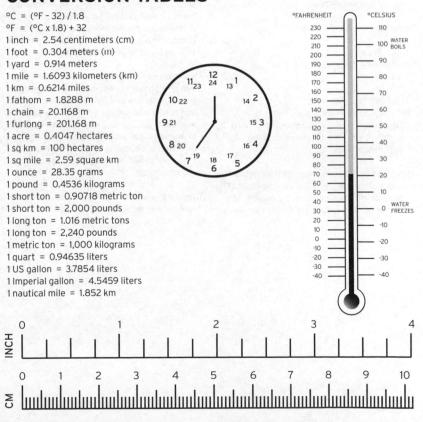

MOON PROVENCE

Avalon Travel
Hachette Book Group
1700 Fourth Street
Berkeley, CA 94710, USA
www.moon.com

Editor: Megan Anderluh
Copy Editor: Barbara Schultz
Graphics Coordinators: Suzanne Albertson,
   Scott Kimball
Production Coordinators: Suzanne Albertson,
   Scott Kimball
Cover Design: Faceout Studio, Charles Brock
Interior Design: Domini Dragoone
Moon Logo: Tim McGrath
Map Editor: Albert Angulo
Cartographer: Karin Dahl
Proofreader: Lai T. Moy
Indexer: Sam Arnold-Boyd

ISBN-13: 978-1-64049-123-6

Printing History
1st Edition — December 2019
5 4 3 2 1

Front cover photo: Martin Pinker, Getty Images
Back cover photo: ZNM, Dreamstime.com

Printed in China by RR Donnelley

Avalon Travel is a division of Hachette Book Group,
Inc. Moon and the Moon logo are trademarks of
Hachette Book Group, Inc. All other marks and logos
depicted are the property of the original owners.